THE STATE OF TEXAS:
Government, Politics, and Policy

SIXTH EDITION

THE STATE OF TEXAS:
Government, Politics, and Policy

SIXTH EDITION

Sherri Mora
Texas State University

With contributions from:

- Patrick Moore, Dallas College–Richland Campus
- Veronica Reyna, Houston Community College
- Thomas Varacalli, Texas State University
- Geoffrey Willbanks, Tyler Junior College

THE STATE OF TEXAS: GOVERNMENT, POLITICS, AND POLICY, SIXTH EDITION

Published by McGraw Hill LLC, 1325 Avenue of the Americas, New York, NY 10019. Copyright ©2024 by McGraw Hill LLC. All rights reserved. Printed in the United States of America. Previous editions ©2022, 2019, and 2017. No part of this publication may be reproduced or distributed in any form or by any means, or stored in a database or retrieval system, without the prior written consent of McGraw Hill LLC, including, but not limited to, in any network or other electronic storage or transmission, or broadcast for distance learning.

Some ancillaries, including electronic and print components, may not be available to customers outside the United States.

This book is printed on acid-free paper.

1 2 3 4 5 6 7 8 9 0 LWI 28 27 26 25 24 23

ISBN 978-1-265-52276-6 (bound edition)
MHID 1-265-52276-6 (bound edition)
ISBN 978-1-265-65718-5 (loose-leaf edition)
MHID 1-265-65718-1 (loose-leaf edition)

Executive Portfolio Manager: *Jason Seitz*
Senior Product Development Manager: *Dawn Groundwater*
Executive Marketing Manager: *Michael Gedatus*
Content Project Managers: *Rick Hecker/George Theofanopoulos*
Senior Buyer: *Laura Fuller*
Content Licensing Specialist: *Brianne Kirschbaum*
Cover Image: *Glow Images*
Compositor: *Aptara®, Inc.*

All credits appearing on page or at the end of the book are considered to be an extension of the copyright page.

Library of Congress Cataloging-in-Publication Data

Names: Mora, Sherri, author. | Ruger, William, author.
Title: The State of Texas : government, politics, and policy / Sherri Mora,
    William Ruger.
Description: Sixth edition. | New York, NY : McGraw Hill LLC, 2024. |
    Includes index.
Identifiers: LCCN 2022038617 (print) | LCCN 2022038618 (ebook) | ISBN
    9781265522766 (hardcover) | ISBN 9781265657185 (spiral bound) | ISBN
    9781265657437 (ebook) | ISBN 9781265655976 (ebook other)
Subjects: LCSH: Texas—Politics and government—Textbooks.
Classification: LCC JK4816 .M67 2023 (print) | LCC JK4816 (ebook) | DDC
    320.4764—dc23/eng/20220921
LC record available at https://lccn.loc.gov/2022038617
LC ebook record available at https://lccn.loc.gov/2022038618

The Internet addresses listed in the text were accurate at the time of publication. The inclusion of a website does not indicate an endorsement by the authors or McGraw Hill LLC, and McGraw Hill LLC does not guarantee the accuracy of the information presented at these sites.

Built for Texas Government Courses . . .

By Texas Government Voices . . .

For Texas Government Students!

 The State of Texas: Government, Politics, and Policy, 6e, combines concise content with effective digital tools that provide a personalized learning experience for every student. Built to align directly with state learning outcomes and core objectives, this highly readable program provides students with the content and tools to make Texas government relevant in their lives.

Developing Foundational Knowledge and Honing Skills

With a comprehensive content program and numerous assignable activities in Connect Texas Government®, *The State of Texas* includes ample material for a full semester course on Texas government. SmartBook®, found in Connect Texas Government, is organized around the Texas Learning Outcomes and Core Objectives, providing the ability to assess directly on those outcomes.

SmartBook™ Tailors Content to the Individual Students

Available within Connect Texas Government, SmartBook has been updated with improved learning objectives to ensure that students gain foundational knowledge while learning to make connections to help them formulate a broader understanding of political events. SmartBook personalizes learning to individual student needs, continually adapting to pinpoint knowledge gaps and focus learning on topics that need the most attention. Study time is more productive, and as a result, students are better prepared for class and coursework. For instructors, SmartBook tracks student progress and provides insights that can help guide teaching strategies.

Writing Assignment

McGraw Hill's Writing Assignment Plus tool delivers a learning experience that improves students' written communication skills and conceptual understanding with every assignment. Assign, monitor, and provide feedback on writing more efficiently and grade assignments within McGraw Hill Connect®. Writing Assignment Plus gives you time-saving tools with a just-in-time basic writing and originality checker. Features include:

- Grammar/writing checking with McGraw Hill learning resources
- Originality checker with McGraw Hill learning resources
- Writing stats
- Rubric building and scoring
- Ability to assign draft and final deadline milestones
- Tablet ready and tools for all learners

Understanding Impact

Understanding Impact features help students understand why key content matters and includes critical thinking questions to help them apply what they learn. Topics in this edition include understanding the impact of Texas's biennial legislative sessions and understanding the impact of court decisions that loosened restrictions on campaign contributions.

Understanding Impact: In this chapter you've heard arguments for and against Texas moving to annual legislative sessions. When Hurricane Harvey hit the Houston area in August 2017, the legislature was not scheduled to meet again for over a year. Additional appropriations couldn't be made and legislative oversight was not possible. Subsequently, the state's response was widely criticized. Do you think arguments against a shift to annual sessions hold up in the face of the human tragedy of Hurricane Harvey? Explain.

How To

How To features provide students with step-by-step guidance for developing skills they need for college and for life. For example, "How to Be Socially and Politically Responsible" and "How to Write Effectively."

How to

How to Be Politically and Socially Responsible

Democracy is about people coming together to improve society. To have a high-quality democracy, citizens must use their political power to guide the government. This includes not only voting but also participating *after* elections.

Step 1: Know where to find election information.
To register to vote, go to the tax assessor's website for your county. You can print and mail a registration form. Once you are registered, you do not need to register again except if you move, if your name changes, or if you complete prison time.

To find election deadlines, ballot information, voting locations, and information on early voting, go to your county clerk's website. This site also has sample ballots for specific races, absentee ballots, and special information for military personnel and voters with disabilities.

As of 2020, Texas no longer has straight-ticket voting. This means you need alternative shortcuts to help you vote. Each political party has its own website with its party platform. Check out third parties, too!

records and at any bills they proposed. The Texas Legislature Online has search options to help you do this. Also, note how or if your representatives respond to you.

Step 2: Fact-check information.
Know your news sources, and recognize shallow policy coverage, clickbait, and infotainment. Check out this resource: False, Misleading, Clickbait-y, and/or Satirical "News" Sources. Learn to identify political spin and fake news. Most important, diversify your news sources so you learn perspectives from across the political spectrum.

Make sure information is valid before you spread it on the Internet. Two main sites for fact-checking are Politifact.com and Snopes.com.

Step 3: Volunteer in the community or in politics.
Take time to discover your neighborhood's needs. Many organizations need volunteers: public schools, food banks, animal shelters, women's shelters, homeless shelters, religious organizations, and others. Start with a volunteer matching site, such as volunteermatch.org if you don't know where to begin.

Informing and Engaging Students on Texas Government . . . as It Happens

Using Connect Texas Government, students can learn the course material more deeply and study more effectively than ever before.

Texas NewsFlash

We ensure that you have the most up-to-date content to share with your students through our NewsFlash activities, which are updated monthly. **NewsFlash** exercises tie current news stories to key Texas government concepts and learning objectives. After interacting with a contemporary news story, students are assessed on their ability to make the connection between real-life events and course content.

Texas Podcasts

You can now create broader interest, engagement, and relevancy in their courses by leveraging political podcasts about Texas government and politics. These assignments, which will be periodically expanded, will ask students to listen to relevant podcasts, demonstrate their understanding of the basic concepts presented, and reflect the broader context of the Texas political system.

Critical Thinking Activities

At the *apply*, *analyze*, and *evaluate* levels of Bloom's taxonomy, **Critical Thinking activities** in Connect Texas Government allow students to engage with the political process and learn by doing. For example, students will understand how Texas is a majority-minority state.

Concept Clips

Concept Clips help students break down key concepts in government. Using easy-to-understand audio narration, visual cues, and colorful animations, Concept Clips provide a step-by-step presentation that aids in student retention. In addition to the concept-based clips, several **Skills Based Clips** equip students for work within and outside the classroom. These skills based clips include the following:

- How to Evaluate News Source
- How to Think Critically
- How to Read a Court Case
- How to Understand Charts and Graphs
- How to Interpret Political Cartoons
- How to Avoid Plagiarism

Focus On

We retained and updated the Focus On features, which present students with engaging examples of how Hispanic, Latino, African American, and LGBTQ individuals and groups play an important role in Texas political life. For example, the Focus On feature in Chapter 1 on "Increasing Religious Diversity in Texas" includes the 2022 Colleyville attack and the rise of antisemitism in Texas.

Focus On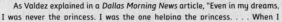

Lupe Valdez: Dallas County Sheriff, 2005–2017

Lupe Valdez came onto the national scene when she ran as the Democratic contender for Texas governor in 2018, but she has a long history of public service before that, notably as the first Latina and one of the first openly LGBTQ county sheriffs in the state.[61]

The child of migrant workers, she was born in San Antonio and split her childhood between San Antonio and a farm in Michigan where her father and older siblings worked. While an undergraduate student in Kansas, she became a corrections officer. Later, she worked for the federal government in various law enforcement capacities. In addition, she went on to earn a master's degree in criminal justice and joined the Army Reserve. It was during these years that she realized her sexual orientation.[62]

Lupe Valdez
Pat Benic/UPI/Alamy Stock Photo

As Valdez explained in a *Dallas Morning News* article, "Even in my dreams, I was never the princess. I was the one helping the princess. . . . When I became aware of my sexuality, the struggle was with God. I came out late because I was too busy trying to get out of where I was. I didn't want to end up in the barrio."[63]

Eventually, she came to terms with her sexuality as a lesbian, and she "said she realizes she was accepted by God."[64]

Retiring from the Department of Homeland Security in 2004, she decided to run for sheriff of Dallas County. She won the primary and then the general election in a close contest.[65]

As sheriff, she believes "her greatest contribution was smashing intolerance in the department." She also was instrumental in improving jail conditions so that in 2010, Dallas County Jail finally passed federal inspection. During her tenure (she was reelected in 2008, 2012, and 2016), she also joined the Democratic National Committee and, at President Obama's behest, joined the fight for immigration reform.[66]

At the end of 2017, she retired to run for governor. Even though Greg Abbott ultimately won reelection, Valdez remains active in Democratic politics in the state.[67]

Critical Thinking Questions
1. Why do you think "smashing intolerance" would be particularly important to Valdez? What types of intolerance did she likely face?
2. What else did Valdez accomplish as county sheriff?

Emphasizing Texas Voices

The Sixth Edition is proud to include the contributions from several Texas faculty members with a wealth of experience in the Texas government classroom:

- Patrick Moore, Dallas College–Richland Campus
- Veronica Reyna, Houston Community College
- Thomas Varacalli, Texas State University
- Geoffrey Willbanks, Tyler Junior College

Content Changes

The Sixth Edition focused on several key areas:

- Impact of the Covid-19 pandemic in Texas
- Greater emphasis on involvement of women in Texas politics

- 2022 federal and state election updates
- New policies and bills passed during the 2021 legislative sessions

Chapter-by-chapter content changes are as follows:

Chapter 1: Introduction to Texas History and Politics

- New section on how the COVID-19 pandemic impacted the Texas economy
- Heavily revised coverage of Texas economy
- Revised Focus On feature Increasing Religious Diversity in Texas to cover the rise in antisemitism in Texas
- Update on how the 2020 U.S. Census and redistricting impacts Texas's representation at the state and national level
- Updated statistics on income and poverty, population density, and Texas's standing among the most populous states

Chapter 2: The American Federal System and the Texas State Constitution

- Updated coverage of state marijuana laws
- New discussion of 2021 amendments to the Texas Constitution and turnout during the 2021 constitutional amendment elections
- Updated comparison of state constitutions

Chapter 3: The Texas Legislature

- New coverage of the 2021 regular legislative session and the three 2021 special sessions
- New section of the 2020 Census and the 2021 redistricting battle
- Streamlined coverage of the 2000 and 2020s battle over redistricting
- Description of the new Texas House Speaker. New material on 2021 bills—numbers, content, process
- New paragraph on the impact of the three-fifths rule
- Updated description of the 2022 primary and general elections
- Updated description of campaign financing in the most recent elections
- Updated data on the demographic makeup of the legislature, years of service in legislature, most senior figures, and turnover rates
- Updated coverage of the legal battle over racial gerrymandering
- Updated information on competitive and noncompetitive districts, the standing committees, the number of constituents for each legislative district, and states with biennial legislatures

Chapter 4: The Executive Department and the Office of the Governor of Texas

- Coverage of the 2022 Texas gubernatorial election results
- New map based of Institutional powers of Governors by State
- Revision of Focus On "A Hispanic Governor for Texas?" introduces new coverage of Joy Diaz's race
- New example of post-gubernatorial and land commissioner career paths
- Heavily revised section on gubernatorial tenure to focus on new trend for longer terms
- Updated information on women governors and term-limits for governors

Chapter 5: The Court System in Texas

- Updated data on the number of courts at each level
- New information on Texas judges who were appointed to their seats, judge selection across the U.S. states, and Texas court workloads
- Updated statistics on demographics of Texas judges, and disciplinary committees

Chapter 6: The Criminal Justice System in Texas

- Updated data on the crime rate, the type of crimes, the number of jails, the number of deaths in Texas jails, suicides, and exonerations
- Updated coverage of attempts at criminal justice reform in the 2021 legislature
- New analysis of the impact of COVID-19 on crime and the imprisonment rate
- New coverage of recent study submitted to Texas legislature on the positive affect education and career-readiness programs have had on reducing the rate of recidivism
- Updated coverage of Texas Board of Pardons and Paroles review of capital cases, the statistics connecting death row convictions with county financial resources
- New map of death row statistics based by state
- Updated coverage of Texas prisoner mental health issues and access to mental health care in Texas
- New example of errors in criminal justice cases

Chapter 7: Local Governments in Texas

- New coverage of Texas laws regarding municipal authority to fill vacant elected positions
- Updated statistics on the percent of mayor-council and council-manager types of city governments
- New coverage of Hispanic Republican mayors elected in recent years
- Updated statistics on voter turnout in local elections

Chapter 8: Public Opinion and the Media in Texas

- Updated poll data on Texas public opinion on the border wall, legalizing marijuana, and trust in media
- Update on legal challenges to Deferred Action for Childhood Arrivals (DACA)
- New figure on Texas approval of the handling of the COVID-19 crisis and an analysis of the correlation between approval/disapproval ratings and the partisan divide
- New figure showing trust in types of media by partisan affiliation
- New figure showing news use across different social media platforms
- New figure showing Americans' podcast listening habits over time
- New figures showing that most people believe that the media is biased, but feel that the media serves a watchdog role keeping political leaders in line

- Updated discussion on net neutrality
- Updated coverage of consolidations in the Spanish-speaking media corporations

Chapter 9: Voting and Political Participation in Texas

- New material on how the 2020 elections impacted the number of voting laws across the states
- Updated coverage on voting laws in other states and voter turnout in 2020, 2021, and 2022 elections
- New section on impact of Voting Laws in Texas includes coverage of attempts to clean voting rolls, detailed explanation of SB1, the 2021 Texas voting law, and the impact of SB1 on the 2022 primary election
- New section on Voter Fraud in Texas distinguishes voter and election fraud, illustrates each with cases, discusses the statistics on the low frequency of voter fraud, and analyzes the five election results that have been overturned. A new figure showing Texas opinion poll on voting fraud
- New coverage of the Latino vote in 2016 and 2020
- New data on voter participation and new examples of protests and the number of participants in these protests
- Updated discussion of trust in elections

Chapter 10: Campaigns and Elections in Texas

- Updated data on PAC contributions across states
- Updated information on electronic voting systems
- Replaced 2002 of personal campaign loans with recent Ted Cruz court case
- Most recent information on number of independent and third-party candidates appearing on the ballot
- Updated data on trends in crossover primary voting
- Updated statistics on filing fees to register to run
- Information about voting poll closures due to staff shortage in 2022

Chapter 11: Political Parties in Texas

- New section on the emerging trend of third parties to become factions within major parties and the impact on major parties
- Clarification on the impact of Australian ballot on the party boss system
- Major revision and update to cover the most recent developments within the Republican Party.
- New section on new developments within the Democratic Party today
- New coverage of Hispanic vote in most recent elections
- Revised analysis of whether Texas will go blue
- Expanded coverage of how Texas eliminated the two-step primary elections
- New paragraph on Cost of Voting Index and Texas's ranking

Chapter 12: Interest Groups and Lobbying in Texas

- Updated analysis of PAC spending
- New coverage of the role of interest groups in the prohibition of teaching critical race theory in public schools

- Update on Affordable Care Act contraception coverage
- New 2021 example of interest groups seeking a gubernatorial veto
- New example feature Republican Attorney General primary candidate Eva Guzman of how a candidate can raise a lot of money but still not win an election
- Updated data on lobbyists

Chapter 13: Public Policy in Texas

- New Understanding Impact featuring K–12 funding
- New coverage of abortion laws and SB8, the Texas law prohibiting abortions after the sixth week of pregnancy
- New policy adoption example featuring the legislatures creation of a Broadband Development Office and the plan to expand broadband services to rural areas in Texas
- New description of the ongoing battle between Texans for Lawsuit Reform and the Texas Trial Lawyers and how that impacts regulation of business in Texas
- Updated coverage of research into whether undocumented immigration benefits the state of Texas financially.
- Updated information on spending on border wall and mobilization of National Guard
- Updated coverage of Biden administration border policy
- Updated coverage of government spending on water resource development

Chapter 14: Financing State Government

- Updated discussion of gross revenue and tax types and levels in comparison to other states
- Updated statistics on nontax revenue for Texas, total federal funds, and total appropriations by function
- Updated comparison of state expenditures on education, public welfare, and health and hospitals
- Revised section on tax revenue from oil and natural gas extraction

Instructor Resources

The Sixth Edition includes the following instructor resources:

Instructor's manual. The instructor's manual provides a wide variety of tools and resources for presenting the course, including learning objectives and ideas for lectures and discussions.

Test bank. Each question has been tagged for level of difficulty, Bloom's taxonomy, and topic coverage. Organized by chapter, the questions are designed to test factual, conceptual, and higher order thinking.

Test Builder. Available within Connect, Test Builder is a cloud-based tool that enables instructors to format tests that can be printed and administered within a Learning Management System. Test Builder offers a modern, streamlined interface for easy content configuration that matches course needs, without requiring a download.

Test Builder enables instructors to:

- Access all test bank content from a particular title
- Easily pinpoint the most relevant content through robust filtering options
- Manipulate the order of questions or scramble questions and/or answers
- Pin questions to a specific location within a test
- Determine your preferred treatment of algorithmic questions
- Choose the layout and spacing
- Add instructions and configure default settings

PowerPoint. The PowerPoint presentations highlight the key points of the chapter and include supporting visuals. All slides are WCAG compliant.

Remote Proctoring. Remote proctoring and browser-locking capabilities are seamlessly integrated within Connect to offer more control over the integrity of online assessments. Instructors can enable security options that restrict browser activity, monitor student behavior, and verify the identity of each student. Instant and detailed reporting gives instructors an at-a-glance view of potential concerns, thereby avoiding personal bias and supporting evidence-based claims.

Learning Outcomes and Core Objectives

GOVT 2306 is one of the foundational component areas within the Core Curriculum identified by the Undergraduate Education Advisory Committee (UEAC) of the Texas Higher Education Coordinating Board (THECB). The UEAC has identified six core objectives, of which four—critical thinking skills, communication skills, social responsibility, and personal responsibility—must be mapped to content in GOVT 2306. Those four core objectives are mapped to specific *The State of Texas* content here and throughout each chapter.

Institutions must assess learning outcomes (provided in the *UEAC's Academic Course Guide Manual*); for example, the student's demonstrated ability to explain the origin and development of the Texas Constitution, consistent with assessment practices required by the Commission on Colleges of the Southern Association of Colleges and Schools (SACSCOC).

These requirements include an explanation of measures, methodology, frequency, and timeline of assessment; an explanation of targets and benchmarks of "Core Objective" attainment; evidence of attainment of the required core objectives; interpretation of assessment information; and the use of results for improving student learning. SACS principles of accreditation 3.3.1.1 requires institutions to identify expected learning outcomes, assess the extent to which it achieves these outcomes, and provide evidence of improvement based on analysis of the results.

Adopting *The State of Texas* and using the provided assessment tools makes SACS compliance easy while meeting the purpose of the Core Curriculum.

Learning Outcomes and Core Objectives Correlation Table

CHAPTER 1	**Learning Outcome:** Explain the history, demographics, and political culture of Texas.	**Thinking Critically**	Texas has always been a state full of immigrants. How have these settlement patterns changed over time and/or how have they stayed the same? How did they change the character and culture of Texas?
	Learning Outcome: Explain the history, demographics, and political culture of Texas.	**Communicating Effectively**	Write a short synopsis of Texas's changing economy and its role in international trade.
	Learning Outcome: Explain the history, demographics, and political culture of Texas.	**Taking Personal Responsibility**	What can you do to become well informed about political issues so that you can make effective decisions at election time?
	Learning Outcome: Explain the history, demographics, and political culture of Texas.	**Being Socially Responsible**	Understanding the relationship between religious affiliations and politics can improve civic knowledge. How would you use this knowledge to engage effectively in your community? Think about your own religious affiliations (if any) and political beliefs and how they compare with those of your neighbors. How might knowing your neighbors' religious affiliations help you better understand their political views?
CHAPTER 2	**Learning Outcome:** Describe separation of powers and checks and balances in both theory and practice in Texas.	**Communicating Effectively**	Analyze the diagram in Figure 2.3 and the division of powers in Table 2.2 to describe the separation of powers and checks and balances in both theory and practice in Texas.
	Learning Outcome: Explain the origin and development of the Texas Constitution.	**Thinking Critically**	What is the impact of a constitutional convention dominated by one party? What were the consequences of the 1875 constitutional convention in the development of the Texas Constitution?
	Learning Outcome: Describe state and local political systems and their relationship with the federal government.	**Being Socially Responsible**	To what extent should the government "promote general welfare"? What does promoting general welfare mean to you? In developing an understanding of state and local political systems and their relationship with the federal government, who do you think should play a greater role—the states or the federal government?
	Learning Outcome: Describe state and local political systems and their relationship with the federal government.	**Taking Personal Responsibility**	As a resident of Texas and a citizen of the United States, identify and discuss examples that reinforce the Full Faith and Credit Clause and the Privileges and Immunities Clause of the U.S. Constitution? Which examples, in your opinion, violate these principles?
CHAPTER 3	**Learning Outcome:** Describe the legislative branch of Texas government.	**Communicating Effectively**	Some people contend that smaller constituencies might allow a wider array of people to participate in state politics, rather than just the "rich" or "well born." How would you argue in favor of or against this statement?
	Learning Outcome: Describe the legislative branch of Texas government.	**Being Socially Responsible**	Each Texas citizen has one Texas state house member and one Texas state senate member to represent him or her. Use this website to find your representatives: https://capitol.texas.gov/. The "Who Represents Me" section allows you to put in your address and locate your state house and senate members.
	Learning Outcome: Describe the legislative branch of Texas government.	**Thinking Critically**	Both demographics and voting patterns have changed in Texas, and some districts have become more competitive. Discuss what these shifts mean for future elections and the composition of the Texas House and Senate. Reference Table 3.4 in your answer.
	Learning Outcome: Describe the legislative branch of Texas government.	**Taking Personal Responsibility**	Many people believe that the success of legislation depends largely on a relative few individuals who make up the leadership in the Texas House and Senate. Do you think the Speaker of the House and the lieutenant governor have too much control over the passage of bills? How can you influence legislation? What can individuals do to affect legislation?

	Learning Outcome		
CHAPTER 4	**Learning Outcome:** Explain the structure and function of the executive branch of Texas government.	**Communicating Effectively**	Analyze Map 4.1. What inferences can you draw from the data? Think about how the data relate to Texas, its neighbors, and other regions of the country.
	Learning Outcome: Explain the structure and function of the executive branch of Texas government.	**Being Socially Responsible**	How does the comptroller promote effective involvement in regional, national, and global communities?
	Learning Outcome: Explain the structure and function of the executive branch of Texas government.	**Taking Personal Responsibility**	What can you do to become more actively engaged in the civic discourse about the role of the State Board of Education?
	Learning Outcome: Explain the structure and function of the executive branch of Texas government.	**Thinking Critically**	The six factors that influence the strength of the power of the governor are the number of elected statewide executives, tenure of office, the governor's appointive powers, the governor's budgetary powers, the governor's veto powers, and the extent to which the governor controls his or her political party. Based on these six factors, what can you conclude about the powers of the governor of Texas?
CHAPTER 5	**Learning Outcome:** Describe the structure and function of the judicial branch of Texas government.	**Communicating Effectively**	Analyze Figure 5.4. Describe the appeals process for a civil case filed in county court.
	Learning Outcome: Describe the structure and function of the judicial branch of Texas government.	**Being Socially Responsible**	What impact, if any, do you think partisan election of judges has on judicial outcomes?
	Learning Outcome: Describe the structure and function of the judicial branch of Texas government.	**Thinking Critically**	Reflecting on the discussion about representation of minorities and women in the Texas judicial system, do you think it is important to have a judiciary that is representative of the general population? Why or why not?
	Learning Outcome: Describe the structure and function of the judicial branch of Texas government.	**Taking Personal Responsibility**	Given what you read in this section, it would seem that citizens have little impact in disciplining and/or removing judges. What do you think is a citizen's responsibility in this matter? How can individuals take greater personal responsibility to ensure that judges perform properly?
CHAPTER 6	**Learning Outcome:** Analyze issues and policies in Texas.	**Communicating Effectively**	Explain the difference between criminal and civil law, including how the standard of proof differs for each. Provide an example of each type of case.
	Learning Outcome: Analyze issues and policies in Texas.	**Taking Personal Responsibility**	Currently, at what age does the state of Texas consider a person an adult in criminal and civil proceedings? At what age do you think the state should require individuals to take personal responsibility? Why?
	Learning Outcome: Analyze issues and policies in Texas.	**Being Socially Responsible**	Why might the use of special courts to punish crimes like prostitution provide a cost savings for the criminal justice system?
	Learning Outcome: Analyze issues and policies in Texas.	**Thinking Critically**	Given the current challenges faced by the criminal justice system, what types of reforms would you recommend? What might be some of the negative or unintended consequences of your recommendations?

CHAPTER 7	**Learning Outcome:** Describe local political systems in Texas.	Communicating Effectively	Compare Figures 7.1, 7.3, and 7.4 with Table 7.2. Discuss the fundamental differences between weak mayor, strong mayor, and council-manager forms of government. Which do you prefer and why?
	Learning Outcome: Describe local political systems in Texas.	Being Socially Responsible	Compare at-large election systems and single-member district systems. An argument in favor of single-member district systems is that they increase minority representation in local government. In your opinion, does increased minority representation increase intercultural competency? Why?
	Learning Outcome: Describe local political systems in Texas.	Taking Personal Responsibility	Local government directly impacts people in their daily lives. What can you do to improve local governance?
	Learning Outcome: Describe local political systems in Texas.	Thinking Critically	Identify some of the problems facing county governments. What solutions would you propose?
CHAPTER 8	**Learning Outcome:** Evaluate public opinion and the role of the media in Texas politics.	Thinking Critically	Review Figure 8.3. Note that Joe Biden (Democrat) was the U.S. president at the time of polling. Why might Texas Democrats and Republicans display different levels of approval of the handling of the Coronavirus crisis?
	Learning Outcome: Evaluate public opinion and the role of the media in Texas politics.	Taking Personal Responsibility	What media sources do you consume? Print? Television? Social media? Which do you access most and least often? How might social media influence you differently than television?
	Learning Outcome: Evaluate public opinion and the role of the media in Texas politics.	Being Socially Responsible	What responsibility do citizens have as social media participants within the context of political campaigns?
	Learning Outcome: Evaluate public opinion and the role of the media in Texas politics.	Communicating Effectively	Explain how the federal government regulates print and electronic media.
CHAPTER 9	**Learning Outcome:** Identify the rights and responsibilities of citizens.	Taking Personal Responsibility	What activities do you engage in that are related to governance? Which forms of political participation do you think are the most effective?
	Learning Outcome: Identify the rights and responsibilities of citizens.	Thinking Critically	How do you think the Texas voter ID law and recent attempts of purging voter rolls affect voter turnout in Texas? Where do you stand on these issues? Explain why you favor or oppose voter ID laws or challenging the status of voters on voter rolls.
	Learning Outcome: Identify the rights and responsibilities of citizens.	Being Socially Responsible	Considering the discussion of political power and the socioeconomic factors that could affect voter turnout, identify effective ways to increase civic knowledge in culturally diverse communities.
	Learning Outcome: Identify the rights and responsibilities of citizens.	Communicating Effectively	Write a one-page summary of the rationalist explanations for low voter turnout.
CHAPTER 10	**Learning Outcome:** Analyze the state and local election process in Texas.	Thinking Critically	Explain the challenges that hinder minor party candidates from succeeding in statewide elections.
	Learning Outcome: Analyze the state and local election process in Texas.	Communicating Effectively	Do you think the Voting Rights Act requirement that Texas provide a bilingual ballot increases voter turnout? Construct an argument in favor of or against this provision of the Voting Rights Act.
	Learning Outcome: Analyze the state and local election process in Texas.	Being Socially Responsible	What responsibility do you think the media have in covering campaigns and elections? Are the media living up to your expectations?
	Learning Outcome: Analyze the state and local election process in Texas.	Taking Personal Responsibility	If you choose to contribute to a candidate's campaign, to what extent is the candidate obligated to you as a contributor? Should your contribution influence public policy? What about corporate contributions?

	Learning Outcome: Evaluate the role of political parties in Texas.	**Communicating Effectively**	Explain how political reforms have weakened political parties.
CHAPTER 11	**Learning Outcome:** Evaluate the role of political parties in Texas.	**Taking Personal Responsibility**	Examine your political values and compare them to the expressed values of both parties. Do your ideas about the role of government, politics, and policy align with one particular party? If so, which one?
	Learning Outcome: Evaluate the role of political parties in Texas.	**Being Socially Responsible**	What effect, if any, do factions have on enhancing or diminishing civic engagement? In your opinion, do factions promote acceptance of diverse opinions?
	Learning Outcome: Evaluate the role of political parties in Texas.	**Thinking Critically**	For a variety of reasons, third parties do not currently have much effect on Texas politics. What measures might be taken to level the playing field for third parties and improve their competitiveness in elections?
CHAPTER 12	**Learning Outcome:** Evaluate the role of interest groups in Texas.	**Thinking Critically**	Review Table 12.1. Are you a participant in a membership organization? If so, how does the organization represent your interests? If not, how are your interests represented at the state and federal levels of government?
	Learning Outcome: Evaluate the role of interest groups in Texas.	**Taking Personal Responsibility**	Socrates suggested "know thyself," and Shakespeare's Hamlet admonished "to thine own self be true." It is important to know what your interests are and how they are represented in government. Consider what you have read in this chapter and determine how interest group efforts align with your personal interests. If they do not, what can you do to ensure that government addresses your interests or the interests of those who share similar values?
	Learning Outcome: Evaluate the role of interest groups in Texas.	**Communicating Effectively**	Review the information about Julian Castro's presidential bid. Identify the reasons that you believe he might have appealed to individual donors and at least one possible reason his candidacy did not take off. Share your ideas with another student.
	Learning Outcome: Evaluate the role of interest groups in Texas.	**Being Socially Responsible**	How can geographic distribution of interest groups improve political awareness between culturally diverse populations?
CHAPTER 13	**Learning Outcome:** Analyze important public policy issues in Texas.	**Taking Personal Responsibility**	How can you affect public policy decisions? At what point in the policy cycle could you voice your preferences? Use Figure 13.1, the policy-cycle graphic, to help you answer these questions.
	Learning Outcome: Analyze important public policy issues in Texas.	**Being Socially Responsible**	To what extent should the government of Texas be responsible for ensuring equal funding for wealthy school districts and poor school districts?
	Learning Outcome: Analyze important public policy issues in Texas.	**Communicating Effectively**	Summarize the legislation that Texas has passed on abortion. Discuss the advantages and disadvantages of state involvement in this policy issue.
	Learning Outcome: Analyze important public policy issues in Texas.	**Thinking Critically**	Given the water-related challenges facing Texas, what measures would you recommend to ensure all Texans have access to water? What might be some negative or unintended consequences of your recommendations?
CHAPTER 14	**Learning Outcome:** Analyze state financing issues and policies in Texas.	**Thinking Critically**	What goods and services do you think state government should provide? Consider the consequences of your answer. What would the possible impact to society be, given your position? Who would benefit, and who would lose out?
	Learning Outcome: Analyze state financing issues and policies in Texas.	**Being Socially Responsible**	Texas taxes prepared food items, but does not tax unprepared food items (such as raw meats and fresh produce). Earlier in this chapter, you learned that individuals can be excluded from receiving services such as electricity if they cannot pay. Keeping this in mind, how does taxing prepared food affect our state's poorest citizens?
	Learning Outcome: Analyze state financing issues and policies in Texas.	**Communicating Effectively**	Consider Table 14.8, which illustrates how specific appropriations are restricted. What percentage of funds is not restricted? How does restricting funds affect budget flexibility?
	Learning Outcome: Analyze state financing issues and policies in Texas.	**Taking Personal Responsibility**	Although few individuals would express a preference for higher taxes, given the information in this chapter about the goods and services the state provides and the revenue data presented in Figure 14.8 and Table 14.9, should Texans advocate for a personal income tax? Why or why not?

BRIEF CONTENTS

CONTENTS

ABOUT THE AUTHOR

Sherri Mora is an Associate Professor of Practice and Undergraduate Program Coordinator for Political Science and Public Administration at Texas State University. She earned advanced degrees in political science, public administration, and education from Texas State University. She has published on teaching and learning in political science and has served on various committees for the Higher Education Coordinating Board since 2004. As an active member of the assessment group, Mora is responsible for core curriculum assessment and programmatic review in the Department of Political Science at Texas State. She has received numerous awards from the university for distinction as a professor, coordinator, and scholar, including the Presidential Distinction Award in Service and the Foundation of Excellence Award.

With Contributions From:

- Patrick Moore, Dallas College–Richland Campus
- Veronica Reyna, Houston Community College
- Thomas Varacalli, Texas State University
- Geoffrey Willbanks, Tyler Junior College

ACKNOWLEDGMENTS

We would like to thank Jamie Falconnier and Lyle Blanco for their exceptional research assistance for the Sixth Edition. We also want to thank the anonymous reviewers of the previous editions whose questions and comments made this a better product.

Additional thanks goes to the following reviewers:

Millie Black, Collin College, Plano
Darrell Castillo, Weatherford College
Daniel Cooper, Lone Star State
Henry Esparza, University of Texas, San Antonio
Brandon Franke, Blinn College
Rodolfo (Rudy) Hernandez, Texas State University, San Marcos
Jennifer E. Lamm, Texas State University
Alan Lehmann, Blinn College
Sharon Manna, North Lake College
David McClendon, Tyler Junior College
Lindsey B. McLennan, Kilgore College
Eric Miller, Blinn College, Bryan
Patrick Moore, Richland College
Chad Mueller, Weatherford College
Martha Musgrove, Tarrant County College, South
Sharon Ann Navarro, University of Texas at San Antonio
John M. Osterman Jr., San Jacinto College, Pasadena
William Parent, Houston Community College, San Jacinto
Paul Philips, Navarro College
Blayne J. Primozich, El Paso Community College, Verde
Prudencio Ramirez, San Jacinto College, Pasadena
Wesley Riddle, Central Texas College, Killeen
Mario Salas, University of Texas at San Antonio
Michael Sanchez, San Antonio College
Raymond Sandoval, Richland College
Jeff Stanglin, Kilgore College
Steven Tran, Houston Community College
Ronald Vardy, Wharton County Junior College

CHAPTER 1

Introduction to Texas History and Politics

- Explain the history, demographics, and political culture of Texas.

Texas is the product of many factors:

- Cultural influences
- A unique geography, including a vast amount of land that borders a foreign nation and has thriving ports
- Complicated historical relations with European powers
- A distinctive experience with the U.S. Civil War and Reconstruction
- Economic shifts from agriculture to industry
- Shifts in political dominance from one party to the other
- Changing demographics as people come to take advantage of economic opportunities

Texas today faces many challenges that are also tied to national events and concerns. To gain a full appreciation for Texas government, we must examine the Texas of the past as well as today's Texas and put them in a framework within which we can understand them—the framework of political culture. By doing this, we can begin to appreciate the special position Texas occupies within the United States, the ways in which it is very much "American," and the ways in which it is uniquely Texan.

Chapter Learning Objectives

- Explain the significance of Texas's six flags.
- Describe the Civil War and Reconstruction in Texas.
- Describe post-Reconstruction Texas.
- Explain the challenges facing Texas today.
- Explain U.S. and Texas political cultures.

Flags of Texas: From Spain to Statehood

Learning Objective: Explain the significance of Texas's six flags.

Settlement of the territory known as Texas began with north Asian groups migrating down from the Bering land bridge into the Americas. These groups spread throughout the Americas, and several eventually occupied the plains, grasslands, and coastal woodlands that are now called Texas. The Caddo settled primarily in the eastern parts of Texas. The Wichita claimed much of the Red River Valley and the lowland grass plains. The Karankawa made their home along the coastal plains, and the western parts of the state were settled by those nations that eventually became part of the great horse cultures in North America: the Comanche, Apache, Kiowa, and Tonkawa. Each of these groups would have an impact on later European settlers.

Over the last 500 years, six Western countries have governed Texas: Spain, France, the Republic of Mexico, the Republic of Texas, the United States of America, and, briefly, the Confederate States of America. This rich history is the origin of the "six flags of Texas." All six of these flags affected the political, social, economic, religious, and cultural development and diversity of Texas.

Spain

Spain was the first of the modern European nations to lay claim to the territory of Texas, although Spanish Texas included only a small part of today's state. Alonso Álvarez de Pineda explored and mapped the Texas coastline as early as 1519, more than 100 years before the Pilgrims landed at Plymouth Rock. However, it was not until 1540 that Francisco Vásquez de Coronado intentionally surveyed the interior of Texas. After Coronado dispelled rumors that the land was brimming with treasures, Spain all but abandoned Texas for almost a century and a half. During this time, Native Americans continued to live and flourish in Texas.

France, Briefly

France was the second European nation to lay claim and bring its flag, briefly, to the territory of Texas. France laid claim to all the territory encompassing the Mississippi River system (bordering much of the territory of Texas in the east and north along the Red River) as well as parts of the Spanish claims in the northwestern territories of Mexico. One settlement attempt, led by René-Robert Cavelier, Sieur de La Salle, began in 1685 when his expedition overshot New Orleans and landed on the Texas coast near Matagorda Bay. Fort Saint Louis, however, was a dismal failure because the expedition was inadequately supplied and La Salle was a poor leader. When La Salle left in 1687, taking an overland route to seek help from New Orleans, his own men killed him. The next year, the Karankawa destroyed the fort and either killed or captured the remaining settlers.

Spain Returns

After the remains of Fort Saint Louis were discovered in 1689, the Spanish crown decided to increase settlement efforts by establishing missions and *presidios* (fortified settlements) in the eastern part of its territory. The goal was to fend off future French claims by bringing Spanish settlers from Mexico into Texas territory. These Spanish settlers were known as Tejanos, and the first area they settled was the Rio Grande Valley. They established settlements along the Rio Grande and as far north and east as San Antonio. Spanish settlements in other parts of the state lasted for only a few years, with the exception of Nacogdoches.

Although permanent Spanish settlement did not penetrate much beyond San Antonio, Spanish influence permeated the entire state. For example, most of the major rivers in Texas have Spanish names, as do other geographic features and a number of cities and counties. Notably, the Spanish introduced horses, sheep, and cattle into Texas. Spanish legal systems also left their legacy on state laws, especially those regarding land ownership and rights. For example, current laws regarding community property and protections against the forced sale of property (to pay off a debt or court-ordered judgment) have their origins in Spanish law.[1] The homestead exemption is another such legacy. This exemption provided family homesteads more protections from creditors and foreclosures if the economy failed. With this protection, the homestead exemption helped populate the rural regions of Texas.[2]

When the United States bought the Louisiana Territory from France in 1803, new settlement and immigration patterns emerged in East Texas. As **Anglos** encroached through Louisiana, Spain continued to promote settlement. But Spanish-Mexican relations deteriorated, and Mexico declared its independence from Spain in 1821.

Anglo

Here, refers to a non-Hispanic white North American of European descent, typically (but not exclusively) English speaking

The Republic of Mexico

The third flag to fly over Texas was that of the Republic of Mexico, which included what had been Spanish Texas. By 1824 Texas, the northeasternmost territory of the new nation had been combined with another province to form the new Mexican state of Coahuila and Texas.[3] The **empresario** land-grant system that had begun under the Spanish continued. Mexico continued to attract settlers into East Texas. Southern U.S. Anglos and the African American enslaved people they brought with them began settling there in the 1820s. These southern white Protestants were decidedly different from the Spanish Catholic settlers who already occupied Texas. Because of Mexico's own history of ethnic diversity, a strong antislavery movement was brewing. When President Antonio López de Santa Anna effectively declared himself dictator of Mexico and issued decrees limiting property rights and economic freedom for Anglos, the simmering conflict led to increased Anglo-Texan calls for rebellion.

Open revolt began in late 1835 when Texan and Mexican forces fought over a small six-pound cannon in Gonzales, Texas. Famously, the defenders of the cannon at Gonzales raised a flag with the words "Come and Take It" underneath a

empresario

A person who contracted with the Spanish or Mexican government to recruit new settlers to Texas in exchange for the ability to claim land

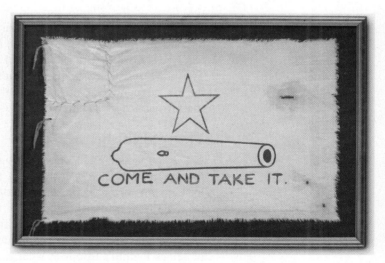

Gonzales flag

Gallery of the Republic

The Battle of the Alamo, Percy Moran, 1912
Library of Congress Prints and Photographs Division [LC-USZCN4-23]

lone star and cannon. A Texan victory fed the fever of revolt, and political leaders began planning for rebellion against Mexico. Internal conflicts in Texas complicated matters. Many of the Catholic Spanish people remained loyal to Mexico, while the more recently arrived Protestant Anglos generally favored independence.

Santa Anna himself took command of the Mexican forces and marched north into Texas to suppress the rebellion and expel the Anglos. His first battle was the siege of the Alamo (an old mission turned fortress) in San Antonio in February 1836. Texan forces under the command of William B. Travis were hopelessly outnumbered and had no real chance to be reinforced. The siege lasted two weeks, ending with the death of all 187 Alamo defenders on March 6, 1836. The brave resistance by the Alamo's defenders provided additional motivation for the independence movement. On March 2, 1836, just before the Alamo's fall, the provisional government of Texas declared its independence from Mexico.

The Republic of Texas

The Republic of Texas flew the fourth national flag. The immediate problem for the new republic was surviving the war with Mexico. The republic did not have an organized army, and the one being assembled had little to no experience. Sam Houston, the general of the Texan army, knew that he needed time to organize and train his troops if Texas was to have a chance at victory. Meanwhile, Santa Anna continued his march north; he captured and killed all 350 of James Fannin's troops at what is now called the Goliad Massacre. It became clear that Santa Anna intended to wipe out the Anglo-American presence in Texas permanently. In what came to be known as the "Runaway Scrape," Texans and Texas forces retreated for several weeks, fleeing ahead of Santa Anna's army toward Louisiana. Finally, on the banks of the San Jacinto River on April 21, 1836, Houston found himself with a tactical advantage; he attacked and defeated Santa Anna's army. Santa Anna was captured and forced to sign the Treaty of Velasco, which recognized Texas's independence from Mexico.

In the aftermath of the revolution, Texas found itself a new country with no real desire to *be* an independent country. With limited resources and infrastructure, the new government was quickly bound by debt, and it struggled to meet its minimum obligations to its citizens. Houston had been elected the first president of Texas, and as one of the first acts of the new republic, he petitioned the government of the United States for statehood. Because the vast majority of Anglo settlers considered themselves Americans, it seemed fitting for Texas to become part of the United States. However, the petition for statehood was denied because of the intensely political and divisive issue of slavery. At that time, if Texas was admitted into the Union as a slave state, a corresponding free state would need to be created. This balancing act was not possible then, so Texas was forced to stand on its own. The United States recognized Texas's independence and set up diplomatic relations.

From 1836 to 1845, the Republic of Texas struggled to survive. Poor relations and border disputes with Mexico to the south and open hostilities with the indigenous people in the west made governing Texas difficult. Lack of revenue and poor infrastructure continued to plague the young republic and made economic development challenging. Nonetheless, Texas promoted settlement of its frontier to Americans and Anglo-Europeans by offering the one thing it did have: land. In the 1840s, an organization called the **Adelsverein Society** aided this appeal for settlers by actively promoting German immigration to Texas. In other words, Texas actively sought out immigration to help stabilize its economy, increase its population, and protect its unpopulated regions from conquest. By 1847, this society had brought more than 7,000 Germans to Texas, most of whom settled in the vicinity of Fredericksburg in what is now known as "Hill Country."[4] By 1850, German settlers made up 5.4 percent of the population.[5]

Adelsverein Society

An organization that promoted German immigration to Texas in the 1840s

CORE OBJECTIVE

Thinking Critically . . .

Texas has always been a state full of immigrants. How have settlement patterns affected Texas? List the several different "waves" of immigration. How have these settlement patterns changed over time and/or how have they stayed the same? How did they change the character and culture of Texas?

The Twenty-Eighth State of the Union

Meanwhile, the idea of Manifest Destiny was gaining popularity in the United States. Advocates of Manifest Destiny believed that the annexation of Texas was necessary to have a nation that stretched from the Atlantic Ocean to the Pacific Ocean. Although the diplomatic efforts to bring Texas into the Union were complex, on December 29, 1845, President Polk signed the act making Texas

WYOMING

NEBRASKA

IOWA

Platte R.

U N I T E D   S T A T E S

COLORADO

KANSAS

MISSOURI

Sold to United States in 1850

Arkansas R.

ARKANSAS

NEW
MEXICO

OKLAHOMA

Pecos R.

Red R.

Rio Grande

Brazos R.

LA

Sabine R.

TEXAS

Colorado R.

MEXICO

*Gulf of
Mexico*

MAP 1.1 Compromise of 1850 Present state
boundaries are shown along with territory transferred to the
federal government as part of this agreement.

the twenty-eighth state of the Union. When Texas
entered the Union, it retained its public debt and its
public lands, forcing the U.S. government to buy all
land that was to be designated as federal. During the
Compromise of 1850 (see Map 1.1), when Texas's
boundary lines were finally settled, the U.S. government purchased lands that were formerly the western
and northwestern parts of Texas (now much of
present-day New Mexico and parts of Colorado,
Wyoming, Kansas, and Oklahoma).[6]

Thus the U.S. flag became the fifth to fly over
Texas. However, Mexico did not give up easily. Still
claiming all of Texas as its own, Mexico had voiced
objections to U.S. annexation of Texas and broke diplomatic relations with the United States in early 1845.
Moreover, Mexican territory at that time extended as
far north as the Great Salt Lake and west to the
Pacific, in direct opposition to the U.S. goal of spreading across the whole continent. Crossing the Rio
Grande on April 25, 1846, Mexican troops attacked
U.S. troops provocatively stationed in a disputed area;
this action prompted the U.S. Congress to declare
war. The resulting Mexican-American War lasted
from 1846 to 1848, ending with a decisive victory for
the United States. In the Treaty of Guadalupe Hidalgo
(in conjunction with the Gadsden Purchase in 1853),
the United States officially gained Texas, California,
and all the land between them. However, Texas had
entered the Union at a time when the very structure
of that Union was becoming tenuous.

Understanding Impact Imagine that you were a member of the United States House of Representatives in 1844 or
1845. Based upon the readings and your knowledge of Texas history, would you vote for the annexation of Texas? What
would have been the strongest arguments *for* and *against* annexation?

The Confederate State of Texas

From 1848 to 1860, settlement of Texas increased dramatically, with more immigrants coming from the southern United States and Europe. Increasingly, Texas's
economy became tied to that of the southern states and the slave system. These
ties were the primary reason Texas seceded from the Union in 1861 and joined
the Confederacy. Texas was not among the first states to secede because its
constitutional requirements were more stringent than those in other southern
states, but in the end, the Confederate flag was the sixth national flag to fly
over Texas.

How to

Read a Map

Maps have been one of the key instruments of exploration, trade, and progress, but many adults have difficulty with map reading—particularly now that so many of us rely on GPS for directions. Being able to read a map allows you to better understand the world in which you live and to acquire valuable historic and geographic knowledge. The ability to comprehend maps is still pivotal while reading textbooks and historical documents, visiting museums and parks, and hiking nature trails. Let's go through the process step by step. Keep in mind that not every map has all the features listed below.

Step 1. Look at the map's orientation.

The first thing to look for is the map's orientation. The compass rose, which sometimes looks like a cross or star, is generally near one of the corners of the map. The compass rose should have four key parts: N (North), S (South), E (East), and W (West). Occasionally, it will point only north, and you will need to deduce the other directions from that. Finding the compass rose is important, since it is rarely helpful to read a map upside down.

Some professional maps of larger areas may even have the longitude and latitude of the area. Longitude measures how far east or west a certain location is; longitudinal lines go from the North to South Pole. Latitude measures how far north or south a certain location is; latitudinal lines are either above or below the Equator.

Step 2. Decide what type of map it is.

Some maps show physical geography: mountains, plains, bodies of water. Others, like Map 1.1, demarcate political borders and the names of political entities such as countries, states, and cities. Still others display historic information, such as a map of troop movements during a battle, or statistical information, such as Map 1.2, which shows population density by Texas county. Some maps even provide thematic information, such as Map 1.3, which classifies U.S. states as having traditionalist, individualistic, or moralistic culture.

Step 3. Examine the map's scale.

A scale is the ratio of what the map is trying to measure. On some maps, an inch or centimeter may measure 1,000 miles. On other maps, it may measure 10 miles. The scale is what allows a given territory to fit on the paper.

Maps sometimes purposefully exaggerate or distort geographic features because paper maps are flat, whereas the actual world is a sphere. Think about what happens when you peel an orange. The peel doesn't lie flat unless you make tears between some of the sections. Those tears are equivalent to the types of distortions it takes to show a round globe on a flat map.

Step 4. Interpret the map key.

The map key, or legend, is a box or chart usually placed near the compass rose. The map key is a directory of all the symbols on the map.

Step 5. Decipher the area you would like to study.

Using the map's orientation, scale, and key, you should be able to find what you are trying to study.

These steps should help you get more out of maps in all sorts of situations—whether you are trying to understand the events of a historic battle or just find the nearest parking lot. The more practice you have reading maps, the more they will teach you.

Civil War and Reconstruction: A Time of Transition

Learning Objective: Describe the Civil War and Reconstruction in Texas.

Few moments in Texas history are more momentous than the state's decision to secede from the Union. The majority of Texans supported secession, including many notable people from the Republic of Texas such as General Albert Sidney Johnston, future governor Francis Lubbock, and future governor Edward

Clark. Many of the secessionists were staunchly in favor of the preservation of slavery, and they feared that the policies of Abraham Lincoln and the newly formed Republican Party would jeopardize the infamous institution. Texas had few Unionists because of the slave question. The most notable Unionist was Sam Houston—the distinguished general and diplomat who guided Texas to independence from Mexico, led the fledging Republic of Texas to join the Union, and served as U.S. senator and governor. Although Houston favored slavery, he still believed that Texas should remain faithful to the Union. Texans evicted Houston from the governorship because he failed to support the Confederacy. The politics around the war were so divisive that many Texans vilified him, friends shunned him, and some people threatened to kill him. Despondent about the future of the place he held so dear, Houston died in 1863. The fact that so many Texans could turn on one of the state's founding leaders only highlights the drama of the Civil War and its later consequences.[7]

Effects of the Civil War

The Civil War was a costly and brutal conflict, but Texas's economy was not as devastated as other Confederate states. Politics and geography combined to create more fortunate circumstances for Texas. The machinations of Emperor Napoleon III of France played a significant role. France had invaded Mexico in 1861. Napoleon's goal was to set up a new government under French protection in Mexico, with Archduke Ferdinand Maximilian of Austria as emperor. Napoleon was openly pro-Confederate but did not want to risk war with the United States. Despite the Confederacy's desperate need for French funds and official recognition, events in Europe combined with U.S. threats to keep the French from fully committing to Confederate support. After the Civil War ended in 1865, the United States stationed 50,000 troops in Texas, primarily along the border with Mexico to oppose the "French intervention." However, conflict did not break out between the United States and Mexico at that time.

Geography also played a role in limiting Texas's exposure to the ravages of war. Anglo southerners had not created many substantial settlements west of the Balcones Escarpment, a natural geological feature that separates the Coastal Plains and pine forest regions of Texas from the middle and High Plains of the state. In fact, white people did not settle in most areas west of this line until after the Civil War, for two reasons. First, the Comanche, Lipan Apache, Kiowa, and Tonkawa already lived in the region. In the 1850s, the U.S. Army tried to control this region by building a series of forts on the edge of the Cross Timbers area. Forts Belknap, Cooper, Phantom Hill, Chadborne, McKavett, and Terrett were part of this plan. During the Civil War, however, the U.S. government abandoned these forts, and the presence of Native American groups in the region reemerged. Indeed, both Union and Confederate forces engaged in skirmishes with Native Americans in Texas during the Civil War. Native American domination of the area continued until 1875, when U.S. forces captured Comanche Chief Quanah Parker in Palo Duro Canyon, near present-day Amarillo. The second geography-related reason settlement was limited was that the dry, arid, treeless plains west of the Balcones Escarpment (Grande Prairie, Cross Timbers, lower plains, and High Plains) were not conducive to the plantation culture that southern Anglos brought with them. This terrain likewise did not offer much food or water for an invading army trying to live off the land.

Battle of Galveston, Harper's Weekly, January 31, 1863
Texas State Library and Archives Commission

Despite Texas's relative fortunate circumstances during the war years from 1861 to 1865, it was the home of some important Civil War events. Foremost among them were the Battle of Sabine Pass and the Battle of Galveston, both fought in 1863. In the former, a small Confederate force prevented a larger Union force, led by General Banks, from moving into Texas. In the latter, Confederate forces on land recaptured Galveston while its naval forces captured the U.S. ship *Harriet Lane,* despite being heavily outnumbered and losing the Confederate vessel *Neptune.* Other noteworthy actions included the Union blockade of the Texas coast, General Henry Sibley's march to El Paso in an attempt to take New Mexico and other federal territories for the Confederacy, and the final land conflict of the war, the Battle of Palmito Ranch (which took place more than a month after Lee's surrender in Virginia). Roughly 90,000 Texans served in the war.[8] The lives lost in battle and the time and money wasted on the conflict devastated Texas and the nation.

Reconstruction in Texas

Immediately after the Civil War, Texas, like many other states of the former Confederacy, found itself deeply in debt and under the military control of the Union army. Reconstruction, which began in 1865, had two primary political goals. First, the Union wanted to restore law and order to a society recovering from war and allow southern states to be readmitted to the Union. Second, the Union sought to finally dismantle the institution of slavery. As historians James M. McPherson and James K. Hogue state, "No single generalization can encompass the variety of ways in which freedom came to the slaves."[9] In Texas, Union General Gordon Granger started the process of emancipation on his arrival at Galveston by issuing General Order Number 3 on June 19, 1865. This order informed Texans that "in accordance with a proclamation from the Executive of the United States, all slaves are free." Importantly, it went on to note that "This involves an absolute equality of personal rights and rights of property between former masters and slaves, and the connection heretofore existing between them becomes that between employer and hired labor." This is the origin of the "Juneteenth" holiday in Texas and other states.[10]

Upon learning of their freedom, former enslaved people were overcome with great jubilation. Many cried, and others danced. The Freedman's Bureau organized the first Juneteenth celebration in Austin in 1867. Since then, many cities and individual families celebrate Juneteenth with barbecues, parties, baseball, concerts, and marches.[11] Some African Americans celebrate Juneteenth not only to commemorate emancipation but also to remember the resilience of African Americans throughout the centuries in facing discrimination and bigotry.[12]

In the aftermath of the Civil War, the United States passed three important constitutional amendments that protected African Americans:

- The Thirteenth Amendment, ratified in 1865, abolished slavery.
- The Fourteenth Amendment, ratified in 1868, declared formerly enslaved people to be American citizens. It mandated that states provide equal protection and due process to all citizens, and it stopped former Confederate leaders from holding federal office (except in cases where Congress voted to lift the ban).
- The Fifteenth Amendment, ratified in 1870, gave Black men the right to vote.

Even though these three amendments became the law of the land, it proved difficult to enforce them without the approval of large parts of the South.

Reconstruction's goals created a culture clash between the two major ideological groups in Texas. The dominant group consisted of Confederate sympathizers (typically southern Democrats) who wanted to maintain the status quo of prewar society as much as possible. The second group was composed of Union supporters, including Republican "**carpetbaggers**," a pejorative term used to describe Republicans who moved to the South to be appointed to political office during Reconstruction, and "scalawags," an equally derisive descriptor of southerners who supported Reconstruction policies. During this time, Republicans in the South were perceived to be outsiders who could not be trusted by "true" (white) southerners.

carpetbagger

People who engage in political activities in a place they do not live. After the American Civil War, people from Union states and elsewhere went to the South to engage in politics and business. Southerners saw them as exploiters and called them "carpetbaggers" because of the type of luggage they typically used.

In 1866, Texas adopted a new constitution that abolished slavery, nullified the ordinances of secession, renounced the right of future secession, and refused to accept responsibility for the state's wartime debt. This constitution was short lived; yet another constitution replaced it in 1869 as a result of the congressional actions and military rule imposed on Texas during Reconstruction. This so-called carpetbagger's constitution was a drastic departure from other Texas constitutions, past and future (see Chapter 2), and granted African Americans the right to vote while also disenfranchising white people who had participated in the Civil War. Texas formally rejoined the Union in 1870.

Republican Edmund Jackson Davis became governor in 1870, but his administration was controversial and unpopular with Texas citizens, who protested taxes and government expenditures during his tenure of office.[13] Southern Democrats were able to regain control of state government with the election of 1874. The new governor, Richard Coke, called for a convention to write yet another constitution. When Texas adopted its new constitution in 1876, the document demonstrated a strong distrust of the institutions of government and a heavy emphasis on the freedoms and liberties of its citizens. The 1876 constitution remains the outline of the fundamental law for the state of Texas, even though it has changed dramatically due to hundreds of amendments over the years. The Coke administration also marked the beginning of one-party Democratic politics in Texas, which lasted about 100 years. Without the legal tools created by the policies of Reconstruction, or the broad political support necessary to win any public office, Republicans began to vanish from the political scene. Democrats were triumphant in Texas. As a result, African Americans lost many rights that they had gained during Reconstruction; as Chapter 9 shows, these rights were not restored until the civil rights movement of the 1960s.

> **Understanding Impact** Some historians and political scientists consider Reconstruction to be a failure because it neither ended regional strife nor secured indefinitely the rights of African Americans. Were these inevitable outcomes? What measures, if any, could have been put in place to establish American unity after the Civil War? What measures were needed to protect African Americans from discrimination?

Post-Reconstruction Texas

Learning Objective: Describe post-Reconstruction Texas.

In 1893, the historian Frederick Jackson Turner famously declared the end of the American frontier.[14] The frontier was a significant symbol and reality for Texans in the nineteenth century. The end of the frontier changed the character of Texas forever. For most of its history, the Lone Star State has had a **land-based economy.** However, that economy has evolved in the many decades following Reconstruction. Texas is no longer simply a rural state with an economy dominated by cattle, cotton, and oil.

land-based economy
An economic system in which most wealth is derived from the use of the land

Land

Early in Texas's history, offers of free land lured many settlers to the region. The Spanish and Mexican governments provided generous land grants to any family willing to settle in the state. Each family could receive one *sitio* or *legua* (Spanish for "league"), the equivalent of about 4,428 acres of land, and a single person could receive 1,500 acres. By the 1820s, it took generous incentives to convince people to settle in Texas, given the hardships of travel and simple survival there. "GTT" ("Gone to Texas") was a common sign left behind by those escaping debt or the long arm of the law. In a letter dated 1855 from Fort Clark, Texas, General P. H. Sheridan said, "If I owned Hell and Texas, I'd rent out Texas and live in Hell."[15]

Land issues also played a role in the Texas revolution in 1836 and annexation of Texas by the United States in 1845. The sheer vastness of Texas—all its acres of land—has played a role in Texas history for generations. Its vastness has enabled the diversification of Texas's economy. The rich soil of East Texas is responsible for the state's timber and a more traditional Southern economy, while other vast areas of Texas land are lush with oil.

Queen of Waco gusher. Spindletop, Beaumont, Port Arthur, and vicinity. Texas oil industry ca. 1901.

Library of Congress Prints and Photographs Division [LC-USZ62-26332]

Transformation of the Texas Economy

From the 1820s to the 1860s, the primary use of Texas's land was for cotton farming. "King Cotton" was the state's major cash crop, helping Texas pay its bills from independence through Reconstruction. In the years following the Civil War, cattle became Texas's economic mainstay. The giant cattle ranches in South and West Texas also helped develop the cowhand culture and mystique of the frontier Texan. In 1901, however, a well in the Spindletop field near Beaumont gushed with oil, and the economy and politics of the state began to change dramatically.

The discovery of oil transformed Texas in three major ways over the next century. First, oil sparked the transition from an agricultural economy to an industrial economy. In addition to jobs directly related to the oil industry, high-tech peripheral jobs and industries developed to support or benefit from the oil industry.[16] Second, it accelerated the growth of Texas's population and brought in new citizens from all over the United States and abroad, looking for work. These new citizens brought with them ideas about government and economics that challenged and diversified the ideas of Texas Democrats and Republicans. Third, oil accelerated the demographic shift from a rural society to an urban society. In 1900, less than 20 percent of Texans lived in urban areas. In 1950, about 63 percent lived in urban areas. By 1990, that number had increased to more than 80 percent.[17]

During the 1970s and early 1980s, the state economy experienced tremendous growth because of an increase in oil prices. But oil was not always reliable. In the mid-1980s, the price of oil declined, and with it the economy of the entire state. To many, the economic recession of the 1980s pointed to a need for more economic diversity. They believed that the old land-based economy, which had been so important in Texas's history, could not carry the state into the twenty-first century.

Passage of the North American Free Trade Agreement (NAFTA), in which the United States, Canada, and Mexico agreed to remove trade barriers between their countries, went into effect in 1994. NAFTA offered the promise of significant economic growth because of increased trade with Mexico. Furthermore, new high-tech industries—especially in Austin, Dallas, and Houston—significantly bolstered the Texas economy. Texas Instruments helped turn the calculator into a common household item in the 1970s, and today's Texas boasts a thriving software, equipment, telecommunications, and semiconductor industry.

Texas has become a leader in scientific and technological research and development. A reliable indicator of technological innovation is the number of international patent applications filed under the Patent Cooperation Treaty. According to the U.S. Patent and Trademark Office, Texas was second among the 50 states in total patents granted in 2020, trailing only California.[18] Although energy and agriculture are still important to the state's economy, many new elements exist today.

The service industry now dominates the Texas economy. According to the U.S. Bureau of Labor Statistics, service-providing industries include trade, transportation, utilities, information and financial activities, real estate, professional and business services, education, health care, and leisure and hospitality, among others. In November 2021, service industries employed roughly 11 million people and more than half of the private-sector workforce in Texas.[19] The state's location, its nearness to Mexico, and its centrality within the continental United States has pushed this sector's growth. Trade has expanded rapidly owing to NAFTA and globalization, and Texas has become a transportation hub. Increased trade has also fueled the growth of professional and business services in accounting, legal services, computer services, construction, engineering, and management. Meanwhile, population expansion has led to a marked increase in the need for health care and education services. Simultaneously, the rise in trade and population has sparked the growth of the leisure and hospitality industry.

Texas has become a major trading power in its own right, leading the 50 U.S. states in exports. When Congress passed NAFTA in 1993, Texas anticipated significant economic growth because of increased trade, primarily with Mexico. Texas has become a major center of international trade. From 2003 to 2020, it led all states in U.S. exports. In 2020, Texas exported $279 billion in goods, whereas California, in second place, exported only $156 billion. Texas by itself accounted for 19.5 percent of all U.S. exports. The state's major trading partners are Mexico and Canada, followed by China, South Korea, Brazil, Japan, and the Netherlands. Still, Mexico's importance is not to be underestimated; that nation alone received more than 31 percent of Texas's exports in 2020. (See Figure 1.1 for major categories of exports.)[20]

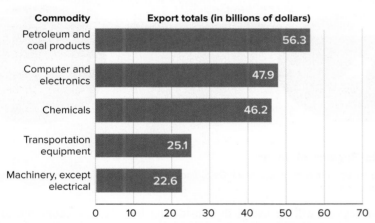

FIGURE 1.1 Top Exports from Texas (in billions of dollars), 2018

Source: State Benefits of Trade, "Office of the United States Trade Representative," https://ustr.gov/map/state-benefits/tx (accessed January 28, 2022)

CORE OBJECTIVE

Communicating Effectively . . .

Write a short synopsis of Texas's changing economy and its role in international trade.

Texas's Economic Regions

The state comptroller's office has divided Texas into 12 **economic regions** as a convenient way to talk about areas of the state.[21] To simplify discussion, this book merges these 12 regions into 6, as shown in Figure 1.2. A basic knowledge

economic regions
Divisions of the state based on dominant economic activity

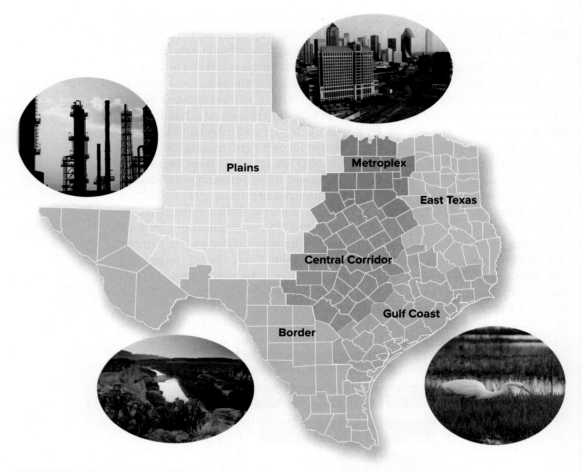

FIGURE 1.2 **Economic Regions of Texas**

Top left: Hal Bergman/E+/Getty Images; top right: floop/iStock/Getty Images; bottom left: ericfoltz/E+/Getty Images; bottom right: gacooksey/E+/Getty Images

of these regions will be useful in considering how Texas's economic diversity affects its government.

The East Texas or Piney Woods region was traditionally dominated by agriculture, timber, and oil. Today, agriculture is less important, and oil is declining, but timber is still important. Some diversification has occurred, with manufacturing becoming more significant.

The Plains region of the state, with Lubbock and Amarillo as its major cities, has historically been dominated by agriculture (especially cotton, wheat, and maize) and by ranching and cattle feedlots. Currently, its economy is shaped by animal production and agriculture, oil and gas extraction, rail and pipeline transportation, and food manufacturing.

The Gulf Coast region, extending from Corpus Christi to Beaumont/Port Arthur/Orange and including Houston, is dominated by petrochemical industries, manufacturing, shipping, and fishing. In recent years, this area has further diversified with the addition of high-tech industries. It is also the area with the highest concentration of organized labor unions in the state.

The border area of South Texas and the Rio Grande Valley, stretching from Brownsville to El Paso, is noted primarily for its agricultural production of citrus fruits and vegetables. In recent years, trade with Mexican border cities has diversified the economy of this region, a process increased by the passage of NAFTA.

The Metroplex, or Dallas–Fort Worth area, is considered the financial center of the state. This region is the most economically diversified, with a combination of banking, manufacturing, high-tech, and aerospace industries.

The Central Corridor, or midstate region, is an area stretching roughly from College Station in the east to Waco in the north and Austin and San Antonio in the southwest. This area is dominated by three large state universities—the University of Texas at Austin, Texas A&M University, and Texas State University—along with high-tech industries in Austin and San Antonio and major military bases in the Waco/Temple/Killeen and San Antonio areas.

Texas Politics: From Democrat to Republican

The Democratic Party dominated Texas politics from the end of Reconstruction until the mid-1970s. In the absence of a strong and viable Republican Party, third parties became the main challengers to the Democratic Party during the **Progressive Era** of American politics. Groups such as the Greenback Party, the Farmers Alliance, and the Populists became known as progressives because they believed in the "doctrine of progress"—the concept that people can improve governing institutions by using science to solve public problems.[22] Each of these groups wanted to use government to positively affect the economy, by either increasing the value of agriculture or reining in the power of business and banking.[23] The Democratic Party successfully responded to these challenges by adopting many progressive reform proposals into its own platform. By the start of the twentieth century, Texas was effectively a one-party state with Progressive Democrats and Conservative Democrats contesting offices. A lack of meaningful competition from Republicans often led to straight-ticket party voting in elections. The term "Yellow Dog Democrat," coined to describe someone who would vote only for Democratic candidates, aptly described the voting habits of many Texans. The term derived from an old saying: "He would vote for a yellow dog if it ran as a Democrat."

From the 1920s through World War II, the oil industry helped shape state and local politics. Most Texas Democrats were conservative. Conservative business interests actually aligned more with the national Republican Party at times, and the state supported Herbert Hoover in 1928—one of only four instances from the end of Reconstruction to the mid-1970s in which a majority of Texas voters favored the Republican candidate in a presidential election.[24] The Great Depression, a severe economic downturn that lasted throughout the 1930s, soured Texans on the Republican Party again because Hoover was in office when the bad times hit. The Democratic New Deal, which offered many forms of relief and reform, brought Texans back into the party fold. Progressive Democrats supporting jobs programs and military development helped attract more liberal-minded citizens to the party.

The next time a majority of Texas voters supported the Republican candidate was in 1952, when Dwight Eisenhower was elected president. He was backed by the "Shivercrats," a faction of Texas Democrats who followed conservative Democratic governor Allan Shivers. Texans supported Eisenhower again in 1956.

As the national Democratic Party increased the federal government's role in the lives of individuals and businesses through the New Deal, the Fair Deal, and Great Society programs, conservative Texas Democrats became disenchanted with the national party and chose not to support it in national races. This coincided with an increase in the number of liberal Democrats joining the

Progressive Era
A movement in the late nineteenth and early twentieth centuries that sought increased federal and state government regulation to help wipe out economic, social, and political ills

civil rights movement
A political movement, primarily in the 1950s and 1960s, that demanded equal civil rights for people of color

party and achieving leadership positions. The **civil rights movement** of the late 1950s and 1960s also pushed socially conservative Democrats away from the Democratic Party and started pulling them toward the Republican Party. John Tower's 1961 election, the first time Texas had sent a Republican to the U.S. Senate since 1870, reflected the beginning of this shift.[25] A majority of Texas voters supported Richard Nixon, a Republican, for president in 1972.

This pattern of supporting Republicans for national political offices eventually evolved into supporting Republican candidates for state offices (for example, Bill Clements for governor in 1978) and, eventually, supporting Republican candidates for local office. Beginning with the election of Ronald Reagan in 1980, a majority of Texans have voted Republican in every presidential election to date.[26] Texas fully transitioned from a predominantly Democratic majority to a fully Republican state-wide majority by 2002. After the 1994 political party realignment, which swept away Democratic majorities in the U.S. House and Senate, Texans voted a large sector of experienced, powerful Democratic officeholders out of public office. Anglo male voters, as well as businesses and conservatives seeking big changes in the state's legal and regulatory system, supported Republican candidates at all levels. By 1998, all statewide elective officeholders were Republicans, and by 2002, the Texas House of Representatives had a Republican majority for the first time in its history due, in part, to redistricting. (See the Chapter 3 section titled "Reapportionment and Redistricting" for an in-depth discussion of redistricting.)

There are other, nonideological reasons for the shift toward a one-party, Republican state. Culturally, there are likely many more individuals who would self-identify as Democrats or who would vote for Democratic candidates than are currently registered or voting. Structurally, however, there are problems with making today's Democratic Party a competitive entity. Many likely Democratic voters either do not register or do not vote (see Chapter 9 for more on why people vote). Some independents might vote Democratic if that party had a better chance of winning statewide seats or legislative control. However, redistricting has virtually guaranteed Republican majorities in the state and federal representative races.

Reaction to the Obama presidency in 2010 and 2012 energized small-government and social conservatives to run for office, and many unseated a number of long-standing Democrats in both the state and U.S. House of Representatives. However, in 2013, Democratic operatives launched "Battleground Texas," a **political action committee (PAC)** whose goal was to revitalize the Democratic Party in the state and ultimately "turn Texas blue."[27]

political action committee (PAC)
A spin-off of an interest group that collects money for campaign contributions and other activities

The success of the Battleground Texas movement has been mixed. On the one hand, Texas remains a reliably Republican state. Republican Texas governor Greg Abbott handily defeated Democratic gubernatorial nominees Wendy Davis in 2014 and Lupe Valdez in 2018. Moreover, all statewide elected officials of the executive branch are Republican. On the other hand, Democrats made gains at both the federal and state level due to enthusiasm sparked by Beto O'Rourke, who challenged Republican Ted Cruz in the 2018 senate race. Cruz won reelection, but O'Rourke came within three points of defeating him. O'Rourke paved the way for potential Democratic gains in traditionally Republican suburbs. For example, Democrat Colin Allred, a former NFL football player, defeated Pete Sessions, a stalwart of the Republican Party, in the race to represent a federal congressional district that includes northeastern Dallas and nearby suburbs.[28]

The election of 2020 produced mixed results for both Republicans and Democrats. Trump carried Texas, but by a smaller margin than his 2016 victory.

John Cornyn, the Republican incumbent for Senate, outperformed Trump by carrying the state by almost 10 points. Overall, Democrats appeared to have made gains in the suburbs, especially with white women. However, the Republicans made significant gains with Hispanic Americans voters, especially in South Texas.

In 2022, Texas will receive two new federal congressional districts. The 37th district was designed to create a safe Democratic seat in Travis County. The 38th district was constructed to create a relatively safe Republican seat in the suburbs of Houston. The majority of the remaining districts at the federal level are Republican-leaning districts. The majority of state level districts are also Republican-leaning which allows the GOP to maintain their hold of the Texas House.[29] In the midterm election, Greg Abbott won a third term as governor by defeating Beto O'Rourke, a 2020 Democratic presidential candidate, by over 10 percentage points.

CORE OBJECTIVE

Taking Personal Responsibility . . .

What can you do to become well informed about political issues so that you can make effective decisions at election time?

Demographics: The Road to Majority-Minority

Demography refers to the statistical characteristics of a population. Typically, data used to develop and describe population statistics come from the United States Census, which the government conducts every 10 years. Regardless of the best efforts of workers, the census is subject to error, particularly in the form of an undercount. Nonetheless, census questions and the information from them provide a means of measuring meaningful features of a population. Population trends reflect much about the political, social, and cultural features of a given region, so they are important indicators for government at all levels. Population data allow governments to plan well, and well in advance, in providing the vital needs for which they are responsible.

demography
The scientific study of a population

Of the 50 states, Texas ranks second not only in total land size but also in terms of population. Moreover, that population has been growing at an explosive rate. In 1970, Texas's population was 11.2 million; by 1990, it had increased to almost 17 million. In 2010, the U.S. Census Bureau calculated the state's official population at 25,145,561. The 2021 estimate jumped to 29,527,941, reflecting an increase of about 5.4 million residents over 11 years.[30] (See Figure 1.3 for a comparison of the Lone Star State's population growth with that of other populous states.) Although birthrates account for part of this growth, it is also attributable to the arrival of newcomers from other states and countries.

This incredible growth has affected Texas's standing in national politics. As a result of the 2010 Census, Texas was awarded four more seats—the biggest gain of any state—in the U.S. House of Representatives.[31] Due to the 2020 Census, Texas gained two federal congressional seats for a total of thirty-eight. Texas was one of six states to gain congressional seats, and the only state to receive two new seats.[32]

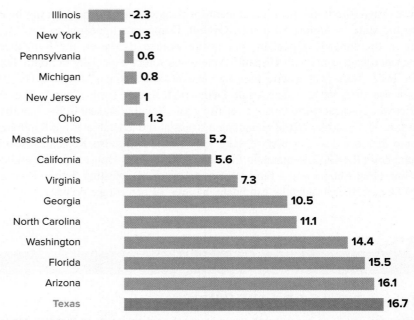

FIGURE 1.3 Percentage Change in Population for the 15 Most Populous States, 2010–2020

Source: Adapted from the U.S. Census Bureau, "State Populations Totals and Estimated Components of Change: 2010–2020," Table 1: Annual Estimates of the Resident Population of the United States, Regions, States, the District of Columbia, and Puerto Richo: April 1, 2020 to July 1, 2020, https://www.census.gov/programs-surveys/popest/technical-documentation/research/evaluation-estimates/2020-evaluation-estimates/2010s-state-total.html (accessed January 24, 2022).

Urban and Rural

As *The Economist* noted, "The imagery of Texas is rural—cattle, cotton, cowboys and, these days, wind turbines whirring against the endless sky. But the reality is increasingly urban."[33] Although definitions of rural and urban can vary, the U.S. Census Bureau uses the following distinction for densely populated areas: "Urbanized Areas (UAs) consist of 50,000 or more people; Urban Clusters (UCs) comprise at least 2,500 but less than 50,000 people, and 'rural' encompasses all population, housing, and territory not included within an urban area."[34] According to the definition used by the U.S. Census, 20.4 percent of Texans lived in rural areas in 1980, 17.5 percent in 2000, and less than 15 percent in 2020.[35] In other words, while the overall population of Texas has increased, the proportion of Texans living in rural areas is declining. The state comptroller's office has projected that over the next 40 years, urban areas will continue to grow much more rapidly than rural areas.[36] In Map 1.2, the urban nature of today's Texas is apparent, with so many Texans living in a handful of populous counties.

As a result of the 2020 Census, Texas has two new congressional districts, District 37 and 38. District 37 consists of a significant portion of Travis County, west of I-35 in Austin. District 38, on the other hand, covers portions of western Houston and some of the city's northwestern suburbs. Thus, both of the seats reflect the drastic population growth in largely urban and suburban areas. District 37 was designed to be a safe Democratic seat and District 38 is likely to be a safe Republican seat.[37]

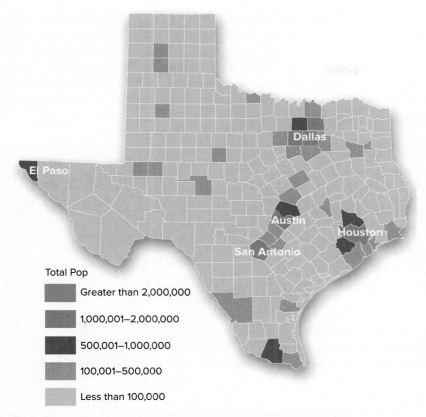

MAP 1.2   Population Density* in Texas by County, 2020

*Population density equals population divided by square mileage of the area in which they live.

Texas Demographic Center. "Redistricting Data for Texas, 2010–2020." https://idser.maps.arcgis.com/apps/MapSeries/index.html?appid=5de0798d9d8646c6a3b6f4bfd2193d93.

Understanding Impact In light of the results of the 2016 presidential election cycle, political scientists are revisiting the difference between urban and rural areas. Urban and rural areas are increasingly voting for different candidates. Why would urban areas vote differently than rural areas? What economic and social issues divide them? What issues could reunite them?

Majority-Minority

Since 2004, Texas has been a **"majority-minority"** state; racial and ethnic minority groups now form a majority of the population and outnumber the non-Hispanic white population.[38] As of 2021, non-Hispanic white Americans made up 41.2 percent of the total state population, making them a numerical, statistical minority.[39] Public school enrollments have been majority-minority for some time. According to the Texas Education Agency, 2001–2002 was the first school year in which Hispanic American students outnumbered whites. By 2020–2021, Hispanic American enrollment was more than half of all students (52.9 percent), and white enrollment had declined to 26.5 percent of the total school population.[40] These changes in majority and minority statistical status have significant implications for state politics and public policy decisions.

majority-minority
Ethnic and racial minority groups make up a majority of the population of the state

Hispanic immigration from Mexico to Texas has steadily increased over the course of the past half century and has become a major factor in state politics. In 1960, Hispanic Americans represented 15 percent of the total population of Texas. The Hispanic population increased to 18 percent by 1970, 21 percent in 1980, and 25 percent in 1990. According to the U.S. Census Bureau, Hispanic or Latino Americans made up 39.7 percent of the state's total population in 2021.[41]

Focus On

How the Government Defines "Hispanic"

Many forms ask respondents to indicate whether or not they are "Hispanic" or "Latino," but what do these terms mean? How do people and the government define "Hispanic" and "Latino"? As with many questions, the answer depends on whom you ask!

First championed by a Hispanic American bureaucrat in the 1970s,[42] U.S. government use of the term "Hispanic" has grown steadily. One of the earliest references was a 1976 law directing various federal departments to collect data regarding "Americans of Spanish origin or descent."[43] This group was originally defined as people who are "of Spanish-speaking background and trace their origin or descent from Mexico, Puerto Rico, Cuba, Central and South America, and other Spanish-speaking

Darren Brode/Shutterstock

countries."[44] The actual term "Hispanic" first appeared on U.S. Census forms in 1980.[45] In 1997, the federal Office of Management and Budget (OMB) revised the definition of "Hispanic" to refer to "persons who trace their origin or descent to Mexico, Puerto Rico, Cuba, Central and South America, and other Spanish cultures." The OMB also began to use "Latino" in conjunction with "Hispanic" at that time. As justification, the OMB cited regional conventions, suggesting that "Hispanic" was often used in the eastern United States and "Latino" preferred in the western United States.[46] (In some contexts, "Latino" may be a more inclusive term reflecting origins anywhere in Latin America—such as Brazil, where Portuguese is the primary language—and not just Spanish-speaking countries. Others have suggested the use of "Latino/Latina" or "Latinx" may be associated with certain age groups or political affiliations.)[47]

Despite the existence of these official governmental definitions, no proof or documentation is required to establish membership in this group. For census purposes, determining whether someone is Hispanic is based solely on self-identification. In other words, if one says one is Hispanic or Latino, then one is considered Hispanic or Latino.[48] According to the federal government's approach, race is a separate classification. The Census Bureau states people "who report themselves as Hispanic can be of any race."[49] This may differ from the perception of many Hispanic Americans. According to a recent study by Pew Research Center, more than half of Hispanic adults surveyed considered their Hispanic background to be part of both their origin and their race.[50] Much of the demographic information in this book is based on census data.

Critical Thinking Questions

1. Why might the federal government collect data regarding particular ethnic groups?
2. In what way is the federal government's definition of the term "Hispanic" appropriate or inappropriate? What might be a better definition?

As the Hispanic population continues to grow, Hispanic Americans have increased voter turnout in the border areas, in some sections of South Texas and the Gulf Coast, and in the San Antonio area. They have elected local officials to city and county government and school boards, to the state legislature, and to Congress. The first Hispanic American either appointed or elected to statewide office was Raul Gonzalez, in 1984, to the Texas Supreme Court.[51] Dan Morales was subsequently elected state attorney general in 1990 and served until 1999. In 2002, Tony Sanchez was the first Hispanic American to become a major-party candidate for governor. The 2012 election of Ted Cruz to the U.S. Senate marked the first time the state sent a Hispanic American to the upper chamber of Congress.[52] In 2015, George P. Bush (whose mother, Columba, is a native of Mexico who became a U.S. citizen in 1979) took office as Commissioner of the General Land Office (the state's fifth-highest elected position), and Carlos Cascos was appointed Texas secretary of state.[53] In the 2018 midterm election, Sylvia Garcia of Houston and Veronica Escobar of El Paso became the first two Hispanic women elected to the House of Representatives in Texas history.[54] In 2020, Republicans made significant gains with Hispanic Americans, especially in the Rio Grande Valley, where Trump received over 40 percent of the vote from Hidalgo, Cameron, and Starr counties.

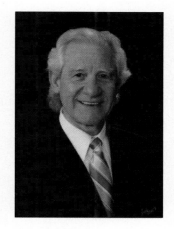

Raul A. Gonzalez Jr.
Raul A. Gonzalez

The Hispanic population has grown as a percentage of total state population since the 1960s, but the African American population has remained fairly constant over that period. The 2019 estimate for African Americans was 12.8 percent of the population.[55] African Americans tend to be concentrated in three metropolitan areas: Houston, Dallas–Fort Worth, and Austin. African Americans have had some political success winning election to local offices (school boards, city councils, and county offices) and the state legislature, in addition to winning a few seats in the U.S. Congress. Currently, in the U.S. House of Representatives there are several powerful and influential African American representatives. Houston's Al Green was the first to call for President Trump's impeachment, and southern Texas's Will Hurd was one of the few Black Republican members of Congress until his retirement from Congress in 2020.[56]

Morris Overstreet was the first African American to be elected to statewide office. From 1990 to 1999, Judge Overstreet served on the Texas Court of Criminal Appeals, the highest court for criminal matters in the state. In 1999, Michael L. Williams was the first African American appointed to the Texas Railroad Commission; he was subsequently elected in three elections. In 2001, Wallace B. Jefferson became the first African American to sit on the Texas Supreme Court. From 2004 to 2013, he served as the first Black chief justice of the Texas Supreme Court. In 2002, Dale Wainwright was also elected to the Texas Supreme Court.[57] In 2002, Ron Kirk, the popular African American mayor of Dallas, ran for a U.S. Senate seat. Although polls showed Kirk to be in a dead heat with Republican John Cornyn, Kirk lost the race by a margin of almost 12 percent (43 percent for Kirk compared to 55 percent for Cornyn).[58]

Asian Americans were less than 1 percent of the population of Texas in 1980 but made up 5.2 percent of the state population by 2019.[59] The state's Asian American population is projected to increase in the years ahead. In fact, the state demographer's office argues that "the non-Hispanic Other group, consisting of mostly Asian Americans, will grow at the fastest rate, when compared to other racial-ethnic categories."[60] Most of Texas's Asian American population is concentrated in the Houston area. In fact, one section of Houston has such a large proportion of Chinese Americans that some of the street signs are in Chinese. However, there are also significant concentrations of Korean Americans in the Dallas–Fort Worth Metroplex and in Killeen. Asian Americans in the Houston area have had some success in electing local officials, including one city council member and a county court of law judge. In 2002, Martha Wong was elected to represent the Houston area in the Texas statehouse. Wong was only the second Asian American to serve in the Texas House and the first Republican of Asian descent. In 2004, Hubert Vo was the first Vietnamese American elected to serve as a state representative, and he continues to represent his Houston area district. The first Asian American elected to the Texas House was Tom Lee from San Antonio. As of 2019, there have been five Asian Americans in the Texas House, including three in the current legislature.[61]

Religion in Texas

Religion in Texas bears the Roman Catholic imprint of its Spanish and Mexican roots as well as the conservative Protestantism of its later Anglo settlers. Approximately 82 percent of Texans affiliate with a religious tradition (see Table 1.1). About 3 in 4 Texans identify as Christians, with Protestants accounting for 50 percent of the population and Catholics accounting for another 23 percent.[62]

The Roman Catholic Church's presence in Texas dates back to the sixteenth century, when almost all of the Spanish settlers were Catholic. Although the influence of Catholicism waned in the nineteenth century with the rise of white Protestant immigration, it is now witnessing a resurgence of political and social clout due to the influx of Latin American immigration. Interestingly, Catholic theology and the political positions of the United States Conference of Catholic Bishops (USCCB) do not neatly align with any particular party. On social issues, the Catholic bishops hold similar views to the Republican Party on abortion and same-sex marriage. However, due to the contemporary debates on sanctuary cities and the rise of undocumented workers, the Catholic bishops have promoted immigration policies that are closer to those of the Democratic Party.[63] As a consequence, sometimes the Catholic Church gets criticized from both sides of the aisle for its political stances.

Due in part to the state's large population of evangelical Protestants and its large metropolitan areas, Texas is home to some of America's largest churches. The Houston area, for example, boasts the largest congregation in the United States: Joel Osteen's Lakewood Church has a weekly attendance in excess of 40,000. According to the Hartford Institute for Religion Research, 207 Protestant churches in Texas have an average weekly attendance of at least 2,000 persons, making them "megachurches."[64]

Religion is also an important feature of Texas politics, and Republican politics in particular. For example, the Governor's Response Against Child Exploitation (GRACE) hosts an annual Week of Prayer to End Human Trafficking with daily nondenominational prayer intentions to combat various aspects of trafficking.[65]

Lakewood Church, the largest congregation in the country, meets in a former sports arena in Houston.

Eric Kayne/Houston Chronicle/AP Images

TABLE 1.1	
Religious Affiliation in Texas	
Evangelical Protestant	31%
Mainline Protestant	13%
Historically Black Protestant	6%
Catholic	23%
Mormon	1%
Jehovah's Witness	1%
Orthodox Christian	< 1%
Other Christian	1%
Jewish	1%
Muslim	1%
Buddhist	1%
Hindu	1%
Other World Religions	< 1%
Other Faiths	1%
Unaffiliated	18%

Source: U.S. Religious Landscape Survey, Pew Research Center, 2014.

Mainline and Evangelical Protestants tend to be Republican. Protestants of the Black church tradition, those who identify as atheist or agnostic, and those who do not identify with an organized religion are overwhelmingly Democratic. Catholics in Texas lean slightly to the Democratic Party (see Figure 1.4).

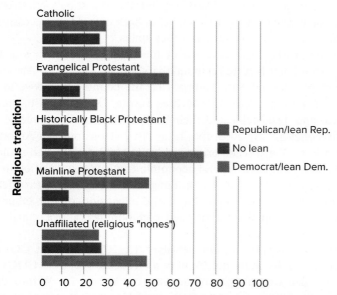

FIGURE 1.4   Party Identification of Texas Voters by Religious Affiliation

Source: Pew Research Center, Religious Landscape Study, "Party Affiliation among Adults in Texas," http://www.pewforum.org/religious-landscape-study/state/texas/partyaffiliation/ (accessed May 15, 2018).

CORE OBJECTIVE

Being Socially Responsible . . .

Understanding the relationship between religious affiliations and politics can improve civic knowledge. How would you use this knowledge to engage effectively in your community? Think about your own religious affiliations (if any) and political beliefs and how they compare with those of your neighbors. How might knowing your neighbors' religious affiliations help you better understand their political views?

Challenges in Texas

Learning Objective: Explain the challenges facing Texas today.

Texas faces national issues that affect all states to some degree, as well as issues specific to the state. The impact of these issues on the state and the state's role in the nation are crucial to understanding today's Texas government.

Challenges to the Texas Economy

Texas's diverse and growth-oriented economy weathered the 2008 financial meltdown-turned-recession better than many other large states. Texas had diversified and transitioned its economy to a combination of energy, agriculture, trade, and an array of professional and business services, utilities, and general services. Due in part to this diversification and the state's relatively business-friendly fiscal and regulatory policies, Texas both entered the recession later and emerged from it more quickly than other states.[66]

During the 2010s, Texas had one of the strongest economies in the United States. The Brookings Institution found that four cities in Texas—Austin, Houston, Dallas–Fort Worth, and San Antonio—led the country in recovering from the recession.[67] Several corporations, such as Toyota, Oracle, Hewitt Packard, PGA of America, and Tesla relocated their headquarters to Texas due to the state's tax-friendly policies.[68] By 2018, five Texas cities—Houston, San Antonio, Austin, Dallas, and Fort Worth—each expanded by 140,000 people within the last eight years.[69] As a consequence, several economic challenges intensified in urban and suburban areas: increased gridlock, congested interstates, gentrification, new construction projects and skyscrapers, the expansion of the suburbs through more housing developments and gated communities, and a sharp increase in home prices.

Then the coronavirus hit. On February 13, 2020, the first COVID-19 case was confirmed in Texas by the Centers for Disease Control (CDC). Governor Greg Abbott declared a state of disaster on March 13. Within days of the announcement, major cities, like Dallas and Houston, began to close bars and to ban in-person dining in restaurants. For much of 2020, evictions were halted, the Southern border with Mexico was closed, social gatherings were limited to ten people, elective medical procedures were postponed, visitation to nursing homes was curtailed, and travelers from out-of-state were expected to quarantine. By April, unemployment in Texas jumped to 12.9 percent. Like many Republican states, Texas tried to re-open earlier than Democratic states. In May 2020, certain businesses, such as restaurants and retail outlets, opened at limited capacity. In June, however, when the number of new COVID-19 cases spiked again, Abbott ordered a state-wide mask mandate. Throughout 2020, tension flared between Abbott, who was concerned about the state of Texas's economy, and many more liberal cities and municipalities, who passed more stringent precautionary safety measures. By December, however, the unemployment rate dropped to 8.1 percent.[70]

The vaccine for coronavirus rolled out in Texas in 2021. By early August, 2021, 15 million Texans received at least one shot of the vaccine.[71] The administration of the vaccine provided an impetus for millions of Americans to return to some semblance of normalcy. Unemployment in Texas decreased to 6.5 percent in May 2021 and then to 5 percent in December 2021. By early 2022, there were 13.06 million nonagricultural jobs within the state of Texas—89,600 more jobs than had existed in February 2020 (the last relatively normal month before the coronavirus impacted greatly the economy). Additionally, the GDP (i.e., the total value of all the services and goods created in Texas) stood at $1.8 trillion as of the third quarter of 2021, bringing it back to pre-pandemic levels.[72] Overall, Texas's economy began to recover despite the prevalence of new strains of coronavirus. Throughout 2022, new problems began to emerge. Texas, like the rest of the country, grappled with supply chain problems, the shortage of certain goods (like baby formula), significant inflation, palpable strains on elementary and secondary education, an increasingly expensive housing market, and a worker shortage for low-paying jobs. The political tensions among conservatives and progressives intensified further due to their different interpretations of how the government responded to the coronavirus during the Biden Administration.

National Issues

The issues of education and income garner perennial attention on the national stage. These issues are interconnected because ample research has demonstrated that individuals with higher educational attainment tend to have higher earnings.[73] On the other hand, low incomes may adversely impact educational attainment because higher education is expensive.

Income and Poverty

Available figures suggest that, on average, incomes in Texas run slightly lower than the national mean, and poverty rates track higher than the national average. According to data from the U.S. Bureau of Economic Analysis, in the third quarter of 2021, the Texas per capita personal income of $58,542 fell slightly below the third quarter's national average of $62,866.[74] Likewise Texas's median household income of $61,874 was lower than the national average of $62,843. In 2021, Texas had a poverty rate of 13.4 percent, compared to 11.4 percent for the U.S. overall.[75]

Education

States are constantly collecting data about and making changes to their educational systems in an effort to improve educational outcomes. Texas is no exception. (See the Chapter 13 section titled "Primary and Secondary Education in

Texas" for a detailed discussion of education policy.) For seven consecutive years, the state has reported rising high school graduation rates. The class of 2020 (the most recent class for which data are available) had an on-time graduation rate of 90.3 percent; in other words, 90 percent of high school students completed their diploma in four years. The Texas Education Agency (TEA), which oversees public K–12 education in Texas, has credited the efforts of teachers and students across the state for this improvement; skeptics have alleged that data manipulation accounts for the impressive statistics.[76] Census Bureau data suggest that Texas continues to lag behind the national average in terms of its proportion of adults aged 25 or older who have graduated from high school or completed a bachelor's degree.[77]

According to Steve Murdock, former Census Bureau chief during the Bush administration and former state demographer of Texas, poverty typically influences educational attainment.[78] This relationship is evident on closer examination of the state's public school dropout numbers. Students who were economically disadvantaged had a graduation rate of 87.5 percent in 2018, while those who were not economically disadvantaged had a graduation rate of 93.5 percent. The dropout rate was higher among Hispanic and African American students than for Asian and white students.[79]

Immigration and In-Migration Today

Texas has been affected by two types of migration: movement of people into Texas from other U.S. states (often called in-migration) and from other countries (immigration).

In-Migration

A look at population trends in the twenty-first century indicates that in-migration to Texas from other states is a reflection of both push and pull forces. In particular, economic, social, and political trends outside the state are pushing people to leave their home states and, in many cases, come to Texas. Many people moved to Texas after the devastation caused by Hurricane Katrina in 2005. However, other factors specific to Texas, such as the relatively inexpensive housing market and appealing natural and business climate in the state, continue to attract, or pull, a significant amount of people. According to State Demographer Lloyd Potter, Texas is growing at a rate of 1,000 people a day. Since 2010, 29 percent of the population growth comes from in-migration.[80]

Migration to Texas from other states over past decades has generally reflected well-established patterns of movement, primarily from the rust-belt states of Ohio, Michigan, and New York, and secondarily from California and Florida. More recently, California and Florida, the nation's most populous and third most populous states, respectively, have tended to outpace the other states in migration to Texas. High-tech workers, in particular, have been drawn to the Texas job market, and the devastation in Florida's housing market due to the recession led to an exodus from that state.[81] In 2019, California and Florida continued to be the most likely states of origin for in-migrants to Texas (see Table 1.2). Other large contributors to the Texas population included

TABLE 1.2

Migration to Texas from Other States, 2019

California	82,235
Florida	41,238
Louisiana	24,513
Georgia	24,209
Illinois	23,747
Oklahoma	23,535
New Mexico	23,425

Source: U.S. Census Bureau, "State-to-State Migration Flows, 2019," https://www.census.gov/data/tables/time-series/demo/geographic-mobility/state-to-state-migration.html (accessed January 28, 2022).

Louisiana, Oklahoma, Colorado, Missouri, Illinois, New York, Virginia, and Arizona.[82]

Immigration

Push and pull factors also affect international migration to Texas. Texas continues to be an attractive location for immigrants both legal and illegal, but such migration will depend in part on political and economic conditions in the United States and other countries. Because of its long contiguous border with Mexico, Texas is a natural draw for Mexican people. Mexico has traditionally been the leading country of origin for both legal and illegal immigrants to the United States. In 2019, the United States admitted 153,502 legal immigrants from Mexico, more than from any other single nation.[83] According to a report by the Department of Homeland Security, 11.4 million unauthorized immigrants resided in the United States in 2018. An estimated 5.4 million Mexican unauthorized immigrants were living in the United States with an estimated 1.9 million unauthorized immigrants living in Texas.[84] In the immediate aftermath of the recession, the number of Mexican immigrants returning to Mexico exceeded the number coming to the United States. By 2018, however, this trend had reversed. During the Trump Administration, a surge of unauthorized immigrants from Mexico and Central Mexico significantly strained border control. A similar surge occurred in the beginning of the Biden Administration. The influx of immigrants, refugees, and asylum seekers seems to correspond with Republican gains among Hispanics in Southern Texas who want tighter border security. Governor Greg Abbott, a critic of the Biden Administration, launched the building of a border wall using state money.[85]

There is also a significant amount of immigration from Asia in Texas. Asian Americans constitute about 5 percent of Texas's population, but they are the fastest-growing ethnic group in the state. In particular, the Asian Indian, Vietnamese, and Chinese populations are growing. There is also a notable share of Filipino, Korean, and Pakistani Americans in Texas. Lila Valencia, a senior demographer with the Texas Demographic Center, predicts that the Asian population will continue to increase rapidly in Texas.[86]

Focus On

Increasing Religious Diversity in Texas

Although Christianity remains the most populous religion, there is increased religious diversity in the United States. About 70 percent of Americans are Christians and about 22 percent are unaffiliated with any religion. Jews constitute about 2 percent of the population, while Muslims, Buddhists, and Hindus each represent less than 1 percent.[87]

Like most Southern states, Texas was a largely Christian state. Texas never had a significant Jewish population, like New York or New Jersey. Texas, for example, has had only one Jewish Speaker of the House: Joe Straus, a moderate Republican from San Antonio.[88] Before the Hart-Cellar Act of 1965, which overturned decades-old restrictions on immigration, there were only a few thousand Muslim, Buddhist, Hindu, and Sikh Americans in Texas. However, these religions

Mohammad Khursheed/Reuters/Newscom

are growing in Texas due to immigration from Asia and in-migration from other states. Currently, there are about 420,000 Muslim Americans and 50,000 Sikhs in Texas. There are also several Buddhist and Hindu temples in urban areas.[89]

Over the last few years, there has been a resurgence of anti-Semitism around the country. On January 15, 2022, a gunman, Malik Faisal Akram, held four people, including a rabbi, hostage at the Beth Israel Synagogue in a Dallas-Fort Worth suburb.[90] Likewise, Muslims in Texas occasionally face various forms of Islamophobia. For example, on January 28, 2017, the Victoria Islamic Center in Victoria, Texas, was burned down by Marq Vincent Perez, who was later convicted in federal court for the hate crime.[91]

The Anti-Defamation League tracks the yearly incidents of anti-Semitism both in Texas and throughout the United States.[92] Likewise, in Texas, Muslim Americans are becoming politically active. Since 2003, Muslim Capitol Day brings thousands of Muslim Americans and their allies to rally and lobby for civil liberties and other pertinent political issues.[93]

Critical Thinking Questions
1. What obstacles and difficulties do members of religious minorities have in Texas and the United States?
2. What can we do as citizens to promote a more inclusive environment for members of religious minorities?

Understanding Impact Now that you have an overview of in-migration and immigration, how have these two movements affected your hometown? Have you witnessed a significant influx of people moving to your neighborhood? How has it influenced your family, friends, school, church, work, and community?

Texas Political Culture

Learning Objective: Explain U.S. and Texas political cultures.

political culture
A system of beliefs and values that defines the role of government and the role of citizens in that government

Certain images come to mind when thinking of Texas: boots, cattle ranching, George Strait, football, and the Alamo, among many others. All of these represent certain aspects of Texas culture. The **political culture** of Texas is something different and more focused than that. Political culture consists of the attitudes, values, and beliefs that most people in a political community have about the proper role of government. This system of beliefs essentially defines the role of government and the role of citizens within that government. Although the average person might not know much about how government works, most people do have views or opinions, even if poorly defined, about what government should and should not do and what their own personal responsibility should be.

Types of Political Culture

In the mid-1960s, Daniel J. Elazar, in his book *American Federalism: A View from the States,* developed a system for classifying different types of political culture in the 50 states. That system is still relevant today. Elazar described three distinctive political subcultures in the United States: moralistic, individualistic, and traditionalistic.[94]

In the **moralistic subculture,** politics "is considered one of the great activities of [people in their] search for the good society . . . an effort to exercise power for the betterment of the commonwealth."[95] In other words, government is viewed as a positive instrument for change and a means of promoting all citizens' general welfare. In the moralistic subculture, politics is regarded as the responsibility of all citizens, who have an obligation to participate in government. Individuals seek leadership roles in government not for personal gain, but from a desire to serve the public. In addition, the government has a right and an obligation to intervene in the private affairs of citizens when deemed necessary for the "public good or the well-being of the community."[96]

moralistic subculture
Government viewed as a positive force to achieve a common good for all citizens

An **individualistic subculture** "emphasizes the conception of the democratic order as a marketplace. In its view, a government is created for strictly utilitarian reasons, to handle those functions demanded by the people it is created to serve."[97] That is, government is not concerned with the creation of a "good society," and government intervention in the private sector should be kept to a minimum. From this perspective, politics is not a profession of high calling, but rather something that should be left to those willing to dirty their hands. Participation is considered a necessary evil but not an obligation of every citizen.

individualistic subculture
Government that benefits the individual rather than society in general

The primary function of the **traditionalistic subculture** is maintenance of the existing political order, and participation is confined to a small, self-perpetuating elite. The public has only limited power and influence. Policies that benefit the public are enacted only when the elite allows them to be. In practice, most policies enacted by government benefit the ruling elite and not the public. Political participation by the public is discouraged. A class-based social structure helps maintain the existing order.

traditionalistic subculture
Government that maintains the existing political order for the benefit of a small elite

Map 1.3 shows Elazar's proposed distribution of political cultures across the nation. As the map indicates, all the old Confederate states have traditionalistic political cultures, and many of the midwestern states have individualistic political cultures. Northern and some far western states have a moralistic political culture.

A look at the attitudes and beliefs of Texas's early settlers provides some insight into the state's political culture. Tejanos and their descendants contributed a strongly traditionalistic culture. This culture had its origins in seventeenth- and eighteenth-century Spanish culture, which was characterized by a dominant landed aristocracy and elite-controlled government. Southern Anglo settlers of East Texas also brought a strong traditionalistic culture with them. This culture was a natural extension of the practice of slavery and persisted even after the

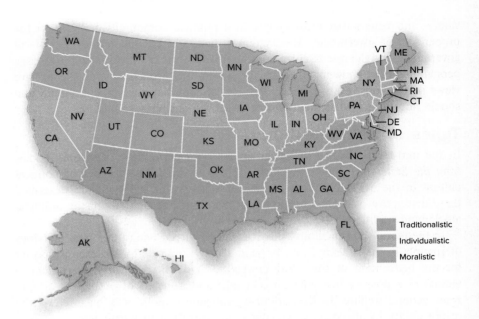

MAP 1.3   Political Culture in the States

Civil War. African American enslaved people were forced to adopt the traditionalistic culture of their Anglo slave owners. Conversely, German and midwestern Anglo settlers in West Texas brought a strong individualistic culture with them. Few, if any, of these settlers had enslaved people, and they came to Texas in search of individual opportunities. Based on this heritage, one might expect to find a blend of traditionalistic and individualistic political cultures in Texas.

In fact, the basic structure of state government in Texas fits the traditionalistic/individualistic model quite well. Government is relatively limited. Power is divided among many elected officials. Executive authority—namely, the office of the governor—is weak, and most power rests with the state legislature. Few state regulations are placed on business, and many of those that do exist benefit specific businesses. Regulation of the environment is modest.

Examining political culture helps us understand the basic structure of state government, the nature of government policy, and the degree to which citizens are involved in government. Although the dominant party has changed, the state's political culture has not. Texas has transitioned from a state dominated by the Democratic Party to a state dominated by the Republican Party, but there have been no significant changes in philosophy, ideology, or policy.

Understanding Impact Texas primarily has a traditionalistic culture with some aspects of individualistic culture. What are the strengths and weaknesses of a traditionalistic culture? Of the three cultures that Elazar enumerates—traditionalistic, individualistic, and moralistic—which one do you think is best, and why?

Populism, Progressivism, and Other Ideologies

The political culture of Texas reflects a deeper ideological position for most Texans, whose ideology is a mix of elements from classical liberalism and social conservatism, with some strains of populism as well. **Classical liberalism,** in general, has both political and economic components and is associated in the United States with the writings of John Locke, Adam Smith, Thomas Jefferson, and James Madison. Politically, classical liberalism focuses on limited government, the rule of law, the protection of individual rights, and a generally free market economy. Classical liberals have often supported representative government and civil liberties (such as freedom of speech, press, assembly, and petition) as means by which citizens could control their government and secure their (natural) rights.

Just as classical liberalism rejects obtrusive government—whether monarchic or even democratic—it also rejected mercantilism in the economic realm. Mercantilism held that, because a country's wealth and power were synonymous and war was inevitable, the government had a right and a duty to regulate the economy and foster economic development. Moreover, mercantilists believed the government could do so effectively. Under mercantilism, European monarchs granted trade and colonial monopolies, subsidized import industries, enacted strict trade and labor regulations, and imposed high tariffs. Classical liberalism viewed such intervention in the economy as a means by which governments and their cronies could buttress their power and influence in opposition to the interests of their people.

Adam Smith, in his book *The Wealth of Nations,* argued that the largely unregulated market would produce wealth on its own as long as government policies offered basic but pivotal services, such as limited taxation and courts of law. Therefore, governmental intrusion into the economy would only thwart the efficient operation of the free market as well as support an overbearing government. Smith's metaphor for the self-regulating market was the "invisible hand."[98] The American Revolution is an example of both the political and economic aspects of the classical liberal approach. Economic liberalism in the United States became dominant with Thomas Jefferson's inauguration. Jefferson favored strong state and local governments and a relatively weak federal government. The Jeffersonian ideal of limited government opposed governmental intervention in the economy; it did not support a role for the federal government in chartering banks—or in spending money on transportation infrastructure, or what would have been termed "internal improvements."

Texan opposition to taxes and government regulation of the economy is reminiscent of the distrust of the federal government that characterized the presidencies of Thomas Jefferson and Andrew Jackson. State government exists, in the view of these people, to provide a healthy business climate and keep taxes and regulations low. To make commerce easier, the state may accept federal help to build roads and bridges. In general, classical liberals in the past—and many Texans today—have held, at least rhetorically, that the government is best that governs least. This philosophy forms the basis of the modern Libertarian Party, as well as some of the planks of the Texas Republican Party. Except for a few periods of reform associated with James Hogg, James Ferguson, and the New Deal, Texas has frequently embraced the economic aspects of classical liberalism. However, many followers of this philosophy have been willing to compromise this faith for political and personal advantage.

At the same time, many Texans also embrace **social conservatism.** In general, they oppose abortion and same-sex marriage. They want robust protections for religious liberty, defend prayer in public schools, and would like to see alternatives

classical liberalism
An ideology that stresses the protection of individual rights, limited government, the rule of law, and a free market economy

social conservatism
An ideology that stresses the dangers of unregulated capitalism and supports relatively conservative social values

In the 2020 presidential primary, Bernie Sanders—the most progressive Democratic candidate in the race—hoped to pull off a win in Texas, but Texas voters opted for the more-moderate candidate, former vice president Joe Biden, shown here with Beto O'Rourke.

Richard W. Rodriguez/AP Images

populism

An ideology that emphasizes the role of government in economic concerns, while simultaneously supporting the government's role in upholding socially conservative values

progressive or modern liberal

An ideology that stresses the positive role of government intervention in the economy for the common and public good

to evolution (for example, creationism or intelligent design) taught in public schools. Many are uncompromising in their beliefs on each of these issues because they see their perspective as grounded in their religious faith.

Another facet of Texas political ideology and culture is **populism.** "Populism" is a difficult term to define, although most political analysts agree that it is an important part of U.S. political history. Populism arose in the 1880s in the southern and western United States. Populists call for the federal and state government to help small businesses, farmers, and ranchers in the face of competition from large U.S. corporations and foreign businesses. Populists, historically, have wanted the federal government to regulate railroad rates and to ensure a money supply equal to the size of the economy. Populists also distrust banks and want the government to provide credit for industrial production and trade unions. They were, historically, also anti-immigrant. Populism, being primarily a rural and small-town movement, supports more conservative religious values. It can also have an anti-intellectual strain, which is voiced as suspicion of experts. The rural anti-union, anti-immigrant, anti-intellectual strain of populism has survived and appears to have merged with social conservatism in Texas and other states.

It is also worth noting that a significant segment of Texans embrace a **progressive or modern liberal** understanding of the relationship between the people and the government. These contemporary liberals or progressives (like Populists before them) are not as skeptical of government intervention in the economy and see the government as a potent force for good. Among other things, they favor a larger social welfare system and more regulation of business while opposing the agenda of social conservatives. Though a minority of Texans, they make up a large part of the modern Democratic Party in Texas and could be a growing force in the state.

Conclusion

The state of Texas has a complex history. In this chapter we have seen how aspects of that history, and in particular the attitudes and beliefs of early settlers to the area, have shaped the state's political culture. Examining government using the framework of political culture helps us understand the basic structure of the government, the nature of government policy, and the degree to which citizens are involved in government. Texas's traditionalistic/individualistic political culture has remained essentially unchanged throughout its history despite major shifts in political party dominance.

Texas occupies a special position within the larger United States today, and its state government must

contend with a number of challenges both common to other states and unique to Texas. Once a primarily rural state with a land-based economy, Texas now has a more diversified economy and is an international trade powerhouse. As it attracts more people through domestic and international channels, the state must deal with unprecedented population growth. That population has shifted toward urban centers, and Texas has become a majority-minority state. These issues provide a backdrop for current policy, and we can use the framework of political culture to understand how state government approaches these challenges.

Summary

LO: Explain the significance of Texas's six flags.

Six nations have ruled either part or all of the territory of Texas during its history: Spain, France, the Republic of Mexico, the Republic of Texas, the United States of America, and the Confederate States of America. After being claimed by Spain and France, Texas was controlled by Mexico until it became an independent republic. Texas joined the United States but then seceded to become a part of the Confederacy. Thus, six different national flags have flown over Texas.

LO: Describe the Civil War and Reconstruction in Texas.

Though it was home to some important Civil War events, Texas for the most part avoided the battles and physical devastation, stemming from invasion and occupation, that affected much of the rest of the Confederacy. During Reconstruction (the period immediately following the Civil War), Republicans controlled state government, slavery was prohibited, and Texas was readmitted to the Union. The backlash against Republican rule during Reconstruction marked the beginning of about 100 years of one-party Democratic dominance in Texas.

LO: Describe post-Reconstruction Texas.

Since Reconstruction, Texas has changed from a land-based economy to a more diversified, primarily service economy. Control of state politics has shifted from the Democratic Party to the Republican Party. In addition,

Texas now has the second-largest population of any state. That population is growing rapidly, is increasingly urban (as opposed to rural), and has become majority-minority (meaning that racial and ethnic minority groups together make up a majority of the state's population).

LO: Explain the challenges facing Texas today.

Like other states, Texas must contend with issues related to poverty, education, and the national economy. One challenge specific to Texas is the large numbers of people moving into the state, both from other U.S. states (a process called in-migration) and from other countries (immigration). Many factors—including the state's fairly resilient and diverse economy, low cost of living, and appealing natural climate—make Texas a strong draw for people outside the state.

LO: Explain U.S. and Texas political cultures.

Political culture is the system of beliefs and values that defines the role of government and the role of citizens in that government. In the United States, many midwestern states have individualistic political cultures, whereas northern and some far western states have a moralistic political culture. Southern (former Confederate) states, including Texas, have traditionalistic political cultures. The traditionalistic subculture is one in which the existing political order is maintained, and political participation is generally confined to a small number of elites.

Key Terms

Adelsverein Society
Anglo
carpetbagger
civil rights movement
classical liberalism
demography
economic regions

empresario
individualistic subculture
land-based economy
majority-minority
moralistic subculture
political action committee (PAC)
political culture

populism
Progressive Era
progressive or modern liberal
social conservatism
traditionalistic subculture

Notes

[1] Texas General Land Office, "History of Texas Public Lands," January 2015, http://www.glo.texas.gov/history/archives/forms/files/history-of-texas-public-lands.pdf.

[2] Jean Stuntz, "Spanish Laws for Texas Women: The Development of Marital Property Law to 1850," *The Southwestern*

Historical Quarterly 104, no. 4 (April 2001): 542–59; Paul Goodman, "The Emergence of Homestead Exemption in the United States: Accommodation and Resistance to the Market Revolution, 1840–1880," *The Journal of American History* 80, no. 2 (September 1993): 470–98.

[3] "Coahuila and Texas," *Handbook of Texas Online*, published by the Texas State Historical Association, http://www.tshaonline.org/handbook/online/articles/usc01 (accessed November 2, 2012).

[4] Terry G. Jordan, *German Seed in Texas Soil: Immigrant Farmers in Nineteenth Century Texas* (Austin: University of Texas Press, 1966).

[5] Robert A. Calvert and Arnold DeLeon, *The History of Texas* (Arlington Heights, IL: Harland Davidson, 1990), 99–100.

[6] T. R. Fehrendbach, *Lone Star: A History of Texas and the Texans* (New York: Collier, 1980), 276–77.

[7] James L. Haley, *Sam Houston* (Norman: University of Oklahoma Press, 2002), chaps. 18–19.

[8] Texas Historical Commission, "Texas in the Civil War," http://www.thc.state.tx.us/public/upload/publications/tx-in-civil-war.pdf; Texas State Historical Association, "Civil War," https://tshaonline.org/handbook/online/articles/qdc02.

[9] James M. McPherson and James K. Hogue, *Ordeal by Fire: The Civil War and Reconstruction*, 4th edition (New York: McGraw-Hill Higher Education, 2009), 428.

[10] Texas State Library and Archives Commission, "Juneteenth," https: www.tsl.texas.gov/ref/abouttx/juneteenth.html.

[11] Joyce King, "How Juneteenth Turned Texas' Shameful Slave Legacy into an International Celebration of Freedom," *Dallas News*, June 14, 2017, https://www.dallasnews.com/opinion/commentary/2017/06/14/black-texans-turned-states-shameful-slave-legacy-international-celebration-freedom.

[12] Vann R. Newkirk II, "The Quintessential Americanness of Juneteenth," *The Atlantic*, June 19, 2017, https://www.theatlantic.com/politics/archive/2017/06/juneteenth-celebration-police-brutality-justice/530898/.

[13] "Texas Governor Edmund Jackson Davis," Texas Archival Resources Online, https://legacy.lib.utexas.edu/taro/tslac/40016/tsl-40016.html.

[14] Frederick Jackson Turner, "The Significance of the Frontier in American History," in *American Progressivism: A Reader*, ed. Ronald J. Pestritto and William J. Atto (Lanham, MD: Lexington, 2008), 67.

[15] Roy Morris, *Sheridan: The Life and Wars of General Phil Sheridan* (New York: Crown, 1992).

[16] Robert A. Calvert and Arnold DeLeon, *The History of Texas* (Arlington Heights, IL: Harland Davidson, 1990), 363.

[17] U.S. Census Bureau, Table 1: Urban and Rural Population: 1900 to 1990, https://www.census.gov/population/censusdata/urpop0090.txt.

[18] U.S. Patent and Trademark Office, "Patent Counts by Origin and Type, Calendar Year 2020," https://www.uspto.gov/web/offices/ac/ido/oeip/taf/st_co_20.htm (accessed January 22, 2022).

[19] U.S. Department of Labor, Bureau of Labor Statistics, "Industries at a Glance, Service-Providing Industries," http://www.bls.gov/iag/tgs/iag07.htm; U.S. Department of Labor, Bureau of Labor Statistics, "Texas Economy at a Glance," http://www.bls.gov/eag/eag.tx.htm#eag_tx.f.1; U.S. Department of Labor, Bureau of Labor Statistics, Southwest Information Office, Texas, http://www.bls.gov/regions/southwest/texas.htm#eag (accessed January 22, 2022).

[20] U.S. Census Bureau, "Foreign Trade: State Exports from Texas," https://www.census.gov/foreign-trade/statistics/state/data/tx.html (accessed January 22, 2022); U.S. Bureau, "Foreign Trade: State Exports from California," https://www.census.gov/foreign-trade/statistics/state/data/ca.html (accessed January 22, 2022).

[21] Glenn Hegar, Texas Comptroller of Public Accounts, "Regional Economic Data," https://comptroller.texas.gov/economy/economic-data/regions/ (accessed May 14, 2018).

[22] Jay M. Shafritz, ed., *The Harper Collins Dictionary of American Government and Politics* (New York: HarperCollins, 1992), 469.

[23] Robert A. Calvert and Arnold DeLeon, *The History of Texas* (Arlington Heights, IL: Harland Davidson, 1990), 228–41.

[24] Texas Secretary of State, "Presidential Election Results," http://www.sos.state.tx.us/elections/historical/presidential.shtml.

[25] Susan Eason, "Tower, John Goodwin," *Handbook of Texas Online*, published by the Texas State Historical Association, http://www.tshaonline.org/handbook/online/articles/ftoss (accessed March 4, 2016).

[26] Ibid.

[27] Texas Ethics Commission, "Active Political Committees (PACS) and Their Treasurers," September 2015, https://www.ethics.state.tx.us/tedd/paclista.htm.

[28] Todd J. Gillman, "Texas Democrats Won 47% of Votes in Congressional Races. Should They Have More Than 13 of 36 Seats?," *The Dallas Morning News*, November 24, 2018, https://www.dallasnews.com/news/politics/2018/11/24/texas-democrats-won-47-of-votes-in-congressional-races-should-they-have-more-than-13-of-36-seats/ (accessed January 11, 2020).

[29] Five Thirty Eight, "What Redistricting Looks Like In Every State" https://projects.fivethirtyeight.com/redistricting-2022-maps/texas/ (accessed January 22, 2022); Patrick Svitek, "Frontrunners for Texas' New Congressional Seats Look to Send Message with Decisive Primary Wins," *The Texas Tribune*, January 26, 2022.

[30] Texas State Historical Association, "Census and Census Records," https://tshaonline.org/handbook/online/articles/ulc01 (accessed January 7, 2020); U.S. Census Bureau, "Texas, Population of Counties by Decennial Census: 1900

to 1990," http://www.census.gov/population/cencounts/tx190090.txt; U.S. Census Bureau, "Quick Facts, Texas," https://www.census.gov/quickfacts/TX (accessed January 7, 2020).

[31] Jeannie Kever, "Census Shows Texas Gains 4 Seats in the U.S. House," *Houston Chronicle*, December 21, 2010, http://www.chron.com/news/houston-texas/article/Census-shows-Texas-gains-4-seats-in-the-U-S-House-1700473.php.

[32] Alexa Ura, "Texas Will Gain Two Seats in Congress As Residents of Color Drive Population Gains," *Texas Tribune*, April 26, 2021, https://www.texastribune.org/2021/04/26/texas-congress-seats-gain/.

[33] "The Trans-Texas Corridor: Miles to Go," *The Economist*, January 7, 2010, http://www.economist.com/node/15213418.

[34] U.S. Census Bureau, "Geography, 2010 Census Urban and Rural Classification and Urban Area Criteria," https://www.census.gov/geo/reference/ua/urban-rural-2010.html.

[35] U.S. Census Bureau, "1980: Census of Population—Texas" https://www2.census.gov/prod2/decennial/documents/1980a_txAB-01.pdf, pg. 8; U.S. Census Bureau, "Geography, Lists of Population, Land Area, and Percent Urban and Rural in 2010 and Changes from 2000 to 2010, Percent Urban and Rural in 2010 by State," https://www.census.gov/geo/reference/ua/urban-rural-2010.html.

[36] Todd Staples, "Texas Rural Impact Report, 2013," Department of Agriculture, https://texasagriculture.gov/Portals/0/Publications/RED/Rural%20Advisory%20Council/TDA%20Rural%20Report%20Final%20%202013.pdf.

[37] Peter Svitek and Abby Livingston, "Longtime U.S. Rep. Lloyd Doggett Will Run in the Austin Area's New Congressional District," *Texas Tribune*, October 18, 2021, https://www.texastribune.org/2021/10/17/lloyd-doggett-austin-congress-2022/; Peter Svitek, "Proposed New Congressional Seat in Houston Gets Prominent GOP Candidate," *Texas Tribune*, September 28, 2021, https://www.texastribune.org/2021/09/28/wesley-hunt-houston-congress/.

[38] Texas Politics Project, "Majority-Minority Jurisdictions," https://texaspolitics.utexas.edu/archive/html/cult/features/0500_03/slide1.html (accessed May 14, 2018).

[39] U.S. Census Bureau, "QuickFacts, Texas," https://www.census.gov/quickfacts/TX (accessed January 25, 2022).

[40] Texas Education Agency, *Enrollment in Texas Public Schools, 2020–2021* June 2021, https://tea.texas.gov/sites/default/files/enroll-2020-21.pdf, ix.

[41] U.S. Census Bureau, "QuickFacts: Texas," https://www.census.gov/quickfacts/TX (accessed January 25, 2022); Texas Education Agency, *Enrollment in Texas Public Schools, 2020–2021* June 2021, https://tea.texas.gov/sites/default/files/enroll-2020-21.pdf.

[42] Rachel Dry, "Grace Flores-Hughes Interview—She Made 'Hispanic' Official," *The Washington Post*, July 26, 2009, http://www.washingtonpost.com/wp-dyn/content/article/2009/07/24/AR2009072402091.html?sid=ST2010031902002.

[43] Jeffrey S. Passel and Paul Taylor, "Who's Hispanic?," Pew Research Center, May 28, 2009, http://www.pewhispanic.org/2009/05/28/whos-hispanic/.

[44] *Joint Resolution Relating to the Publication of Economic and Social Statistics for Americans of Spanish Origin or Descent*, Public Law 94–311, *U.S. Statutes at Large* 90 (1976): 688. Accessible at http://uscode.house.gov/statviewer.htm?volume =90&page=688.

[45] D'Vera Cohn, "Census History: Counting Hispanics," Pew Research Center, March 3, 2010, http://www.pewsocialtrends.org/2010/03/03/census-history-counting-hispanics-2/; U.S. Department of Commerce, Bureau of the Census, "Twenty Censuses: Population and Housing Questions 1790–1980," October 1979, https://www.census.gov/history/pdf/20censuses.pdf.

[46] Office of Management and Budget, "Revisions to the Standards for the Classification of Federal Data on Race and Ethnicity," *Federal Register*, October 30, 1997. https://www.whitehouse.gov/omb/fedreg_1997standards.

[47] U.S. Census Bureau, "Equal Employment Opportunity, Hispanic Heritage Month," https://www.census.gov/eeo/special_emphasis_programs/hispanic_heritage.html; Rachel Dry, "Grace Flores-Hughes Interview—She Made 'Hispanic' Official," *The Washington Post*, July 26, 2009, http://www.washingtonpost.com/wp-dyn/content/article/2009/07/24/AR2009072402091.html?sid=ST2010031902002.

[48] U.S. Census, "Hispanic Origin," http://www.census.gov/population/hispanic/; Jeffrey S. Passel and Paul Taylor, "Who's Hispanic?," Pew Research Center, May 28, 2009, http://www.pewhispanic.org/2009/05/28/whos-hispanic/.

[49] U.S. Census Bureau, "Hispanic Origin." http://www.census.gov/topics/population/hispanic-origin/about.html.

[50] Ana Gonzalez-Barrera and Mark Hugo Lopez, "Is Being Hispanic a Matter of Race, Ethnicity or Both?," Pew Research Center, June 15, 2015, http://www.pewresearch.org/fact-tank/2015/06/15/is-being-hispanic-a-matter-of-race-ethnicity-or-both/.

[51] State Bar of Texas, "Texas Legal Legends," http://www.texasbar.com/AM/Template.cfm?Section=Texas_Legal_Legends (accessed May 8, 2018).

[52] Texas Secretary of State, "2012 General Election, Election Night Returns," https://team1.sos.state.tx.us/enr/results/nov06_164_state.htm; Fox News Latino, "Election 2012: Ted Cruz Wins Senate Seat in Texas, Makes History," November 6, 2012, http://latino.foxnews.com/latino/politics/2012/11/06/election-2012-ted-cruz-wins-senate-seat-in-texas/ (accessed May 8, 2018).

[53] Texas Secretary of State, "Statewide Elected Officials," http://www.sos.state.tx.us/elections/voter/elected.shtml; Texas Secretary of State, "Biography of Secretary of State Carlos H. Cascos," http://www.sos.state.tx.us/about/sosbio.shtml.

[54] Julian Aguilar, "Texas Sending Its First Latinas to Congress: Veronica Escobar and Sylvia Garcia," *Texas Tribune,* November 6, 2018, https://www.texastribune.org/2018/11/06/sylvia-garcia-veronica-escobar-first-latina-texas-midterm-election/ (accessed January 8, 2020).

[55] U.S. Census Bureau, "QuickFacts, Texas," https://www.census.gov/quickfacts/TX (accessed January 8, 2020).

[56] Claire Allbright, "U.S. Rep. Al Green Push for Trump's Impeachment Dies in Lopsided 364–58 Vote," *Texas Tribune*, December 6, 2017, http://www.yourbasin.com/news/us-rep-al-green-push-for-trumps-impeachment-dies-in-lopsided-364-58-vote/876481217 (accessed May 29, 2018); Tim Alberta, "Will Hurd Is the Future of the GOP," *Politico,* May 5, 2017, https://www.politico.com/magazine/story/2017/05/05/congressman-will-hurd-texas-republican-profile-215102 (accessed May 29, 2018).

[57] Texas Historical Commission, "Wallace B. Jefferson," https://www.thc.texas.gov/about/commissioners/jefferson-wallace-b (accessed January 8, 2019); Darra Cunningham, "Black History: 1st African American Judge to Be Elected to State-wide Office," *ABC7 News,* https://abc7amarillo.com/news/local/black-history-1st-african-american-judge-to-be-elected-state-wide (accessed January 8, 2019); Anna M. Tinsley, "Michael Williams Stepping Down as Texas Education Agency Chief," *Fort Worth Star-Telegram,* October 15, 2015, https://www.star-telegram.com/news/politics-government/article39290817.html (accessed January 8, 2019); Greenberg Trauig, LLP, "Dale Wainwright, Former Texas Supreme Court Justice, Joins Greenberg Traurig to Chair the Texas Appellate Practice Group," *PR Newswire,* February 21, 2017, https://www.prnewswire.com/news-releases/dale-wainwright-former-texas-supreme-court-justice-joins-greenberg-traurig-to-chair-the-texas-appellate-group-300410916.html (accessed January 8, 2020).

[58] Texas Secretary of State, Race Summary Report, "2002 General Election," http://elections.sos.state.tx.us/elchist95_state.htm.

[59] U.S. Census Bureau, "QuickFacts: Texas," https://www.census.gov/quickfacts/TX (accessed January 8, 2020).

[60] Office of the State Demographer, "Texas Population Projections, 2010 to 2050," accessed May 8, 2018, http://osd.texas.gov/Resources/Publications/2014/2014-11_ProjectionBrief.pdf.

[61] Corrie MacLaggan, "Texas House Race Draws Focus to Vietnamese Voters," *Texas Tribune,* January 10, 2014, https://www.texastribune.org/2014/01/10/texas-house-race-draws-focus-vietnamese-bloc/ (accessed January 9, 2020);

Renzo Downey and Dan Keemahill, "Does the 86th Texas Legislature Reflect You?," *Austin Statesman,* April 12, 2019, https://www.statesman.com/news/20190412/does-86th-texas-legislature-reflect-you (accessed January 9, 2020).

[62] 2014 U.S. Religious Landscape Study, Pew Research Center. http://www.pewforum.org/religious-landscape-study/state/texas/.

[63] United States Conference of Catholic Bishops, "Immigration," http://www.usccb.org/issues-and-action/human-life-and-dignity/immigration/; Paul Stinson, "Texas Bishops Cut Ties with Texas Right to Life," *America*, March 2, 2018, https://www.americamagazine.org/politics-society/2018/03/02/texas-bishops-cut-ties-texas-right-life.

[64] Hartford Institute for Religion Research, Database of Megachurches in the United States, http://hirr.hartsem.edu/cgi-bin/mega/db.pl?db=default&uid=default&view_records=1&ID=*&sb=4&State=TX (accessed May 8, 2018).

[65] Office of the Texas Governor, "GRACE - Governor's Response Against Child Exploitation" https://gov.texas.gov/organization/cjd/cstt-grace (accessed January 28, 2022).

[66] Keith R. Phillips and Jesus Cañas, "Recession Arrives in Texas: A Rougher Ride in 2009," *Southwest Economy* (Federal Reserve Bank of Dallas), first quarter 2009, http://www.dallasfed.org/assets/documents/research/swe/2009/swe0901b.pdf; Susan Combs, "Comptroller's Weekly Economic Outlook," *The Texas Economy*, November 2, 2012, http://www.thetexaseconomy.org/economic-outlook/.

[67] Fred Dews, "4 Texas Metros in Top 10 for Economic Recovery Since Recession," *Brookings Now*, April 2, 2014, https://www.brookings.edu/blog/brookings-now/2014/04/02/4-texas-metros-in-top-10-for-economic-recovery-since-recession/.

[68] Sharon Jayson, "Welcome Home, North Texas Tells Companies," U.S. News and World Report February 8, 2019, https://www.usnews.com/news/best-states/articles/2019-02-08/corporations-move-in-to-north-texas-suburbs; Nico Grant and Bloomberg, "Oracle Moves Its Headquarters to Texas, Adding to Silicon Valley Exodus," *Fortune,* December 11, 2020, https://fortune.com/2020/12/11/oracle-moves-headquarters-to-texas-austin/#:~:text=Oracle%20moves%20its%20headquarters%20to%20Texas%2C%20adding%20to%20Silicon%20Valley%20exodus&text=Oracle%20said%20it%20has%20moved,where%20they%20do%20their%20jobs.

[69] Texas Demographic Center, "2018 Estimated Population of Texas, Its Counties, and Places," Table 2, https://demographics.texas.gov/Resources/publications/2019/20191205_PopEstimatesBrief.pdf (accessed January 10, 2020).

[70] Elvia Limon, "Here's How the COVID-19 Pandemic Has Unfolded in Texas Since March," *The Texas Tribune,* December 18, 2020, https://www.texastribune.org/2020/07/31/coronavirus-timeline-texas/; Anna Novak, et al.

"How Coronavirus Impacted the Texas Economy," *The Texas Tribune*, June 26, 2021, https://apps.texastribune.org/features/2020/texas-unemployment/.

71 Colleen Deguzman and Mandi Cai, "COVID-19 Is Spreading Fast Among Texas' Unvaccinated. Here's Who They Are and Where They Live," *Texas Tribune*, August 3, 2021, https://www.texastribune.org/2021/08/03/unvaccinated-texas-demographics/; Texas Health and Human Services, "Percentage of Population Vaccinated for COVID-19," https://tabexternal.dshs.texas.gov/t/THD/views/COVID-19VaccineinTexasDashboard/Summary?%3Aorigin=card_share_link&%3Aembed=y&%3AisGuestRedirectFromVizportal=y (accessed January 28, 2022).

72 Anna Novak et al., "How Coronavirus Impacted the Economy," *The Texas Tribune*, June 26, 2021, https://apps.texastribune.org/features/2020/texas-unemployment/; Sneha Dey, "Texas Now Has More Jobs Than It Did Before the Pandemic Hit," *The Texas Tribune*, January 28, 2022, https://www.texastribune.org/2022/01/28/texas-unemployment-jobs-pandemic/; U.S. Department of Commerce, Bureau of Economic Analysis, "Regional Data: GDP and Personal Income—Texas," https://apps.bea.gov/itable/iTable.cfm?ReqID=70&step=1#reqid=70&step=1&isuri=1 (accessed January 28, 2022).

73 U.S. Department of Labor, Bureau of Labor Statistics, "Earnings and Unemployment Rates by Educational Attainment, 2015," http://www.bls.gov/emp/ep_chart_001.htm.

74 U.S. Department of Commerce, Bureau of Economic Analysis, "Regional Data: GDP and Personal Income, Texas," https://apps.bea.gov/itable/iTable.cfm?ReqID=70&step=1#reqid=70&step=1&isuri=1 (accessed January 28, 2022).

75 U.S. Census Bureau, "QuickFacts: Texas," https://www.census.gov/quickfacts/fact/table/TX/PST045219 (accessed January 28, 2022); U.S. Census Bureau, "QuickFacts: United States," https://www.census.gov/quickfacts/fact/table/US/PST045219 (accessed January 28, 2022).

76 Texas Education Agency, "Secondary School Completion and Dropouts in Texas Public Schools, 2019–2020," https://tea.texas.gov/sites/default/files/dropcomp-2019-20.pdf, pg. xi.

77 U.S. Census Bureau, "QuickFacts, Texas," http://www.census.gov/quickfacts/table/PST045215/48.

78 Jake Berry, "Democrats Say Texas Graduation Rate Fell to 50th under Rick Perry," *Tampa Bay Times*, September 8, 2011, http://www.politifact.com/truth-o-meter/statements/2011/sep/08/new-hampshire-democratic-party/democrats-say-texas-graduation-rate-fell-50th-unde/ (accessed May 8, 2018).

79 Texas Education Agency, "Secondary School Completion and Dropouts in Texas Public Schools, 2019–2020," https://tea.texas.gov/sites/default/files/dropcomp-2019-20.pdf, pg. xii.

80 Maria Mendez, "Where Is Texas' Growing Population Coming From?," *Texas Tribune,* May 8, 2019, https://www.texastribune.org/2019/05/08/texas-keeps-growing-where-are-newest-transplants-coming/ (accessed February 17, 2020).

81 William H. Frey, "A Rollercoaster Decade for Migration," The Brookings Institution, December 29, 2009, http://www.brookings.edu/research/opinions/2009/12/29-migration-frey (accessed May 8, 2018).

82 U.S. Census Bureau, "State-to-State Migration Flows, 2018," https://www.census.gov/data/tables/time-series/demo/geographic-mobility/state-to-state-migration.html (accessed January 10, 2020).

83 Department of Homeland Security, *Yearbook of Immigration Statistics 2019*, Table 2, https://www.dhs.gov/immigration-statistics/yearbook/2019/table2 (accessed January 28, 2022).

84 Bryan Baker, "Estimates of the Unauthorized Immigrant Population Residing in the United States: January 2015-January 2018," U.S. Department of Homeland Security, 1, 4, 5.

85 Ana Gonzalez-Barrera, "More Mexicans Leaving Than Coming to the U.S.," Pew Research Center, November 19, 2015, http://www.pewhispanic.org/2015/11/19/more-mexicans-leaving-than-coming-to-the-u-s/; Ana Gonzalez-Barrera, "Before COVID-19, More Mexicans Came to the U.S. Than Left for Mexico For the First Time In Years," Pew Research Center, July 9, 2021, https://www.pewresearch.org/fact-tank/2021/07/09/before-covid-19-more-mexicans-came-to-the-u-s-than-left-for-mexico-for-the-first-time-in-years/; Tunku Varadarjan, "The Republican Mayor of McAllen Represents the Changing Political Map of Texas," *Wall Street Journal*, February 25, 2022, https://www.wsj.com/articles/gop-mayor-mcallen-texas-javier-villalobos-hidalgo-county-2020-election-2022-midterms-hispanic-vote-rio-grande-valley-11645820166; Eleanor Klibanoff and Uriel J. Garcia, "Governor Greg Abbott Inaugurates First Stretch of State-Funded Border Barrier in Starr County," *The Texas Tribune*, December 18, 2021, https://www.texastribune.org/2021/12/18/texas-mexico-border-wall-greg-abbott/.

86 Joy Diaz and Terri Langford, "As the Asian American Population Grows in Texas, So Does Its Political Power," *Texas Standard*, September 7, 2020, https://www.texasstandard.org/stories/as-the-asian-american-population-grows-in-texas-so-does-its-political-power/.

87 Pew Research Center, "Religious Landscape Study—Adults in Texas," https://www.pewforum.org/religious-landscape-study/state/texas/ (accessed February 25, 2022).

88 Nathan Guttman, "Five Things About Joe Straus, The Last Moderate Republican Left in Texas," *Forward*, July 20, 2017, https://forward.com/news/377506/5-things-about-joe-straus-the-last-republican-moderate-left-in-texas/.

[89] Joy Diaz and Caroline Covington, "How Ramadan Has Become a Thread in the Multicultural Fabric of Texas," *The Texas Standard,* April 16, 2021, https://www.texasstandard.org/stories/how-ramadan-has-become-a-thread-in-the-multicultural-fabric-of-texas/#:~:text=Muslims%20are%20a%20fast%2Dgrowing,the%20late%201970s%20and%20'80s; "Texas Sikhs are Part of Your Community: Discover Their History in Texas," *Texas Hill Country,* January 15, 2020, https://texashillcountry.com/texan-sikhs-community-history/.

[90] Alaa Elassar, Michelle Watson, and Alanne Orjoux, "FBI Identifies Hostage-Taker at Texas Synagogue," *CNN,* January 17, 2022, https://www.cnn.com/2022/01/16/us/colleyville-texas-hostage-situation-sunday/index.html.

[91] Christina Caron, "Texas Man Found Guilty of Hate Crime in Mosque Fire," *The New York Times,* July 17, 2018, https://www.nytimes.com/2018/07/17/us/mosque-arson-guilty-verdict.html (accessed February 16, 2020).

[92] Antidefamation League, "Audit of Anti-Semitic Incidents: Year in Review 2020," https://www.adl.org/2020-audit-h (accessed February 25, 2022).

[93] Alexa Ura and Alex Samuels, "At Texas Muslim Capitol Days, Supporters Form Human Shield around Demonstrators," *Texas Tribune,* January 31, 2017, https://www.texastribune.org/2017/01/31/texas-capitol-rally-muslim-advocacy-day-draws-1000/ (accessed February 16, 2020).

[94] Daniel J. Elazar, *American Federalism: A View from the States* (New York: HarperCollins, 1984; originally published 1966).

[95] Daniel J. Elazar, *American Federalism: A View from the States* (New York: HarperCollins, 1984; originally published 1966), 90.

[96] Daniel J. Elazar, *American Federalism: A View from the States* (New York: HarperCollins, 1984; originally published 1966).

[97] Daniel J. Elazar, *American Federalism: A View from the States* (New York: HarperCollins, 1984; originally published 1966), 86.

[98] Adam Smith, *The Wealth of Nations* (New York: Bantam Classics), 572.

CHAPTER 2

The American Federal System and the Texas State Constitution

Texas Learning Outcomes

- Describe state and local political systems and their relationship with the federal government.

- Describe separation of powers and checks and balances in both theory and practice in Texas.

- Explain the origin and development of the Texas Constitution.

A **constitution** establishes the fundamental rules by which nations and states govern. Constitutions instruct, though not always explicitly, what a government can and cannot do. The American federal system, through the U.S. Constitution, structures how power is distributed within the national government as well as with and between the states.

Texas and the other 49 states operate within what is called a **federal system of government.** Federalism distributes power between the national government and the states. This system promotes sharing power and responsibility between levels of government.

constitution

The basic document that provides a framework for government and limits what the government can do

federal system of government

The division of powers between a national government and regional governments

Chapter Learning Objectives

- Describe the principles of constitutional government.

- Explain the American federal system of government.

- Describe the characteristics common to state constitutions.

- Describe the development of Texas's constitutions before and after 1876.

- Describe how political culture drives institutions.

- Explain how state constitutions, including Texas's, are amended and revised.

- Discuss common criticisms of Texas's constitution.

The American Federal System of Government

Learning Objective: Explain the American federal system of government.

The Federal Structure

The primary objectives of a written constitution are to structure government, to assign it power, and to limit its power. The U.S. Constitution distributes power between the national and state governments. It grants and denies powers to those governments. In some cases, the U.S. Constitution grants powers exclusively to the national government and, in other cases, exclusively to the states. There are also instances where the Constitution grants powers to both the national and the state governments. The same can be said for denied powers. Some are denied to the national government, others are denied to the states, and some are denied to both.

Division of Powers between National and State Governments

Figures 2.1 and 2.2 present a clear summary of the division of powers between the national and state governments. Although the division of powers may seem

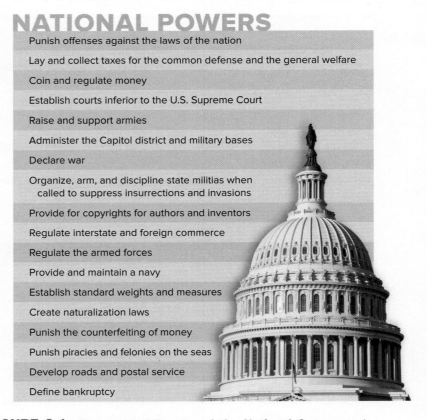

NATIONAL POWERS

Punish offenses against the laws of the nation

Lay and collect taxes for the common defense and the general welfare

Coin and regulate money

Establish courts inferior to the U.S. Supreme Court

Raise and support armies

Administer the Capitol district and military bases

Declare war

Organize, arm, and discipline state militias when called to suppress insurrections and invasions

Provide for copyrights for authors and inventors

Regulate interstate and foreign commerce

Regulate the armed forces

Provide and maintain a navy

Establish standard weights and measures

Create naturalization laws

Punish the counterfeiting of money

Punish piracies and felonies on the seas

Develop roads and postal service

Define bankruptcy

FIGURE 2.1 Enumerated Powers of the National Government

Pxlar8/iStock/Getty Images

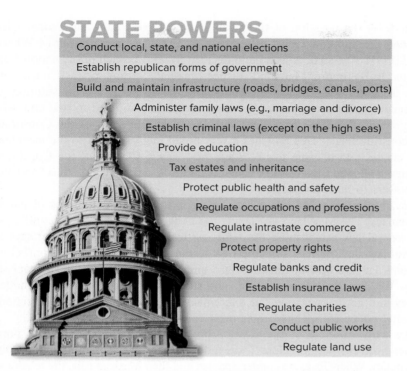

STATE POWERS

Conduct local, state, and national elections

Establish republican forms of government

Build and maintain infrastructure (roads, bridges, canals, ports)

Administer family laws (e.g., marriage and divorce)

Establish criminal laws (except on the high seas)

Provide education

Tax estates and inheritance

Protect public health and safety

Regulate occupations and professions

Regulate intrastate commerce

Protect property rights

Regulate banks and credit

Establish insurance laws

Regulate charities

Conduct public works

Regulate land use

FIGURE 2.2 Constitutionally Delegated and Reserved Powers of the State
Harvey Loyd/Stockbyte/Getty Images

straightforward, these figures belie the true complexity of our federal system of government. It is complicated, and the meaning of each power has been subject to interpretation by the federal courts. If we examine four areas of the U.S. Constitution and the courts' interpretations, we gain a much better understanding of American federalism. These four areas are the Necessary and Proper Clause versus the Tenth Amendment; the Interstate Commerce Clause; the Equal Protection and Due Process Clause of the Fourteenth Amendment; and the power to tax and spend to promote the general welfare.

"Necessary and Proper" Clause versus the Tenth Amendment

Article 1, Section 8, paragraph 18 of the United States Constitution, known as the **Necessary and Proper Clause,** states that Congress shall have the power "To make all Laws which shall be necessary and proper for carrying into Execution the foregoing Powers, and all other Powers vested by this Constitution in the Government of the United States, or in any Department or Officer thereof." Thus, beyond the Enumerated Powers identified in Figure 2.1, this clause seems to grant considerable power to the national government. However, the **Tenth Amendment** states: "The powers not delegated to the United States by the Constitution, nor prohibited by it to the States, are reserved to the States respectively, or to the people." This seems to grant most powers not expressly granted to the federal government to the states or the people. The meanings of these two sections of the Constitution were the cause of conflict early in the history of the United States.

Necessary and Proper Clause (Elastic Clause)
Statement in Article 1, Section 8, paragraph 18 of the U.S. Constitution that says Congress can pass any law necessary and proper to carry out other powers

Tenth Amendment
Amendment of the U.S. Constitution that delegates or reserves some powers to the state governments or to the people

In 1819, the question of the meaning of the Necessary and Proper Clause reached the Supreme Court in the case of *McCulloch v. Maryland* (4 Wheaton 316 [1819]). The state of Maryland decided to tax a branch of the national bank located in Baltimore, Maryland. Justice Marshall, writing for the Court, stated, "Let the end be legitimate, let it be within the scope of the Constitution, and all means which are appropriate, which are plainly adopted to that end, which are not prohibited but consistent with the letter and spirit of the Constitution are constitutional." This provides a very broad interpretation to the meaning of this clause, and it came to be called the "Elastic Clause" of the Constitution because it allowed Congress to decide the means to carry out ends, thus "stretching" its powers to meet its needs.

In addition, the *McCulloch* case also contributed to definitions of national supremacy. The Maryland law taxing the bank was found to be in conflict with the federal law establishing the bank. Article 6 of the Constitution says that federal law shall be the "supreme Law of the Land." State laws in conflict with national law are thus unconstitutional, and federal law would prevail over state laws. Without this interpretation, any state could choose to ignore national policy and go its own way. The supremacy clause provided for the creation of national policy with which states must comply.

An early example of the relationship between national and state powers comes from the period before Texas independence and has to do with immigration policy. When Texas was under Spanish and then Mexican rule, the relationship between the state and the national government concerning immigration became a source of tension. While under Spanish rule, Moses Austin obtained a permit from the Mexican provincial government to settle Anglo families in the state. When Mexico gained independence later that same year, the new government under the leadership of Agustín de Iturbide did not recognize the permit. Instead, the Mexican government passed a new law that created a system of land contractors to bring in families, with emphasis placed on Catholic immigrants. Stephen F. Austin (Moses's son) received special permission for his first colony. In 1824, when the Mexican empire fell and become a republic with a federal structure, a new national law gave individual states within Mexico authority to determine immigration policy within their own borders. Austin then worked with the state government of Coahuila y Tejas to maintain contracts to bring in settlers. National supremacy versus state power in this policy area continued to evolve over time.[1]

Interstate Commerce Clause

Another troubling area for the U.S. government was the question of interstate commerce. During the nineteenth century and much of the twentieth, the Supreme Court placed a very narrow interpretation on the **Interstate Commerce Clause** and applied it only to goods that were transported across state lines, leaving most regulation of commerce to the states. For example, in the past many states prohibited cattle from Texas from being shipped into their states because the herds were often infected with tick fever. This case addresses the issue of the legitimacy of trade barriers. If the prohibition on the importation of an item is truly to protect health, morals, and safety, and not a barrier imposed to restrict trade, it will be allowed by the appropriate department of state government. For example, if the reason for the barriers is to protect the

Interstate Commerce Clause

Article in U.S. Constitution that gives Congress the exclusive power to regulate commerce between the states; Congress and the courts determine what is interstate commerce health of cattle or oranges, then states may erect such barriers. If it is simply to protect a state's internal economy (such as protecting ranchers against out-of-state competition), the barrier is not allowed. Again, determination is up to the courts. The courts decide when barriers have been erected for legitimate purposes and when barriers are a restraint on interstate trade.

There are many areas of seeming contradiction when it comes to interstate commerce. The courts' interpretation of the Interstate Commerce Clause has continued to evolve case by case. For example, some industries are regulated and others are not. The conclusion is that interstate commerce has become largely whatever the courts say it is. Critics of an expansive view of the commerce clause charge that it undermines the notion of the Constitution establishing a government of specific enumerated powers while strengthening the federal government at the expense of the states and individual liberty.

Equal Protection and Due Process Clauses of the Fourteenth Amendment

The U.S. Bill of Rights provides for the protection of civil liberties and individual rights. Initially, the Bill of Rights applied only to actions of the national government that affected citizens. For example, the First Amendment states, "Congress shall make no laws respecting an establishment of religion." It says Congress—not Congress and the states.

In the aftermath of the Civil War, Congress passed and the states approved the Fourteenth Amendment, which for the first time ascribed rights to national as well as state citizenship, and extended some of the basic protections outlined in the Bill of Rights to African American freed persons that even state and local governments had to respect:

> No State shall make or enforce any law which shall abridge the privileges or immunities of citizens of the United States; nor shall any State deprive any person of life, liberty or property, without due process of law, or deny to any person within its jurisdiction the equal protection of the law.

The **Equal Protection Clause** and the **Due Process Clause** mean that state and local governments must treat people equally and in accordance with established rules and procedures.

After World War I, the federal courts gradually began to apply the basic rights provided in the Constitution to the states. There were three primary areas where states were required to provide protection for citizens: civil liberties, criminal proceedings, and election laws.

Civil liberties include freedom of speech and religion. States may no longer require prayer in public schools or allow segregated schools. Criminal procedures include protection against self-incrimination (the so-called Miranda warnings) and the right to legal counsel in criminal procedures. Election laws overturned restrictive voter registration laws and white primaries. States were also forced to apportion legislative districts equally by population. (You will learn about these issues in more detail in later chapters.)

This gradual expansion of basic rights also expanded the role of the national government into areas that had traditionally been reserved to the states. Although state power may have been reduced, individual rights and liberties were expanded.

Equal Protection Clause
Clause in the Fourteenth Amendment of the U.S. Constitution that requires states to treat all citizens equally

Due Process Clause
Clause in the Fifth and Fourteenth Amendments of the U.S. Constitution that requires states to treat all citizens equally and specifies that states must follow certain rules and procedures

How to

Read Critically

Critical reading is more than just reading for information. It means asking questions about the content and reading with an eye toward analysis and interpretation. When you read critically, you think about who wrote the text and why, what the author's purpose might be, and how the text affects the world beyond the page.

Let's use Section 1 of the Fourteenth Amendment as an example:

> All persons born or naturalized in the United States, and subject to the jurisdiction thereof, are citizens of the United States and of the state wherein they reside. No State shall make or enforce any law which shall abridge the privileges or immunities of citizens of the United States; nor shall any state deprive any person of life, liberty, or property, without due process of law; nor deny to any person within its jurisdiction the equal protection of the laws.[2]

Step 1: What is the context?

Ask yourself: Who wrote this text and why?

In this case, the context is the U.S. Constitution, specifically the amendments that came after the original Bill of Rights. A quick Internet search reveals that the Fourteenth Amendment is one of the Reconstruction amendments that the U.S. Congress wrote and ratified after the Civil War. Because this amendment came after Union victory and reunification, it likely reflects values that the Union held.

Step 2: What do you believe is the main idea of the text?

Read all the text. At this point, don't pause if you get confused or see a word you don't know. Then, ask yourself what you think the text is saying in general. It's perfectly fine to not really know. Guess. Only after you've written down what you think is it time to dig in a bit deeper.

This extract seems to be talking about who can be a citizen of the United States. It also discusses limits on states' power over citizens' freedoms and rights.

Step 3: What does each part of the text say specifically?

Look up words or expressions you don't understand. Restate what you think each idea is. Let's take this text piece by piece:

> All persons born or naturalized in the United States, and subject to the jurisdiction thereof,

are citizens of the United States and of the state wherein they reside.

This seems to be a definition of citizenship. Everyone who is born within U.S. borders or who goes through the naturalization process is a U.S. citizen. Checking a dictionary shows that *jurisdiction* means "power, authority, or control."

> No State shall make or enforce any law which shall abridge the privileges or immunities of citizens of the United States;

To *abridge* is to shorten, reduce, or deprive. This part of the text seems to be saying that no individual state should try to take away any "privileges or immunities" that the federal government grants its citizens.

> nor shall any state deprive any person of life, liberty, or property, without due process of law;

This means that no state can take away anyone's life, freedom, or possessions unless there is legal justification. Note that the text doesn't just say citizen; it says *any person*.

> nor deny to any person within its jurisdiction the equal protection of the laws.

Again, note the use of *any person*. The text says that no one person or group should have higher standing or better legal protection than others.

Step 4: What does the entire text mean?

Reading critically means asking in-depth questions: What is the purpose of the text? What values does it express, and do you agree or disagree with those values? What impact did the author or authors probably want it to have beyond the page?

Here are a few specific questions to think about when reading this text:

- What is the relationship between the values the authors express and the historical context (the aftermath of the Civil War and the liberation of enslaved persons)?
- How does this text relate to the original text of the Constitution and the Bill of Rights? Why did the authors create this amendment?

Reading critically is all about asking questions. Even if you're not sure which ones to ask, start with figuring out the main point. Once you work that out, you can begin to engage with the text more deeply.

Power to Tax and Spend to Promote the General Welfare of Citizens

Article 1, Section 8 grants Congress the right to tax and spend to promote general welfare. The national government lacks the power to provide many basic services to citizens. Congress cannot, for example, operate schools and hospitals, build roads, or do many things state governments can. These powers are reserved to the states. The national government has only interstate police powers; however, the national government may provide money to state and local governments to provide these basic services.

In this area, the national government has had great impact on state and local authority. Congress can provide money to state and local governments and set standards for how the money can be spent. Congress supplies money to state governments to build and maintain roads and highways. When states accept this money, they must agree to some standards. Most college students are aware of these standards as applied to highway funds: States must agree to set a drinking age of 21 if they accept federal money. Texas raised the minimum legal drinking age from 18 to 21 in 1986.

The attitude of many state and local officials is that the national government should provide funds and then end its involvement in state affairs. They believe that the rules are often burdensome, inflexible, and unnecessary. There are probably cases where this is true; however, the positive side of these requirements is that they have led to improved uniformity in standards. For example, if you drive on an interstate highway anywhere in the United States (including Hawaii) there is a uniformity of highway signs and rules. Also, national requirements have led to improvements in accounting standards. State and local governments that accept federal money must comply with generally accepted accounting principles (GAAP).

CORE OBJECTIVE

Being Socially Responsible . . .

To what extent should the government "promote general welfare"? What does promoting general welfare mean to you? In developing an understanding of state and local political systems and their relationship with the federal government, who do you think should play a greater role—the states or the federal government?

A federal system has a number of advantages. A key one, as Supreme Court Justice Louis Brandeis noted in 1932, is that states can be "laboratories" of democracy. In particular, he argued, "It is one of the happy incidents of the federal system that a single courageous state may, if its citizens choose, serve as a laboratory; and try novel social and economic experiments without risk to the rest of the country."[3] Another advantage, as the Supreme Court argued in *Bond v. United States* (2011), is that "By denying any one government complete jurisdiction over all the concerns of public life, federalism protects the liberty of the individual from arbitrary power."[4] A law professor has pointed out other advantages:

- Federalism can accommodate a diversity of preferences in a heterogeneous society.
- The most appropriate level of government can be used for a particular purpose.
- States can compete, and their citizens can move to places that have an attractive mix of public policies.[5]

Understanding Impact Think about some of the areas where states compete. It is fairly common, for example, for people to say they want to move from a state with high taxes to one with low sales or property taxes or one without a state income tax. Another way in which states compete is in the amount and kind of regulations placed on business. What do you think are the advantages and disadvantages of this competition? Do you agree that it is a good thing?

The Evolution of American Federalism

The real strength of the American federal system is flexibility. The relationship between the national government and state governments has changed with time and political trends, and this flexibility is likely to continue. Several models are used to describe this changing relationship over time.

During most of the nineteenth and early twentieth centuries, a system called dual federalism operated. Under this model, there were rather specific areas of influence. The national government had primary delegated powers as defined in the Constitution, and the state governments provided most basic services to citizens. There was little financial assistance from the national government to states. Some have compared this to a layer cake with clearly defined areas of influence. Although this is called dual federalism, for much of the nineteenth century, states were dominant. After the Civil War, the idea of states' rights over national power began to decline.

The second model used to describe federal-state relations is often called cooperative federalism. This relationship, compared to a marble cake in which there is no clear line between what the national government does and what the states do, began during the 1930s with the Great Depression. The federal government began to supply more money to state and local governments. A cooperative relationship existed between the national and state governments in order to provide services to meet the increasing needs of citizens as the idea of what a government should provide to its people gradually expanded during a time of severe economic hardship.

During the 1960s, some saw a changed relationship with what came to be called creative federalism. President Johnson sought to create a Great Society through a massive expenditure of money to end poverty and lift all citizens in society. Under President Nixon, the system was referred to as new federalism. It involved giving state governments more discretion in program administration and so-called revenue sharing. President Reagan sought to give the states more power in spending grant money while reducing the amount of money available to state and local governments. Some viewed this as a return of both power and responsibilities to the states.

Under President Clinton, with emphasis from the Republicans in Congress, federal-state relations were described as undergoing a devolution of power. This basically means that states were given even greater authority on both program construction and administration.

When it comes to decisions about spending money, the evolution in the United States has been from one where the national government specified programs and provided money to support them to one where state and local governments are given greater power and authority to determine how federal programs are administrated in their states. Whereas federal grants to states declined as a percentage of federal expenditures during the Reagan administration, they grew under both Bush presidencies and under Clinton.

Federal grants are a form of financial assistance from a federal agency for a specific program or purpose. For example, the Texas Railroad Commission receives money annually from the Federal Recovery and Reinvestment Fund. About 24 percent of state expenditures are from the federal government. Of course, although states have greater power now than previously, they can still be coerced. Some grants, called **categorical grants,** have federal strings attached that specify to states where the money can and cannot be spent. This phenomenon is called coercive federalism. (We examine state financing more closely in Chapter 14.)

Relations between States in the Federal System

It is also important to understand the relations that exist between states, and between states and individuals. Article 4, Section 1 of the Constitution, known as the **Full Faith and Credit Clause,** states, "Full Faith and Credit shall be given in each state to the public Acts, Records and Judicial Proceedings of every other state." For example, if your last will and testament is probated in a Texas court, other states must recognize that court action.

This seems like an obvious requirement because it enables citizens to know that the rights they enjoy in their home state will be honored in another. However, this is not as simple as it seems. There are three good examples in the past 70 years where this clause in the Constitution was tested. The first is divorce. In the 1950s, it was difficult, in most states, to obtain a divorce. The state of Nevada was an exception. It granted divorces very easily. At first, some states refused to accept what were often negatively called "quickie divorce mill" decisions, but eventually all states had to recognize these divorces.

Second, in the 1980s, some states refused to enforce child custody and support payments following divorce. There were cases where one parent in a divorce would move to another state and refuse to abide by the child custody or payment agreements. Eventually, federal courts forced all states to enforce these court decrees from other states.

A third, and more recent, example is the issue of same-sex marriage. The U.S. Congress passed, and President Clinton signed into law, the federal Defense of Marriage Act (DOMA) in 1996. At the time, the argument that people should be allowed to marry same-sex partners was not widely accepted. Yet, over the following decade and a half, more and more states, and the District of Columbia, were legalizing same-sex marriage of their own accord. However, Sections 2 and 3 of DOMA prevented the federal government from legally recognizing these marriages and allowed DOMA-supporting states to ignore marriage licenses and any other state's definition of marriage.[6] Advocates of same-sex marriage argued that states were violating the Full Faith and Credit Clause by refusing to recognize same-sex marriages performed in other states.

Several cases challenging DOMA and Proposition 8 in California, which banned same-sex marriage, were up for review in the 2012–2013 term. In June 2013, the Supreme Court, in *U.S. v. Windsor*, struck down Section 3 of DOMA (the prohibition on federal government recognition) as unconstitutional. At the same time, the Court dismissed Proposition 8 on procedural grounds instead of ruling on its constitutionality. This effectively left a previous lower district court ruling on the proposition intact (originally *Perry v. Schwarzenegger* in 2010), a ruling that overturned the proposition on constitutional grounds. Later in 2013, a U.S. district court dismissed Pennsylvania's argument that same-sex marriage is a state issue rather than a federal one, clearing the way for the Supreme Court to weigh in on the constitutionality of Pennsylvania's same-sex marriage ban. Similar cases were also concurrently underway in other states.

categorical grants
Grants that may be used to fund specific purposes as defined by the federal government

Full Faith and Credit Clause
Clause in Article 4 of the U.S. Constitution that requires states to recognize the judgments, legislation, and public records of other states

State Representative Celia Israel (D-District 50) speaks to approximately 150 people gathered at the north steps of the Texas State Capitol building in Austin, Texas, in 2015 to support the recent U.S. Supreme Court ruling on same-sex marriage.

Jeff Newman/ZUMA Press, Inc/Alamy Stock Photo

All of this back and forth led to a landmark decision by the Supreme Court on June 26, 2015. In *Obergefell v. Hodges*, the Court determined that the Fourteenth Amendment not only protected marriage as a fundamental right but also "extend[ed] to certain personal choices central to individual dignity and autonomy, including intimate choices that define personal identity and beliefs."[7] As a result, marriage as a federally protected institution can no longer be defined as between one man and one woman. Any law, state or federal or otherwise, requiring such is now unconstitutional and rendered defunct.

The U.S. Constitution, in Article 4, Section 2, Clause 2, says that in some areas a state must treat citizens of other states the same way as it treats its own citizens. This is more formally known as the **Privileges and Immunities Clause.** States cannot violate basic rights or protected privileges of any individual federal citizen who happens to be a nonresident or a citizen of other states.[8] When the Supreme Court, for example, struck down Section 2 and Section 3 of DOMA in the decisions *U.S. v. Windsor* and *Obergefell v. Hodges*, it meant that all states must both recognize and permit marriage licenses for same-sex couples regardless of their residency. If a state must now recognize and permit marriages between its own same-sex citizens, it must also do so for citizens of other states.

It is understood, however, that in other areas, residents and nonresidents *can* be treated differently. One particularly relevant example is out-of-state tuition at public universities. Differential rates can be charged for residents of Texas and residents of other states. The justification for different rates is that because state universities are publicly funded, residents of Texas rightfully should pay a lower tuition rate because they have been subsidizing higher education through taxes. This also applies to driver's licenses, hunting licenses, law licenses, and professional licenses.

Of course, it can be difficult to determine what falls under the privileges and immunities of citizenship and what does not. It can also be unclear who has the right to decide. There is a long history spanning the judicial and legislative branches, from colonial times to today and onward.[9]

Privileges and Immunities Clause

Clause in Article 4 of the U.S. Constitution that prevents states from discriminating against citizens of other states and requires those citizens to be treated in like manner

CORE OBJECTIVE

Taking Personal Responsibility . . .

As a resident of Texas and a citizen of the United States, identify and discuss examples that reinforce the Full Faith and Credit Clause and the Privileges and Immunities Clause of the U.S. Constitution. Which examples, in your opinion, violate these principles?

Conclusion to Federalism

Learning Objective: Explain the American federal system of government.

As we have seen, one of the real strengths of the American federal system is its flexibility and ability to change with the times. This is obvious if you examine the U.S. Constitution and observe how little the document has been altered in the past 230-plus years (see Table 2.1). A few of the structural amendments are often pointed to as examples. The Sixteenth Amendment gave the national

TABLE 2.1

Amendments to the Federal Constitution

Civil Liberties and Voting Rights		Structural Amendments	
Number	**Subject Matter**	**Number**	**Subject Matter**
1–8	Various civil liberties	10	Reserved powers
9	Other liberties that may exist	11	Sovereign immunity
13	End to slavery	12	Electoral College voting
14	Equal protection, due process of law	20	When the president takes office—lame duck amendment
15	Race and voting	22	Two terms for president
16	Income tax	25	Presidential disability
17	Direct election of senators	27	Congressional pay
19	Women's right to vote		
23	D.C. vote for president		
24	End poll tax as requirement for voting		
26	18-year-old right to vote		
18 & 21	Prohibition and repeal of prohibition on sale of alcohol		

government great financial resources and led to greater national influence over state spending decisions and policies. Many of the civil and voting rights amendments have had a greater impact on federal-state relations. The Fourteenth Amendment applied many of the first eight amendments to the states. Amendments were aimed at ending violations of civil and voting rights practiced by the states (for example, women's right to vote and the issue of poll taxes).

Admittedly some changes were more profound than others. However, most were evolutional in nature and did not cause major structural changes. American federalism is a flexible system that will allow for change to meet future needs and challenges.

> **Understanding Impact** Within our federal system of government, we are obligated to follow both federal and state laws. Some argue that the state should enact laws in most policy areas because state legislators are more closely aligned with the will of the people in that state. Others argue that some policy areas are so important that the federal government should act to secure good outcomes for citizens in all states. Understanding how our federal system works allows individuals to take an active role in guiding federal and state government action that affect our lives. Which policies do you think should be managed at the state level?

Principles of Constitutional Government

Learning Objective: Describe the principles of constitutional government.

In addition to the U.S. Constitution, all 50 states have their own written constitutions. In the previous chapter, we discussed the political culture of Texas, and the Texas Constitution is very much an embodiment of both the traditionalistic and individualistic subcultures. The current (and seventh) constitution, ratified in 1876, reflects the conservative nature of the state, the distrust of government, and the desire to limit the government's ability to act.

History, culture, traditions, basic principles, and ideas affect constitutions. Later in this chapter, you will see how the individualistic and traditional political culture of Texas influenced the current state constitution. Still, all constitutional forms of government share certain characteristics, be they at the national or state level. The principles of popular sovereignty, social contract theory, and division of power underpin both the U.S. and Texas Constitutions.

popular sovereignty

The idea that power granted in state constitutions rests with the people

The first principle, **popular sovereignty,** is the idea that, at root, power rests with the people[10] and, theoretically, legitimate constitutions should articulate the will of the people. For example, U.S. state constitutions are written by a popularly elected convention of citizens and not by state legislatures. Thus, the citizens must also approve any changes in state constitutions—except in Delaware, where the state legislature can amend the state constitution without voter approval. The current Texas Constitution emphasizes the idea of popular sovereignty in its preamble and bill of rights.

social contract theory

The idea that all individuals possess inalienable rights and willingly submit to government to protect these rights

Second, constitutions are contracts or compacts between the citizens and the government and cannot be violated. This principle is embodied in **social contract theory,** the notion that all individuals possess inalienable rights and willingly submit to government to protect these rights. In essence, the constitution binds the government and the people, providing the framework within which interaction occurs. The laws passed by legislatures must fit within the framework of the constitution.

Third, constitutions structure government, divide and assign power, and limit government's power. Many assume that government can do anything not prohibited by its constitution, and thus it is necessary to expressly limit the power of government. The current Texas Constitution is very much an example of limitations set on the power of state government. The men who assembled in the Texas constitutional convention of 1875 had as their primary aim limiting the power of state government due to the perceived abuses of Radical Republican Governor Edmund J. Davis. The actions of the Radical Republicans in the U.S. Congress and in Texas during Reconstruction may have intensified the desires of these men to weaken and limit government, but they were predisposed to this philosophy even before the Civil War. Although the Texas Constitution embraces all three principles, the idea of a limited government, in particular, is wholeheartedly embraced.

Understanding Impact The principles of constitutional government establish a framework for action. Government derives its power from the people and we, in turn, consent to be governed. Thus, the role of the individual in our constitutional government is very important. To ensure that government functions consistent with the will of the people, individuals should be informed. What actions can you take to engage in the process and make your preferences known?

Characteristics Common to State Constitutions

Learning Objective: Describe the characteristics common to state constitutions.

separation of powers

Power divided among the legislative, executive, and judicial branches of government

Separation of Powers

Besides the ideals of popular sovereignty, compact or contract theory, and limited government, state constitutions share other common characteristics. First, all state constitutions embrace the idea of **separation of powers** provided in the

U.S. Constitution. Power is divided among an elected executive, an elected legislature, and the judiciary. The separation of powers provides a check on the actions of government. Fear of concentration of power in a single person led the framers of the U.S. Constitution to separate powers and provide for a system of **checks and balances.** Similarly, framers of the current Texas Constitution sought to distribute powers broadly among the branches of Texas government. Figure 2.3 shows a diagram of the separation of powers among the three branches of the federal government, and Table 2.2 clearly articulates the powers of the legislature, the governor, and the judiciary in Texas.

checks and balances
Power granted by the Constitution to each branch of government giving it authority to restrain other branches

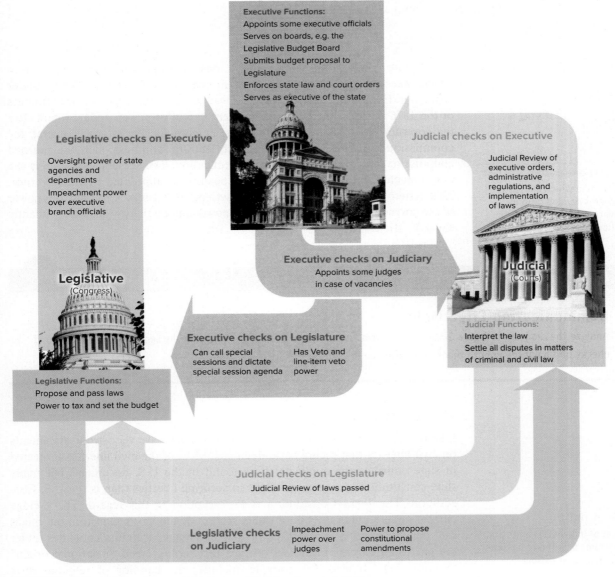

Texas Government Separation of Powers with Checks and Balances

FIGURE 2.3 Separation of Powers with Checks and Balances

(top): Mike Norton/Purestock/SuperStock; (bottom left): Pixtal/age fotostock; (bottom right): Hisham Ibrahim/Photographer's Choice/Getty Images

TABLE 2.2

Separation of Powers in Texas Government

The Legislature	The Governor	The Judiciary
Power to propose and pass laws (includes power to propose constitutional amendments)	Limited appointment power of some executive officials and judges in cases of vacancies	Interpret the law (includes settling all disputes in matters of criminal and civil law)
Power to tax and set the budget	Submit budget proposal to legislature	Popularly elected
Oversight power of state agencies and departments	Serve on boards, such as the Legislative Budget Board	
Power to impeach judges and executive branch officials	Can call special sessions and dictate special session agenda	
	Veto and line-item veto power	

All state constitutions embrace the idea of separation of power. Fear of strong executive authority, which had been experienced in Texas under Governor Edmund J. Davis and the Radical Republicans, led the framers of the 1876 Texas Constitution to fragment executive power. Today, voters elect the governor, the lieutenant governor, the comptroller, the attorney general, the commissioner of the land office, the agricultural commissioner, the railroad commissioners, and the state board of education. The secretary of state is the only non-elected executive official; the position is appointed by the governor. This system is called a **plural executive system,** and it serves to limit the power of the governor by distributing executive power among the various independently elected officials.

plural executive system
System in which executive power is divided among several statewide elected officials

CORE OBJECTIVE

Communicating Effectively . . .

Analyze the diagram in Figure 2.3 and the division of powers in Table 2.2 to describe the separation of powers and checks and balances in both theory and practice in Texas.

Bill of Rights

Like the U.S. Constitution, most state constitutions have very strong statements on civil liberties that secure basic freedoms. Most of the civil liberties protected in state constitutions duplicate those found in the U.S. document, but many state constitutions are more generous in securing liberties than is the U.S. Constitution. The Texas Constitution is no exception in this regard. The average citizen, upon reading the **bill of rights** section of the Texas Constitution, might well conclude that it is a very permissive document. It grants equalities under the law to all citizens regardless of "sex, race, color, creed or national origin" (Section 3a).[11] It also, for example, includes the banning of religious tests (Section 4) and explicit rights for those accused of a crime (Section 10).

bill of rights
A list of individual rights and freedoms granted to citizens within a constitution

Supreme Law of the State

Article 6 of the U.S. Constitution contains the **Supremacy Clause.** This makes the U.S. Constitution the supreme law of the land, and no federal or state **statute** may violate it. Because laws follow a hierarchy (owing to our federal system of government, discussed at the beginning of this chapter), federal law preempts state law, and state law preempts local law. Similarly, state law may not violate the state constitution, and state statutes are superior to local government **ordinances.**

A recent example of local ordinances potentially conflicting with a state statute involves the state issuing permits to citizens for carrying concealed handguns. Many local governments (cities, counties, and metropolitan transit authorities) passed regulations prohibiting the carrying of concealed handguns in some public places. Many of these gun laws have been struck down, though not all. Typically, local gun laws have been upheld only when they do not contradict state law, such as when local laws prohibit what the state prohibits, but more strictly. For example, in *Cincinnati v. Baskin* (2006), the defendant argued local law (prohibiting semiautomatic firearms with 10+ round capacity) was in violation of state law (prohibiting semiautomatic firearms with 31+ round capacity). Whereas state law was found to be general law, the local law was determined to not be in conflict and was therefore applicable to the defendant.[12] In 2015, the 84th Texas Legislature passed legislation permitting the "license to carry" firearms, also known as "open carry." This legislation (discussed more fully in Chapter 13) prohibits municipalities from regulating "the transfer, private ownership, keeping, transportation, licensing, or registration of fire arms."[13] In this policy area, local governments are very limited in their ability to act.

The legalization of marijuana is another area where the federal government and state and local government come into conflict. In 2018, the federal government declared hemp (if it "contains less than 0.3% of THC") a common agricultural product.[14] This caused problems because it is difficult to tell hemp and marijuana apart. This means that when law enforcement officers find what looks to be marijuana on an individual, they can be at a loss to prove it without specialized equipment to determine THC content.[15] Texas followed the federal government in legalizing low-THC hemp. Further, in 2021, Texas passed two laws: SB 181 which removed a required driver's license suspension for minor drug possession, leaving it up to judges' discretion based on the offender's past history; and, HB 1535 which eased restrictions on medical marijuana use and allowed products with up to 1% THC content.[16] Still, within the state, it varies county by county whether or not a person will be arrested for a small amount of cannabis, even if that small amount can't be tested locally for THC content. As of 2022, it is an ongoing issue.[17]

Supremacy Clause
A clause that makes constitutional provisions superior to other laws

statutes
Laws passed by state legislatures

ordinances
Laws passed by local governments

Understanding Impact The Texas Constitution, like other state constitutions, establishes the superiority of state law over local laws. All Texans reside in either an urban or rural community, which passes laws that impact many aspects of our daily lives. Therefore, we are more closely connected to these lower levels of jurisdiction. What roles do individuals play in securing their local interests within the larger state government structure?

Evolution of the Texas Constitution: 1824–1876

Learning Objective: Describe the development of Texas's constitutions before and after 1876.

Examining the constitutions that have governed Texas since Anglo settlement began gives us a greater understanding of how political culture affects the formal structure of government. Throughout history, each transitional period for the region that became Texas (incorporating under Mexico, gaining independent nation status, becoming part of the United States, and moving through the troubled period before and after the Civil War) required the creation of a new constitution. Still, each new constitution shared not only the common features detailed earlier but also the significant influence of Texas's history and culture.

Constitutions under the Republic of Mexico

The first constitution to govern Anglos in Texas was the Republic of Mexico's Constitution of 1824. This constitution was federalist in concept, dividing governing authority between the nation and the states, breaking with the Spanish centralist tradition of a strong national government.[18] Under the provisions of the 1824 Constitution, the state of Coahuila y Tejas was formed. The new state was required to enact a state constitution that passed in 1827. It provided for a unicameral legislature, and Texas elected two representatives to the state legislature. This constitution, which lacked a bill of rights, provided a government structure with which the Anglos were mostly comfortable. Anglos simply disregarded sections of the constitution they found disagreeable—such as those designating Catholicism as the state religion and those that did not recognize slavery.[19]

Early Texas flag depicting dissatisfaction with the suspension of the Republic of Mexico's 1824 Constitution

The suspension of the Mexican national constitution of 1824, and with it the state constitution of 1827, by Mexican president Santa Anna, was a factor that led to the Texas revolution. One of the early Texas flags, supposedly flown at the Alamo, had the number 1824 superimposed on a red, green, and white emblem of the Mexican flag. This was a demand that the Constitution of 1824 be restored.[20]

The Republic of Texas Constitution of 1836

In 1836, when Texas declared itself a republic independent of Mexico (Map 2.1), it adopted a new constitution. This document was a composite of the U.S. Constitution and the constitutions of several southern states. It provided for a **unitary system of government,** rather than a federal form of government discussed

unitary system of government

A system of government where all functions of government are controlled by the central/national government

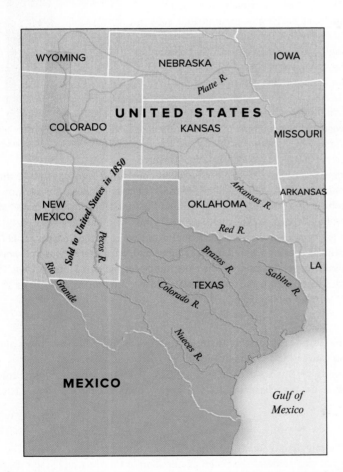

MAP 2.1   Republic of Texas From 1836 until 1845, Texas was an independent nation known as the Republic of Texas. In the treaty forced on Mexico by Texas, Mexico ceded land stretching to the headwaters of the Rio Grande. Although this land was never fully occupied by the government of the Republic, Texas claimed land in what is now part of the states of New Mexico, Oklahoma, Kansas, Colorado, and Wyoming.

Source: Texas State Library and Archives Commission

Focus On

The Tejano Contribution to Texas's Founding

José Antonio Navarro played an important part in the evolution of Texas from Mexican province to independent republic to statehood.

Born on February 27, 1795, into an elite San Antonio family, Navarro lived a relatively privileged life until his father's death in 1808.[22] Around this same time, there was increasing unrest in Texas as Mexican rebels began clashing with the Spanish army. Navarro, along with his mother's family, actively supported the rebellion.[23] The loss at the Battle of Medina in 1813 forced Navarro, his uncle José Francisco Ruiz, and others to flee to Louisiana.

After Navarro returned to Texas in 1816,[24] he became friendly with Stephen F. Austin. Together Navarro and Austin subtly, yet decisively, ensured that slavery would thrive in Mexican Texas[25] and actively pushed for Anglo settlement.[26] Initially, the Mexican government wanted Anglos to help settle Texas, but as Anglos started to sharply outnumber Tejanos, the government's position reversed and a law was passed restricting North American immigration to the province in 1830.[27] In December 1832, the *ayuntamiento* of San Antonio (a council of elite Tejanos that included Navarro) agreed, in defiance of the Mexican government, to encourage North American immigration because of various benefits, such as increased trade, protection against Native American raids, and infrastructure building.[28]

Witold Skrypczak/Alamy Stock Photo

As one of only three Tejano delegates to the Independence Convention, Navarro signed the Texas Declaration of Independence, an act that would have been considered treasonous had the Texas revolution failed. After the Texas Revolution, many Anglos became hostile to indigenous Tejanos. Navarro was able to sidestep this prejudice to a degree due to his history of service to Texas and his friendship with a number of Anglo leaders. Navarro's unwavering loyalty led many Texans, Anglos included, to see him as a hero.[29]

When the annexation of Texas drew near, Navarro was elected to represent Bexar County at the Constitutional Convention of 1845.[30] Notably, he was the only Hispanic person elected in any county and, once there, "was instrumental in having the word 'white' stricken from the requirements for voting in the constitution for the new State of Texas."[31]

Navarro served two terms in the state senate before retiring in 1849.[32] In recognition of his service to Texas, Navarro County was named in his honor.[33] He died on January 13, 1871.[34]

Navarro's Legacy Today

Navarro's home in San Antonio is part of the Casa Navarro State Historic Site.[35] Navarro's collected papers are at the Briscoe Center for American History at the University of Texas at Austin.[36]

In addition, the nonprofit group Friends of Casa Navarro sponsors an annual scholarship for university students. You can find out more about it on the Historic Site's web page, hosted by the Texas Historical Commission.[37]

Critical Thinking Questions

1. What were Navarro's contributions to the founding of Texas as a republic and as a state?
2. Why do you think Navarro was able to sidestep some of the racial persecution of the time and stay a leader?

earlier. Signs of distrust of government by the traditionalistic southerners who wrote the document are evident. They limited the president to one three-year term of office and prohibited consecutive reelection. The president was also prohibited from raising an army without the consent of the congress. There were other features, such as freedom of religion and property rights protection, that had been absent in the 1824 and 1827 Mexican constitutions. Slavery, which had not been recognized by the Mexican government, was legalized.[21]

Statehood Constitution of 1845

The first Texas state constitution was adopted when Texas joined the Union in 1845. This document also reflected the traditionalistic southern culture, with a few notable exceptions that were adaptations of Spanish law. Women were granted property rights equal to those of men, especially in marriage, where women were given half the value of all property acquired during the marriage (communal property). In addition, a person's homestead was protected from forced sale to pay debts. These ideas were later adopted by many other states. The 1845 constitution also provided for limited executive authority, biennial sessions of the legislature, and two-year terms for most officials. Most of these features were included in later constitutions.

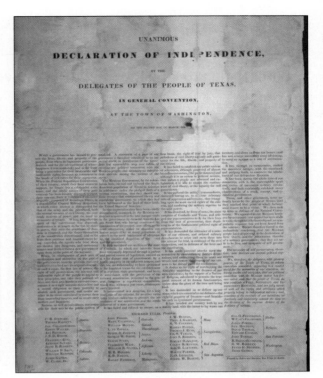

The Declaration of Independence 1836

Texas State Library and Archives Commission

The Civil War and Reconstruction Constitutions of 1861, 1866, and 1869

In 1861, when Texas joined the Confederacy, another state constitution was adopted. It was essentially the same as the 1845 document but with an added prohibition against the freeing of slaves, a provision to secede from the Union, and a provision to join the Confederacy.

In 1866, a third state constitution was approved as a condition for rejoining the Union following the Civil War. This document abolished slavery, nullified the ordinances of secession, renounced the right of future secession, and repudiated the wartime debts of the state. This constitution was short lived and overturned by Reconstruction acts of the U.S. Congress.

Texas adopted a new constitution in 1869. This fourth state constitution, which was approved under the supervision of the federal government's military rule, is called the Reconstruction constitution or the "carpetbagger's constitution." It represented a radical departure from past and future documents and reflected the centralization aspirations of the national Republicans. The 1869 constitution provided a four-year term for the governor, who had the authority to appoint most state and many local officials. The constitution abolished county courts and removed much local authority and control from the planter class. Public schools were centralized under state control and funded with a poll tax and the sale of public lands. African Americans were given the right to vote, and white Americans who had participated in the "rebellion" (the Civil War) lost the right to vote.[38]

Black Delegates Push for Political Advancement

In the aftermath of the American Civil War, there was a solid push to improve the rights of Black Texans. Historian James Marten notes that "by early 1868, fifty thousand freedmen had registered to vote, and in February over 80 percent turned out to cast their ballots almost unanimously in favor of what everyone predicted would be a Radical-dominated constitutional convention."[39] From there, 9 Black men were chosen as delegates to that convention along with 81 white men. Those 9 delegates along with 5 others later elected as state legislators would come to comprise the core of Black leadership in the state.[40]

During the convention's two sessions, there were four large blocs of interests, the largest of which related to Unionist interests and therefore desired to include basic civil rights. The 9 Black delegates as a bloc tentatively allied with the Unionists and more fully allied with another bloc of Radical Republicans. The fourth bloc represented East Texas and was completely opposed to Black civil rights.[41]

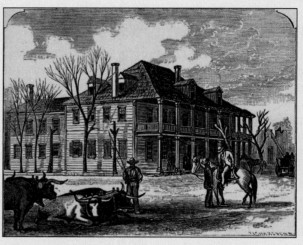

George T. Ruby, a free-born Black, was one of the leading members of the 9 Black delegates to the constitutional convention.

Smith Collection/Gado/Archive Photos/Getty Images

Due to intense differences both among and within the blocs, the convention ended without a formal document. However, what did come out of the convention was put before voters and largely approved, becoming the Constitution of 1869.[42] The three most important adopted elements that came from the 9 delegates and their allies were as follows:

1. "That the right to hold office be extended to all men without regard to race, color, or creed"
2. That "illegitimate Black children, or children of slave parents, [shall be made] legitimate with all the legal rights of inheritance upon the marriage of their parents"
3. That "all men [be allowed] to vote except those disqualified by the United States Constitution"[43]

The third item sparked the most controversy and brought fraction to the convention and even among the 9 because it allowed ex-Confederates to vote. Many white Radicals and 4 of the 9 refused to sign the final document. They feared that permitting ex-Confederates to vote would allow those interests to regain political supremacy in the state.[44] This fear would prove somewhat true as Black political participation declined in the following decade, and the Constitution of 1876 reflected white resentment toward Reconstruction.

Critical Thinking Questions

1. What were the 9 Black delegates' contributions to the Texas Constitution of 1869?
2. How did the work of these original 9 Black delegates pave the way for future reform within the state?

The Constitution of 1876

The current Texas Constitution was written in 1875 at the end of Reconstruction and approved by the voters in 1876. None of the delegates present at the 1875 constitutional convention had participated in writing the 1869 constitution.

These men were landowners who had strongly objected to the centralist government under Reconstruction. As T. R. Fehrenbach put it, these men were

> mostly old Texans: John Henry Brown, Sterling C. Robertson, sons of empresarios, Rip Ford (Texas Ranger), John H. Reagan (Ex-Postmaster General of the Confederacy), and a bevy of generals who has [*sic*] worn the grey. Of the ninety members, more than twenty held high rank in the C.S.A. [Confederate States of America] This was a restoration convention. . . . It was a landowners' group, including forty members of the Grange. . . . This was an antigovernment instrument: too many Texans had seen what government could do, not for them but to them. It tore up previous frameworks, and its essential aim was to try and bind all state government within tight confines.[45]

The new constitution reflected the antigovernment sentiments of the traditionalistic/individualistic political culture of the state. It reimposed shorter terms of office, reestablished many statewide and local elected offices, and severely restricted the government's authority to act. This constitution restricted the powers of the legislature and the governor.[46]

Delegates to the 1875 Constitutional Convention
Texas State Library and Archives Commission

CORE OBJECTIVE

Thinking Critically . . .

What is the impact of a constitutional convention dominated by one party? What were the consequences of the 1875 constitutional convention in the development of the Texas Constitution?

Culture Drives Institutions

Learning Objective: Describe how political culture drives institutions.

The various Texas constitutions have all reflected the political climate of the state, demonstrating how political culture drives institutions. During the annexation period, many Texans distrusted government. Their political culture was influenced by their attitudes about the former Mexican government, as well as their deep-rooted southern traditional beliefs. Consistent with the dominant views of the day, the 1845 constitution provided for limited government with little centralized power. The Civil War and post–Civil War constitutions of 1861 and 1866 continued these principles of limited government. The present 1876 constitution not only reinstated but also expanded the ideas of limited government. Only the Reconstruction constitution of 1869, which provided for a strong centralized government, was a departure from these ideas. Its swift repeal at the end of Reconstruction indicates how southern whites utterly rejected these concepts.

Many Texans today would not accept these concepts, either. In 1999, voters rejected two amendments that would have expanded the power of the governor to appoint and remove minor state officials.[47] In addition, voters have rejected annual sessions of the legislature on several occasions, and there is a consistent voice for decentralization of decisions down to the local level. In short, the current Texas Constitution is very compatible with the political climate of the state. However, institutions also can independently impact political outcomes as well as shape political culture in the future. The Spanish constitutions (1824 and 1827) contributed several key elements, including community property rights for women, which were a clear departure from English common law.

Understanding Impact The political culture of Texas has influenced the development of the state's constitution and the role of government in our lives. Texas is becoming increasingly diverse with individuals from many cultural backgrounds living in the state. Does your cultural background align with the political culture of limited government?

Important Sections of the Texas Constitution

Learning Objective: Describe the development of Texas's constitutions before and after 1876.

There are 17 articles in the Texas Constitution in addition to a preamble and appendix. Because the Texas Constitution contains over 92,000 words, to discuss all sections in depth would be exhaustive.[48] However, quite a few sections stand out as essential. A number of them are reflective of sections found in the U.S. Constitution, but the Texas Constitution is significantly more detailed.

Article I: Bill of Rights

The first article in the Texas Constitution is the bill of rights. Much like the U.S. Constitution, the Texas Constitution provides protection for freedom of speech and religion and protects the rights of the accused. Additional elements can be found in the Texas Constitution. For example, an equal rights amendment was inserted into the Texas Constitution in 1972, guaranteeing equality based on sex, race, color, creed, and national origin. The Texas Constitution ensures that the writ of habeas corpus will not be suspended and gives protection to crime victims. In 2021, voters amended the Texas Constitution to prevent the state and other organizations from closing in-person religious services due to the Covid-19 pandemic.[49]

These rights add many of the elements of law found in the federal government and in other state constitutions. Some elements and amendments conflict, however. One such conflicting amendment, added in late 2005, is Section 32, which defines marriage as a union between one man and one woman.[50] This amendment was struck down as unconstitutional by the U.S. Supreme Court in February 2015 and is no longer operational.[51]

Article II: The Powers of Government

Article II discusses separation of powers specifically. The Texas Constitution makes it clear that the system contains separate checks, as compared to the more implied structure noted in the U.S. Constitution, by stating "no person, or collection of persons, being of one of these departments, shall exercise any power properly attached to either of the others, except in the instances herein expressly permitted."[52]

Article III: Legislative Department

Article III refers to the legislative branch. The Texas Constitution divides the Texas state legislature into two branches: a senate and a house of representatives. The senate is to be composed of 31 members, and the house of representatives is to be 150 members. The constitution provides for the election system, terms of office of members, and required qualifications of both branches. Much like the U.S. Constitution, the qualifications for senators and representatives are minimal. The legislature is to meet every two years for 140 days. Unlike the U.S. Constitution, the Texas Constitution lays out in significant detail the rules of procedure that legislators must follow. Article III, Section 24 provides the amount of compensation for legislators at $600 per month, with per diem expenses allowed. The Texas Ethics Commission, an agency whose membership is outlined in Article III, sets the per diem amount and can choose to recommend a higher salary for legislators.

Article IV: Executive Department

Article IV describes the executive branch, which consists of the governor, lieutenant governor, comptroller of public accounts, commissioner of general land office, and the attorney general, who are all elected. The secretary of state is appointed by the governor. Under Article IV, the Texas legislature sets the annual salary of the governor. The governor's term is set at four years, and the constitution establishes no term limits. The governor is given the right to call a special session (which differs from an extraordinary session), during which members of the "Legislature may not consider any subject other than the appointment of electors at that special session."[53] The Texas Constitution purposefully provides for a fragmented executive branch and limits the powers of the governor. This is in keeping with much of the history and culture of the state, in which a general distrust of centralized power led to a preference for limited government.

Article V: Judicial Department

Article V refers to the judicial branch. This is one of the branches whose structural elements are distinct from the design of the federal branches. The judicial department consists of multiple courts and, rather than having a single high court, the Texas Constitution provides for two high courts: the Supreme Court (eight justices and one chief justice) and the Court of Criminal Appeals (eight judges and one presiding judge). The Texas legislature has the right to create additional courts as it sees fit. Article V provides the requirements for judges. For example, a justice on the Texas Supreme Court must be "licensed to practice law in this state and [must be], at the time of election, a citizen of the

United States and of this state, and [have] attained the age of thirty-five years, and [have] been a practicing lawyer, or a lawyer or judge of a court of record together at least ten years."[54] It should be noted, however, that not all judges need be lawyers. For example, county judges and justices of the peace are excluded from this requirement. In addition, the Texas Constitution provides for the election, rather than appointment, of judges. This has been a political concern wherein some citizens argue that the partisan election of judges may lead judges to base decisions on political reasons to ensure reelection. However, others argue that the election of judges provides for more direct involvement by the people in the democratic process.

Additional Articles

Article VI concerns suffrage and provides the list of persons not allowed to vote in the state, including those who are under 18 years of age, individuals deemed mentally incompetent by the court, and persons convicted of felonies. Article VII focuses on education and provides for a system of free public schools as well as various systems of funding for primary and secondary schools. Article VII also provides for the establishment of state universities. Articles IX and XVI define the creation and structure of counties in the state. These portions of the constitution are incredibly detailed, and the structure provided for counties leads to a fairly inflexible system to which counties are required to conform. Article XVII provides the means for amending the Texas Constitution.

Understanding Impact In addition to structuring state government, assigning it power, and limiting its power, the Texas Constitution provides the rules by which the state government acts. It is beneficial for individuals to know how state government functions since the outcomes of government action affect us every day. What can do you to become better informed about government action?

Comparing the Structure of State Constitutions

Learning Objective: Describe the characteristics common to state constitutions.

Although they have some common characteristics, vast differences exist among state constitutions. According to legal experts and political theorists, there are some ideal characteristics that constitutions should possess. Ideally, a constitution should be brief and explicit, embody only the general principles of government, and provide the broad outlines of government subject to interpretation, especially through the court's power of judicial review. Constitutions should not be too detailed and specific, but should be broad and flexible. Furthermore, constitutions should provide broad grants of power to specific agencies and hold government officials accountable for their actions. Last, formal amendments to the constitution should be infrequent, deliberate, and significant.

Although it is worth identifying the qualities of an ideal constitution, it is important to understand that an "ideal" constitution does not necessarily equal good governance. The culture in which political institutions operate has a much more significant impact on governance. A good constitution serves to reinforce cultural expectations, but it is not sufficient in and of itself.

The U.S. Constitution meets these "ideal characteristics." There are only 4,543 words in the original document. It broadly outlines the basic principles of government and has been amended only 27 times. All but 8 of these amendments involved issues of civil liberty, voting, and electoral questions. Very few of these amendments have altered the basic structure of the federal government. The document is flexible enough to allow for change without altering the basic document.

Few state constitutions can meet the ideal standards of brevity and a small number of amendments. This is especially true of the Texas Constitution. Table 2.3 details information about all 50 state constitutions as of January 1, 2021. Several conclusions are obvious from examining this table. First, most states have had several constitutions. Only 19 states are still operating under their first constitution, and most of these are newer states in the West. Maine and Massachusetts are the only states of the "original 13" still operating under their first constitutions. Because of the Civil War and its aftermath, former Confederate states have had multiple constitutions.

Second, most state constitutions are lengthy. Alabama's is the longest, with 402,852 words, including the amendments. The average state constitution is about 40,028 words. Some writers have pointed out that state constitutions have to be longer than the U.S. document because of the nature of state responsibility. Although this is true, it can also be argued that most state documents are of excessive length for other reasons, which are discussed later.

Third, most state constitutions have been amended more often than the U.S. Constitution; the average is about 133 times. Alabama is again the leader with 977 amendments. Fourth, state constitutions have a limited life span when compared with the U.S. Constitution. The average life span for a state constitution is 95 years.[55]

If we compare the Texas Constitution to the "average" state constitution, we find that it is longer than most, at 92,345 words, and has more amendments. It has been amended 507 times as of January 1, 2021.[56] As previously noted, Texas drafted a new constitution each time its status changed and has created five constitutions over its history. Only six states have drafted more constitutions, and Louisiana, with 11, has drafted the most. One can easily conclude that most state constitutions, including Texas's, do not meet the criteria for an ideal constitution. Most are lengthy, detailed documents that require frequent alteration and might be more accurately described as statutory or legislative acts rather than constitutional law. This is especially true of the document that governs Texas.

Several other generalizations can be made about state constitutions. First, most create weak executives and strong legislatures. (This is discussed later in the text.) Second, all state constitutions contain articles on taxation and finance that limit how funds can be spent. Often, taxes are **earmarked** for specific purposes (a common example is the gasoline tax for state highways). Third, all but a few constitutions prohibit deficit expenditures unless approved by voters in the form of a bond election. Finally, most state constitutions contain large amounts of detail. For example, the original Texas Constitution has a homestead protection provision that contains a detailed list of items that cannot be forcibly sold for payment of debts. The list included the numbers of chickens, ducks, cows, pigs, dogs, and horses that were exempt.

earmarked revenue
Money dedicated to a specific expenditure; for example, the excise tax on gasoline funds highway infrastructure

TABLE 2.3

Comparisons of State Constitutions, January 1, 2021

State or Other Jurisdiction	Number of State Constitutions	Dates of Adoption	Effective Date of Present Constitution	Estimated Length (number of words)	Number of Amendments	
					Submitted to Voters	Adopted
Alabama	6	1819, 1861, 1865, 1868, 1875, 1901	Nov. 28, 1901	402,852	1,316	977
Alaska	1	1956	Jan. 3, 1959	13,479	43	29
Arizona	1	1911	Feb. 14, 1912	47,306	280	156
Arkansas	5	1836, 1861, 1864, 1868, 1874	Oct. 30, 1874	77,663	211	110
California	2	1849, 1879	July 4, 1879	76,930	914	540
Colorado	1	1876	Aug. 1, 1876	84,239	359	167
Connecticut	2	1818, 1965	Dec. 30, 1965	16,544	35	33
Delaware	4	1776, 1792, 1831, 1897	June 10, 1897	25,445	0*	151
Florida	6	1839, 1861, 1865, 1868, 1886, 1968	Jan. 7, 1969	48,440	191	141
Georgia	10	1777, 1789, 1798, 1861, 1865, 1868, 1877, 1945, 1976, 1982	July 1, 1983	41,684	109	85
Hawaii	1	1950	Aug. 21, 1959	21,498	140	114
Idaho	1	1889	July 3, 1890	24,626	215	127
Illinois	4	1818, 1848, 1870, 1970	July 1, 1971	16,401	23	15
Indiana	2	1816, 1851	Nov. 1, 1851	11,610	81	49
Iowa	2	1846, 1857	Sept. 3, 1857	11,089	59	54
Kansas	1	1859	Jan. 29, 1861	14,097	129	99
Kentucky	4	1792, 1799, 1850, 1891	Sept. 28, 1891	27,234	78	43
Louisiana	11	1812, 1845, 1852, 1861, 1864, 1868, 1879, 1898, 1913, 1921, 1974	Jan. 1, 1975	76,730	293	203
Maine	1	1819	March 15, 1820	16,313	207	174
Maryland	4	1776, 1851, 1864, 1867	Oct. 5, 1867	43,198	270	234
Massachusetts	1	1780	Oct. 25, 1780	45,283	148	120
Michigan	4	1835, 1850, 1908, 1963	Jan. 1, 1964	31,164	78	34
Minnesota	1	1857	May 11, 1858	12,016	218	121

TABLE 2.3 *(continued)*

Comparisons of State Constitutions, January 1, 2021

State or Other Jurisdiction	Number of State Constitutions	Dates of Adoption	Effective Date of Present Constitution	Estimated Length (number of words)	Number of Amendments	
					Submitted to Voters	Adopted
Mississippi	4	1817, 1832, 1869, 1890	Nov. 1, 1890	26,229	166	128
Missouri	4	1820, 1865, 1875, 1945	March 30, 1945	85,673	196	128
Montana	2	1889, 1972	July 1, 1973	12,790	61	35
Nebraska	2	1866, 1875	Oct. 12, 1875	34,934	357	233
Nevada	1	1864	Oct. 31, 1864	31,915	243	144
New Hampshire	2	1776, 1784	June 2, 1784	13,238	291	147
New Jersey	3	1776, 1844, 1947	Jan. 1, 1948	28,071	92	76
New Mexico	1	1911	Jan. 6, 1912	33,198	308	174
New York	4	1777, 1822, 1846, 1894	Jan. 1, 1895	49,360	305	229
North Carolina	3	1776, 1868, 1970	July 1, 1971	17,177	51	41
North Dakota	1	1889	Nov. 2, 1889	18,746	284	161
Ohio	2	1802, 1851	Sept. 1, 1851	59,858	294	177
Oklahoma	1	1907	Nov. 16, 1907	84,956	376	200
Oregon	1	1857	Feb. 14, 1859	49,430	506	259
Pennsylvania	5	1776, 1790, 1838, 1873, 1968	1968	26,078	39	33
Rhode Island	2	1842, 1986	Dec. 4, 1986	11,407	15	13
South Carolina	7	1776, 1778, 1790, 1861, 1865, 1868, 1895	Jan. 1, 1896	27,421	690	500
South Dakota	1	1889	Nov. 2, 1889	28,840	245	124
Tennessee	3	1796, 1835, 1870	Feb. 23, 1870	13,960	66	43
Texas	5	1845, 1861, 1866, 1869, 1876	Feb. 15, 1876	92,345	686	507
Utah	1	1895	Jan. 4, 1896	21,010	185	129
Vermont	3	1777, 1786, 1793	July 9, 1793	8,565	212	54
Virginia	6	1776, 1830, 1851, 1869, 1902, 1970	July 1, 1971	24,009	62	54
Washington	1	1889	Nov. 11, 1889	32,578	183	108
West Virginia	2	1863, 1872	April 9, 1872	33,324	126	75
Wisconsin	1	1848	May 29, 1848	15,102	198	148
Wyoming	1	1889	July 10, 1890	26,349	131	101

*In Delaware, proposed amendments are voted on by the state senate and house of representatives, not by the people. An amendment succeeds if it achieves a two-thirds majority in both bodies.

Source: Book of the States 2021, "Council of State Governments," Table 1.3. https://issuu.com/csg.publications/docs/bos_2021_issuu.

Amending and Revising State Constitutions

Learning Objective: Explain how state constitutions, including Texas's, are amended and revised.

All state constitutions provide procedures for amending and revising the document. Except in the state of Delaware, two steps are involved in changing constitutions: proposing amendments and gaining citizen approval. In Texas, two-thirds of each house of the legislature must propose amendments, and a majority of the voters who vote on the amendment must approve it.

Some states provide a variety of methods for proposing or recommending changes to the constitution. All state constitutions allow the legislature to propose changes. Most other states require an extraordinary majority vote of both houses to propose an amendment. Seventeen states require only a majority; 18 states require a two-thirds vote of the state legislature; 9 states require a three-fifths vote of the state legislature; and 6 states use variations thereof.[57]

A second method of proposing amendments to constitutions is by voter initiative. **Initiative** requires the collection of a prescribed number of signatures on a petition within a set time. Seventeen states allow initiative. Most states with initiative are western states that entered the Union in the late nineteenth century or early twentieth century, when initiative was a popular idea. Only five states that allow for constitutional amendments by initiative are east of the Mississippi River. Texas does not have initiative. The Texas Republican Party pushed the idea of initiative for many years, but in 1996, it was dropped from the party platform.

Most states, including Texas, allow the legislature to submit to the voters the question of calling a **constitutional convention** to propose amendments. This method is normally used for general revision and not for single amendments. Fourteen states have some provision for automatically submitting the question of a general convention to the voters periodically. If the voters approve, a convention is elected, it assembles, and it proposes amendments for voter approval.

Constitutional commissions are most often created by acts of the legislature, although there are other methods. These commissions usually submit a report to the legislature recommending changes. If the legislature approves, the proposed amendments are submitted to the voters. In Florida, the commission can bypass the legislature and go directly to the voters. Texas last used a commission in 1973, when the legislature created a 37-member commission to consider substantive and comprehensive revision to the Texas Constitution. After 8 months of meetings and 19 public hearings, the Constitutional Revision Commission submitted recommendations to the 63rd Texas legislature.[58] Many issues, such as "right to work" provisions, were contentious and necessitated compromise. Other provisions, including bringing the multitude of local government clauses together in one article, represented vast improvements. Ultimately the committee's recommendations were rejected by the legislature on July 30, 1974, having failed to garner a two-thirds majority by three votes.

initiative

A process that allows citizens to propose changes to the state constitution through the use of petitions signed by registered voters; Texas does not allow constitutional revision through initiative

constitutional convention

An assembly of citizens that may propose changes to state constitutions through voter approval

Patterns of Constitutional Change

If we examine state constitutional amendment processes, several patterns emerge. The first involves the frequency of change. State constitutions are amended more frequently than the U.S. Constitution. One reason is that state constitutions deal with a wider range of functions. About 63 percent of state amendments deal with issues not covered in the U.S. Constitution. A good example of this is education. Even if we remove issues not covered in the U.S. Constitution, the rate of amendment is still 3.5 times the national rate.[59] Change is also related to length. Longer state constitutions are more likely to be amended.[60]

The second pattern involves the method used to amend. As indicated, most amendments (90 percent) are proposed by state legislatures. States that require large legislative majorities for initiation have fewer amendments proposed and approved. Most amendments proposed by legislatures also receive voter approval. Voters have approved about 61 percent of all amendments proposed since their state's constitution adoption.[61]

In the 18 states that allow voters to initiate amendments, two patterns emerge: more amendments are proposed, and the voter approval success rate for initiative-generated amendments is about half the rate for those proposed by state legislatures (32 percent versus 64 percent).[62] This tells us that the initiative process does not screen out amendments that lack broad public support. Proposal by legislature does. Amendments that gain support from supermajorities (majorities at a specified level above a simple majority of 50 percent) are more likely to be politically acceptable. The legislature serves as a screening process to rule out unacceptable amendments.

Amending the Texas Constitution

All amendments to the Texas Constitution have been proposed by a two-thirds vote of each house of the state legislature. From 1876 through 2020, the legislature has proposed 686 amendments for voter approval. The voters have approved 507 and have rejected 179 (a 73.9 percent approval rate).[63]

Voter turnout for amendments tends to be quite low, for a variety of reasons. Most amendments appear on the ballot in November of odd-numbered years, when no statewide offices are up for election. Texas submits more amendments in odd-numbered years than most states. Since 1972, Texas has formally adopted 295 constitutional amendments. Of these, three were in even-numbered years.[64] Voter turnout for odd-year elections is lower than for even-year elections. In odd-year elections, less than 10 percent of the voting-age population participates (see Table 2.4).[65] This means that as few as 5 percent (plus one voter) could approve an amendment to the constitution. In 2005, there was a slight increase due to the anti–gay marriage amendment that was on the ballot.

Second, statewide voter turnout rates are often skewed by election schedules in counties with large cities. For example, Harris County could have a greater impact on statewide elections if many city and school board elections are held in the same election cycle as constitutional amendments. The Harris County vote could be significant if turnout statewide is very low. A strongly contested race for mayor of Houston could inflate the turnout rate in that city and affect statewide election results. The Harris County vote often constitutes about

TABLE 2.4

Voter Turnout in Odd-Year Constitutional Amendment Elections

Year	Percentage of Voting-Age Population Voting
2021	6.79%
2019	9.19
2017	4.50
2015	8.30
2013	6.14
2011	3.77
2009	5.77
2007	6.31
2005	13.82 (Anti–gay marriage amendment)
2003	9.31
2001	5.57
1999	6.69
1997	5.32
1997	8.45 (Special election)
1995	5.55
1993	8.52
1991	16.60 (School tax reform)
1989	9.33
1987	18.60 (School tax reform)
1985	8.24
1983	6.91
1981	8.07

Source: Adapted from Texas Secretary of State, http://www.sos.state.tx.us/elections/historical/70-92.shtml.

30 percent of the total statewide votes cast on these amendments, despite the fact that registered voters in Harris County make up approximately 15 percent of the total number of registered voters in the entire state.

Third, **ballot wording** can also contribute to voter confusion and apathy about the political process. The state legislature dictates the ballot wording of all amendments. Sometimes this wording can be misleading or noninstructive unless the voter has studied the issue before the election. This example from the 2019 constitutional election is illustrative:

> The constitutional amendment prohibiting the imposition of an individual income tax, including a tax on an individual's share of partnership and unincorporated association income.[66]

The state already lacks an income tax. The proposition is asking whether or not the state should close the door on the *possibility* of implementing one. Do voters favor or not favor the ability to possibly adopt an income tax in the future? The wording requires voters to understand that it is closing the door on possibility, not closing the door on an income tax right now. The amendment passed by a large majority.

ballot wording

Description of a proposed amendment as it appears on the ballot; can be intentionally noninstructive and misleading to voters in order to affect voter outcome

Another example of ballot-wording bias occurred in an amendment exempting personal property in Texas ports—the "freeport" amendment—that failed in 1987. The ballot read: "rendering to the exemption from ad valorem taxation, certain tangible personal property temporarily located within the states." In contrast, in 1989 the ballot read: "The constitutional amendment promoting economic growth, job creation and fair tax treatment for Texans who export goods." The 1989 amendment passed by a large majority. Ballot wording is apparently an important factor in the passage or rejection of amendments.

Fourth, the number of amendments and the subject matter of most amendments are not of interest to most voters, thus discouraging voter turnout. For example, in 2021, the voters were asked to approve eight amendments to the constitution. The subjects of many (though, not all) of these amendments were financial: to allow charitable raffles at rodeo events, to allow counties to issue bonds for infrastructure funding in designated underdeveloped zones, to expand property tax exemptions to include spouses of fatally injured members of the military, to limit property taxes on spouses of deceased persons with registered disabilities and so on.[67] The seemingly trivial or irrelevant subject matter in these elections contribute to low voter interest and turnout. Only those people most affected by an amendment are likely to understand it and to vote. Most voters stay home because there is little else to bring them out to the polls on Election Day.

Finally, voter ignorance of the issues is also a factor, although numerous sources provide ballot information. Issues are commonly reported in newspapers, on the nightly news, and on public radio broadcasting. Many county websites provide sample ballots beginning about a month in advance of an election. Unfortunately, many people remain uninformed regardless of the numerous avenues through which information can be accessed. This issue is discussed in detail in Chapter 9.

Thus, odd-year elections, the impact of counties with large cities, confusing or noninstructive ballot wording, issues that interest few voters, and voter ignorance all contribute to low voter turnout (see Table 2.5). A very small number of voters, stimulated by personal interests and supported by an active interest group, can amend the constitution without a majority of the voters becoming involved. Often, many voters are not even aware that an election is being held.

Several other observations can be made regarding the amendment processes in Texas. First, most amendments face little opposition. Texans have approved 507 amendments and rejected 179.[68] Most are supported by an organized interest group willing to spend money, gain support, and work hard for passage. Second, interest groups attempt to have their particular concerns protected in the constitution. A vested interest, protected in the constitution, is more difficult to alter than one protected by state law alone because state law can be changed easily in the next session of the legislature. The process of constitutional change requires a two-thirds vote of the legislature plus electoral approval.

A good example of such a protection in the constitution is the Permanent University Fund (PUF). The University of Texas (UT) and Texas A&M University are the only state schools that benefit from this fund, which has a value of approximately $11 billion. Other state universities have long felt that they deserved a share of this protected fund. Texas A&M and the University of Texas wanted to protect their funds and formed a coalition with non-PUF schools to support

TABLE 2.5	
Reasons for Low Voter Turnout in Constitutional Amendment Elections	
Reason	**Consequence**
Odd-year election	Fewer citizens vote when elections occur in odd years, particularly when there are no other statewide elections on the ballot.
Counties with larger cities skew turnout	If larger cities have issues on the ballot, particularly city offices, more citizens of those cities will turn out than citizens in other areas of a state, thereby giving those particular city citizens greater influence over amendment approval or disapproval.
Poorly worded amendments	Amendment proposals with poor or misleading wording can increase voter apathy due to lack of understanding or can cause voters to vote for an amendment they do not actually want.
Little public interest	Many amendments are not perceived to be of concern to the daily life of a typical voter, such as those on land grants or other government financial matters.
Voter ignorance	Even though there are numerous media outlets for information on upcoming amendment elections, few voters are aware of what any given amendment election is about. This can be attributed to lack of voter interest in learning about these issues and also to the media and political outlets themselves.

an amendment that created the Higher Education Assistance Fund (HEAF). This fund provides money to non-PUF universities. In the end, higher education funding for all state universities became protected in the state constitution.[69]

Understanding Impact Roughly, just over a quarter of Texas college students attend the UT and Texas A&M University systems.[70] The PUF generates income based on land grants, income that goes into a fund that the board of regents can use to pay off debt or provide individual schools money for programs, support, and maintenance. In contrast, the state legislature oversees HEAF and funds it through appropriations from general revenue.[71] How do you feel about the state, through constitutional amendment, creating a specific and self-sustaining funding source (PUF) for only two school systems? Does the creation of the HEAF balance out the state's support and financing of its public higher education institutions?

Criticisms of the Texas Constitution

Learning Objective: Discuss common criticisms of Texas's constitution.

A number of criticisms can be levied against the Texas Constitution. These include length, wording, unclear organization, excessive detail, inflexibility, and constant change.

The Texas Constitution is the second-longest state constitution in the nation, with much of its length in the form of amendments. For example, Article I, Bill of Rights, contains 34 sections, and Article VIII, Taxation and Revenue, contains 29 sections.[72] Much of it is written in language that is unclear and that some consider outdated. For example, Article IV, Section 3 on election returns states:

> The returns of every election for said executive officers, until otherwise provided by law, shall be made out, sealed up, and transmitted by the returning officers prescribed by law, to the seat of Government, directed to the Secretary of State, who shall deliver the same to the Speaker of the House of Representatives, as soon as the Speaker shall be chosen, and the said Speaker shall, during the first week of the session of the Legislature, open and publish them in the presence of both Houses of the Legislature.

In addition to the difficult language, the Texas Constitution is not well organized. Thus, it has a table of contents and an index.

Whereas such detail might not seem problematic at first, the purpose of a constitution is to provide a broad foundation upon which a state government can rest. Although the Texas Constitution contains some broad foundational aspects, many of its components are so specific and detailed that they would be better placed in a legislative enactment. For example, Article VIII, Taxation and Revenue, addresses topics such as homestead exemptions, assessment of lands designated for agricultural use, and ad valorem tax relief for items such as mobile drilling equipment and green (raw) coffee beans. Although these items may be important for government to address, their placement in the constitution, in contrast to being part of a statute or agency regulation, illustrates that many parts of the Texas Constitution are focused on specifics rather than on broad foundations.

The criticism that the Texas Constitution is inflexible and constantly changing seems contradictory. However, the inflexibility comes from the excessive detail. Broad statements allow for a wider use of discretion in interpreting and implementing constitutional provisions. The extreme detail found in a number of sections is one reason it is more difficult for government actors to use their discretion in interpretation and implementation. For example, Article IX, Counties, lays out in detail such items as hospital districts, tax rates, and airport authorities. Counties become limited in what they can do under the Texas Constitution. Of course, some people see this as an advantage. They believe that a constitution that frustrates the use of power by governmental authorities limits government and preserves their freedom.

The constant change comes from the stream of new amendments. These also contribute to excessive length. The changes tend to be incremental, meaning that the Texas Constitution as a whole has not been drastically revised since the 1876 version. Although many reformers believe the constitution needs comprehensive revision, it is unlikely that such change can take place in the brief biennial legislative session in a state whose citizens tend to distrust government.

Understanding Impact The Texas Constitution is criticized for being too lengthy, unclear, overly detailed, inflexible, and requiring frequent change. Given that constitutional amendments are commonly placed on off-year ballots, few Texans vote on these measures. Since the state constitution sets the rules for government action, individuals in the state should provide input. How can you ensure that you have a voice in establishing these rules?

Conclusion to the Texas Constitution

Learning Objective: Describe the development of Texas's constitutions before and after 1876.

Many legal scholars have pointed out the need for a general revision of the current Texas Constitution. In the 1970s, a serious effort at total revision was unsuccessful. A commission of legal experts, acting as a constitutional commission, made recommendations to the state legislature for major changes. The state legislature, acting as a constitutional convention in 1974, deadlocked and adjourned without making any recommendations for change. The next regular session of the Texas legislature, in 1975, proposed eight separate amendments to the voters. In November 1975, the voters rejected all amendments by a two-to-one margin.

In 1999, two prominent members of the Texas legislature introduced a bill calling for general revision of the Texas Constitution. Then-senator Bill Ratliff, Republican from East Texas, and Representative Robert Junell, Democrat from San Angelo, were the chairs of budget-writing committees in the senate and house in that session. Their bill called for some substantial changes in the current constitution. This proposal, which would have reduced the size of the current constitution to some 19,000 words in 150 sections, died in committee in both houses.

The 76th Legislature (1999) created the Select Committee on Constitutional Revision, and Speaker of the House James Laney (Democrat) appointed Representative Joe Driver (Republican) as chair. This committee held hearings in various locations in the state and suggested changes to eliminate outdated sections and update wording. The committee saw no need for a general revision of the document or the calling of a constitutional convention or commission.

The piecemeal process of amending the constitution every two years will likely continue. Significant political forces in the state lack interest in more thorough reform. Strong political leadership from someone like the governor would be necessary. Gov. Greg Abbott has not indicated any interest in supporting reform efforts; supporting controversial issues such as revision of the constitution has little appeal or political payoff. Currently, no statewide leader has been particularly vocal about supporting revision. In short, the political will to significantly change the constitution does not exist.

Second, the political culture of the state and the basic conservative nature of state politics do not support broad change. The current constitution supports the traditional, individual political culture of the state. The document serves select groups of people and protects their interests and privileges, and these groups have the resources to maintain those protections. Senator Ratliff's and Representative Junell's 1999 proposal avoided many of the major controversies by leaving intact important interests that are well protected by the constitution.

Third, opposition from lobby groups whose interests are currently protected by the document would make change difficult. In his opening address to the constitutional convention assembled in 1974, the vice chair of the convention, Lt. Gov. William Hobby, made the following observation:

> The special interests of today will be replaced by new and different special interests tomorrow, and any attempt to draft a constitution to serve such interests would be futile and also dishonorable.[73]

This convention adjourned without approving a new, rewritten constitution to be submitted to the voters. The special interests in the state had prevailed. The entire effort was, indeed, "futile and also dishonorable."

Fourth, one could cite a general lack of interest and support for change among citizens. Constitutional revision does not excite most citizens. The average Texan probably does not see the need for revision. Some proud Texans would take offense at the suggestion that the state document is flawed. The document drafted at the end of Reconstruction in the 1870s will probably continue to serve Texans for many years. The prospects for general revisions do not seem great. Evidence of this can be found in the 1999 election. In that year, the voters rejected three amendments that might be considered mildly progressive. Two of these amendments would have provided that the adjutant general of the national guard and the commissioner of health and human services were to serve at the pleasure of the governor. Another would have created a Judicial Compensation Commission providing procedures that are standard in most state constitutions today. And 20 years later, in 2019, voters rejected the possibility of legally considering an income tax.

Understanding Impact Consider how the current power of special interests might advance or obstruct the political issues that you care about. Does what you have learned in this chapter make you more interested in constitutional reform aimed at reducing the influence of such special interests? Why or why not? What might be done to motivate the citizens of Texas to care more about this issue?

Summary

LO: Describe the principles of constitutional government.

History, culture, traditions, basic principles, and ideas affect constitutions. Several important principles underpin the general idea of constitutional government. The first is the idea of popular sovereignty. This idea holds that, at root, power rests with the people and, theoretically, legitimate constitutions should articulate the will of the people. Second, constitutions are contracts or compacts between the citizens and the government (for example, social contract theory) and cannot be violated. Third, constitutions structure government, divide and assign power, and limit government power.

LO: Explain the American federal system of government.

The federal system of government provides for the national (federal) government and respective state governments to share powers. It balances power and responsibilities between the national and state governments. The federal system grants some powers exclusively to the national government and some exclusively to the states. In other cases, it grants powers to both the national and the state governments. The same can be said for denied powers. The federal system of government denies some powers to the national government, denies others to the states, and denies still others to both.

LO: Describe the characteristics common to state constitutions.

All state constitutions embrace the idea of separation of powers provided in the U.S. Constitution. Most state constitutions have very strong statements on civil liberties that secure basic freedoms. In addition, a constitution should be brief and explicit, embody only the general principles of government, and provide the broad outlines of government subject to interpretation. Constitutions should not be too detailed or specific. Instead, they should be broad and flexible. They should provide broad grants of power to specific agencies and hold government officials accountable for their actions. Formal amendments to the constitution should be infrequent, deliberate, and significant.

LO: Describe the development of Texas's constitutions before and after 1876.

During this period, there are four main constitutions to take note of: the Constitutions of 1824 (Republic of Mexico), 1836 (Republic of Texas), 1845 (Texas, as a new state in the Union), and 1876 (Texas, as a state in the Union, post-Reconstruction, current). The first governed Anglos in Texas and was federalist in concept, dividing governing authority between the nation and the states. It designated Catholicism as the state religion and did not recognize slavery. The second constitution (1836) was a composite of the U.S. Constitution and the constitutions of several southern states, providing for a unitary form of government and limiting the president to one three-year term with prohibitions against consecutive reelection. It also included freedom of religion and property rights protection that had been absent before. Slavery was legalized. The third constitution (1845) included a few adaptions of Spanish law, such as women being granted property rights equal to those of men. It also provided for limited executive authority, biennial sessions of the legislature, and two-year terms for most officials. The fourth and current Texas Constitution (1876) reimposed shorter terms of office, reestablished many statewide and local elected offices, and severely restricted the government's authority to act. Otherwise,

it maintains many of the characteristics of the 1845 constitution.

LO: Describe how political culture drives institutions.

The various Texas constitutions have all reflected the political climate of the state, demonstrating how political culture drives institutions. For example, during the annexation period, many Texans distrusted government. Their political culture was influenced by their attitudes about the former Mexican government, as well as their deep-rooted southern traditional beliefs. Consistent with that, the 1845 constitution provided for limited government with little centralized power.

LO: Explain how state constitutions, including Texas's, are amended and revised.

All state constitutions allow the legislature to propose changes. A second method of proposing amendments to constitutions is by voter initiative. Initiative requires the collection of a prescribed number of signatures on a petition within a set time. Texas does not have initiative. Most states, including Texas, allow the legislature to submit to the voters the question of calling a constitutional convention to propose amendments. These commissions usually submit a report to the legislature recommending changes. All amendments to the Texas Constitution have been proposed by a two-thirds vote of each house of the state legislature. General voter turnout on these proposals has been traditionally low.

LO: Discuss common criticisms of Texas's constitution.

Common criticisms include length, wording, unclear organization, excessive detail, inflexibility, and constant change. The Texas Constitution is the second-longest state constitution in the nation, with much of its length in the form of amendments. The inflexibility comes from the excessive detail. Constant change comes from the frequent adoption of amendments. In addition, broad statements allow for a wider use of discretion in interpreting and implementing constitutional provisions.

Key Terms

ballot wording	constitution	Equal Protection Clause
bill of rights	constitutional convention	federal system of government
categorical grants	Due Process Clause	Full Faith and Credit Clause
checks and balances	earmarked revenue	initiative

Interstate Commerce Clause
Necessary and Proper Clause
(Elastic Clause)
ordinances
plural executive system

popular sovereignty
Privileges and Immunities Clause
separation of powers
social contract theory
statutes

Supremacy Clause
Tenth Amendment
unitary system of government

Notes

1 Eugene C. Barker, "Mexican Colonization Laws," *Handbook of Texas Online*, https://www.tshaonline.org/handbook/entries/mexican-colonization-laws (accessed February 11, 2022).

2 https://www.law.cornell.edu/constitution/amendmentxiv (accessed February 11, 2022).

3 *New State Ice Co. v. Liebmann,* 285 U.S. 262 (1932), https://caselaw.findlaw.com/us-supreme-court/285/262.html (accessed February 11, 2022).

4 http://www.law.cornell.edu/supct/html/09-1227.ZO.html (accessed February 11, 2022).

5 Alexander T. Tabarrok, "Arguments for Federalism," Hastings Law School, University of California, San Francisco, September 20, 2001.

6 http://www.glaad.org/marriage/doma (accessed February 11, 2022).

7 U.S. Supreme Court, Syllabus: *Obergefell et al. v. Hodges, Director, Ohio Department of Health, et al.,* http://www.supremecourt.gov/opinions/14pdf/14-556_3204.pdf (accessed February 11, 2022).

8 "Congress's Power to Define the Privileges and Immunities of Citizenship," *Harvard Law Review*, February 10, 2015, http://harvardlawreview.org/2015/02/congresss-power-to-define-the-privileges-and-immunities-of-citizenship.

9 "Congress's Power to Define the Privileges and Immunities of Citizenship," *Harvard Law Review*, February 10, 2015, http://harvardlawreview.org/2015/02/congresss-power-to-define-the-privileges-and-immunities-of-citizenship.

10 Donald S. Lutz, "Toward a Theory of Constitutional Amendment," *American Political Science Review* 88 (June 1994): 355–70.

11 Texas Constitution, art. 1, sec. 3a.

12 *Cincinnati v. Baskin,* 112 Ohio St.3d 279, 2006-Ohio-6422, http://www.supremecourt.ohio.gov/rod/docs/pdf/0/2006/2006-Ohio-6422.pdf (accessed February 11, 2022).

13 Texas Department of Public Safety, "Texas License to Carry a Handgun Laws and Selected Statutes," 2016, http://www.dps.texas.gov/InternetForms/Forms/LTC-16.pdf (accessed January 9, 2020).

14 Malen Blackmon, "Marijuana Is Now Legal . . . ish in Texas," *Dallas Observer,* August 23, 2019, https://www.dallasobserver.com/arts/texas-cannabis-laws-remain-confusing-but-we-think-they-lean-toward-legal-11739333 (accessed February 11, 2022).

15 Malen Blackmon, "Marijuana Is Now Legal . . . ish in Texas," *Dallas Observer,* August 23, 2019, https://www.dallasobserver.com/arts/texas-cannabis-laws-remain-confusing-but-we-think-they-lean-toward-legal-11739333 (accessed March 8, 2022).

16 See https://capitol.texas.gov/BillLookup/History.aspx?LegSess=87R&Bill=SB181 and https://capitol.texas.gov/billlookup/History.aspx?LegSess=87R&Bill=HB1535 (accessed February 11, 2022).

17 Marin, Daniel, "Texas is evolving on marijuana, so what would it take to change the laws," *kxan.com,* January 15, 2022, https://www.kxan.com/news/texas-politics/texas-is-evolving-on-marijuana-so-what-would-it-take-to-change-the-laws/ (accessed March 8, 2022).

18 T. R. Fehrendbach, *Lone Star: A History of Texas and the Texans* (New York: Collier, 1980), 146–47.

19 Jesus del la Teja, *A Revolution Remembered: The Memoirs and Selected Correspondence of Juan N. Seguin* (Austin, TX: State House Press, 1991), 88; Josefina Zoraida Vazquez, "The Colonization and Loss of Texas: A Mexican Perspective," in *Myths, Misdeeds, and Misunderstandings: The Roots of Conflict in U.S.-Mexican Relations*, ed. O. Rodriguez, E. Jaime, and Kathryn Vincent (Wilmington, DE: Scholarly Resources Inc., 1997), 50.

20 T. R. Fehrendbach, *Lone Star: A History of Texas and the Texans* (New York: Collier, 1980), 206.

21 T. R. Fehrendbach, *Lone Star: A History of Texas and the Texans* (New York: Collier, 1980), 222–23.

22 "People & Events: Jose Antonio Navarro (1795–1871)," January 30, 2004, http://www.shoppbs.pbs.org/wgbh/amex/alamo/peopleevents/p_navarro.html (accessed February 11, 2022).

23 Ibid.

24 Stanley E. Siegel, "Navarro, Jose Antonio," *Handbook of Texas Online*, June 15, 2010, https://www.tshaonline.org/handbook/entries/navarro-jose-antonio.

25 David R. McDonald, *José Antonio Navarro: In Search of the American Dream in Nineteenth-Century Texas*, Watson Caufield and Mary Maxwell Arnold Republic of Texas Series, 2013, p. 1765. [Google Books version]. http://books.google.com/books?id=mbwLIze2vEAC.

[26] "People & Events: Jose Antonio Navarro (1795–1871)," January 30, 2004, http://www.shoppbs.pbs.org/wgbh/amex/alamo/peopleevents/p_navarro.html (accessed February 11, 2022).

[27] David J. Webster, *Foreigners in Their Native Land: Historical Roots of the Mexican Americans* (Albuquerque: University of New Mexico Press, 2003), 83–84.

[28] Ibid.

[29] "People & Events: Jose Antonio Navarro (1795–1871)," January 30, 2004, http://www.shoppbs.pbs.org/wgbh/amex/alamo/peopleevents/p_navarro.html (accessed February 11, 2022).

[30] Ibid.

[31] Ibid.

[32] Ibid.

[33] Stanley E. Siegel, "Navarro, Jose Antonio," *Handbook of Texas Online,* June 15, 2010, https://www.tshaonline.org/handbook/entries/navarro-jose-antonio; "History," https://www.cityofcorsicana.com/600/History (accessed February 11, 2022).

[34] Ibid.

[35] "Casa Navarro State Historic Site," http://www.thc.texas.gov/historic-sites/casa-navarro-state-historic-site (accessed February 11, 2022).

[36] https://txarchives.org/utcah/finding_aids/02978.xml#scopecontent (accessed February 11, 2022).

[37] "Scholarship Award," http://www.thc.texas.gov/historic-sites/casa-navarro/scholarship-award (accessed February 11, 2022).

[38] T. R. Fehrendbach, *Lone Star: A History of Texas and the Texans* (New York: Collier, 1980), 411–14.

[39] James Marten, *Texas Divided: Loyalty and Dissent in the Lone Star State, 1856–1874* (Lexington: University Press of Kentucky, 1990), 161.

[40] Ibid.

[41] Merline Pitre, "The Evolution of Black Political Participation in Reconstruction Texas," *East Texas Historical Journal* 26, no. 1 (1988): 36–45.

[42] "Texas Constitutional History," https://dlc.dcccd.edu/txgov1-2/texas-constitutional-history (accessed January 17, 2020).

[43] Ibid.

[44] Ibid.

[45] Constitutional amendments ballot general election, November 7, 1978, tax relief amendment, H.J.R. 1.

[46] *The Book of the States 2019*, http://knowledgecenter.csg.org/kc/system/files/1.3.2019.pdf.

[47] "Texas 1999 Ballot Measures," https://ballotpedia.org/Texas_1999_ballot_measures (accessed March 8, 2022).

[48] *The Book of the States*, Table 1.3, "General Information on State Constitutions" (as of January 1, 2021), https://issuu.com/csg.publications/docs/bos_2021_issuu (accessed March 8, 2022).

[49] *Texas Constitution*, art. 1, http://www.statutes.legis.state.tx.us/Docs/CN/htm/CN.1.htm; Ballotpedia, "Texas Proposition 3, Prohibition on Limiting Religious Services or Organizations Amendment(2021)," https://ballotpedia.org/Texas_Proposition_3,_Prohibition_on_Limiting_Religious_Services_or_Organizations_Amendment_(2021) (accessed February 11, 2022).

[50] *Texas Constitution*, art. 1. sec. 32, http://www.statutes.legis.state.tx.us/Docs/CN/htm/CN.1.htm.

[51] Lauren McGaughy, "Court Affirms Same-Sex Marriage Nationwide; Texas Stay Lifted," *Houston Chronicle*, June 26, 2015, http://www.chron.com/news/politics/texas/article/Supreme-Court-legalizes-same-sex-marriage-6341493.php (accessed March 8, 2022).

[52] *Texas Constitution*, art. 2, sec. 1, http://www.statutes.legis.state.tx.us/Docs/CN/htm/CN.1.htm.

[53] *Texas Constitution*, art. 4, sec. 8(b), http://www.statutes.legis.state.tx.us/Docs/CN/htm/CN.1.htm.

[54] *Texas Constitution*, art. 5, sec. 2(b), http://www.statutes.legis.state.tx.us/Docs/CN/htm/CN.1.htm.

[55] Donald S. Lutz, "Toward a Theory of Constitutional Amendment," *American Political Science Review* 88 (June 1994): 359.

[56] *The Book of the States 2021*, Table 1.3, https://issuu.com/csg.publications/docs/bos_2021_issuu (accessed February 11, 2022).

[57] *The Book of the States, 2021*, Table 1.4, https://issuu.com/csg.publications/docs/bos_2021_issuu (accessed March 8, 2022).

[58] Mary Lucia Barras and Houston Daniel, "Constitutional Convention of 1974," Texas State Historical Association, *Handbook of Texas Online,* https://www.tshaonline.org/handbook/entries/constitutional-convention-of-1974.

[59] Donald S. Lutz, "Toward a Theory of Constitutional Amendment," *American Political Science Review* 88 (June 1994): 359; Bowser, Jennie Drage, "Constitutions: Amend With Care," *State Legislatures Magazine* (September 2015): https://www.ncsl.org/research/elections-and-campaigns/constitution-amend-with-care.aspx (accessed March 8, 2022).

[60] Donald S. Lutz, "Toward a Theory of Constitutional Amendment," *American Political Science Review* 88 (June 1994): 359.

[61] *The Book of the States 2021*, Table 1.3, https://issuu.com/csg.publications/docs/bos_2020_web (accessed February 11, 2022).

[62] Donald S. Lutz, "Toward a Theory of Constitutional Amendment," *American Political Science Review* 88 (June 1994):

360; Ballotpedia, "Amending state constitutions," https://ballotpedia.org/Amending_state_constitutions (accessed March 8, 2022).

[63] *Book of the States 2021*, Table 1.3, https://issuu.com/csg.publications/docs/bos_2021_issuu (accessed March 8, 2022).

[64] Texas Legislative Council, "Amendments to the Texas Constitution since 1876: Current through November 7, 2019," June 2021. https://tlc.texas.gov/docs/amendments/Constamend1876.pdf (accessed February 11, 2022).

[65] Texas Secretary of State, "Turnout and Voter Registration Figures (1970-Current)," http://www.sos.state.tx.us/elections/historical/70-92.shtml.

[66] Proposition 4 - HJR 38, https://www.sos.state.tx.us/elections/voter/2019novballotlang.shtml (accessed February 11, 2022).

[67] Huang, Kalley; Astudillo, Carla; Zhang, Andrew, "Texas 2021 constitutional amendment election results," *Texas Tribune*. November 3, 2021, https://apps.texastribune.org/features/2021/texas-election-results-2021-constitutional-amendments/ (accessed March 8, 2022).

[68] *The Book of the States 2021,* Table 1.3, https://issuu.com/csg.publications/docs/bos_2021_issuu (accessed March 8, 2022).

[69] More information is at https://www.utsystem.edu/puf (as of February 2022).

[70] https://reportcenter.highered.texas.gov/reports/data/applicants-acceptance-and-enrollment-2017-2020 (accessed February 11, 2022).

[71] Legislative Budget Board, *Financing Public Higher Education in Texas: Legislative Primer*, 31–32, http://www.lbb.state.tx.us/Documents/Publications/Primer/3148_Financing_Public_Higher_Ed_Texas_Aug_2016.pdf (accessed February 11, 2022).

[72] *Texas Constitution* through November 2021, https://statutes.capitol.texas.gov/ (accessed February 11, 2022).

[73] *Houston Chronicle*, January 8, 1974.

CHAPTER 3

The Texas Legislature

Texas Learning Outcome

- Describe the legislative branch of Texas government.

In his autobiography, Sam Houston exhorted Texans to "Govern wisely, but as little as possible." This quotation captures both the importance of the Texas legislature in state politics and the distaste many Texans have for government. The framers of the 1876 Texas constitution distrusted government generally, but they were especially leery of executive authority and gave more power to the legislature than to the executive. (The drafters of the U.S. Constitution held a similar point of view.) This does not mean that the office of governor is insignificant in state politics; governors play an important role. However, what power the governor of Texas has comes mostly from informal sources. Courts and state agencies are also important, but the legislature is the most important institution in state government.

Legislative action is essential for many things. Money cannot be spent, taxes cannot be levied, state laws cannot be enacted or changed, and, in most states, the constitution cannot be amended without the approval of the legislature. Without actions by the legislature, most state governments would quickly come to a halt. In recent years, the federal government has shifted more responsibility to state governments in some areas—regulating possession of marijuana, for example—while reducing their power in other areas, most notably in health care policy and in defining marriage. State governments have also taken the lead on some issues. In its 2021 session, for example, the Texas legislature allocated $1.8 billion for border security, $750 million of which is targeted for the building of a security barrier between Mexico and Texas, a responsibility traditionally assigned to the federal government.[1] State legislatures, therefore, continue to fulfill an important policy-making role in the American system.

Chapter Learning Objectives

- Describe the structure, size, and general characteristics of the Texas legislature.

- Explain legislators' qualifications and member demographics.

- Explain how legislators are elected, including the single-member district method of election.

- Describe reapportionment and redistricting issues in Texas.
- Discuss various leadership positions in the Texas legislature.
- Describe the Texas legislature's functions and procedures.

The Structure and Size of the Texas Legislature

Learning Objective: Describe the structure, size, and general characteristics of the Texas legislature.

bicameral

Legislative body that consists of two houses

As defined in the Texas Constitution (Article III, Section 1), the Texas legislature is **bicameral,** meaning it has two chambers: the senate and the house of representatives. The Texas Senate has 31 members elected for four-year overlapping terms (Article III, Section 3), meaning that half the membership is elected every two years. In the election that follows reapportionment (usually the second year of each decade), all seats in the senate are up for election. The members draw lots to determine who will stand for reelection in another two years (half of the senate) or in another four years (the other half). Following the 2020 Census and subsequent redistricting, the entire Texas Senate stood for election in November 2022.

The Texas House of Representatives now has 150 members elected for two-year terms (Article III, Section 4). The first house, elected following the adoption of the 1876 constitution, had 93 members. After 1880, a new house seat was added for every 50,000 inhabitants until the membership reached 150 representatives.[2]

State legislatures vary in size. Alaska has the smallest senate, with 20 members, and Minnesota has the largest, with 67 senators. Lower house membership ranges from 40 in Alaska to 400 in New Hampshire.[3] The median size for state senates is 38; for the lower houses it is 100.

The Texas House and Senate are both quite small relative to the state's population. As of 2021, there were about 952,514 constituents per state senate district and 196,852 constituents for each house district.[4] Only California has more constituents per state senator, for example.[5] As Texas has 31 state senators and 36 U.S. House members, a Texas state senator represents more people than does a U.S. congressperson from Texas!

Texas state Capitol building, Austin, Texas

Mike Norton/Purestock/SuperStock

The size of legislatures raises several issues. Large bodies might better pro-mote the representation of local concerns and diverse interests within the state. However, statewide interests might get less attention. Another downside of large legislatures is that they can become inefficient at decision making or, in part because of that inefficiency, be dominated by a few members (especially legis-lative leaders). This could certainly be said of Texas, where the relatively small senate has historically been considered to be genteel and free of individual domination, and the relatively large house is less genteel and has historically been dominated by the speaker. Yet larger bodies would ensure that the senate and especially the house would be more democratic and closer to the people because each state legislator would represent fewer constituents and a smaller geographic area. As one member of the founding generation of the United States noted, smaller constituencies might also allow a wider array of people to par-ticipate in state politics, rather than just the "rich" or "well born."[6]

> **Understanding Impact** Given Texans' historical resistance to too much government, it is easy to understand why citizens would hesitate to increase the size and cost of the legislature. On the other hand, having more represen-tatives would mean each would represent fewer people, theoretically making them responsive to local priorities. Do you think Texas should expand the size of its legislature? Or should we keep the comparatively small body envisioned by the framers of Texas's constitution?

CORE OBJECTIVE

Communicating Effectively . . .

Some people contend that smaller constituencies might allow a wider array of people to participate in state politics, rather than just the "rich" or "well born." How would you argue in favor of or against this statement?

General Characteristics of the Legislature

Learning Objective: Describe the structure, size, and general characteristics of the Texas legislature.

Sessions and Session Length

Though it is jokingly said that the framers of the Texas Constitution wanted the legislature to meet for 2 days every 140 years, they settled on the current system, in which the Texas legislature meets in **biennial sessions** (every two years) for 140 days in odd-numbered years, beginning in January (in accordance with Article III, Sec-tion 5 and Article III, Section 24[b] of the Texas Constitution). While the national trend has been moving away from biennial sessions toward annual sessions, Texas (along with Montana, Nevada, and North Dakota) has resisted that trend.[7]

biennial sessions
Legislature meets every two years

Voters in Texas rejected a proposed change to annual sessions in 1969 and again in 1972. In keeping with the traditionalistic/individualistic political culture of the state (see Chapter 1), there is some concern that the more often the legislature meets, the more damage it can do.

At the end of the 140-day session, the Texas legislature must adjourn **(sine die).** It cannot call itself into special session (sometime called **extraordinary session**) or otherwise extend a session. This lack of ability to call special sessions makes the limit on the regular session even more meaningful. The legislature must finish its work in the prescribed time and then adjourn. All but 11 states limit the length of legislative sessions.[8] However, the Texas legislature's inability to call itself into special session differs from the national trend. Special sessions can be called by either the governor or the legislature in 36 states, and only by the governor in 14 states, including Texas.[9]

In Texas, only the governor may call **special sessions** (Article IV, Section 8). These sessions may not last more than 30 days each. However, there is no limit on the number of special sessions the governor may call. Governor Bill Clements holds the record, having called six special sessions following the 1989 regular legislative session. In Texas, the governor determines the subject matter of the session (Article III, Section 40). This gives the governor tremendous power to set the legislature's agenda during special sessions, as well as a bargaining chip to persuade the legislature to do what the governor wants. Having completed a grueling 140 days—and there are indeed long hours and late nights in "crunch time" near the end of the session—no legislator wants to come back for a special session. And no legislator wants to answer to taxpayers for the expense of bringing legislators back for a special session. They are therefore much more likely to accede to the governor's priorities when they are under threat of being forced to come back for another 30 days.

The Texas legislature's inability to call itself into special session also gives the governor stronger veto powers. If the governor vetoes a bill after the legislature has adjourned, the veto stands. This, in part, helps explain why so few gubernatorial vetoes are overridden.

sine die
Legislature must adjourn at end of regular session and cannot continue to meet

extraordinary session
A specially called meeting of the legislature, outside the regular session, to discuss specified matters

special sessions
In Texas, sessions called by the governor to consider legislation proposed by the governor only

Murat Taner/The Image Bank/Getty Images

States such as Texas that limit the number of days in regular session often must resort to special sessions. Budgetary problems, reapportionment issues, school finance, and prison funding have forced the governor to call special sessions in past decades.

In 2021, Governor Abbott called three special sessions. After the 2021 regular session failed to adopt what Republicans called election integrity measures, Abbott called a special session with this as the primary goal. Democratic legislators argued that these measures, as laid out in Senate Bill 1 (SB 1) would make it harder for Texans of color and those with disabilities to participate in elections. Realizing that they did not have the votes to stop, Democratic legislators chose to flee the state to break quorum, making it impossible for the legislature to do business. Two-thirds of House members must be present to make a quorum, without which no business can be conducted.[10] This tactic successfully killed the bill, and everything else, in the first special session.

Spending a month on the run in a Washington, D.C., hotel took a toll, though, and when Gov. Abbott called a second special session, enough Democrats returned to Austin that a quorum was restored.[11] The Republican majority was able to pass SB 1 with only a few compromises.[12]

As the second special session was chiefly focused on voting legislation, Abbott called a third session to deal with his other priorities. In this session, the legislature adopted the state's newly redistricted maps and barred transgender athletes from participating in high school sports in their gender identity.[13] Though some Republican goals, such as legislatively banning vaccine and mask mandates and steeper property tax cuts, were not achieved, they did have an overall successful legislative year.

Many critics of Texas's biennial sessions may point to 2021's three special sessions as evidence that the state needs to change to annual sessions. However, this would not come without trade-offs.

As we will see in Chapter 14, the tax structure in Texas is closely tied to economic conditions in the state. Predicting state revenues for two-year periods is extremely difficult. However, biennial sessions help the legislature avoid reacting rashly in any particular situation because there is often time to reflect on a problem. Moreover, the nature of perceived problems may change, especially in the economic realm. Therefore, biennial sessions may insulate politicians from being pressured to chase yesterday's economic news, given the lag time before policy can be developed and have a meaningful impact. Advantages and disadvantages of annual and biennial sessions are presented in Table 3.1.

In 1960, only 19 state legislatures met annually; today, 46 states hold annual sessions.[14] California, Michigan, New York, and Pennsylvania have full-time legislatures, where legislators have large staffs. The largest number of states (26) fall within a hybrid legislative session, in which legislators spend approximately two-thirds of a full-time job as legislators. Texas falls within this category, along with Florida, Oklahoma, Minnesota, and Louisiana. While it seems odd to say that a legislator who is in session only every other year spends the equivalent of two-thirds of a full-time job, that estimate includes not just time in session but also time on committee responsibilities during the interim (which many Texas legislators have), time spent on constituent service (which goes on year-round), and time campaigning.[15] Montana, Wyoming, North Dakota, and Texas are the only remaining states meeting biennially rather than annually.[16]

Since becoming a state, Texas has embraced biennial sessions and has used annual sessions only during Reconstruction. The switch to an annual session would require majority approval of Texas voters through a constitutional amendment. Texas voters rejected five such proposed amendments between 1949 and 1975.[17] In the 87th legislative session in 2021, Texas legislators introduced more than 7,000 pieces of legislation (6,927 house and senate bills plus resolutions) in the regular session, and 1,147 of those became law.[18] They introduced another 962 in the three special sessions, of which 24 became law.[19] Plus they adopted a $248 billion biennial budget.[20] Although the 2021 legislature took an extra three special sessions to complete their work, that level of productivity bolsters the argument that annual sessions are unnecessary.

TABLE 3.1

Advantages and Disadvantages of Annual and Biennial Legislative Sessions

Arguments in Favor of Annual Sessions	Arguments in Favor of Biennial Sessions
The responsibilities of a legislature have become so burdensome that they can no longer be discharged on an alternate-year basis.	There are enough laws. Biennial sessions constitute a safeguard against fast and reckless legislative action.
More frequent meetings may raise the status of the legislature, thereby helping to check the flow of power to the executive branch.	Yearly meetings of the legislature will contribute to legislative harassment of the administration and its agencies.
Annual sessions make it easier for legislators to oversee the administration and hold administrators accountable for carrying out legislative policies.	Individual legislators and interim study commissions can put the interval between sessions to good use, since there is never enough time during a session to study proposed legislation.
States may respond more rapidly to new federal laws which require state participation.	The biennial system gives legislators more time to renew relations with constituents, to mend political fences, and to campaign for reelection.
The legislature cannot operate effectively in fits and starts. Annual sessions may help make the policy-making process more timely and orderly.	Annual sessions are more expensive because the legislators and other assembly personnel meet twice as often.
Annual sessions would lessen the need for special sessions.	

Source: Table adapted from National Conference of State Legislatures, http://www.ncsl.org/legislatures-elections/legislatures/annual-vs-biennial-legislative-sessions.aspx.

Understanding Impact In this chapter you've heard arguments for and against Texas moving to annual legislative sessions. When Hurricane Harvey hit the Houston area in August 2017, the legislature was not scheduled to meet again for over a year. Additional appropriations couldn't be made and legislative oversight was not possible. Subsequently, the state's response was widely criticized. Do you think arguments against a shift to annual sessions hold up in the face of the human tragedy of Hurricane Harvey? Explain.

Qualifications and Demographics

Learning Objective: Explain legislators' qualifications and member demographics.

Let's look at the formal and informal qualifications for election to an office in state government. States typically impose requirements including age, citizenship, state residency, district residency, and qualified voter status. Texas has requirements generally in line with other states.

A Texas state house member must be a U.S. citizen, at least 21 years of age, and must have lived in the state for at least two years and for a minimum of 12 months in the district they will represent (Article I, Section 7). To be a Texas state senate member, a person must be a U.S. citizen, at least 26 years old before the date of the general election, and must have been a Texas resident for at least five years and a district resident for at least 12 months (Article III, Section 6). To stand for office, candidates do not have to be registered to vote; however, they must be "qualified voters."[21] The Texas Constitution bars individuals who have been "convicted of bribery, perjury, forgery, or other high crimes" from voting.[22] Therefore, candidates for the state legislature cannot have been convicted of a felony (unless they have been pardoned or had their rights restored by the governor, which is rare).

CORE OBJECTIVE

Taking Personal Responsibility . . .

Each Texas citizen has one Texas state house member and one Texas state senate member to represent them. Use this website to find your representatives: https://capitol.texas.gov/. The "Who Represents Me" section allows you to put in your address and locate your state house and senate members.

Formal requirements are minimal and do not constitute much of a barrier to holding office. More important are the informal qualifications that may influence who is elected. These include income, education, occupation, knowledge of state politics and current events, communication skills, a desire for public service, and the ability to raise money for campaigns. State legislators tend to be less diverse than the general population. According to a recent study of state legislatures across the country, legislators tend to be older, male, well educated, and professionals (often in business).[23]

Cultural changes in the state over recent decades have increased the diversity of the Texas legislature. The number of officeholders who are members of ethnic minority groups has grown, both in Texas and across the nation. This is partly because of reapportionment and redistricting (which we will discuss in detail later in this chapter). However, women and people of color are still underrepresented in the Texas legislature when compared with their proportions of the state population. In the 87th Texas Legislature (2021), people of color made up over 58 percent of Texas's population,[24] yet they accounted for only 39 percent of the legislative seats.[25]

The number of female lawmakers has also grown dramatically. The first U.S. women to serve in a state legislature were elected to the Colorado General Assembly in 1894 (following Colorado women's winning the right to vote in 1893).[26] Texas women did not gain full voting rights until 1920, when the Nineteenth Amendment to the U.S. Constitution took effect. Because they were not "qualified voters," women could not be elected to the Texas legislature before 1920.[27] The first woman elected to the state legislature was Edith Wilmans of Dallas, who served one term in the Texas House starting in 1923.[28] From that point on, few women served until the 1970s.

Focus On

The First Hispanic Woman in the Texas Legislature

Texas House of Representatives

Hispanic men have served in leadership roles since Texas was a Mexican province and an independent republic. The first Hispanic woman to serve in the Texas state legislature was elected in 1976. Irma Rangel, a Democrat, represented her district for 26 years and became a champion of educational opportunity for her native region of South Texas.

Born in 1931 in Kingsville, along Texas's Gulf Coast, Rangel was the daughter of small-business owners. After graduating from college, she began her career in education, first as a teacher, then as a principal. Rangel later earned a law degree and accomplished several milestones in her legal career. She was one of the first Hispanic women to clerk for a federal district judge, one of the first Hispanic women to serve as an assistant district attorney in Texas, and then (after returning to her hometown) became the first female Hispanic attorney to practice in Kingsville.[29]

During her tenure as a member of the Texas House of Representatives, Rangel's primary focus was education. She chaired the House Committee on Higher Education, and she secured more than $450 million in funding for border-area colleges and universities, as well as funding for the first professional school in the South Texas region—a college of pharmacy that now bears her name.[30] In 1997, she coauthored and spearheaded the effort to pass HB 588, which came to be known as the "Top Ten Percent Plan." This legislation "guarantees admission to Texas public universities and colleges for all Texas high school students who graduate in the top ten percent of their class."[31] Rangel favored the policy because it would increase admissions for students who are economically disadvantaged or members of historically underrepresented groups at Texas universities.

Rangel died in 2003. She is in the "Texas Women's Hall of Fame,"[32] and the Public Policy Institute at the University of Texas at Austin was renamed for her in 2009.[33]

Critical Thinking Questions

1. How did Rangel's "Top Ten Percent Plan" affect students who are economically disadvantaged or members of historically underrepresented groups in terms of college admissions?
2. What are some reasons for and against the idea that legislators should share the demographic characteristics of their constituents?

The number of women legislators in Texas has increased from 1 woman in each chamber in 1971 to a total of 48 in 2021, with 38 women serving in the house and 10 women serving in the senate. This is 27 percent of all seats in the state legislature,[34] which remains below the national average of women in state legislatures, 30.6 percent,[35] and is far less than women's 50 percent of the Texas population. (Note: There was one unfilled House seats in the 86th Texas Legislature.) Map 3.1 ranks the 50 states in terms of percentage of female legislators.

Most legislators do not report "legislator" as their full-time occupation, and a recent survey by the National Conference of State Legislatures showed that the number who describe themselves as full-time legislators has been declining nationwide (perhaps because of some voters' contempt for politicians).[36] Some professions, including law, allow a person time to devote to legislative duties. The percentage of attorneys in the Texas legislature is much higher than the

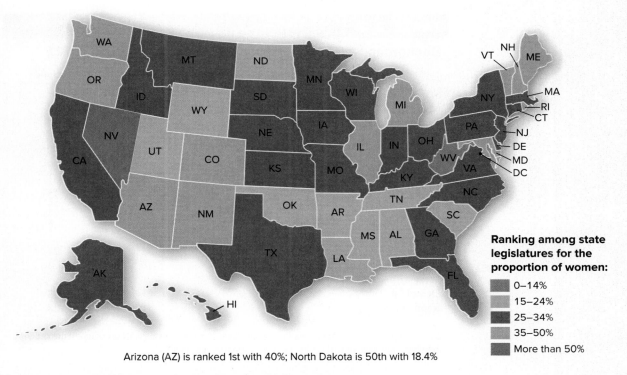

Arizona (AZ) is ranked 1st with 40%; North Dakota is 50th with 18.4%

Ranking among state legislatures for the proportion of women:

- 0–14%
- 15–24%
- 25–34%
- 35–50%
- More than 50%

MAP 3.1   Percentage of Women Legislators by State

Source: Adapted from National Conference of State Legislatures, "Women in State Legislatures for 2021," https://www.ncsl.org/legislators-staff/legislators/womens-legislative-network/women-in-state-legislatures-for-2021.aspx.

national average. According to a recent study, 14 percent of legislators nation-wide were lawyers, whereas roughly one-third of Texas legislators were lawyers.[37] A higher-than-average percentage of businesspeople are in the Texas legislature, and a lower-than-average percentage of teachers. This is because in Texas, unlike some other states, a state legislator may not hold other compensated public employment. Texas teachers can be paid to teach while also being paid to serve on the "governing body of a school district, city, town, or local governmental district," but they cannot be paid to serve in the state legislature.[38] Table 3.2 provides a demographic breakdown of the 86th Legislature.

Understanding Impact Texas is the second-largest state in the union and is among the most diverse in population, economy, and geography. These factors would seem to argue for more diversity among legislators, but that is difficult to achieve as long as they are paid only for part-time work, which makes it difficult or impossible for many people even to consider running for election. Should Texas move to a full-time legislature to help it better reflect the diversity of the state?

Salary

Some citizens believe that, because the legislature meets for only 140 days every two years, it is part time and members should be paid accordingly. Legislative pay reflects this attitude. As set by the constitution (Article III, Section 24), Texas

TABLE 3.2

Background of Members of the Texas Legislature, 2021

	House	Senate
Sex		
Male	111	21
Female	38	10
Age		
Under 30	0	0
30–39	16	0
40–49	43	1
50–59	44	15
60–69	29	7
70+	17	8
Incumbency		
Incumbents (and previously elected)	132	27
Newcomers	16	4
Party Affiliation		
Democrat	67	13
Republican	82	18

Source: Adapted from Legislative Reference Library of Texas, https://lrl.texas.gov/legeLeaders/members/memberStatistics.cfm. (Some information not available)

pays the 181 members of the legislature $7,200 a year, plus another $221 per day while in session. In years when the legislature meets, the total compensation is $7,200 in salary plus $30,940 in per diem (in other words, per day) pay, for a total of $38,140.[39] The Texas Ethics Commission sets the per diem rate.[40] Most legislators maintain a second home in Austin while the session is going on, so the per diem pay is not high. Housing and lodging costs in Austin are among the highest in the state. In years when the legislature is not in session, legislators receive their $7,200 in salary and may receive some additional per diem pay for off-session committee work.

Texas legislators' basic salaries have not increased since 1975.[41] Compared to the 10 most populous states, Texas legislators are paid the least.[42] Voters have rejected several attempts to increase legislator pay, and this low pay contributes to the small number of legislators who consider themselves full-time lawmakers. Most legislators must have other sources of income. Many are attorneys or successful businesspeople, as mentioned previously. Low monetary compensation is very much in keeping with the traditionalistic political culture of the state, according to which only the elite should serve in the legislature; the low pay excludes most citizens, who can't take months away from their jobs, from being legislators.

Texas legislators are allowed to use campaign contributions to pay "reasonable household expenses in Austin," which includes rent and telephone services. They may also use contributions to pay expenses related to serving as a state representative, which includes meals, gas, parking, tolls, and mobile phone access.[43] Legislators can also accept gifts from registered lobbyists, so long as the gift is not tied to the legislator taking an official act. Lobbyists are limited to spending $500 for entertainment (such as sporting events or concerts), as well as gifts. However, so long as the lobbyist is present, unlimited spending is allowed for food and beverages; travel and lodging for a fact-finding trip, seminar, or conference; and tickets or other expenses for attendance at political fundraisers or charitable events.

Although many believe that lobbyists are the only ones providing gifts, legislators use campaign funds to shower constituents, staffers, and even one another with gifts. Campaign spending on gifts has decreased over the last decade, but house and senate members spent around $1 million on presents, with $375,000 being spent during the 2016–2017 legislative session, most of which was spent on one another.[44]

Over the years, lobbyists have provided legislators with interesting gifts. Legislators over the years have received .22-caliber semiautomatic rifles, Nikon binoculars, and even highchairs.[45]

Many states provide retirement benefits for legislators. In Texas, legislators' retirement pay is linked to the salary of state district judges. Somewhat circularly, the salary of district judges is set by the Texas legislature. Therefore, legislators are able to increase their own retirement pay by voting to raise district judges' pay.[46] Recognizing the political sensitivity of increasing their own benefits, however, Texas lawmakers have struggled with how to improve incentives for retention of judges without raising judicial base pay, which would increase legislators' own retirement benefits. During the 86th Legislature, they arrived at a solution by offering judges longevity increases without raising their base pay, thus avoiding the political problem of raising legislators' retirement earning.[47] Legislators may retire at 50 years of age with 12 years of service or at 60 years of age with 8 years of service. Currently, a retired lawmaker who served 8 years would receive $25,760 in benefits annually, and $38,640 after 12 years.[48] Tom Craddick, who was first elected in 1969 and continues to be the longest-serving member of the legislature, would receive $140,000 as an annual pension, as the annual benefit is capped at the $140,000 salary of state district judges.[49]

This relatively generous benefit may prompt some members to retire after achieving the minimum time requirement. They can count on cost-of-living pay raises as the legislature increases the salaries of district judges. Some increases can also come from cost-of-living adjustments given to all state retirees. In short, as an active member of the legislature, you are worth only $600 per month. Retire after at least eight years in office, and your pay increases substantially. Another benefit state legislators receive is health care and life insurance benefits. After the lawmaker retires, the state pays 100 percent of their premium and part of the premium for dependents.[50]

Staff and Facilities

The Texas legislature provides generous support for staff assistance. According to the most recent figures available, Texas trailed only New York in the total number of permanent and session-only staff.[51] Most members keep full-time offices in their district, and many do so in the state capital as well. At the beginning of each session, both the house and senate adopt resolutions establishing members' monthly allowance for salary and office expenses.

In addition, standing committees have staff salary support during and between legislative sessions. The Texas Legislative Council has a large professional staff to assist the legislature. It has produced a very informative website (http://www.tlc.state.tx.us/) that provides easy access for citizens during and between legislative sessions. The house also has the House Research Organization, which provides professional assistance to the legislature. The state Capitol building provides each senator and house member with excellent office and committee hearing space.

Single-Member versus Multimember Districts

Learning Objective: Explain how legislators are elected, including the single-member district method of election.

single-member district (SMD)

District represented by one elected member to the legislature

Members of legislative bodies are most often elected from **single-member districts.** Under this system, each legislative district has one member in the legislative body. In Texas there are 31 senatorial districts and 150 house districts. Voters living in these districts elect one state senator and one state house member. This system allows for geographic representation—all areas of the state choose representatives to the state legislature. Maps 3.2 and 3.3 show the senate and house districts for the entire state.

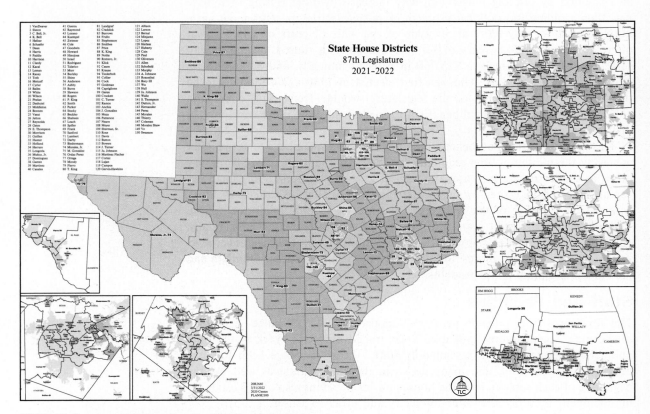

MAP 3.2   Texas State House Districts, 2021

Based on "Texas Redistricting," https://redistricting.capitol.texas.gov/Current-districts#st-house-section.

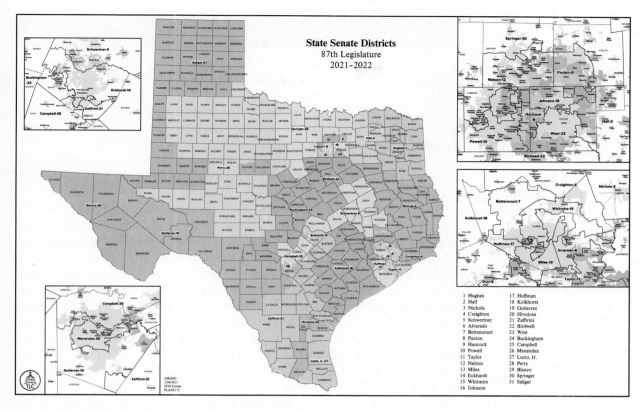

MAP 3.3 **Texas State Senate Districts, 2021**

Based on "Texas Redistricting," https://redistricting.capitol.texas.gov/Current-districts.

In a single-member district system, a party or a candidate has to win only a plurality of the vote in a district to win one seat. In other words, the candidate does not have to win more than 50 percent of the vote. They just need to win more votes than any other candidate. Single-member districts can be drawn to the advantage of ethnic and political minorities within the county. In countywide districts with multiple seats, a majority of the voters in the county can control all the seats, potentially excluding members of ethnic and racial minority groups from representation. Alternatives exist in other states, such as **multimember districts** in which more than one official is elected to represent the interests of a district. These multimember districts promote broader representation.

multimember districts
Districts represented by more than one member elected to the legislature

Understanding Impact Multimember districts are credited by some with increasing likelihood of electing female candidates and candidates from racial and ethnic minority groups, and with potentially providing a pathway for third-party candidates to win election. On the other hand, with multiple members per district, each member's personal accountability for representing constituents would be diminished. Do you think Texas should consider adopting multimember districts? Why or why not?

Reapportionment and Redistricting

Learning Objective: Describe reapportionment and redistricting issues in Texas.

In Texas, the number of state senators is constitutionally set at 31; therefore, there are 31 (single-member) state senate districts. Likewise, the Texas Constitution stipulates there shall be 150 members in the House of Representatives; therefore, there are 150 (single-member) state house districts. How those representatives are divvied up and what determines the boundary lines for each district are highly controversial matters.

The U.S. Constitution requires that Congress reapportion the seats in the U.S. House of Representatives among the states following each federal census, every 10 years. In other words, Congress determines how many representatives each state will have in the House, based on current population figures. The Texas Constitution similarly requires the state legislature to reapportion the seats following each federal census.[52] Two terms are usually used to describe this process: **reapportionment** and **redistricting.** The term *reapportionment* refers to the process of allocating representatives to states; *redistricting* is the drawing of district boundary lines within states. Table 3.3 presents the number of constituents per legislative district in the five most populous U.S. states, as of the U.S. Census Bureau's 2021 population estimate. Each of the 150 house members in Texas represents about 196,853 people, and each of the 31 state senators represents approximately 952,913 people.

Apportioning seats in any legislative body is an extremely political process. Each interest group within the state tries to gain as much as possible from the process. Existing powers, such as the majority party in the legislature, will try to protect their advantages. Incumbent legislators will try to ensure their reelection. The primary issues raised by reapportionment are equity of representation, representation of racial and ethnic minorities, and **gerrymandering,** which is drawing district boundary lines for political advantage.

reapportionment
The process of allocating representatives to districts

redistricting
The drawing of district boundaries

gerrymandering
Drawing district boundary lines for political advantage

Equity of Representation

The issue of *equity of representation* is not new; it is perhaps as old as legislative bodies. Thomas Jefferson noted the problem in the Virginia legislature in the

TABLE 3.3

Average Constituents per State Legislative District

	2021 Population	House	Senate
California	39,237,836	490,437	980,946
Texas	**29,527,941**	**196,853**	**952,913**
Florida	21,781,128	181,509	544,528
New York	19,835,913	132,239	314,856
Pennsylvania	12,964,056	63,862	259,281

Sources: Population—Census data, https://data.census.gov/cedsci/table?tid=PEPPOP2021.NST_EST2021_POP&hidePreview=false; State legislatures, https://www.ncsl.org/Portals/1/Documents/Elections/Legis_Control_February_2022.pdf

eighteenth century.[53] During most of the nineteenth century, legislative apportionment most often resulted in equity. In other words, each representative represented an equal number of citizens. Some states had provisions that limited the number of seats a single county could have. In the early twentieth century, population shifted from rural to urban areas, and gradually the rural areas were overrepresented in many state legislatures. In the 1960s, only two states (Wisconsin and Massachusetts) had rural/urban representation in the legislature that accurately reflected population distributions in the state.[54]

From 1876 until the 1920s, the Texas legislature made an effort to reapportion the seats after each census. This process was made easier by the addition of one seat for each increase of 50,000 in the population. (The 1876 Constitution initially set state house membership at 93 but allowed for expansion to bring house membership to a maximum of 150 representatives.)[55] However, in 1930 and 1940 the legislature failed to reapportion legislative seats, and no new seats were added. Thus, by 1948 Texas legislative seats had not changed since 1921 despite the fact that major population shifts from rural to urban areas had occurred.[56] Shifts in population created a serious disparity in representation between rural and urban areas of the state. Most urban counties were vastly underrepresented.

Texas amended its constitution in 1948 to create the **Legislative Redistricting Board (LRB).** This board was given the authority to redistrict the seats in the Texas House and Senate if the legislature failed to do so. The LRB is made up of the lieutenant governor, the speaker of the house, the attorney general, the comptroller of public accounts, and the commissioner of the general land office.[57]

Legislative Redistricting Board (LRB)

State board composed of elected officials that can draw new legislative districts for the house and senate if the legislature fails to act

The creation of the LRB forced the legislature to act in 1951 and 1961. Representation shifted from rural to urban areas, but large urban counties were still underrepresented. This underrepresentation was due in part to a 1936 amendment to the Texas Constitution that limited the number of representatives any county could have to seven until the population reached 700,000, and then the county could have one additional representative for each 100,000 population.[58] For example, in 1952, had apportionment been based on population alone, each state representative would have represented about 50,000 people. This means that Dallas County would have increased from 7 to 12 representatives, Harris County (Houston) from 8 to 16, and Bexar County (San Antonio) from 7 to 10. However, the number of citizens within legislative districts remained unequal. The constitution also prohibited any county from having more than one state senator, no matter how large the county's population.

In 1962, in *Baker v. Carr,* the U.S. Supreme Court decided that these kinds of inequalities in the apportionment of legislative districts denied voters "equal protection of the law" and said that "as nearly as practicable, one man's vote" should be "equal to another's."[59] Two years later, in *Reynolds v. Sims,* the Court ruled that both houses of state legislatures had to be apportioned based on population. In addition, state legislative districts needed to be roughly equal in population. The Court rejected the analogy to the U.S. Senate, which is based on geographic units, stating "Legislators represent people, not trees or acres. Legislators are elected by voters, not farms or cities or economic interests."[60]

Baker v. Carr

Court case that required state legislative districts to contain about the same number of citizens

Reynolds v. Sims

Court case holding that issues of representation are justiciable, and that one person's vote should be roughly equal in weight to another person's

These two cases forced all states to redistrict based on population, following the "one person, one vote" rule. Over time, the general rule that developed with regard to reapportionment was that the "maximum population deviation between the largest and smallest [legislative] district" must be "less than 10 percent."[61] As of 2015, the largest and smallest senate districts in Texas deviated from the ideal district population by about 4 percent, for a total range of about 8 percent. The largest and smallest house districts deviated from the ideal district population by about 5 percent, for a total range of just under 10 percent.[62]

In 1965, a federal district court ruled that the provisions in the Texas Constitution that limited a county to seven house seats and one senate seat were unconstitutional.[63] This forced the apportionment of both houses of the Texas legislature to be based on population. The political consequences of these court decisions shifted power from rural to urban areas.

For many decades, computers have efficiently handled the task of drawing districts with approximately equal numbers of people. However, a recent case before the U.S. Supreme Court raised this issue again. In *Evenwel v. Abbott* (2016), the plaintiffs argued that Texas's practice of making legislative districts equal in terms of total population violates the "one person, one vote" rule. They contended that, instead, there should be an equal number of eligible voters in each district.[64] If this alternative view had been upheld, states would have been required to change their apportionment and redistricting practices, because noncitizens and children (among others) would have been excluded from relevant population counts when apportioning representatives.[65] In April 2016, the Supreme Court unanimously rejected this challenge, asserting that "total-population apportionment promotes equitable and effective representation."[66]

Minority Representation

The second issue that redistricting raises is representation of racial and ethnic minorities. According to current law, not only should legislative districts be approximately equal in population, but they should also allow for representation of racial and ethnic minorities. This issue was first raised in Texas when the state used multimember districts in some large urban counties. Court decisions invalidated these districts in the early 1970s.[67]

The 1981 session of the legislature produced a redistricting plan that advanced representation of previously underrepresented groups in both houses. However, Bill Clements, the Republican governor, vetoed the senate plan, and the Texas Supreme Court invalidated the house plan. This forced the Legislative Redistricting Board to draw new districts. The new plan was challenged in federal courts and by the U.S. Justice Department, which ruled that the plan violated the federal Voting Rights Act because it did not achieve maximum racial and ethnic minority representation. African Americans and Hispanics believed that the plan diluted their voting strength. A new plan, drawn up by federal courts, maximized representation by creating districts that contained a majority of racial and ethnic minorities—"majority-minority" districts.

Similar battles took place in the 1990s and into the 2000s. Racial and ethnic minority voters became better represented, and non-white candidates gained more seats in the state legislature (as did Republicans, who in 1996 managed to take control of the Texas Senate for the first time in more than 100 years). In 2008, there were 16 African Americans in the Texas legislature. This represented 9 percent of the total seats, which was equivalent to the average proportion of African American legislators across all 50 states.[68] The trend in Texas over recent decades has been a slowly increasing number of representatives who are people of color. In 2009, there were 37 Hispanic state legislators in Texas, which was 20 percent of the total seats—the third-highest percentage of any state in the country (after New Mexico and California).[69] The number of Hispanic legislators increased to 41 by 2015. The majority of these were Democrats, with only 5 Republicans. In 2015, there were 19 African Americans, 17 of whom were Democrats, and 3 Asian American legislators (2 Democrats and 1 Republican).[70] As of 2021, 110 members, or 61.5 percent, of the legislature is white, compared to 41.2 percent of the Texas population overall; 46 members, or 25.7 percent, is Hispanic, compared to 39.7 percent of the population; 19 members, or 10.6 percent, are African American, compared to 12.9 percent of the population; and 4 members, or 2.2 percent are Asian, compared to 5.2 percent of the population. Men hold 73.3 percent and women hold 26.7 percent of the seats, despite a 50-50 split in the overall population.[71] (These numbers do not equal a total of 181 members because there is one vacant seat and one member's racial or ethnic identity could not be confirmed.)

Political and Racial Gerrymandering

Political gerrymandering is the drawing of legislative districts to achieve the political advantage of one political party over another. The practice of creating districts with the intent of achieving a particular racial makeup is **racial gerrymandering.** The practice of gerrymandering dates to the early days of our nation. In 1812, Governor Elbridge Gerry of Massachusetts drew a legislative district shaped somewhat like a salamander. A political cartoonist for a Boston newspaper dressed up the outlines of the district with eyes, wings, and claws and called it a "Gerrymander."

With the rise of the Republican Party in Texas, political gerrymandering has intensified. Until 2003, Republicans repeatedly charged that the Democrats reduced the number of potential Republican districts, especially in suburban areas. In the 1980s, Republicans forged alliances with racial and ethnic minority groups. Republicans supported the creation of racially gerrymandered majority-minority districts, and the groups that benefited supported those Republican efforts. As we shall see subsequently, the creation of majority-minority districts has aided the Republicans as well as racial and ethnic minorities.

A legal challenge to the practice of racial gerrymandering was reviewed by the U.S. Supreme Court in 1996 in *Bush v. Vera*. This challenge was aimed at U.S. congressional districts, rather than state house and senate districts, but the ruling could be applied to the latter as well. In striking down three newly created majority-minority U.S. congressional districts in Texas, the Supreme Court affirmed a lower-court finding that these districts were "formed in utter disregard for traditional redistricting criteria" of compactness and regularity and that the district shapes were "ultimately unexplainable" in terms other than race, resulting in "unconstitutional racial gerrymandering."[72] Justice O'Connor, who drafted the Court's majority opinion, explained that "deviations from traditional districting principles . . . cause constitutional harm insofar as they convey the message that political identity is, or should be, predominantly racial."[73] The Court did

political gerrymandering
Drawing legislative districts to the advantage of a political party

racial gerrymandering
Legislative districts that are drawn to the advantage of a minority group

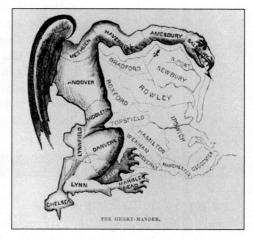

The original Gerrymander in Massachusetts, 1812
Bettmann/Getty Images

Hunt v. Cromartie

Court case that ruled while race can be a factor, it can not be the primary factor in determining the makeup of legislative districts

not object to states' considering race when drawing district lines or to their intentionally creating majority-minority districts; however, using race as the predominant factor in drawing districts, while subordinating other considerations, was found to be unconstitutional.[74]

In April 1999, the U.S. Supreme Court, in **Hunt v. Cromartie,**[75] allowed the use of political gerrymandering in drawing legislative districts. Having affirmed in an earlier case that race could not be the primary factor in determining the makeup of legislative districts, the Court found that drawing district boundaries based on political affiliation or partisan makeup was justifiable and constitutional. Therefore, creating a "safe" Democratic or Republican seat was permissible.

Because political party affiliation and race are often correlated, it can be unclear to what extent racial rather than political considerations influenced creation of legislative districts. Still, since *Hunt*, there have been several challenges against the legality of certain legislative districts. The most famous case study of racial gerrymandering happened in North Carolina after the 2010 midterm election. The constitutionality of North Carolina's first and twelfth federal congressional districts was challenged out of the belief that they were drawn primarily on the basis of race. The case went before the Supreme Court. In *Cooper v. Harris* (2017), the Supreme Court, in a 5–3 decision, found that North Carolina relied too heavily on race while drawing the district. Conservative Supreme Court justice Clarence Thomas, the only African American on the Court, joined the more liberal wing of the Court in the decision.[76]

Legal jousting over racial gerrymandering is not over. In *Merrill v. Milligan* (2022), the Supreme Court used the shadow docket, an emergency measure that allows the Court to reach decisions without hearing full arguments, to uphold the use of district maps in Alabama that a lower court had ruled were an unconstitutional racial gerrymander. The Court will hear a full argument on the merits in its next term starting in October 2022, but until then the challenged maps remained in use.[77]

The fine art of gerrymandering has been with us since the development of political parties and will surely remain a part of the political landscape for years to come. Both political parties engage in gerrymandering. Districts gerrymandered by Democrats in Maryland and Illinois and by Republicans in North Carolina and Texas have all resulted in litigation. For the last 18 years, gerrymandering in Texas has attracted national attention. As the next sections will show, political gerrymandering in Texas has led to interparty tension, intraparty disputes, political theatrics, closed-door politicking, and a string of lower-court district and Supreme Court cases.[78]

CORE OBJECTIVE

Being Socially Responsible . . .

To what extent should legislators use race when redistricting? Do you think redistricting is an appropriate tool to provide representation to racial and ethnic minority or other underserved populations? Why or why not?

Redistricting in 2001

In the reapportionment following the 2000 census, Texas gained two additional seats in the U.S. House of Representatives for a total of 32. Because the state legislature could not agree on how to redistrict, a special three-judge court was left to draw a new map of Texas districts. Although the map had appeared to slightly favor Republicans, Democrats managed to win 17 of the 32 congressional seats.

In response, U.S. House Majority Leader Tom DeLay (a Republican from Sugar Land, Texas), taking advantage of the fact that Republicans had a majority in the state legislature for the first time in 130 years, proposed an unprecedented mid-decade redistricting.

2003 and the Texas Eleven

In the 2003 session, following DeLay's suggestion, Republicans used their new-found control of the legislature to redraw the state's 32 U.S. congressional districts. The Texas House approved a new map, but Democrats managed to block its adoption in the senate in the regular session of the legislature.

Governor Rick Perry called a special session of the legislature to consider re-redistricting. The house again quickly passed a new congressional map. Eleven senate Democrats, who saw little hope of stopping the Republican majority from adopting the House plan, fled to New Mexico to break the two-thirds quorum required for the senate to conduct business.

This tactic stopped redistricting for the first special session, but the stalemate was broken when Senator John Whitmire, a Democrat from Houston, broke the boycott and returned to Texas. Governor Perry called another special session, which passed a new congressional map over the objections of Democrats.

Using this new map in the 2004 election, Republicans gained five U.S. congressional seats and controlled the Texas delegation to Congress. Republicans, who had entered the decade with a 15 out of 32 seats in the U.S. House, ended with 21 out of 32 seats.

Redistricting in 2011

The 2010 census showed that Texas's population had increased by more than four million people since the year 2000.[79] As a result, Texas gained 4 seats in reapportionment, for a total of 36 seats in the U.S. House of Representatives. Three maps needed to be redrawn in 2011: the congressional districts of Texas, the state of Texas House of Representative districts, and the state of Texas Senate districts.

Initial maps created three additional Republican seats and one additional Democratic seat. Because Texas has a past history of discrimination against voters who are members of minorities, the 1965 Voting Rights Act required Texas to gain federal approval, called preclearance, for the new redistricting maps.[80] Because most of Texas's growth had come from the Hispanic population, and Hispanics tend to vote for Democrats, some considered the 3-1 Republican split to be discriminatory.

In 2012, a federal court determined that the maps drawn by the Texas legislature did not qualify for preclearance. The state appealed this decision to the U.S. Supreme Court.

In June 2013, in the landmark case *Shelby County v. Holder*, the U.S. Supreme Court struck down the portion of the Voting Rights Act, Section 4(b), which laid out the formula used to determine which jurisdictions were subject to preclearance.[81] Without a formula in place to identify jurisdictions subject to preclearance, neither Texas nor any other previously covered jurisdiction needed to get federal approval for its district maps.

Because of the *Shelby County* decision, Texas no longer needs preclearance for its redistricting maps from the U.S. Department of Justice. However, the legality of maps can still be challenged in federal courts. In 2017, as part of ongoing litigation, a federal district court held that some districts outlined in the Texas maps were racially discriminatory. The court found that U.S. congressional districts 27 and 35, and several state house districts in Dallas, Nueces, Bell, and Tarrant counties, were crafted with the intent to minimize the impact of minority votes.[82]

Attorney General Ken Paxton appealed the district's court decision to the U.S. Supreme Court. In *Abbott v. Perez* (2018), the court reversed the district court and affirmed the legality of the current maps, holding that the court had violated a presumption of good faith on the part of the legislature. Justice Sonia Sotomayor, the only Latina justice, dissented, arguing that the maps violated the voting rights of people of color.[83]

Outside of Texas, the U.S. Supreme Court held in two 2019 cases that partisan gerrymandering, as distinct from racial gerrymandering, is a political question beyond the reach of the judiciary, in part because no "limited and precise standard" exists to determine when partisan gerrymandering is "too partisan."[84]

Redistricting is an important contributor to election outcomes in both Texas and national politics. District boundaries are not, however, the only factor. Personalities, issues, and campaigns still matter. In the 2018 midterm elections, Democrats gained two seats in the Texas Senate and 12 seats in the Texas House.[85]

Redistricting in 2021

Following the 2020 census, Texas gained two more seats in its U.S. House delegation, for a total of 38 seats. The Republican-controlled Texas legislature, in its third special session of 2021, adopted new district maps. The resulting maps are not likely to change the partisan balance in Texas's U.S. House delegation, but did reduce the number of competitive districts, districts in which either party is likely to win, from five to one.[86]

Unsurprisingly, not everyone is happy with Texas's new maps. Both the League of United Latin American Citizens (LULAC) and the U.S. Department of Justice filed lawsuits challenging the Texas maps, asserting that they were discriminatory in that they did not take account of population growth among racial and ethnic minorities.[87] Ninety-five percent of Texas's population growth was among people of color, but the new maps do not, it is claimed, reflect this demographic trend.[88] The trial date in the LULAC lawsuit was tentatively set for late September 2022, guaranteeing that the current challenged maps would be used in November 2022 elections.

Because of the continuing nationwide controversy over redistricting, some states have moved away from allowing state legislatures to develop election maps and have placed this task in the hands of redistricting commissions separate from the legislature. Although these are different in each state, they have in common that they are intended to diminish partisanship in the redistricting process, producing more equitable redistricting and more competitive elections. Fifteen states have given primary responsibility for redistricting to these commissions. Time will tell if they fulfill their promise and produce positive benefits for democracy.[89]

How to

Think Critically about Issues

As the discussion of redistricting and reapportionment demonstrates, political issues can be very complex. They affect people's lives in important and sometimes unforeseen ways. Because of this complexity, people often have conflicting opinions about political issues. When dealing with political issues such as redistricting and reapportionment, you will find it easier to defend your opinions if you formed them by using critical thinking skills.

Step 1: Ask questions about the issue to make sure you understand the basics.
Do you know what all the terms related to this issue mean? For example, how would you define *redistricting* and *reapportionment*? What is the history behind these two practices? What are different methods of redistricting and reapportionment? Are there related issues, such as gerrymandering? If so, how would you explain the relationship between the issues?

Step 2: Analyze the positions that people take.
What are redistricting and reapportionment meant to accomplish? Different groups may want conflicting outcomes. What are the main proposals for the best methods of redistricting and reapportionment? Think about the benefits of each method and the problems each might cause. What do you think is the correct outcome for redistricting and reapportionment? Which method is most likely to bring about the result that you favor?

Step 3: Look for assumptions and biases.
Who benefits most from each method being proposed? Are there assumptions and biases that influence people's positions? For example, people may be affected by prejudice, a desire for power, or the possibility of economic gain. Are your own feelings about the issue influenced by bias or untested assumptions?

Step 4: Consider claims and evidence.
Before forming a final opinion, look at what advocates of the various proposals claim will be the outcome. Do they contend that a particular method of redistricting will bring about more equal representation for minority populations? If so, what is their evidence to support that claim? Have they demonstrated, for instance, that the method has been tried in another state and produced the desired results?

Step 5: Evaluate the information you have gathered and draw your own conclusions.
First, develop your own criteria, or standards, for what the best outcome would look like. Then, reexamine the claims, arguments, and evidence that you have gathered. Based on all these things, judge which methods of redistricting and reapportionment would bring about the outcome that you believe is most desirable. To do this, you will need to draw a conclusion by looking closely at the facts, making connections between those facts, and being willing to change your mind if the facts don't support your previously held opinion.

Critical thinking is the objective analysis of facts and evidence to form a judgment about something that matters. It is an essential life skill that is not just for forming political opinions. You will need critical thinking in your work life and as you make significant personal decisions. The more you exercise critical thinking, the better you will become at making wise decisions that can affect almost every area of your life.

The Texas Legislative Redistricting Board, whose primary responsibility is to draw these maps, is made up entirely of elected officials. It is hard to imagine that Texas politicians will move in the direction of a commission independent of the legislature.

Understanding Impact In this chapter, we've seen that courts have consistently upheld the legality of political gerrymandering—and that it can be difficult to discern when its racial effect would be sufficient to render gerrymandering unconstitutional. Why do you think the Supreme Court has consistently allowed political gerrymandering? Should districts instead be drawn in as "compact" a way as possible, without allowing political or other considerations? Explain.

Getting Elected

Learning Objective: Explain how legislators are elected, including the single-member district method of election.

Now that we know something about who is elected to state legislatures, we'll turn our attention to what it takes to win an election. As we'll discuss in Chapter 10, running for office can be costly. Many candidates for the state legislature face little or no opposition in either the primary or general election. Even when candidates do not face opposition, however, they are likely to collect large amounts of money from various groups, especially from **political action committees (PACs)**.

political action committee (PAC)
A spin-off of an interest group that collects money for campaign contributions and other activities

In the 2020 election cycle, 382 candidates competed for 150 seats (plus special elections) in the Texas House. Over $137.5 million was contributed, for an average of $360,178 per candidate. The amount collected ranged dramatically. Dade Phelan, new speaker of the house, collected $4.7 million; Lina Ortega, incumbent candidate for house District 77, raised the least of any successful house candidate, but still collected $48,394. In the Texas state senate, 55 candidates competed for 17 seats, raising a total of $30.4 million for an average of $554,000 per candidate. The largest amount raised in the senate was $3.1 million raised by Eddie Lucio, Jr. in his race for Senate District 27. The highest amount raised by a losing candidate was $2.7 million raised by Peter Flores, who lost his race although he was the incumbent in Senate District 19. The lowest amount raised by a winning candidate in the senate was Carol Alvarado, the incumbent in District 6, with a total of $540,375.[90]

Much of this money comes from contributors who live outside the senator's or representative's district.[91] Races in both the house and senate are financed by PACs and large contributors. In some cases, candidates for state legislature receive contributions from out-of-state sources as well. Based on long-standing house statute, members of the Texas legislature are prohibited from accepting campaign contributions during the legislative session (as well as in the 30 days before a session starts and for 20 days after adjournment).[92] This statute does not apply to special legislative sessions.

Competition for House and Senate Seats

As previously noted, in the one-party Democratic era in Texas (1870s to 1970s), most of the competition for offices took place within the Democratic Party primary. Today, competition is more likely in the general election, but many seats are still in relatively safe districts.

In the 2020 election, 48 Texas House candidates, almost of third of the 150 total seats, ran unopposed. This was 1 more than ran unopposed in 2018. Of these unopposed candidates, 26 were Democrats and 22 were Republicans. In 8 races (4 each for Democrats and Republicans), the only competition was a third party candidate presenting no realistic opposition.[93]

In the Texas Senate, there were 16 senate seats up for reelection in 2020. Only 1 senate seat, held by District 28 Republican Charles Perry, was uncontested. Of the 15 contested seats, 10 involved Republican and Democratic candidates, 2 had Democratic and Libertarian candidates, and 3 had a Republican, a Democrat and a Libertarian.[94]

Party voting is a measure of the strength of a political party in each legislative district, based on voter support for the party's candidates in previous elections. This measure also indicates the level of party competition. Studies of party competition for seats in the U.S. House and Senate define **noncompetitive districts** as any district in which either party receives 55 percent or more of the votes. A district in which party vote is between 44 and 54 percent is considered competitive.[95] The measure used here to gauge party competitiveness is the combined vote received by either party for all offices/candidates in the district in the previous general election. This is the composite party vote. Thus, a house or senate district in which the Republican Party candidates for statewide office collectively received 55 percent or more of the votes is considered a safe Republican district. Table 3.4 shows the number of competitive and noncompetitive seats in the Texas House and Senate from the 2020 general election.

In addition to party competition, we can also describe districts by their racial composition, the percentages of racial and ethnic minority residents compared to other residents of the district. If we compare these two variables (party competition and minority population in the district) using some simple statistics, we can see that most Texas House and Senate seats fall into two categories: noncompetitive Republican Anglo districts and noncompetitive Democratic racial and ethnic minority districts. The creation of majority-minority districts results in the creation of safe Republican districts. Because African American and Hispanic support for Democratic candidates is always very high, concentrating members of these communities in districts also concentrates Democratic Party support in these districts. Many remaining districts are therefore noncompetitive Republican districts. Other studies have found the same is true for U.S. congressional districts.[96]

One reason for the low level of competition in Texas legislative races is racial and political gerrymandering. Competition in gerrymandered districts is most likely to occur in the primary or when there is no incumbent. Competition in the general elections is less likely. Safe Democratic districts exist primarily in South Texas, where there are high concentrations of Hispanics, and East Texas, the traditional Democratic stronghold. Republicans are strong in the Panhandle and the Hill Country. Metropolitan areas of the state include both safe Democratic and safe

noncompetitive districts
Districts in which a candidate from either party wins 55 percent or more of the vote

TABLE 3.4

Competitive and Noncompetitive Seats in the Texas House and Senate, 2020 Election

	Safe Democratic	Safe Republican	Competitive	Unopposed*
House	27 (18%)	50 (33.3%)	25 (16.7%)	48 (32.0%)
Senate	7 (43.75%)	7 (43.75%)	1 (6.25%)	1 (6.25%)

*"Unopposed" means a candidate ran without opposition from the other major party but may or may not have been opposed by a third-party candidate; unopposed candidates were also included in the "safe" count for their respective party.

Source: Adapted from "Texas Election Results," *The New York Times*, https://www.nytimes.com/interactive/2020/11/03/us/elections/results-texas.html.

Republican districts, with Democrats in the inner city and Republicans in the suburbs. The trend of suburbs voting Republican may be challenged as Texas politics evolve, as was made plain by the 2018 defeat of incumbent Republican Pete Sessions by Democratic challenger Colin Allred in a race for U.S. House district 32, which is largely made up of north Dallas suburbs. Allred held his seat in 2020, getting nearly the same percentage of the vote that he earned in 2018.

CORE OBJECTIVE

Thinking Critically . . .

Both demographics and voting patterns have changed in Texas, and many districts have become more competitive. Discuss what these shifts mean for future elections and the composition of the Texas House and Senate. Reference Table 3.4 in your answer.

Most members who seek reelection are reelected. Unless legislators are in a competitive district, they can generally stay as long as they like. Most voluntarily retire after a few years of service.

Term Limits

term limits

Limitations on the number of times a person can be elected to the same office in state legislatures

Although turnover in state legislatures nationwide is quite high, many states have adopted formal **term limits** for state legislators in order to legally limit long tenures in any particular seat. This trend was particularly pronounced in the 1990s, when many states enacted term limits either by constitutional amendment or by statute, for both house and senate seats. These limits were approved despite the fact that self-limiting of terms was working for many years. For example, "nationally, 72 percent of the house members and 75 percent of the senators who served in 1979 had left their respective chamber by 1989."[97] Currently, 15 states impose term limits on legislators.[98] The Texas legislature is not term limited.

The two most senior members of the Texas legislature as of 2021 are Senator John Whitmire (39 years) and Representative Tom Craddick (52 years). As of 2021, about 57 percent of members of the house had fewer than 8 years of service; in the senate, it is only 9.7 percent. As for 20-plus years of service, the percentage in the house is 8.0, and the percentage in the senate is 19.4 (see Table 3.5).[99]

TABLE 3.5

Years of Service of Members of the 87th Legislature

	House		Senate	
	Number	Percent	Number	Percent
20+	12	8.0%	6	19.4%
14–19	13	8.7%	3	9.7%
8–13	39	26.0%	11	35.5%
1–7	67	44.7%	8	25.8%
1st	19	12.7%	3	9.7%

Source: Texas Legislative Reference Library, https://lrl.texas.gov/legeLeaders/members/seniority.cfm

> **Understanding Impact** It is frequently argued that term limits are desirable because legislators who spend many years in their seats become too comfortable, and lose touch with "the people." On the other hand, experienced legislators who understand how government works and who have built relationships with experts inside and outside government may be better able to get the hard work of legislating done, on behalf of their constituents and the state. Do you think the benefit of experience outweighs the potential downside of legislators serving for too long? Explain.

Turnover in State Legislatures

Turnover refers to the number of new members of the legislature each session. One might suspect, based on the general lack of competition for Texas legislative seats, that there would be low turnover of the membership. However, this is not the case. Turnover is high in Texas, as it is in all state legislatures, and normally it is higher for the lower house than for the upper chamber.[100]

In the 1980s and 1990s, some states had very high turnover because of the imposition of term limits. Excluding those years, the average turnover in state legislatures around the country is around 25 percent for the lower house and about 15 percent for the upper house.[101] Table 3.5 lists the number of years of service for members of the Texas legislature. At the start of the 2020 session, there were 20 first time members in the house and 3 new members of the senate.[102]

Turnover rates in Texas are very high. Turnover is not due mainly to electoral defeat; most members voluntarily retire from service. Retirement around the country is prompted by generous retirement benefits for eligible members, relatively low pay, the lack of professional staff assistance, redistricting, the requirements of the job, the demands on one's family, fundraising demands, and the rigors of seeking reelection.[103] Some use the office as a stepping-stone to higher office and leave to become members of Congress or to take statewide office. In Texas, the retirement benefits are excellent for those serving a relatively low number of years in the legislature, so leaving office can be financially wise.

Why is turnover a significant issue in state legislatures? It can be argued that high turnover contributes to the amateurish nature of state legislatures (which could be good or bad, depending on your view). In recent years, this has been especially significant in those states with term limits. If 20 to 25 percent of the members are new each session, these new members are learning the rules and finding their way. This allows a few "old-timers" to control the legislative process.

turnover
The number of new members of the legislature each session

Leadership Positions in the Texas Legislature

Learning Objective: Discuss various leadership positions in the Texas legislature.

In any legislative body, those holding formal leadership positions have considerable power to decide the outcome of legislation. In the Texas legislature, power is very much concentrated in the hands of two individuals: the speaker of the house and the lieutenant governor.

Speaker of the House

speaker of the house
Member of the Texas House, elected by the house members, who serves as presiding officer and generally controls the passage of legislation

The members of the house elect the speaker of the Texas House of Representatives, by majority vote, for a two-year term. The election of the **speaker of the house** is the members' first formal act in each legislative session. The secretary of state presides over the election, and only occasionally is the outcome of this election in doubt. The identity of the speaker is generally known far in advance of the beginning of the session, and this individual spends considerable time lining up supporters before the session begins. In all but a few cases, the person elected is a long-time member of the house and has support from current members. When one-third of the members are new, the person elected speaker may also have to gain support from some of these new members. It is illegal for candidates for speaker to formally promise members something in exchange for their vote, but key players in the election of the speaker often receive choice committee assignments.

Incumbent speakers are almost always reelected. A new speaker is typically chosen only after the death, retirement, or resignation of a sitting speaker. Traditionally, speakers served for two terms and retired or moved to higher offices. From 1951 to 1975, no speaker served more than two terms. In 1975, Billy Clayton broke with this tradition and served for four terms. Gib Lewis, who succeeded Clayton, served for five terms, as did Pete Laney.[104]

Tom Craddick was first elected speaker for the 2003 session. He was the first Republican speaker since Reconstruction. After serving three terms as speaker, Craddick was not reelected in 2009. In the 2008 election, the Republicans retained a bare majority (76 to 74). Before the 2009 session even began, a long-standing "Anybody but Craddick" movement among legislators who resented his autocratic style gained momentum and ultimately led to his replacement by San Antonio–area legislator Joe Straus as the speaker for the 81st Legislature. Straus was speaker through 2018.

Speaker Straus earned the ire of conservative Republicans.[105] Straus succeeded in getting the 2017 session to pass big-ticket school finance and property tax legislation, but not legislation favored by social conservatives.[106] Straus did not seek reelection and was replaced by Dennis Bonnen for the 2019 session. Bonnen had a successful first term, but he became embroiled in a scandal involving one of the conservative groups that was not satisfied with the results of the 2019 legislative session. Bonnen was caught on tape asking the group to target Republicans in the following election. By the end of the summer, Bonnen had announced that he would not run for reelection.[107] Republican Dade Phelan was elected to serve as speaker for the 2021 session.[108]

House Parliamentarian Sharon Carter and Speaker of the House Dade Phelan go over a stack of bills on the last full day of the 2021 legislative session. Shortly after this, House Democrats dramatically walked out to prevent the passage of a bill that would make it harder to post bail.

Eric Gay/AP Images

As one of "the Big Three" in Texas government, alongside the Governor and Lt. Governor, the speaker is extremely powerful. Generally, speakers have the power to direct and decide what legislation passes the house. The speaker gains power from the formal rules adopted by the house at the beginning of each session. These rules allow the speaker to do the following:

1. Appoint the chairs of all committees.
2. Appoint most of the members of each standing committee. About half of these committee seats are assigned based on a limited seniority system. In reality, backers of the speaker often use their seniority to choose a committee assignment in line with the speaker's priorities, freeing the speaker of the need to reward them with a seat and thus allowing the speaker to use appointments to place preferred members in other strategic committee slots.
3. Appoint members of the calendar and procedural committees, conference committees, and other special and interim committees.
4. Serve as presiding officer over all sessions. This power allows the speaker to recognize members on the floor who want to speak, generally interpret house rules, decide when a vote will be taken, and decide the outcome of voice votes.
5. Refer all bills to committees. As a rule, bills go to subject matter committees. However, the speaker has discretion in deciding what committee will receive a bill. Some speakers used the State Affairs Committee as their "dead bill committee." Bills assigned to this committee usually had little chance of passing. Also, the speaker can assign a bill to a favorable committee to enhance its chances of passing.

Few bills pass the house without the speaker's approval. For example, in the third special session of the 87th Legislature in summer 2021, Governor Abbott included a call to increase the penalty for illegal voting, which had been reduced as part of SB 1, Texas's voting overhaul that had passed in the second special session. However, Speaker Phelan announced that he did not support "relitigating" voting regulation, ending any chance of passing the Governor's and Lt. Governor's priority.[109]

Lieutenant Governor

Unlike the speaker of the house, the **lieutenant governor** is elected by the voters in a statewide general election and serves a four-year term. The lieutenant governor does not owe their election to the legislative body, is not formally a senator, and cannot vote in the senate except in cases of a tie. One might assume that the office was not a powerful legislative office, and in most states this is true. The lieutenant governor in Texas, however, has powers very similar to those of the speaker. Lieutenant governors can do the following:

1. Appoint the chairs of all senate committees.
2. Select all members of all senate committees. No formal seniority rule applies in the senate.
3. Appoint members of the conference committees.
4. Serve as presiding officer of the senate and interpret rules.
5. Refer all bills to committees.

lieutenant governor
Presiding officer of the Texas Senate; elected by the voters of the state

At first glance, it may appear that the lieutenant governor in Texas is even more powerful than the speaker. After all, the lieutenant governor does not owe their election to the senate, and the lieutenant governor has all the powers that the speaker has. The reality, however, is different. The powers of the lieutenant governor are assigned by the formal rules of the senate, which are adopted at the beginning of each session. What the senate gives, it can take away. Lieutenant governors must play a delicate balancing role of working with powerful members of the senate, often compromising in the assignment of chairs of committees and committee membership. The same is true for all other powers. Thus, the lieutenant governor must forge an alliance with key senators to effectively use these powers.

In most states, the lieutenant governor has not traditionally been a powerful leader. Five states (Arizona, Maine, New Hampshire, Oregon, and Wyoming) do not even have a lieutenant governor.[110] More than half of all lieutenant governors serve as the presiding officer in their state senate,[111] though some attend a senate session only when their vote is needed to break a tie. In states without a lieutenant governor, the senate elects one of its members to be the presiding officer, called the pro tempore, president of the senate, or speaker of the senate.[112] In only a few states is the lieutenant governor able to appoint committee members and assign bills to committees.[113] Most lieutenant governors are figureheads who stand in when the governor is outside the state or incapacitated, and if the governor's office is vacated due to death, resignation, or removal, the lieutenant governor succeeds as governor. Thus, the office of lieutenant governor in Texas is quite different from, and is more powerful than, the office in most other states.[114]

Lieutenant Governor Dan Patrick
Eric Gay/AP Images

extra legislative powers
Legislative leaders serve on boards outside of the legislature

In addition to their legislative duties, the speaker and the lieutenant governor have other **extra legislative powers.** They appoint members of other state boards, or they serve as members of such boards. For example, they appoint the members of the Legislative Budget Board, which writes the state budget, and they serve as the chair and vice chair of this board. These are important powers because these boards make policy. The state budget, for instance, is a policy statement in monetary terms. The budget decides what agencies and programs will be funded and in what amounts. It is easy for elected officials to make speeches and promises. However, their actual priorities are revealed in how they choose to spend taxpayers' money.

The speaker and the lieutenant governor also serve as members of the Legislative Redistricting Board. This board meets if the legislature fails to redraw house or senate districts. The decision of this board is subject to change only by court action.

The current lieutenant governor of Texas is Dan Patrick, who took office in 2015 and who previously made a name for himself as a conservative radio talk-show host. Though both Patrick and Governor Abbott are Republicans, in Texas the lieutenant governor is elected separately from the governor rather than on the same ticket as the governor's designated running mate.[115] Therefore, the governor and lieutenant governor sometimes come from different political parties. This has been the case recently, in fact, as Democrat Bill Hobby served as lieutenant governor alongside Republican governor Bill Clements, and Democrat Bob Bullock was lieutenant governor during most of Republican governor, and later president, George W. Bush's time in the governor's mansion.

> **Understanding Impact** The Texas legislature has traditionally been a body that displayed less partisanship than, for example, the U.S. Congress. That is changing, however, and sharper partisan conflict is becoming more common in Austin. Because the governor and lieutenant governor are elected separately, they can and, at times, have come from different parties. Do you think that having the top two statewide elected officials in the Texas government from different parties would be a problem today? Should Texas change how these two officials are elected, to avoid partisan dysfunction?

Committees in the House and Senate

Learning Objective: Discuss various leadership positions in the Texas legislature.

Most of the work of the legislature is done in **standing committees** established by house and senate rules. Besides the standing committees, there are also subcommittees of the standing committees, **conference committees** to work out differences in bills passed by the two houses, temporary committees to study special problems, and interim committees to study issues between sessions of the state legislature.

Of these, the standing committees are the most important. They are subject-matter specific and are established at the beginning of each legislative session by the house and the senate. In the 87th Legislature, there were 15 in the senate and 34 in the house.[116] These are listed in Table 3.6. The chairs of these standing committees have powers similar to those of the speaker and lieutenant governor at the committee level. They decide the times and agendas for meetings of the committee. In doing so, they decide the amount of time devoted to bills and which bills get the attention of the committee. A chair who strongly dislikes a bill can often prevent that bill from passing. Even if the bill gets a hearing, the chair can decide to give that bill to a subcommittee that might kill it. As in most legislative bodies, power in Texas is heavily concentrated in the individuals who make up the house and senate leadership and who control the agendas and actions of the legislature. Few bills can pass the legislature without the support of these individuals.

standing committees
Committees of the house and senate that consider legislation during sessions

conference committees
Joint committees of the house and senate that work out differences in bills passed in each chamber

> **Understanding Impact** Committee chairs, like other legislative leaders, have immense power to control not simply what legislation becomes law, but what even receives a full hearing. This kind of top-down power relationship has been criticized for placing too much influence in too few hands, and thus being undemocratic. Do you agree? How might the committee structure of the Texas legislature be changed to ensure that the voices of more people are heard in the legislative process?

CORE OBJECTIVE

Taking Personal Responsibility . . .

Many people believe that the success of legislation largely depends on a relatively few individuals who make up the leadership in the Texas House and Senate. Do you think the speaker of the house and the lieutenant governor have too much, too little, or the right amount of control over the passage of bills? How can you influence legislation? What can individuals do to affect legislation?

TABLE 3.6

Standing Committees of the Texas House and Senate, 87th Legislature

Senate Committees	House Committees
Administration	Agriculture & Livestock
Business & Commerce	Appropriations
Criminal Justice	Business & Industry
Education	Calendars
Finance	Corrections
Health & Human Services	County Affairs
Higher Education	Criminal Jurisprudence
Jurisprudence	Culture, Recreation & Tourism
Local Government	Defense & Veterans' Affairs
Natural Resources & Economic Development	Elections
Nominations	Energy Resources
State Affairs	Environmental Regulation
Transportation	General Investigating
Veteran Affairs	Higher Education
Water, Agriculture & Rural Affairs	Homeland Security & Public Safety
	House Administration
	Human Services
	Insurance
	International Relations & Economic Development
	Judiciary & Civil Jurisprudence
	Juvenile Justice & Family Issues
	Land & Resource Management
	Licensing & Administrative Procedures
	Local & Consent Calendars
	Natural Resources
	Pensions, Investments & Financial Services
	Public Education
	Public Health
	Redistricting
	Resolutions Calendars
	State Affairs
	Transportation
	Urban Affairs
	Ways & Means

Sources: Adapted from Texas Senate, https://www.senate.texas.gov/committees.php; House of Representatives, https://house.texas.gov/committees/.

Functions

Learning Objective: Describe the Texas legislature's functions and procedures.

Lawmaking

The Texas legislature has, as one of its main functions, the responsibility to create, alter, and enact laws for the state. The Texas legislature's two branches carry out these functions. This is the main duty and function of legislative bodies in general. In Texas, legislators fulfill this function by passing bills and resolutions.

Bills

A bill is a proposed law or a proposed change to a current law. Revenue bills must begin in the House of Representatives (Article III, Section 33).[117] Outside of that restriction, any bill can begin in the house or the senate, but it must pass both chambers to become law. Companion bills are very common in Texas. This happens when a member of the house and a member of the senate file an identical bill at the same time. The purpose is to save time, especially in a session that lasts only 140 days.

During the 87th regular legislative session, lawmakers filed 7,327 house and senate bills and resolutions. Of these, both house and senate passed 1,161, and the governor vetoed 20 of those.[118] During the three special sessions of the 87th legislature, an additional 1,034 bills and resolutions were introduced, and 24 passed both chambers and were signed by the governor. SB 2222 is one of the 1,161 bills that passed in the regular session. It was filed on April 21, 2021, passed both chambers, was signed by the governor on June 18, 2021; it mandates that windshields of cars used by the Texas Highway Patrol be bullet-resistent.[119]

Bills generally become effective September 1 following the legislative session, unless classified as emergency bills, which require a two-thirds vote in both chambers to become effective immediately with the governor's signature (Article III, Section 39). During the 87th session, 329 bills became effective immediately. These bills taking immediate effect ranged from HB 54, which prohibits film crews following state or local law enforcement to produce reality TV shows, to SB 279, which requires that suicide prevention contact information be included on secondary school student identification cards.[120]

Because Texas must have a balanced budget (Article III, Section 49; Article VIII, Section 22), each bill must have a fiscal note. The fiscal note explains the cost of the bill to the state if it is adopted. For example, the fiscal note for HB 1525, which makes changes to public education management and finance, commits Texas taxpayers to spending $475,196,008 in the 2021–23 biennium, with similar costs in future years.[121]

Resolutions

Resolutions are another method of lawmaking. Members of the Texas legislature can file three types: (1) concurrent resolutions, (2) joint resolutions, and (3) simple resolutions.

Concurrent resolutions must pass both the house and senate and generally require the governor's signature. A concurrent resolution is used to convey the sentiment of the legislature, request information from a state agency, or call on Congress for some action. For example, during the 87th session, SCR 41 urged Congress to adopt the "Keep Nine" amendment to the U.S. Constitution and send it to the states for ratification. This amendment would establish a constitutional requirement that the Supreme Court have nine members.[122]

Concurrent resolutions can also be congratulatory or used for memorials. One example from the 87th legislature is HCR 61, which designated the Texas star mushroom as the official State Mushroom of Texas![123]

Joint resolutions require passage of both the house and senate, but they do not require the governor's signature. In Texas, lawmakers use joint resolutions to propose constitutional amendments. Before proposed constitutional amendments become effective, the voters of Texas must approve each by a majority vote. In November 2021, voters approved all eight proposed constitutional amendments that came out of the 87th session. Amendments included allowing charity raffles at professional rodeo events, forbidding the state to place limitations on religious services (including during pandemics, for example), and requiring 10 years of experience practicing law in Texas to be eligible to serve as a judge on certain courts.[124]

Because the Texas legislature meets in the spring of odd-numbered years, typically joint resolutions proposing constitutional amendments are passed in the spring and appear on the ballot in November of that year. In 2021, however, two joint resolutions were adopted in special sessions of the legislature. As these were passed after the deadline for placement on the November ballot, Governor Abbott scheduled a special election for May 2022 for voters to consider two constitutional amendments, both dealing with property taxes.

Simple resolutions are used as a method of dealing with measures that concern only one chamber. They need to pass only one chamber and do not require the governor's signature. Lawmakers use simple resolutions primarily to adopt chamber rules and to honor constituents of the legislators. These resolutions do not have to be read or debated. For example, HR 1973 recognized April 2021 as Parkinson's Disease Awareness Month.

In the next section, we'll look at the complicated process legislation follows to become law.

Budget and Taxation

One of the most essential laws that Texas legislators enact is the biennial budget. The Legislative Budget Board submits a recommended budget to the legislature. The governor's office also submits an executive budget. The legislature then uses these two documents to help create and enact the budget that will be in place for the state until the next legislative session. The Senate Finance Committee and House Appropriations Committee begin the process of creating the budget bill for the legislature. The budget bill follows a similar process as other bills in the legislature, but it passes to the state comptroller before it goes to the governor. The comptroller must certify that the budget spends no more than the state's anticipated revenue for the biennium.[125]

The Texas legislature establishes the state sales tax, which is the main source of revenue for the state because Texas has no state income tax. Additional taxes can be established, such as franchise taxes on businesses or "sin" taxes on activities the legislature may want to discourage, such as buying alcohol and tobacco.

Oversight

Another key responsibility of the legislature is to keep track of what state agencies are doing, assess their performance, and determine whether they provide necessary functions. The legislature has several ways to examine these state agencies in order to fulfill this "oversight" duty. One way is by using committees. A committee may call representatives of agencies to testify at a hearing. Although this tactic is common in the federal government, it is less effective for the Texas legislature because of the limited legislative session. Another way to oversee

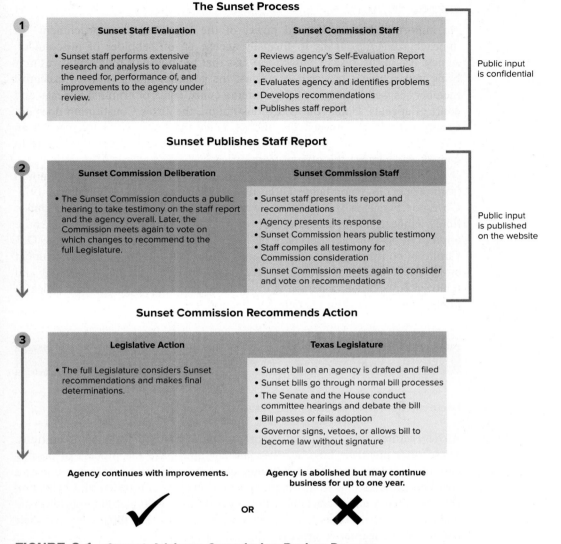

FIGURE 3.1   Sunset Advisory Commission Review Process

state agencies is through financial mechanisms—for example, the actions taken by the Legislative Budget Board and by the Legislative Audit Committee. A final means of oversight is the Sunset Advisory Commission. The commission reviews about 130 state agencies on a rotating basis to determine whether there is a continued need for the agency under review. This works out to each agency being reviewed, on average, about every 12 years. The commission then makes a recommendation to the legislature on whether to continue or abolish the agency. See Figure 3.1 to learn how this process works.[126]

Understanding Impact As you've seen in this section, oversight of state agencies can be difficult in Texas, largely because of time constraints imposed by biennial sessions. Are the people of Texas well served by this system? Do you think this makes a powerful argument to move to annual legislative sessions? How else might state agencies be more effectively overseen by the people's representatives?

Impeachment

An important but rarely used power of the legislature is impeachment. To impeach someone means to formally accuse an officeholder of misconduct. Article XV of the Texas Constitution says that the house of representatives may bring impeachment proceedings against the governor and all elected executive members as well as judges of the supreme court, court of criminal appeals, and court of appeals. Unlike the U.S. Constitution, the Texas Constitution does not specify what is an impeachable offense. Once the house votes to impeach an official, the trial must be held in the senate and requires a two-thirds vote to convict and remove the official from office.

In Texas, only two officials have been impeached, convicted, and removed from office: Governor James Ferguson in 1917 and Judge O.P. Carillo in 1975. Governor Ferguson was indicted on nine charges of misapplication of public funds, embezzlement, and diversion of a special fund after vetoing the entire appropriations for the University of Texas.[127] The senate convicted Judge O.P. Carillo of conspiring with others to charge and collect money from government entities for rentals of equipment that did not exist.[128] Once convicted and removed from office, a person is disqualified from holding any other office of public trust in the state (Article XV, Section 4).

Procedures

Learning Objective: Describe the Texas legislature's functions and procedures.

All legislatures have formal rules of procedure that govern their operations. These rules prescribe how bills become law and make the process of passing laws more orderly and fair. A bill must clear many hurdles before it becomes a law. This prevents bills from becoming law without careful review and helps provide consistency and predictability in the law. In the traditionalistic/individualistic political culture of Texas, these rules tend to protect the ruling elite and their control of the legislative process.

Formal Rules: How a Bill Becomes a Law

Figure 3.2 lists the formal procedures in the Texas House and Senate for passing a bill. Each bill, to become law, must clear each step during the legislative session. Over half of the bills that are introduced fail to pass. Few bills of major importance are passed in any given legislative session.

At each stage in the process, a bill can receive favorable or unfavorable actions. Within each step, a bill can die by action or inaction. There are many ways to kill a bill, but only one way to pass a bill.

There are eight primary steps in how a bill becomes a law. Let's follow the path a bill must navigate to become law, starting, in this example, in the house. Bills intended to raise revenue must start in the house.

1. **Introduction** This step includes assignment of the bill number and "first reading" of the bill number and caption, giving notice of the bill's topic.

The Texas Legislative Process for House Bills and Resolutions

This diagram displays the sequential flow of a bill from the time it is introduced in the house of representatives to final passage and transmittal to the governor.

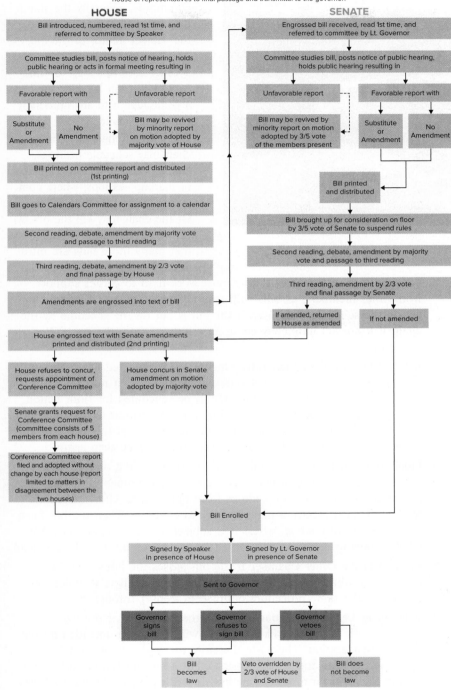

FIGURE 3.2   Basic Steps in the Texas Legislative Process This diagram displays the sequential flow of a bill from the time it is introduced in the Texas House of Representatives to final passage and transmittal to the governor. A bill introduced in the senate follows the same procedure, flowing from senate to house.

Texas House of Representatives

Jay Janner/Austin American-Statesman/AP Images

2. **Referral to Standing Committee** The speaker refers each bill to committee, generally the standing committee appropriate to the subject matter of the bill. As noted earlier, sometimes the speaker uses this step to effectively kill a bill by referring it to a committee with an "unfriendly" committee chair.

3. **Committee Action** The committee chair may schedule hearings, where public input is obtained, or markup sessions, where committee members revise the bill. Or the chair may kill the bill by taking no action. Remember that many more bills are introduced than the legislature can consider in a session. Legislators must work hard to garner support from other members, as bills with insufficient support are unlikely to get on the schedule. And even if the bill is put on the schedule by the chair, if it doesn't ultimately get a majority vote from the committee, it still dies.

4. **Referral to Calendars Committee** Once a bill is reported favorably out of committee (meaning that it gets a majority vote), it must pass the gauntlet of the Calendars Committee to be scheduled for floor action. This committee is generally chaired by a member loyal to the speaker, so if the speaker does not support a particular bill, at this point it may enter what turns out to be a black hole and never be seen again.

5. **Floor Action** If a bill does make it to the floor, it first undergoes a second reading, during which it is subject to amendment and various potential parliamentary procedures from opponents. After the second reading, it must receive a majority vote to continue. Then the bill must still have a third reading, where it is subject to the same actions. Any bill that fails to get a majority on either second or third reading is dead.

6. **Referral to the Other Chamber** If the bill passes the house with a majority on third reading, it is sent to the senate, where it undergoes essentially the same procedure outlined in steps 1 through 5.

7. **Subsequent Legislative Action** Let's say the bill makes it through the senate successfully. Most likely the bill will have been amended during senate consideration. There are therefore two versions of the bill (the house version and the senate version), but a bill must pass both chambers in identical form to become law. In our example, the bill that was amended in the senate will first be sent back to the house, which will have a chance to take one of two actions: (a) vote to accept the senate amendments and send the bill to the governor or (b) send the bill to conference committee, which will try to negotiate a compromise version

of the bill. If conferees fail to reach a compromise, or if the compromise bill does not get a majority vote in both the house and senate, the bill will still die.

8. **Action by the Governor**[129] If the bill makes it this far, it is ready to go to the governor, who can take one of the actions described under the heading "The Governor."

In the Texas Senate, bills are brought to the floor in the order in which they are reported on. At the beginning of each term in the senate, someone traditionally introduces a "blocker bill," which is moved out of committee quickly and therefore becomes the first on the agenda. As a result, from the beginning of the session, this blocker bill is always the next bill that must be considered. For another bill to be considered ahead of the blocker bill, the senate must vote to suspend its regular order of business. For 70 years, it took the support of two-thirds of the senate to move a bill past the blocker. In other words, 21 senators had to agree to suspend the regular order of business and bring the bill to the floor for debate.

The 84th Legislature broke with precedent and changed this rule. According to the new rule, three-fifths of the senate must support consideration to bring a bill to the floor.[130] That lowered the threshold to only 19 senators to move legislation forward. Lieutenant Governor Patrick, who championed the rule change, argued it would allow the senate "to pass legislation that has been blocked for many years."[131] Opponents argued that it would make the senate more partisan, for as long as one party has at least 19 members of the 31 senators, those 19 would not need to seek the support of members of the opposing party to get their legislation through. One example of a bill that passed after the change was "campus carry" legislation, allowing licensed gun owners to carry weapons on most higher education campuses.[132]

The three-fifths rule's impact has been unclear. In the 2021 87th legislature, the Texas Senate passed several conservative priorities despite having only 18 Republicans—one short of the 19 required to bring bills to the floor on a strictly partisan basis. Passage of HB 25, the bill that required transgender youth to competing on sports teams according to the sex they were assigned on their birth certificates, was passed when a Democrat crossed the aisle and voted in favor.[133] For SB 1, the election bill, votes were taken when two Democratic senators were away from the senate floor because of COVID-19, so 18 Republican senators satisfied the three-fifths requirement.[134]

Once a bill becomes law it remains in effect until nullified by subsequent legislation or by the courts at the state or the federal level. For example, in 1925, Texas passed a law banning abortions in the state. In 1973, the U.S. Supreme Court legalized abortion in *Roe v. Wade*. This ruling nullified the 1925 law. However, in 2022, the U.S. Supreme Court overturned the *Roe* decision in *Dobbs v. Jackson Women's Health Organization*, leaving abortion policy up to the states. Texas Attorney General Ken Paxton issued an advisory that the 1925 law could still create legal liability for abortion providers, and the Texas Supreme Court concurred.[135] Furthermore, the Texas legislature passed a "trigger bill" in 2021[136] that would snap into effect 30 days after a U.S. Supreme Court decision overturning Roe went into effect. The 30-day period expired, and the trigger law went into effect, on August 25, 2022.[137]

Understanding Impact The Texas Senate's three-fifths rule, formerly the two-thirds rule, was intended to ensure that legislation was a compromise that earned support from members of both parties before floor consideration. Opponents of the rule believed if they were in the majority they should be able to pass legislation without obstruction. Do you think legislatures should have rules encouraging cooperation and compromise? Or is a requirement for a three-fifths supermajority unreasonable in today's political climate?

The Governor

The governor has 10 days to sign or veto a bill after receiving it. The only exception is during the final 10 days of the session; then the governor has 20 days. If the governor does nothing, the bill automatically becomes law. This reflects the traditional political culture of limiting the governor's power. If the governor vetoes a bill, they must provide the legislature with a veto message explaining how the bill violates the Texas Constitution or other state laws.

According to the Texas Constitution, the legislature can override a governor's veto with a two-thirds vote in each chamber. In practice, this is very unlikely because most bills go to the governor in the final days of the session, which leaves no time for overrides, because by the time the governor vetoes the bill the legislative session will have ended.

In Texas, the governor does not have "pocket veto" power. This means that in Texas, any bill that goes unsigned and does not receive a veto becomes law. If the governor wants to prevent a bill from becoming law, then they must actively veto it. During the 86th session, Governor Abbott vetoed 58 bills of all types, with no overrides occurring.

Legislative Workload and Logjams

Most bills pass the legislature in the final days of the session. This scenario gives the impression that the legislature "goofs off" for most of the session and then frantically passes bills just before adjournment, producing laws that are rushed and ill-considered.

In Texas, it is true that most legislation—about 80 percent of all bills—passes in the final two weeks of the session. Does this result in poor quality and inferior legislation? The answer is, probably not. Understanding the process of agenda setting makes this process clearer.

First, bills may be introduced in either chamber. However, only members of the house can file bills in the house, and only senate members can file bills in the senate. Legislators may start introducing bills on the first Monday after the general election preceding the regular session, a process known as pre-filing. They may continue to file bills until the 60th day of the 140-day session. After the 60th day, only local bills, emergency appropriations, emergency matters submitted by the governor, and bills with a four-fifths vote of the house may be introduced. Thus, for the first 60 days, the agendas for both houses are being set.[138]

After the 60th day, the legislature begins to clear these agendas. As indicated, most bills die in committees and are never assigned to a calendar. Killing a bill in committee happens regularly during the session. The bill is dead if it does not make it out of committee. This leaves only about a third of all bills for further consideration late in the session.

The formal rules of the house and senate are important factors in determining how and what kind of legislation gets passed. It is difficult to pass legislation and

Focus On

The Pink Wave

When Erin Zwiener showed up to take her seat representing Texas House District 45 in the 86th session of the Texas legislature in January 2019, she brought along more than just her laptop. Zwiener was accompanied by Lark, her six-month-old daughter.[139]

Erin Zwiener grew up around Austin, went to Montana and Arizona for her education, spent some time in New Mexico, where she was a three-time *Jeopardy* winner, and moved back to Texas with her husband in 2016. She'd had a political epiphany while in Montana, realizing everyone's voice is meaningful and, with work, can be effective.[140]

Then one day at home in the Texas Hill country, Zwiener was on Facebook and saw a post from her state representative, Jason Isaac, a four-term rep who was first elected in the 2010 Tea Party wave. She replied, asking his position on SB 4, Texas's anti–"Sanctuary City" legislation. A tense exchange followed, ending with Isaac calling her a troll and blocking her. That's all it took. Zwiener was then and there committed to challenging Isaac in the next election.[141]

Zwiener's campaign was more eventful than she could have imagined. She was featured in *Time* magazine's article chronicling the "Pink Wave" of women running for election in 2018.[142] As if that weren't enough for the political neophyte, one day Zwiener, who was pregnant throughout her campaign, was participating in a protest against family separation at the U.S.-Mexico border when she went into labor.[143]

Having been elected to the legislature, Zwiener was faced with balancing the intense workload generated by the legislative session with new motherhood. It is not unusual for a committee meeting to start at 10 A.M. one day and run until 5 A.M. the next day. Such a workload is daunting for anyone, but especially so for the mother of an infant.[144] Part of Zwiener's answer is bringing Lark to work. Not only does Zwiener say she can't afford a full-time nanny, but, she adds, "Every time I look at my daughter I'm reminded of why I'm doing this."[145]

The Pink Wave of which Zwiener was a part stretched across the nation, achieving significant increases in representation for women in state legislatures and the U.S. Congress. And judging by Zwiener's first term, these women are not slowing down after winning their seats. Zwiener managed to pass several bills into law, an accomplishment many freshman legislators don't manage. As a bisexual woman, she was also a founding member of the Texas House LGBTQ caucus.

In its biennial "Best and Worst Legislators" issue, the venerable *Texas Monthly* magazine said, "Zwiener was described by many as the most savvy freshman and potential future leader of the House Democrats."[146]

Critical Thinking Questions

1. If you are dissatisfied with the way the state is being managed, what is the best way to respond? In what other ways besides running for office can an individual make a difference?

2. Texas legislators have formed numerous caucuses among their membership, including bipartisan affiliation, race and ethnicity, and, now, LGBTQ status. Are these kinds of organizations helpful, or do they do more to emphasize our differences rather than our similarities?

---

easy to kill a bill. Although the Texas legislature is not dramatically different from most other legislatures in this respect, in Texas these rules have historically protected the status quo of the state's traditionalistic/individualistic political culture.

Effective legislators must, of course, understand the formal rules and parliamentary procedures followed in the legislature. However, **informal rules** can be just as important to exerting influence and getting bills passed. Legislators should strike an appropriate balance between collegiality and insistence on principle. Legislators should not "showboat" and should be willing to share credit. Legislators should study to ensure that they are well informed on issues. They should, in other words, be reliable colleagues. Members who fail to work effectively with other members will find they have no backers when they are looking for cosponsors for their priorities.

informal rules
Set of norms or values that govern legislative bodies

Legislative Roles

Learning Objective: Describe the Texas legislature's functions and procedures.

Members of the legislature play many roles during legislative sessions. We have already discussed formal leadership roles. Each speaker approaches the job differently. Historically, most speakers have tightly controlled the house and dominated the legislative process. The two most recent speakers, though, have both worked mostly behind the scenes and let members take more visible roles. Joe Straus, who served five terms as speaker, through the 85th legislative session, was a mild-mannered and bipartisan speaker. Straus, however, would occasionally use his power to stop bills he disliked, even if it meant going against his own party.[147]

The speaker for the 87th Legislature, Dade Phelan, was a consensus choice in the house, with only 2 members voting against his election. He vowed to lead by letting members do the work of the house.[148] Conservatives were suspicious of Phelan from the start of his term, questioning the conservative bona fides of anyone who would work to build a coalition with Democrats.[149] By the end of the term and special sessions, the house had passed several conservative policy priorities, including the "heartbeat bill" restricting abortions after 6 weeks gestation, restrictions on transgender athletes, election legislation, permitless handgun carry, and restrictions on social media companies, which are believed to be unfriendly to conservative political perspectives. Still, Phelan came under criticism, as other priorities failed, including legislatively banning vaccine and mask mandates, a ban on taxpayer-funded lobbying, and larger property tax cuts.[150]

Great differences can also exist in lieutenant governors' leadership styles. Some have worked primarily in the background to forge compromises to accomplish their goals. Others have been aggressive and dogmatic.

Dan Patrick, who became lieutenant governor in 2015, has been a controversial figure. One of Texas's leading social conservatives, Patrick has used his position to influence politics not only in the senate but also throughout the state. Patrick has been a relatively successful leader in the regular sessions, but he has caused some internal rifts between moderates and conservatives within the Republican Party, particularly in his dealings with the speaker of the house, with whom he maintains fraught relationships. This was most apparent in Patrick's dealings with Speaker Joe Straus, who blocked many of Patrick's big-ticket social conservative priorities.[151] Similar tensions appeared in 2021 between Patrick and Speaker Phelan.[152]

Leadership in legislative bodies can take many forms. In addition to formal leadership roles, some members develop reputations as experts in particular areas of legislation and are leaders in those areas. For instance, a person who is a recognized expert on taxation can use this reputation to forge coalitions and pass tax legislation.

Representational Roles

delegates
Representational role of member stating that he or she represents the wishes of the voters

Constituencies have expectations about the roles of their legislators. For centuries, members of legislatures have argued about the representational role of a legislator. Whom do legislators represent? Are they **delegates,** sent to reflect or mirror the interests and wishes of voters, or are they **trustees,** entrusted by the voters to make decisions based on their best judgment? The delegate role is perceived as being more democratic—as doing what the people want. The trustee role can be characterized as elitist—as doing what one person thinks is best. The trustee role may be beneficial, as the legislator is elected to study issues closely, and has a professional staff to help, so they may be more knowledgeable of nuances of legislation that are not known to citizens back home.

In reality, members may play both delegate and trustee roles, depending on the issue before them. For example, in 1981 the Texas legislature passed a bill prohibiting commercial fishers from catching redfish in some waters in the Gulf of Mexico. Sport fishers wrote and advanced the bill. Representatives from coastal communities in Texas voted as delegates—from the perspective of commercial fishermen and against the bill. Representatives from the Panhandle, however, were free to vote as trustees. In matters affecting the livelihood of Panhandle ranchers but not coastal fisheries, these representatives might reverse their voting roles.

Each session offers similar examples. In the 87th Legislature, for example, HB 4667 granted a plot of state-owned land to the city of Eagle Pass, to be used for a police substation. Constituents of the senator from District 19, Roland Gutierrez, were the beneficiaries of this act, so he acted as a delegate in this case. In agreeing to give state property to District 19, other senators were taking a broad view and acting as trustees.[153] No legislator wants to be portrayed in their next campaign as frivolously disposing of state property, nor do they want to alienate a colleague or deprive a district of something it needs. Legislators' position on HB 4667, therefore, was impacted by their perspective of their own role as either a delegate or a trustee.

Which role representatives play largely depends on how the issues affect their district. The problem with this is that local interests can take the forefront, leading legislators to neglect long-term statewide or larger public interests.

Partisan Roles

Party has traditionally not been a strong factor in the Texas legislature. Members of both parties are given committee assignments. Texas differs from states with a tradition of strong partisanship, where party leadership roles are important, formal leadership positions are assigned on the basis of party, and party leaders try to ensure that party members support party positions on issues.

In recent years, conservative Republicans and Democrats organized the Texas Conservative Coalition to fight what they view as liberal ideas. Other caucuses represent Hispanics and African Americans. In 1993, the Republicans formed a caucus to promote the election of Pete Laney, a Democrat, as speaker. As a reward, they were assigned several committee chairs. However, partisan factors have played a much larger role in the Texas legislature in recent years.

The 2017 special session saw formation of the Texas Freedom Caucus, a hardline conservative group,[154] and brought attacks on then-Speaker Joe Straus. The same conflict between more conservative and more moderate wings of the Republican Party erupted in the 2021 legislature, when some conservative legislative priorities championed by Governor Abbott and Lieutenant Governor Dan Patrick failed to be enacted into law. Patrick said of Speaker Phelan's management of the conservative legislative agenda, the "clock ran out on the house because it was managed poorly."[155]

trustees
Representational role of a member that states that the member will make decisions based on his or her own judgment about what is best for voters

Understanding Impact As has been described in this section, recent years have seen Texas legislators take more partisan stances, in some cases forming caucuses to advocate for particular partisan issues. Although legislators are expected to represent partisan interests of the constituents who elected them (delegate role), they also have a responsibility to work for the good of the whole state (trustee role). What impact do you think the new partisanship will have on the Texas legislature? Will it be bogged down and unable to compromise? Or will it be able to accomplish political priorities that were stalled because both parties were not on board?

Legislative Professionalism versus Citizen Legislatures

Learning Objective: Explain legislators' qualifications and member demographics.

legislative professionalism

Legislatures with higher pay, longer sessions, and high levels of staff support are considered more professional

citizen legislatures

Legislatures characterized by low pay, short sessions, and fewer staff resources

In this chapter, we have often compared the Texas legislature to the legislatures of other states. For example, we noted that few states have as many constituents per house and senate district as Texas, and that Texas is one of only four states to have biennial sessions. Political scientists have also compared state legislatures in terms of their level of **legislative professionalism.** According to political scientist Peverill Squire, legislative professionalism can be measured using data on "pay, session length, and staff resources."[156] States with higher legislative pay, longer sessions (such as no limits on the length of regular sessions), and more staff support are considered more professional. One could say that states with part-time legislators who get lower pay, shorter or biennial sessions, and fewer staff resources are less professional or, more positively, "**citizen legislatures.**"[157] Compared to all other states, Texas ranks as the nineteenth most professional in the Squire Legislative Professionalism Index.[158] New Hampshire has the least professional legislature (or the strongest citizen legislature), and California has the most professional.

Understanding Impact Texas's "citizen legislature" was designed that way out of distaste for strong central government. Since the Constitution of 1876 was adopted, however, Texas has grown in ways unimaginable to the constitution's drafters. Now it could be argued that lack of legislative professionalism in America's second most populous state gives too much power to lobbyists, to whom minimally staffed legislators turn for information and legislative support. Still, many continue to support this legislative structure, remembering Sam Houston's advice to "govern as little as possible." Do you think Texas should "professionalize" its legislature? How might you update lawmaking in Texas?

Conclusion

Thomas R. Dye comes to three conclusions on state legislatures, all of which could be said to apply to the Texas legislature.[159] First, Dye observes that

State legislatures reflect socioeconomic conditions of their states. These conditions help to explain many of the differences one encounters in state legislative politics: the level of legislative activity, the degree of inter-party competition, the

extent of party cohesion, the professionalism of the legislature . . . [and] the level of interest group activity.[160]

What Dye means is that legislators are mindful of social and economic conditions in the state, as those conditions strongly influence the quality of life felt by legislators' constituents. Policies created by the legislature thus reflect those conditions, because legislators are responding to pressures from their constituents. This certainly applies to Texas.

Second, legislatures function as "arbiters of public policy rather than initiators" of policy change.[161] State legislatures wait for others—state agencies, local governments, interest groups, and citizens—to bring issues to them for resolution. Someone other than members of the legislature write most bills introduced. The rules make it much easier to delay legislation than to pass it. Leadership most often comes from others outside the legislature, often the governor. With a few exceptions this applies to Texas.

Third, legislatures "function to inject into public decision making a parochial influence."[162] By this Dye means that state legislatures tend to represent local legislative interests and not statewide interests. Legislators are recruited, elected, and reelected locally. Local interests will always be predominant in determining how legislators vote on proposed legislation; legislators will act as delegates when local interests are at stake. Sometimes no one seems to represent statewide interests. This conclusion certainly applies to Texas. Statewide interests often get lost in the shuffle to protect and promote local interests.

Summary

LO: Describe the structure, size, and general characteristics of the Texas legislature.

The Texas state legislature is bicameral (meaning it consists of two chambers: a senate and a house of representatives). The Texas Senate has 31 members, and the Texas House of Representatives has 150 members. Both chambers are quite small relative to the state's population. The Texas legislature meets biennially (every two years) for a 140-day regular session, and only the governor can call special sessions. Texas legislators receive relatively low pay compared to legislators in other states.

LO: Explain legislators' qualifications and member demographics.

A Texas House member must be a U.S. citizen, at least 21 years of age, and must have lived in the state for at least 2 years and in the district they will represent for a minimum of 12 months. A Texas state senator must be a U.S. citizen, at least 26 years old, and must have been a Texas resident for at least 5 years and a district resident for at least 12 months. The state legislature is less diverse than the general population. Texas legislators tend to be older, male, well-educated professionals.

LO: Explain how legislators are elected, including the single-member district method of election.

Texas uses the single-member district method of election, in which each legislative district elects one member to the legislative body. Voters in each of Texas's 31 state senatorial districts and 150 state house districts elect one senator and one congressperson. This system promotes geographic representation because all areas of the state choose representatives to the state legislature.

LO: Describe reapportionment and redistricting issues in Texas.

Reapportionment is the process of allocating representatives to states and is completed by the U.S. Census Bureau, whereas redistricting is the drawing of district boundary lines, and is the responsibility of the state legislature. U.S. House seats are reapportioned following each federal census (every 10 years), and district maps generally must be redrawn as a result. Redistricting especially is a highly political matter, as each interest group within the state tries to gain as much as possible from the process. In Texas, this process has generated a great deal of controversy, including multiple lawsuits that the U.S. Supreme Court ultimately decided.

LO: Discuss various leadership positions in the Texas legislature.

In the Texas legislature, power is concentrated in the hands of the speaker of the house and the lieutenant governor. The speaker of the house is presiding officer in the Texas House of Representatives and generally controls the passage of legislation. The lieutenant governor is presiding officer in the Texas Senate. In addition, committee chairs, themselves appointed by the speaker and the lieutenant governor, can have a great deal of influence over the legislature's agenda and actions.

LO: Describe the Texas legislature's functions and procedures.

The function of the Texas legislature is to create, alter, and enact laws for the state. Some of the legislature's most important responsibilities are passing the state budget and overseeing state agencies. The rules of the Texas legislature have traditionally had a conserving force on legislation, meaning that they tend to maintain the status quo and prevent bills from becoming law without careful review.

Key Terms

Baker v. Carr
bicameral
biennial sessions
citizen legislatures
conference committees
delegates
extra legislative powers
extraordinary session
gerrymandering
Hunt v. Cromartie
informal rules

legislative professionalism
Legislative Redistricting Board
  (LRB)
lieutenant governor
multimember districts
noncompetitive districts
political action committee (PAC)
political gerrymandering
racial gerrymandering
reapportionment
redistricting

Reynolds v. Sims
sine die
single-member districts
speaker of the house
special sessions
standing committees
term limits
trustees
turnover

Notes

[1] James Barragan, "Bill tripling Texas' border security budget and allocating $750 million to wall construction becomes law," *Texas Tribune*, September 17, 2021, https://www.texastribune.org/2021/09/17/texas-border-wall-security-budget-abbott/.

[2] Texas Constitution, 1876, art. III, sec. 2.

[3] Council of State Governments, *The Book of the States, 2012* (Lexington, KY: Council of State Governments, 2012), 118; National Conference of State Legislatures, "Number of Legislators and Length of Term in Years," http://www.ncsl.org/research/about-state-legislatures/number-of-legislators-and-length-of-terms.aspx.

[4] https://www.census.gov/quickfacts/TX, calculations by author

[5] https://www.thegreenpapers.com/Census10/FedRep.phtml?sort=Sena#table

[6] On this and other points related to the size of the legislature, see Anti-Federalist writings such as Brutus's "III" from the *New York Journal*, November 15, 1787, or Cato's "Letter V" from the *New York Journal*, November 22, 1787. These particular quotations come from Brutus, the pseudonym often attributed to Robert Yates.

[7] At the end of World War II, only 4 states held annual sessions. By 1966, 20 states met annually, and that number more than doubled by 1974. More recently, Oregon convened its first annual session in 2011. See Rich Jones, "State Legislatures," *The Book of the States, 1944–95*, 99; National Conference of State Legislatures, "Annual versus Biennial Legislative Sessions," http://www.ncsl.org/research/about-state-legislatures/annual-versus-biennial-legislative-sessions.aspx.

[8] National Conference of State Legislatures, "Legislative Session Length," http://www.ncsl.org/research/about-state-legislatures/legislative-session-length.aspx.

[9] National Conference of State Legislatures, "Special Sessions," May 6, 2009, http://www.ncsl.org/research/about-state-legislatures/special-sessions472.aspx.

[10] Farah Eltohamy, "What it means to break quorum and what you need to know about the Texas House Democrats' dramatic departure," *Texas Tribune*, July 14, 2021, https://www.texastribune.org/2021/07/14/texas-democrats-walkout-quorum/

[11] Patrick Svitek and Cassandra Pollock, "How the quorum break got broken: Texas Democrats splintered during second session break," *Texas Tribune,* September 10, 2021, https://www.texastribune.org/2021/09/10/texas-house-democrats-quorum-break/

[12] Alexa Ura, "The hard-fought Texas voting bill is poised to become law. Here's what it does," *Texas Tribune*, August 30, 2021, https://www.texastribune.org/2021/08/30/texas-voting-restrictions-bill/.

[13] James Barragan and Cassandra Pollock, "Five takeaways from Texas' third special legislative session," *Texas Tribune*, October 19, 2021, https://www.texastribune.org/2021/10/19/texas-special-session-legislature/

[14] National Conference of State Legislatures, "Annual versus Biennial Legislative Sessions."

[15] National Conference of State Legislatures, "Full- and Part-Time Legislatures," June 14, 2017, https://www.ncsl.org/research/about-state-legislatures/full-and-part-time-legislatures.aspx.

[16] https://www.ncsl.org/research/about-state-legislatures/legislative-sessions-a-primer.aspx#:~:text=Today%2C%2046%20legislatures%20meet%20in,regular%20session%20every%20other%20year

[17] Kate Galbraith, "Biennial Blues?," *Texas Tribune*, December 31, 2010, https://www.texastribune.org/2010/12/31/defying-national-trend-texas-clings-biennial-legis/.

[18] Legislative Reference Library of Texas, "87th Legislature statistics," https://lrl.texas.gov/whatsNew/client/index.cfm/2021/6/21/Bill-Statistics-After-SigningVeto-Period-87th-Legislature

[19] Legislative Reference Library of Texas, "87th Legislature statistics," https://lrl.texas.gov/whatsNew/client/index.cfm/Bill-statistics

[20] Cassandra Pollock, "Texas lawmakers send $248 billion two-year budget to Gov. Greg Abbott," *Texas Tribune*, May 27, 2021, https://www.texastribune.org/2021/05/27/texas-legislature-budget-approved/

[21] Texas Secretary of State, "Qualifications for Office," http://www.sos.state.tx.us/elections/candidates/guide/qualifications.shtml.

[22] Texas Constitution, art. VI, sec. 1 (see http://www.statutes.legis.state.tx.us/Docs/CN/pdf/CN.6.pdf).

[23] Karl Kurtz, "Who We Elect: The Demographics of State Legislatures," *State Legislatures* magazine, December 2015, http://www.ncsl.org/research/about-state-legislatures/who-we-elect.aspx.

[24] U.S. Census Bureau "Quick Facts - Texas," July 1, 2021, https://www.census.gov/quickfacts/TX

[25] Alexa Ura and Carla Astudillo, "In 2021, white men are still overrepresented in the Texas Legislature," *The Texas Tribune*, January 11, 2021, https://apps.texastribune.org/features/2020/2021-texas-legislature-representation/

[26] Laura Chapin, "Colorado Led the Way on Women's Suffrage," *U.S. News & World Report*, August 21, 2010, http://www.usnews.com/opinion/blogs/laura-chapin/2010/08/21/colorado-led-the-way-on-womens-suffrage.

[27] Janice C. May, "Texas Legislature," *Handbook of Texas Online*, https://tshaonline.org/handbook/online/articles/mkt02 (accessed April 16, 2016).

[28] Legislative Reference Library of Texas, "Women Members of the Texas Legislature, 1923–Present," http://www.lrl.state.tx.us/legeLeaders/members/Women.cfm.

[29] Britney Jeffrey, "Rangel, Irma Lerma," *Handbook of Texas Online*, https://tshaonline.org/handbook/online/articles/fra85.

[30] Sonia R. Garcia et al., *Politicas: Latina Public Officials in Texas* (Austin: University of Texas Press, 2008), 48.

[31] Sonia R. Garcia et al., *Politicas: Latina Public Officials in Texas* (Austin: University of Texas Press, 2008), 44.

[32] Texas Woman's University, Texas Women's Hall of Fame, "Rangel, Irma L." http://www.twu.edu/twhf/tw-rangel.asp.

[33] University of Texas at Austin, Irma Rangel Public Policy Institute, "Irma Rangel," http://www.utexas.edu/cola/ppi/irma-rangel.php.

[34] Legislative Reference Library, "Membership Statistics for the 87th Legislature," https://lrl.texas.gov/legeLeaders/members/memberStatistics.cfm

[35] https://www.ncsl.org/legislators-staff/legislators/womens-legislative-network/women-in-state-legislatures-for-2021.aspx

[36] Karl Kurtz, "Who We Elect: The Demographics of State Legislatures," *State Legislatures* magazine, December 2015, http://www.ncsl.org/research/about-state-legislatures/who-we-elect.aspx.

[37] Karl Kurtz, "Who We Elect: The Demographics of State Legislatures," *State Legislatures* magazine, December 2015, http://www.ncsl.org/research/about-state-legislatures/who-we-elect.aspx; Alexa Ura and Darla Cameron, "In Increasingly Diverse Texas, Legislature Remains Mostly White and Male," *Texas Tribune*, January 10, 2019. https://apps.texastribune.org/features/2019/texas-lawmakers-legislature-demographics/.

[38] National Conference of State Legislatures, "Dual Employment: Regulating Public Jobs for Legislators," October 1, 2015, http://www.ncsl.org/research/ethics/50-state-table-dual-employment.aspx; Texas Legislature, *A joint resolution proposing a constitutional amendment to allow current and retired public school teachers and retired public school administrators to receive compensation for serving on the governing bodies of school districts, cities, towns, or other local governmental districts, including water districts.* H.J.R. 85, 77th Reg. Sess. (May 27, 2001), *The Legislature of the State of Texas*, http://www.lrl.state.tx.us/scanned/session-Laws/77-0/HJR_85.pdf.

[39] Texas Ethics Commission, "Commission Rules," Chapter 50, https://www.ethics.state.tx.us/rules/commission/ch50.php.

[40] Legislative Reference Library of Texas, "Answers to Frequently Asked Questions about the Texas Legislature," http://www.lrl.state.tx.us/genInfo/FAQ.cfm#legPay.

[41] Texas State Historical Association, "Texas Legislature," http://www.tshaonline.org/handbook/online/articles/mkt02.

[42] National Conference of State Legislatures, "2019 Legislator Compensation," https://www.ncsl.org/research/about-state-legislatures/2019-legislator-compensation.aspx.

[43] Texas Ethics Commission, "Use of Per Diem," March 5, 2015, https://www.ethics.state.tx.us/guides/Gperdiem.htm (accessed June 8, 2018).

[44] Allie Morris, "Bibles, Boots, and Booze: Lawmakers Go Big with Campaign Cash Gifts," *San Antonio Express-News*, December 20, 2017, https://www.expressnews.com/news/local/article/Bibles-boots-and-booze-Lawmakers-go-big-with-12445037.php.

[45] Emily Ranshaw, "For Lobbyists, They're Gifts That Keep On Giving," *Texas Tribune*, February 6, 2013, https://www.texastribune.org/2013/02/06/lobbyists-shower-lawmakers-state-staffers-gifts/ (accessed June 8, 2018).

[46] Robert T. Garrett, "Texas Lawmakers Move to Indirectly Boost Their Own Pensions," *Dallas Morning News*, May 13, 2013,

http://www.dallasnews.com/news/politics/state-politics/
20130513-texas-lawmakers-move-to-indirectly-boost-their-
own-pensions.ece.

[47] Robert T. Garrett, "What Texas Lawmakers May Sacrifice
to Get Judges a Pay Raise," *Dallas Morning News*, May 14,
2019, https://www.dallasnews.com/news/politics/2019/
05/14/what-texas-lawmakers-may-sacrifice-to-get-judges-a-
pay-raise/.

[48] Ross Ramsey, "Legislators with Benefits, Even When They
Stray," *The New York Times*, April 12, 2012, http://www.
nytimes.com/2012/04/13/us/texas-legislators-with-benefits-
even-when-they-stray.html; Employees Retirement System
of Texas, "Retirement Benefits for Elected State Officials,"
January 2016, https://www.ers.state.tx.us/Employees/
Retirement/Types_of_Retirement/; According to the
current formula (state district judge salary—currently
$140,000—multiplied by 0.023), the pension provides
$3,220 for every year in office.

[49] Ross Ramsey, "Legislators with Benefits, Even When
They Stray," *The New York Times*, April 12, 2012,
http://www.nytimes.com/2012/04/13/us/texas-legislators-
with-benefits-even-when-they-stray.html; National
Conference of State Legislatures, "State Legislative
Retirement Benefits," https://www.ncsl.org/Portals/1/
Documents/legismgt/2016_Leg_Comp_Retirement_
Benefits.pdf.

[50] Employee Retirement System of Texas, https://ers.texas.gov/
Contact-ERS/Additional-Resources/Guides-and-handouts/
Retirement/Booklet_2017_ESO_FINAL.pdf.

[51] National Conference of State Legislatures, "Size of State
Legislative Staff," https://www.ncsl.org/Documents/
legismgt/StaffingData1979-2015.pdf.

[52] Texas Constitution, art. III, sec. 26.

[53] Leroy Hardy, Alan Heslop, and Stuart Anderson, *Reapportionment Politics* (Beverly Hills, CA: Sage, 1981), 18.

[54] Gordon E. Baker, *The Reapportionment Revolution: Representation,
Political Power and the Supreme Court* (New York: Random
House, 1966).

[55] Texas Legislative Council, "Overview: Texas House Districts
1846–1982," Texas Redistricting, http://www.tlc.state.tx.us/
redist/history/overview_house.html.

[56] Wilbourn E. Benton, *Texas: Its Government and Politics*, 2nd ed.
(Englewood Cliffs, NJ: Prentice Hall, 1966), 141.

[57] Texas Constitution, art. III, sec. 28.

[58] Texas Constitution, art. III, sec. 26a.

[59] *Baker v. Carr,* 369 U.S. 186 (1962).

[60] *Reynolds v. Sims,* 377 U.S. 533 (1964).

[61] *Evenwel v. Abbott*, 578 U.S. ____ (2016); Opinion accessible
at http://www.supremecourt.gov/opinions/15pdf/14-940_
ed9g.pdf.

[62] Texas Legislative Council, "District Population Analysis
with County Subtotals, Senate Districts: Plans 172,"
http://www.tlc.state.tx.us/redist/districts/senate.html;
Texas Legislative Council, "District Population
Analysis with County Subtotals, House Districts:
Plan H358," http://www.tlc.state.tx.us/redist/districts/
house.html.

[63] *Kilgarlin v. Martin*, 1965.

[64] SCOTUSblog, *Evenwel v. Abbott*, http://www.scotusblog.com/
case-files/cases/evenwel-v-abbott/.

[65] Garrett Epps, "Who Gets to Be Represented in Congress?,"
The Atlantic, December 3, 2015, http://www.theatlantic.
com/politics/archive/2015/12/evenwel-supreme-court-
districting/418437/.

[66] *Evenwel v. Abbott*, 578 U.S. ____ (2016), http://www.
supremecourt.gov/opinions/15pdf/14-940_ed9g.pdf.

[67] *Graves v. Barnes*, 343 F.Supp. 704 (W.D. Tex. 1972); *White v.
Regester*, 412 U.S. 755 (1973).

[68] National Conference of State Legislatures, "African-
American Legislators 2009," http://www.ncsl.org/
research/about-state-legislatures/african-american-
legislators-in-2009.aspx.

[69] National Conference of State Legislatures, "2009 Latino
Legislators," http://www.ncsl.org/research/about-state-
legislatures/latino-legislators-overview.aspx.

[70] Alexa Ura and Jolie McCullough, "The 84th Texas
Legislature, by the Numbers," *Texas Tribune,* January 14,
2015, https:// www.texastribune.org/2015/01/14/
demographics-2015-texaslegislature/ (accessed
May 8, 2018).

[71] Alexa Ura and Carla Astudillo, "In 2021, white men are still
overrepresented in the Texas Legislature," *Texas Tribune*,
January 11, 2021, https://apps.texastribune.org/features/
2020/2021-texas-legislature-representation/.

[72] *Bush v. Vera,* 517 U.S. 952 (1996), http://www.supremecourt.
gov/opinions/boundvolumes/517bv.pdf.

[73] Ibid.

[74] Ibid.

[75] *Hunt v. Cromartie*, 562 U.S. 541 (1999).

[76] Adam Liptak, "Justices Reject 2 Gerrymandered North
Carolina Districts, Citing Racial Bias," *The New York
Times*, May 22, 2017, https://www.nytimes.com/2017/05/22/
us/politics/supreme-court-north-carolina-congressional-
districts.html.

[77] Amy Howe, "In 5-4 vote, justices reinstate Alabama voting
map despite lower court's ruling that it dilutes Black
votes," *SCOTUSblog*, February 7, 2022, https://www.
scotusblog.com/2022/02/in-5-4-vote-justices-reinstate-
alabama-voting-map-despite-lower-courts-ruling-that-it-
dilutes-black-votes/

[78] Christopher Ingraham, "How Maryland Democrats Pulled Off Their Aggressive Gerrymander," *The Washington Post*, March 28, 2018, https://www.washingtonpost.com/news/wonk/wp/2018/03/28/how-maryland-democrats-pulled-off-their-aggressive-gerrymander/?utm_term=.7d34d20abe79; Christopher Ingraham, "America's Most Gerrymandered Congressional Districts," *The Washington Post*, May 15, 2014, https://www.washingtonpost.com/news/wonk/wp/2014/05/15/americas-most-gerrymandered-congressional-districts/?utm_term=.fbebb3356664.

[79] Paul Mackun and Steven Wilson, "Population Distribution and Change: 2000 to 2010," U.S. Census Bureau, 2010 Census Briefs, March 2011, http://www.census.gov/prod/cen2010/briefs/c2010br-01.pdf.

[80] U.S. Department of Justice, "Jurisdictions Previously Covered by Section 5," https://www.justice.gov/crt/jurisdictions-previously-covered-section-5.

[81] *Shelby County v. Holder*, 570 U.S. ___ (2013).

[82] Maggie Astor, "Two Congressional Districts Are Unconstitutional, Court Rules," *The New York Times*, August 15, 2017, https://www.nytimes.com/2017/08/15/us/texas-districts-unconstitutional.html.

[83] Alexa Ura, "Texas Redistricting Fight Returns to the U.S. Supreme Court. Here's What You Need to Know," *Texas Tribune,* April 23, 2018, https://www.texastribune.org/2018/04/23/texas-redistricting-fight-returns-us-supreme-court/; Robert Barnes, "Supreme Court Is Divided over Texas Redistricting Maps," *The Washington Post,* April 24, 2018, https://www.washingtonpost.com/politics/courts_law/supreme-court-is-divided-over-texas-redistricting-maps/2018/04/24/ae769fa4-47dd-11e8-9072-f6d4bc32f223_story.html?noredirect=on&utm_term=.0245eaa7f43a.

[84] *Rucho v. Common Cause,* https://www.supremecourt.gov/opinions/18pdf/18-422_9ol1.pdf; *Lamone v. Benisek,* https://www.oyez.org/cases/2018/18-726.

[85] Emma Platoff, "Four Top Takeaways from the 2018 Texas Midterm Elections," *Texas Tribune*, November 7, 2018, https://www.texastribune.org/2018/11/07/what-happened-texas-midterm-election-results/.

[86] What Redistricting Looks Like in Every State - Texas, Fivethirtyeight.com, https://projects.fivethirtyeight.com/redistricting-2022-maps/texas/

[87] U.S. Department of Justice, "Justice Department Files Lawsuit Against the State of Texas to Challenge Statewide Redistricting Plans," https://www.justice.gov/opa/pr/justice-department-files-lawsuit-against-state-texas-challenge-statewide-redistricting-plans#:~:text=The%20United%20States'%20complaint%20contends,minority%20group%20in%20that%20it, League of United Latin American Citizens, "LULAC Takes Federal Court Action Against Texas Voter Suppression," https://lulac.org/news/pr/LULAC_TAKES_FEDERAL_COURT_ACTION_AGAINST_TEXAS_VOTER_SUPPRESSION/index.html

[88] Ross Ramsey, "Analysis: Texas' population has changed much faster than its political maps," *Texas Tribune*, December 8, 2021, https://www.texastribune.org/2021/12/08/texas-redistricting-demographics-elections/

[89] National Conference of State Legislatures, "Redistricting Commissions: State Legislative Plans," December 10, 2021, https://www.ncsl.org/research/redistricting/2009-redistricting-commissions-table.aspxx.

[90] "Election Overview," FollowTheMoney.org, https://www.followthemoney.org/tools/election-overview?s=TX&y=2020 (accessed March 5, 2022).

[91] Patrick Svitek, "With More Competitive Races Than Usual, Texas Saw Deluge of Outside Spending," *Texas Tribune*, November 6, 2018, https://www.texastribune.org/2018/11/06/texas-elections-outside-spending/.

[92] National Conference of State Legislatures, "Limits on Campaign Contributions during the Legislative Session," http://www.ncsl.org/research/elections-and-campaigns/limits-on-contributions-during-session.aspx.

[93] Texas Secretary of State, "Texas Election Results, 2020 General Election," https://results.texas-election.com/races.

[94] Ibid.

[95] Gary C. Jacobson, *The Politics of Congressional Elections*, 3rd ed. (New York: HarperCollins, 1992).

[96] Kevin A. Hill, "Does the Creation of Majority Black Districts Aid Republicans? An Analysis of the 1992 Congressional Election in Eight Southern States," *Journal of Politics* 57 (May 1995): 348–401.

[97] *The Book of the States 1994-95,* 27.

[98] National Conference of State Legislatures, "The Term-Limited States," November 12, 2020, https://www.ncsl.org/research/about-state-legislatures/chart-of-term-limits-states.aspx.

[99] Legislative Reference Library of Texas, "Senate and House Seniority," https://lrl.texas.gov/legeLeaders/members/86Senority.pdf (accessed January 30, 2020); Texas House of Representatives, "Seniority Order— Member Class," https://capitol.texas.gov/tlodocs/houseReports/seniorityOrder.pdf.

[100] Samuel C. Patterson, "Legislative Politics in the States," in *Politics in the American States*, 6th ed., ed. Virginia Gray and Herbert Jacob (Washington, D.C.: Congressional Quarterly Press, 1996), 179–86.

[101] *The Book of the States 2004.*

[102] Ibid.

[103] Lawrence W. Miller, "Legislative Turnover and Political Careers: A Study of Texas Legislators," 1969–75 (Ph.D. dissertation, Texas Tech University, 1977, 43–45).

[104] *Presiding Officers of the Texas Legislature, 1846–2002* (Austin: Texas Legislative Council, 2002).

[105] Michael Quinn Sullivan, "Shining Light on Texas House Speaker Joe Straus," http://www.breitbart.com/Breitbart-Texas/2014/02/16/Shining-Light-On-House-Speaker-Joe-Straus.

[106] Cassandra Pollock, "'The Right Man at this Point in Texas History': How Dennis Bonnen Led the Texas House," *Texas Tribune*, May 30, 2019, https://www.texastribune.org/2019/05/30/texas-house-speaker-Dennis-Bonnen-first-term/

[107] Cassandra Pollock, "Texas House Speaker Dennis Bonnen Won't Seek Reelection after Recording Scandal," *Texas Tribune*, October 22, 2019, https://www.texastribune.org/2019/10/22/Dennis-Bonnen-to-not-seek-reelection-to-Texas-House/.

[108] Cassandra Pollock, "Texas House elects Dade Phelan speaker as 2021 legislative session gets underway," *Texas Tribune*, January 12, 2021, https://www.texastribune.org/2021/01/12/dade-phelan-elected-house-speaker/

[109] Neelam Bohra, "Gov. Greg Abbott calls for stiffer penalty for illegal voting — weeks after he signed a bill lowering it," *Texas Tribune*, September 30, 2021, https://www.texastribune.org/2021/09/30/texas-greg-abbott-voting/

[110] National Lieutenant Governors Association, "Roster of Lieutenant Governors," http://www.nlga.us/lt-governors/roster/.

[111] National Lieutenant Governors Association, "Responsibilities of the Office of Lieutenant Governor," http://www.nlga.us/lt-governors/.

[112] In Tennessee and West Virginia, the president of the senate simultaneously holds the title of lieutenant governor.

[113] *The Book of the States 1998–99,* 48, table 2.13.

[114] This has not always been the case. J. William Davis, in his book *There Shall Also Be a Lieutenant Governor,* traces the concentration of power in this office to the actions of Allan Shivers and Ben Ramsey during the 1940s and 1950s. Over a period of several years, the office of lieutenant governor gained power in the senate. See J. William Davis, *There Shall Also Be a Lieutenant Governor* (Austin: University of Texas, Institute of Public Affairs, 1967).

[115] National Lieutenant Governors Association, "Methods of Election," http://www.nlga.us/lt-governors/office-of-lieutenant-governor/methods-of-election/.

[116] The Senate of Texas, "Committees of the 87th Legislature," https://www.senate.texas.gov/committees.php; Texas House of Representatives, "House Committees," https://house.texas.gov/committees/ .

[117] Texas Constitution, art. III, sec. 33, https://tlc.texas.gov/docs/legref/TxConst.pdf.

[118] Texas Legislative Council, "87th Legislature Statistics," https://lrl.texas.gov/whatsNew/client/index.cfm/2021/6/21/Bill-Statistics-After-SigningVeto-Period-87th-Legislature.

[119] Texas Legislature Online, Legislation, SB21, https://capitol.texas.gov/BillLookup/History.aspx?LegSess=86R&Bill=SB21 (accessed February 1, 2020).

[120] Legislative Reference Library of Texas, "87th Legislature (2021)–Effective Dates for Bills," https://lrl.texas.gov/sessions/effDates/billsEffective87.cfm

[121] Texas Legislature Online, Legislation, HB 1525, Fiscal Note, https://capitol.texas.gov/tlodocs/87R/fiscalnotes/pdf/HB01525F.pdf#navpanes=0

[122] Texas Legislature Online, https://capitol.texas.gov/BillLookup/history.aspx?LegSess=87R&Bill=SCR41

[123] Texas Legislature, HCR19, Text, https://capitol.texas.gov/BillLookup/Text.aspx?LegSess=86R&Bill=HCR19.

[124] Kalley Huang, Carla Astudillo, and Andrew Zhang, "Texas 2021 constitutional amendment election results," *Texas Tribune*, November 3, 2021, https://texastribune.org/features/2021/texas-election-results-2021-constitutional-amendments/.

[125] Texas Comptroller's Office, "The Texas Budget Process: A Primer," https://comptroller.texas.gov/transparency/budget/primer.php.

[126] Sunset Advisory Commission, "Sunset in Texas 2020–2021," https://www.sunset.texas.gov/public/uploads/u64/Sunset%20in%20Texas%202017-2019.pdf .

[127] Texas Politics Project, University of Texas at Austin, "James E. Ferguson," https://texaspolitics.utexas.edu/archive/html/exec/governors/12.html (accessed June 11, 2018).

[128] Legislative Reference Library, "O.P. Carrillo Impeachment Collection," https://lrl.texas.gov/whatsNew/client/index.cfm/2014/4/23/OP-Carrillo-Impeachment-Collection.

[129] Texas House of Representatives, "How a Bill Becomes a Law," http://www.house.state.tx.us/about-us/bill/; Texas Legislative Council, "Bill to Law," https://tlc.texas.gov/BillToLaw.

[130] Texas Legislative Council, "Guide to Texas Legislative Information (Revised)," March 2015, http://www.tlc.state.tx.us/pubslegref/gtli.pdf.

[131] Aman Batheja, "Without Two-Thirds Rule, Senate Moving Patrick's Priorities," *Texas Tribune*, May 19, 2015, http://www.texastribune.org/2015/05/19/loss-two-thirds-rule-senate/.

[132] Aman Batheja, "Senate's Procedural Change Has an Impact, but Not a Dramatic One," *Texas Tribune*, May 19, 2015,

https://www.texastribune.org/2015/05/19/loss-two-thirds-rule-senate/.

133 Allyson Waller, "Texas bill restricting transgender student athletes' sports participation heads to Gov. Greg Abbott," *The Texas Tribune*, October 17, 2021, https://www.texastribune.org/2021/10/15/texas-transgender-student-athletes/; *Senate Journal*, October 15, 2021, p. 170, http://www.journals.senate.state.tx.us/sjrnl/873/pdf/87S310-15-F.PDF#page=2

134 Chuck Lindell, "Texas Democrat's filibuster of GOP voting bill ends after 15 hours; SB 1 passes," *Austin American-Statesman*, August 12, 2021, https://www.statesman.com/story/news/2021/08/12/texas-sb-1-voting-bill-passes-despite-filibuster-carol-alvarado/8105541002/

135 Erin Douglas and Eleanor Klibanoff, "Abortions in Texas have stopped after Attorney General Ken Paxton said pre-Roe bans could be in effect, clinics say," *The Texas Tribune*, June 24, 2022, https://www.texastribune.org/2022/06/24/texas-clinics-abortions-whole-womans-health/

136 "Human Life Protection Act of 2021," https://capitol.texas.gov/BillLookup/History.aspx?LegSess=87R&Bill=HB1280

137 Nadine El-Bawab, "Texas abortion 'trigger' law allowing criminal, civil penalties set to go into effect in August," *ABC News*, July 27, 2022, https://abcnews.go.com/US/texas-abortion-trigger-law-allowing-criminal-civil-penalties/story?id=87485720

138 Texas Legislative Council, "Dates of Interest, 86th Legislature," https://tlc.texas.gov/docs/legref/Dates-of-Interest.pdf. (accessed February 2, 2020).

139 "Interview: Texas House District 45 Incumbent Erin Zwiener," *Austin American-Statesman*, February 7, 2020, https://www.statesman.com/news/20200207/interview-texas-house-district-45-incumbent-erin-zwiener.

140 Charlotte Alter, "A Year Ago, They Marched. Now a Record Number of Women Are Running for Office," *Time Magazine*, January 18, 2018, https://time.com/5107499/record-number-of-women-are-running-for-office/ (accessed February 27, 2020).

141 Christy Millweard, "State Representative Brings 6-Month-Old Daughter to Work at the Capitol," KVUE.com, January 17, 2019, https://www.kvue.com/article/news/politics/texas-legislature/state-representative-brings-6-month-old-daughter-to-work-at-the-capitol/269-a15bfe29-b1c5-49c8-bab9-7ba19f9446d9 (accessed February 26, 2020).

142 Charlotte Alter, "A Year Ago, They Marched. Now a Record Number of Women Are Running for Office," *Time*, January 18, 2018, https://time.com/5107499/record-number-of-women-are-running-for-office/ (accessed February 27, 2020).

143 Kelly McLaughlin, "A First-Time Candidate in Texas Who Campaigned at the Hospital after Going into Labor during a Border-Separation Protest Won a Seat in the State's House of Representatives," *Business Insider*, November 7, 2018, https://www.businessinsider.com/midterms-texas-erin-zwiener-wins-after-going-into-labor-during-campaign-2018-11 (accessed February 27, 2020).

144 Alana Rocha, Justin Dehn, Richard Loria, Todd Wiseman, and Woojae Julia Song, "What the 'Wave of Women' Elected in 2018 Looks Like in the 2019 Texas Legislature," *Under the Dome*, March 18, 2019, https://www.texastribune.org/2019/03/18/under-the-dome-episode-7-texas-women-legislature/ (accessed March 24, 2020).

145 Christy Millweard, "State Representative Brings 6-Month-Old Daughter to Work at the Capitol," KVUE.com, January 17, 2019, https://www.kvue.com/article/news/politics/texas-legislature/state-representative-brings-6-month-old-daughter-to-work-at-the-capitol/269-a15bfe29-b1c5-49c8-bab9-7ba19f9446d9 (accessed February 26, 2020).

146 "2019: The Best and Worst Legislators," *Texas Monthly*, https://www.texasmonthly.com/politics/2019-the-best-and-worst-texas-legislators/ (accessed March 23, 2020).

147 Manny Fernandez and David Montgomery, "Bathroom Bill Tests Clout of Rare Moderate in Increasingly Conservative Texas," *The New York Times*, July 18, 2017, https://www.nytimes.com/2017/07/18/us/bathroom-bill-texas-abbott-straus.html.

148 Cassandra Pollock, "Texas House elects Dade Phelan speaker as 2021 legislative session gets underway," *Texas Tribune*, January 12, 2021, https://www.texastribune.org/2021/01/12/dade-phelan-elected-house-speaker/.

149 Cassandra Pollock, "Texas GOP Chair says party will not "support or accept" Republican Rep. Dade Phelan as next House speaker," *Texas Tribune*, November 9, 2020, https://www.texastribune.org/2020/11/09/texas-gop-allen-west-dade-phelan-house-speaker/

150 James Barragan and Cassandra Pollock, "Five takeaways from Texas' third special legislative session," *Texas Tribune*, October 19, 2021, https://www.texastribune.org/2021/10/19/texas-special-session-legislature/

151 Patrick Svitek, "Tensions Mount between Dan Patrick and the Texas House," *Texas Tribune*, March 3, 2017, https://www.texastribune.org/2017/03/03/house-senate-tensions/.

152 Patrick Svitek and Cassandra Pollock, "Leadership tensions, potential special session loom as Texas legislative session hits uncertain end," *Texas Tribune*, May 27, 2021, https://www.texastribune.org/2021/05/27/texas-legislature-special-session/.

153 Texas Legislature Online, HB 4667, https://capitol.texas.gov/BillLookup/Text.aspx?LegSess=87R&Bill=HB4667

[154] Cassandra Pollock, "Texas State Rep. Jonathan Stickland Resigns from Hardline Conservative House Freedom Caucus," *Texas Tribune*, May 6, 2019, https://www.texastribune.org/2019/05/06/jonathan-stickland-resigns-texas-house-freedom-caucus/

[155] Cassandra Pollock and Shawn Mulcahy, "With feelings raw over voting bill's demise, Texas Legislature wraps up—for now," *Texas Tribune*, May 31, 2021, https://www.texastribune.org/2021/05/31/texas-adjourns-special-session/.

[156] Peverill Squire, "Measuring State Legislative Professionalism: The Squire Index Revisited," *State Politics & Policy Quarterly* 7, no. 2 (Summer 2007): 211–27.

[157] William Ruger and Jason Sorens, "The Citizen Legislature," Goldwater Institute Policy Brief, June 22, 2011.

[158] Peverill Squire, "A Squire Index Update," *State Politics & Policy Quarterly* 17, no. 4 (2017): 361–71.

[159] Thomas R. Dye, *Politics in States and Communities,* 7th ed. (Englewood Cliffs, NJ: Prentice Hall, 1991), 192–93.

[160] Thomas R. Dye, *Politics in States and Communities,* 7th ed. (Englewood Cliffs, NJ: Prentice Hall, 1991), 192.

[161] Thomas R. Dye, *Politics in States and Communities,* 7th ed. (Englewood Cliffs, NJ: Prentice Hall, 1991), 193.

[162] Ibid.

CHAPTER 4

The Executive Department and the Office of the Governor of Texas

- Explain the structure and function of the executive branch of Texas government.

T he governor is the most salient political actor in state government. Whether the true power center of the state is embodied in the occupant of the office or elsewhere, the office is the focal point of state government and politics. The expectation is that governors will be leaders in their states.

Chapter Learning Objectives

- Summarize the formal and informal qualifications for the governor of Texas.
- Explain the provisions for succession of a governor.
- Explain the provisions for removal of a governor.
- Explain the governor's formal powers.
- Explain the governor's informal powers.

Qualifications

Learning Objective: Summarize the formal and informal qualifications for the governor of Texas.

Formal Qualifications

In most states the formal qualifications to be governor are minimal. All but three states (Kansas, Massachusetts, and Vermont) set a minimum age requirement, and exactly half of all states require a candidate to be a resident of the state preceding the election. The time period each state specifies varies widely, from no set time to seven years. Most states also require governors to be U.S. citizens and qualified voters.[1]

In Texas the formal qualifications are simple: One must be at least 30 years of age, a citizen of the United States, and a resident of the state for 5 years preceding election (Article IV, Section 1). There is no requirement to be a registered voter. In fact, in the 1930s, W. Lee O'Daniel ran for governor, stressing that he was not a "professional politician." To prove his point, he made an issue of not being a registered voter.

Informal Qualifications

Experience

informal qualifications
Additional qualifications beyond the formal qualifications required for men and women to be elected governor; holding statewide elected office is an example

Informal qualifications are more important. Nationwide, most governors have held elected office before becoming governor. An examination of the 933 people who have served as governor in the United States between 1900 and 1997 reveals that the most common career path to that office is to begin in the state legislature, move to statewide office, and then move to the governor's office. Others who have been elected governor have served as a U.S. senator or representative, and a few have served in local elected offices (such as mayor). Some governors gain experience as appointed administrators or party officials. Indeed, fast-forwarding to currently held governorships (2022), this trend holds: 14 have been a lieutenant governor, 12 were in their state senate, 10 were in their state house of representatives, 11 have been in the U.S. House of Representatives, and 14 held other elected executive branch offices.[2] It remains clear that having held elected office is an important informal qualification for becoming governor.

The national statistics generally apply to most Texas governors. Table 4.1 lists the men and women who have served since 1949 and their prior office

TABLE 4.1

Previous Public Office Experience of Texas Governors, 1949–2026

Governor	Term of Office	Previous Offices
Allan Shivers	1949–1957	State senator, lieutenant governor
Price Daniel	1957–1963	U.S. senator
John Connally	1963–1969	U.S. secretary of the navy*
Preston Smith	1969–1973	State representative and senator, lieutenant governor
Dolph Briscoe	1973–1979	State representative
Bill Clements	1979–1983 1987–1991	U.S. deputy secretary of defense*
Mark White	1983–1987	State attorney general
Ann Richards	1991–1994	County office, state treasurer
George W. Bush	1995–2001	None
Rick Perry	2001–2014	State representative, agricultural commissioner, and lieutenant governor
Greg Abbott	2015–2026	Attorney general, Texas Supreme Court jurist

* Appointed office. No electoral experience before becoming governor.

Sources: James Anderson, Richard W. Murray, and Edward L. Farley, *Texas Politics: An Introduction,* 6th ed. (New York: HarperCollins, 1992), 166–88; Legislative Reference Library, "Governors of Texas, 1846–Present," http://www.lrl.state.tx.us/legeLeaders/governors/govBrowse.cfm.

Focus On

A Hispanic Governor for Texas?

In December 2021, journalist and public school teacher Joy Diaz threw her name into the Democratic race for governor. Diaz ran on an "outside platform"—as a political outsider with no previous experience in government. She argued that Texas needed to government needed to rely on experts, rather than state politicians, to make policy decisions. The state should reach out to teachers to run education programs and to local governments along the border to handle immigration issues.

Dias lost to better known and well-funded candidate Beta O'Rourke in the Texas Democratic primary election, but her dream of becoming the first Hispanic governor is not far fetched. Other Hispanic gubernatorial candidates have had notable success.

Sandra Dahdah/ZUMA Press, Inc./Alamy Stock Photo

During the 2002 governor's race, the state came very close. Tony Sanchez, a business executive and politician from Laredo, was the first Hispanic to run for governor in the statewide election. Before the election, he served as board regent for the University of Texas at Austin and also worked, albeit unsuccessfully, to get a Hispanic to run for president of the UT Health Science Center in San Antonio. Moving into election season, Sanchez won the Democratic primary with 60 percent of the vote and faced off against Rick Perry, who had been unopposed in the Republican primary.[3]

During the election, many Democrats hoped that the state's Hispanic population would turn out in larger numbers and become a more distinct bloc in favor of the Democratic Party.[4] Unfortunately for Democrats and Sanchez, there was less Hispanic mobilization for their party than desired. Sanchez lost the election, winning only 40 percent of the vote.[5] In addition, although Hispanic turnout improved somewhat from the 2000 election, there was not enough movement to indicate a surge.[6] Hispanic turnout has been historically low as a percentage of Hispanic population and remains so.[7] (See Chapter 9 for more information on Hispanic voter turnout.)

Still, both the Democratic and Republican Parties have been making inroads, capturing votes as well as candidates from the grassroots up. Although Hispanic voter turnout remains low, Rafael Anchia (as well as Lupe Valdez who ran for governor in 2018 and Joy Díaz who campaigned in 2022) are part of a rising group of Hispanic politicians who have very real potential to capture the governor's office in the near future. This group also includes current Texas land commissioner George P. Bush and former secretary of housing and urban development Julian Castro.

Critical Thinking Questions
1. What do you think it will take to mobilize and expand the Hispanic electorate?
2. In your opinion, why might the Hispanic vote be important for candidates seeking statewide office?

experience. Only two had not held elected office. Rick Perry followed a rather typical pattern. He served in the state legislature, as agricultural commissioner, and as lieutenant governor prior to becoming governor when George W. Bush resigned to assume the office of president of the United States. Perry was elected governor in his own right in 2002, 2006, and 2010. He did not run for a fourth term. Current governor Greg Abbott (R) served under Perry as attorney general. He previously served on the Texas Supreme Court, as appointed by George W. Bush, and as a state district judge in Harris County.

Race and Ethnicity

Besides electoral experience, there are many other informal qualifications. Nationwide, most people who have served as governor have been white, wealthy, well-educated, Protestant males. Only three African Americans—Douglas Wilder of Virginia, David Paterson of New York, and Deval Patrick of Massachusetts—have been elected as governor. None currently serve. Several Hispanics have served as state governors, including Tony Anaya, Jerry Abodaca, Bill Richardson, Susan Martinez, and Michelle Lujan Grisham (current) in New Mexico; Bob Martinez in Florida; Paul Castro in Arizona; and Brian Sandoval in Nevada. In addition, as of 2022, one Asian American (David Ige in Hawaii) and one member of the Cherokee Nation (Kevin Stitt in Oklahoma) currently serve as governor.[8]

Women

More women have served as governors in recent years. In 1924, Wyoming elected the first woman governor, Nellie T. Ross, who served one term. She succeeded her husband, who died in office. Also in 1924, Texans elected Miriam A. Ferguson governor. "Ma" Ferguson was a "stand-in" for her husband, Jim Ferguson, who had been impeached, removed from office, and barred from seeking reelection. Miriam Ferguson was reelected in 1932. Similarly, in 1968 Lurleen Wallace was elected governor of Alabama as a stand-in governor for her husband, George Wallace, who could not be reelected because of term limits. Although Ferguson and Wallace were stand-in governors for husbands ineligible for reelection, several women have been elected in their own right. Aside from Ferguson, Texas has had one other female governor, Ann Richards. She was elected in 1990 and served from 1991 to 1995.

As of January 2022, 28 states have elected a total of 40 women as governors (see Map 4.1). Arizona is the first state where three women have held the office in succession, though currently it is held by a man. The number of women serving as governor will undoubtedly increase. As of this writing, 9 women are serving as governors, 19 women are serving as lieutenant governors, and 67 women are serving in other statewide elected executive offices. For women as well as men, service in statewide office is a good stepping-stone to the governor's office.[9]

CORE OBJECTIVE

Communicating Effectively . . .

Analyze Map 4.1. What inferences can you draw from the data? Think about how the data relate to Texas, its neighbors, and other regions of the country.

Wealth

Historically, the men who have served as governor of Texas have generally had one thing in common—wealth. A few, such as Dolph Briscoe and Bill Clements, were very wealthy. If not wealthy, most have been successful in law, business, or politics before becoming governor. Ann Richards was something of an exception to these informal qualifications. She was neither wealthy nor from a wealthy

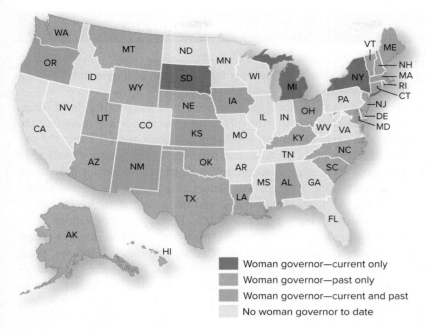

MAP 4.1   Women Governors

Source: Center for American Women and Politics, "Women in Statewide Elective Executive Office 2022," 2022, https://cawp.rutgers.edu/facts/levels-office/statewide-elective-executive/women-statewide-elective-executive-office-2022.

family, and she had no business or law experience. Governor Bush is an example of past governors in terms of background, with a famous family name and family wealth. Governor Perry, while claiming the status of a sharecropper's son, came from a family with a moderate middle-class background.

> **Understanding Impact** The informal qualifications to serve as governor identified in this section tend to disadvantage individuals without prior political experience, nonwhite individuals, women, and the nonwealthy. Are you concerned that the majority of Texas governors have been white, wealthy males? What are your thoughts on improving the likelihood that women or those with nonwhite racial or ethnic background be elected as governor?

Salary

Nationwide, governors receive much higher pay than state legislators. The Council of State Governments identifies the salaries of all state governors. Maine is the lowest at $70,000, while California is the highest at $209,747.[10] The Texas governor's salary of $153,750 per year has been consistently above the average, which is roughly $140,000.[11] Texas also provides the governor with a home in Austin, an automobile with a driver, an airplane, and reimbursement for travel expenses (Article IV, Section 5). Texas governors also receive a budget for entertaining and for maintaining the governor's mansion. Compared with members of the state legislature, the governor in Texas is extremely well paid. Given the demands and responsibilities of the job, however, the governor is not overpaid compared with executives of large corporations who earn much more.

Succession to Office and Acting Governor

Learning Objective: Explain the provisions for succession of a governor.

Most states provide for a successor if the governor dies or leaves office. In 45 states, the lieutenant governor advances to the office if it is vacant for any reason. In the 5 states without lieutenant governors, another officeholder, usually either the secretary of state or leader of the state senate, succeeds to the governor's office. In 17 states, including Texas, the lieutenant governor and the governor are elected separately. In 26 states, the governor and lieutenant governor are elected jointly. In 8 of those states, the lieutenant governor and the governor are jointly elected on a party ticket based on the winning candidates in the primary elections.[12]

In Texas, the lieutenant governor becomes governor if the office is vacated. Following the lieutenant governor, the order of succession is as follows: president pro tempore of the Texas Senate, the speaker of the house, and the attorney general. In the unlikely event that the attorney general is no longer able to discharge the duties of governor, the Texas Constitution stipulates that succession follows the chief justices of the Court of Criminal Appeals in ascending order (Article IV, Section 16).

acting governor

When a governor leaves a state, the position is held by the lieutenant governor, who performs the functions of the office

When governors leave their states, lieutenant governors become **acting governors.** Sometimes problems arise with this arrangement. For instance, in 1995, Arkansas governor Jim Guy Tucker had problems with Senate President Pro Tempore Jerry Jewell, who was acting as governor in the absence of the lieutenant governor. Jewell "granted two pardons and executive clemency to two prison inmates."[14] Also, the Arkansas lieutenant governor, a Republican named Mike Huckabee, "signed a proclamation for a Christian Heritage Week after Tucker declined to do so earlier."[15]

In Texas, former governor Rick Perry may hold the record as serving the most time as acting governor when Governor George W. Bush was campaigning for president outside the state. Lieutenant Governor David Dewherst also served as acting governor for a great deal of time while Governor Perry was out of state running for the Republican presidential nomination in 2012. When serving as acting governor, the lieutenant governor in Texas receives the same pay as the governor.

Lieutenant Governor of Texas Dan Patrick In the 2014 election, Dan Patrick beat out incumbent David Dewhurst in the Republican primary and then won by a wide margin in the general vote in November.[13] Patrick won again in November 2018. More recently, he won the general election in November 2022. Although Texas elects its lieutenant governors separately from its governors, it rarely has a split party executive.

Pat Sullivan/AP Images

Postgubernatorial Office

For some governors, the office is a stepping-stone to other offices. Some go on to the U.S. Senate, and several have been elected president of the United States. In Texas, former governor W. Lee O'Daniel served as a U.S. senator from 1941 to 1949, and George W. Bush became president in 2001.

Postgubernatorial administrative service in the federal government is also common. Presidents often call upon former governors to head departments. Under

President Donald Trump, former Texas governor Rick Perry became the U.S. secretary of energy (2017–2019), former Georgia governor Sonny Perdue is the U.S. secretary of agriculture (2017–current), and former South Carolina governor Nikki Haley was the U.S. ambassador to the United Nations (2017–2018).[16] More recently in 2021, President Biden nominated Vermont governor Phil Scott to the Council of Governors for a two-year term.

However, for many governors the office is the peak of their political careers, and they retire to private life after leaving office. More recently, a 2009 study of all the states' latest former governors found that 42 percent retired to private life, two-thirds of whom entered into business. Only 20 percent moved on to other forms of public service.[17] This statistic is true for most Texas governors. George W. Bush was the first Texas governor since 1941 to go on to higher elected office. In addition, while many governors have attempted to enter into presidential politics, few have made that leap in recent years.[18]

> **Understanding Impact** In Texas, eight lieutenant governors have succeeded to the office of the governor. Four of these men, W. P. Hobby, Coke Stevenson, R. Allan Shivers, and Rick Perry, later ran for the office and were elected. What factors do you think influence the likelihood that a lieutenant governor who inherits the office will succeed in subsequent gubernatorial elections?

Removal from Office

Learning Objective: Explain the provisions for removal of a governor.

All states except Oregon have a procedure for removing governors by a process generally called impeachment.[19] Technically, the lower house of the legislature adopts articles of impeachment; then a trial on these articles of impeachment is held in the senate. If the senate finds the governor guilty by a two-thirds vote, he or she is removed from office. Together the two steps—the adoption of articles of **impeachment** and **conviction** by the senate—are commonly called impeachment (Article XV). Sixteen U.S. governors have had impeachment trials, and nine have been removed from office.[20] Technically, impeachment is a judicial process, but it is also a very political process. Impeached governors have generally been guilty of some wrongdoing, but they are often removed for political reasons.

Four impeachments illustrate the highly political nature of the process. Governor Jim Ferguson of Texas (1915–1917) is one example. Ferguson was indicted by the Texas House, technically for misuse of state funds, and he was convicted and removed from office by the senate. In reality, he was impeached because of his fight with the University of Texas board of regents. When Ferguson could not force the board to terminate several professors who had been critical of him, or force the resignation of board members, he used his line-item veto authority to veto the entire appropriations bill for the University of Texas.[21] This veto led to his impeachment. Ferguson tried to prevent his impeachment by calling the legislature into special session. Because only the

impeachment

The process by which some elected officials, including governors, may be impeached (accused of an impeachable offense) by the lower house adopting articles of impeachment

conviction

Following adoption of articles of impeachment by the lower legislative house, the senate tries the official under those articles; if convicted, the official is removed from office

James E. Ferguson (D) was the 26th governor of Texas for three years until his impeachment in 1917. While the judgment technically prevented him from further public office, he would go on to try for both the governorship and the presidency, the former with his wife as the official candidate. They won the governorship in 1924, but they did not win reelection.

Library of Congress Prints & Photographs Division [LC-DIG-ggbain-16894]

recall
The removal of the governor or an elected official by a petition signed by the required number of registered voters and by an election in which a majority votes to remove the person from office

governor may decide the agenda of a special session, Governor Ferguson told the legislature it could consider any item it wanted, except impeachment. This ploy did not work, and he was removed from office. Courts later upheld Ferguson's impeachment.

A few years after the Ferguson affair in Texas, Oklahoma impeached two consecutively elected governors. These two impeachments were as political as the one in Texas. In 1919, during what is called the Red Summer, hundreds of African Americans died in dozens of race riots across the country. Later, in 1921, the most notable race riot occurred in the Greenwood area of Tulsa, Oklahoma. Thirty-five square blocks of this segregated African American community were burned and destroyed, and more than 40 people were killed. The next year, John C. Walton was elected governor as a member of the Farmer-Laborite Party. Walton tried to break up the Ku Klux Klan in the state, and this led to his impeachment. The lieutenant governor, Martin Trapp, served out the remainder of Walton's term but was unable to run for reelection because Oklahoma had a one-term limit at that time. Henry S. Johnson was elected governor in 1926 as a pro-KKK candidate and refused to use his office to quell Klan activity in the state. Johnson used the National Guard to try to prevent the legislature from meeting to consider his impeachment. The legislature was kept out of the state Capitol building and had to meet in a hotel in Oklahoma City. Johnson was convicted and removed from office. He had been indicted on 18 counts and found not guilty on all charges but one—"general incompetence"—for which he was impeached.[22]

The impeachment of Evan Mecham in Arizona in 1988 was equally political. Mecham made a number of racist remarks and had become a source of embarrassment in the state. Technically, he was impeached for misuse of state funds during his inaugural celebration. All these governors had technically committed some malfeasance of office, but they were impeached for largely political reasons.

Nineteen states also allow **recall** of the governor; Texas does not. Many Texas home-rule cities allow recall of city councils and mayors. Recall involves having petitions signed by a specific number of voters, followed by an election where, if a majority approves, the governor can be recalled or removed from office. Two governors have been recalled. Lynn J. Frazier of North Dakota was recalled in 1921, the same time when governors were being impeached in Texas and Oklahoma. In 2003, Gray Davis of California was recalled. In 2011, the voters of Wisconsin voted against recalling Governor Scott Walker. More than 60 percent of Wisconsin voters disapproved the idea of using a recall to remove a governor.[23] In 1988, Governor Mecham of Arizona was spared a recall election when impeached by the legislature.[24] With so few examples of recall, it is impossible to make any generalizations about the politics of it.

Understanding Impact Advocates of impeachment argue that the process, controlled by the state legislature, strengthens the independence of the governor against overreaction by the state's citizens or well-funded special interests. Conversely, those that support the recall process argue that it allows voters to exercise some control over governors who fail to act in the public's best interest. Which process, impeachment or recall, do you think would best serve the citizens of Texas?

Formal Powers of the Governor

Learning Objective: Explain the governor's formal powers.

Most governors do not have extensive formal powers, but the few they do have can be measured using six variables: election of other statewide executives, tenure of office, appointment powers, budgetary powers, veto powers, and control over party. By examining each of these variables, we can compare the formal powers of governors and, more specifically, assess the powers of the Texas governor (Article IV).

Election of Other Statewide Executives

The ability of the Texas governor to control administrative functions through formal appointive and removal powers is exceptionally weak. The voters elect many important state administrators. Texas is, therefore, a good example of the **plural executive system** structure. Map 4.2 provides a comparison of the number of elected executive officials in all states. Texas voters elect the lieutenant governor (discussed in Chapter 3), attorney general, comptroller of public accounts, state land commissioner, agricultural commissioner, the railroad commission, and the state board of education.

The election of people to head administrative units of government is a concept dating to the 1820s. In the aftermath of Reconstruction in the 1870s, the

plural executive system
System in which executive power is divided among several statewide elected officials

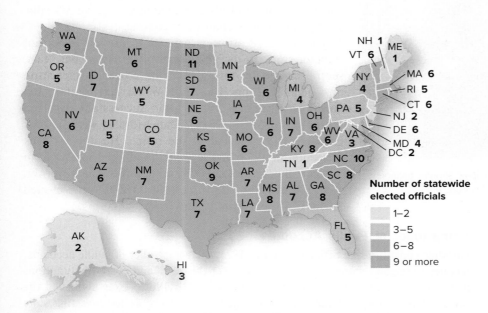

MAP 4.2   Total Number of Major Statewide Elected Officials for Each State, Executive Branch

Source: Council of State Governments, *The Book of the States 2021* (Lexington, KY: Council of State Governments, 2021), Table 4.9.

current Texas Constitution reintroduced the idea of electing almost all office-holders and limiting the governor's ability to appoint them.

Office of the Attorney General

attorney general

Chief counsel to the governor and state agencies; limited criminal jurisdiction

The 1876 Texas Constitution created this office. The **attorney general** is the legal counsel to the governor, the legislature, and most of the other agencies, boards, and commissions in state government (Article IV, Section 22). The attorney general's office, with some 4,000 state employees, is responsible for representing the state in litigation, enforcing state and federal child support laws, providing legal counsel to state officials, and enforcing state laws. Criminal functions of the office are primarily limited to those cases appealed to federal courts.[25] The most common examples of these criminal cases are death penalty appeals. Occasionally, the attorney general's office may assist local criminal prosecutors when invited to do so. Although the functions of the attorney general are usually civil and not criminal in nature, this does not prevent most candidates who run for the office from emphasizing their commitment to law enforcement and being tough on criminals.

Most of the resources of this office are devoted to collection of child support payments, collection of delinquent state taxes, administration of the Crime Victims' Compensation program, and investigation of Medicare fraud. Despite this rather mundane list of functions, the office has important political functions. The most important of these is to issue so-called AG (attorney general) opinions on legal questions. Many times, when the legislature is in session, its members will ask the AG for an opinion on a pending piece of legislation. These AG opinions can affect the course of legislation. Often, a negative AG opinion will kill a bill's chances of passing.

The office of attorney general is also an important stepping-stone to the governor's office. In recent years, several candidates for governor have been former attorneys general (John Hill, Mark White, Jim Mattox, and most recently Greg Abbott, who successfully assumed the governorship in 2015). Dan Morales was the first Hispanic to be elected to the office. He did not seek reelection in 1998, and in 2002 he ran and lost a bid to become the Democratic Party nominee for governor. John Cornyn, the AG from 1998 to 2002, was elected to the U.S. Senate in 2002.

Current governor Greg Abbott served as attorney general before being elected to the governor's office.

Bob Levey/Getty Images

Comptroller of Public Accounts

comptroller of public accounts

Chief tax collector and investor of state funds; does not perform financial audits

Another constitutional office created in 1876, the **comptroller of public accounts,** has been assigned many additional duties over the years and currently functions as the chief fiscal and revenue forecasting office. In 1966, Texas abolished the office of treasurer, and the comptroller became responsible for investing state funds (Texas Government Code Title 4, Subtitle A, Chapter 403).

In many states and in the private sector, the term is "controller," rather than "comptroller" as used in Texas. Generally, in government the controller has a pre-audit responsibility for ensuring that funds can be spent for specific functions. An audit is an inspection or examination of financial accounts. A pre-audit is a preliminary step to make sure everything is in order before the official audit takes place. In Texas, the comptroller not only has the pre-audit responsibility but also serves as the chief tax collector (a function normally associated with the office of treasurer), revenue forecaster, and investor of state funds.

The comptroller is responsible for collecting more than 60 taxes and other fees for the state and collects the sales tax for 1,218 cities, 254 counties, and many other special districts.[26] The property tax division also conducts annual audits of property appraisal districts in the state to ensure uniformity in appraisals. This uniformity is important to improve the equity of state aid to local school districts. (See Chapter 7 on local government.)

Former governor Bob Bullock was comptroller for many years. During his tenure, the office expanded the information and management functions and developed a fiscal forecasting model essential to projecting revenues in a two-year budget cycle. John Sharp, who succeeded Bullock as comptroller, continued and expanded the information management programs of the office. Also under Sharp, the office developed the Texas Performance Review teams to evaluate the effectiveness of government operations and ensure the most efficient use of state funds. These reviews were estimated to have saved the state more than $1.3 billion in the 1998–1999 biennium fiscal years. Similar management information and efficiency audits are available to assist local governments. Most of these programs were kept in place by Sharp's successor, Carole Keeton Strayhorn (1999–2007), as well as Susan Combs (2007–2015) and Glenn Hegar (2015–current).

The office also provides information to the private sector. The State of Texas Econometric Model is used to forecast state economic growth, keep track of business cycles, and generally provide information on the health of the economy of the state. Finally, the office is responsible for investing state funds.

CORE OBJECTIVE

Being Socially Responsible . . .

How does the comptroller promote effective involvement in regional, national, and global communities?

Commissioner of the General Land Office

Texas is one of only five states to have an elected **land commissioner (LC)**.[27] In Texas, the office was created under the 1836 constitution to administer state-owned land. When Texas entered the Union in 1845, the agreement between the former republic and the U.S. government was that Texas kept its public debt and its public land. When Texas became a state, most of the land was state owned. Today the state of Texas owns and manages 20.3 million acres, including open beaches and submerged land 10.3 miles into the Gulf of Mexico.

The office of the LC is responsible for leasing state lands and generating funds from oil and gas production. The office is also responsible for overseeing the Veterans' Land Board and Veterans' Land Fund, which loans money to Texas veterans to buy rural land. Finally, the land office is responsible for

land commissioner (LC)
Elected official responsible for administration and oversight of state-owned lands and coastal lands

maintaining the environmental quality of the state's open beaches along the Gulf Coast (Article XIV).

Some land commissioners go on to run for more powerful offices. David Dewhurst, the LC from 1999 to 2003 later served as lieutenant governor from 2003 to 2015.

Commissioner of Agriculture

The Texas Department of Agriculture (TDA) was created by statute in 1907. A commissioner of agriculture, elected in a statewide election, heads the department. The TDA has the dual, and sometimes contradictory, roles of promoting agricultural products and production, and regulating agricultural practices, while also protecting the public health from unsafe agricultural practices (Texas Agricultural Code, Chapter 11). For example, the TDA must both promote cotton production and sales in the state, and regulate the use of pesticides on the crop.

The TDA has six major functions: marketing of Texas agricultural products, development and promotion of agricultural products, pesticide regulation, pest management, product certification and safety inspection, and inspection and certification of measuring devices (including gasoline pumps, electronic scanners, and scales).

Although the agriculture commissioner is not as publicly visible as the other statewide elected officials, it is an important office to a large section of the state's economy—those engaged in agriculture. Texas's economy has become more diversified in recent years, but agriculture is still a significant player. Major agribusinesses and others in agriculture in the state pay close attention to who serves as the agriculture commissioner.

The Texas Railroad Commission

Texas Railroad Commission (RRC)
State agency with regulation over some aspects of transportation and the oil and gas industry of the state

The **Texas Railroad Commission (RRC)** was created in 1891 under the administration of Governor James S. Hogg to regulate the railroad monopolies that had developed in the state. The commission was also given regulatory authority over terminals, wharves, and express companies. The commission consists of three members who are elected in statewide elections for six-year staggered terms, with one member elected every two years. The member up for election, by convention, always serves as chair of the commission (Texas Natural Resource Code, Title 3, Chapter 81).

In the 1920s, when oil and natural gas production developed in the state, the task of regulating the exploration, drilling, and production of oil and natural gas was assigned to the RRC in part because it was the only state regulatory agency at the time. When motor truck transport developed in the state, regulation of the trucking industry was also assigned to the RRC. In part because of federal rules and regulations, the original role of regulating railroads and the later role of regulating trucking have diminished to minor roles, reduced primarily to concern with safety issues. The regulation of the oil and gas industry is the RRC's primary function today.

Many have been critical of the RRC over the years because of close ties between the elected commissioners and the oil and gas industry they regulate. (See Chapter 12 on interest groups.) Large campaign contributions from oil and gas PACs have raised questions about the commission being co-opted by the industry it regulates. Also, like the agriculture commissioner, the RRC has the dual role of promoting oil and gas production in the state, and regulating the safety and environmental aspects of the industry (for example, promoting the development of pipelines to carry petroleum products as well as overseeing the safety of such pipelines). A similar conflict may exist between the RRC's task of regulating and promoting the mining of minerals (especially lignite coal) in the state.

The role of the RRC that most directly affects citizens in the state is that of setting the rates that local natural gas companies charge. The RRC must approve the rates those companies charge residential and commercial customers. The RRC also regulates the safety of natural gas systems.

It has been suggested that the name of this agency be changed to better reflect its function. Proponents of change argue that the present name is confusing to voters and does not reflect everything it does.

The State Board of Education

Unlike the other offices discussed in this section, the governing body for public elementary and secondary education in the state has varied greatly in form and structure over the years. Originally, in 1884, an elected school superintendent governed Texas schools. In 1929 an appointed state board was created. In 1949, the Gilmer-Aikin Act created the Texas Education Agency (TEA) with an appointed superintendent of education. An elected state board was added in the 1960s. In 1984, the elected board was reduced from 21 members who were elected from congressional districts in the state to 15 members appointed by the governor. In 1986, the board was again changed, and members were elected from 15 districts. The current board, called the State Board of Education, nominates a person to the governor to be commissioner of education (Article VII, Section 8).

In recent years, the authority of the state board has been greatly reduced by actions of the state legislature. The political battle over the power of the state board revolved around conservative Christian success in electing members to the board, setting curriculum standards, and selecting textbooks. One of the main issues has been the teaching of evolution in biology classes. Some members of the board want the curriculum to reflect a creationist approach to human existence. Public infighting among members of the board diminished its effectiveness. The legislature has removed several functions, most significantly the selection of textbooks, from the state board, in part because of the infighting and control by this faction.

CORE OBJECTIVE

Taking Personal Responsibility . . .

What can you do to become more actively engaged in the civic discourse about the role of the State Board of Education?

Tenure of Office

tenure of office

The ability of governors to be reelected to office and the term length

Tenure of office is both the legal ability of governors to succeed themselves in office and the term length. Historically, the tenure of governors has been less than that for most other statewide elected state officials, in part because of term limits.[28] Term limits for governors have been a fixture since the beginning of the U.S. Republic. In the original 13 states, 10 of the governors had one-year terms. States first moved to two-year terms, then four-year terms. In the 1960s, states borrowed from the Twenty-Second amendment of the U.S. Constitution the idea of limiting the chief executive (governors, in the case of states) to two four-year terms.[29] Southern states were the last to move to longer terms. Many southern states once prohibited the governor from serving consecutive terms in office. Today, only Virginia retains this provision. Map 4.3 provides a comparison of gubernatorial term limits.

Tenure is an important determinant of power. If governors can be continually reelected, they retain the potential to influence government until they decide to leave office. When term limits prevent governors from being reelected, they suffer as "lame ducks" toward the end of their terms. Long tenure also enables governors to carry out their programs. Short terms (two years) force governors to continually seek reelection and make political compromises. However, the upside is that they have to remain connected to the electorate. Only two states retain the two-year term—Vermont and New Hampshire.

Longer tenure is also an important factor in the governor's role as intergovernmental coordinator. Building up associations with officials in other states and in Washington is important and takes time. Short tenure makes it difficult for governors to gain leadership roles in this area and has the effect of shortchanging the state that imposes them.[30]

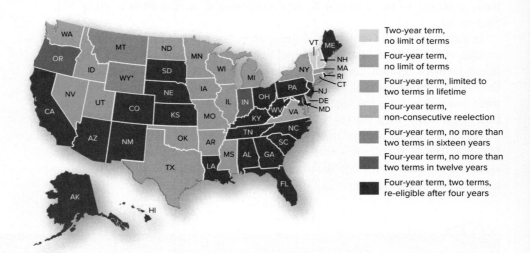

*Wyoming had imposed term limits through a ballot measure in 1992, but in 2013 the Wyoming Supreme Court declared it unconstitutional, determining that only a constitutional amendment could legitimately define any such changes.

MAP 4.3 Term Limits for Governors as of 2021

Source: The Council of State Governments, *The Book of the States 2021,* Table 4.1, https://issuu.com/csg.publications/docs/bos_2021_issuu (accessed March 7, 2022).

The Texas governor has the strongest form of tenure—four-year terms with no limit on the number of terms. Texas originally had a two-year terms. From 1874 until 1953, no person served more than four years as governor in Texas.[31] In 1975, Texas changed to a four-year term.

However, few Texas governors have served more than four years in office. Bill Clements served for eight nonconsecutive years. George W. Bush was the first governor to be elected to two consecutive four-year terms. However, Bush served only six years because he was elected president in 2000. Former governor Perry was the first governor to be elected to three consecutive four-year terms. Upon finishing his final term in January 2015, he had served a total of 14 years. As a result of Governor Perry's long tenure, many Texans have called for gubernatorial term limits.

Governor's Appointment Powers

If the governor can appoint and remove the heads of most state agencies, he or she can better control the administration of programs. Historically, governors have not had strong appointive powers. For most of the nineteenth century, the traditional method of selecting the heads of state agencies was by election. This is called Jacksonian statehouse democracy. President Andrew Jackson expressed ultimate faith in the ballot box for selecting administrators. Toward the end of the nineteenth century, there was a proliferation of agencies headed by appointed or elected boards and commissions. The governor was just one of many elected state officials and had little formal control over state administration.[32] Governors often share power with many other elected individuals. Such arrangements are known as plural executive structures. Figure 4.1 shows a diagram of the administrative structure of the Texas state government and is divided into three categories: statewide elected offices, single-head agencies appointed by the governor, and boards and commissions appointed by the governor.

VOTERS IN STATE ELECT	GOVERNOR APPOINTS		
	Agency Heads	Boards and Commissions	
Lieutenant Governor	Secretary of State	General Government	Licensing and Professional Examining Boards
Attorney General	Adjutant General of the National Guard	Health and Human Services	Public Safety and Criminal Justice
Comptroller of Public Accounts	Director of Housing and Community Affairs	Higher Education Boards of Regents	Natural Resources
Commissioner of the General Land Office	Director of Office of State-Federal Relations	Other Education	Employee Retirement Boards
Commissioner of Agriculture	Executive Director of Texas Education Agency	Business Regulation	Interstate Compact Commissions
Railroad Commission (three members)	Commissioner for Health and Human Services	Business and Economic Development	Water and River Authorities
State Board of Education (fifteen members)	Eight other minor agencies	Regional Economic Development	Judicial

FIGURE 4.1 The Administrative Structure of State Government in Texas

Equally important to the appointive power is the power to remove administrators, which is discussed in a later section of this chapter. Without the power of removal, the appointive powers of the governor are greatly diminished. Beginning in the early twentieth century, the powers of the governor to appoint and remove officials increased in some states. This expansion of executive authority has increased in the past three decades in many states.[33] This has not been the pattern for much of the South or for the office of governor in Texas. In 2001 the voters in Texas even rejected an amendment that would have made the adjutant general of the Texas National Guard subject to removal by the governor. The traditionalistic political culture does not support the idea of strong executive authority, even for relatively minor offices.

Of the 174 currently active agencies in Texas,[34] the governor appoints a few agency heads; the most significant is the secretary of state, who serves as the chief record keeper and election official for the state. The governor also appoints the executive directors of the departments of Commerce, Health and Human Services, Housing and Community Affairs, Insurance, and the Office of State-Federal Relations. The governor appoints the head of the Texas National Guard and appoints the executive director of the Texas Education Agency from recommendations made by the elected Texas State Board of Education. The governor also appoints the chief counsels for the Public Utility Commission, the Insurance Commission, and the State Office of Administrative Hearings.

Thus, significant portions of state government are beyond the direct control of the governor because several agency heads are elected. In terms of numbers, most agencies are controlled by independent boards and commissions over which the governor has minimal direct control. These independent state agencies are usually governed by three-, six-, or nine-member boards or commissions appointed by the governor for six-year, overlapping, staggered terms. Usually, one-third of the membership is appointed every two years. In total, the number of governing and policy-making positions filled by gubernatorial appointment is about 1,500 per 4 years.[35] If the governor stays in office for two terms (eight years), she or he will have appointed all members of these agencies and boards and can have indirect influence over them. (See Table 4.2, which covers Governor Greg Abbott's first year and a half in office.) The governing board chooses the heads of these agencies. A good example of this is the president of a state university, who is selected by the board of regents, whose members are appointed by the governor. The governor often exercises influence with his or her appointees on the board of regents. In 2002, it was rumored that Governor Perry strongly supported the selection of retiring senator Phil Gramm for president of Texas A&M University. All of Governor Perry's appointees supported Gramm. (Although Phil Gramm was not appointed president of Texas A&M, his wife Wendy, an accomplished academic in her own right, was appointed to the A&M Board of Regents, and she served from 2001 to 2005.[36])

The governor also appoints people to non-policy-making and governing boards that make recommendations to the governor or other state officials. Although not discussed in detail in this chapter, many of these non-policy-making boards recommend changes in policy and programs; others are simply window dressing and allow the governor to reward supporters. Most often, these non-policy-making boards do not require senate approval.

TABLE 4.2

Texas Governor Appointments to Policy-Making and Governing Boards, Commissions, and Agencies as Required by Statute

Type of Agency	Number of Agencies
Economic Development	14
Financial	16
Health Care	12
Higher Education	15
Human Services	19
Humanities	13
Legal	9
Natural Resources	31
Public Education	14
Public Safety	9
Regulatory Industry	21
Regulatory Professional	34
State Oversight	38
Transportation	12
Total	257

Source: Office of the Texas Governor, https://gov.texas.gov/organization/appointments/positions, accessed 3/29/2022.

Some gubernatorial appointments are subject to approval by a two-thirds vote of the senate. In these cases, the governor must clear his or her appointments with the state senator from the appointee's home district. This limits the discretion of the governor. This process is known as **senatorial courtesy.** If the senator from an appointee's home district disapproves of the appointment, the senate might not confirm the appointee. Senatorial courtesy does not apply to all gubernatorial appointments, especially the non-policy-making boards.

Other factors also limit the governor's discretion. For example, some boards require geographic representation. Members of river authority boards must live in the area covered by the river authority. Good examples of this are the Trinity River Authority and the Lower Colorado River Authority. Other boards require specified professional backgrounds. Membership on the Texas Municipal Retirement System, for instance, is limited to certain types of city employees—such as firefighters, police, and city managers.[37]

The governor also faces political limits on his or her ability to appoint people. Interest groups pay close attention to the governor's appointments to these boards and commissions, and try to influence the governor's choices. The governor may have to bend to demands from such groups. Chapter 12 discusses this subject in detail.

In Texas, the appointive power of the governor, even with these formal limitations, allows the governor to indirectly influence policy by appointing people with similar policy views to serve on these boards and commissions. It is unlikely that a governor will select men and women with whom he or she differs on major policy issues. This broad appointive power allows the governor to influence policy even after leaving office because some of the appointees remain on these boards and commissions after the governor's term

senatorial courtesy
The favor of the governor clearing his or her appointments with the state senator from the appointee's home district

ends. Ann Richards used her appointive powers to increase the number of women and minorities serving on these boards and commissions. Richards's successor, George W. Bush, appointed some women and minorities but tended mainly to appoint white businessmen to these positions. Former governor Perry, for the most part, appointed white business leaders as well. Current governor Greg Abbott has tended to place Republican and conservative law-makers into high-level judgeships as well as to favor white men overall; for example, three of his five picks for the Texas Supreme Court have been white men, and all five are Repblican.[38]

In some states, a single person, appointed and serving at the pleasure of the governor, heads most agencies. The structure is much like that of the federal government, where the president appoints members of his own cabinet and they serve at his or her pleasure. Only a handful of state agencies in Texas meet this model.

Secretary of State

secretary of state (SOS)
Chief election official and keeper of state records; appointed by the governor

The **secretary of state (SOS)** is a constitutional office, appointed by the governor with approval of the state senate. The constitution and state statutes assign many duties to this office, which can be lumped into three broad categories: elections, record keeping/information management, and international protocol. As the chief election official, the SOS is responsible for overseeing voter registration, preparing election information, and supervising elections. The SOS issues rules, directives, and opinions on the conduct of elections and voter registration. These duties allow the secretary some latitude in the interpretation and application of the state election code. For example, the SOS has some latitude in how vigor-ously he or she encourages citizens to register and vote (Article IV, Section 21).

A second duty of the SOS is to serve as the official keeper of state records. This includes records on business corporations and some other commercial activities. The office also publishes the *Texas Register,* which is the source of official notices or rules, meetings, executive orders, and opinions of the attorney general that are required to be filed by state agencies. Through the protocol functions of the office, the SOS provides support services to state officials who interact with representatives of foreign countries.

In a few cases, the office of secretary of state has been an important stepping stone to higher office. It is a highly visible office, so the secretary is often in the public eye, especially with the duties as chief election official. It is without doubt the most important single-head agency appointment that the governor makes. The most noted example is Mark White (1973–1977), who became attor-ney general and later governor. Former governor Bush picked his secretary of state, Alberto Gonzales (1998–1999), to become White House counsel in his administration from 2001 to 2005.[39]

Commissioner for Health and Human Services

This office was created in 1991 to coordinate a number of health-related pro-grams and agencies. The governor appoints the commissioner for a two-year term with the approval of the state senate. The commissioner has oversight responsibility over eight separate health and welfare programs, which are directed by boards, councils, or commissions. The commissioner is not directly respon-sible for the administration of these programs but has oversight and review functions. Those programs include aging; alcohol and drug abuse; the blind, deaf, and hard of hearing; early childhood intervention; juvenile probation; mental health and retardation; rehabilitation; and departments of Health, Human Services, and Protective and Regulatory Services. Although this office has little direct administrative control, it can and often does affect policy. The commissioner is a spokesperson for the governor in health and welfare matters.[40]

Office of State-Federal Relations

The governor appoints the executive director of the Office of State-Federal Relations. As the name suggests, this office coordinates relations between state and federal officials. The office has existed since 1971 and is the primary liaison between the governor's office and federal officials. To some degree, the person who holds this office becomes an advocate for the state in dealing with the Texas congressional delegation and federal agencies.[41]

Adjutant General of the National Guard

This office was created by the Texas Constitution and is responsible for directing the state military force under the direction of the governor. The governor serves as commander-in-chief of the guard. The **military powers** of the governor are quite limited and come into play only in times of natural disaster or civil unrest. The governor appoints the adjutant general of the National Guard and can direct the guard to protect the lives and property of Texas citizens. The most common use of this power is during natural disasters, when the guard is employed to help evacuate people, protect property, and supply food and water to victims. During the November 2020 election, the National Guard helped with election security and was on stand-by in case of any civil unrest. The size of the National Guard (nationwide and in Texas) is determined and funded by Congress as a reserve force to the regular army.

military powers
Powers giving the governor the right to use the National Guard in times of natural disaster or civil unrest

As with other appointees, the governor may appoint the head of the National Guard but may not remove him or her except on approval of the state senate.[42] In the 1999 November election, Texas voters rejected a constitutional amendment that would have allowed the governor to appoint and remove the head of the National Guard. This decision reflects the continued reluctance of Texans to place too much power in the hands of the governor.

Other Single-Head Agencies

The remaining state agencies to which the governor makes a single appointment are not of great significance in terms of policy or politics. This is not to say that they are insignificant, but simply of less importance or visibility. These agencies often receive little or no attention from the average citizen or the press. They include the Department of Housing and Community Affairs, Department of Commerce, State Office of Administrative Hearings, Insurance Commissioner, and Public Utility Commission Council. In addition, five interstate compact commissions govern the rivers in Texas.[43] The governor appoints the executive director of each of these commissions.

Boards and Commissions

In addition to these elected and appointed officials, the governor also appoints about 1,500 members to 303 state **boards and commissions.** These administrative

boards and commissions
Governing body for many state agencies; members appointed by the governor for fixed term

units carry out most of the work of state government. The board or commission usually appoints the head of the agency (such as the chancellor of a university or the executive director of a state agency) and in varying degrees is responsible for policy and administration of the agency. Most operate independently from other agencies of state government, except the legislature.

This means state government in Texas is decentralized. For example, 18 separate agencies provide health and welfare services. In addition to the Department of Agriculture, the General Land Office, and the Railroad Commission—all having some control over environmental and natural resources—and at least seven other agencies with independent boards or commissions have some authority in this area. These include the Texas Commission of Environmental Quality, the Texas Parks and Wildlife Department, the Soil and Water Conservation Board, and the Water Development Board.

In this conservative state with a strong belief in the free market there are, nonetheless, 38 separate professional licensing and examining boards. Many professions have a state agency that licenses and regulates them. Just a few examples are accountants, architects, barbers, chiropractors, cosmetologists, dentists, exterminators, funeral directors, land surveyors, medical doctors, two kinds of nurses, pharmacists, physical therapists, podiatrists, and veterinarians.

Most often a professional group asks for regulation by the state. When such a group advocates government regulation and licensing, it claims its primary interest to protect the public from incompetent or dishonest practitioners. This may be partially true; however, regulation also lets interested parties develop rules that favor the group and that limit entry into the profession—at a cost to consumers. Two good examples are the water-well drillers and landscape architects. (See Chapter 12 on interest groups.) Also, professionals always argue that the people the governor appoints to the boards should know about the profession they are governing. Knowledge is one factor, but the danger is that these boards and commissions, dominated by members of the profession, will be more interested in making rules and regulations favorable to the group than in protecting the public. Because of this fear, in recent years, the appointment of at least some members of the board from outside the profession has become the norm—for example, non-physicians are on the State Board of Medical Examiners.

Twelve college governing boards oversee the institutions of higher education in the state. These boards are required to coordinate their activities and gain approval for some activities and programs from the State Higher Education Coordinating Board. Within these broad guidelines, each university governing board is relatively free to set policy, approve budgets, and govern their universities. Again, governance is decentralized, with only minimum control from the state and almost none from the governor.

Appointment and Campaign Contributions

Governors have also been known to appoint their campaign supporters to governing boards and commissions. People who were loyal supporters, especially those giving big campaign contributions, often receive appointment to prestigious state boards and commissions. University governing boards are especially desired positions. From 2015 to 2019, for example, two donors to Governor Abbott's campaigns were appointed to positions that put them on ERCOT's

TABLE 4.3

Appointees Who Donated the Most Money to Governor Greg Abbott's Campaigns

Appointee	Government Entity	Donation
Syed "Javaid" Anwar	Higher Education Coordinating Board	$1,334,191.75
Kelcy L. Warren	Parks and Wildlife Commission	1,086,302.66
Robert and Mary Louise Albritton	A&M University System Board of Regents	1,005,000.00
John L. Nau III	Historical Commission	984,058.81
Stanley "Reed" Morian	Parks and Wildlife Commission	820,576.54
Thomas "Dan" Friedkin	Parks and Wildlife Commission	786,807.61
Stuart W. Stedman	Higher Education Coordinating Board	651,250.00
Tilman J. Fertitta	University of Houston System Board of Regents	616,000.00
Stephanie F. Tucker (and husband)	Humanities Texas	482,000.00
Robert S. "Steve" Hicks	University of Texas System Board of Regents	456,008.01

Source: Office of the Texas Governor, https://gov.texas.gov/.

board of regents.[44] Listed in Table 4.3 are the 10 highest contributions Governor Abbott has received from individuals who were appointed to state boards and commissions during his tenure.

Removal Powers

The other side of the power to appoint is the power to remove persons from office. U.S. presidents may remove many of their appointees, but state governors are often very restricted by the state constitution, statutes creating the agency, or term limits set for appointees. Some states allow the governor to remove a person only for cause. This requires the governor to make a case for wrongdoing by the individual. Of course, the governor can force the resignation of a person without formal hearings, but the political cost of such forced resignations can be quite high and beyond what the governor is willing to pay.

In Texas, the removal power of the governor is very weak. Before 1981, Texas state law was silent on the issue of removal. In 1981, the constitution was amended to allow governors, with a two-thirds vote of the senate, to remove any person they personally appointed. Governors may not remove any of their predecessors' appointees. To date, no person has been formally removed from office using this procedure, but it does provide the governor with some leverage to force an appointee to resign. It might also be used to force a policy change favored by the governor. It does not, however, allow the governor to control the day-to-day administration of state government.

In 2010 Governor Perry became openly involved in the removal of some members of these appointed boards when he demanded the resignation of a member of the Texas Tech Board of Regents who was supporting his rival, Senator Kay Bailey Hutchison, in the Republican primary.

How to

Interpret a Table

Tables summarize and simplify information. They present names, numbers, percentages, and amounts in a way that is easy to read. Let's use Table 4.3 to work through the process of interpreting a table.

Step 1: What is the title of Table 4.3?
The title of the table tells you how the elements within the table are related. Table 4.3 has the title "Appointees Who Donated the Most Money to Governor Greg Abbott's Campaigns." The title presents the relationship between the campaign contributions Governor Abbott received and the appointments he made to state boards and commissions.

Step 2: What are the column headings?
The column headings or subheadings identify what data the table is reporting. In Table 4.3 the column headings show (1) the "Appointee" category expressed as the

name of the individual appointed, (2) the "Government Entity" the individual was appointed to, and (3) the "Donation" the individual contributed in a dollar amount.

Step 3: What is the relationship among the headings?
For example, Syed "Javaid" Anwar who was named by the governor to the Higher Education Coordinating Board gave the governor a donation of $1,334,191.75.

Step 4: What conclusions can you draw from Table 4.3?
Though it is possible to make several observations about the data included in the table, it is important to look for the big picture. This information suggests that in choosing whom to appoint to Texas executive bodies, Governor Abbot gave preference to and chose those who were high-dollar donors to his election campaigns.

Current governor Greg Abbott came under fire more recently in December 2019 for removing two appointees from the state's disciplinary board, the body responsible for disciplining state judges. They had voted to penalize a judge who refused to grant same-sex marriages. The governor's office did not officially state one way or another whether this decision was motivated by their vote.[45]

Budgetary Powers

budgetary powers
The ability of a governor to formulate a budget, present it to the legislature, and execute or control the budget

Along with tenure of office and appointive/executive authority, **budgetary powers** are an important determinant of executive authority. Control over how money is spent is at the heart of the policy-making process. Some writers define a budget as a statement of policy in monetary terms. If the governor can control budget formation and development (the preparation of the budget for submission to the legislature) and budget execution (deciding how money is spent), the governor can have a significant influence on state policy. Four kinds of constraints can undercut the governor's budgetary authority:

- The extent to which the governor must share budget formation with the legislature or with other state agencies
- The extent to which funds are earmarked for specific expenditures and the choice on how to spend money is limited by previous actions
- The extent to which the governor shares budget execution authority with others in state government
- The limits on the governor's use of a line-item veto for the budget

In 27 U.S. states, the governor has full responsibility in budget-making power; in the other states, like Texas, responsibility is shared.[46] In states where the governor is given authority for budget formation, agencies must present their requests for expenditures to the governor's office, which combines them and presents a unified budget to the legislature. In some states, the governor is limited regarding how much he or she can reduce the budget requests of some state agencies. If the governor can change the requests of agencies, this gives him or her tremendous control over the final form of the budget submitted to the legislature. A common practice of state governments is to earmark revenue for specific purposes. For example, funds received through the gasoline tax are commonly earmarked for state highways. This also limits the discretion of the governor.

Budget-execution authority is more complex. Governors and others control budget execution in a variety of ways. If the governor controls the appointment of the major department heads of state government, he or she will have some discretion in how money is spent. The governor may decide not to spend all the money appropriated for a state park, for example. Administrative discretion over how money is spent is a time-honored way to expand executive authority over the budget.

Another area where governors can often exercise control over budgets is veto authority. The Texas governor has a **line-item veto** that allows him or her to exercise great influence over the budgetary process. All but six U.S. governors have line-item veto authority.[47] The legislature determines what a line item is. It can be a department within an agency or the entire agency. In the 2015 Texas legislative session, Governor Abbott item-vetoed more than $227 million in the biennial budget. Many thought Abbott exceeded his authority, but Attorney General Ken Paxton supported the governor's position. In 2017, Abbott vetoed $120 million. In 2019, he did not use the line-item veto at all. In 2021, he vetoed just over $168 million.[48]

The legislature can override this veto by a two-thirds vote of each house. However, as we saw in Chapter 3, appropriations bills generally pass in the last days of the session, so the legislature has adjourned by the time the governor vetoes items. Because the legislature cannot call itself back into session ("extraordinary" sessions), overriding a line-item veto is impossible. The governor may call special sessions, but he or she controls the agenda. If the governor thought there was a chance of a veto override, this would not be included in the agenda of the special session.

Thus, the line-item veto is a very important power of the Texas governor, but more important than the actual veto is the threat of a veto. Historically, governors have used this threat to discipline the legislature. It is not uncommon for the governor to threaten to veto a local line item, such as an item creating a new state park in a legislator's district. The governor can use this threat to veto local appropriations in order to gain legislative support for items important to the governor but unrelated to the park. Typically governors do not veto many bills. Although exceptions occasionally occur, as a general rule, threats are more important than the actual veto.

In Texas, the governor's budgetary powers are exceptionally weak, except in the area of the line-item veto. The governor is not constitutionally mandated to submit a budget. This power is given to the **Legislative Budget Board (LBB),** an agency governed by the speaker of the house and the lieutenant governor. State agencies must present budget requests to the LBB, and the LBB produces a

line-item veto
The ability of a governor to veto part of an appropriations bill without vetoing the whole bill

Legislative Budget Board (LBB)
State agency that is controlled by the leadership in the state legislature and that writes the state budget

budget and submits it to the legislature. Historically, governors have submitted budget messages to the legislature, often in the form of reactions to the LBB proposed budget.

In Texas, many funds are earmarked by the previous actions of the legislature. One estimate from the LBB is that more than 80 percent of all funds are earmarked for specific expenditures, such as highways, teachers' retirement, parks, and schools. This is discussed in Chapter 14.

The Texas governor has very limited authority over budget execution. Outside the governor's immediate office, control over the budget rests with other state agencies over which the governor has little or no control. Only in cases of fiscal crisis can the governor exercise any influence. A constitutional amendment approved in 1985 created the Budget Execution Committee, composed of the governor, the lieutenant governor, the comptroller, the speaker of the house, and chairs of the finance and appropriations committees in the senate and house. The Budget Execution Committee can exercise restraints over the budget if there is a fiscal crisis, such as a shortfall in projected revenue.

Legislative Powers

legislative power
The formal power, especially the veto authority, of the governor to force the legislature to enact his or her legislation

partial veto
The ability of some governors to veto part of a nonappropriations bill without vetoing the entire bill; a Texas governor does not have this power except on appropriations bills

The line-item veto can be viewed as a budgetary power, but it is also a **legislative power.** There are also other types of vetoes. All governors possess some form of veto authority, but this varies among the states. (See Table 4.4.) Forty-two states have formalized **partial vetoes,** where the legislature can recall a bill from the governor so that it can address objections that the governor has raised and thereby avoid a veto.[49] Texas has a limited partial veto process; the governor can state objections to a bill before it is passed and thus seek to affect changes in legislation. Formalizing this process would increase veto power to the office of governor and give the governor more say in the legislative process.

Requirements for overriding a governor's veto also vary widely among the states. Most states require a two-thirds vote to override, although a few allow a simple majority.[50] In Texas, the governor has very strong veto authority. The

TABLE 4.4

Veto Authority of State Governors with Override Provisions

Type of Veto	No. of Governors
General veto and item veto: two-thirds legislative majority needed to override	38
General veto and item veto: simple legislative majority needed to override	4
General veto, no item veto: special legislative majority to override*	6
General veto, no item veto: simple legislative majority to override	2

*Most common is three-fifths vote. Not all occurred by three-fifths vote, so depending on the precise method, the data change slightly.

Sources: Thad L. Beyle, "Governors: The Middlemen and Women in Our Political System," in *Politics in the American States,* 8th ed., ed. Virginia Gray and Russell L. Hanson (Washington, D.C.: Congressional Quarterly Press, 2004); *The Book of the States 2021,* Table 3.16, https://issuu.com/csg.publications/docs/bos_2021_issuu.

office possesses a general veto and line-item veto, with a two-thirds vote of each house required for override. Very few vetoes have been overturned. From 1876 to 1968, only 25 of 936 vetoes were overridden in the legislature. Most of these vetoes occurred before 1940. This low number of veto overrides is primarily due to late passage of bills and adjournment of the legislature. Only 1 veto has been overturned in recent years, and it was not a significant bill. In 1979, during his first term, Bill Clements vetoed 52 bills. The legislature, in an attempt to catch the governor's attention, overrode the veto on a bill that limited the ability of county governments to prohibit hunters from killing female deer.[51] Since 1979, the legislature has not overridden any vetoes.

In 14 other states besides Texas, the legislature may not call a "special" session. These are usually called *extraordinary sessions* to distinguish them from *special sessions,* which are called by the governor. States where the legislature cannot call extraordinary sessions add to the power of the governor to veto bills. In the 2001 session of the Texas legislature, Governor Perry set a new record by vetoing 82 bills. If the Texas legislature could have called an extraordinary session, there is little doubt that it would have called one and overridden some of those vetoes.

Thus, the veto authority of the Texas governor is significant. Accomplishing a two-thirds override (in both house and senate) is very difficult. If the legislature has adjourned, it is impossible. For these reasons, there have been few overrides.

Some governors have a pocket veto, meaning that they can veto a bill by not signing it. The governor just "puts the bill in a pocket" and forgets about it. The Texas governor does not have a pocket veto. If the legislature is in session, the governor has 10 days to sign a bill or it becomes law without his or her signature. If the legislature has adjourned, the governor has 20 days to sign a bill or it becomes law without a signature. Sometimes governors do not like a bill but do not want to veto it. Letting the bill become law without a signature can be a way of expressing displeasure short of an actual veto. Some U.S. governors have also used the line-item veto to eliminate more than a line item in an appropriations bill.

Governor's Control over Party

Governors are expected to be leaders of their political party and in most states are recognized as such. In the one-party era in Texas, the Democratic candidate for governor picked the state party chair and controlled the state party organization. Often such control was based on a personal following rather than a well-organized party structure. Governor Bill Clements, a Republican, used his election to build the party in the state, especially during his second term. He managed enough control over the Republican Party and its elected house members to thwart Democratic control of the legislature on some issues.

Today, governors might influence the choice of party leadership, but they do not control the party. George W. Bush found himself in the uncomfortable position of having to work with a state party chair chosen by the social conservatives. Governor Bush would probably have made a different choice for party chair. He did not attend the meeting of the Republican Party convention in 2000. He claimed to be very busy campaigning for president. This may have been the first time a sitting governor did not attend his or her state's party convention.

Focus On

Ann Richards

Although headlining the Democratic National Convention in 1988 was a high-profile event, Ann Richards had been making a splash on the Texas political stage since 1978 when she ran for and won the county commissioner seat in Travis County. She would go on to be reelected as the Travis County commissioner to another term and then serve as the Texas treasurer in 1982 and again in 1986 before finally being elected as the Texas governor.[52]

Ann Richards was a strong and active proponent of the women's movement in the 1970s and used her charisma and talents to help fellow women and friends launch their political careers. Assisting in running state congressional campaigns and several democratic gubernatorial campaigns, Richards started to become uneasy about the societal pressure put on women to stay home and raise the family. In 1972, the opportunity arose to buck the traditional role of women in society with a run for county office, which her husband had declined when he was approached by the Travis County Democratic leadership. With the encouragement of her husband and family, Ann Richards went on to win the position beating a three-term incumbent, becoming the first female county commissioner in Travis County history.[53]

Ann Richards celebrates her victory on election night, November 6, 1990, becoming the state's 45th governor.

Shelly Katz/The LIFE Images Collection/Getty Images

When Richards took office as Travis County commissioner, her politics went from a theoretical form to a more practical method. As a county commissioner, she used her newfound authority to help change the lives of minorities and women in Travis County. Richards took her role as the county commissioner seriously and expanded human services programs throughout the county. As she became less of a political outsider and more of an insider, Richards was approached by a friend inquiring whether she wanted to run for statewide office as the Texas state treasurer. This was a race she would win (twice) and go on to demonstrate the ability to modernize the state's office and run a competent and skillful workforce in order to adequately handle the state's money and banking relations. Mimi Swartz of *Texas Monthly* stated, "No one could ever, would ever, accuse Ann Richards of being an impostor. She did her job too damn well."[54]

After being reelected in 1986 as the Texas state treasurer and fulfilling her duties to that office, Richards started to explore the possibility of a bid for the governor's office. Knowing the potential of a contentious primary process, which was then just as heated a campaign as the general election, Richards started to collect and recruit for her run as Texas governor. With her band of friends and supporters behind her, Ann Richards went on to beat the Republican candidate by 2.55 percent, just 99,239 votes.[55] While in office, Richards would appoint women and minorities to positions, surpassing the number appointed by her predecessors combined. She worked on prison reform at the state level and worked to overhaul the education system.[56] Richards also made efforts to bring Texas's financial future back into line and approved the introduction of the state lottery to Texas.[57] All Richards worked toward was what she dubbed a "new Texas" in which all benefited—especially minorities and women—from the workings of government.[58]

Ann Richards died on September 13, 2006, from complications relating to esophageal cancer. Richards's legacy as a fighter and proponent for minority and women's rights was reflected by the Austin City County in the renaming of the Congress Avenue Bridge by the City of Austin to the "Ann W. Richards Congress Avenue Bridge" on November 16, 2006.[59]

Critical Thinking Questions

1. How did Ann Richards's experience in other executive offices inform her performance as governor?
2. What is Ann Richards's legacy today?

It indicated the level of disagreement between the governor and the party leaders. As the two-party system matures in Texas, party leadership by the governor will have to become more of a fixture in state politics. Except when he was in a primary election with a tough opponent, Governor Perry did not embrace the social conservatives' program or the party platform, in part because of personal beliefs.

Administrative Agencies of State Government

In addition to the office of governor, a number of state agencies make up what might be called the state bureaucracy. The term "bureaucracy" often implies a hierarchy of offices with levels of power leading to a centralized controlling authority. This term does not describe the overall structure of state government in Texas because there is no overall central governing, controlling authority. Government authority in Texas is decentralized and resides within many independent state agencies. In addition, many independent boards, commissions, and agencies operate independently of the governor. Power is decentralized among many officials. This structure of power is in keeping with the traditionalistic and individualistic political culture of the state.

State Employees

Most of the funds appropriated by the state legislature go to pay for human resources. This is the largest single expenditure for all state governments. Figure 4.2 shows a breakdown of the four largest state agency categories in

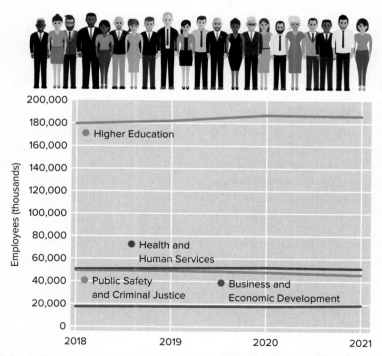

FIGURE 4.2   Employment in the Top 10 State Agency Categories by General Appropriation

Source: Texas State Auditor's Office, https://hr.sao.texas.gov/Reports/Category/FTE/
Jamesjames2541/iStock/Getty Images

Texas by total number of full-time-equivalent employees. Texas has no general civil service system or central personnel agency. Each agency creates its own set of rules and regulations regarding personnel practices and procedures. Most states, however, have a central personnel system and some form of civil service system that formulates personnel policies and procedures. In keeping with the decentralized nature of state government, the personnel system in Texas is also decentralized. More than three-quarters of Texas state employees work in the five major functional areas of state government: corrections, highways, public welfare, hospitals, and higher education.

The number of state employees has declined slightly in recent years due in part to the performance review audits conducted by former comptroller John Sharp. Texas had the second-highest number of full-time-equivalent state government employees (290,001), superseded only by California (369,611).[60] It is not surprising, then, that the state of Texas is the largest single employer in Texas.

Legislative Agencies

In addition to the executive agencies, there are also several legislative agencies. The leadership in the Texas House and Senate controls these units. Their purpose is to provide legislative oversight of the executive agencies and to help the legislature make laws.

Legislative Budget Board

The Legislative Budget Board (LBB) is primarily responsible for preparing the state budget. It is composed of the lieutenant governor, the speaker of the house, four senators, and four representatives. All agencies that receive state funds from the state budget must submit their requests for appropriations to the LBB. The LBB reviews these requests and proposes a budget to the state legislature. Unlike most other states, in Texas the governor plays a very limited role in budgeting.[61]

Texas Legislative Council

The speaker of the house, the lieutenant governor, four senators, and four state representatives control this agency and appoint its executive director. The agency was created in 1949 to assist the legislature in drafting bills, conducting research on legislation, producing publications, and providing technical support services. This is a highly professional agency that produces information for the legislature, which is made available to the public in various ways.[62]

Legislative Audit Committee and State Auditor's Office

The Legislative Audit Committee consists of the lieutenant governor, the speaker of the house, and the chairs of these committees: senate finance, state affairs, house appropriations, and ways and means. This committee appoints the state auditor, who is responsible for auditing state agencies and assisting the legislature in its oversight functions.[63]

Legislative Reference Library

This organization assists the legislature in doing research and serves as a depository of records for the legislature. Located in the state capitol, the library is open to other state agencies and members of the public also engaged in legislative research.

The Texas Legislative Reference Library was originally created in 1909 as the Legislative Reference Division of the Texas State Library. In 1969, the Reference Division was separated out into its own library directly under the authority of the Texas legislature. The library houses an extensive collection of print and online media, including documents going back to the 1850s.
Matthew Bollom

Judicial Agencies

Several agencies, which can be called judicial agencies, are under the supervision of the state supreme court (for civil matters). Except for budgeting of money by the legislature, these agencies are relatively free of legislative oversight. The state bar, which licenses attorneys, receives no state appropriations. The remaining agencies are responsible for court administration (Office of Court Administration), operations of the state law library, and certification of legal licenses and specializations.

Judicial Powers

Governors also have limited **judicial powers** to grant pardons, executive clemency, and parole. Historically, governors have misused this power. This has led to the creation of some checks on governors' ability to exercise this authority. In Texas, James "Pa" Ferguson was accused of misusing this power, especially during the second term of his wife, "Ma" Ferguson (1933–1935). It was charged that Jim Ferguson sold pardons and paroles to convicted felons.[64] These charges led to the creation of the Texas Board of Pardons and Paroles. Today this seven-member board,[65] appointed by the governor, recommends the action the governor can take in such matters and serves as a check on the process. Independent of board action, the governor may grant only one 30-day stay of execution for any condemned prisoner. This board must recommend all other actions by the governor.

In the Fergusons' defense, many of the pardons went to people who were in prison because they had violated the Prohibition laws. Former lieutenant governor Hobby put it this way: "Prohibition's laws filled the prisons and ruined lives. . . . The Fergusons may have rightly concluded that the state was better served by these men . . . supporting their families."[66]

In 2010, Governor Haley Barber of Mississippi attracted national attention by pardoning some 200 individuals as he was leaving office. This has led to much discussion about limiting a governor's power to pardon.

judicial powers
The ability of a governor to issue pardons, executive clemency, and parole of citizens convicted of a crime

Ex Officio Boards and Commissions

A number of state agencies are headed by boards whose membership is completely or partially made up of designated state officials who are members because of the position they hold. Examples of these officials are the statewide elected officials—governor, lieutenant governor, speaker of the house, attorney general, and land commissioner. Examples of these agencies are the Bond Review Board, the Legislative Redistricting Board, and the Budget Execution Committee.

Multi-Appointment Boards

Finally, some state agencies have governing boards whose members are appointed by more than one elected official. This is to prevent any one individual from dominating the selection process and the outcome of decisions. An example of such an agency is the Texas Ethics Commission, which has four members appointed by the governor, two by the lieutenant governor, and two by the speaker of the house. This commission oversees campaign contributions and lobbying activities.

Democratic Control and Bureaucratic Responsiveness

The concept of democratic control requires that state agencies be responsible to the people—that is, that state agencies respond to demands that citizens place on them. With Texas state administrative agencies operating quite independently of each other, and overall administrative control being absent from state government, agencies are often able to respond only to clientele groups they serve and not the public generally. (See Chapter 12 on interest groups for a more complete discussion of agency capture.)

In other states, accountability in a more general sense is ensured by giving the governor broader power to appoint agency heads (rather than independent boards and commissions) who serve at the pleasure of the governor. Also, some states have given the governor broad budgetary control over state agencies. Agencies are required to submit budget requests to the governor, who produces a state budget that is submitted to the state legislature. As discussed previously, in Texas the governor plays a small role in the budgetary process; the Legislative Budget Board performs this function.

State government in Texas is so fragmented and responsibility so divided that holding anyone responsible for state government is impossible. Although citizens may blame the governor when things go wrong, and governors may claim credit when things go right, in truth the governor is responsible for very little and deserves credit for much less than most claim. An example of this is a governor who claims to have created hundreds of jobs in the state when, in fact, a governor has very little to do with the economy or job creation.

Sunset Review

Sunset Advisory Commission

Agency responsible for making recommendations to the legislature for change in the structure and organization of most state agencies

Given the lack of overall central control in state government and the limited and weak authority of the governor, in 1977 the Texas legislature created the 10-member **Sunset Advisory Commission** to review most state agencies every 12 years and recommend changes. This commission consists of five state senators, five representatives, and two public members.

The sunset process is the "idea that legislative oversight of government operations can be enhanced by a systematic evaluation of state agencies."[67]

The process works by establishing a date on which an agency of state government is abolished if the legislature does not pass a law providing for its continuance. The act does not apply to agencies created by the Texas Constitution, and some state agencies are exempt, such as state universities. Sunset asks the basic question: "Do the policies that an agency carries out need to be continued?"[68]

In the years that sunset review has existed in Texas, 44 state agencies have been abolished. Most were minor state agencies with few functions. Most notable were the Boll Weevil Commission, the Battleship Texas Commission, and the Stonewall Jackson Memorial Board. More important than abolition is the review process. By forcing a review of an agency every 12 years, the legislature has the opportunity to recommend changes to improve the efficiency and effectiveness of state government. In many cases, functions of state agencies are transferred to other agencies, and agencies are combined or merged. Sunset review has also forced into the limelight many agencies that operated out of the public's attention, especially agencies that license professions. Sunset review resulted in the appointment of nonprofessionals to these agencies in an effort to promote the broader interests of the public over the narrower interests of the agency and its clientele. Table 4.5 lists the activities of the Texas Sunset Advisory Commission over the past 30 years.

TABLE 4.5

Overview of Sunset Activities in Texas, 1979–2021

Year	Session	Reviews	Agencies Continued	Agencies Abolished	Functions Transferred
1979	66	26	13	7	6
1981	67	28	23	3	2
1983	68	32	29	3	0
1985	69	31	23	6	1
1987	70	20	17	1	1
1989	71	30	22	3	2
1991	72	30	20	3	5
1993	73	31	22	1	5
1995	74	18	14	0	2
1997	75	21	18	0	2
1999	76	25	22	1	1
2001	77	25	19	1	1
2003	78	29	23	1	2
2005	79	29	21	2	4
2007	80	20	14	1	1
2009	81	27	20	2	2
2011	82	29	19	2	4
2013	83	24	19	0	1
2015	84	20	14	0	4
2017	85	24	14	1	4
2019	86	32	21	5	5
2021	87	19	14	2	1
Total		546	407	44	52
			74.5%	8%	9.5%

Source: Texas Sunset Advisory Commission, "Past Review Cycles," June 2021, https://www.sunset. texas.gov/reviews-and-reports/past-review-cycles.

Powers of the Texas Governor in Comparative Context

If we take the six indicators of power—election of other statewide executives, tenure of office, governor's appointment powers, budgetary powers, veto powers, and governor's control over party—and compare the Texas governor with the other 49 U.S. governors, the Texas office is comparatively weak in formal powers because of the limitations placed on administrative and budgetary powers, although the office is strong on tenure and veto authority (see Table 4.6). The formal weakness in the office of governor is very much in keeping with the traditionalistic, individualistic political culture of the state. As was discussed earlier, the present constitution was written in a time when limited government was very much on the minds of the framers of the constitution. Having experienced strong executive authority during Reconstruction, these framers wanted to limit the governor's ability to act, especially in budgetary and administrative matters. They succeeded. In recent years the powers of the Texas governor have been increased somewhat, but the office is still very weak on the budgetary and administrative dimensions. Given this formal weakness, Texas governors must use all their informal powers of persuasion and their political skills if they are to succeed. Also, in recent years the voters have rejected constitutional amendments that would have expanded the governor's ability to appoint and remove agency heads.

Understanding Impact During times of crisis, the power of the chief executive tends to increase. We have seen this occur across the county as governors took action to combat the COVID-19 pandemic. California governor Newsome declared a state of emergency on March 4, 2020, and later imposed a shelter-in-place order that required a large portion of the state's population to remain at home. About a week later, Texas governor Abbott declared a state of disaster and subsequently issued executive orders limiting social interaction to mitigate the spread of the virus. Governors continued to use their powers to mitigate spread throughout the pandemic. What actions do you think governors should take to ensure the safety of citizens during a crisis?

CORE OBJECTIVE

Thinking Critically . . .

The six factors that influence the strength of the power of the governor are the number of elected statewide executives, tenure of office, the governor's appointive powers, the governor's budgetary powers, the governor's veto powers, and the extent to which the governor controls his or her political party. Based on these six factors, what can you conclude about the powers of the governor of Texas?

Informal Powers

Learning Objective: Explain the governor's informal powers.

Although the office of Texas governor is formally very weak, it can be strong politically. The governor's primary political resource is the ability to exert influence. The governor is the most visible officeholder in the state and can

TABLE 4.6

Summary of Institutional Powers of Governors by State

Alabama	2.8
Alaska	4.1
Arizona	3.4
Arkansas	3.6
California	3.2
Colorado	3.9
Connecticut	3.6
Delaware	3.5
Florida	3.6
Georgia	3.2
Hawaii	3.4
Idaho	3.3
Illinois	3.8
Indiana	2.9
Iowa	3.8
Kansas	3.3
Kentucky	3.3
Louisiana	3.4
Maine	3.6
Maryland	4.1
Massachusetts	4.3
Michigan	3.6
Minnesota	3.6
Mississippi	2.9
Missouri	3.6
Montana	3.5
Nebraska	3.8
Nevada	3.0
New Hampshire	3.2
New Jersey	4.1
New Mexico	3.7
New York	4.1
North Carolina	2.9
North Dakota	3.9
Ohio	3.6
Oklahoma	2.8
Oregon	3.5
Pennsylvania	3.8
Rhode Island	2.6
South Carolina	3.0
South Dakota	3.0
Tennessee	3.8
Texas	**3.2**
Utah	4.0
Vermont	2.5
Virginia	3.2
Washington	3.6
West Virginia	4.1
Wisconsin	3.5
Wyoming	3.1
50 average	**3.5**

Source: Thad L. Beyle, "Governors," in *Politics in the American States*, 9th ed., ed. Virginia Gray and Russell L. Hanson (Washington, D.C.: Congressional Quarterly Press, 2008).

command the attention of the news media, holding press conferences and announcing new decisions on policy issues. Such news conferences usually are well covered and reported by the press and other media. This enables the governor to have an impact on the direction of state government. The governor can also stage events that are newsworthy to emphasize things she or he is interested in changing.

The popularity of the governor in public opinion polls is also an important aspect of informal leadership. Governors who consistently rank high in popularity polls can use this fact to overcome opposition to their policies and reduce the likelihood of opposition, both to policies and electoral challenges. A governor who is weak in public opinion polls becomes an easy target for political opponents.

In very general ways, governors are judged on their leadership abilities. Some governors develop reputations as being indecisive, whereas others become known as effective, decisive leaders. The characterization attached to the governor will affect his or her ability to be effective. The media will begin to repeat the reputational description of the governor, and if this happens often enough, the reputation will become "fact." Therefore, developing a good image is very important.

The power and respect accorded to governors have varied greatly over time. During the colonial period, there was very little; some have argued that the American Revolution was a war against colonial governors. The experiences of southern states following Reconstruction led to a return of weak governors in the South. An old Texas saying states, "The governor should have only enough power to sign for his paycheck." In recent times, the power and prestige of the office have increased, as evidenced by recent presidential politics. In both Democratic and Republican Parties, many presidential candidates have been former governors. In the past 40 years, only presidents George H. W. Bush, Barack Obama, Donald Trump and Joe Biden have not served as governors prior to being elected president. Today the office of governor has assumed new significance because of a change in attitude toward the role of the federal government. Over the past 50 years, every Congress promised to return power and responsibility to state governments and to allow states more flexibility in administering programs funded by the federal government. Even without the renewed significance of the office, and even though many governors have little formal power, governors are important players in state politics.

Roles

chief legislator

The expectation that a governor has an active agenda of legislation to recommend to the legislature and works to pass that agenda

Citizens expect governors to play many roles. First, the governor is expected to be the **chief legislator,** formulating long-term policy goals and objectives. In this capacity the governor recommends policy initiatives to state legislators and coordinates with state agencies that administer programs and implement policies. Although governors do not formally introduce bills, passing legislation requires the support of legislative leaders to carry their program forward. Often governors spend considerable time and energy developing these relationships. If the governor is of one party, and the other party dominates the legislature, it is more difficult to pass legislation.

The governor must act as **party chief.** As the most important party official in the state, the governor leads the party and aids its development and growth. This role is important in promoting the party's position on political issues and shaping its policy initiatives. The governor is the most visible member of the party, helping legislators and other elected officials in their reelection efforts, raising money for the party, and creating a favorable image of the party in the state.

In addition, the governor serves as the ceremonial leader of the state. The **ceremonial duties** can be demanding. The governor receives many invitations to speak, make presentations, and cut ribbons. Some governors become trapped in the safe, friendly environment of ceremonial duties and neglect or avoid the other duties of their office. For governors with an agenda for action, getting caught in a "ceremonial trap" is a diversion from more important and difficult objectives. Governors can, however, use ceremonial duties as communication opportunities to promote their programs. They must carefully choose which invitations to accept and which to delegate to others or decline. Ceremonial appearances, such as a commencement speaker, provide an opportunity to generate favorable press coverage and support for one's programs. Former Governor Bush used these opportunities to promote his state programs and his race for the presidency.

In recent years, a new role for the governor has been added to that list—**crisis manager.** Governors are expected to react to crises, such as natural or human-made disasters. How well the governor reacts to these situations may very well have an impact on reelection chances. For example, during Hurricane Katrina in Louisiana, Governor Blanco was not viewed as a strong leader, thus influencing her decision not to seek reelection in 2007. Since March 2020, Texas Governor Greg Abbott has received both praise and criticism over his response to the COVID-19 pandemic. After initial shutdowns in spring and summer 2020, Abbott eased restrictions and has been vocal about not wanting to issue any more lockdowns, instead calling for personal responsibility and vaccine adoption as soon as possible.

Finally, the governor is expected to be the chief **intergovernmental coordinator,** working with federal officials and officials in other states. The governor must also work with the state congressional delegation of U.S. senators and representatives, the president, and cabinet officials to promote the interests of the state.

In Texas, like many other states, the formal powers of the governor are very weak. Without explicit authority, the governor must develop and use the power and prestige of the office to persuade others to accept his or her legislative agenda. This informal leadership trait, the power to persuade others, is perhaps the most important and necessary "power" the governor must develop. Governor Perry used his considerable charm and tenure to persuade the legislature to go along with his programs; over time, his influence and power in the office increased.

party chief
The expectation that the governor will be the head of his or her party

ceremonial duties
The expectation that a governor attends many functions and represents the state; some governors become so active at this role that they get caught in a ceremonial trap and neglect other duties

crisis manager
The expectation that a governor will provide strong leadership in times of a natural or human-made disaster

intergovernmental coordinator
The expectation that a governor works smoothly with other state governments

The Governor's Staff

In Texas, the trend in recent years has been to expand the staff of the governor's office. In 1963, when he became governor, John Connally made the first use of a professional staff of advisors. Previous governors often appointed only a handful of individuals who were loyal to them politically but were not necessarily highly professional. Other governors since Connally have added to the governor's staff. Today an organizational chart is necessary to maintain lines of authority and responsibility. Currently, the governor has a staff of about 277.[69]

Each governor is going to make different use of her or his staff. In recent years most have used their staff to keep track of state agencies over which the governors themselves have little or no direct control. The staff also gathers information and makes recommendations on changes in policy that affect most areas of state government. A message from a member of the governor's staff to a state agency is taken seriously. A report issued by the governor's office automatically attracts the attention of significant state leaders and the news media. Often the governor must use the information gathered to wage a public relations war with the legislature or state agencies. In Texas, the increases in the size, professionalism, and complexity of the governor's staff have become necessary to offset the limited formal control the governor has over state government.

Understanding Impact In the previous section, you learned that the formal powers of the Texas governor are relatively weak when compared to the power conferred on governors of other states. In this section you learned that the informal powers of the governor have evolved over time and the position has achieved new relevance. Do you believe the governor's informal powers have strengthened the power of the office, or does our governor still occupy a relatively weak position in state government? Give reasons for your answer.

Conclusion

Even though governors in most states do not have much formal power, the office has great importance in state politics. In recent years, the importance of the office has increased. Of the past six U.S. presidents, three have been state governors before their move to the White House (Ronald Reagan in California, Bill Clinton in Arkansas, and George W. Bush in Texas). The office has become increasingly visible in both state and national politics. The need for strong leadership in this office will continue to increase.

Texas is now the second-largest state in population and one of the leading states in industrial growth. The governor's lack of formal power makes the task of governing this large, diverse, and economically important state challenging. Some reform of the powers of the governor is still needed, but it is doubtful that such changes will occur. The political culture of the state does not support that change. Leadership will have to come from force of will and personality, not from formal changes in structure. Interest groups do not support transferring power from state agencies they can dominate to agencies under the control of a single individual appointed by the governor. Although the Sunset Advisory Commission has had a positive impact on some agencies, general reorganization of state government is not likely anytime soon.

Summary

LO: Summarize the formal and informal qualifications for the governor of Texas.

While there are certain formal qualifications including citizenship, age, and residency, required by law in Texas, gubernatorial candidates are subject to a much broader range of informal qualifications that can sway the electorate. Political experience, race and ethnicity, gender, and wealth all factor into a candidate's electability.

LO: Explain the provisions for succession of a governor.

Each state elects and provides for the succession of its executive officials according to its own rules. Texas elects the governor and lieutenant governor separately and could, therefore, have a split executive, though this seldom happens. If a governor leaves the state or is removed from office, Texas and most other states dictate that the lieutenant governor move into the governorship.

LO: Explain the provisions for removal of a governor.

Outside of an election, a governor can be removed by either impeachment or recall. Impeachment is the more common (possible in all states except Oregon), whereas recall is allowable in only 15 states, Texas not included. Whereas impeachment is inherently a political process, the state must prove real wrongdoing on the part of the governor in a court of law. Recall, however, is a special vote where the electorate can remove a governor from office.

LO: Explain the governor's formal powers.

Most governors do not have extensive formal powers, but the few they do have can be measured using six variables: election of other statewide executives, tenure of office, appointment powers, budgetary powers, veto powers, and control over party. The Texas governor has relatively weak appointive powers but does enjoy four-year terms and no term limits. Texas governors' budgetary powers are especially weak, except in the area of the line-item veto, which is considered a legislative power and is very strong in Texas. Governors also have very limited judicial authority through pardons and other similar actions. Overall, the office of governor in Texas is relatively weak with a few strong abilities.

LO: Explain the governor's informal powers.

The governor's primary political resource is the ability to exert influence. The governor is the most visible officeholder in the state and can command the attention of the news media, holding press conferences and announcing new decisions on policy issues. Of course, this also means the governor is vulnerable to political attacks and can be subject to electoral disapproval.

Key Terms

acting governor	informal qualifications	party chief
attorney general	intergovernmental coordinator	plural executive system
boards and commissions	judicial powers	recall
budgetary powers	land commissioner (LC)	secretary of state (SOS)
ceremonial duties	Legislative Budget	senatorial courtesy
chief legislator	Board (LBB)	Sunset Advisory Commission
comptroller of public accounts	legislative power	tenure of office
conviction	line-item veto	Texas Railroad
crisis manager	military powers	Commission (RRC)
impeachment	partial veto	

Notes

[1] *The Book of the States 2021,* Table 4.2, https://issuu.com/csg. publications/docs/bos_2021_issuu.

[2] Center on the American Governor, Rutgers University, "Fast Facts about American Governors," https:// governors.rutgers.edu/wp-content/uploads/2022/01/ GOV-experience-2022.pdf (accessed February 28, 2022).

[3] Ballotpedia, "Texas Gubernatorial Election, 2002," https:// ballotpedia.org/Texas_gubernatorial_election,_2002.

[4] Melissa del Bosque, "The Race for the Hispanic Vote," *Texas Observer*, April 26, 2011, https://www.texasobserver.org/ the-race-for-the-hispanic-vote/.

[5] Ballotpedia, "Texas Gubernatorial Election, 2002," https:// ballotpedia.org/Texas_gubernatorial_election,_2002;

Elizabeth Cruce Alvarez, ed., *Texas Almanac*, 2004–2005 (Dallas: Texas State Historical Association, 2004), http://texashistory.unt.edu/ark:/67531/metapth162511/ m1/399/.

[6] James G. Gimpel, "Latinos and the 2002 Election: Republicans Do Well When Latinos Stay Home," January 2003, Center for Immigration Studies, http://cis.org/2002Election-Latinos%2526Republicans.

[7] Melissa del Bosque, "The Race for the Hispanic Vote," *Texas Observer,* April 26, 2011, https://www.texasobserver.org/ therace- for-the-hispanic-vote/.

[8] Center on the American Governor, Eagleton Institute on Politics, "Fast Facts about American Governors," Rutgers, the State University of New Jersey, https://governors. rutgers.edu/fast-facts-about-americas-governors/ (accessed February 28, 2022).

[9] Center for American Women and Politics, "Women in Statewide Elective Executive Office 2022," 2022, https:// cawp.rutgers.edu/facts/levels-office/statewide-elective-executive/women-statewide-elective-executive-office-2022.

[10] *The Book of the States 2021*, Table 4.3, https://issuu.com/csg. publications/docs/bos_2021_issuu.

[11] Ibid.

[12] Ballotpedia, "Lieutenant Governor," https://ballotpedia.org/ Lieutenant_Governor_(state_executive_office) (accessed March 3, 2022).

[13] Texas Secretary of State, "Election Results Archive," https:// www.sos.state.tx.us/elections/historical/elections-results-archive.shtml (accessed February 7, 2020).

[14] *The Book of the States 1994–1995,* 66, http://knowledgecenter. csg.org/kc/category/content-type/bos-archive.

[15] Ibid.

[16] Russell Berman, "The Donald Trump Cabinet Tracker," *The Atlantic*, March 28, 2018, https://www.theatlantic.com/ politics/archive/2018/03/trump-cabinet-tracker/510527/.

[17] Todd Donovan, Daniel A. Smith, and Christopher Z. Mooney, "Governors and Their Careers," in *State and Local Politics: Institutions and Reform* (Stamford, CT: Cengage Learning, 2012), 290.

[18] Alan Greenblatt, "'Being Governor Ain't What It Used to Be': How Their Road to the White House Became an Uphill Climb," Governing.com, https://www.governing.com/ archive/gov-governors-president-trump-2020-hickenlooper-bullock.html (accessed March 28, 2022).

[19] *The Book of the States 2019*, Table 4.8, http://knowledgecenter. csg.org/kc/category/content-type/bos-2019. Oregon is the only state without any such provisions. The District of

Columbia, Guam, and the U.S. Virgin Islands can only use the recall procedure, where citizens can remove an official before the end of his or her term.

[20] Ballotpedia, "Gubernatorial Impeachment Procedures," https://ballotpedia.org/Gubernatorial_impeachment_ procedures. (accessed February 7, 2020).

[21] Wilbourn E. Benton, *Texas: Its Government and Politics*, 2nd ed. (Englewood Cliffs, NJ: Prentice Hall, 1966), 222–24.

[22] Victor E. Harlow, *Harlow's History of Oklahoma*, 5th ed. (Norman, OK: Harlow, 1967), 294–315.

[23] Kevin Hechtkopf, "Early Wisconsin Recall Exit Polls: 60 Percent Say Recalls Are Only for Official Misconduct," *CBS News*, June 5, 2012, https://www.cbsnews.com/ news/early-wisconsin-recall-exit-polls-60-percent-say-recalls-are-only-for-official-misconduct/ (accessed April 2, 2018).

[24] Daniel R. Grant and Lloyd B. Omdahl, *State and Local Government in America* (Madison, WI: Brown & Benchmark, 1987), 260.

[25] Texas Attorney General's Office, "About the Attorney General," https://www.texasattorneygeneral.gov/about-office (accessed March 7, 2022).

[26] Texas Comptroller of Public Accounts, "Taxes," http:// comptroller.texas.gov/taxes/; *Texas Almanac*, "Facts," https://www.texasalmanac.com/articles/texas-facts.

[27] Ballotpedia, "Natural Resources Commissioner," https:// ballotpedia.org/Natural_Resources_Commissioner_(state_ executive_office).

[28] S. M. Morehouse, *State Politics, Parties and Policy* (New York: Holt, Rinehart & Winston, 1981), 206.

[29] Thad L. Beyle, "Governors: The Middlemen and Women in Our Political System," in *Politics in the American States*, 6th ed., ed. Virginia Gray and Herbert Jacob (Washington, D.C.: Congressional Quarterly Press, 2004), 230.

[30] Thad L. Beyle, "Governors: The Middlemen and Women in Our Political System," in *Politics in the American States*, 6th ed., ed. Virginia Gray and Herbert Jacob (Washington, D.C.: Congressional Quarterly Press, 2004), 231.

[31] *Texas Almanac 1994–1995*, 519. Retrieved June 3, 2020, from https://texashistory.unt.edu/ark:/67531/metapth162513/ m1/518/

[32] Thad L. Beyle, "Governors: The Middlemen and Women in Our Political System," in *Politics in the American States*, 6th ed., ed. Virginia Gray and Herbert Jacob (Washington, D.C.: Congressional Quarterly Press, 2004), 221.

[33] Ibid.

[34] Texas State Library and Archives Commission, "State Agency List: TRAIL List of Texas State Agencies," https://www.tsl.texas.gov/apps/lrs/agencies/index.html.

[35] Office of the Governor, "Governor's Appointment Responsibility," https://gov.texas.gov/organization/appointments.

[36] "Governor Perry's Patronage," *Texas for Public Justice*, September 2010, www.tpj.org.

[37] Ibid.

[38] CBS DFW, "Texas Governor Abbott Has Been Filling Courts with GOP Judges Voters Rejected," March 7, 2019, https://dfw.cbslocal.com/2019/03/07/texas-governor-abbott-courts-gop-judge-rejects/ (accessed March 7, 2022); Peggy Fikac, "Analysis: Abbott Favors Donors, White Men for Appointments," *Houston Chronicle,* January 7, 2018, https://www.houstonchronicle.com/news/houston-texas/houston/article/Analysis-Abbott-favors-donors-white-men-for-12480587.php (accessed March 7, 2022); https://ballotpedia.org/Judges_appointed_by_Greg_Abbott (accessed March 28, 2022).

[39] For more information, see Texas Secretary of State, http://www.sos.state.tx.us/about/index.shtml.

[40] For more information, see Texas Health and Human Services, https://hhs.texas.gov/about-hhs.

[41] For more information, see Texas Office of State-Federal Relations, https://gov.texas.gov/organization/osfr.

[42] For more information, see the Office of the Adjutant General, https://tmd.texas.gov/office-of-the-adjutant-general.

[43] Texas Commission on Environmental Quality, "Interstate River Compact Commissions," https://www.tceq.texas.gov/permitting/compacts/interstate.html.

[44] Collier, Dillon; Parker, Kolten, "Political contributions link ERCOT board to Abbott and the state committee now investigating the troubled entity." February 24, 2021. ksat.com (accessed March 7, 2022).

[45] Emma Platoff, "Appointees Claim Gov. Greg Abbott Ousted Them from Board for Voting to Sanction Judge Who Refused to Perform Same-Sex Marriages," *Texas Tribune,* December 5, 2019, https://www.texastribune.org/2019/12/05/did-greg-abbott-ax-appointees-sanctioning-judge-who-refused-gay-marria/ (accessed March 7, 2022).

[46] *The Book of the States 2021*, Table 4.4, https://issuu.com/csg.publications/docs/bos_2021_issuu.

[47] Ibid.

[48] https://www.texastribune.org/2017/04/14/will-abbott-wield-new-veto-power-budget-standoff; https://www.texastribune.org/2019/06/15/texas-gov-greg-abbott-signs-250-billion-budget/; https://lrl.texas.gov/scanned/vetoes/87/SB1.pdf (accessed March 7, 2022).

[49] *The Book of the States 2021*, Table 3.16, https://issuu.com/csg.publications/docs/bos_2021_issuu.

[50] Ibid.

[51] James Anderson, Richard Murray, and Edward L. Farley, *Texas Politics: An Introduction* (New York: HarperCollins, 1992), 122.

[52] Biography.com Editors, "Ann Richards Biography," Biography.com, July 23, 2019, https://www.biography.com/political-figure/ann-richards.

[53] Texas State Historical Association, https://www.tshaonline.org/handbook/entries/richards-dorothy-ann-willis-ann (accessed March 7, 2022).

[54] Mimi Swartz, "Meet the Governor: Ann Richards," *Texas Monthly,* October 1990, https://www.texasmonthly.com/news-politics/meet-the-governor-ann-richards/.

[55] Dave Leip, "1990 Gubernatorial General Election Results—Texas," uselectionatlas.org, https://uselectionatlas.org/RESULTS/state.php?year=1990&fips=48&f=0&off=5&elect=0.

[56] Austin History Center, "Ann Richards," Austin Public Library, https://library.austintexas.gov/ahc/ann-richards-54629.

[57] The Texas Politics Project, Texas Politics–Governors: Ann Richards," https://texaspolitics.utexas.edu/archive/html/exec/governors/31.html.

[58] Ibid.

[59] The City of Austin, *Closed Caption Log, Council Meeting,* November 16, 2006, https://www.austintexas.gov/edims/document.cfm?id=192845.

[60] U.S. Census Bureau, "State Government Employment and Payroll Data: March 2020," in *2020 Annual Survey of Public Employment and Payroll,* https://www.census.gov/programs-surveys/apes/data/datasetstables/2020.html.

[61] For more information, see the Legislative Budget Board website, http://www.lbb.state.tx.us/history.aspx.

[62] For more information, see the Texas Legislative Council website, https://tlc.texas.gov/about.

[63] For more information, see the Texas State Auditor's Office website, https://sao.texas.gov/About/.

[64] Deborah K. Wheeler, *Two Men, Two Governors, Two Pardons: A Study of Pardon Policy of Governor Miriam Ferguson*, Unpublished copyrighted paper, presented at State Historical Society Meeting, March 1998, Austin.

[65] Texas Board of Pardons and Paroles, "Board Member Responsibilities," https://www.tdcj.texas.gov/bpp/brd_members/brd_members.html.

[66] Bill Hobby, "Speaking of Pardons, Texas Has Had Its Share," *Houston Chronicle*, February 18, 2001, 4c.

[67] Texas Legislative Budget Board (permanent joint committee within the Texas legislature), *Fiscal Size-Up 2002-03*, 242,

https://www.lbb.texas.gov/Documents/Publications/Fiscal_SizeUp/Fiscal_SizeUp_2002-03.pdf.

[68] Texas Sunset Advisory Commission, *Guide to the Texas Sunset Process*, 1997, Austin, 1997, 1.

[69] Ibid.

CHAPTER 5

The Court System in Texas

Texas Learning Outcome

- Describe the structure and function of the judicial branch of Texas government.

Texans share with citizens in the rest of the United States a conflicting view of how courts should function in a democratic society. In part, this conflicted understanding arises from the two primary sources of law: legislatures and courts.

When we say "law" in the context of a legislature, we mean a present, binding requirement imposed on all citizens in a given category, such as all citizens under the age of 21, or all divorced parents, or all people who drive vehicles, or all people who work. The law in this sense applies to all people in a category of citizens, without exceptions. It embodies majority rule, or *majoritarianism.*

Courts also create law, but they do so by evaluating individuals on a case-by-case basis. Under our common law system, each opinion that a court hands down enjoys equal status with a statute as "law." But the courts ask a different question than the legislature does: Given that a statute has created a general requirement, are there special circumstances that should lead the court to deal with a particular individual differently? For example, a party could argue that if a general law was applied to them, it would violate their constitutional rights. Courts, therefore, write decisions that will later apply to everyone who is in the same category of citizens as the party in court, but they analyze the law in a way that accounts for individual circumstances or that take into account a higher law. Legal scholars sometimes refer to this approach to the law as *countermajoritarianism:* where special circumstances exist that make the application of the general law to a specific individual illegal. In these situations, courts carve out an exception despite the will of the majority expressed in the statute.

These two conflicting roles of the law translate into contradictory views of how law should function, both in Texas and in the country. First, citizens think the court system should be above politics. Courts are expected to act in nonpolitical ways, interpreting our nation's Constitution as individual challenges arise. That is, regardless of generally applicable legislation that theoretically embodies the majority will, the courts should evaluate each case without preexisting assumptions about who should prevail in a specific case. This is the countermajoritarian role of the courts. Justice is often portrayed as a blindfolded statue holding the scales of justice in one hand. Most Americans firmly believe that courts should be blind to political bias. Fairness, it would seem, requires neutrality.[1]

Second, Americans want state courts to be responsive to the electorate, "especially if they play prominent roles in molding and implementing public policy."[2] But how can courts be simultaneously above politics and responsive to the electorate?

Surprisingly, most citizens do not see a conflict between these two ideas. They think that courts should both dispense pure justice and do so according to the wishes of the electorate. Courts are placed in this position because they make decisions on matters ranging from domestic and family law to criminal law, and they serve as the final arbitrator of highly political decisions. In playing the dual roles of decision maker and policy maker, courts function very differently from other institutions.

Some conservative judges and legal scholars, though, would argue that even if courts frequently play this dual role in practice, they really should not be engaging in the policy-making role. Instead, they should focus on interpreting the law based on the original text and its meaning. For example, the late U.S. Supreme Court justice Antonin Scalia frequently argued against judges engaging in policy making from the bench. He believed it was proper to leave this role to the legislature.

Chapter Learning Objectives

- Distinguish between civil cases and criminal cases within the legal system.
- Discuss judicial federalism.
- Explain the structure of state courts, including trial and appellate courts.
- Describe methods of judicial selection.
- Describe judicial selection in Texas.
- Compare and contrast judicial selection methods, including the "appointive-elective" system.
- Describe the challenges to the judiciary in Texas.
- Describe ways in which judges are disciplined and removed.
- Explain the courts' approach to decision making.

The Legal System

Learning Objective: Distinguish between civil cases and criminal cases within the legal system.

Types of Law

The American legal system can be broadly divided into different branches of law. The most common types of legal cases that states' courts adjudicate are civil, criminal, and family. Civil cases are disputes between individual citizens and involve the idea of responsibilities, not guilt. Under civil law, all individuals who believe they have cause or have been injured by others may file a civil lawsuit. Courts decide whether the case is valid and deserves a hearing in the court. The standard of proof in a civil case is typically determined by "the preponderance of the evidence," meaning that it is likely something occurred in a particular way. A judge or a jury may decide a civil case. The default is a bench trial, or trial by judge. However, a written request can be filed with the court clerk for a jury trial (Texas Constitution, Article V, Section 10). If the request is made within a reasonable time frame before the trial is set to begin, then a jury will be selected (see Texas Rules of Civil Procedure Rule 216a). The winning party in a civil lawsuit receives some form of compensation or relief.[3] However, people found guilty in a civil case do not go to jail or prison for their crimes.

Criminal cases are those cases brought against individuals for violations of law—crimes against society. In these cases, representatives of the state prosecute individuals. The standard of proof in criminal cases is much stricter, requiring that the state proves someone's guilt "beyond a reasonable doubt." Individuals accused of a crime have the right to a trial by jury. If the person is found guilty, the penalty for a crime is a monetary fine, imprisonment, or both.[4]

Family law includes cases related to marriage, divorce, child custody, and age of consent, among other issues. In cases that involve family violence, criminal charges may also arise. A judge or a jury determines the outcome of family law cases. The procedure is similar to civil cases, but narrowed by the particular family issue involved. The Texas Family Code (Section 105.002) prohibits juries in cases of adoption and in certain parenting situations.

Figures 5.1, 5.2, and 5.3 present a breakdown of caseloads by type for district and county courts in Texas.[5]

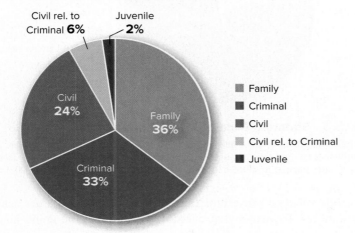

District Court Workload

FIGURE 5.1   District Court Workload, 2020

Source: Adapted from Office of Court Administration, *Annual Statistical Reports, Fiscal Year 2020.*
See: Activity Details for District Courts, http://www.txcourts.gov/media/1451853/fy-20-annual-statistical-report_final_mar10_2021.pdf.

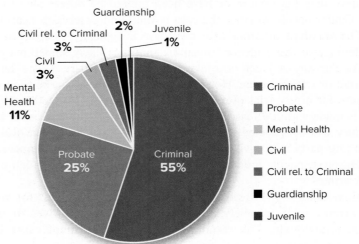

FIGURE 5.2   Constitutional County Court Workload, 2020

Source: Adapted from Office of Court Administration, *Annual Statistical Reports, Fiscal Year 2020.*
See: Activity Details for Constitutional County Courts, http://www.txcourts.gov/media/1451853/
fy-20-annual-statistical-report_final_mar10_2021.pdf.

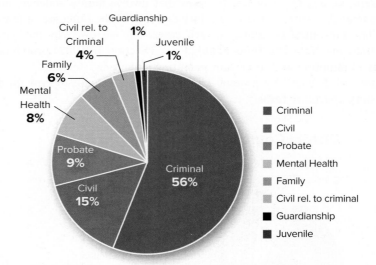

FIGURE 5.3   Statutory County Court Workload, 2020

Source: Adapted from Office of Court Administration, *Annual Statistical Reports, Fiscal Year 2020.*
See: Activity Details for Statutory County Courts and Activity Details for Constitutional County Courts,
http://www.txcourts.gov/media/1451853/fy-20-annual-statistical-report_final_mar10_2021.pdf.

What stops a federal prosecutor from bringing criminal charges against anyone they want to? To answer that question, let's look at the grand jury next.

Grand Jury

Although any citizen may file a civil suit in court, a citizen who may face criminal prosecution can require allegations to be screened by a body that reviews criminal cases. The U.S. Constitution requires the use of **grand juries** to be a screening mechanism to prevent arbitrary actions by federal prosecutors (Fifth Amendment). Some states use the grand jury system for some criminal cases. In recent years the use of a formal hearing before a judge, which is called an **information or an administrative hearing,** has become more common. The judge reviews the facts and decides whether enough evidence exists to try the case.

Texas uses both grand juries and administrative hearings. A citizen may waive their right to review by a grand jury and ask that a judge review the charges. In Texas, grand juries consist of 12 citizens that district judges choose in one of two ways. The district judge may appoint a grand jury commission that consists of 3 to 5 people.[6] Each grand jury commissioner supplies the judge with 3 to 5 names of citizens qualified to serve on a grand jury. From these names, the judge selects 12 citizens to serve as a grand jury. In the other method, the district judge can have 20 to 75 prospective grand jurors summoned in the same manner used for petit juries (described in the next section). From this group, the district judge selects 12 citizens, who are called grand jurors.[7] In both methods, the judge will also select up to four alternates.

Most grand juries serve for six months. They often screen major criminal cases to decide whether enough evidence exists to go to trial. Grand juries are supposed to serve as filters to prevent arbitrary actions by prosecuting attorneys, but they do not always serve this function. The district attorney often dominates grand juries. Most grand jury members are laypeople who have never served before, and they frequently follow the advice of the prosecuting attorney. Although grand juries may conduct investigations on their own, few do. Those that do conduct investigations are sometimes termed "runaway grand juries" by the media.

Thus, a grand jury might not always serve the function of protecting citizens from arbitrary action by prosecutors. For this reason, a person may ask for an administrative hearing before a judge. During grand jury proceedings, the accused may not have an attorney present during the hearing; during an administrative hearing, however, the attorney is present and can protect the accused.

In Texas, the prosecuting attorney leads minor criminal cases in county courts. The county court judge, who determines whether the case should go to trial, holds an "administration" hearing. Criminal cases in the county court are generally less serious than those led in district courts. County court criminal cases usually relate to driving under the influence or driving while intoxicated, minor theft, drug use, assault, and traffic violations.

Petit Jury

Both criminal and civil cases can be decided by a petit (pronounced *petty*) jury. For **petit juries,** the Texas Government Code allows jurisdictions to draw on two sources for jury selection. A jury pool may be selected randomly from voter registration lists or from a list of licensed drivers.[8] In criminal and civil cases, the defendant has the right to a trial by jury but may waive this right and let the judge decide the case.

On average in Texas, more than a million cases are filed in county courts each year, and fewer than 5,000 result in jury trials. Most cases end in a plea bargain and never go to trial. The person charged agrees to plead guilty in exchange for a lesser sentence. The judge hearing the case can accept or reject the agreement.

grand juries
Juries of citizens that determine if a person will be charged with a crime

information or an administrative hearing
A hearing before a judge who decides if a person must stand trial; used in place of a grand jury

petit juries
Juries of citizens that determine the guilt or innocence of a person during a trial; pronounced *petty* juries

If all criminal cases were subject to jury trials, the court system would have to be greatly expanded. Many additional judges, prosecuting attorneys, and public defenders would be needed. In addition, many more citizens would have to serve on juries. The cost of this expanded process would be excessive, and even though many citizens support "getting tough on criminals," they would balk at paying the bill.

Understanding Impact Less than half of a percent of all cases in Texas go to jury trial. What impact does this trend have on defendants in trials? What impact does it have on taxpayers?

Judicial Federalism

Learning Objective: Discuss judicial federalism.

Article 3 of the United States Constitution established the Supreme Court and gave Congress the authority to create other, lower federal courts. Article 6 of the U.S. Constitution makes federal law the *supreme law of the land.* Any direct conflicts between federal and state law must be resolved in favor of federal authority. States create their own courts. As a result, each of the 50 states has a complete court system that exists side by side with the federal courts. Federal courts hear cases involving federal laws, and state courts hear cases involving state laws. Although some cases might be held in either state or federal court, most cases go to state courts rather than federal ones.

Few other countries have **dual court systems.** Ours developed because of the United States' federal system of government. State courts existed during the colonial period and continued after the adoption of the U.S. Constitution in 1789. State courts act primarily in areas where the federal government lacks authority to act.

dual court system

A judicial structure where there are two systems in place: federal and state. The federal court system deals with matters subject to federal law, as well as with interstate and international disputes. The state court system deals with almost everything else that falls within a given state's borders

The Structure of State Courts

Learning Objective: Explain the structure of state courts, including trial and appellate courts.

Most states provide for three levels of courts: trial courts, appellate courts, and a supreme court. The structure of courts in Texas is more complicated, as shown in Figure 5.4. Texas has several levels of trial courts and appellate courts. Trial courts include the justices of the peace, municipal courts, county courts, district courts, and special-purpose courts, such as probate, juvenile, and domestic relations courts. Texas has 14 intermediate appellate courts and 2 "supreme" appellate courts: 1 for civil cases (the Texas Supreme Court) and 1 for criminal cases (the Texas Court of Criminal Appeals).

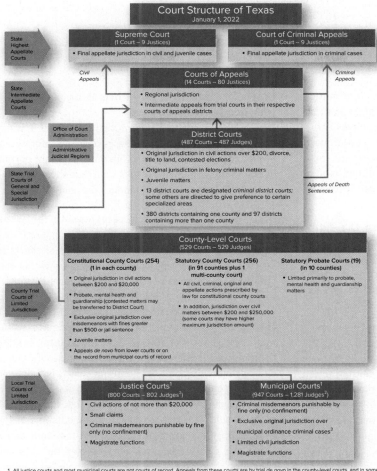

FIGURE 5.4   Court Structure of Texas

Source: Adapted from Texas Courts Online, http://www.txcourts.gov/media/1453418/court-structure-chart-january-2022.pdf

Trial and Appellate Courts

There are two kinds of state courts: trial courts and appellate courts.

- **Trial courts** are local. Jurisdiction is limited to a geographic area, such as a county.[9]
- Only one judge presides over a trial court, and each court is considered a separate court.
- Citizens participate in trial court activity. They serve as members of juries and as witnesses during trials.
- Trial courts are primarily concerned with establishing the facts of a case (such as determining whether a person is guilty).
- Trial courts announce decisions immediately after the trial ends.[10]

trial courts

Local courts that hear cases; juries determine the outcome of the cases heard in the court

How to

Interpret Figures

A figure is a visual way to communicate information. Displaying information in a figure can make it easier for a reader or viewer to understand complex structures and relationships. Within a figure, information appears in its component parts, and the figure shows how each part is related. Visual literacy, like reading a text, takes practice. Use the following steps to interpret Figure 5.4.

Step 1: Determine what information the figure shows.

Before examining the figure in detail, look at the title to find out what information it is presenting. The title of Figure 5.4 is "Court Structure of Texas," so you can expect to see information on Texas state courts.

Step 2: Decide which parts of the figure are most important.

You read most text from left to right, but you can view a figure from top to bottom, side to side, bottom to top, center outward, or center inward. Review the figure from different directions. In Figure 5.4, colored arrows indicate the level of state courts. Examining the figure from the bottom up, you will note that the figure identifies specific courts within each color-coded level. These color-coded courts, displayed by level, are the most important elements of the figure.

Step 3: Identify the information the figure provides for each element.

Examine the secondary information the figure provides about each court. For example, review the information listed under "Municipal Courts" in the lower-right portion of the figure. The subtitle tells you that there are 947 courts of this type with 1,281 judges presiding in them.

Step 4: Determine the relationship between elements in the figure.

Figure 5.4 shows arrows between the levels of courts to identify the relationship between the courts within this structure. These arrows show the path a court case travels within the court structure. For example, a case may originate in local trial courts (justice or municipal), county trial courts (constitutional county courts, statutory county courts, or statutory probate courts), or state trial courts (district courts). Where a case originates depends on the type of case and the court's jurisdiction. If a case begins in district court and its outcome is appealed, the directional arrow shows that the courts of appeal would hear the case next. If the outcome of the case is appealed at that level, the directional arrow shows the case would then go to either the supreme court (for civil or juvenile cases) or the court of criminal appeals (for a criminal case).

---

appellate courts
Higher-level courts that decide on points of law and not questions of guilt or innocence

Appellate courts have structures and purposes that differ from trial courts.

- Appellate courts are centralized, often at the state level.
- More than one judge presides over an appellate court.
- Citizen participation is virtually absent.
- Most importantly, appellate courts decide points of law, not points of fact.

An appeal of a murder conviction from a trial court to a higher court is not based on points of fact (Is the person guilty?) but on points of law (Did everyone follow legal procedures?). Trial courts establish guilt; appellate courts decide whether proper procedures have been followed. For example, in Texas, all death penalty cases are automatically appealed to the Texas Court of Criminal Appeals (Texas Constitution, Article V, Section 5). The issue is not the guilt or innocence of the person but whether the trial court properly followed all procedures and whether the defense adequately defended the person charged.

Magistrate or Minor Courts

All states provide for some type of minor or magistrate court, usually called the justice of the peace (JP). These courts hear cases involving misdemeanors, most often traffic violations and minor civil cases. In Texas there are two courts at this level. The Texas Constitution creates justices of the peace (Article V, Sections 1, 18), and the state legislature creates municipal courts by statute.

Municipal court judges are either appointed by city councils or elected. Some jurisdictions require municipal court judges to be attorneys; others do not. Further, some municipal courts are so-called courts of record, which means that a court reporter transcribes all the court's hearings and trials. As a result, appeals to county courts from these courts of record have a transcript the higher court can review for errors. Most municipal courts create no such record, however, so the county court considers any case brought up on appeal "de novo." (The term comes from Latin; *novo* means "new" in that language.) In other words, the appeal starts with a blank slate, as if no court has heard the claim before.

Municipal courts hear all cases involving violations of city ordinances, most often traffic violations. Like JP courts, they can hear other misdemeanor offenses. These courts also have magistrate functions involving preliminary hearings for people charged with serious offenses. In preliminary hearings, these people find out about the charges against them, learn what their rights are, and find out how much bail would cost. As magistrates, municipal judges can issue arrest warrants.

JPs are not required to be attorneys, and these courts do not create a record of their proceedings for a county court to review. All appeals from a JP court are de novo, meaning there is a new trial at the county level. JPs in small communities without coroners can perform essential coroner functions, and they can issue search-and-arrest warrants. JP courts also perform **magistrate functions** and hear minor criminal cases, most of which involve traffic tickets issued by the Texas Highway Patrol or county deputy sheriffs. JP courts also serve as small claims courts in Texas.[11] Municipal courts do not. Jurisdiction in small claims is limited to $20,000 or less. Of the cases in the JP courts in fiscal year 2020 (September 2019 to August 2020), 84 percent were criminal misdemeanor cases, with most of those being traffic cases (79 percent), whereas only 21 percent were civil cases.[12] This rate is on par with most years.

magistrate functions
Preliminary hearings for persons charged with a serious criminal offense

CORE OBJECTIVE

Communicating Effectively . . .
Analyze Figure 5.4. Describe the appeals process for a civil case filed in county court.

County Courts

In Texas, there are two main kinds of county courts: constitutional county courts and county courts at law. The state constitution creates a county court in each of the 254 counties in the state (Article V, Section 15), and the state legislature has created 256 statutory county courts at law and 19 probate courts.[13] County courts at law are created in large urban counties. In those counties, the constitutional county court ceases to function as a court, and the "county judge" becomes almost exclusively an administrative officer or county executive but retains the title of judge and some limited judicial functions. The state constitution determines the jurisdiction of constitutional county courts (Article V, Section 16). The jurisdiction of county courts at law is set by the act passed by the legislature creating the court and varies from court to court. The general levels of jurisdiction appear in Figure 5.4.

County courts primarily hear intermediate criminal and civil cases. Most criminal cases are misdemeanors. On average, more than one million cases are pled in Texas county courts each year. The most common type of cases are driving while intoxicated (DWI), worthless checks, violation of drug laws, and traffic appeals cases from city and justice courts.

County courts also serve as appellate courts for cases heard by JP and municipal courts. All JP and most municipal courts in Texas are trial de novo courts and not courts of record. In **trial de novo courts,** no record of the proceeding is kept, and cases may be appealed for any reason. It is common in Texas to appeal traffic tickets to the county court, which has heavy caseloads. If a person has the resources to hire a lawyer, there is a good chance the ticket will be "forgotten" in case overload.

trial de novo courts
Courts that do not keep a written record of their proceedings; cases on appeal begin as new cases in the appellate courts

District Courts

In most states, major trial courts are called district or superior courts. These courts hear major criminal and civil cases. Examples of major criminal cases (felonies) are murder, armed robbery, and car theft. Whether a civil case is major is generally established by the dollar amount of damages claimed in the case.

In Texas as of January 2022, there were 487 district courts.[14] The state legislature created each one. Large urban counties generally have several district courts. In rural areas, district courts may serve several counties. The jurisdiction of these courts often overlaps with county courts, and cases may be heard in either court. Other cases must begin in district courts.

Appellate Courts

Eight states, in addition to the District of Columbia, do not have courts of appeal, and 30 states have only one court of appeal.[15] The other states, primarily large urban states, have several courts of appeal.[16] Texas has 14 courts of appeal with 80 judges elected by districts in the state.[17] Only California has more judges and courts at this level. These courts hear all civil appeals cases and all criminal appeals except those involving the death penalty, which go directly to the court of criminal appeals.

Supreme Courts

All states have a supreme court, or court of last resort. Oklahoma, like Texas, has two supreme courts.[18] Oklahoma copied the idea from Texas when it entered the Union in 1907. The highest court in Texas for civil matters is the Texas Supreme Court (Article V, Sections 2, 3), and the highest court for criminal cases is the Texas Court of Criminal Appeals (Article V, Sections 4, 5). Each court consists of nine judges who are elected statewide for six-year overlapping terms.

> **Understanding Impact** In this section you learned about the complexity of the state court structure. Depending on the type of case, civil or criminal, and jurisdiction, a case may originate in one of three levels: local, county, or district. Court costs increase at higher levels, as do other legal expenses. How do costs affect Texans who find themselves accused of a crime?

Judicial Selection

Learning Objective: Describe methods of judicial selection.

Under the U.S. Constitution, the president appoints all federal judges, and they serve for life. A lifetime appointment means that a judge continues to serve during good behavior and can be removed only for cause. States use a variety of methods to select judges.

Eight of the original 13 states allow some judges to be appointed by the governor and serve for life. Two states, also among the original 13, allow the legislature to elect judges.[19] Some states use **partisan elections** to select certain judges. Candidates must run in a primary and in a general election. Still other states elect particular state judges in **nonpartisan elections**. And finally, some states use the **merit system, or Missouri system.** Under this plan, the governor appoints judges from a list submitted by a screening committee of legal officials. After appointment, a judge serves for a set term and is then subjected to a retention election in which the voters decide whether the judge retains the office.

partisan election
Method used to select all judges (except municipal court judges) in Texas by using a ballot in which party identification is shown

nonpartisan election
Election in which party identification is not formally declared

merit system, or Missouri system
A system of electing judges that involves appointment by the governor and a periodic retention election

Appointment by the Governor

When judicial selection is by gubernatorial appointment, there is great potential for selection of judges who are competent, but the process itself does not ensure competence. Governors can use judicial appointments to reward friends and repay political debts. All U.S. presidents, some more than others, have used their judicial appointive powers to select federal judges with political philosophies similar to their own. Governors do the same thing. In such cases, people sometimes raise questions of judicial competence.

Governors are not likely to select unqualified people for judicial appointments; however, governors might not be able to convince the best candidates to agree to serve. The appointive system probably rules out the completely incompetent, but it does not necessarily result in the appointment of the most competent people to serve as judges. Once appointed, judges are not as responsive to voters and can exercise great independence in their decisions.

Election by the Legislature

Election by the legislature is a system left over from colonial America, when much power rested with the state legislature. Only South Carolina and Virginia use this system.[20] It tends to select former legislators as judges. In South Carolina, the number of judges who were former legislators was traditionally very close to 100 percent, and many people view judicial appointment as a capstone to a successful legislative career.[21]

South Carolina experienced discontent over questions of judicial independence. Attempts at reform there culminated in 1996 with an amendment to the state constitution instituting a Judicial Merit Selection Commission. The commission is an intermediary between judicial candidates and the General Assembly (the term used for South Carolina's legislature).

Instead of direct General Assembly review and appointment,

> a Judicial Merit Selection Commission reviews the qualifications of all applicants and nominates the three most qualified candidates. These three nominees are then voted on by the General Assembly, and the nominee with the highest votes is appointed to the bench.[22]

The result has been an increase in judicial independence from the legislature, evidenced by an increase in cases in which the Court has overruled itself. In addition, new rules include a required one-year separation between legislative service and nomination for appointment to the judiciary.[23]

The establishment of the Judicial Merit Selection Commission in South Carolina created a quasi-hybrid method of judicial selection that infused legislative selection with a merit component.

Now let's look at how Texas elects judges.

Partisan Election

In partisan elections of judges, party identification appears on the ballot. Texas uses this system. Originally—that is, during the state's founding and up until the mid-1800s—the executive appointed federal and state judges, who were subject to legislative confirmation and oversight. But as the idea of judicial accountability began to grow in popularity,[24] states began to move to elections as their primary method of selection. A problem soon developed, however. All these elections were partisan, and judges, therefore, were potentially subject to political demands.[25]

In response, states began to branch out, either returning to appointive measures or developing other methods: nonpartisan elections and the merit plan.[26] Still, partisan elections remain the most-used system for trial judges (see Figure 5.5). Indeed, in states with this system, judges are strongly responsive to the citizenry,[27] though this responsiveness can come at the cost of independence in their interpretation of the law.

Sandra Day O'Connor, the first woman to sit on the Supreme Court, was sworn into office in 1981. Although she retired in 2005, her legacy continues in the judicial selection plan that she proposed. The O'Connor plan consists of four elements: judicial nominating commission, gubernatorial appointment, judicial performance evaluation, and retention elections.

David Hume Kennerly/3rd Party-Misc/Getty Images

Nonpartisan Election

Texas is seriously considering nonpartisan election of judges, in which no party affiliation is listed next to the candidate's name on the ballot. This system would reduce the cost of campaigns and force voters to base their decisions on something other than party label. It would not necessarily result in the selection of more competent judges, but it would prevent the kind of large-scale partisan changes in judgeships that happened in Harris County in 1994 and Dallas County in 2008. (See the section "Challenges to the Judiciary in Texas.") Beginning in 2020, Texas prohibited straight-ticket voting, so voters now have to mark the ballot for each judicial race.

The Merit, or Missouri, Plan

Texas is also considering the merit, or Missouri, plan as a way of selecting judges. Under this system, the governor would appoint judges from a list of acceptable (and, it is to be hoped, competent) candidates supplied by a judicial panel and perhaps ranked by the state bar association. Once appointed, the judge would serve for a set term and then stand for retention in an election. In this retention election, voters could choose to either retain or remove the judge from office. As of 2021, twenty-five states use it in at least one appellate or trial court, and twenty-one use it for their supreme courts.[28]

The merit plan seems strong on the issues of competency and responsiveness; however, there is little evidence that it results in the selection of more competent judges.[29] There is also evidence that it is weak on responsiveness. In retention elections, the judge does not have an opponent.[30] Voters vote to retain or remove. Several writers have pointed out that it is difficult to defeat someone with no one.[31] In the states that use this system, most judges are retained; fewer than 1 percent are ever removed.[32] One study showed that between 1964 (when the system was first used) and 1984, only 22 of 1,864 trial judges were defeated.[33] When judges are removed, it is usually because of either an organized political effort to remove them from office or gross incompetence. This remains true today.

Some states have variations on these plans. In Illinois, judges are elected using a partisan ballot, but they must win 60 percent of the vote in a retention election to remain in office. In Arizona, judges in rural counties are elected in nonpartisan elections, but judges in the most populous counties are appointed. These variations might also be considered in Texas.

In short, no perfect system exists for selecting judges. Also, there is no evidence that any one of these judicial selection methods results in the selection of judges with "substantially different credentials."[34] The only exception is that in the states where the legislature elects judges, more former legislators serve as judges.

The method of selection also varies between courts within some states. For example, in some states, appellate court judges are chosen by a merit system while the voters elect trial court judges. Table 5.1 and Figure 5.5 show the

TABLE 5.1

Methods of Selecting Judges

Method of Selecting Judges	Number of State Courts Using Method
Appellate Court Judges	
Legislative election	5
Appointment by governor	2
Partisan election	21
Nonpartisan election	23
Merit plan	25
Other/Combination	14
Trial Court Judges (including municipal level)	
Legislative election	4
Appointment by governor	0*
Partisan election	54
Nonpartisan election	17
Merit plan	40
Other/Combination	43

Source: Data from Council of State Governments, *The Book of the States 2021* (Lexington, KY: Council of State Governments, 2021), Tables 5.6 and 5.7.

*Note this means gubernatorial appointment only.

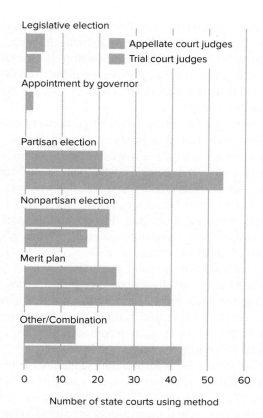

FIGURE 5.5 Method of Selecting Judges

Source: Data from Council of State Governments, *The Book of the States 2021* (Lexington, KY: Council of State Governments, 2021), Tables 5.6 and 5.7.

number of state appellate and trial courts using each selection method. Many states have moved away from partisan election of supreme court and appellate court judges and use either a nonpartisan election or a merit system. However, partisan elections are still a large percentage of the selection process in trial courts, particularly when taking all levels of state trial courts into account.

Table 5.2 shows how states initially select judges to the supreme court. Some states use different methods to select appellate court judges.

Understanding Impact Why is it particularly important to select competent judges? Explain your reasoning.

Judicial Selection in Texas

Learning Objective: Describe judicial selection in Texas.

Partisan Elections

In Texas, trial court judges are elected in partisan elections for four-year terms (Texas Constitution, Article V, Sections 7, 15, 18, 30), and appellate court judges

TABLE 5.2

Judicial Selection of State Supreme Court Judges

Partisan Election	Nonpartisan Election	Missouri Plan	Appointment
Alabama	Arkansas	Alaska	California
Illinois	Georgia	Arizona	Maine
Louisiana	Idaho	Colorado	New Hampshire
Michigan	Kentucky	Connecticut	New Jersey
New Mexico	Minnesota	Delaware	Puerto Rico
North Carolina	Mississippi	Florida	Tennessee
Ohio	Montana	Hawaii	
Pennsylvania	Nevada	Indiana	
Texas	North Dakota	Iowa	
	Oregon	Kansas	
	Washington	Maryland	
	West Virginia	Massachusetts	
	Wisconsin	Missouri	
		Nebraska	
		New York	
		Oklahoma	
		Rhode Island	
		South Dakota	
		Utah	
		Vermont	
		Wyoming	

Table shows how judges are normally selected. Some judges in partisan and nonpartisan systems may get their initial seat by appointment of the governor. Note that South Carolina and Virginia elect supreme court judges legislatively.

Source: Data from Council of State Governments, *The Book of the States 2021* (Lexington, KY: Council of State Governments, 2021), Table 5.6.

are elected in partisan elections for six-year terms (Article V, Section 4). The only exceptions to this are municipal court judges, who are usually appointed by the mayor or the city council.

The question of judicial selection has been an issue in Texas for almost two decades. In 1995, the Texas Supreme Court established the Commission on Judicial Efficiency to make recommendations on the method of judicial selection, and other issues, to the 1997 session of the Texas legislature, but the legislature took no action on the recommendations. Between 1999 and 2011, several bills were introduced to change judicial selections, but none passed. In 2019, a bill was introduced by Republican House representatives to change to a system of governor appointment with Senate approval, but the bill died in committee.[35]

Although the election of judges can be problematic, most Texans do not like the idea of giving up their right to elect judges. Other issues in Texas judicial selection include voting by familiar name rather than qualifications, judicial campaign contributions, and lack of minority representation in judicial elections. Indeed, in 2017, a bill passed outlawing straight-ticket voting beginning in 2020, which forces voters to manually select their desired candidate.[36]

Focus On

The Impact of High Judicial Election Costs

The election process of judges in Texas and the money poured into campaigns by special interest groups raise questions about the integrity and representativeness of the Texas bench. The arguments in favor of partisan elections are that they are the most democratic decision-making process for the judiciary, give greater accountability to communities and jurisdictions, and limit independence to prevent the judiciary from having greater power than the legislative and executive branches.[37] Critics of the current election process in Texas claim the dominance of special interest contributions, the sharp increase of campaign costs, and the polarizing nature of partisan elections are reason enough to reform the judicial election process.[38]

With the U.S. Supreme Court's decision in *Citizens United v. FEC*, the rise in special interest money in politics has become more prevalent throughout the electoral process, including in state judicial elections.

Chief Supreme Court Justice John Roberts speaking at the U.S. District of Columbia Circuit Court.

Keith Srakocic/AP Images

In Texas, approximately 9 percent of the total campaign contributions of the three Texas Supreme Court races in the 2018 midterms were funded by special interest groups.[39] Critics of the *Citizens United* decision decry the use of unlimited spending in U.S. elections and politics but say it is especially damaging to our judiciaries, giving a small group of wealthy donors more power over the vast majority of the electorate.[40]

Self-described philanthropist Salem Abraham[41] is an outspoken critic of partisan judicial ballots and special interest spending and has been leading a reform effort, specifically regarding the Texas Supreme Court. Abraham, along with a group of his employees, began to analyze the relationship between special interest contributions—specifically by law firms in Texas—and the political bias of having a case taken up by the Texas Supreme Court and the judicial bias of having a reversal in one's favor. What Abraham's team found was nine specific law firms have donated over $3 million to Texas Supreme Court justices from 2006 to 2016, and if a petitioner of the court was being represented by one of these nine firms, there was a 27.6 percent greater chance of having their case brought before the court and a 5.6 percent higher likelihood of having some reversal.[42] While linkage does not always spell correlation, the appearance of a conflict is enough to call justice into question.

The high cost of elections may contribute to another problem with courts—a lack of diversity—by making it harder for candidates who are members of ethnic or racial minority groups to be elected to judicial positions. As of September 1, 2021, of 3,194 possible judge positions, only 186 (5.8 percent) were held by African Americans and only 550 (17.2 percent) were held by Hispanics.[43] In each case, that is roughly half the proportion of the general population held by the group. The *Citizens United* decision is still too recent to draw firm conclusions, but according to a paper published by the Brennan Center for Justice in 2019, early findings suggest that candidates of color raise substantially less money than do white candidates. Further, special interest groups are less likely to run ads supporting candidates of color than white candidates, and they spend more on ads attacking candidates of color than on ads attacking white candidates.[44]

A recent example of this disparity comes from the 2018 election. In 2018, Kathy Cheng (Taiwanese American female Democrat) ran against Jeff Brown (white male Republican incumbent) for the Texas Supreme Court (Place 6).

(Continued...)

Cheng raised $64,536 whereas Brown raised $713,428. Brown received significant donations from the Texas Republican Party and other lawyers and industry interest groups.[45] Cheng, on the other hand, was not nearly as well supported by the Texas Democratic Party. Her funding primarily came from herself and other individuals along with some assistance from Texas for Fairness and Justice and North Texas Asian Democrats.[46] Her case isn't at all unusual in the state.

These trends suggest that the high costs of elections and the influx of special interest money might make the already-existing problem of a nonrepresentative judicial branch even worse.

Critical Thinking Questions
1. Do you think Salem Abraham's research indicates actual bias or just the appearance of bias? Explain your reasoning.
2. What problems might be created by having a judiciary that looks less and less like the population it must judge?

CORE OBJECTIVE

Being Socially Responsible . . .
What impact, if any, do you think partisan election of judges has on judicial outcomes?

Appointive-Elective System

Reformers, some of whom were elected through the current partisan system, have called for change to Texas's judicial selection process. Both nonpartisan and merit systems have been suggested. Some have pointed out that the state already has an **appointive-elective system.** The Texas governor can fill any seat for district or appellate court that becomes vacant because of death or resignation or any new district court position that the legislature creates. Vacancies in the county courts and justice of the peace courts are filled by the county governing body, the County Commissioners Court. Persons appointed to fill vacancies serve until the next regular election for that office, when they must stand for regular election.

Historically, many judges in Texas initially receive their seats on the courts by appointment. The data are not complete for all time periods, but enough are available to show that this is a common practice. Between 1940 and 1962, about 66 percent of the district and appellate judges were appointed by the governor to their first term on the court. Today, the vast majority of municipal court judges are appointed while other trial court judges are predominantly elected. In terms of the state's two highest courts, the Supreme Court is currently mostly appointed while the Court of Criminal Appeals is currently mostly elected. Table 5.3 shows data on appointments of sitting judges in 2021.

appointive-elective system
In Texas, the system of many judges gaining the initial seat on the court by being appointed and later standing for election

TABLE 5.3

Texas Judges Serving in 2021 Who Were Appointed to Their Initial Seat on the Court

	Appointed		Elected	
	Number	Percent	Number	Percent
Supreme Court	7	88%	1	13%
Court of Criminal Appeals	1	11%	8	89%
Court of Appeals	25	56%	55	44%
District Courts	122	26%	345	74%
Criminal District Courts	2	15%	11	85%
County Courts at Law	59	23%	199	78%
Probate Courts	2	11%	16	89%
Constitutional County Courts	52	20%	202	80%
Justice of the Peace Courts	226	28%	572	72%
Municipal Courts	1,628	99%	16	1%

Source: Data from Office of Court Administration, Annual Statistical Reports, Fiscal Year 2021. See Profile of Appellate and Trial Judges, https://www.txcourts.gov/media/1452755/judge-profile-september-2021.pdf.

Is There a Best System for Judicial Selection?

Learning Objective: Compare and contrast judicial selection, including the "appointive-elective" system.

The debate in Texas over judicial selection will continue in future sessions of the legislature. Judicial selection revolves around three basic issues. Citizens expect judges to be (1) competent, (2) independent and not subject to political pressures, and (3) responsive, or subject to democratic control.[47] Each method that the states use to select judges has strengths and weaknesses regarding each of these issues (see Table 5.4).

TABLE 5.4

Strengths and Weaknesses of Judicial Selection Methods

Method of Selection	Issue		
	Competence	Independence	Responsiveness
Election by legislature	Mixed	Strong	Weak
Appointment by the governor	Strong	Strong	Weak
Partisan election	Weak	Weak	Strong
Nonpartisan election	Mixed/Weak	Mixed/Weak	Strong
Merit/Missouri Method	Moderate	Moderate	Weak

Source: Ann O. Bowman and Richard C. Kearney, *State and Local Government* (Boston: Houghton Mifflin, 1990), 286–97.

Challenges to the Judiciary in Texas

Learning Objective: Describe the challenges to the judiciary in Texas.

Familiar Names Can Skew Judicial Elections

Several events have brought the issue of judicial selection to the forefront in Texas today. The first of these is electoral problems. Although elections are the heart of any democracy, they are imperfect instruments for deciding the qualifications of the persons seeking office. This is especially true for judicial offices, for which qualifications are extremely important. The average voter in Texas will be asked to vote for judges for the Texas Supreme Court and the Court of Criminal Appeals and, in large urban counties, several district judges, county judges, and JPs. Most voters go to the election booth with scant knowledge about the qualifications of judicial candidates, and they often end up voting by **name familiarity.**

Straight-Ticket Voting

Another electoral problem that has surfaced in recent years is straight-ticket voting (STV). Texas, until the end of 2019, was one of the few states that allowed this practice. (The remaining STV states are Alabama, Indiana, Kentucky, Michigan, Oklahoma, South Carolina, and Utah.)[48] The **straight-ticket voting system** allows a voter to vote for all candidates in a party by making a single mark. In 1984, many incumbent Democratic judges lost their seats in large urban counties to unknown Republican challengers because of Republican straight-ticket voting. In Harris County in 1994, only 1 incumbent Democrat was reelected, and Republicans defeated 16 Democrats because of straight-ticket voting. In 2008, voters reversed this and returned Democrats to most judicial offices in Harris County. Many of the Republicans elected lacked judicial experience, and some had no courtroom experience.

More recent cases of straight-ticket voting have caused some to call for non-partisan election of state judges. In every session since 1995, bills have been introduced that called for the nonpartisan election of district judges and a merit system for appellate judges. Yet another suggestion has been to prohibit straight-ticket voting in judicial races, which the legislature has considered in past sessions. This would force voters to mark the ballot for each judicial race.

In the 2017 legislative session, Texas passed House Bill 5 to get rid of straight-ticket voting starting in 2020.[49] There has been controversy, however, surrounding the change. The state of Michigan, for example, abolished straight-ticket voting in 2016. Later, a district court judge determined that the act "disproportionally affected African-Americans," so straight-ticket voting went back into effect.[50] There are worries about how eliminating straight-ticket voting in Texas will affect voting among ethnic and racial minority groups and down-ballot races, but the actual effect on voting patterns and election outcomes remains to be seen.

Campaign Contributions

Another electoral issue is campaign contributions. Under the Texas partisan election system, judges must win nomination in the party primary and in the

name familiarity
Practice of voting for candidates with familiar or popular names; a significant issue in Texas judicial elections

straight-ticket voting system
System that allows voters to vote for all candidates of a single political party by making a single mark and that has resulted in an increase in the number of Republican judges

Does money influence the judiciary?

spxChrome/E+/Getty Images

general election. Two elections, stretching over 10 months (January to November), can be a costly process. In 2018, for example, Texas Supreme Court justices Jimmy Blacklock and John Devine raised over $1 million to secure their reelection.[51]

Money for election efforts often comes from law firms that have business before the same judges who receive the money. Other money comes from interest groups, such as the Texas Medical Association, which wants to limit malpractice tort claims in cases before the courts. The Public Broadcasting System's *Frontline* television series ran a program titled "Justice for Sale" about the Texas courts and money. This report detailed how eight justices on the supreme court in 1994 received more than $9 million, primarily from corporations and law firms. In the 2020 election cycle, the majority of contributions came from business (energy, finance, insurance, and real estate), lawyers, and lobbyists.[52]

Since the mid-1990s, corporate donations have steadily grown, often matching or outpacing contributions made by lawyers and other interests. Many of these special interests had cases pending in the courts. According to a report published in 2011 by the Center for American Progress, a majority of cases held by the Texas Supreme Court between 1992 and 2010 were found in favor of corporate defendants. A 2016 update to that report found more of the same.[53]

The basic question raised by these contributions is their impact on judicial impartiality. Do these contributions influence judges' decisions? A 1999 poll conducted by the Texas Supreme Court found that 83 percent of Texans think money influences judges.[54] In 2006, a Texans for Public Justice study found that the Texas Supreme Court is more likely to hear cases filed by large contributors. Because of the volume of cases, the high court accepted only about 11 percent of all petitions filed, but they were seven and a half times more likely to hear cases filed by contributors of $100,000 and ten times more likely from contributors of $250,000.[55] More recently, in 2019, the state created a committee to study the effect of money on judicial selection (House Bill 3040). In December 2020, the committee released its report and made a few recommendations (such as increasing qualification minimums), but was conflicted over choosing a different judicial election system overall.[56] Respect for the law declines when people lose confidence in the courts. This situation should concern all citizens.

Understanding Impact As you know, Texas selects judges by partisan election. This section points out that campaign contributions may affect judicial impartiality. Why should this issue matter to you?

Gender and Minority Representation in the Texas Judiciary

When asking how the gender, race, or ethnicity of Texas judges compares with these same traits in the state's general population, it is important to remember why the question is relevant. Many studies have asked whether such differences between judges and citizens appearing in their courts result in biased decisions.[57] We will likely never know the extent to which such bias exists or what forms it takes.

Approximately 49.7 percent of the state's general population is male.[58] However, over 60 percent of Texas judges are male.[59] Despite this disparity, the number of female judges in the state is significant and growing. Even as early as 1995, some major metropolitan areas in Texas saw a significant increase in the number of female judges. At that time, for example, almost half of the 59 sitting district court judges in Harris County were female.[60] As of 2021, 50 percent of justices serving on Texas Courts of Appeals were female,[61] and women have filled two or three of the nine seats on the Texas Supreme Court at different times in recent history.[62] Three women serve on the Texas Supreme Court, and 4 of the 9 justices on the Texas Court of Criminal Appeals are women as of the November 2020 election. Approximately 37 percent of all Texas judges are female.[63]

Texas Supreme Court justice Eva A. Guzman, sworn into office at the Texas Capitol on January 11, 2010, is a well-respected judge who grew up in an impoverished Houston home. She won another six-year term in the November 2016 election.

Erick Schlegel/AP Images

Focus On

The First Hispanic Justice on the Texas Supreme Court

In March 1940, Raul A. Gonzalez Jr. was born to two migrant farmworkers from Mexico in Weslaco, Texas. From an interview in 2004, he remembers the following:

> As children, we worked out in the fields along with our parents, and my grandfather, and my aunts and uncles, and nieces and nephews harvesting crops. We harvested everything that they grew in the Valley: tomatoes, onions, cabbage, and cotton.[64]

He noted that his parents, particularly his mother, instilled in him the importance of education.

> Well before I graduated high school, when I was probably about 12, 13, or 14 years old, my Mom planted in all of our heads that if we were ever going to break the cycle of poverty, it was going to be through education. So she really encouraged us to do as best we could in school.[65]

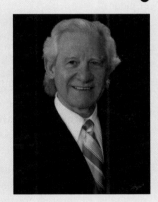

Raul A. Gonzalez

After graduating from high school and spending the subsequent summer harvesting tomatoes and apricots in California, Gonzalez moved to Austin to study government at the University of Texas at Austin. He became intensely involved with the Texas Young Democrats student club, picketing, participating in marches, and other forms of civil rights activism. He graduated in 1963 and, from there, moved on to the University of Houston to study law where he earned a juris doctorate in 1966.[66]

(Continued...)

Over the next several years, he worked as an assistant city attorney in Houston, an attorney for the Houston Legal Foundation, an assistant U.S. attorney for the Southern District of Texas in Brownsville, and as a Diocesan attorney for the Catholic Diocese in Brownsville. He also maintained a private practice for several years while serving in these other positions.[67]

In 1978, however, his career as an attorney shifted to a career in the judiciary when Texas governor Dolph Briscoe appointed him as a judge to the 103rd Judicial District. In rapid succession, subsequent Texas governors Clements and White appointed Gonzalez to increasingly high positions within the Texas judiciary. In 1984, Gonzalez was appointed as associate justice to the Texas Supreme Court. Because Texas elects its judges, Gonzalez won the following elections that secured these judicial positions.[68]

As the first Hispanic to be elected to the Texas Supreme Court, Gonzalez served for 14 years, from 1984 to 1998.[69] In the early years of his tenure, he was, many times, the lone voice of dissent. Although all justices in 1984 were Democrats, most did not share his worldview. He notes, in the same interview from 2004:

> When I came to the Court, the members were all Democrats and by and large, were of a different philosophy than me. They were more progressive and liberal than I am. And there were some who didn't know what to make of me, like "Who is this guy, and where did he come from?" I was very honored to be there. I never dreamed I would be a justice of the Texas Supreme Court. I saw it as a calling or vocation and I was going to do the best I could and speak my mind.[70]

In later years, he would to go on to write both majority and dissenting opinions and, as the court changed over time, his dissents drew more support from other judges.[71]

One of the major issues during his time on the court was a controversy over the possible "buying" of judges. After the Texas Supreme Court ruled to uphold a lower court ruling in 1985 in favor of Pennzoil against Texaco, "granting the largest damage award in history—$10.53 billion, plus interest,"[72] there were accusations of partiality, particularly in light of how judges are selected in partisan elections. In a 1987 *60 Minutes* episode titled "Is Justice for Sale in Texas," host Mike Wallace investigated the issue, noting that many of the "biggest [judicial nominee] campaign contributors are the lawyers who practice before the very judges they helped elect."[73]

Gonzalez has been supportive of the more recent push toward merit selection of judges, even desiring a constitutional amendment in Texas to allow its application.[74] Texas, however, remains firmly committed to the partisan election of judges.

Since retiring from the Texas Supreme Court in 1998 after many successful years, Gonzalez returned to private life but remains active in private practice and consulting.[75]

The Supreme Court Today

Since Justice Gonzalez's retirement, a few more Hispanics have served on the Supreme Court. Alberto R. Gonzales took Raul Gonzalez's place and stayed on until January 2001, when he left to become White House Council for President George W. Bush. Xavier Rodriguez served briefly in 2001 and 2002 until becoming a U.S. District Court judge in the Western District of Texas. David Michael Medina served from 2004 to 2012 when he lost the Republican runoff election.

Currently, Eva Guzman is the only serving Hispanic. She began her tenure in 2009 when appointed by Governor Rick Perry. She continues to serve, having won reelection in 2016.

Critical Thinking Questions

1. Do you think having Hispanic representation on the Texas Supreme Court changes outcomes?
2. Why is it important for there to have been a Hispanic justice and more Hispanic justices in the future?

In 2021, despite the fast-growing Hispanic population in the state, only 33 percent of all Texas judges identify as nonwhite.[76] Seventeen percent of all judges in the state are identified as Hispanic.[77] In the general population, by comparison, 41.2 percent of Texans identified themselves as white and non-Hispanic.[78] Even more sharply, 39.7 percent of the Texas population identified itself as Hispanic or Latino.[79]

Perhaps the most striking disparity between the composition of Texas judges and the state's general population can be seen among African Americans, who constitute 12.9 percent of the Texas population.[80] Only 5.9 percent of all Texas judges are Black.[81] Though recent appointments to the Supreme Court have increased the visibility of African American judges, the racial makeup of the defendants and judges in the criminal court system continues to draw criticism.[82]

CORE OBJECTIVE

Thinking Critically . . .

Reflecting on the discussion about representation of minorities and women in the Texas judicial system, do you think it is important to have a judiciary that is representative of the general population? Why or why not?

Removing and Disciplining Judges

Learning Objective: Describe ways in which judges are disciplined and removed.

Most states provide some system to remove judges for misconduct. Impeachment, a little-used and very political process, is provided for in 47 states, including Texas. Eight states allow for recall of judges by the voters. One state, New Hampshire, allows the governor to remove a judge after a hearing. In 17 states, the legislature can remove judges by a supermajority (most commonly two-thirds) vote. This typically takes the form of one chamber impeaching and the other chamber voting to remove. Some states, however, require both chambers to reach supermajority. In recent years, the trend in the states has been to create a commission on judicial conduct to review cases of misconduct by judges and remove them from office.[83] To date, all states have some kind of investigating body.[84] Also, the method of removal of judges can depend on the level of the judgeship—for instance, trial judges versus appellate judges.

The discipline or removal of judges from the bench can take several routes in Texas. First and foremost in practical terms is the State Commission on Judicial Conduct (Article V, Section 1), which receives complaints about judges at all levels in the judiciary. This 13-member commission conducts hearings and decides whether "the judge in question is guilty of willful or persistent conduct that is inconsistent with the proper performance of a judge's duties."[85] The commission can privately reprimand, publicly censure, or recommend that the state supreme court remove the judge. One observer has noted that sometimes "the commission persuades judges to resign voluntarily in lieu of disciplinary action."[86] In fiscal year 2021, citizens filed 1,724 cases with the commission, from which the commission issued 96 disciplinary actions. Of the judges the commission reprimanded, 19 percent were justices of the peace.[87]

In addition, the Texas Constitution creates avenues to remove judges from office and empowers the Texas legislature to create other such processes by statute. The Texas Supreme Court can remove a judge for "partiality, or oppression, or official misconduct," or if the judge's "habits . . . render him unfit to hold . . . office" (Article XV, Section 6). By two-thirds vote of the Texas legislature, the governor can remove a judge from office for "neglect of duty," "habitual drunkenness," or "oppression in office" (Article XV, Section 8). A two-thirds vote of the state senate can remove a judge in an impeachment process (Article XV, Section 2). District judges may remove county judges and justices of the peace (Article V, Section 24).

The State Commission on Judicial Conduct provides a real check on the actions of judges. Furthermore, if Texas adopts the merit, or Missouri, plan, this commission would probably increase in importance.

CORE OBJECTIVE

Taking Personal Responsibility . . .

Given what you read in this section, it would seem that citizens have little impact in disciplining and/or removing judges. What do you think is a citizen's responsibility in this matter? How can individuals take greater personal responsibility to ensure that judges perform properly?

Understanding Impact Why do you think misdeeds such as drunkenness, partiality, and oppression in office are considered serious enough to remove a judge from office? What harm could a judge who commits those misdeeds do?

Court Decision Making

Learning Objective: Explain the courts' approach to decision making.

The courts' approach to decision making is quite different from that of the executive and legislative branches.[88] Unlike the legislature or governor, who can initiate policy changes, courts evaluate individual disputes that arise in cases that parties file with them. Cases that Texas courts decide may have an important effect on different sectors of the state's population. All schoolchildren, all property taxpayers, or all landowners, for example, may be affected by a single decision involving schoolchildren, taxpayers, or landowners. Most cases do not involve policy questions, however, but deal only with controversies between individuals. Another way of expressing the role of the courts is that they resolve individual conflicts by interpreting and enforcing existing rules and laws. But in doing so, they may create law that plays an important role in the lives of far more people than the individuals who actually participated in the case.

Parties who want a court to resolve their dispute must satisfy *strict rules of access.*[89] Although any citizen may approach the legislature or the governor, courts have rules that limit access to them. Individuals must have "standing." This means the case must involve real controversies between two or more parties, and someone must have suffered real damage. Courts do not deal in hypothetical or imaginary controversies. In short, they do not play "what if" ("What if I hit this person? What will the court do?").

Courts must follow *strict procedural rules* that determine when and how to present facts and arguments.[90] These rules prevent the introduction of some evidence in a criminal case. For example, if police gather evidence through an illegal search, the court may not allow the prosecution to use that evidence.

Generally, a court's decisions affect only the cases that particular court is considering and not other cases before other courts.[91] However, a court's decision serves as **precedent** for parties in the future with a similar dispute.[92] For example, if a trial court rules that a city ordinance in one city is invalid, this does not invalidate all similar ordinances in other cities. At a later time, however, someone in another city may challenge a similar ordinance on similar legal grounds, in which case the earlier decision will serve as legal precedent for invalidating the ordinance in the second case. The court must evaluate each case separately and then decide whether earlier decisions apply to the present case.

The rulings of appellate and supreme courts serve as especially important precedents for future legal decisions. Under the principle of **stare decisis**—"to stand by that which was decided before"—courts must follow principles announced in former cases and diverge from these only when they can show good cause for doing so. In this way, appellate courts affect how trial courts make decisions; however, each case in a lower court might be affected slightly differently.

Courts also differ from other branches of government in that, to the extent possible, they seek to evaluate cases with **objectivity**.[93] Unlike governors and legislators, courts may not appear to be political in their decision making, even though political considerations might affect judges' decisions. Judges must base their decisions on the federal and state constitutions, statutes, and earlier court decisions. A court's decision may have unintended or even deliberate political consequences, but the law binds a court's decision-making process to a greater extent than in the executive and legislative branches.

Thus, courts differ from governors and legislators in the way they make decisions. They must maintain a passive role, enforce rules that restrict access to the courts, uphold strict rules of procedure, confine their decisions to the specifics of the cases before them, and maintain the appearance of objectivity. By doing this, courts help reinforce the legitimacy of their decisions and their place as the final arbitrators of conflict. This in turn reinforces the concept that the rule of law, not the rule of arbitrary actions by individuals, governs.

precedent
An earlier legal decision by a court that can be used to decide similar cases in the future

stare decisis
The principle that court decisions depend on previous rulings of other courts; the term is Latin for "to stand by that which was decided before"

objectivity
The appearance that courts make impartial decisions and not political ones

---

Understanding Impact The principles of precedent and stare decisis help courts be consistent in the way they apply the law and judge cases. Why does consistency in the judicial branch matter?

Conclusion

In the twenty-first century, the court system in Texas faces many challenges. Methods of selecting judges will continue to be controversial. Texas has a partisan election system but uses an "appointive-elective" process where the governor can fill any seat for district or appellate court that becomes vacant because of death or resignation, or any new district court position the legislature creates. Problems in the electoral process and issues of representativeness pose challenges for the Texas judiciary. Some change in process has occurred as as result of HB 5 which prohibited straight-ticket voting as of 2020.

Summary

LO: Distinguish between civil cases and criminal cases within the legal system.

Civil cases are those between individual citizens and involve the idea of responsibilities, not guilt. Criminal cases are those cases brought against individuals for violations of law—crimes against society. Any citizen may file a civil suit in court. Citizens who may face criminal prosecution can require allegations to be screened by a body that reviews criminal cases. These cases must go before a grand jury (as required by the U.S. Constitution). But it is becoming common for people to request a formal administrative hearing before a judge. In these hearings, the judge reviews the facts and decides whether enough evidence exists to try the case.

LO: Discuss judicial federalism.

Article 3 of the United States Constitution established the Supreme Court and gave Congress the authority to create other, lower federal courts. Article 6 of the U.S. Constitution makes federal law the supreme law of the land. Any direct conflicts between federal and state law must be resolved in favor of federal authority. States create their own courts. As a result, 50 separate jurisdictions have complete court systems that exist side by side with the federal courts. Federal courts hear cases involving federal laws, and state courts hear cases involving state laws.

LO: Explain the structure of state courts, including trial and appellate courts.

Most states provide for three levels of courts: trial courts, appellate courts, and a supreme court. Trial courts are local courts that hear cases; juries determine the outcome of the cases heard in the court. Appellate courts are higher-level courts that decide on points of law and not questions of guilt or innocence. Texas has several levels of trial courts and appellate courts. Trial courts include the justices of the peace, municipal courts, county courts, district courts, and special-purpose courts, such as probate, juvenile, and domestic relations courts. Texas has 14 intermediate appellate courts and 2 "supreme" appellate courts: 1 for civil cases (the Texas Supreme Court) and 1 for criminal cases (the Texas Court of Criminal Appeals).

LO: Describe methods of judicial selection.

The states use a variety of methods to select judges. These methods include appointment by the governor, election by legislature, partisan elections, nonpartisan elections, and selection based on merit. Some states have variations on these plans. The method of selection also varies between courts within some states. In short, no perfect system exists for selecting judges.

LO: Describe judicial selection in Texas, including the "appointive-elective" system.

In Texas, trial court judges are elected in partisan elections for four-year terms, and all appellate court judges are elected in partisan elections for six-year terms. The only exceptions to this are municipal court judges; the mayor or the city council usually appoint them. Texas has an appointive-elective system in which many judges gain their initial seat on the court by being appointed and later stand for election to retain the seat.

LO: Describe the challenges to the judiciary in Texas.

Problems in the electoral process and issues of representativeness pose challenges for the Texas judiciary. Many voters go to the election booth with scant knowledge about the qualifications of judicial candidates, and they often end up voting by name familiarity. Texas used to be one of nine states using straight-ticket voting, which allows a voter to vote for all candidates in a party by making a single mark. This method can affect the selection of qualified candidates. Although straight-ticket voting has been prohibited as of 2020, it is unclear how this change will affect the judiciary. Judicial elections are very costly for candidates. Campaign contributions from businesspeople, lawyers, and lobbyists call into question judicial impartiality. Gender and minority representation in the Texas judiciary is inconsistent with the state's population. There is a concern that a lack of representativeness may result in biased decisions.

LO: Describe ways in which judges are disciplined and removed.

Most states provide some system to remove judges for misconduct. Impeachment, a little-used and very political process, is provided for in 47 states, including Texas. Eight states allow for recall of judges by the voters. One state, New Hampshire, allows the governor to remove a judge after a hearing. In 17 states, the legislature can remove judges by a supermajority (most commonly two-thirds) vote. To date, 49 states have established judicial conduct commissions. Also, the method of removal of judges can depend on the level of the judgeship—for instance, trial judges versus appellate judges.

LO: Explain the courts' approach to decision making.

Courts evaluate disputes between individuals not involving policy questions and resolve them by interpreting and enforcing existing rules and laws. But in doing so they may create law that plays an important role in the lives of far more people than the individuals who actually participated in the case. Courts are governed by strict procedural rules that determine when and how facts and arguments can be presented.

Key Terms

appellate courts
appointive-elective system
dual court system
grand juries
information or an administrative
    hearing

magistrate functions
merit system, or Missouri system
name familiarity
nonpartisan election
objectivity
partisan election

petit juries
precedent
stare decisis
straight-ticket voting system
trial courts
trial de novo courts

Notes

[1] Herbert Jacob, "Courts: The Least Visible Branch," in *Politics in the American States*, 6th ed., ed. Virginia Gray and Herbert Jacob (Washington, D.C.: Congressional Quarterly Press, 1996), 254.

[2] Ibid.

[3] "The Differences between a Criminal Case and a Civil Case," https://www.findlaw.com/criminal/criminal-law-basics/the-differences-between-a-criminal-case-and-a-civil-case.html.

[4] Ibid.

[5] Office of Court Administration, *Annual Statistical Reports, Fiscal Year 2020*, http://www.txcourts.gov/statistics/annual-statistical-reports/.

[6] Interview with District Court Judge John Delaney, Brazos County Courthouse, November 1995.

[7] *Texas Code of Criminal Procedure*, arts. 19.01–20.22.

[8] Texas Family Code section 62.001(a).

[9] Herbert Jacob, "Courts: The Least Visible Branch," in *Politics in the American States*, 6th ed., ed. Virginia Gray and Herbert Jacob (Washington, D.C.: Congressional Quarterly Press, 1996), 253.

[10] Herbert Jacob, "Courts: The Least Visible Branch," in *Politics in the American States*, 6th ed., ed. Virginia Gray and Herbert Jacob (Washington, D.C.: Congressional Quarterly Press, 1996), 256–58.

[11] Texas State Law Library, "Small Claims Cases," updated March 15, 2022, https://guides.sll.texas.gov/small-claims (accessed March 21, 2022).

[12] Office of Court Administration, Texas Judicial Council, "FY 2020 Annual Statistical Report: Court-Level Trends," 2020, https://www.txcourts.gov/media/1451853/fy-20-annual-statistical-report_final_mar10_2021.pdf.

[13] Office of Court Administration, "Court Structure of Texas as of January 1, 2022," Texas Judicial Branch, https://www.txcourts.gov/media/1453418/court-structure-chart-january-2022.pdf.

[14] Texas Judicial Branch, "Court Structure of Texas," January 1, 2022, https://www.txcourts.gov/media/1453418/court-structure-chart-january-2022.pdf.

[15] Council of State Governments, *The Book of the States 2021* (Lexington, KY: Council of State Governments, 2022), Table 5.2; *Ballotopia*, "Intermediate Appellate Courts," https://ballotpedia.org/Intermediate_appellate_courts (accessed March 21, 2022).

[16] Council of State Governments, *The Book of the States 2021* (Lexington, KY: Council of State Governments, 2022), Table 5.2.

[17] Office of Court Administration, Texas Judiciary Council, "Court Structure of Texas," https://www.txcourts.gov/media/1453418/court-structure-chart-january-2022.pdf.

[18] Council of State Governments, *The Book of the States 2021* (Lexington, KY: Council of State Governments, 2022), Table 5.6.

[19] Delaware, New Jersey, Connecticut, Massachusetts, Maryland, New Hampshire, New York, and Rhode Island have some judges who are appointed by the governor and can be removed only for cause. See Herbert Jacob, "Courts: The Least Visible Branch," in *Politics in the American States*, 6th ed., ed. Virginia Gray and Herbert Jacob (Washington, D.C.: Congressional Quarterly Press, 1996), 268, Table 7.2. Also see *The Book of the States 1994–1995*, 190–93, Table 4.4. There are some slight variations between the Jacob table and the table in *The Book of the States*. This is probably due to interpretations by the

writers. Because of minor variations among states, classification differences are possible. Updated information up to 2021 is from *The Book of the States 2021,* Table 5.6.

20 Ballotpedia, "Judicial Selection in the States," https://ballotpedia.org/Judicial_selection_in_the_states (accessed March 23, 2022).

21 Herbert Jacob, "The Effect of Institutional Differences in the Recruitment Process: The Case of State Judges," *Journal of Public Law* 33, no. 113 (1964): 104–19.

22 Kimberly C. Petillo, "The Untouchables: The Impact of South Carolina's New Judicial Selection System on the South Carolina Supreme Court, 1997–2003," *Albany Law Review* 67 (2004): 937–38, https://web.archive.org/web/20120113203701/http://www.albanylawreview.org/archives/67/3/SouthCarolinaHighCourtStudy.pdf (accessed April 10, 2016).

23 Ibid.

24 This occurred for a number of reasons. Matthew J. Streb writes that "Scholars have put forth several reasons behind the surge in state-elected judiciaries, including concern over an independent judiciary after the Supreme Court's controversial ruling in *Marbury v. Madison*, resistance to English common law, imitation by the states, the fact that impeachment was difficult to enact, the belief that judges at the local level should be responsive to their communities, and the legal profession's belief that the judiciary needed more independence from state legislatures" (Matthew J. Streb, "The Study of Judicial Elections," in *Running for Judge: The Rising Political, Financial, and Legal Stakes of Judicial Elections*, ed. Matthew J. Streb [New York: New York University Press, 2007], 9).

25 Ibid.

26 Matthew J. Streb, "The Study of Judicial Elections," in *Running for Judge: The Rising Political, Financial, and Legal Stakes of Judicial Elections*, ed. Matthew J. Streb (New York: New York University Press, 2007), 10.

27 Michael DeBow et al., "The Case for Partisan Judicial Elections," January 1, 2003, The Federalist Society for Law & Public Policy Studies, https://fedsoc.org/commentary/publications/the-case-for-partisan-judicial-elections (accessed March 25, 2022).

28 Ballotpedia, "Assisted Appointment (judicial selection)," https://ballotpedia.org/Assisted_appointment_(judicial_selection) (accessed March 25, 2022).

29 Bradley Canon, "The Impact of Formal Selection Processes on Characteristics of Judges Reconsidered," *Law and Society Review* 13 (May 1972): 570–93.

30 Richard Watson and Rondal G. Downing, *Politics of the Bench and Bar: Judicial Selection under the Missouri Nonpartisan Court Plan* (New York: Wiley, 1969).

31 Thomas R. Dye, *Politics in States and Communities*, 8th ed. (New York: Pearson, 1994), 236.

32 William Jenkins, "Retention Elections: Who Wins When No One Loses," *Judicature* 61 (1977): 78–86; R. D. Gill, "Beyond High Hopes and Unmet Expectations: Judicial Selection Reforms in the States," *Judicature* 96 (2013): 278–95.

33 William K. Hall and Larry T. Aspen, "What Twenty Years of Judicial Retention and Elections Have Told Us," *Judicature* 70 (1987): 340–47.

34 Craig F. Emmert and Henry R. Glick, "The Selection of Supreme Court Judges," *American Politics Quarterly* 19 (October 1988): 444–65.

35 https://capitol.texas.gov/BillLookup/History.aspx?LegSess=86R&Bill=HB4504 (accessed March 25, 2022).

36 Jolie McCullough, "Gov. Abbott Signs Bill to Eliminate Straight-Ticket Voting Beginning in 2020," *Texas Tribune,* June 1, 2017, https://www.texastribune.org/2017/06/01/texas-gov-greg-abbott-signs-bill-eliminate-straight-ticket-voting/ (accessed March 25, 2022).

37 Matthew J. Streb, "The Study of Judicial Elections," 2007, https://www.academia.edu/1389795/The_Study_of_Judicial_Elections.

38 "Partisan Elections of Judges," Ballotpedia, https://ballotpedia.org/Partisan_election_of_judges.

39 Douglas Keith, Patrick Berry, and Eric Valasco, *The Politics of Judicial Elections 2017–2018: How Dark Money, Interest Groups, and Big Donors Shape State High Courts*, Brennan Center for Justice at New York University School of Law, https://www.brennancenter.org/sites/default/files/2019-12/2019_11_Politics%20of%20Judicial%20Elections_FINAL.pdf.

40 "Citizens United Explained," Brennan Center for Justice, https://www.brennancenter.org/our-work/research-reports/citizens-united-explained.

41 "Salem Abraham," *Bloomberg*, https://www.bloomberg.com/profile/person/15919538.

42 Emma Platoff, "Speaking Statistically, This GOP Donor Wants to Convince You That Money Buys Justice in Texas," *Texas Tribune*, February 24, 2020, https://www.texastribune.org/2020/02/24/wealthy-panhandle-financier-wants-change-way-texas-elects-judges/.

43 "Profile of Appellate and Trial Judges as of September 1, 2021," Texas Judicial Branch, https://www.txcourts.gov/media/1452755/judge-profile-september-2021.pdf.

44 Laila Robbins, Alicia Bannon, and Malia Reddick, *State Supreme Court Diversity,* Brennan Center of Justice at New York University School of Law, July 23, 2019, https://www.brennancenter.org/our-work/research-reports/state-supreme-court-diversity.

45 "Jeff Brown," Follow the Money, https://www.followthemoney.org/entity-details?eid=6679625.

46 "Kathy Cheng," Follow the Money, https://www.followthemoney.org/entity-details?eid=16072592&default=candidate.

47 Francesco Ferraro, "Ajudication and Expectations: Bentham on the Role of Judges," *Utilitas* 25, no. 2 (2013): 140–60; James

Gibson, *Electing Judges: The Surprising Effects of Campaigning on Judicial Legitimacy*, Chicago Studies in American Politics (Chicago, IL: Chicago University Press, 2012).

[48] National Conference of State Legislatures, "Straight Ticket Voting States," http://www.ncsl.org/research/elections-and-campaigns/straight-ticket-voting.aspx (accessed March 5, 2020).

[49] Jolie McCullough, "Gov. Abbott Signs Bill to Eliminate Straight-Ticket Voting Beginning in 2020," *Texas Tribune,* June 1, 2017, https://www.texastribune.org/2017/06/01/texas-gov-greg-abbott-signs-bill-eliminate-straight-ticket-voting/.

[50] National Conference of State Legislatures, "Straight Ticket Voting States," http://www.ncsl.org/research/elections-and-campaigns/straight-ticket-voting.aspx (accessed March 5, 2020).

[51] Ballotpedia, https://ballotpedia.org/Texas_Supreme_Court_elections,_2018 (accessed March 5, 2020); Vote Smart, https://justfacts.votesmart.org/ (accessed March 5, 2020).

[52] Ballotpedia, https://ballotpedia.org/Texas_Supreme_Court_elections (accessed March 25, 2022).

[53] Billy Corriher, "Big Business Taking over State Supreme Courts: How Campaign Contributions to Judges Tip the Scales Against Individuals," Center for American Progress, August 2012, https://www.americanprogress.org/wp-content/uploads/issues/2012/08/pdf/statecourts.pdf; Billy Corriher, "Big Business Is Still Dominating State Supreme Courts," Center for American Progress, September 2016, https://www.americanprogress.org/issues/courts/reports/2016/09/01/143420/big-business-is-still-dominating-state-supreme-courts/ (accessed March 5, 2020).

[54] Texans for Public Justice, "Courtroom Contributions Stain Supreme Court Campaigns," http://info.tpj.org/reports/courtroomcontributions/courtroomcontributions.pdf.

[55] Texans for Public Justice, "Billable Ours: Texas Endures Another Attorney Financed Supreme Court Race," http://info.tpj.org/reports/supremes06/supremes06.pdf.

[56] Emma Platoff, "Advocates Have Long Tried to Change Judicial Selection in Texas. Is Dan Patrick Their Newest Obstacle?," *Texas Tribune,* January 15, 2020, https://www.texastribune.org/2020/01/15/judicial-selection-reform-obstacle-dan-patrick/; Emma Platoff, "State Leaders Again Want to Review How Texas Elects Judges. Will They End Partisan Judicial Elections?," *Texas Tribune,* July 15, 2019, https://www.texastribune.org/2019/07/15/texas-partisan-judicial-elections-reform-abbott-support/ (accessed March 5, 2020); https://www.txcourts.gov/media/1450219/201230_tcjs-final-report_compressed.pdf.

[57] See, for example, Sherrilyn A. Ifill, "Judging the Judges: Racial Diversity and Representation on State Trial Courts," *Boston College Law Review* 39, no. 1 (1998), http://lawdigitalcommons.bc.edu/bclr/vol39/iss1/3.

[58] U.S. Census Bureau, "QuickFacts: Texas," https://www.census.gov/quickfacts/TX (accessed March 25, 2022).

[59] Texas Judicial Branch, Office of Court Administration, "Profile of Appellate and Trial Judges as of September 1, 2021," https://www.txcourts.gov/media/1452755/judge-profile-september-2021.pdf.

[60] Sherrilyn A. Ifill, "Judging the Judges: Racial Diversity and Representation on State Trial Courts," *Boston College Law Review* 39, no. 1 (1998), http://lawdigitalcommons.bc.edu/bclr/vol39/iss1/3.

[61] Texas Judicial Branch, Office of Court Administration, "Profile of Appellate and Trial Judges."

[62] Texas Office of Court Administration, "Texas Supreme Court," http://www.txcourts.gov/supreme/ (three female justices 2001–2005).

[63] Texas Judicial Branch, Office of Court Administration. "Profile of Appellate and Trial Judges as of September 1, 2021," https://www.txcourts.gov/media/1452755/judge-profile-september-2021.pdf.

[64] Robert B. Gilbreath and D. Todd Smith, "An Interview with Former Justice Raul A. Gonzalez," *The Appellate Advocate* XVII, no. 1 (Summer 2004): 25–33, http://www.hptylaw.com/media/article/24_rob.pdf.

[65] Ibid.

[66] Robert B. Gilbreath and D. Todd Smith, "An Interview with Former Justice Raul A. Gonzalez," *The Appellate Advocate* XVII, no. 1 (Summer 2004): 25–33, http://www.hptylaw.com/media/article/24_rob.pdf; Jamail Center for Legal Research, "Raul A. Gonzalez, Jr. (b. 1940)," in *Justices of Texas 1836–1986*. Tarlton Law Library, University of Texas School of Law, https://tarlton.law.utexas.edu/justices/profile/view/38.

[67] Jamail Center for Legal Research, "Raul A. Gonzalez, Jr. (b. 1940)," in *Justices of Texas 1836–1986*. Tarlton Law Library, University of Texas School of Law, https://tarlton.law.utexas.edu/justices/profile/view/38.

[68] Ibid.

[69] Ibid.

[70] Robert B. Gilbreath and D. Todd Smith, "An Interview with Former Justice Raul A. Gonzalez," *The Appellate Advocate* XVII, no. 1 (Summer 2004): 25–33, http://www.hptylaw.com/media/article/24_rob.pdf.

[71] Ibid.

[72] Tamar Lewin, "Pennzoil-Texaco Fight Raised Key Questions," *The New York Times*, December 19, 1987, http://www.nytimes.com/1987/12/19/business/pennzoil-texaco-fight-raised-key-questions.html?pagewanted=all.

[73] Mike Wallace, "Is Justice for Sale in Texas?" [Television Broadcast], *60 Minutes*, 1987, CBS Broadcasting. Retrieved from a copy of the broadcast uploaded to YouTube: [Hawthorne, Blake] (2015, May 6), 1987 60 Minutes Is

Justice For Sale in Texas. [Video File], https://www.youtube.com/watch?v=ob3_-Ilf6Vw.

[74] Robert B. Gilbreath and D. Todd Smith, "An Interview with Former Justice Raul A. Gonzalez," *The Appellate Advocate* XVII, no. 1 (Summer 2004): 25–33, http://www.hptylaw.com/media/article/24_rob.pdf.

[75] Jamail Center for Legal Research, "Raul A. Gonzalez, Jr. (b. 1940)," in *Justices of Texas 1836–1986*. Tarlton Law Library, University of Texas School of Law, https://tarlton.law.utexas.edu/justices/profile/view/38.

[76] Texas Judicial Branch, Office of Court Administration. "Profile of Appellate and Trial Judges As of September 1, 2021," https://www.txcourts.gov/media/1452755/judge-profile-september-2021.pdf.

[77] Ibid.

[78] U.S. Census Bureau, "QuickFacts: Texas," https://www.census.gov/quickfacts/TX (accessed March 25, 2022).

[79] Ibid.

[80] Ibid.

[81] Texas Judicial Branch, Office of Court Administration. "Profile of Appellate and Trial Judges As of September 1, 2021," https://www.txcourts.gov/media/1452755/judge-profile-september-2021.pdf.

[82] University of Texas at Austin, Liberal Arts Instructional Technology Services, "Characteristics of the Judiciary," https://web.archive.org/web/20170218054752/http://www.laits.utexas.edu/txp_media/html/just/0403.html (last updated September 6, 2016).

[83] National Center for State Courts, "Methods of Judicial Selection: Removal of Judges," https://web.archive.org/web/20211206073359/http://judicialselection.com/judicial_selection/methods/removal_of_judges.cfm?state (accessed March 25, 2022).

[84] The Council of State Governments, *The Book of the States 2021*, Table 5.8, https://issuu.com/csg.publications/docs/bos_2021_issuu (accessed March 25, 2022).

[85] Commission on Judicial Conduct, *Annual Report*, 1994 (Austin: Commission on Judicial Conduct, State of Texas, 1994); "TRIBPEDIA: State Commission on Judicial Conduct," *Texas Tribune*, https://www.texastribune.org/tribpedia/state-commission-on-judicial-conduct/about/ (accessed September 6, 2016).

[86] Diane Jennings, "State Commission on Judicial Conduct Has the Job of Judging Texas' Judges," *Dallas Morning News*, December 14, 2009 (updated November 26, 2010).

[87] Texas State Commission on Judicial Conduct, *Annual Report for Fiscal Year 2021*, pp. 21 and 24, http://www.scjc.texas.gov/media/46863/scjc-2021-annual-report.pdf (accessed March 25, 2022).

[88] Thomas R. Dye, *Politics in States and Communities*, 8th ed. (New York: Pearson, 1994), 227.

[89] Thomas R. Dye, *Politics in States and Communities*, 8th ed. (New York: Pearson, 1994).

[90] Ibid.

[91] Ibid.

[92] "Precedent," https://www.law.cornell.edu/wex/precedent.

[93] Thomas R. Dye, *Politics in States and Communities*, 8th ed. (New York: Pearson, 1994), 228.

CHAPTER 6

The Criminal Justice System in Texas

Texas Learning Outcome

- Analyze issues and policies in Texas.

Texans' attitudes toward crime and punishment, in many ways, reflect a tradition of "frontier justice," which arose when no formal legal system was in place and people took justice into their own hands. Over time, this informal system of justice has been transformed by Texas's current constitution, amendments to it, and other statutory changes enacted by the legislature into a complex, multilevel court system to address both criminal and civil matters (see Chapter 5). The justice system provides for public safety and the common good, not only through the courts but also through the Department of Public Safety, which enforces the law, and the Department of Criminal Justice, which houses and supervises over half a million inmates and parolees, as well as a variety of other local law enforcement agencies.[1] Texas's justice system is large and, from the perspective of the average Texan, can be difficult to navigate.

Texas's criminal justice system is shaped by the sophisticated and challenging nature of providing justice as well as the complicated labyrinth of Texas's multilevel court system. Any large system of this type will at times face difficulty satisfying the underlying, simple philosophy held by most citizens of the state that justice should be swift and equitable. Individuals interact with the criminal justice system in a myriad of ways and for equally numerous reasons. For example, people in Texas might interact with the law enforcement community to report a crime or be subject to policing if suspected of committing one. Others might be involved with the court system to answer criminal charges, to address personal family matters, to settle financial questions arising from economic disputes between individuals or businesses, or to resolve dilemmas over discrimination or even political contests. Citizens expect government to pursue justice on behalf of victims when crimes have been committed, just as they expect judges and juries to deliver fair rulings after weighing arguments and considering evidence and the law. There are, however, many criticisms leveled at Texas's criminal justice system (aside from the difficulty citizens face as they seek to navigate the complex, fragmented, and overlapping jurisdictions within it). These include issues with policing, the number and complexity of laws, the high cost of legal assistance, sentencing, and the perception that justice may not be equal for all.

This chapter expands on the information covered in Chapter 5 through a deeper exploration of the concept of law and a further discussion of punishment and problems associated with the processes of delivering justice in Texas. It examines the state's various policing agencies and how they enforce the law and implement the findings of juries and judges on behalf of citizens. Attention is given to the legal procedures associated with both criminal and civil trials and how Texas deals with juvenile offenders. The chapter also examines the concepts of correction and rehabilitation in Texas—including incarceration, parole, and probation—to understand how the criminal justice system's policies and procedures impact justice and how justice is perceived by society. The chapter concludes with a look at issues with the criminal justice system raised by reformers and whether and how Texas has attempted to deal with them.

Chapter Learning Objectives

- Discuss crime and punishment in Texas.

- Recall the differences between criminal and civil law, and explain criminal justice policy in Texas.

- Describe the state of Texas's juvenile justice system and its procedures.

- Explain the state of Texas's correction system, including its approach to rehabilitation and use of the death penalty.

- Describe the challenges the state of Texas faces in its criminal justice system.

Elements of the Criminal Justice System

Learning Objective: Discuss crime and punishment in Texas.

Learning Objective: Recall the differences between criminal and civil law, and explain criminal justice policy in Texas.

In Texas, as elsewhere, the criminal justice system serves many broad purposes, including promoting public safety, punishing criminal activity, recompensing victims, deterring future criminal action, and rehabilitating offenders so they do not break the law again upon returning to society. The many elements of that system include the courts, policies enacted by the legislature, and correctional facilities and programs. For many individuals, their first (and perhaps only) point of contact with the criminal justice system is through law enforcement or police.

Law Enforcement and Policing

According to the federal Bureau of Justice Statistics (BJS), law enforcement preserves order and ensures compliance with the law, primarily through "the activities of prevention, detection, and investigation of crime and the apprehension of criminals."[2] Texas law enforcement agencies operate at the state, county, and municipal levels as well as in other special jurisdictions, and law enforcement officers include highway patrol troopers, sheriffs, city police officers, campus police officers, and many others.

The Texas Department of Public Safety (DPS) is the chief law enforcement agency in the state. It is the fourth-largest such agency in the United States (after the California Highway Patrol, the New York State Police, and the Pennsylvania State Police) in terms of the number of full-time, sworn personnel.[3] DPS is overseen by the Public Safety Commission, whose five members are appointed by the governor. DPS divisions include the Texas Highway Patrol (which is primarily responsible for supervising vehicular traffic but whose troopers are fully authorized to enforce criminal law throughout the state), the Criminal Investigations Division, the Driver License Division, the Division of Emergency Management, and the Texas Rangers, among others.[4] In addition to coordinating border security, the Texas Rangers investigate major crimes as well as serial and unsolved crimes, charges of public corruption, and shootings involving police officers.[5]

The primary law enforcement agency at the county level is the County Sheriff's Office. As required by the state constitution (Article V, Section 23), each of Texas's 254 counties has a sheriff who is elected by county voters to a four-year term. Additional staff in the sheriff's office might include deputies, reserve deputies, guards, and clerks.[6] While these officers carry out "traditional law enforcement functions," such as making traffic stops, responding to calls for assistance, and patrolling, sheriff's office personnel also provide security for courthouses, serve warrants and other official papers, and run county jails.[7] Although the sheriff's office has authority over the entire county, sheriffs typically do not operate in incorporated areas or within city limits where municipal police departments have jurisdiction.[8]

Texas also has a considerable number of local police departments, most of which are operated by city governments. Some of these, including the Houston, Dallas, and San Antonio police departments, are among the largest in the nation in terms of number of sworn officers.[9] Texas law allows municipalities to establish a police force to maintain public safety, police officers are appointed by the governing body of the city or municipality, and they perform many of the same law enforcement functions as do sheriffs' offices.[10]

Aside from these state and local agencies, additional agencies provide law enforcement for particular jurisdictions or geographic areas. These special jurisdictions include public school districts, public colleges and universities, other state-owned buildings, natural resources (such as parks and wildlife), and transportation systems (including airports, mass transit, and port facilities), all of which may have their own police force.[11]

Of course, police and other law enforcement agents could not do their jobs without an established set of laws to enforce. Thus, the state legislature, in its law-making capacity, also plays an important role in the criminal justice system. By enacting and amending state law or code, legislators not only lay out the rules

A law enforcement agent stands guard at the Alamo, one of Texas's most important historical sites.

Richard Nowitz/National Geographic Creative/Alamy Stock Photo

of the state but also specify what constitutes a rule violation, the punishment that will be applied, and the duties law enforcement and the courts have when they address such rule violations.

Criminal Law and Civil Law

The function of courts is to hear matters of legal controversy and deliver justice to the parties involved. In criminal cases, the parties include a government attorney who prosecutes a defendant and seeks punishment on behalf of society or a victim. The government must prove the defendant is guilty of having committed the alleged offense. The defendant enters a plea and generally seeks to be found "not guilty."[12] **Criminal law** applies in cases involving a violation of the **Texas Penal Code,** the statutory law that establishes "a system of prohibitions, penalties, and correctional measures to deal with conduct that unjustifiably and inexcusably causes or threatens harm to those individual or public interests for which state protection is appropriate."[13] The penal code lists and defines the offenses and **graded penalties** associated with offenses against a person, family, society, or public office, in addition to providing guidance for law enforcement to protect against arbitrary treatment of people suspected, accused, or convicted of offenses.

Equally important, however, is the **Texas Code of Criminal Procedure,** which describes the rules associated with the criminal justice process in Texas. Created by the Texas Supreme Court, this code contains specific rights afforded the accused during trial, sentencing, and punishment phases, and details the procedures that must be followed by government representatives taking part in these processes. Anyone who has read the U.S. Constitution would find the first chapter of the Texas Code of Criminal Procedure familiar; there are many similarities to the Bill of Rights. For example, Article 1.04 protects the accused's right to due process, and Article 1.06, like the Fourth Amendment, guarantees Texans the expectation of privacy in their person, papers, and homes, free from governmental intrusion without a search warrant. The Texas Penal Code and the Code of Criminal Procedure together form the framework for delivering justice in criminal trials in Texas.

The Texas Penal Code grades offenses, based on severity, into two categories: felonies and misdemeanors. **Felony** offenses are divided into five categories that range from the most serious: capital felonies; first-, second-, and third-degree felonies; and state jail felonies. Felony offenses carry penalties ranging from death (for capital offenses) to a minimum of 180 days' confinement in jail (for state jail felonies). **Misdemeanors** are considered less serious crimes, punishable by fine, incarceration, or both. Table 6.1 lists the categories of offenses from the Texas Penal Code, examples of the offenses, and the typical punishment imposed for a guilty verdict.

Because Texas uses enhanced sentencing for repeat and habitual offenders, the accused's prior convictions (both felonies and misdemeanors) can play a major role when a judge or jury imposes punishment. The practice of **enhanced punishment,** applied to defendants who have been convicted previously, involves elevating the charges and increasing the penalty to that associated with the next most serious crime. For example, in 2020, Robert Jade Lopez-Parker, a 47-year-old man, was sentenced to a 99-year prison sentence for sexually assaulting a 54-year-old woman with disabilities in Lubbock. Enhanced punishment was

---

criminal law

Statutory law that defines both the violation and the penalty the state will seek to have imposed upon the defendant

Texas Penal Code

The statutory law that defines criminal offenses and punishments in Texas

graded penalties

Punishments that differ based upon the seriousness of the crime

Texas Code of Criminal Procedure

The rules created by the Texas Supreme Court to govern the proceedings of trials in Texas

felony

A serious criminal offense, punishable by death or incarceration

misdemeanor

Less serious criminal offense, punishable by fine, incarceration, or both fine and incarceration

enhanced punishment

The application of the next most serious penalty for repeat offenders

TABLE 6.1

Categories of Crime and Maximum Punishments

Offense	Example	Maximum Punishment
Capital Felony	Murder of a first-responder; murder of a child under the age of 10; murder for hire; murder during the commission of another crime; mass murder	Life imprisonment without the possibility of parole OR execution
First-Degree Felony	Murder; aggravated sexual assault; theft of $300,000+; sale of more than 4 grams of heroin or cocaine	5–99 years imprisonment; $10,000 fine
Second-Degree Felony	Manslaughter; sexual assault; arson; robbery; theft of $150,000+	2–20 years imprisonment; $10,000 fine
Third-Degree Felony	Kidnapping; tampering with consumer products; theft of $30,000+; drive-by shootings	2–10 years imprisonment; $10,000 fine
State Jail Felony	Criminally negligent homicide; auto theft; theft of $2,500+; forgery; credit or debit card abuse	180 days to 2 years in jail; $10,000 fine
Class A Misdemeanor	Public lewdness; assault; burglary of a vehicle; theft of $750+; theft of cable service	1 year in jail; $4,000 fine
Class B Misdemeanor	DUI; indecent exposure; theft of over $100; prostitution;	180 days in jail; $2,000 fine
Class C Misdemeanor	Gambling; aiding suicide; leaving a child unattended in a vehicle; theft of less than $100; smoking in a public elevator; public intoxication	$500 fine

Source: Texas Penal Code, https://statutes.capitol.texas.gov/?link=PE, http://www.statutes.legis.state.tx.us/docs/PE/htm/PE.12.htm.

applied to his sentence when prosecutors entered into evidence a previous sexual assault incident and his subsequent failure to register previously as a sex offender.[14] Laws that allow harsher punishment for repeat or habitual offenders have been called recidivist statutes, habitual offender laws, or three-strikes laws. **Recidivism** refers to the rate at which criminal offenders commit another crime after they leave the state's custody. Though the intent of recidivist statutes is certainly to target and discourage repeat offenders,[15] enhanced punishment is typically reserved for violent offenders or serious offenses involving minors. However, Texas does not require any of an individual's prior convictions to be violent in order for enhanced punishment to apply.[16] Some reformers have argued that these types of laws have led to excessive or disproportionate sentencing. Marc Mauer of the Sentencing Project argues that this excessive sentencing is financially wasteful. He argues that the money that pays for long sentences should be diverted to policing, drug treatment, and other projects that might decrease crime.[17]

Texas also uses mandatory minimum sentences. The state legislature has passed laws dictating a fixed amount of time in prison for individuals convicted of certain crimes. Supporters of mandatory minimums argue that these compulsory sentences increase public safety by keeping criminals off the streets for

recidivism
The rate at which criminal offenders commit crime after they leave the state's custody

longer periods of time and by discouraging others from committing similar crimes. However, mandatory minimums have been controversial because they take discretion away from judges, who cannot consider other factors (such as an offender's prior record or mitigating circumstances) in these cases, and because they often lead to sentences that some consider to be out of proportion to the crime committed.[18] Still, mandatory minimums, in certain situations, remain popular. In 2019, Governor Abbott signed into law HB 2502, a bipartisan bill that established a mandatory minimum of a 120-day prison sentence for anyone who receives probation for failing to stop and aid someone in a hit-and-run car accident.[19] It is worth noting that Texas has fewer mandatory minimums than do a lot of other states (including large, populous states like California and Florida).

The vast majority of crime in Texas involves property. As part of the FBI's Uniform Crime Reporting program, DPS collects data on the number of certain "index crimes" reported across the state. Of the 782,974 index crimes reported in Texas in 2020, property crimes (such as burglary and motor vehicle theft) made up 83.3 percent. Violent crime, including murder, rape, and aggravated assault, represented 16.7 percent of reported index crimes in 2020. Overall, the total number of index offenses decreased 2.8 percent from 2019 to 2020.[20]

Aside from the sheer volume of crimes reported, another way to analyze trends is by looking at the crime rate. This statistic is based on population and is defined as the number of crimes committed for every 100,000 residents. The Texas crime rate for 2020 was calculated as 2,666.7 offenses per 100,000 persons.[21] This represented a 4.0 percent decrease from 2019.

civil law

Defines private relationships as well as financial matters or damages to property committed by businesses or other individuals to a person

Civil law has to do with private relationships (rather than violations of the penal code) and can address financial matters, including financial wrongs that citizens or businesses might commit against others. In civil cases, the party who claims to have been harmed by another's conduct and seeks a remedy is referred to as the petitioner or plaintiff. The other party, who is being sued by the plaintiff, is called a respondent or defendant. In civil trials, the plaintiff must prove that the defendant has caused the plaintiff harm.[22] The respondent answers the charges of harm and seeks to be found "not responsible." Just as criminal cases are governed by the Texas Code of Criminal Procedure, civil cases are governed by the Texas Rules of Civil Procedure.

Civil law cases generally fall into one of four categories: family law, tort law, contract law, and property law.[23] Common examples of family law cases decided in civil court are divorces and child custody cases. Another type of civil case, involving tort law, may arise when an individual files suit against another individual or a corporation. An example would be if an individual alleged that a product manufactured by a corporation had caused the individual harm. Contract law includes things like property owner-tenant disputes and other contractual disagreements. For example, if a tenant fails to pay rent or violates the terms of the lease in some other manner, the landlord can serve notice to the tenant to vacate the property. If the tenant fails to vacate, the property owner can file for eviction in the local justice court.[24]

Depending on the amount of money or the value of property in dispute, there may be multiple options for filing suit because of overlapping jurisdiction of justice, county, and district courts (see Chapter 5, Figures 5.1, 5.2, and 5.3). For example, in matters involving $200 to $10,000, a suit may be filed in either

Focus On

Navigating the Criminal Justice System in Spanish

For most people, navigating the criminal justice system is intimidating even without the presence of a language barrier. Many Spanish-speaking Texans do not speak English well enough to easily interface with law enforcement and may find it difficult to understand the process or to be understood, especially in court proceedings. Therefore, they depend on interpreters (who work with signed or spoken languages) and translators (who work with written language).[25]

In *Miranda v. Arizona* (1966), the U.S. Supreme Court made it standard operating procedure for law enforcement to inform individuals of their rights (specifically, the right to speak with a lawyer and avoid self-incrimination) when they are in police custody or being interrogated.

A court of law.

ZUMA Press, Inc./Alamy Stock Photo

This instruction is called the Miranda warning.[26] In Texas, Spanish-speaking individuals typically have their Miranda warning read to them in Spanish. In addition, they may be given a card to read with a Spanish-language translation of the Miranda warning printed on it.[27] However, there is no universally agreed-upon Miranda translation (in fact, the Supreme Court did not provide exact wording for the English version either), and different translations have been found to vary considerably. Cases have been overturned on the grounds that the accused did not have a proper understanding of their rights. As a result, in 2016 the American Bar Association recommended that a standardized Spanish Miranda translation be developed and used nationwide.[28]

Texas law also provides for the use of interpreters in civil and criminal court proceedings. If it is determined that either a party to the proceeding (such as the defendant) or a witness "can hear but does not comprehend or communicate in English," the court will appoint an interpreter for that individual.[29] Interpreters must be licensed to provide real-time, verbatim translations of court proceedings, and they must "give an oath or affirmation to make a true translation."[30]

Critical Thinking Questions

1. In what way does communicating through an interpreter allow individuals to participate effectively in legal proceedings? What are the potential pitfalls?
2. What are the possible positive and negative impacts of a standardized Miranda translation in Spanish?

---

justice, county, or district court. Moreover, two or more district courts may overlap in terms of the geographic area over which they have jurisdiction, and many courts hear both civil and criminal cases. However, patterns have emerged in terms of the kind of case typically filed in a given court. In 2020 the vast majority of family cases were heard in district courts. Debt cases tended to be handled by justice courts.[31]

It is important to note that civil cases can follow from criminal cases. Namely, a guilty verdict in a criminal trial may lead to a subsequent civil trial wherein monetary damages are awarded to a plaintiff. For instance, an individual may be charged with and convicted of assault in a criminal proceeding. The victim of the assault may then seek damages, via a civil proceeding, for medical bills as well as pain and suffering.

burden of proof

The obligation associated with providing evidence sufficient to support the assertion or claim made by the individual bringing suit in a court of law

exculpatory evidence

Material evidence that could assist the accused in proving that they were innocent of the offense charged

Aside from the differences described previously, there are also differences between criminal and civil law in terms of proving a case in court. The standard for providing evidence in support of an argument is called the **burden of proof.** The burden of proof in civil matters requires that the party bringing suit persuade the judge (or in some cases a jury) by only a "preponderance of evidence" in order to prevail. In criminal law, the standard of proof is much higher, but that is because the stakes are higher. The government, after charging an individual with a criminal offense, is required to provide sufficient evidence that demonstrates to a judge or jury "beyond a reasonable doubt" that the individual being accused actually committed the crime. Whereas the plaintiff must prove that the defendant caused the plaintiff harm in a civil trial, in criminal trials, the burden of proving guilt rests on the state. In addition, the rules associated with providing evidence are different for criminal and civil trials. Because the state has significant resources at its disposal, it is required to share with the defense any information or evidence that could assist the accused. The Brady Rule, established by a 1963 U.S. Supreme Court decision, requires the government to disclose to the accused any **exculpatory evidence** that could materially affect the judge's or jury's determination of guilt.[32]

CORE OBJECTIVE

Communicating Effectively . . .

Explain the difference between criminal and civil law, including how the standard of proof differs for each. Provide an example of each type of case.

Criminal Justice Policy

Texas has a reputation as a "tough on crime" state. That reputation is well deserved. The strictness of Texas's criminal justice policies is reflected in the state's incarceration or imprisonment rate. The imprisonment rate is the number of prisoners with longer than one-year sentences who are under the jurisdiction of state and federal correctional authorities, per 100,000 residents. According to the Bureau of Justice Statistics, Texas's imprisonment rate in 2020 was 455, down significantly from 529 the prior year. COVID was primarily responsible for the drop, since the pandemic delayed both trials and sentencing. Texas's rate was fifth highest of all states. At the other end of the spectrum, Massachusetts's rate was lowest at 103.[33] These data indicate that, as a percentage of population, Texas locks up more of its residents than most other states do.

However, Texas's incarceration rate is high in part because the state's crime rate is high. Texas had the sixteenth-highest violent crime rate in the country in 2019.[34] As shown in Table 6.1, violent crimes are typically felonies and carry longer prison sentences. Therefore, a high violent crime rate would be expected to result in a high incarceration rate.

Despite the state's reputation as "tough on crime," Texas has recently witnessed some fairly significant reform efforts and garnered national attention as a leading criminal justice reform state. These reforms included increased use of drug courts (which channel nonviolent drug offenders into treatment programs rather than jail), changes to its juvenile justice system, and the shutting down of prisons.[35] Perhaps surprisingly, these reforms have been supported by conservative Republicans, such as former governor Rick Perry and state legislator Jerry Madden, as well as conservative groups such as the Texas Public Policy Foundation (whose "Right on Crime" initiative led by Marc Levin has addressed issues such as overcriminalization, civil asset forfeiture, and policing and prison reform) and the Texas Association of Business. These reformers were allied with Democrats, including state senators John Whitmire and Rodney Ellis, both strong proponents of prison reform. Although more-elevated motives are certainly at play (namely, concern about the dignity of individuals and the impact of excessive sentencing and high incarceration rates on families and communities), conservative reformers have noticed that high incarceration rates carries a daunting price tag for state taxpayers and negatively impacts labor markets. After the 86th Legislature failed to pass pivotal legislation in 2019, several Republican and Democratic legislators established the Criminal Justice Reform Caucus to examine potential legislation for the 87th Legislature in 2021. However, little was achieved. Several bipartisan bills in the Texas House were later tabled in the Texas Senate.[36]

> **Understanding Impact** The incarceration rate in Texas is slowly but steadily decreasing. As people reenter civil society after serving their sentences, what problems and hurdles will they face? What programs should the state establish? What are some ways that you might be able to help those recently released from prison?

Juvenile Justice

Learning Objective: Describe the state of Texas's juvenile justice system and its procedures.

As of 2021, 25.5 percent of the Texas population was under 18 years of age.[37] Both state and federal law in the United States treat juveniles differently from adults. Citizens are considered juveniles until they reach the so-called age of majority, which in Texas is age 17 for civil and criminal responsibility before the law.[38] "Juvenile justice" applies not only to those minors charged with civil or criminal wrongdoing but also to those who, through no fault of their own, are wards of the state.

Government's Duties to Minors

Texas state and local governments are charged with at least three general legal duties in cases involving minors. The first is **in loco parentis,** which means that the state must act in the place of the parent to protect the interests of the child, even without a formal legal relationship.[39] The second is **parens patriae,** which refers to the inherent power of the state to protect persons legally incapable of protecting themselves before the law.[40] The third is the "police powers doctrine,"

in loco parentis
Latin for "in the place of a parent"

parens patriae
Latin for "parent of the fatherland"

defined as the state's duty to protect the health, safety, and welfare of its citizens.[41] The state acts as a caretaker for minors, a defender of their legal interests, and is at the same time the guardian of public safety.

Because these duties are complex and difficult to carry out, Texas juvenile justice encompasses a large network of state and local authorities charged with meting out justice while also safeguarding the interests of minors. This network includes judges who determine whether a minor faces full criminal responsibility as an adult; state agencies that provide needed detention and living facilities; and caseworkers, lawyers, and other experts who must act in the best interests of minors while also giving consideration to parents or legal guardians and crime victims. The agency responsible for coordinating and overseeing juvenile justice programs in the state is the Texas Juvenile Justice Department.

Until 2011, two separate state agencies bore the responsibility of administering the juvenile justice system: the Texas Youth Commission, which managed detention centers and halfway houses throughout the state, and the Texas Juvenile Probation Commission, which oversaw the entire system at the local level and coordinated state-local communication. Unfortunately, these agencies were plagued by a long-standing record of abuse and misconduct, so they lost the public's trust. One example of this occurred at the Mountain View State School for Boys, which opened in 1962. In the early 1970s, this facility incarcerated juveniles who had previously been held at the nearby Gatesville State School and were deemed dangerous. Both were run by the Texas Youth Council (the precursor to the Texas Youth Commission).[42] Conditions at the Mountain View School were harsh, and abuse perpetrated by staff members and inmates alike was widespread. Some juveniles had been involuntarily committed to the Council (often without due process), whereupon they were housed in dormitories like Mountain View and largely forgotten.[43]

In 1971, a class-action lawsuit was filed on behalf of the inmates against the Texas Youth Council. In *Morales v. Turman,* Judge William Wayne Justice found that the state schools' operations violated the Eighth Amendment's prohibition against cruel and unusual punishment and ordered Texas to shutter both Gatesville and Mountain View. Additionally, he ordered Texas to establish "a system of community-based treatment alternatives" for juveniles and to institutionalize only those not appropriate for some "alternative form of rehabilitative treatment."[44] In his order, Justice cited a quote from *Kent v. U.S.* (1966) that he likened to conditions faced by delinquent children in Texas:

> While there can be no doubt of the original laudable purpose of juvenile courts. . . . There is evidence, in fact, that there may be grounds for concern that the child receives the worst of both worlds: that [the child] gets neither the protections accorded to adults nor the solicitous care and regenerative treatment postulated for children.[45]

Mountain View was closed in 1975, and its inmates were transferred to other facilities across the state.[46] In 1983, the Texas Youth Council was renamed the Texas Youth Commission and, under federal supervision that was a condition of its legal settlement, began attempts to overhaul the juvenile justice system in Texas.[47] However, this effort was unsuccessful, and the system floundered on further allegations of misconduct. Between 2004 to 2008, there was a quelled riot at the Evins Regional Juvenile Center, child sexual abuse scandals at two facilities run by the Texas Youth Commission, and yet another civil rights lawsuit filed against the commission by students in its care. During the 2011 legislative session, Senator John Whitmire, chair of the Senate Committee on Criminal Justice, proposed SB 653, which abolished both the Texas Youth Commission and the Texas Juvenile Probation Commission and transferred their responsibilities to a newly established agency, the Texas Juvenile Justice Department. The bill passed and was signed into law by Governor Perry.[48] Today, the newly reconstituted Texas Juvenile Justice Department (TJJD) is directed by a 13-member board appointed by the governor.[49]

The current juvenile justice system bears the imprint of Judge Justice's orders. Traditionally, Texas has considered juvenile justice to be part of family law. In 1995, the legislature revised and amended the Family Code to create the Juvenile Justice Code (now Title III of the Texas Family Code, Chapters 51 through 61).[50] This revision established a more "localized" approach to handling juveniles, with rehabilitation as the primary goal. When a youth is charged with a violation, the county or local district court generally prosecutes the case. In fact, some counties have dedicated district courts or county courts at law that deal exclusively with juvenile cases. Harris County has three such "juvenile district courts"; Dallas County has two.[51] At that point, the county's juvenile probation department implements any punishment or treatment imposed by the court. Every county provides juvenile probation services, although some juvenile probation departments serve more than one county.[52] Each probation department operates under the guidance of the county's juvenile board, and each board may create an advisory council of citizens who provide guidance to the board, including a prosecuting attorney, mental health and medical professionals, and a representative from the educational community.[53]

In other words, all phases of a juvenile case—including intake, predisposition investigation, prosecution, and possible probation—are handled at the county level to the greatest extent possible. Only those individuals who have "exhausted their options in the county" or "committed the most serious offenses" are sent to TJJD.[54] If juveniles are found guilty and are to be detained at a TJJD facility, they can appeal the court's decision. That appeal proceeds directly to the Texas Supreme Court, as discussed in Chapter 5.

Understanding Impact: Many Americans have their own preconceived opinions about how young people should be raised, educated, and punished. These opinions affect how they view the thorny topic of juvenile justice. How should young people in juvenile centers be treated? What responsibilities do state organizations, like the TJJD, have to the young people in juvenile centers? What responsibilities does the TJJD have to society and the victims of juvenile crime?

Procedures Involving Juveniles

The Juvenile Justice Code applies only to children aged 10–17; children younger than 10 cannot be prosecuted for a crime.[55] Juveniles who do commit offenses—whether they be misdemeanors or felonies—are arrested and

TABLE 6.2

Juvenile Offenses Tried in Court

CINS Offenses	Delinquent Conduct Offenses
Any finable offense	Felonies or jailable misdemeanors
School expulsion for conduct code violations	Contempt of court or violation of a court order
Prostitution or sexting	DUI
Running away	

Source: Texas Family Code, Sec. 51.03(a) and (b).

generally referred to juvenile court. Two types of offenses result in a child's referral to juvenile court: conduct indicating a need for supervision (CINS) or delinquent conduct. According to the Texas Juvenile Justice Code, conduct indicating a need for supervision is defined as an act that, if committed by an adult, would either be punishable by a fine or would not be considered a violation at all (such as running away from home). Delinquent conduct, on the other hand, involves a violation of the penal code and would result in imprisonment if committed by an adult.[56] Some examples of these offenses are listed in Table 6.2.

The process associated with a juvenile criminal trial is almost the same as that for an adult. However, one notable difference is that a hearing is held to determine whether or not the juvenile will be tried as an adult. In Texas, the juvenile court must waive its jurisdiction over the case in order for a minor to be tried as an adult. In making this decision, the juvenile court judge can consider whether the crime was committed against a person or property, whether the minor had a prior record, whether the minor's mental state at the time of the crime indicated criminal intent, whether the minor committed several crimes in the same transaction, and similar issues.[57]

Some studies have shown that, in practice, there is not much difference between minors tried as adults versus those tried in juvenile court; the process of distinguishing between the two populations and certifying some minors as adults appears somewhat arbitrary.[58] It is worth noting that minors tried as adults are not necessarily the "worst" offenders in the juvenile system in terms of violent or repeated offenses. Compared to other juvenile offenders, however, those tried as adults do face more serious consequences later in life from long sentences and criminal records that are more difficult to keep confidential.[59]

Even if tried as an adult, minors cannot be sentenced to life imprisonment without parole or to death if they committed the crime before the age of 18.[60] Before 2005, Texas and 19 other states had the dubious distinction of allowing a death sentence for juveniles. In *Roper v. Simmons* (2005), however, the U.S. Supreme Court barred the death penalty for defendants who were under the age of 18 at the time of their crime, thereby resulting in the sentences of 29 juveniles on Texas's death row being commuted to life without parole.[61] In 2012, the Supreme Court ruled in *Miller*

Under certain circumstances, juveniles may be tried as adults.

Andrew Lichtenstein/Corbis News/Getty Images

v. Alabama that the sentence of life without parole also constituted cruel and unusual punishment for juveniles and could not be applied to those under 18 at the time their crime was committed.[62] Texas applied this ruling retroactively and commuted the sentences of juvenile offenders who had been convicted prior to the *Miller* ruling.

Another difference between adult and juvenile trials involves terminology. The term "adjudication" is used to refer to the trial phase of a juvenile case. It also refers to a finding of guilt or conviction for the alleged offense. Similarly, a "disposition hearing" in a juvenile case is the equivalent of the sentencing phase in an adult trial. In addition, juvenile cases differ from adult cases in the sense that there is often a hard cap or limit on the length of punishment. If a minor is put on probation, that probation must end by the individual's eighteenth birthday. Juveniles sent to a TJJD facility are either released by their nineteenth birthday or transferred to an adult facility, depending on the type of sentence imposed and their behavior while in TJJD custody.[63]

During fiscal year 2017 (the most recent year for which statistics have been released), 802 juveniles were placed in the custody of the Texas Juvenile Justice Department. The vast majority of these (92.5 percent) were male, most had at least two prior felony adjudications or were on probation at the time they committed their crime (66 percent and 68.2 percent, respectively), and 83 percent were members of an ethnic or racial minority group. More of these offenders came from Harris County (24.8 percent) than from any other single county in the state.[64]

State lawmakers have undertaken reforms to both improve the system and decrease the number of youths detained. For example, a bill passed in 2007 made it illegal for minors convicted of misdemeanors (minor offenses) to be sent to a detention facility. To encourage community-based treatment, the legislature increased funding for juvenile probation departments and cut the budget for state-run facilities. The state was subsequently able to close eight juvenile detention facilities.[65] In 2015, a new law decriminalized truancy; interestingly, this did not lead to a drop in public school attendance. However, many cities in Texas can still enforce local juvenile daytime curfew laws.[66] Apart from these reforms, there is also evidence that the juvenile crime rate has decreased in Texas. For instance, the number of referrals to juvenile probation departments fell sharply from 2020 to 2021 by about 27 percent.[67] Despite the checkered past of juvenile justice in Texas and the uncertainty associated with the newness of the Texas Juvenile Justice Department, these trends suggest there is reason for cautious optimism regarding the future of the new state agency as it carries out wide-ranging and difficult responsibilities.

CORE OBJECTIVE

Taking Personal Responsibility . . .

Currently, at what age does the state of Texas consider a person an adult in criminal and civil proceedings?

At what age do you think the state should require individuals to take personal responsibility? Why?

Correction and Rehabilitation

Learning Objective: Explain the state of Texas's correction system, including its approach to rehabilitation and use of the death penalty.

The Texas Department of Criminal Justice (TDCJ) is a vast organization that had a $3.6 billion budget for fiscal year 2020.[68] TDCJ is responsible for the detention and supervision of over a half million adult inmates, parolees, and individuals on community supervision (also known as probation). TDCJ is governed by the gubernatorially appointed, nine-member Texas Board of Criminal Justice, which hires an executive director to run the agency.[69] The department oversees the operation of many types of facilities, including state prisons, state jails, private prisons, transfer and prerelease facilities, as well as medical, psychiatric, and geriatric facilities. As of February 2022, the state had a total of 99 operational units.[70]

The State Prison System

Texas has one of the highest rates of incarceration in the nation; as of 2020, it was 455 per 100,000. (Table 6.3 lists the states with the 10 highest incarceration rates.) There were 134,345 sentenced prisoners in Texas in 2020—more than in any other state. Still, Texas saw a sharp drop in the number of prisoners due to the effects of COVID. For example, Texas witnessed a 13 percent decrease from 2019.[71]

Having the largest prison population of any state and the sixth-highest incarceration rate comes with challenges. Foremost among those is maintaining enough space to house all the state's inmates. Prison overcrowding has been a

TABLE 6.3	
2020 Incarceration Rate per 100,000 Residents by State (top 10 states)	
State	**Rate**
Mississippi	584
Louisiana	581
Oklahoma	559
Arkansas	529
Arizona	495
Texas	**455**
Georgia	433
Kentucky	414
Idaho	398
Alabama	398

Source: U.S. Department of Justice, Bureau of Justice Statistics, "Prisoners in 2020," Table 7: "Imprisonment Rates of U.S. Residents, Based on Sentenced Prisoners Under the Jurisdiction of State or Federal Correctional Authorities, by Sex, Age, and Jurisdiction, 2019 and 2020," https://bjs.ojp.gov/content/pub/pdf/p20st.pdf (accessed February 12, 2022).

chronic problem in Texas, at times reaching crisis levels. In 1980, U.S. District Court Judge William Wayne Justice ruled, in *Ruiz v. Estelle,* that conditions in Texas prisons constituted "cruel and unusual punishment" and thus violated the U.S. Constitution.[72] The court ordered changes to many aspects of the state's prison system. As part of this process, Texas began a massive prison construction program to relieve overcrowding. One journalist called this enterprise "the greatest expansion of prison beds in the history of the free world."[73] The prison population grew from 36,769 inmates in 1983 to a peak of 173,649 inmates in 2010.[74] In the 2010s, the population began to decrease. Texans began to see the cost of maintaining a high number inmates to be too expensive. In 2019, the number of inmates truncated to 158,429. Then, it further decreased to 135,906 in 2020 due, in large part, to COVID.[75]

Managing the Prison Population

Of course, one way to reduce the prison population is to increase the number of individuals on parole. According to the TDCJ, parole is defined as "the release of an offender, by decision of a parole panel, to serve the remainder of his or her sentence under supervision in the community."[76] The Texas Board of Pardons and Paroles is the entity responsible for determining if offenders have been sufficiently rehabilitated to be paroled and, based on a combined score of "static" and "dynamic" factors, rates their potential risk to society. Inmates serving life sentences for capital crimes must serve at least 40 years before they are considered eligible for parole. Those who are convicted of other violent offenses must serve at least half their sentence, and those convicted of nonviolent crimes must serve a minimum of one-quarter of their sentence.[77] Releasing offenders on parole is associated with a considerable cost savings over keeping them in prison. Table 6.4 shows the average costs in 2020 of incarceration. (Note that the figures for juveniles, also included here, are significantly more dramatic in terms of cost.)

The creation of the "state jail felony" represented another attempt to manage the Texas prison population. In 1993, the state legislature created this new, fifth category of felony offenses.[78] The concept behind the new state jail division was

TABLE 6.4

Daily Cost per Person for Various Correctional Programs, 2020

Texas Department of Criminal Justice

Prison	$ 69.27
Parole Supervision	$ 4.64
Community Supervision	$ 3.98

Texas Juvenile Justice Department

State Residential Facilities	$616.70
Parole Supervision	$ 50.55
Juvenile Probation Supervision	$ 15.14

Source: Legislative Budget Board, "Criminal and Juvenile Justice Uniform Cost Report, Fiscal Years 2019–2020," January 2021, p. 2, https://www.lbb.texas.gov/Documents/Publications/Policy_Report/6292_CJDA_Uniform_Cost.pdf (accessed February 12, 2022).

twofold. First, state jails would relieve overcrowding in state penitentiaries. Second, nonviolent drug and property offenders, previously convicted of third-degree felonies, would be separated from more violent offenders in state prisons and offered a greater opportunity for rehabilitation, as "rehabilitation programming [was] meant to be the cornerstone of the state jail system."[79] Texas has made great strides since 2007 in reducing recidivism among prison inmates, but it has seen much less success with inmates in its state jail facilities, for whom the percentage rearrested and reincarcerated is significantly higher.[80]

Another approach to reducing incarceration, recidivism, and related costs has been the use of "specialty courts." According to TDCJ, nonviolent offenders made up 37.6 percent of Texas's incarcerated population in 2020.[81] Specialty or problem-solving courts are "trial courts with specialized dockets that often hear only nonviolent cases for either certain types of defendants or offenses."[82] Common types of specialty courts are drug courts, veteran treatment courts, mental health courts, prostitution courts, and DWI courts. An offender convicted in one of these specialty courts is diverted from incarceration and given a treatment plan (with required participation) and community supervision. The first such specialty court in the state was a drug court established in 1990.[83] The proliferation of these nontraditional courtrooms caught the attention of the state legislature, which decided that special statutory language should be written to better capture what these courts were doing and how they were doing it, as well as establish accountability by creating a Specialty Courts Advisory Council. Texas has 184 specialty courts, many of which are in the more populous areas of the state, such as Bexar, Dallas, El Paso, and Harris Counties.[84]

CORE OBJECTIVE

Being Socially Responsible . . .

Why might the use of special courts to punish crimes like prostitution provide a cost savings for the criminal justice system?

Private Prisons

Private prisons emerged as another attempt to address the problem of a growing prison population and limited space in state prisons. Rather than building, staffing, and maintaining new state prisons, Texas opted to contract with for-profit prison corporations. These private corporations then built and operated the new facilities, with oversight provided by the TDCJ. In other cases, private corporations were contracted to operate facilities built for the state. As Table 6.5 illustrates, TDCJ currently provides oversight for a number of private correctional facilities, jails, residential halfway houses, and substance abuse facilities (SAFs), among others.[85]

Beginning in the late 1980s, the state of Texas, like many other states, began negotiating contracts with private prison corporations in an effort to help relieve prison overcrowding and save tax dollars, even as it was still constructing new state-owned prisons. The resulting boom in prison construction produced such

TABLE 6.5

Selected Private Facilities under State Contract, 2022

Type	Contractor	Number of Units (beds)
Correctional	Management & Training Corp.	7 (4,618)
State Jail	Various	3 (4,080)
Multi-Use Facility	East Texas Multi-Use Facility	1 (2,236)
Residential Reentry Centers	Various	8 (2,015)
Residential Substance Abuse Facilities (SAFs)	Various	17 (1,556)
In-Prison Treatment Programs	Various	19 (8,877)

Source: Texas Department of Criminal Justice, Private Facility Contract Monitoring/Oversight Division, "Contracted Facilities as of January 31, 2022," https://www.tdcj.texas.gov/divisions/pf/pf_unit_list.html (accessed May 16, 2022).

an oversupply that prison beds in Texas were rented out for use by inmates from other states.[86] Though not as robust as it was in the 1990s, the private prison industry continues in Texas today; many prisoners are housed through contracts with the federal government. Moreover, the federal government, specifically Immigration and Customs Enforcement, or ICE, had contracted with several private prison corporations to run immigrant detention centers, some of which are located in Texas.[87]

Many of these private prisons were built in rural areas. Smaller rural counties, searching for additional revenue sources or opportunities for economic development, partnered with private corporations to construct new prisons. Potential benefits to the county included the creation of new jobs because members of the community found employment at the prison. These new jobs, in turn, brought growth to established businesses. Such projects also promised a relatively passive revenue stream for the county. The county would offer revenue bonds to finance construction and, once paid off, the county would own a prison facility that would be staffed and operated by an outside contractor. In addition, repairs to infrastructure were included as part of the contracts, along with new construction projects for the community. In fact, rural counties that contracted to build private prisons initially experienced increased revenues, allowing them to expand budgets based on this injection of new money and improving their economic outlook.[88]

Unfortunately, the private prison industry has had its share of scandal and corruption. Allegations of physical abuse, neglect, inhumane conditions, and dangerous understaffing have been made at these prisons. One example is found in Willacy County, which built three detention centers, the largest of which was the Willacy County Correctional Center. This facility, built in 2006 and operated by Management & Training Corporation (MTC), initially generated about $2.5 million a year in revenue for the county. Known as "Tent City" because of its use of Kevlar tents, the prison had space to house up to 3,000 inmates. However, it lost its federal contract following a *Frontline* documentary detailing physical and sexual abuse there. After a riot in early 2015 that lasted about five hours, the 2,800 federal prisoners housed there were transferred, and the prison was shut down. When the prison closed, Willacy County faced a budget shortfall due to the loss of prison-related revenue as well as debt payments for construction of the prison, the outstanding balance of which was $128 million. Bond service payments amounted to almost $250,000 a month. Ultimately, the county faced difficult decisions that required layoffs for county government employees, including jail staff, and reductions in operational hours for the courts and other agencies. The economy of Willacy County, however, has partially rebounded because it opened El Valle, a 1,000-bed immigrant detention center. It is also trying to diversify its economy by expanding its use of wind turbines for farming.[89]

Because of a number of issues, it is difficult to compare private and public prisons in terms of cost and outcomes. According to data provided by the TDCJ and the Legislative Budget Board, the daily cost per inmate is lower for privately operated prisons ($46.25 in 2018) than for state-operated facilities. However, such comparisons are muddied by the fact that certain expenses for privately operated facilities, including inmate medical care and facility repairs, are paid by the state of Texas and are therefore not included in private facilities' cost estimates.[90] Comparing outcomes—including such variables as staff and inmate injuries, escapes, number of inmate complaints, and facility accreditation—is equally problematic. Studies specifically comparing recidivism rates for public and private prisoners have been criticized for design flaws.[91]

Arguments have been made on both sides regarding the use of private prisons. On the one hand, some argue that operating costs are lower for private prisons than for public prisons. Another important justification for using private prisons is to relieve overcrowding in state facilities. Conversely, critics have questioned whether the profit motive distorts how private prison operators fulfill their duties. For instance, correctional programs that focus on rehabilitation and reducing recidivism run counter to the incentive of private prison corporations to keep all of their beds occupied. Therefore, critics worry that for-profit prisons are more likely to resolve this inherent conflict of interest by doing what is best for their profit margins rather than what is best for prisoners.[92]

Local Government Jails

Although not part of the state penal system, local jails also house and care for prisoners. According to state statute, each county is required to provide a "safe and suitable" jail.[93] County jails house inmates scheduled to serve time in the state system; they also incarcerate people who commit misdemeanors within the county's jurisdiction. The Texas legislature created the Texas Commission on Jail Standards to ensure that counties maintain minimum standards for construction and the custody, rehabilitation, and treatment of inmates in their care. As of January 2022, there were 61,397 individuals incarcerated in Texas's county jails.[94]

Cities operate detention facilities as well. Municipalities are authorized under the Local Government Code to operate jails,[95] and cities in Texas may use their jails or holding cells to detain state statute violators who are being processed or waiting to be interviewed or interrogated before being transferred to a county jail. Generally, city jails incarcerate individuals for violations of municipal ordinances, which are fine-only penalties, when the individual cannot or chooses not to pay the fines. If cities do not have a facility to do so, they may enter into an agreement with the county to detain individuals who fail to pay fines.

TABLE 6.6

Custodial Deaths in City and County Jails in Texas, 2005–2021

City Jails		County Jails	
Houston	301	Harris	401
San Antonio	192	Bexar	161
Dallas	155	Dallas	129
Fort Worth	89	Tarrant	83

Source: Texas Justice Initiative, "Explore the Data—Deaths in Custody, 2005–2021," https://texasjusticeinitiative.org/datasets/custodial-deaths (accessed February 12, 2022).

Although privately operated municipal jails are subject to the same standards as county jails, publicly operated municipal jails have no regulatory body to oversee their operations. Moreover, no other state laws or rules govern the operation of city jails. There have been attempts during previous legislative sessions to expand the authority of the Texas Commission on Jail Standards to provide oversight and regulation for all municipal jails, but these bills faced extreme opposition, primarily from city officials who argued that it would be cost prohibitive to make the necessary improvements to meet current standards.[96]

Recently, local jails have come under increased scrutiny because of inmate deaths while in custody. In Texas, there were 188 deaths in municipal jails between 2005 and 2021.[97] Several wrongful death suits have been filed in recent years by family members of individuals who died while in custody. Table 6.6 indicates the four cities and counties where the most custodial deaths occurred during this period, according to the Texas Attorney General's Custodial Death Report. During 2021, there were 12 deaths in municipal jails.[98]

The "Three R's": Recidivism, Rehabilitation, and Reform

As noted previously, Texas's criminal justice system experienced an unprecedented expansion at the end of the twentieth century. The incarcerated population ballooned, scores of prisons were built, and state spending on corrections skyrocketed from 1980 to 2000. Faced with a dire forecast that even more prison beds would be needed in the future, Texas lawmakers, looking for a solution to their anticipated budgetary woes, analyzed the system with the goal of curbing that trend.[99]

Since 2005, the legislature has enacted a number of reforms focused on rehabilitation and alternatives to incarceration. First, the legislature incentivized probation departments to reduce probation revocations by offering them increased funding. During the 2007 session, the legislature appropriated nearly $250 million for treatment and diversion facilities, including mental illness and substance abuse treatment. This initiative was estimated to have saved the state $2 billion and averted what was projected by TDCJ to be a 17,000-bed shortfall by 2012. Bills passed in 2011 created additional incentives for improvements in the system. For example, individuals under community supervision could reduce their time on probation by demonstrating "exemplary behavior." Another legislative change allowed people, who are in state jails due to felony convictions and were not considered previously for early release, to serve the last few months of their jail sentence on probation if they participated in rehabilitation programs.[100]

The state's shift in approach has had a dramatic effect. The prison population, which peaked in 2010, has declined.[101] The state's incarceration rate, second highest in the country in 2004, has fallen to sixth. In 2011, due to surplus capacity at other facilities, Texas closed a public prison for the first time in the state's history. Then, the effects of COVID hastened the closing of two prison units permanently in 2020, and several other units temporarily in 2021.[102] Recidivism has also decreased. According to one study, the recidivism rate for inmates released in Texas in 2007 (and followed for three years) was 11 percent lower than the rate for inmates released in 2005 and 22 percent lower than the rate for 2000 releases. However, a report of the Legislative Budget Board in 2021 shows that recidivism rates are beginning to plateau and stabilize again.[103] The state's crime rate has also fallen. Since 2009 in particular, the crime rate has declined. In 2020, the crime rate decreased by 4.0 percent from 2019 to 2020, largely because fewer property crimes were committed. However, there was still an increase in violent crimes (especially murder and aggravated assault) from 2019 to 2020 by 6.6 percent.[104]

Thanks to legislative reforms, Texas has shown that an increased focus on rehabilitation programs, rather than just expanding prison capacity, can cut costs and decrease incarceration by reducing recidivism. These programs provide many offenders with the skills required to transition to being productive members of society.

Substance abuse treatment is one of the many programs provided in an effort to reduce recidivism. Because many offenders struggle with drug and alcohol addiction, inmates are assessed for substance abuse as part of the **intake** process. Appropriate inmates are then transferred to units that offer specific programs operated by TDCJ's rehabilitation division. The Substance Abuse Felony Punishment Facility (SAFPF) and the In-Prison Therapeutic Community (IPTC) are both six-month programs, with aftercare and follow-up supervision. The SAFPF is a "diversion" program, operated by TDCJ, to which offenders can be sentenced in lieu of prison. Alternatively, the Board of Pardons and Paroles may require a parolee's participation in the program as a condition of parole.[105]

Another service aimed at reducing recidivism is education. According to the most recent demographic profile of inmates received by the TDCJ, average educational attainment scores among offenders in custody reflected an eighth-grade education. Since 1969, the Windham School District has provided education for inmates at TDCJ facilities. Its purpose is to assist inmates in obtaining their high school diploma or General Educational Development (GED) certificate or vocational training, with the goal of easing their transition back into society. Windham was the first school district in the nation expressly for offenders and is still in operation today.

In 2021, the Windham School District, in a report to the Texas legislature, stated that students who participated in their Cognitive Intervention Program were 16.2 percent less likely to recidivate and those who participated in their Career and Technical Education Program were 25.5 percent less likely to recidivate. Students who participated in these programs were also more likely to find

intake

The procedures involved with the arrest and detention of an individual before a bail hearing work.[106] During the 2020–2021 academic year, 7,941 students (15.8 percent) of the 50,013 released from the Texas Department of Criminal Justice received a High School Equivalency (HSE) certificate.[107]

The Death Penalty

One area in which Texas has remained tough on crime is the death penalty. This form of punishment was effectively suspended in the United States in 1972 (*Furman v. Georgia*) when the U.S. Supreme Court found that many state laws regarding the death penalty were applied in an arbitrary or discriminatory fashion.[108] In 1976, however, the Court established guidelines under which states could reinstate the death penalty (*Gregg v. Georgia*). Since 1976, most executions in the United States (81.6 percent) have taken place in southern states,[109] which is perhaps unsurprising considering the dominant traditionalistic culture of the South.

Texas reinstated the death penalty in 1976 and is currently the leading state in terms of the number of death sentences handed out and the number of prisoners executed. From the time of reinstatement until February 2022, Texas carried out 573 of the nation's 1,542 executions.[110] Texas accounts for 37.1 percent of the country's executions. In 2021, Texas executed 3 people.[111] Table 6.7 shows states with prisoners currently on death row. (Some of these states have a moratorium on executions, have abolished the death penalty since these sentences were handed down, or have otherwise not carried out an execution in several years.)

TABLE 6.7

Death Row Inmates by State, October 2021

State	Number Waiting to Be Executed	State	Number Waiting to Be Executed
California	695	Arkansas	30
Florida	333	Kentucky	27
Texas	198	Oregon	24
Alabama	170	Missouri	21
North Carolina	139	Nebraska	12
Ohio	135	Kansas	9
Pennsylvania	130	Indiana	8
Arizona	118	Idaho	8
Louisiana	65	Utah	7
Nevada	65	U.S. Military	4
Tennessee	49	Montana	2
Oklahoma	46	New Hampshire	1
United States Federal Government	45	South Dakota	1
Georgia	42		
Mississippi	38		
South Carolina	37		

Source: Death Penalty Information Center, "Death Row Prisoners by State: October 1, 2021," https://deathpenaltyinfo.org/death-row/overview (accessed February 13, 2022).

Gate to Death Row at the Ellis Unit in Huntsville

Per-Anders Pettersson/Hulton Archive/Getty Images

When a Texas jury concludes that a criminal defendant murdered someone under especially heinous circumstances, as defined by the Texas Penal Code, that jury can condemn that defendant to death. Such a crime is called capital murder. Proponents of the death penalty argue that it deters crime (particularly murder), restores justice when a life has been taken, provides retribution for society and the victim's family, and costs less than imprisoning the convicted person for life. Critics argue that the death penalty does very little to deter future violent crime, that it constitutes "cruel and unusual punishment," that governments have no moral right to deprive someone of life, that death penalty cases cost more to prosecute than life imprisonment, and that innocent people may be put to death when the criminal justice system makes mistakes.

In Texas prior to 2005, a defendant convicted of capital murder could be sentenced only to death or life imprisonment (which included the possibility of parole after 40 years). However, in 2005 the legislature passed and then-governor Perry signed SB 60, which provided juries a third option when assessing punishment for a capital offense. Juries can now sentence a person to death, life in prison, or life without parole.[112] This third option allows juries to permanently confine an individual who might pose a "threat to the community" if released, while allowing them to avoid imposing a death sentence. This may be particularly relevant to concerns about "irrevocable mistakes" within the system.[113] Reexamination of older cases has cast doubt on some death penalty convictions, suggesting that Texas has likely put innocent people to death. One particularly well-publicized case was that of Cameron Todd Willingham, who was charged for setting a fire that killed his three daughters. Since his execution in 2004, new evidence emerged that suggests that Willingham was innocent.[114] Since 1973, 16 inmates on Texas's death row have been **exonerated**.[115]

exoneration
The official absolution of a false criminal conviction and release from incarceration

Understanding Impact In *Callins v. Collins* (1994), Justice Blackmun and Justice Scalia debated the nature of capital punishment. Justice Blackmun claimed that the way in which capital punishment is administered is unconstitutional. He argued it was akin to cruel and unusual punishment, which is banned by the Eighth Amendment. Justice Scalia, based on his interpretation of the Due Process Clause, retorted that there was nothing constitutionally wrong with the death penalty so long as the accused received due process under the law. The Court did not grant Callins's request for an appeal, and he was later executed.[116] Do you believe the death penalty is constitutional? If so, what clause justifies it? What clause condemns it? Is the Constitution silent on the issue?

Texas, the Death Penalty, and the Harris County Factor

What factors contribute to the large number of death sentences in Texas, and in Harris County (Houston) in particular? First, the statutes in Texas for assigning a death sentence are among the least complicated in the nation. Following a trial in which guilt is determined, the punishment phase of the trial begins. The jury must answer two questions: (1) Did the defendant act intentionally? and (2) Is the defendant a future threat to society? If a person commits murder while committing another crime (such as rape or robbery); kills more than one person; kills a police officer, firefighter, or child; or is a murderer for hire—and committed any of these crimes intentionally—that person can receive the death sentence. These standards make it easy for juries to answer "yes" and render a death sentence.

Second, the Texas Court of Criminal Appeals (to which all death penalty cases in Texas are appealed) rarely reverses a death sentence. In 2020, the Court of Criminal Appeals upheld 3 of the 8 death penalty cases brought before it.[117] Judge Sharon Keller has served as presiding justice of the court since 2000. During her election campaign, Judge Keller stated that failure to execute condemned murderers was a violation of human rights.[118] She garnered widespread criticism when, in September 2007, defense attorneys representing convicted murderer Michael Richard (who was scheduled to be executed that night) were attempting to file last-minute paperwork to stay their client's execution but were experiencing technical problems. The attorneys asked for additional time to file the paperwork but were told by Judge Keller: "We close at five." The attorneys missed the deadline, and Richard's execution proceeded hours later.[119]

Third, the U.S. Fifth Circuit Court of Appeals, a federal court that hears appeals from Texas, also rarely overturns cases. The purpose of appellate courts is to check on procedures and processes in lower courts and make sure no mistakes were made.

Finally, the Texas Board of Pardons and Paroles, often the final recourse for those with failed appeals, is even less likely to make sentencing changes when reviewing convictions. During fiscal year 2020, the board reviewed 7 capital cases and recommended clemency (commutation of sentence, pardon, or reprieve of execution) for only one person.[120] The governor of Texas has limited authority with respect to powers of pardon, clemency, and parole. Although the governor can choose to grant a **reprieve** for an individual scheduled for execution—providing a 30-day temporary stay of execution—the Board of Pardons and Paroles decides which inmates will be granted parole and makes recommendations to the governor on matters respecting executive clemency. The governor, on the recommendation of the board, may grant a full **pardon** wherein the individual convicted of a crime receives no punishment. The board might also recommend that the governor **commute** or reduce the sentence received.

In Texas, Harris County places more defendants on death row than any other county. With a population of almost 4.7 million as of 2020, the county forms part of the greater metropolitan area of Houston, the fourth-largest city in the nation.[121] The county's huge size alone, however, does not seem to explain the large number of people it sentences to death. In fact, Harris County has sentenced more people to death than all other large urban Texas counties

reprieve
The temporary 30-day stay of execution the governor may grant

pardon
Grants forgiveness by the state for a conviction and requires that the convicted receive no punishment; does not erase the criminal record

commute
The reduction in punishment for an individual convicted of a crime

combined. Between December 1982 and February 2022, Texas executed 573 individuals; of these, 131 came from Harris County. The next highest counties are Dallas (Dallas) with 62, Bexar (San Antonio) with 46, and Tarrant (Forth Worth) with 44. Below that, the number of executions per county decreases sharply, the next highest county is Nueces (Corpus Christi) with 16.[122]

One explanation for the large number of death sentences in Harris County has to do with financial resources. Death penalty cases are costly; smaller, rural counties often lack the money to prosecute them. Even large urban counties often find that death penalty cases strain their budgets. Harris County is an exception, however, because the annual budget for its district attorney's office in fiscal year 2021–2022 was over $95.5 million, and it has a staff of nearly 300 assistant district attorneys.[123] Dallas County, the jurisdiction with the next highest number of death penalty convictions, had a 2022 annual budget of about $61.2 million and roughly 240 assistant district attorneys.[124] Harris County also has a total of 16 criminal courts, whereas Dallas County has 11.[125] Traditionally, many of the criminal court judges in Harris County are former prosecutors in the Harris County District Attorney's Office.

Concerns exist about the large number of death sentences handed down by Texas courts, including accessibility of legal representation for those accused of capital crimes, the appeals procedure, and prosecution-oriented courts. Nevertheless, a majority of Texans support the death penalty. In the most recent national poll conducted by Gallup in October 2021, 54 percent of those surveyed approved of the death penalty for convicted murderers while 43 percent were not in favor of it. In an April 2020 survey specific to Texas, 63 percent of residents either strongly or somewhat support the death penalty.[126] Table 6.8 provides a breakdown of responses by Texans polled about the death penalty. Texans favor the death penalty more strongly than the nation as a whole.

Whether or not the death penalty is effective in deterring crime is controversial. A fairly recent study by sociologist Kenneth Land and colleagues, which focused on Texas and claimed a small reduction in the number of homicides after executions, set off intense debate.[127] However, this and other studies of the death penalty's deterrent effect have been criticized as seriously flawed (and therefore inconclusive).[128] According to a widely cited survey of specialists,

TABLE 6.8

Public Opinion on the Death Penalty in Texas, 2020

Which of the following characterizes your opinion on the death penalty for those convicted of violent crimes?

Strongly support	40%
Somewhat support	23%
Somewhat oppose	12%
Strongly oppose	13%
Don't know/No opinion	12%

Source: The Texas Politics Project at the University of Texas at Austin, "Texas Statewide Survey," Q. 43, https://static.texastribune.org/media/files/2678e64f3f22edf2cee906e12ca3f1c2/ut-tt-2021-04-summary-all.pdf?_ga=2.198854764.2123450611.1620253780-591199111.1615555411 (accessed February 14, 2022).

88 percent of criminologists "[do] not believe that the death penalty is a deterrent" when they were asked to consider their knowledge of the empirical research.[129] One argument against the deterrent value is the long time span between sentencing and execution. In Texas, the average time from sentencing to execution is 10.87 years. David Lee Powell spent the longest amount of time on Texas's death row—31 years—before being executed in 2010.[130] Therefore, the consequences of homicidal behavior are not immediately apparent to the general public.

Poverty and Access to Legal Services

Some basic statistics illustrate the impact of economic status on the ability to obtain legal representation or participate effectively in the legal system. In 2021, according to the U.S. Census Bureau, 29,527,941 people lived in Texas. Of these, 13.4 percent were estimated to be living below the federally defined poverty threshold.[131] As of 2019, the federal poverty threshold for a single individual under the age of 65 was $14,097; for two people under the age of 65 without children, this figure increased to $18,145.[132] For such individuals, legal and attorneys' fees can represent a significant percentage of annual income.

Anyone, from an infant to a person who is elderly, may require some form of legal services. For example, issues requiring legal representation may arise from the quality of care given to an infant or health issues related to a person who is elderly. Moreover, Texans below the poverty line are not the only ones who cannot afford an attorney. Legal aid services for the poor often use 125 percent of the federal poverty threshold as their guideline for free legal services, for example. This means that millions of Texans living below or near the federal poverty threshold have difficulty paying for legal services.

Texas addresses these citizens' need for legal representation with a patchwork of public and private resources at the state and local levels. Through the Interest on Lawyers Trust Accounts (IOLTA) program, money generated from interest-bearing accounts (held by attorneys for their clients) is diverted to provide legal aid for the poor.[133] Free or reduced-fee legal representation is referred to as *pro bono,* short for *pro bono publico,* or "for the public good." Private law firms sometimes require their attorneys to devote a percentage of their time to pro bono work, often coordinated through the State Bar of Texas's Legal Access Division or its Care Campaign.[134] University legal clinics and nonprofit organizations provide representation to a small number of indigent (very poor) clients on a wide range of civil and criminal matters, such as immigration, environmental protection, family and domestic abuse matters, criminal defense, and death penalty defense.[135] The state bar and local bar associations offer referral services to attorneys who may work for reduced rates if a client is economically disadvantaged.[136] Courts can appoint defense counsel in criminal cases. In 1995, the Texas legislature passed a law requiring that poverty-stricken people who are condemned be provided tax-paid attorneys for automatic *habeas corpus* ("you shall have the body") appeals.

The Texas Access to Justice Commission is a state agency that funds indigent legal services for thousands of clients—primarily for problems related to marriage, child custody, domestic abuse, and other issues. This agency, which is supported by the state legislature and its own fundraising efforts, makes grants to fund legal assistance and recruits lawyers to work pro bono.[137] Whether in civil or criminal matters, Texas provides little assistance to indigent citizens for their legal needs. The state has relatively low indigent criminal defense spending when compared to other states. The Texas Indigent Defense Commission reports that Texas spent $35.2 million in 2020.[138] The result is that tens of thousands of Texans who earn low incomes are not receiving adequate legal aid.[139]

Problems and Reform: Implications for Public Policy

Learning Objective: Describe the challenges the state of Texas faces in its criminal justice system.

Throughout its history, Texas has earned a reputation as a "tough on crime" state, but systems—even those as large as the Texas criminal justice system—can change. Supreme Court rulings, shifting public attitudes, and shrinking budgets are all factors that drive policy changes in states, and Texas is no exception. In an effort to rein in the size of the state's criminal justice system, the Texas legislature has instituted a number of reforms, ranging from using specialty courts to channel nonviolent offenders into treatment programs rather than jail, to shutting down prisons, to overhauling the entire juvenile justice system.[140] In general, these policy prescriptions have changed the focus from punishment to rehabilitation.

Despite the successes of recent years, there is still room for improvement. This section details several problem areas where reformers are focusing their attention on both the federal and state levels.

Overcriminalization

Overcriminalization is the notion that laws defining criminal behavior have proliferated to include "vast areas of [nonviolent] conduct," and as such, represent an overreach of criminal justice power.[141] According to one source, there are over 4,000 federal criminal laws, an additional 300,000 federal regulatory offenses, and more than 1,700 state crimes with which Texans can be charged. In addition, in many cases it is no longer required that the accused have intent or prior knowledge of doing anything wrong (a legal concept called *mens rea,* or "guilty mind") in order to be convicted of a crime.[142] This phenomenon led attorney Harvey Silverglate to write that most Americans commit three felonies in the course of a normal day, without even knowing they have done so.[143]

Sentencing Reform

A number of harsh sentencing practices, including mandatory minimum sentences and enhanced punishment for repeat offenses, grew out of efforts to get "tough on crime" during the 1980s and 1990s. Many have argued that such sentences can be disproportionate to the crimes committed and have generated numerous unintended negative consequences (such as the growth of the prison population and destruction of families).[144] For example, a famous federal case involving mandatory minimums was that of Weldon Angelos, who was convicted of selling about $1,000 worth of marijuana while in possession of a gun. Because the sale of narcotics while in possession of a firearm triggered a mandatory minimum sentence, Angelos (who had no prior record) was sentenced to 55 years in prison. The federal judge who imposed the sentence called it "utterly unjust" and wrote to President Obama, asking for a reduction of Angelos's sentence.[145] Angelos was released in 2016 after serving 13 years.

The Fair Sentencing Act (FSA), passed by the U.S. Congress in 2010, was part of reform efforts in this area. Among other things, the FSA "eliminated the mandatory minimum sentence for simple possession of crack cocaine."[146] Previously, the minimum sentence for this crime was five years for first-time offenders.

Many police departments throughout the country have adapted the use of military vehicles.
Tom Mihalek/EPA/Shutterstock

Police Militarization

Police militarization refers to the trend for police departments to increasingly use military vehicles, weapons, and gear as well as military tactics (such as violent no-knock raids) in performing their regular duties. This trend has been exacerbated by federal programs that allow state and local law enforcement agencies to obtain surplus military equipment.[147] Proponents argue that such programs, equipment, and tactics provide greater safety for law enforcement officers and allow equipment that might otherwise go unused to be repurposed. Critics of this trend argue that it can lead to feelings of insecurity and a hazardous escalation of violence in communities and that it contributes to a mindset among police officers that they are "at war" with an enemy, rather than serving and protecting normal citizens.[148]

Civil Asset Forfeiture

According to the American Civil Liberties Union (ACLU), civil asset forfeiture "allows police to seize—and then keep or sell—any property they allege is involved in a crime."[149] When this mechanism is invoked, the government takes property belonging to an individual citizen or business without benefit of a trial or due process. Initially, law enforcement engaged in this practice to deprive criminal enterprises (such as drug traffickers) of resources, but the practice has since been abused by law enforcement agencies, some of which have allegedly used seized property as a means of funding their own departments' operations.[150]

Understanding Impact The Due Process Clause in the Fourteenth Amendment of the United States states that "no state shall . . . deprive any person of life, liberty, or property without due process of law." Do you think civil asset forfeiture violates the principle of the Fourteenth Amendment? Or is it protected under the state's police power? Explain.

Mental Illness in Prison

In the latter twentieth century, deinstitutionalization (the movement of people suffering from mental illness out of large, state-run psychiatric hospitals), as well as reduced federal and state funding for mental health programs, led to increased numbers of people suffering from severe mental illness living within communities. Evidence suggests that significant numbers of that population have since been incarcerated in prisons and jails. This thesis has been called "progressive transinstitutionalism."[151] In 2018, the Bureau of Justice Statistics reported that 26 percent of people in local jails and 14 percent of prisoners in state and federal facilities struggled with mental health issues.[152] This situation led investigative journalist Mary Beth Pfeiffer to call prisons "the de facto custodians of people with mental illness."[153]

People with mental illness come into contact with law enforcement for a number of reasons, ranging from major crimes to petty violations such as vagrancy, panhandling, or other unacceptable behaviors in public. In 2016, 35,305 offenders received mental health care from the state.[154] Moreover, inmates with mental illness have higher rates of recidivism. Many argue that these cases are dealt with more appropriately and effectively by medical and mental health professionals, rather than by incarceration, not to mention the potential for decreased costs. The amount of money spent on corrections intake alone for detainees with mental illness has been estimated at $138.7 million annually for six of the state's largest counties.[155]

Thus far, the state has experimented with pretrial diversion programs, which divert individuals who suffer from mental illness to community-based mental health services that not only better serve their needs but are also more cost-effective. A small number of Texas's specialty courts have been designated as mental health courts.[156] Houston mayor Sylvester Turner quoted a Legislative Budget Board estimate that community mental health services cost about $12 a day per patient, as opposed to $137 a day for incarceration.[157] During the 2013 legislative session, Harris County received $5 million in annual funding to pilot a "jail diversion" program.[158] By March 2016, the program had diverted over 750 people from the criminal justice system, saving an estimated $3 million a year for Harris County taxpayers. In October 2018, Harris County expanded this program by partnering with the Judge Ed Emmett Mental Health Diversion Center, which provided services for 1,000 persons with mental health issues within its first six months.[159] For many years, Bexar County has had its own jail diversion program, which serves as a model for other, similar programs. Since its inception, it has served thousands of people suffering from mental illness, diverting them from jail to treatment, and has saved Bexar County millions of dollars.[160]

Some would argue that, in order to fully address this problem, the state needs to spend more on mental health in general. According to a 2021 report by Mental Health America, Texas ranks second to last of all the states in access to mental health care.[161] If the thesis of progressive transinstitutionalism is valid, the state's cost savings on mental health care may have merely shifted to the criminal justice system.

Fine and Fee Practices

Many people are detained in local jails simply because they cannot pay the fines and costs associated with misdemeanor offenses (such as traffic tickets).

Although it is against state law for people to be jailed for inability to pay fines, evidence suggests this occurs nonetheless. Under Texas law, judges are required to perform a poverty assessment to determine a defendant's financial situation. If the defendant is indigent, the judge may offer a payment plan or, in lieu of fines, impose community service.[162] The judicial system garnered negative publicity in 2015 when an investigative report claimed that 9 out of 20 Texas courts had no record of having conducted poverty hearings. In addition, in 100 cases where defendants had been jailed for five days or more, no poverty hearings were documented by the El Paso municipal court.[163]

A related issue is bail and pretrial release. According to a 2018 study, 74 percent of the jail population were awaiting trial and had not been convicted.[164] Many are detained because they cannot make the bail payment necessary to be released from custody until their trial. The Conference of Chief Justices found that

> defendants who are detained can suffer job loss, home loss, and disintegrated social relationships, and, according to the Bureau of Justice Assistance, "receive more severe sentences, are offered less attractive plea bargains and are more likely to become 'reentry' clients because of their pretrial detention regardless of charge or criminal history."[165]

Supporters of reforms argue that excessive bail and pretrial confinement conflict with the judicial principle of "innocent until proven guilty," not to mention the high cost to taxpayers. Pretrial confinement costs roughly $69 per day per inmate.[166] Both the legislative and judicial branches are studying this issue.[167]

Suicide

In 2018, the single leading cause of death in local jails was suicide, which accounted for about 30 percent of inmate deaths nationwide.[168] In Texas, 24 percent of inmates who died in city and county jails over a 16-year period committed suicide, as shown in Figure 6.1. In contrast, only about 7 percent of state prison deaths during the same period were attributed to suicide.[169]

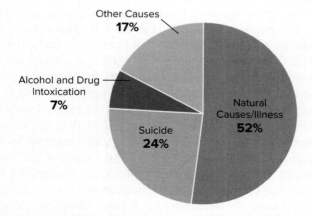

FIGURE 6.1 Deaths in Texas City and County Jails, 2005–2021

Source: Texas Justice Initiative, "Explore the Data: Deaths in Custody, 2005–2021, Municipal and County Jails," https://texasjusticeinitiative.org/datasets/custodial-deaths (accessed February 15, 2022).

Experts propose that the primary reason the suicide rate is higher in city and county jails is the initial "shock of confinement" that detainees experience; they recommend that the best practice to reduce suicide rates would be an initial interview with medical personnel during the intake process.[170] The Texas Commission on Jail Standards amended its rules on admission such that "'health tags' which may identify the inmate as having special medical or mental health needs shall be noted in the inmate's medical record and brought to the attention of health personnel and/or the supervisor on duty."[171] The Texas Commission on Jail Standards maintains a list of noncompliant jails on its website. As of March 2020, there were 14 noncompliant jails.[172]

A highly publicized suicide in a Texas county jail was that of Sandra Bland in 2015. In July 2015, Bland, a 28-year-old African American female, was pulled over by DPS officer Brian Encinia for failing to signal a lane change. The traffic stop quickly turned into an altercation wherein Bland was thrown to the ground and arrested. Three days after her arrest, Bland was found hanging in her cell in the Waller County jail. Her death was ruled a suicide. The Commission on Jail Standards inspected the Waller County jail and found deficiencies in its procedures. Trooper Encinia was later fired and charged with perjury related to Bland's arrest. To avoid the perjury charge, Encinia handed in his law enforcement license. The family of Sandra Bland negotiated a $1.9 million settlement in a wrongful death suit against the county and DPS. Although Waller County did not admit responsibility for Bland's death, the terms of the settlement included changes the county agreed to make to its jail practices.[173]

Technology and Crime

American fascination with crime dramas has generated a spate of television programs that stretch the boundaries of belief when compared to the actual processes associated with investigating and prosecuting offenses. In the space of one hour, detectives are able to solve a murder, the district attorney prosecutes, and the case is resolved. In actuality, the investigation and prosecution of a crime, particularly a serious violent crime, can take months or even years. After the initial evidence is gathered, crime labs analyze it. The science and technology associated with doing so evolves quite rapidly.

The Texas Forensic Science Commission—composed of nine members appointed by the governor, seven of whom are scientists—was created in 2005 and ensures the integrity of lab results used in criminal trials. It is responsible for investigating charges of professional negligence or misconduct with regard to forensic analysis. It also accredits crime labs in Texas and establishes the policies and procedures under which crime labs operate.[174] This agency, in collaboration with the FBI Crime Lab, brings together regional state labs for discussion and training to ensure that the most up-to-date scientific knowledge drives the investigation and analysis of evidence. For example, in August 2015 the Texas Forensic Science Commission (TFSC) notified the Texas criminal justice community of concerns about a protocol for interpreting mixed DNA evidence and the fact that forensic errors could impact current and past cases.[175] In response to changes in technology or specific complaints, the TFSC may reexamine cases already decided based on outdated methods of analysis. If a review of the case "identifies potential issues with the laboratory report and/or expert testimony rendered at trial," the TFSC notifies relevant parties.[176]

Exoneration

Exoneration refers to the official absolution of a false criminal conviction and may involve release from prison or jail. Nationwide, there were 2,955 exonerations between 1989 and February 2022, with 400 of these in Texas (more than in any other state). In 2020, Texas had 15 exonerations; only Illinois and Michigan had more exonerations that year.[177]

A notable case of wrongful conviction and posthumous exoneration is that of Timothy Cole. In 1985, a female student at Texas Tech was abducted and raped. In photo and in-person lineups, the victim identified Timothy Cole, a 24-year-old African American male who was also a student at Tech, as

Inmate Jerry Wayne Johnson (center) stands next to a picture of Timothy Cole at the hearing conducted to clear Cole's name.

Harry Cabluck/AP Images

her attacker. She testified against him in court, and even after several of Cole's friends testified that he was at home studying at the time of the rape, he was convicted and received a 25-year sentence. In 1995, Jerry Wayne Johnson, who was serving a life plus 99-year sentence for two rapes, wrote to judges, the Lubbock County prosecutor, and Cole's lawyer claiming that he had in fact committed the rape for which Cole was serving time. No action was taken based on Johnson's letters. In 1999, Cole died in prison of an asthma attack. In 2000, another letter of confession written by Johnson was dismissed. In 2008, the Innocence Project obtained DNA proving that Johnson committed the rape. Cole was officially exonerated in 2009, and a posthumous pardon was signed by then-governor Perry the next year. The Texas legislature enacted the Timothy Cole Act, which provides $80,000 in compensation to a wrongfully incarcerated individual for each year served; Cole's family received more than $1 million.[178]

Race, Gender, and the Criminal Justice System

Women are underrepresented in the criminal justice system relative to their percentage of the total state population. According to 2020 data from the TDCJ, women made up only 7.1 percent of the state's prison population, despite the fact that they make up about half of the Texas population overall.[179] Statistics show that women commit crime at a lower rate than men. In Texas, fewer adult women than men were arrested for index crimes in 2020 (145,667 versus 451,114).[180]

Nationally, racial and ethnic minority groups make up a disproportionate percentage of prison and jail populations compared to their numbers in the total population.[181] This is also true in Texas. For fiscal year 2018, TDCJ reported that the state prison population was 33.0 percent white, 33.3 percent African

American, and 33.0 percent Hispanic Americans (whereas their proportions in the state population were 41.2 percent white, 12.9 percent African American, and 39.7 percent Hispanic Americans).[182]

Data suggest that members of ethnic and racial minority groups, and particularly African Americans, are overrepresented in crime statistics compared to their proportion of the population. For instance, according to Texas Department of Public Safety's annual report, African Americans made up 26.2 percent of all individuals arrested for tracked crimes (twice their percentage of the population), and 36.8 percent of those arrested for the same crimes were of Hispanic ethnicity.[183] Multiple theories have been put forth to explain the overrepresentation of African Americans in the criminal justice system. Some have argued that African Americans are arrested, convicted, and imprisoned at higher rates due to discrimination and bias throughout the criminal justice system (including policing and the courts).[184] A 2016 Harvard Law School study of counties with a high output of death penalty sentences (which included Harris County, Texas) laid the blame not only on "overzealous prosecutors" and "inadequate defense" but also on racial bias. The study noted that "all 18 men who have been newly sentenced to death in Harris County since November 2004 have been people of color."[185]

Racial tensions have also been evident in the national conversation about police use of deadly force. The 2014 police shooting of Michael Brown in Ferguson, Missouri, along with the accompanying protests and publicity surrounding that incident, focused national attention on this issue. The following year, in 2015, 986 people in the United States were shot and killed by police. The killing of African Americans, in particular, by law enforcement officers generated an immense public outcry and sparked numerous protests.[186] During the summer of 2016, the debate about race as a factor in policing practices again reached a boiling point. The first week of July 2016 marked a particularly violent series of racially charged events. Two African American men—Alton Sterling in Baton Rouge, Louisiana, and Philando Castile in St. Paul, Minnesota—were killed by police within a matter of days. The movement Black Lives Matter and other groups organized protests across the country, one of which took place in Dallas. During that protest, five Dallas police officers were killed by a sniper, who was later killed by police. During the summer of 2020, the national conversation about race resurfaced after the death of George Floyd in Minneapolis.[187] Floyd was arrested for using counterfeit money. While Floyd was handcuffed, a white police officer kneeled on Floyd's neck for eight minutes. His death served as a catalyst for reflection on how members of ethnic and racial minority groups, and more specifically African Americans, experience encounters with police officers, as well as on the relationship that law enforcement and the larger criminal justice system have with the communities they serve.

Misconduct in the Justice System

District attorneys serve the state and the people. They bring charges, present evidence, and argue for the conviction of individuals charged with crimes. As prosecutor, they present the state's case to a jury and coordinate with the defense to ensure that the accused receives a fair trial. The Texas Code of

Focus On

Race and Imprisonment

Although African Americans constitute only 13.4 percent of the U.S. population, they are disproportionately imprisoned in the criminal justice system.[188] As of 2020, there were 389,500 Black sentenced prisoners under the jurisdiction of state or federal correctional authorities; there were only 358,900 White prisoners.[189]

High rates of incarceration, particularly for African American men, increased for several factors. First, in response to the protests of the late 1960s, Richard Nixon's administration adopted a "hard on crime" narrative, which pushed for longer and more stringent sentences to deter further crime. Second, presidents Ronald Reagan and George H. W. Bush advocated for a "war on drugs," which led police officers to target particular drug offenses, especially those prevalent in the Black community.[190]

A peaceful assembly for social reform.
Mike Stone/Reuters/Newscom

Third, criminologist George L. Kelling and political scientist James Q. Wilson pioneered the concept of "broken windows," which claimed that crime was more likely to occur when a neighborhood had broken windows or other visible signs of disarray. Kelling and Wilson encouraged the police to walk the beat and make arrests to protect the neighborhoods.[191] All three of these factors particularly affected those in poor urban areas with large African American populations.

Michelle Alexander's *The New Jim Crow: Mass Incarceration in the Age of Colorblindness* argues that these policies were racially motivated. She argues that they constitute a "new Jim Crow" in which "it is perfectly legal to discriminate against criminals in nearly all the ways that it was once legal to discriminate against African Americans."[192] Columnist Ta-Nehisi Coates, in an article in *The Atlantic*, also fears that these policies are causing damage to the Black family.[193]

Even so, one recent development over the last decade is a decrease in incarceration. From 2010 to 2020, the imprisonment rate of sentenced Black adults has declined by 31.5 percent.[194] Eli Hager of the Marshall Project provides a few potential reasons why the incarceration rate for African Americans, particularly Black men, is continuing to decline. First, crime and arrests are declining overall. Second, the government's war on drugs is being redirected to meth and opioids, which are used more heavily by whites. Third, many American cities have embarked on significant criminal justice reform.[195]

Critical Thinking Questions
1. Do you think criminal justice laws are racially motivated?
2. How have these laws affected Black families?

Criminal Procedure states that the primary duty of a district attorney is "not to convict, but to see that justice is done." Further, Article 2.01 mandates that prosecuting attorneys "shall not suppress facts or secrete witnesses capable of establishing the innocence of the accused."[196] Unfortunately, instances of misconduct do occur. When prosecutors fail to follow procedure, it is referred to as misconduct. Misconduct can involve many types of wrongdoing, including intentionally denying or hiding evidence from the defense,

Michael Morton (right) and his legal team hold a press conference after it was determined that the attorney who prosecuted him withheld evidence.

Patrick Dove/San Angelo Standard-Times/AP Images

encouraging witnesses to lie under oath, or using their office to intimidate witnesses for the defense.

One especially prominent and egregious case of prosecutorial misconduct involved Michael Morton, who in 1987 was convicted of murdering his wife and sentenced to life in prison. It was later determined that exculpatory evidence, including a bloody bandana discovered about 100 yards from Morton's house, was withheld from the defense. In 2011, partly due to efforts by the Innocence Project, DNA testing conducted on the bandana proved that another individual (who, in the intervening time had been convicted of a similar murder) had been present at the crime scene.

Morton was released and exonerated in 2011 after serving almost 25 years. The district attorney responsible for prosecuting the case was subsequently charged with ethical violations, gave up his license to practice law, and served 10 days in jail.[197] This case caused such uproar that the 2013 legislature passed SB 1611, the Michael Morton Act, which requires that all evidence pertaining to a criminal case, whether or not it is perceived as relevant to guilt or punishment, is disclosed to the defense.[198]

Though sensational when it is uncovered, prosecutorial misconduct is uncommon. The Texas District and County Attorneys Association, after analyzing 91 suspected cases of misconduct, found only 6 cases of "actual prosecutorial misconduct" during a four-year period, representing less than 1 percent of all trials in Texas during the period studied.[199]

Misconduct can be committed, and errors introduced into cases, by other parties in the legal system. For instance, in 2016, City of Austin found that the Austin Police Department DNA lab failed to follow proper scientific procedures while calculating the odds of DNA results. The malfeasance has forced several cases to be reexamined over the last few years.[200]

CORE OBJECTIVE

Thinking Critically . . .

Given the current challenges faced by the criminal justice system, what types of reforms would you recommend? What might be some of the negative or unintended consequences of your recommendations?

How to

Locate Primary Sources

A primary source is a firsthand account of a topic, such as a historical or legal document. Locating primary sources is a skill that can assist you in a variety of ways. In school, primary sources are always welcome in research papers and student projects. In the workforce, you may be required to look at many types of primary sources—ranging from federal, state, or local budgetary databases to old newspaper clippings. Perhaps most importantly, the study of primary sources can help you as a citizen develop opinions and arguments grounded on factually accurate data. In all three cases, primary sources allow you to make judgments for yourself and not be dependent on the analysis of another person. In fact, the more you study primary sources, the more you are able to judge the opinions of other commentators. Primary sources, in other words, empower individuals on many levels.

Due to the federal structure of the United States, the government produces a plethora of primary sources. Let's look at locating primary sources at each level.

Step 1: Finding Primary Sources at the Federal Level

There are two easy ways to look up primary sources at the federal level. The first, and most efficient, way is through the Internet. Every major federal institution has a robust website. Usually, these websites provide tabs and links to various forms of data. Here are a few quick links to get you started:

- Office of the Law Revision Council, U.S. Code: uscode.house.gov
- Supreme Court of the United States Cases: supremecourt.gov
- Congressional Legislation: congress.gov
- *Federal Register,* the daily newspaper of the government: federalregister.gov
- National Archives: archives.gov
- United States Census: census.gov

The second way to look up primary sources is to go to your university library. Some university libraries have a librarian who specializes in government research. University libraries will have several different types of resources. In the book stacks, many libraries have bound copies of government documents. University libraries also have access to online search engines where scholars

have posted their quantitative data in Excel documents. A good database will have thousands of such documents. One of the most impressive databases in political science is the Inter-university Consortium for Political and Social Research (ICPSR). Be forewarned, however, that the resources of university libraries greatly vary. You need to take the initiative to talk to a university librarian about what resources are available to you.

Step 2: Finding Primary Sources at the State Level

The Texas Public Information Act empowers the public in order to make sure the people have access to information in the state. The attorney general oversees the implementation of the act. The *Public Information Act Handbook 2022* is available for free at this link: https://www.texasattorneygeneral.gov/sites/default/files/files/divisions/open-government/publicinfo_hb.pdf

Another way to find primary sources is through the state's websites. The websites of Texas state institutions tend to be relatively well developed and provide a wide array of information. Here are a couple of important links:

- Texas House of Representatives: www.house.state.tx.us
- Texas Senate: senate.texas.gov
- Office of the Texas Governor: gov.texas.gov
- Texas Supreme Court: www.txcourts.gov/supreme
- Court of Criminal Appeals: www.txcourts.gov/cca

Hundreds of Texas agencies exist, and they all have websites with an abundance of information.

Step 3: Finding Primary Sources at the Local Level

Finding primary sources at the local level is a bit trickier because some information may be available on the municipality or city website, whereas other information may be available on the county website. Start your Internet search with the city web page. Although the quality of the websites vary, you usually will be able to access information about the budget, elected leaders, local law enforcement, utilities, and a directory of law code, among several other things.

Look up the web page to your city and county. What struck you? What information does the website make easily accessible? Did visiting this website help you become more actively engaged?

Conclusion

Historically, Texas's criminal justice system has reflected the political culture of the state. In a traditionalistic political culture, citizens expect government to maintain order and the status quo; as a result, there may be a heavy emphasis on punishment and incarceration for those who break the law. In recent years, however, Texas has relied less on incarceration and more on alternatives to imprisonment. This shift in approach from punishment toward rehabilitation has yielded initial success in the form of reduced recidivism, greater cost savings, and a smaller prison population (not to mention a lower crime rate). Other potential areas of reform still persist.

Summary

LO: Discuss crime and punishment in Texas.

Crime has decreased in the United States over the past several decades, although less in Texas than in the United States as a whole. Many factors contribute to the crime rate. Most crimes are committed in larger cities. Also, a strong relationship exists between age, sex, and race and criminal arrests.

LO: Recall the differences between criminal and civil law, and explain criminal justice policy in Texas.

Criminal law involves violations of the Texas Penal Code, a system of state laws dealing with conduct that causes or threatens harm to individual or state-protected public interests. Civil law has to do with private relationships (rather than violations of the penal code) and can address financial matters, including wrongs committed by individuals or businesses against others. In criminal law, the standard of proof is higher ("beyond a reasonable doubt") than for civil cases (which require only a "preponderance of evidence"). Historically, Texas has had a "tough on crime" approach to criminal justice policy, primarily focused on punishment through incarceration. More recently, however, it has been the site of some fairly significant reform efforts.

LO: Describe the state of Texas's juvenile justice system and its procedures.

The Texas Juvenile Justice Department is the agency responsible for coordinating and overseeing juvenile justice programs in the state. This system has been overhauled to reflect a focus on rehabilitation as an alternative to incarceration. Juvenile cases are handled locally whenever possible, with county courts and local probation departments shouldering the bulk of the responsibility for them. A distinguishing feature of juvenile cases is that a hearing must take place to determine whether or not the juvenile will be tried as an adult.

LO: Explain the state of Texas's correction system, including its approach to rehabilitation and use of the death penalty.

The Texas Department of Criminal Justice (TDCJ) is a vast organization responsible for the detention and supervision of adult inmates, parolees, and individuals on community supervision (parole). It operates state prisons, state jails, and other facilities in addition to overseeing the operation of private prisons within the state. (Although they are not part of the state correctional system, local jails also detain prisoners.) Recently, Texas has attempted to curb its growing prison population and reduce recidivism by focusing on rehabilitation and alternatives to incarceration. Texas is still tough on crime in its use of the death penalty. It leads all other states in the number of death sentences imposed and number of executions carried out.

LO: Describe the challenges the state of Texas faces in its criminal justice system.

Despite the success of recent reform efforts, Texas continues to face challenges with regard to its criminal justice system. Some areas of continued concern include overcriminalization, excessive sentencing, police militarization, civil asset forfeiture, mental illness and suicide among the incarcerated, fine and fee practices, technological advances in evidence analysis, exoneration, race, and professional misconduct.

Key Terms

burden of proof
civil law
commute

criminal law
enhanced punishment
exculpatory evidence

exoneration
felony
graded penalties

in loco parentis

intake

misdemeanor

pardon

parens patriae

recidivism

reprieve

Texas Code of Criminal Procedure

Texas Penal Code

Notes

[1] Danielle Kaeble, Lauren Glaze, Anastasios Tsoutis, et al., "Correctional Populations in the United States, 2014," Bureau of Justice Statistics, last modified January 21, 2016, http://www.bjs.gov/content/pub/pdf/cpus14.pdf.

[2] Bureau of Justice Statistics, "Terms & Definitions: Law Enforcement," http://www.bjs.gov/index.cfm?ty=tdtp&tid=7.

[3] Brian A. Reaves, "Census of State and Local Law Enforcement Agencies, 2008," Bureau of Justice Statistics, July 2011, http://www.bjs.gov/content/pub/pdf/csllea08.pdf.

[4] Texas Department of Public Safety, http://www.dps.texas.gov/about.htm.

[5] Texas Department of Public Safety, "Texas Rangers," http://www.dps.texas.gov/TexasRangers/.

[6] Texas Constitution, art. 5, sec. 23, http://www.statutes.legis.state.tx.us/Docs/CN/htm/CN.5.htm; Texas Local Government Code Sec. 85.003-85.005, http://www.statutes.legis.state.tx.us/Docs/LG/htm/LG.85.htm.

[7] Brian A. Reaves, "Census of State and Local Law Enforcement Agencies, 2008," Bureau of Justice Statistics, July 2011, http://www.bjs.gov/content/pub/pdf/csllea08.pdf; Texas Association of Counties, "Sheriff," https://county.org/texas-county-government/texas-county-officials/Pages/Sheriff.aspx.

[8] William B. Travis, Denton County Sheriff's Office, https://dentoncounty.gov/Departments/Sheriff; Comal County Sheriff's Office, "Frequently Asked Questions," http://www.co.comal.tx.us/so/Questions.html.

[9] Brian A. Reaves, "Census of State and Local Law Enforcement Agencies, 2008," Bureau of Justice Statistics, July 2011, http://www.bjs.gov/content/pub/pdf/csllea08.pdf.

[10] Texas Local Government Code Sec. 341.001, http://www.statutes.legis.state.tx.us/Docs/LG/htm/LG.341.htm.

[11] Brian A. Reaves, "Census of State and Local Law Enforcement Agencies, 2008," Bureau of Justice Statistics, July 2011, http://www.bjs.gov/content/pub/pdf/csllea08.pdf.

[12] United States Courts, "Criminal Cases," http://www.uscourts.gov/about-federal-courts/types-cases/criminal-cases.

[13] Texas Penal Code, Sec. 1.02.

[14] Gabriel Monte, "Man Sentenced to 99 Years in Prison for 2018 Sexual Assault of Disabled Woman in Lubbock," *Lubbock Avalanche-Journal,* February 7, 2020, https://www.lubbockonline.com/news/20200207/man-sentenced-to-99-years-in-prison-for-2018-sexual-assault-of-disabled-woman-in-lubbock (accessed March 2, 2020).

[15] *Rummel v. Estelle,* 445 U.S. 263 (1980).

[16] Texas Penal Code, Sections 12.42–12.46, http://www.statutes.legis.state.tx.us/docs/PE/htm/PE.12.htm.

[17] Marc Mauer, "Long-Term Sentences: Time to Reconsider the Scale of Punishment," *UMKC Law Journal* 87, no. 1 (2018): 124.

[18] Derek M. Cohen, "Texas' Mandatory Sentencing Enhancements," Texas Public Policy Foundation, June 2016, http://www.texaspolicy.com/library/doclib/Texas-Mandatory-Sentencing-Enhancements.pdf.

[19] Chase Karacostas and Stacy Fernandez, "Texas Raises Sentencing for Hit-and-Run Car Accidents to Equivalent of DWI Manslaughter," *Texas Tribune,* September 20, 2019, https://www.texastribune.org/2019/09/20/render-aid/ (accessed March 2, 2020).

[20] Texas Department of Public Safety, *Crime in Texas: The Texas Crime Report for 2020,* https://www.dps.texas.gov/sites/default/files/documents/crimereports/20/2020cit.pdf, pg. 2 (accessed February 1, 2022).

[21] Ibid.

[22] United States Courts, "Civil Cases," http://www.uscourts.gov/about-federal-courts/types-cases/civil-cases.

[23] "Civil Law," *Legal Dictionary,* http://legaldictionary.net/civil-law/.

[24] Harris County Justice of the Peace Courts, "Information about Justice Court Cases," http://www.jp.hctx.net/evictions/filing.htm.

[25] Texas Judicial Branch, "Interpretation & Translation," http://www.txcourts.gov/lap/.

[26] United States Courts, "Facts and Case Summary—*Miranda v. Arizona,"* http://www.uscourts.gov/educational-resources/educational-activities/facts-and-case-summary-miranda-v-arizona.

[27] *Bernabe v. Texas,* No. 03-10-00773-CR (2012), https://cases.justia.com/texas/third-court-of-appeals/03-10-00773-cr.pdf.

[28] Richard Rogers, Amor A. Correa, Lisa L. Hazelwood, et al., "Spanish Translations of Miranda Warnings and the Totality of the Circumstances," *Law and Human Behavior 33,* no. 1 (February 2009): 61–69; Shaun Rabb, "Lawyers Want Universal Spanish Translation for Miranda Rights," Fox4News.com, August 12, 2016, http://www.fox4news.com/news/189600908-story.

[29] Texas Government Code, Sec. 57.002, http://www.statutes.legis.state.tx.us/Docs/GV/htm/GV.57.htm; Texas Code of Criminal Procedure, Art. 38.30, http://www.statutes.legis.state.tx.us/Docs/CR/htm/CR.38.htm#38.30.

[30] Texas Government Code, Sec. 57.001, http://www.statutes. legis.state.tx.us/Docs/GV/htm/GV.57.htm; Texas Rules of Evidence, Rule 604 (April 1, 2015), http://www.txcourts. gov/media/921665/tx-rules-of-evidence.pdf.

[31] Office of Court Administration, "Annual Statistical Report for the Texas Judiciary: Fiscal Year 2020," https://www. txcourts.gov/media/1451853/fy-20-annual-statistical-report_ final_mar10_2021.pdf, pg. 5,8 (accessed February 1, 2022).

[32] *Brady v. Maryland,* 373 U.S. 83 (1963).

[33] E. Ann Carson, "Prisoners in 2020 - Statistical Tables," U.S. Department of Justice, Bureau of Justice Statistics, December 2021, https://bjs.ojp.gov/content/pub/pdf/ p20st.pdf, pg. 1, 8 (accessed February 1, 2022).

[34] Federal Bureau of Investigation, "2016 Crime in the United States," Table 3: Crime in the United States by State, 2016, https://ucr.fbi.gov/crime-in-the-u.s/2016/ crime-in-the-u.s.-2016/tables/table-3.

[35] Editorial Board, "Texas Leads the Way in Needed Criminal Justice Reforms," *The Washington Post,* January 28, 2014, http://www.washingtonpost.com/opinions/texas-leads- the-way-in-needed-criminal-justice-reforms/2014/01/28/ 83919b72-879d-11e3-916e-e01534b1e132_story.html; Office of the Governor Rick Perry, "Drug Courts," https://web.archive.org/web/20140518192648/ http:// governor.state.tx.us/priorities/security/public_safety/ drug_courts/; Olivia Nuzzi, "Prison Reform Is Bigger in Texas," *The Daily Beast,* April 12, 2014, http://www. thedailybeast.com/articles/2014/04/12/prison-reform-is- bigger-in-texas.html.

[36] Bill Hammond, "Why Texas Businesses Back Reforming the State's Criminal Justice System," *Dallas Morning News,* January 19, 2014, https://www.dallasnews.com/opinion/ commentary/2014/01/20/why-texas-businesses-back- reforming-the-states-criminal-justice-system/ (accessed March 2, 2020); Brant Bingamon, "Criminal Justice Goes Unreformed by a Dismal 87th Texas Legislature," *The Austin Chronicle,* June 4, 2021, https://www.austinchronicle. com/news/2021-06-04/criminal-justice-goes-unreformed- by-a-dismal-87th-texas-legislature/ (accessed February 16, 2022).

[37] U.S. Census Bureau, "QuickFacts: Texas," https://www.census. gov/quickfacts/TX (accessed February 12, 2022).

[38] Texas Family Code, Sec. 51.041(a).

[39] See, for example, definition of "in loco parentis" in the *Free Legal Dictionary,* http://legal-dictionary.thefreelegaldictionary. com/in+loco+parentis.com.

[40] See, for example, definition of "parens patriae" in the *Free Legal Dictionary,* http://legal-dictionary.thefreelegaldictionary. com/prens+patriae.com.

[41] See, for example, definition of the "police power doctrine" in the *Free Legal Dictionary,* http://legal-dictionary. thefreelegaldictionary.com/Police+powers.com.

[42] William T. Field, "Mountain View School for Boys," *Handbook of Texas Online,* http://www.tshaonline.org/handbook/ online/articles/jjm01.

[43] University of Texas Tarlton Law Library, The William Wayne Justice Papers, "Juvenile Incarceration: *Morales v. Turman,*" http://tarlton.law.utexas.edu/william-wayne-justice/ morales-v-turman; William S. Bush, *Who Gets a Childhood?: Race and Juvenile Justice in Twentieth-Century Texas* (Athens: University of Georgia Press, 2010).

[44] *Morales v. Turman,* 383 F.Supp. 53 (1974), https://tarltonapps. law.utexas.edu/exhibits/ww_justice/documents_3/Morales_ opinion_3_1974.pdf.

[45] Ibid.

[46] Ibid.

[47] Laurie E. Jasinski, "Texas Youth Commission," *Handbook of Texas Online,* http://www.tshaonline.org/handbook/online/ articles/mdt35.

[48] Texas Legislature Online, "History," SB 653, http://www.legis. state.tx.us/billlookup/History.aspx?LegSess=82R&Bill=SB653.

[49] Texas Juvenile Justice Department, "Governing Board," http:// www.tjjd.texas.gov/index.php/board#introduction (accessed March 2, 2020).

[50] Texas Family Code, Chapter 51, http://www.statutes.legis.state. tx.us/Docs/FA/htm/FA.51.htm.

[51] Harris County District Courts, http://www.justex.net/courts/ Juvenile/JuvenileCourts.aspx; Dallas County Court System, http://www.dallascounty.org/department/courts/juvenile.php.

[52] Texas Juvenile Justice Department, "Texas Juvenile Probation Departments," http://www.tjjd.texas.gov/publications/other/ alljuveniledepartments.aspx.

[53] Texas Human Resources Code, Sec. 152.0010, http://www. statutes.legis.state.tx.us/Docs/HR/htm/HR.152.htm.

[54] Texas Juvenile Justice Department, "Overview of the Juvenile Justice System in Texas," http://www.tjjd.texas.gov/about/ overview.aspx.

[55] Texas Family Code, Sec. 51.02, http://www.statutes.legis.state. tx.us/Docs/FA/htm/FA.51.htm.

[56] Texas Family Code, Sec. 51.03, http://www.statutes.legis.state. tx.us/Docs/FA/htm/FA.51.htm; Texas Juvenile Justice Department, "Overview of the Juvenile Justice System in Texas."

[57] Texas Family Code, Sec. 54.02.

[58] Michele Deitch, *Juveniles in the Adult Criminal Justice System in Texas,* LBJ School of Public Affairs, University of Texas at Austin, Special Project Report, March 2011, http://www.utexas. edu/lbj/sites/default/files/file/news/juvenilestexas–final.pdf.

[59] Michele Deitch, *Juveniles in the Adult Criminal Justice System in Texas,* LBJ School of Public Affairs, University of Texas at Austin, Special Project Report, March 2011, http://www. utexas.edu/lbj/sites/default/files/file/news/juvenilestexas– final.pdf. See also provisions relating to expunging or keep- ing confidential the criminal records of minors: Texas

Government Code, Sec. 411.081 (orders of nondisclosure), Texas Family Code, Sec. 58.003 (sealing juvenile records); Texas Family Code, Sec. 58.203 (automatic restriction of access to juvenile records except by law enforcement officers).

[60] Death penalty: see Tarlton Law Library, Jamail Center for Legal Research, "Texas Death Penalty Law: Resources and Information about the Death Penalty Law in Texas," http://www.tarltonguides.law.utexas.edu/texas-death-penalty. See also Texas Penal Code, Sec. 8.07(c). Life sentence: see *Miller v. Alabama,* United States Supreme Court, June 2012.

[61] *Roper v. Simmons* (03-633), 543 U.S. 551 (2005); Charles Lane, "5–4 Supreme Court Abolishes Juvenile Executions," *The Washington Post,* March 2, 2005, http://www.washingtonpost.com/wp-dyn/articles/A62584-2005Mar1.html.

[62] *Miller v. Alabama,* 567 U.S. _____ (2012); accessible at https://www.supremecourt.gov/opinions/11pdf/10-9646g2i8.pdf.

[63] Texas Juvenile Justice Department, "Overview of the Juvenile Justice System in Texas," http://www.tjjd.texas.gov/about/overview.aspx.

[64] Texas Juvenile Justice Department, "TJJD Commitment Profile for Fiscal Years 2013–2017," Youth Characteristics, New Admissions FY 2013-2017, https://www2.tjjd.texas.gov/statistics/youth-characteristics1317.pdf (accessed February 12, 2022).

[65] Tony Fabelo, Nancy Arrigona, Michael D. Thompson, et al., "Closer to Home: An Analysis of the State and Local Impact of the Texas Juvenile Justice Reforms," January 2015, Council of State Governments Justice Center and the Public Policy Research Institute, https://csgjusticecenter.org/wp-content/uploads/2015/01/texas-JJ-reform-closer-to-home.pdf.

[66] Haley Holik and Deborah Fowler, "Kids No Longer Get Arrested for Truancy and Guess What? They Still Go to Class," *Dallas Morning News,* March 23, 2017. https://www.dallasnews.com/opinion/commentary/2017/03/23/kids-no-longer-get-arrested-for-truancy-and-guess-what-they-still-go-to-class/ (accessed March 2, 2020); Kate McGee, "Despite State Decriminalizing Truancy, Austin Students Can Still Get Charged for Skipping," KUT 90.5 Austin's NPR Station, https://www.kut.org/post/despite-state-decriminalizing-truancy-austin-students-can-still-get-charged-skipping (accessed March 2, 2020).

[67] Texas Juvenile Justice Department's Annual Report to Governor and Legislative Budget Board, "Community Juvenile Justice Appropriations, Riders, and Special Diversion Programs," 12, http://www.tjjd.texas.gov/index.php/document-library/send/338-reports-to-the-governor-and-legislative-budget-board/3043-annual-report-2021 (accessed February 12, 2022).

[68] Texas Board of Criminal Justice, "Agency Operating Budget 2022," Texas Department of Criminal Justice, December 1, 2021, https://www.tdcj.texas.gov/documents/bfd/FY2022_Operating_Budget_LBB.pdf (accessed February 12, 2022).

[69] Texas Department of Criminal Justice, "Texas Board of Criminal Justice Overview," http://www.tdcj.state.tx.us/tbcj/index.html.

[70] Texas Department of Criminal Justice, "Unit Directory," https://www.tdcj.texas.gov/unit_directory/ (accessed February 12, 2022).

[71] U.S. Department of Justice, Bureau of Justice Statistics, "Prisoners in 2020," Tables 4, 7, https://bjs.ojp.gov/content/pub/pdf/p20st.pdf (accessed February 12, 2022).

[72] *Ruiz v. Estelle,* 503 F.Supp. 1265 (S.D. Tex. 1980), https://tarltonapps.law.utexas.edu/exhibits/ww_justice/documents_3/Ruiz_opinion_1_1980.pdf.

[73] Robert Draper, "The Great Texas Prison Mess," *Texas Monthly,* May 1996, http://www.texasmonthly.com/articles/the-great-texas-prison-mess/.

[74] Paul M. Lucko, "Prison System," *Handbook of Texas Online,* http://www.tshaonline.org/handbook/online/articles/jjp03; Jolie McCullough, "Dip in Texas Prison Population Continues Trend," *Texas Tribune,* September 25, 2015, https://www.texastribune.org/2015/09/25/slight-dip-in-texas-prisoner-population-trend/.

[75] U.S. Department of Justice, Bureau of Justice Statistics, "Prisoners in 2020," Table 2, https://bjs.ojp.gov/content/pub/pdf/p20st.pdf (accessed February 12, 2022).

[76] Texas Board of Pardons and Paroles and Texas Department of Criminal Justice Parole Division, "Parole in Texas: Answers to Common Questions," 2005, http://www.tdcj.state.tx.us/bpp/publications/PIT_eng.pdf.

[77] Texas Board of Pardons and Paroles, "Revised Parole Guidelines," http://www.tdcj.state.tx.us/bpp/parole_guidelines/parole_guidelines.html (accessed May 27, 2016).

[78] Texas Penal Code, Sec. 12.35, http://www.statutes.legis.state.tx.us/docs/PE/htm/PE.12.htm.

[79] Texas Senate Committee on Criminal Justice, Charge 5, Interim Report to the 77th Legislature, http://www.lrl.state.tx.us/scanned/interim/76/c868_5.pdf.

[80] Legislative Budget Board, "Statewide Criminal and Juvenile Justice Recidivism and Revocation Rates," p. 2, http://www.lbb.state.tx.us/documents/publications/policy_report/4914_recidivism_revocation_rates_jan2019.pdf (accessed March 3, 2020).

[81] Texas Department of Criminal Justice, "Fiscal Year 2020 Statistical Report," p. 1, https://www.tdcj.texas.gov/documents/Statistical_Report_FY2020.pdf (accessed February 12, 2022).

[82] Legislative Budget Board, "Specialty Courts," http://www.lbb.state.tx.us/Documents/Publications/Issue_Briefs/3015_Specialty_Courts_0701.pdf.

[83] Ibid.

[84] For a comprehensive list, see "Texas Specialty Courts," https://www.txcourts.gov/media/1444764/specialty-courts-by-county-sept-2019.pdf (accessed February 12, 2022).

[85] Texas Department of Criminal Justice, "Private Facility Contract Monitoring/Oversight Division, Contracted Facilities as of February 02, 2016," http://tdcj.state.tx.us/divisions/pf/pf_unit_list.html.

[86] John MacCormack, "Private Prison Boom Goes Bust: In State, More Than a Dozen of the Lockups Have Failed," *San Antonio Express News,* August 22, 2015, http://www.expressnews.com/news/local/article/Private-prison-boom-goes-bust-6459964.php.

[87] John Burnett, "Texas Judge Refuses to License Child Care Facility in Immigrant Detention Center," NPR, May 6, 2016, http://www.npr.org/sections/thetwo-way/2016/05/06/476976133/texas-judge-refuses-to-license-childcare-facility-in-immigrant-detention-center.

[88] John MacCormack, "Private Prison Boom Goes Bust: In State, More Than a Dozen of the Lockups Have Failed," *San Antonio Express News,* August 22, 2015, http://www.expressnews.com/news/local/article/Private-prison-boom-goes-bust-6459964.php.

[89] Sarah Childress, "'Predictable' Riot at Texas Prison Followed Years of Complaints," *Frontline,* February 25, 2015, http://www.pbs.org/wgbh/frontline/article/predictable-riot-texas-prison-willacy-years-complaints/; John MacCormack, "Private Prison Boom Goes Bust: In State, More Than a Dozen of the Lockups Have Failed," *San Antonio Express News,* August 22, 2015, http://www.expressnews.com/news/local/article/Private-prison-boom-goes-bust-6459964.php; David Martin Davies, Reynaldo Leanons Jr., and Max Parrott, "Texas Matters: How Did a Small Texas County Become Prisonville USA?," Texas Public Radio, December 20, 2019, https://www.tpr.org/post/texas-matters-how-did-small-texas-county-become-prisonville-usa; Fernando de Valle, "Wind Turbines Diversifying Willacy's Farm-Based Economy," *Brownsville Herald,* April 17, 2019, https://www.brownsvilleherald.com/news/valley/wind-turbines-diversifying-willacy-s-farm-based-economy/article_ae42e7e0-611d-11e9-bd22-ff85a141204a.html (accessed March 3, 2020).

[90] Legislative Budget Board, "Criminal and Juvenile Justice Uniform Cost Report, Fiscal Years 2019 and 2020," January 2021, Figure 5, https://www.lbb.texas.gov/Documents/Publications/Policy_Report/6292_CJDA_Uniform_Cost.pdf (accessed February 12, 2022).

[91] Sasha Volokh, "Are Private Prisons Better or Worse Than Public Prisons?," *The Washington Post,* February 25, 2014, https://www.washingtonpost.com/news/volokh-conspiracy/wp/2014/02/25/are-private-prisons-better-or-worse-than-public-prisons/?utm_term=.09cedd6c6d9c.

[92] Adrian T. Moore, "Private Prisons: Quality Corrections at a Lower Cost," *Reason* Policy Study No. 240, http://reason.org/files/d14ffa18290a9aeb969d1a6c1a9ff935.pdf; Joseph Margulies, "This Is the Real Reason Private Prisons Should Be Outlawed," *Time,* August 24, 2016, http://time.com/4461791/private-prisons-department-of-justice/.

[93] Texas Local Government Code, 351.001-002, http://www.statutes.legis.state.tx.us/Docs/LG/htm/LG.351.htm.

[94] Texas Commission on Jail Standards, "Incarceration Rate Report–Highest to Lowest" January 1, 2022, https://www.tcjs.state.tx.us/wp-content/uploads/2022/01/IncarcerationRateRptCurrent.pdf (accessed February 12, 2022).

[95] See Local Government Code 341.902 and 361.

[96] Brandi Grissom, "City Jails Unregulated Despite Deaths, Complaints," *Texas Tribune,* September 17, 2010, https://www.texastribune.org/2010/09/17/city-jails-unregulated-despite-deaths-complaints/.

[97] Texas Justice Initiative, "Explore the Data: Deaths in Custody, 2005-2021, Type of Custody, Jail: Municipal," https://texasjusticeinitiative.org/data/ (accessed February 12, 2022).

[98] Texas Justice Initiative, "Explore the Data: Deaths in Custody, Type of Custody, Jail: Municipal," https://texasjusticeinitiative.org/datasets/custodial-deaths (accessed February 12, 2022).

[99] Reid Wilson, "Tough Texas Gets Results by Going Softer on Crime," *The Washington Post,* November 27, 2014, https://www.washingtonpost.com/blogs/govbeat/wp/2014/11/27/tough-texas-gets-results-by-going-softer-on-crime/; Olivia Nuzzi, "Prison Reform Is Bigger in Texas," *The Daily Beast,* April 12, 2014, http://www.thedailybeast.com/articles/2014/04/12/prison-reform-is-bigger-in-texas.html.

[100] Marc Levin, "Adult Corrections Reform: Lower Crime, Lower Costs," Texas Public Policy Foundation, September 2011, http://rightoncrime.com/wp-content/uploads/2011/09/Texas-Model-Adult.pdf.

[101] Jolie McCullough, "Dip in Texas Prison Population Continues Trend," *Texas Tribune,* September 25, 2015, https://www.texastribune.org/2015/09/25/slight-dip-in-texas-prisoner-population-trend/.

[102] Jolie McCullough, "Dip in Texas Prison Population Continues Trend," *Texas Tribune,* September 25, 2015, https://www.texastribune.org/2015/09/25/slight-dip-in-texas-prisoner-population-trend/; Texas Department of Criminal Justice, "The Texas Department of Criminal Justice To Close Two Prison Units in 2020," TDCJ News, https://www.tdcj.texas.gov/news/TDCJ_to_close_two_units_2020.html (accessed February 13, 2022); Jayson Hawkins, "Texas Prisons Close Amid Pandemic," *Prison Legal News,* May 1, 2021, https://www.prisonlegalnews.org/news/2021/may/1/texas-prisons-close-amid-pandemic/#:~:text=The%20agency%20had%20also%20shut,shuttered%20prisons%20housed%20men%20only.

[103] Council of State Governments Justice Center, "States Report Reductions in Recidivism," September 2012, https://csgjusticecenter.org/documents/0000/1569/9.24.12_Recidivism_Reductions_9-24_lo_res.pdf; Legislative Budget Board, "Statewide Criminal and Juvenile Justice Recidivism and Revocation Rates," January 2021, Figures 1 and 2,

https://www.lbb.texas.gov/Documents/Publications/
Policy_Report/6293_CJDA_Recidivism-Revocation.pdf
(accessed February 13, 2022).

[104] Texas Department of Public Safety, "Crime in Texas," Table
ES 1: Crime Rates by Offense, 2, https://www.dps.texas.
gov/sites/default/files/documents/crimereports/20/2020cit.
pdf (accessed February 13, 2022).

[105] Texas Department of Criminal Justice, "Rehabilitation
Programs Division, Substance Abuse Treatment Program,"
https://www.tdcj.texas.gov/divisions/rpd/rpd_substance_
abuse.html.

[106] Windham School District, "Rider 6 Response," January 2021,
1-2, https://wsdtx.org/images/PDF/legislative_required_
reports/87/2021_WSD_Rider_6_Report.pdf (accessed
February 13, 2022).

[107] Windham School District, "Pioneering Success: Annual
Performance Report School Year 2020-2021," pg. 6,
https://wsdtx.org/images/PDF/APR/2021/Annual
PerformanceReport2021highresweb.pdf (accessed
February 13, 2022).

[108] Cornell University Law School Legal Information Institute,
Furman v. Georgia, https://www.law.cornell.edu/supremecourt/
text/408/238#writing-USSC_CR_0408_0238_ZS; Michael
H. Reggio, "History of the Death Penalty," *Frontline: The
Execution* (PBS), http://www.pbs.org/wgbh/pages/frontline/
shows/execution/readings/history.html.

[109] Death Penalty Information Center, "Number of Executions by
State and Region Since 1976," http://www.deathpenaltyinfo.
org/number-executions-state-and-region-1976.

[110] Death Penalty Information Center, "Number of Executions by
State and Region Since 1976," http://www.deathpenaltyinfo.
org/number-executions-state-and-region-1976 (accessed
February 13, 2022).

[111] Ibid.

[112] Texas Legislature Online, Bill Analysis SB 60, http://
www.legis.state.tx.us/tlodocs/79R/analysis/pdf/SB00060F.
pdf#navpanes=0.

[113] ProCon.org, "Top 10 Pros and Cons: Should the Death
Penalty Be Allowed?," http://deathpenalty.procon.org/
view.resource.php?resourceID=002000.

[114] Innocence Project, "Cameron Todd Willingham: Wrongfully
Convicted and Executed in Texas," http://www.
innocenceproject.org/cameron-todd-willingham-
wrongfully-convicted-and-executed-in-texas/.

[115] Death Penalty Information Center, "Exoneration by the
Numbers - Exoneration by State," https://deathpenaltyinfo.
org/policy-issues/innocence/innocence-by-the-numbers
(accessed February 13, 2022).

[116] *Callins v. Collins,* 510 U.S. 1141 (1994).

[117] State of Texas Office of Court Administration, "Annual
Statistical Report for the Texas Judiciary, Fiscal Year 2020,"

44, https://www.txcourts.gov/media/1451853/fy-20-annual-
statistical-report_final_mar10_2021.pdf (accessed
February 14, 2022).

[118] James Kimberly, "Once on Death Row, It Might Not Matter,"
Houston Chronicle, February 9, 2001, https://www.chron.
com/news/article/Once-on-death-row-it-might-not-matter-
2007654.php

[119] Michael Hall, "The Judgment of Sharon Keller," *Texas
Monthly,* August 2009, http://www.texasmonthly.com/
articles/the-judgment-of-sharon-keller/.

[120] Texas Board of Pardons and Paroles, "Annual Statistical
Report, FY 2020," 23, https://www.tdcj.texas.gov/bpp/
publications/FY_2020_Annual_Statistical_Report.pdf
(accessed February 14, 2022).

[121] U.S. Census Bureau, "QuickFacts: Harris County," https://
www.census.gov/quickfacts/harriscountytexas (accessed
February 14, 2022).

[122] Texas Department of Criminal Justice, "Death Row Information: Executed Offenders," https://www.tdcj.state.tx.us/
death_row/dr_executed_offenders.html (accessed
February 14, 2022).

[123] Harris County Budget Management Department, "Fiscal
Year 2021-22 General Fund Adopted Budget," http://
budget.harriscountytx.gov/doc/Budget/budgetbook/
FY2021_22_Adopted_Budget.pdf (accessed February 14,
2022).

[124] Dallas County Office of Budget and Evaluation, "Dallas
County FY 2022 Budget," https://www.dallascounty.org/
Assets/uploads/docs/budget/fy2022/FY2022-BudgetBook-
Detail-OnlineVersion-Adopted-FINAL.pdf (accessed
February 14, 2022).

[125] Harris County Criminal Courts at Law, http://www.ccl.hctx.
net/criminal/ (accessed February 14, 2022); Dallas County
Criminal Courts, https://www.dallascounty.org/government/
courts/county_criminal/ (accessed February 14, 2022).

[126] Gallup, "Death Penalty: Are You in Favor of the Death Penalty for a Person Convicted of Murder?" https://news.gallup.
com/poll/1606/death-penalty.aspx (accessed February 14,
2022); University of Texas/Texas Tribune Poll, "Texas
Statewide Survey," Q. 43, https://static.texastribune.org/
media/files/2678e64f3f22edf2cee906e12ca3f1c2/ut-tt-2021-
04-summary-all.pdf?_ga=2.198854764.2123450611.
1620253780-591199111.1615555411 (accessed February 14,
2022).

[127] Kenneth C. Land, Raymond H. C. Teske Jr., and Hui Zheng,
"The Short-Term Effects of Executions on Homicides:
Deterrence, Displacement, or Both?," *Criminology* 47,
no. 4 (November 2009): 1009–43.

[128] Death Penalty Information Center, "Discussion of Recent
Deterrence Studies," http://www.deathpenaltyinfo.org/
discussion-recent-deterrence-studies.

[129] Michael L. Radelet and Traci L. Lacock, "Do Executions Lower Homicide Rates? The Views of Leading Criminologists," *Journal of Criminal Law & Criminology 99,* no. 2 (2009): 489–508, http://www.deathpenaltyinfo.org/files/DeterrenceStudy2009.pdf.

[130] Texas Department of Criminal Justice, "Death Row Information," https://www.tdcj.state.tx.us/death_row/dr_facts.html.

[131] U.S. Census Bureau, "QuickFacts: Texas," https://www.census.gov/quickfacts/TX (accessed February 14, 2022).

[132] U.S. Census Bureau, "Poverty Thresholds by Size of Family and Number of Children, 2021," https://www.census.gov/data/tables/time-series/demo/income-poverty/historical-poverty-thresholds.html (accessed February 14, 2022).

[133] Interest on Lawyers Trust Accounts, http://www.iolta.org/.

[134] State Bar of Texas, "Access to Justice," https://www.texasbar.com/AM/Template.cfm?Section=Access_To_Justice_Home.

[135] For university legal clinics, see the University of Texas and Saint Mary's University, www.stmarytx.edu/law/index.php?site=centerforlawandsocialjustice and https://www.sll.texas.gov/self-help/where-to-go-for-help/legal-clinics/. An example of a nonprofit organization is the Texas Civil Rights Project, http://www.texascivilrightsproject.org.

[136] The Lawyer Referral and Information Service of the State Bar, https://www.texasbar.com/AM/Template.cfm?Section=Lawyer_Referral_Service_LRIS_.

[137] Texas Access to Justice Commission, "FAQ," http://www.texasatj.org/faq.

[138] Texas Indigent Defense Commission, "Summary of Funding for All Counties: All Counties," https://tidc.tamu.edu/public.net/Reports/SummaryReport.aspx (accessed February 14, 2022).

[139] Mark Curriden, "Dearth of Legal Aid for Low-Income Texans 'Really Dire,'" *Texas Lawbook,* https://www.bizjournals.com/dallas/news/2019/11/22/legal-aid-texans.html (accessed February 29, 2020).

[140] Editorial Board, "Texas Leads the Way in Needed Criminal Justice Reforms," *The Washington Post,* January 28, 2014, http://www.washingtonpost.com/opinions/texas-leads-the-way-in-needed-criminal-justice-reforms/2014/01/28/83919b72-879d-11e3-916e-e01534b1e132_story.html; Office of the Governor Rick Perry, "Drug Courts," https://web.archive.org/web/20140518192648/http://governor.state.tx.us/priorities/security/public_safety/drug_courts/; Nuzzi, "Prison Reform Is Bigger in Texas," *The Daily Beast,* April 12, 2014, http://www.thedailybeast.com/articles/2014/04/12/prison-reform-is-bigger-in-texas.html.

[141] Mortimer B. Zuckerman, "Get a Little Less Tough on Crime," *U.S. News & World Report,* May 9, 2014, http://www.usnews.com/opinion/articles/2014/05/09/its-time-for-prison-reform-and-an-end-to-mandatory-minimum-sentences; Erik Luna, "The Overcriminalization Phenomenon," *American University Law Review 54,* no. 3 (2005): 703–43, http://digitalcommons.wcl.american.edu/aulr/vol54/iss3/5.

[142] Right on Crime, "Overcriminalization," http://rightoncrime.com/category/priority-issues/overcriminalization/.

[143] See Harvey Silverglate, *Three Felonies A Day: How the Feds Target the Innocent* (New York: Encounter Books, 2009).

[144] Derek M. Cohen, "Texas' Mandatory Sentencing Enhancements," Texas Public Policy Foundation, June 2016, http://www.texaspolicy.com/library/doclib/Texas-Mandatory-Sentencing-Enhancements.pdf.

[145] Byron Pitts, Jackie Jesko, and Lauren Effron, "Former Federal Judge Regrets 55-Year Marijuana Sentence," *ABC News,* February 18, 2015, http://abcnews.go.com/US/federal-judge-regrets-55-year-marijuana-sentence/story?id=28869467; Matt McDonald, "Former Federal Judge Writes to White House Requesting Reduced Sentence for Jailed Utah Man," February 9, 2016, *Fox 13,* http://fox13now.com/2016/02/09/former-federal-judge-writes-to-white-house-requesting-reduced-sentence-for-jailed-utah-man/.

[146] United States Sentencing Commission, "2015 Report to the Congress: Impact of the Fair Sentencing Act of 2010," http://www.ussc.gov/research/congressional-reports/2015-report-congress-impact-fair-sentencing-act-2010.

[147] Texas Department of Public Safety, "The Texas 1033 Military Surplus Property Program," http://www.dps.texas.gov/LawEnforcementSupport/texas1033.htm.

[148] American Civil Liberties Union, "Police Militarization," https://www.aclu.org/issues/criminal-law-reform/reforming-police-practices/police-militarization; Daniela Guzman, "From Warfighter to Crimefighter—The U.S. 1033 Program, and the Risk of Corruption and Misuse of Public Funds, Association of Certified Financial Crime Specialists," http://www.acfcs.org/from-warfighter-to-crimefighter-the-us-1033-program-and-the-risk-of-corruption-and-misuse-of-public-funds/; also see ACLU, "War Comes Home: The Excessive Militarization of American Policing," June 2014, https://www.aclu.org/sites/default/files/assets/jus14-warcomeshome-report-web-rel1.pdf.

[149] American Civil Liberties Union, "Asset Forfeiture Abuse," https://www.aclu.org/issues/criminal-law-reform/reforming-police-practices/asset-forfeiture-abuse (accessed August 23, 2016).

[150] American Civil Liberties Union, "Asset Forfeiture Abuse," https://www.aclu.org/issues/criminal-law-reform/reforming-police-practices/asset-forfeiture-abuse (accessed August 23, 2016); "Right on Crime, Civil Asset Forfeiture," Texas Public Policy Foundation, http://rightoncrime.com/category/priority-issues/civil-asset-forfeiture/.

[151] "Deinstitutionalization: A Psychiatric 'Titanic,'" *Frontline* (PBS), excerpted from E. Fuller Torrey, *Out of the Shadows: Confronting America's Mental Illness Crisis* (New York: Wiley, 1997), http://www.pbs.org/wgbh/pages/frontline/shows/asylums/special/excerpt.html.

[152] Ed Lyon, "Imprisoning America's Mentally Ill," *Prison Legal News* February 4, 2019, https://www.prisonlegalnews.org/news/2019/feb/4/imprisoning-americas-mentally-ill/.

153 Mary Beth Pfeiffer, "Cruel and Unusual Punishment," *The New York Times,* May 7, 2006, http://crazyinamerica.com/html/articles.html#Anchor-62428.

154 Texas Department of Criminal Justice, "Biennial Report of the Texas Correctional Office on Offenders with Medical and Mental Impairments, Fiscal Year 2015-2016," p. 8, https://www.tdcj.texas.gov/documents/rid/TCOOMMI_Biennial_Report_2017.pdf (accessed March 3, 2020).

155 Kate Murphy and Christi Bar, "Overincarceration of People with Mental Illness: Pretrial Diversion across the Country and the Next Steps for Texas to Improve Its Efforts and Increase Utilization," Texas Public Policy Institute, June 2015, p. 5, http://www.texaspolicy.com/library/doclib/Overincarceration-of-People-with-Mental-Illness.pdf.

156 Texas Specialty Courts, http://gov.texas.gov/files/cjd/Specialty_Courts_By_County_May_2016.pdf.

157 Sylvester Turner, "Texas Facing Mental Health Crisis," January 22, 2014, http://www.chron.com/opinion/outlook/article/Texas-facing-mental-health-crisis-4214980.php.

158 *An act relating to the creation of a mental health jail diversion pilot program.* SB. 1885, Texas State Legislature, 2013, http://www.capitol.state.tx.us/tlodocs/83R/billtext/pdf/SB01185F.pdf.

159 Mihir Zaveri, "Pilot Program Gives Hope to Inmates with Mental Health Needs," *Houston Chronicle,* March 15, 2016, http://www.chron.com/news/houston-texas/houston/article/Pilot-program-gives-hope-to-inmates-with-mental-6892205.php; Harris Center for Mental Health and IDD, "Harris County Mental Health Jail Diversion Program," https://www.theharriscenter.org/About/News/Agency-News/ArticleId/37/harris-county-mental-health-jail-diversion-program (accessed March 3, 2020).

160 The Center for Health Care Services, "Blueprint for Success: The Bexar County Model, 2011," http://www.jtvf.org/wp-content/uploads/Feb-22-2011-Convening/fina-jail-text%20(2).pdf. See also Alexander Cowell, Arnie Aldridge, Nahama Brone, et al., "A Cost Analysis of the Bexar County, Texas, Jail Diversion Program," 2008, http://www.naco.org/sites/default/files/documents/Cost%20Benefit%20Study.pdf.

161 Elvia Limon, "Q&A with NAMI Texas' Executive Director about Mental Health During the Pandemic," *Texas Tribune,* November 25, 2020, https://www.texastribune.org/2020/11/25/mental-health-COVID-AMA/

162 Texas Code of Criminal Procedure, Art. 45.046.

163 Kendall Taggart and Alex Campbell, "Their Crime: Being Poor. Their Sentence: Jail," BuzzFeed.com, October 7, 2015, https://www.buzzfeed.com/kendalltaggart/in-texas-its-a-crime-to-be-poor?utm_term=.ytODVAALNv#.yxVx855opN.

164 Marc Levin and Michael Haugen, "Open Roads and Overflowing Jails: Addressing High Rates of Rural Pretrial Incarceration," Right on Crime, Texas Public Policy Foundation https://files.texaspolicy.com/uploads/2018/08/16104511/2018-04-RR-Rural-Pretrial-Incarceration-CEJ-Levin-Haugen-1.pdf (accessed March 4, 2020).

165 Conference of Chief Justices, "Resolution 3," 2013, http://ccj.ncsc.org/~/media/microsites/files/ccj/resolutions/01302013-pretrial-release-endorsing-cosca-paper-evidencebased-pretrial-release.ashx.

166 Legislative Budget Board, "Criminal and Juvenile Justice Uniform Cost Report, FY 2019– 2020," January 2021, https://www.lbb.texas.gov/Documents/Publications/Policy_Report/6292_CJDA_Uniform_Cost.pdf (accessed February 15, 2022).

167 Ross Ramsey, "Analysis: Legislators Seeking a More Efficient Approach to Jail Policies," *Texas Tribune,* January 25, 2016, https://www.texastribune.org/2016/01/25/analysis-criminal-justice-reformers-take-police-an/.

168 E. Ann Carson, "Mortality in Local Jails, 2000-2018," U.S. Department of Justice, 1, https://bjs.ojp.gov/content/pub/pdf/mlj0018st.pdf (accessed February 15, 2022).

169 Texas Justice Initiative, "Deaths in Custody," https://texasjusticeinitiative.org/data/ (accessed March 4, 2020).

170 Klaus-Peter Dahle, Johannes C. Lohner, and Norbert Konrad, "Suicide Prevention in Penal Institutions: Validation and Optimization of a Screening Tool for Early Identification of High-Risk Inmates in Pretrial Detention," *International Journal of Forensic Mental Health* 4, no. 1 (2005): 53–62.

171 Texas Administrative Code, Title 37, Chapter 265.

172 Texas Commission on Jail Standards, "Non-Compliant Jails," https://www.tcjs.state.tx.us/non-compliant-jails/ (accessed March 4, 2020).

173 Dane Schiller, "Findings of Sandra Bland Jail Death Probe Released," *Houston Chronicle,* April 14, 2016, http://www.chron.com/news/houston-texas/article/Findings-of-Sandra-Bland-jail-death-probe-7243359.php; K. K. Rebecca Lai, Haeyoun Park, Larry Buchanan, et al., "Assessing the Legality of Sandra Bland's Arrest," *The New York Times,* July 22, 2015, http://www.nytimes.com/interactive/2015/07/20/us/sandra-bland-arrest-death-videos-maps.html?_r=0; Christine Hauser, "Sandra Bland's Family Settles $1.9 Million Civil Suit, Lawyer Says," *The New York Times,* September 15, 2016, http://www.nytimes.com/2016/09/16/us/sandra-bland-family-settlement-19-million-lawsuit.html; Manny Fernandez and David Montgomery, "Perjury Charge Dropped against Ex-Trooper in Sandra Bland Case," *The New York Times,* June 28, 2017, https://www.nytimes.com/2017/06/28/us/sandra-bland-death-brian-encinia-texas-texas.html.

174 Texas Forensic Science Commission, "About Us," http://www.fsc.texas.gov/about (accessed August 28, 2016).

175 Texas Forensic Science Commission, "Letter to Legal Community Stakeholders," August 21, 2015, http://www.fsc.texas.gov/sites/default/files/documents/Unintended%20Effects%20of%20FBI%20Database%20Corrections%20on%20Assessment%20of%20DNA%20Mixture%20Interpretation%20in%20Texas%20NOTICE.pdf.

176 Texas Forensic Science Commission, "Fourth Annual Report, November 2014–November 2015," p. 17, http://www.fsc.

texas.gov/sites/default/files/2015%20FSC%20Annual%20 Report%20Posted.pdf.

[177] National Registry of Exonerations, "Exonerations by State," http://www.law.umich.edu/special/exoneration/Pages/ Exonerations-in-the-United-States-Map.aspx; The National Registry of Exonerations, "Annual Report," March 30, 2021, Table 1, https://www.law.umich.edu/special/exoneration/ Documents/2021AnnualReport.pdf (accessed February 15, 2022).

[178] National Registry of Exonerations, "Timothy B. Cole," https:// www.law.umich.edu/special/exoneration/Pages/casedetail. aspx?caseid=3114. Note that Texas Civil Practice and Remedies 103.001 (2016) may also require a pardon even after a dismissal or an acquittal in order to be eligible for compensation for wrongful incarceration.

[179] Texas Department of Criminal Justice, "Statistical Report Fiscal Year 2020," 1, https://www.tdcj.texas.gov/documents/ Statistical_Report_FY2020.pdf (accessed February 15, 2022).

[180] Department of Public Safety, "Crime in Texas 2020," 30-37, https://www.dps.texas.gov/sites/default/files/documents/ crimereports/20/2020cit.pdf (accessed February 15, 2022).

[181] Kimberly Kindy, Marc Fisher, Julie Tate, et al., "A Year of Reckoning: Police Fatally Shoot Nearly 1,000," *The Washington Post,* December 26, 2015, http://www.washingtonpost.com/ sf/investigative/wp/2015/12/26/2015/12/26/a-year-of- reckoning-police-fatally-shoot-nearly-1000/.

[182] Texas Department of Criminal Justice, "Statistical Report Fiscal Year 2020," https://www.tdcj.texas.gov/documents/Statistical_ Report_FY2020.pdf; U.S. Census Bureau, "QuickFacts: Texas," https://www.census.gov/quickfacts/TX (accessed February 15, 2022).

[183] Texas Department of Public Safety, "Crime in Texas, 2020," pg. 39, 41, https://www.dps.texas.gov/sites/default/files/documents/ crimereports/20/2020cit.pdf (accessed February 16, 2022).

[184] Alex R. Piquero and Robert W. Brame, "Assessing the Race– Crime and Ethnicity–Crime Relationship in a Sample of Serious Adolescent Delinquents," *Crime & Delinquency* 54, no. 3 (July 2008): 390–422.

[185] Fair Punishment Project, "Too Broken to Fix: Part I. An In- depth Look at America's Outlier Death Penalty Counties," August 2016, http://fairpunishment.org/wp-content/ uploads/2016/08/FPP-TooBroken.pdf.

[186] Sandhya Somashekhar and Steven Rich, "Final Tally: Police Shot and Killed 986 People in 2015" *The Washington Post,* January 6, 2016.

[187] Evan Hill et al. "How George Floyd was killed in Police Custody." *New York Times,* May 31, 2020.

[188] U.S. Census Bureau, "QuickFacts: United States," https:// www.census.gov/quickfacts/fact/table/US/PST045218 (accessed February 16, 2022).

[189] E. Ann Carson, "Prisoners in 2020," U.S. Department of Justice, December 2021, Table 3, https://bjs.ojp.gov/content/ pub/pdf/p20st.pdf (accessed February 16, 2022).

[190] Committee on Causes and Consequences of High Rates of Incarceration, *The Growth of Incarceration in the United States* (Washington, D.C.: National Academies Press, 2014), 70.

[191] George L. Kelling and James Q. Wilson, "Broken Windows: The Police and Neighborhood Safety," *The Atlantic,* March 1982, https://www.theatlantic.com/magazine/archive/1982/ 03/broken-windows/304465/ (accessed March 1, 2020).

[192] Michelle Alexander, *The New Jim Crow: Mass Incarceration in the Age of Colorblindness* (New York: New Press, 2010), 2.

[193] Ta-Nehisi Coates, "The Black Family in the Age of Mass Incarceration" *The Atlantic,* October 2015, https://www. theatlantic.com/magazine/archive/2015/10/the-black- family-in-the-age-of-mass-incarceration/403246/ (accessed March 1, 2020).

[194] E. Ann Carson, "Prisoners in 2020," U.S. Department of Jus- tice, Office of Justice Programs, Bureau of Justice Statistics, December 2020, Table 3, https://bjs.ojp.gov/content/pub/ pdf/p20st.pdf (accessed February 16, 2022).

[195] Eli Hager, "A Mass Incarceration Mystery: Why Are Black Imprisonment Rates Going Down? Four Theories," *The Marshall Project,* December 15, 2017, https://www.themarshall- project.org/2017/12/15/a-mass-incarceration-mystery (accessed March 1, 2020).

[196] Texas Code of Criminal Procedure, Art. 2.01.

[197] Pamela Coloff, "Jail Time May Be the Least of Ken Anderson's Problems," *Texas Monthly,* November 14, 2013, http:// www.texasmonthly.com/articles/jail-time-may-be-the-least- of-ken-andersons-problems/#sthash.nz5UEobF.dpuf; Inno- cence Project, "Michael Morton," http://www. innocenceproject.org/cases/michael-morton/.

[198] *An act relating to discovery in a criminal case.* SB 1611 (2013), Texas state legislature, http://www.legis.state.tx.us/tlodocs/ 83R/billtext/html/SB01611F.HTM.

[199] "Setting the Record Straight on Prosecutorial Misconduct," Texas District and County Attorneys Association (TDCAA), 2012.

[200] Alex Caprariello, "Hundreds of DNA Criminal Cases From Shuttered Austin Police DNA Lab under Review," *KXAN,* June 8, 2021, https://www.kxan.com/news/crime/ hundreds-of-dna-criminal-cases-from-shuttered-austin-police- dna-lab-under-review/.

CHAPTER 7

Local Governments in Texas

Local governments in Texas and throughout the United States are hiding in plain sight. Evidence of local government is all around us: paved streets, sidewalks, clean water, fire stations, police cars, parks, and schools. Yet many citizens are either unaware of or uninterested in the operations and procedures of local governments and local government elections. Most citizens show as little interest in the former as the latter. Voter turnout in local government elections is consistently the lowest year in and year out when compared to federal and state elections.

Austin City Hall
Peter Tsai Photography/Alamy Stock Photo

Over 85 percent of Texans live in urban areas and rely on local governments for a host of services, and they have been increasing their demands for a greater range of services. Local governments, in short, provide some of the services that make our modern lives possible. Even the roughly 15 percent of Texans who live in rural areas rely on services from county governments and special districts. It is important for us, as Texans, to understand how local governments work and affect our lives.[1]

Chapter Learning Objectives

- Define types of local government.
- Define general law cities and home rule cities.
- Explain municipal elections in Texas, including a discussion of voter turnout.

- Describe county governments in Texas, including weaknesses and possible reforms.

- Discuss special purpose districts.

Federalism Revisited

Learning Objective: Define types of local government.

The United States is characterized by its highly decentralized system of government. This lack of centralization has its roots in the historic fear of a strong national government and the principles of federalism enshrined in the U.S. Constitution. Federalism is the political principle that assigns different functions to different levels of government. In Chapter 2 we focused on the relationship between the central government and the various state governments in our federalist structure. Local governments add another layer. Decentralization and the lack of intergovernmental coordination are trends in Texas government and throughout the United States. Nationwide, there are 90,095 local government units, and Texas has a little more than 5,000 of them. Counts for 2017 on the number of local governments by category are presented in Table 7.1.

Creatures of the State

In a federal system in which multiple levels of government share authority over the same territory, states have **police powers**—in other words, the authority to regulate the health, safety, and morals of their citizens. These powers come from the Tenth Amendment of the U.S. Constitution, and states exercise them by

police power
The ability afforded states under the Tenth Amendment of the U.S. Constitution to regulate behavior and enforce order within their geographic territories

TABLE 7.1

Number of Local Governments in the United States and Texas, 2017

	United States	Texas
Counties	3,031	254
Cities	19,495	1,218
Townships	16,253	—
School districts	12,754	1,073
Special districts	38,542	2,798
Totals	90,095	5,343

Source: U.S. Census Bureau, *2017 Census of Governments: Organization,* Table ORG02. Note that the Census of Governments occurs every five years, https://www.census.gov/data/tables/2017/econ/gus/2017-governments.html.

making and enforcing laws. Enforcement here includes not just what we usually think of as police powers (actual police forces; the people in uniform) but also legal sanctions and other methods of nonphysical coercion. States are allowed to form local governments to help them use their police powers. Constitutionally, municipalities and other local governments are legal **creatures of the state.** This means municipal and other local governments are constrained by the same legal limits as are states and lack any legal existence independent of state action. In this sense, the relationship between a state and the local governments within its boundaries is **unitary** in design. On the other hand, unitary governments, while also able to form creatures of the state, strictly dictate what those governments can and cannot do. Unlike in a federal system where states are granted all those powers not expressly given to the national government, unitary systems are much more centralized. State-level governments receive only those powers that the central governing authority expressly grants them. The same principle goes for municipalities and other local governments.

In our federal system, the states have substantial discretion in the authority they grant their local governments, and local governments within each state have different types of authority. We can categorize local governments by the amount of authority the states grant them. General-purpose governments have broad discretionary authority to act on a range of issues; to control their own spending, revenue, and personnel; and to establish and modify their own governmental structures. Conversely, limited-purpose governments have rather narrow authority to act and have little leeway over revenue, spending, and personnel; the state sets the structure of these governments.[2]

Examples of limited-purpose government in Texas include school districts and counties. A school district has one function: education. Its taxing authority is limited to the property tax, and a state agency controls many personnel issues. Texas counties are also limited-purpose governments. State law severely restricts county authority and revenue sources, and all 254 Texas counties share the same government structure.

Municipalities are the most visible example of general-purpose governments in Texas. Home rule Texas cities (see the following section) have the authority to pass any ordinance not expressly forbidden by the state constitution or state laws, and they have multiple sources of revenue. Texas home rule cities have greater discretion in deciding their government structure, and the state has limited authority over cities' personnel decisions. Consequently, not all local governments are created equal, although all are legal creatures of their states. Cities, counties, special districts, and school districts all have their unique aspects.

creatures of the state
State governments create local governments, and all of local governments' powers come from the state government; there are no inherent rights for local governments independent of what the state grants them

unitary system of government
A system of government where all functions of government are controlled by the central/national government

---

Understanding Impact A federal system divides power between the nation and the states. In Texas, there are two broad categories of local government—general purpose and limited purpose—based on the amount of authority granted by the state. Cities in Texas are categorized as general-purpose government and exercise broad authority within their jurisdiction. Counties, school districts, and other special districts such as fire, transportation, and utility are limited in their activities, though these entities provide many critical services to citizens. Which category of local government do you think is most important based on the types of activities and services provided? Why?

General Law Cities and Home Rule

Learning Objective: Define general law cities and home rule cities.

general law city
City governed by a city charter, which state statutes created

home rule city
City governed by a city charter that local citizens created

City governments are municipal corporations, granted a corporate charter by their state. The term "municipality" derives from the Roman *municipium,* which means a "free city capable of governing its local affairs, even though subordinate to the sovereignty of Rome."[3] A city's charter is its constitution, which provides the basic organization and structure of the city government and outlines the general powers and authority of its government and officials. Cities in Texas are chartered as either a **general law city** or a **home rule city.** The charters for general law cities are spelled out in state statutes, and those cities must choose from the seven charters provided in these statutes.[4] According to the Texas Municipal League, roughly 75 percent of all Texas cities are under general law, with only 385 cities under home rule.[5]

Thanks to a state constitutional amendment in 1912, Texas cities with populations of at least 5,000 may be chartered as home rule cities.[6] Most cities with such populations choose to be home rule cities. Home rule affords local citizens a greater range of governmental structure and organization and allows such cities to pass ordinances not prohibited by state law. Although there is no specific grant of power to cities in the state constitution, cities can pass any ordinance that does not conflict with state law or violate the state constitution. For example, no state law establishes the number of city council members, but the state constitution does establish a ceiling of four years for terms of office.

Prohibitions on local government action can be implicit or explicit. For instance, there is no explicit prohibition against cities passing an ordinance banning open alcohol containers in vehicles. Several Texas cities passed such ordinances in the 1980s before there was a state law against open containers. However, state courts ruled that the regulation of alcohol was a state function and, by *implication,* Texas cities could not pass ordinances banning open alcohol containers in vehicles.

The home rule provisions of the Texas Constitution allow great latitude in governing local affairs. Once adopted, home rule charters may be amended solely with the approval of the city voters. Usually a charter review commission or the city council proposes amendments; but "under Section 9.004 of the Local Government Code, citizens can force the city council to call an election on a proposed charter amendment by simply filing a petition signed by five percent of the qualified voters or 20,000, whichever is less."[7]

Yet, at times, state law allows home rule councils to amend their charters, without the vote of their citizens, on specific issues. For example, the Texas legislature periodically passes a law permitting city councils to change their municipal election date to November.

In addition, in 2013, Texas voters agreed on Proposition 7, amending the constitution to allow municipalities to fill a short-term vacancy in their governing body. Usually vacancies are filled during special elections. This change allows cities to avoid the costs of these elections when the term is 12 months or less, without harming their democratic process.[8]

Incorporation: The Process of Creating a City

incorporation
Process of creating a city government

The process of establishing a city is known as **incorporation** because, legally, cities are municipal corporations. Local citizens need to petition the state and ask to be incorporated as a city. Second, an election is held, and a simple majority of the voters need to approve the establishment of a city with explicitly drawn territorial boundaries. Then the state issues a municipal corporate charter.

In Texas, for incorporation to proceed, first, a minimum population of 201 citizens must be living within a two-square-mile area.[9] Second, 10 percent of the registered voters and 50 percent of the property owners in the area to be incorporated must sign petitions asking that an election be held. If the petition is deemed valid, then the county judge calls an election. If a simple majority of the voters approve incorporation, then the city receives a general law charter and holds a second election to elect city officials.[10]

There are some limits regarding where cities can be established. By Texas law, all cities have **extraterritorial jurisdiction (ETJ)** that extends beyond the city limits.[11] General law cities have only one-half mile of ETJ, but the distance increases as the cities' populations increase, and they may extend for five miles for cities with populations above 250,000. ETJ provides a city some measure of regulatory control over the growth (zoning, construction, and so on) of surrounding areas. It is illegal for a city to be incorporated within the ETJ of an existing city unless the existing city approves. This provision was intended to prevent smaller towns from impeding the growth of existing cities within their own ETJs.

extraterritorial jurisdiction (ETJ)
City powers that extend beyond the city limits to an area next to the city limits

Annexation

Annexation has become increasingly contentious in Texas and elsewhere. Cities annex for a number of reasons. First, cities annex so that they will not be surrounded by other incorporated cities. Annexation of one city by another requires the consent of the annexed city, which happens rarely, so encirclement means the end of growth. Second, and connected to the first, cities annex to protect and enhance their tax base. New land means new property taxes, new sales taxes, and a larger population. Finally, cities annex to become more important politically. Larger populations mean greater political clout, more federal grant money, and more representatives elected to the state legislature and the U.S. Congress.

Cities may expand by annexing land within their ETJ. Annexation is the process by which cities legally add adjoining unincorporated territory to the total land area of the city. Texas cities have broad annexation powers. The city council, by majority vote, can unilaterally annex land, and the residents living in the area being annexed typically have no voice or vote in the process (however, this is changing). This provision in state law, coupled with the ETJ provisions, provides Texas cities with room to expand. In every session of the Texas legislature, many bills are introduced to restrict Texas cities' ability to annex land.

Indeed, the rapid growth in Texas cities created counterpressure from people who had been enjoying the benefits of a nearby city without paying for those benefits before their property was annexed. In 1999, the Texas legislature passed an annexation law that required cities to give a three-year notice before annexation formally begins, to create a service plan and deliver those services within two and a half years, and to arbitrate with the residents of the proposed annexed area.[12] However, in 2009, the attorney general issued an opinion stating that the three-year requirement does not pertain to "sparsely populated areas."[13]

In 2017 and 2019, the state passed Senate Bill 6 and House Bill 347, respectively, which gave those in the ETJ a voice in the annexation process. For home rule cities in counties with more than 500,000 residents, there is an additional step: resident approval. There are two major provisions in the bill: one for areas with fewer than 200 residents and another for areas with more than 200 residents. For the former, the city must get signatures from more than 50 percent of registered voters. If those registered voters own 50 percent or less of the land in question, then the petition must include signatures from more than 50 percent of the landowners.[14] For the latter, those with more than 200 residents, the city must hold an election in the area in question where registered voters can decide whether to approve annexation. In addition, as in the previous provision, if all registered voters own 50 percent or less of the land in question, then the petition must include signatures from more than 50 percent of the landowners.[15] This is a much stricter policy than anything Texas has seen before.[16]

Still, even in the face of these limitations, it is inevitable that cities will be even more important to Texas in the future.

Understanding Impact Cities in Texas are expanding in area and growing in population. In 1910, 75.9 percent of Texans lived in rural areas. By 2010, that percentage decreased to 15.3 percent, whereas the urban population of Texas grew to 84.7 percent. The Texas Demographic Center predicts that 94.6 percent of the state's population growth between 2010 and 2050 will occur in metropolitan counties. With more Texans living in metropolitan counties, resources for rural counties are likely to decline. Consider the impact this phenomenon will have on Texas families who have lived in rural areas of the state, many for several generations.[17]

Types of City Government

Learning Objective: Define types of local government.

Most cities in the United States use two basic forms of city government: mayor-council and council-manager, 38 and 40 percent, respectively.[18] The mayor-council system has two variations: the strong mayor system and the weak mayor system. Only a few cities nationwide use a third form of local government, the commission. No city in Texas uses it, but it once played an important role in the development of local government in Texas.[19]

Council-Manager Government

council-manager form of government

Form of government where voters elect a mayor and city council; the mayor and city council appoint a professional administrator to manage the city

The **council-manager form of government** is the most popular form of government in Texas today. It arose during the Progressive era (1901–1920) out of concern about the corruption and inefficiency of large cities dominated by political machines. Figure 7.1 outlines the structure of the council-manager form. Amarillo was the first Texas city to adopt it in 1913, and Phoenix, Dallas, and San Antonio are the largest adopter cities today. Except for Houston, all major cities in Texas use the council-manager form of government.[20] Under this system, the voters elect a small city council (usually seven members), including a mayor. The council hires a city manager, who has administrative control over city government. The city manager appoints and removes the major heads of departments of government and is responsible for budget preparation and execution.

The mayor and city council are responsible for establishing the mission, policy, and direction of city government. More specifically, the mayor and council generate policy, while all administrative authority rests with the city manager. The

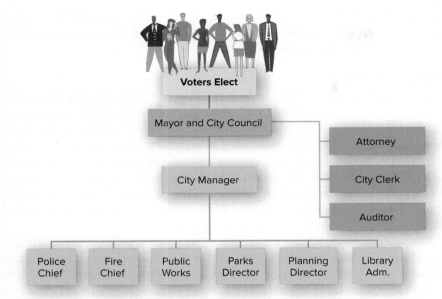

FIGURE 7.1   Council-Manager Form of City Government

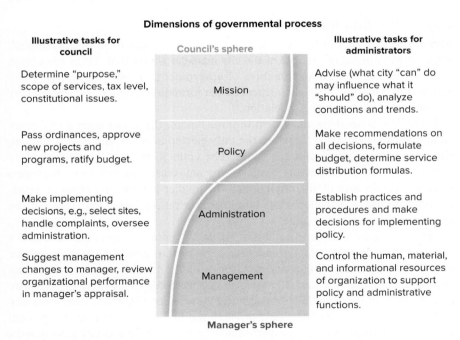

FIGURE 7.2   Roles in the Council-Manager Form of Government

mayor and council roles in administration and management are greatly reduced. Figure 7.2 shows the roles of the council and mayor on the four dimensions of city government: mission, policy, administration, and management. In Figure 7.2, the curved line shows the division between the council's and the manager's spheres of activity (the council's tasks are to the left of the line, and the manager's to the right). This division roughly approximates a "proper" degree of separation and sharing; shifts to the left or right would indicate improper incursions. The council and mayor dominate the areas of mission and policy, and the city manager dominates the areas of administration and management.

Role of the Mayor

People often misunderstand the role of the mayor in city governments because of the variations in the roles of the office. In most Texas cities, the mayor is the presiding officer of the council and most often has a vote on all issues. (A small number of Texas cities have the mayor vote only in case of a tie vote.) The mayor usually lacks any type of veto, though a few cities such as El Paso[21] do extend veto power to the office. Passing a law requires a majority vote of the total council membership, not just a majority of those present. The mayor in this form is the "head of state," the symbolic leader and the embodiment of his or her city, but is not the head of government.

The council, including the mayor, selects only four city government officials: the manager, the attorney, the clerk (sometimes called secretary), and the municipal judge. (Some cities elect the municipal judge.) The city council passes ordinances (also called laws), sets policies for the government, and provides guidelines to the city staff on issues such as the budget, taxes, fees, and spending. The council is considered part-time, so members are paid only a nominal salary or none at all.

Role of the City Manager

city manager

Person hired by the city council to manage the city; is the chief administrative officer of the city

Because so many cities in Texas use the council-manager form of government, some understanding of the role of the **city manager** is essential. Texas has always been a leader in the use of this form of government. O. M. Carr, the first city manager in Amarillo, strongly influenced the formation of the International City Managers (Management) Association.[22]

Under the council-manager form of government, the voters elect a city council and mayor. Generally, these are the only elected officials in city government, although a few cities elect a city judge. The council, in turn, appoints the city manager and may remove the manager for any reason at any time; managers serve at the pleasure of the city council. In smaller general law cities in Texas, the position might be called a city administrator rather than a manager, but the duties are essentially the same.

Most managers are trained professionals. Today many managers have a master's degree in public administration and have served as an assistant city manager for several years before becoming city manager. All but a few city managers are members of the International City Management Association (ICMA) and, in Texas, are also members of the Texas City Management Association (TCMA). These organizations have codes of ethics and help promote the ideas of professionalism in local government management. This expertise and professionalism sets city governments apart from county governments in Texas, where the voters elect almost all officeholders and professionalism is often absent. Because city managers appoint and can remove all major department heads and are in charge of the day-to-day management of city government, they can instill a high level of professionalism in the city staff.[23]

Although the manager's primary role is to administer city government, managers affect councils' policy decisions. Managers provide information and advice to the council on the impact of policy changes in city government. Professional managers attempt to provide information that is impartial so the council can make an informed decision. Councils sometimes delegate this policy-making process to city managers, either openly or indirectly, by failure to act. When this happens, councils are neglecting their duty of office and are not serving the citizens who elected them. Over the past 100 years, the council-manager form of government has functioned well in Texas. Texas cities have a national reputation of being well managed and highly professional in their operations.

Weaknesses of the Council-Manager Form

The council-manager form has some weaknesses. First, the council members are part-time and usually serve for a short time. Second, because the city manager is not directly answerable to the voters, citizens may believe they lack influence. Third, owing to political coalitions on a council, a city manager may be able to ignore large parts of the community when it comes to provision of simple city services such as sidewalks and serviceable streets. Finally, a powerful city manager can skew and hide information from the council so as to control council policy decisions before they are even made.

Mayor-Council Government

Mayor-council government is the more traditional form that developed in the nineteenth century. There are two variations of mayor-council government—weak executive and strong executive (see Figures 7.3 and 7.4). Under the **weak mayor form of government** (also known as the weak executive form), the formal powers of the mayor are limited in much the same way that the Texas governor's formal powers are limited. First, the mayor shares power with other elected officials and with the city council. Second, the mayor has only limited control over budget formation and execution. Third, the number of terms the mayor can serve is limited. Fourth, the mayor has little or no veto authority.[24]

Under a strong executive or **strong mayor form of government,** the mayor can appoint and remove the major heads of departments, controls budget formation and execution, is not limited by short terms or term limits, and can veto actions of the city council.

weak mayor form of government
Form of government where the mayor shares power with the council and other elected officials

strong mayor form of government
Form of local government where most power rests with the mayor

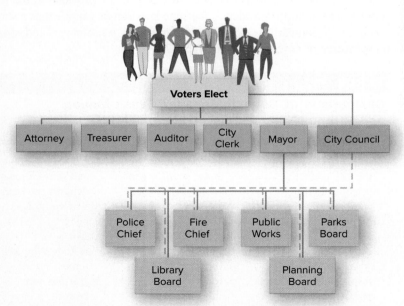

FIGURE 7.3   Weak Mayor-Council Form of City Government

Voters Elect

Mayor — City Council

Chief of Staff

Police Chief | Fire Chief | Public Works | City Clerk | Parks Director

Municipal Courts | Planning Administration

Library Administration | Finance Department

FIGURE 7.4   Strong Mayor-Council Form of City Government

Sylvester Turner is the current (and 62nd) mayor of Houston. He assumed the office after winning against Bill King in 2015 and continued to a second term after winning against Tony Buzbee in 2019.

Robyn Beck/AFP/Getty Images

Houston and nearby Pasadena are the two largest home rule cities using the mayor-council form.[25] Many home rule cities in Texas blend strong and weak mayoral powers. The Houston mayor, for example, can appoint and remove department heads and is responsible for budget formation and execution. However, the office has no veto authority, has a short term (two years), and is limited to three terms. Many more mayor-council forms exist in the general law cities in Texas than in the home rule cities. Formally, however, all have very weak mayors. Their powers are provided in the state statutes, and no form provided in the state laws can be classified as a strong executive. A comparison of the council-manager, weak-mayor, and strong-mayor forms of government is in Table 7.2.

TABLE 7.2

Comparison of Council-Manager, Weak-Mayor, and Strong-Mayor Forms of Government

Council-Manager Form	Weak-Mayor Form	Strong-Mayor Form
A city manager hired by the city council is responsible for administration. City manager appoints and removes department heads. City manager is responsible for budget preparation and execution.	Power of the mayor is limited and divided among city council and other elected officials. Mayor has limited control over budget. Mayor has term limits. Mayor has no veto authority.	Mayor can appoint and remove major department heads. Mayor controls budget. Mayor is not restricted by term limits. Mayor has veto power.

CORE OBJECTIVE

Communicating Effectively . . .

Compare Figures 7.1, 7.3, and 7.4 with Table 7.2. Discuss the fundamental differences between weak-mayor, strong-mayor, and council-manager forms of government. Which do you prefer and why?

Focus On

Hispanic Representation in Local Government

Broadly speaking, there are two types of political representation: descriptive and substantive. Descriptive representation means that a representative body *looks* like its constituency. In other words, the demographics of government officials mirror the demographics of the population they represent. Substantive representation means constituents' interests (expressed in voting, polls, letters, emails, phone calls, and so on) are *reflected* in the political and policy decisions of their local, state, and nationally elected representatives.[26]

Mayor Javier Villalobos of McAllen during his 2021 campaign.

Villalobos Campaign

Much of the debate surrounding representation in local government has focused on descriptive representation, with the hope that it will then lead to substantive representation. Research in this area supports that notion.[27] One problem, however, is how few Hispanic Americans (and members of other ethnic and racial minority groups) attain positions of executive authority within municipal governments. Austin's city council, for example, like most city councils in the United States, has been dominated by white males for most of its history. In 1975, the city elected its first Hispanic American council member, John Treviño, and there have been only a handful of Hispanic American members since.[28] In Fort Worth, there is currently only one Hispanic American council member for a city that is over one-third Hispanic American.[29] Even more jarring, Houston is roughly 45 percent Hispanic American with one current Hispanic American council member.[30]

In terms of city mayors, there have been well-known Hispanic Americans elected in Texas, such as Henry Cisneros and Julián Castro of San Antonio. In addition, in 2021, several Hispanic American Republicans won mayoral seats such as Javier Villalobos of McAllen.[31]

A 2013 study found that "only 4.6 percent of cities that have 30,000 people or more have Latino mayors."[32] Despite the wins of Villalobos and others in recent years, descriptive representation still falls short when compared to overall population percentages.[33]

Current Trends

Still, representation is improving. The number of elected Hispanic American officials grows every year. The National Association of Latino Elected Officials (NALEO) found that between 2004 and 2014, Hispanic Americans in elected offices nationwide grew by 25 percent.[34] In addition, according to NALEO's 2021 National Directory, there are approximately 2,349 Latino municipal officials in the United States, 813 of whom are in Texas.[35]

Critical Thinking Questions

1. What is the difference between descriptive and substantive representation?
2. Why might executive-level descriptive representation of Hispanic Americans in municipal governments be lagging behind overall population numbers?

Commission Form of Government

commission form of government
A form of local government where voters elect department heads who also serve as members of the city council

No home rule city in Texas uses the **commission form of government,** but it deserves mention because of its impact on local Texas governments. The city of Galveston popularized this form of government in the early part of the twentieth century. In 1901, a major hurricane destroyed most of Galveston and killed an estimated 5,000 people. At the time, Galveston was the only major port on the Texas Gulf Coast and was a kingpin in the cotton economy of the state. It was in the interests of all Texans to have the city and port rebuilt. A delegation of Galveston citizens approached the Texas legislature for funds to help in the rebuilding effort. Then-governor Joseph D. Sayers was opposed to state funding without some state control. The governor proposed that he be allowed to appoint five commissioners to oversee the rebuilding of the city, and he threatened to line-item veto any appropriations without this control. The legislature balked at the idea of locally appointed officials because of the experiences during Reconstruction under the administration of Edmund J. Davis. John Nance Garner, who served as vice president for two terms under Franklin Delano Roosevelt, was speaker of the Texas House at that time and said that without the threat of a line-item veto, it would be impossible to find five citizens in Galveston who supported the commission form of government. The governor and legislature compromised; initially, the governor appointed three commissioners, and the voters elected two. Later, all were elected.[36]

The new commission in Galveston quickly rebuilt the port city. This efficiency attracted nationwide attention. Many other cities adopted this new form of government, assuming that its form had caused the efficiency. It was a very simple form (see Figure 7.5) when compared to the older weak mayor system and the long ballot of elected officials that went with that system. In most commission forms, the voters elected five commissioners. Each commissioner was elected citywide by the voters as the head of a department of city government

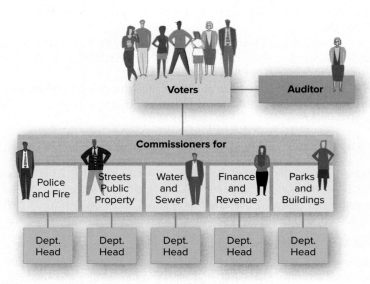

FIGURE 7.5   Commission Form of City Government

and was also a member of the city commission (the legislative body). Thus, the system combined executive and legislative functions into a single body of government.

This combination seemed to allow for quick action, but it also created many problems. Between 1901 and 1920, many cities adopted the commission form of government, but after 1920, very few cities adopted it, and many began to abandon the form. By the end of World War II, few commission governments remained. Even Galveston abandoned the form in the 1950s.[37] Several fundamental weaknesses in the form caused these abandonments.

Weaknesses of the Commission Form of Government

The first weakness was that voters did not always elect competent administrators. Citizens voted for candidates based on apparent qualifications. For example, a failed banker might run for finance commissioner and stress their banking experience.[38] Voters might have no way of knowing that their banking experience had been a failure and would, instead, vote based on their apparent qualifications. The failed banker's bank might be happy to see them depart and not challenge their qualifications.

Second, the combination of legislative and executive functions, although efficient, eliminated the separation of powers and its checks and balances. Commissioners were reluctant to scrutinize the budget and actions of other commissioners for fear of retaliation. Logrolling (exchanging political favors) set in: "You look the other way on my budget and programs, and I will on yours."

Third, initially the commission had no leader. The commissioners rotated the position of mayor among themselves. This "mayor" presided over meetings and served as the official representative of the city but was not in a leadership position. This lack of a single, strong leader was a major shortcoming in the commission government. One writer describes it as a ship with five captains.[39] Later variations called for a separately elected mayor with budget and veto authority.

Impact on the Evolution of Local Government

The major contribution of the commission form of government was that it served as a transition between the old weak mayor form, with many elected officials and a large city council, and the council-manager form, with no elected executives and a small city council. Many cities altered their charters, stripping the administrative power from the commissioners and assigning it to a city manager. Many Texas cities retained the term "commission" as a name for the city council. Lubbock retained the five-member commission until the 1980s, when it was forced to increase the size of the council and use single-member district elections.

Understanding Impact City governments in Texas are generally organized as council-manager or mayor-council. Mayor-council forms are commonly classified as "weak mayor" or "strong mayor." Visit your city's website to discover how it is organized. How does your city's form of government affect its ability to serve its citizens?

Municipal Elections

Learning Objective: Explain municipal elections in Texas, including a discussion of voter turnout.

The two most common municipal election types are at-large election systems and single-member district systems. Texas uses two other systems: cumulative voting and preferential voting.

Texas Municipal Election Systems

At-Large Election Systems

In the beginning of the twentieth century, many cities, led by early commissions, chose to move away from the single-member district system and began to elect council members at large, by all voters in the city. There are several variations of the **at-large election system,** which are summarized in Figure 7.6.

at-large election system
System where all voters in the city elect the mayor and city council members

---

At-large by place

This is the most common such system used in Texas. In this system, candidates file for at-large ballot positions, which are usually given a number designation—Place 1, Place 2, and so on. Voters cast one vote for each at-large ballot position, and the candidate with a majority is elected to that place on the city council.

At-large by place with residence wards required

In this system, candidates file for a specific place as in an at-large by place system; however, these candidates must live in a section, area, or ward of the city to file for a specific place. Mayors can live anywhere in the city. All voters in the city elect them at large.

At-large no place

This is the least common system used in Texas. In this system, all candidates seeking election to the council have their names placed on the ballot. If there are ten candidates seeking election and five open seats, each voter is instructed to cast one vote each for five candidates. The top five vote getters are elected. With this method, it is not uncommon for a candidate to win with only a plurality (less than a majority) of the vote.

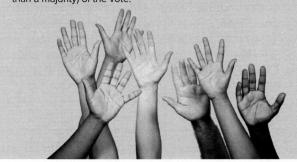

FIGURE 7.6   Variations of At-Large Voting Systems
RapidEye/iStock/Getty Images

At-large by place is the most common form of at-large voting in Texas. In this system, candidates file for at-large ballot positions, which are usually given a number designation—Place 1, Place 2, and so on. Voters cast one vote for each at-large ballot position, and the candidate with a majority is elected to that place on the city council.

At-large by place with residence wards required is a system by which candidates file for a specific place, just as in at-large by place. However, each place on the ballot is assigned to a specific geographic area, and a candidate must live within that section, area, or ward of the city to file for a specific place. Abilene, Texas, uses this form.[40] The city is divided into two wards with three council seats in each ward. The mayor can live anywhere in the city, and the mayor and council are elected at-large by all city residents.[41]

At-large no place is the least common system in Texas. Under this system, all candidates seeking election to the council have their names placed on the ballot. If 10 candidates are seeking election for 5 open seats, each voter is instructed to cast one vote each for 5 candidates. The top 5 candidates with the most votes win. With this method, it is not uncommon for a candidate to win with only a plurality (less than a majority).[42]

Last, some cities use a combination of at-large and single-member district systems. Houston is a prime example. Voters elect 11 council members from single-member districts while 5 council members and the mayor are elected at large by all voters within the city.[43]

Single-Member District Election Systems

In **single-member district (SMD)** elections, each city council seat is assigned to a specific district. The city is divided into election districts of approximately equal populations, and the voters in these districts elect a council member. In a true single-member district system, only the mayor is selected at large. Usually, candidates for a particular council seat must live within the district for which they are running. Though some municipalities use multimember district systems, all district elections in Texas are single-member district systems.

Prior to 1975, almost no Texas cities used the SMD system. When the 1965 Voting Rights Act took effect, the language surrounding racial discrimination in polls was targeted at specific districts in specific states with known problems. Section 4, for example, targeted those election sites with disenfranchising tactics (such as literacy tests) and required federal intervention.[44] Section 5, the centerpiece of the legislation, subjected those targeted states and counties to preauthorization requirements for any election-related legislation and to federal monitors during election time.[45] But going into the 1970s, with southern states attempting to circumvent the law with at-large voting (to limit the concentration and effect of Black voters), Congress began to make changes. One of the outcomes was the growth of single-member districts across the United States. At the federal level, it was believed that in a single-member district a minority group could be the majority, thereby electing their desired candidate.[46] Since the Voting Rights Act was amended in 1975 and applied to Texas, many cities have changed from an at-large system to single-member districts. Most of the major cities have been forced to change to SMD for at least some of the city council seats. Though Section 4 of the Voting Rights Act has since been struck down in a Supreme Court decision in 2013 (*Shelby County v. Holder*), SMDs remain.

single-member district (SMD)
District represented by one elected member to the legislature

In cities that have changed from at-large to SMD systems, the number of minority candidates elected to the city council has increased substantially. There is some evidence that SMD council members approach their role differently than at-large council members do. A study of council members in Houston, Dallas, San Antonio, and Fort Worth found that council members from SMDs showed greater concern for neighborhood issues, engaged in vote trading, increased their contacts with constituents in their districts regarding service requests, and became more involved in administrative affairs of the city.[47]

Although SMD council members might view their job as representing their districts first and the city as a whole second, no evidence shows that the distribution of services changes dramatically. District representation may be primarily symbolic. Symbolism can be significant, though, because support for local governments can increase as minority groups believe they have representation on city councils and feel comfortable contacting their council member.

CORE OBJECTIVE

Being Socially Responsible . . .

Compare at-large election systems and single-member district systems. An argument in favor of single-member district systems is that they increase minority representation in local government. In your opinion, does increased minority representation increase intercultural competency? Why?

Cumulative and Preferential Voting Systems

cumulative voting system

A system where voters can concentrate (accumulate) all their votes on one candidate rather than casting one vote for each office up for election

In a **cumulative voting system,** each voter has votes equal to the number of seats open in the election. If five seats are open, then each voter has five votes and may cast all five votes for one candidate (cumulating their votes), one vote each for five candidates, or any combination or variation. Several cities and school districts have adopted this system as an alternative to single-member districts. This system is preferred by voting rights activists as a means of increasing minority representation. The Amarillo Independent School District adopted the method in 2000[48] and became the largest government body using the system in Texas. It remains so with 4,500 employees as of February 2022.[49]

preferential voting system

A system that allows voters to rank order candidates for the city council

The **preferential voting system** is also referred to as the instant-runoff system. It allows voters to rank their candidates for city council. All candidates' names are listed on the ballot, and the voter indicates the order of their preferences (first, second, third, and so on). Using a complicated ballot-counting system, the most-preferred candidates are elected. Although no city in Texas uses this form today, Gorman and Sweetwater used it in the past.

Advocates of the cumulative voting system and the preferential voting system argue that they allow minority interests to vote for candidates without having to draw single-member districts and possibly risk the accompanying gerrymandering (see Chapter 3). Some evidence shows, as in the case of the Amarillo Independent School District, that these alternative systems result in more minority candidates being elected.[50]

Regardless of the system used to elect city council members, some city charters allow for a person to be elected with a plurality of the vote—less than a majority.

In Texas, if the city council term of office is longer than two years, a majority vote is required. This may necessitate a runoff election if no one has a majority.

Nonpartisan Elections

Another facet of municipal elections in Texas is that they are all technically nonpartisan. In **nonpartisan elections,** candidates run and appear on the ballot without any party designation. The Texas Election Code allows home rule cities to conduct partisan elections, but no city in Texas does so.[51]

nonpartisan election
Election in which party identification is not formally declared

Nonpartisan elections were a feature of the reform movement in the early part of the past century and were aimed at undercutting the power of partisan big-city political machines. Reformers said that there is no Democratic or Republican way to collect garbage, pave streets, or provide police and fire protection, so partisanship should not be a factor in city decisions.

Texas cities adopted the nonpartisan system largely because the state was a one-party Democratic state for more than 100 years, and partisanship, even in state elections, was not a factor as long as candidates ran as Democrats. However, using a nonpartisan ballot does not eliminate partisanship from local politics. Partisanship simply takes new forms, and people apply new labels.

For decades in several Texas cities, "nonpartisan organizations" successfully ran slates of candidates and dominated city politics. Most noted among these organizations were the Citizens Charter Association in Dallas, the Good Government League in San Antonio, and the Business and Professional Association in Wichita Falls and Abilene.[52] The influence of these groups has declined, but slate making is not unknown today in Texas politics. Partisanship has been a factor in city elections recently in San Antonio, Houston, and Dallas, especially in mayoral races. Without a doubt, partisanship will be a factor in city politics in the years ahead. Candidates often run with attachment to partisan movements. In the mid-2010s, for example, many Republican candidates ran in local elections as "Tea Party Approved." The Tea Party is not a political party, but its social conservative views most closely align with the Republican Party. Although local elections are explicitly nonpartisan, it is quite easy for voters to understand a candidate's political leanings, especially in large cities such as Dallas, Houston, and San Antonio.[53]

> **Understanding Impact** Municipal elections are nonpartisan, meaning that candidates run for office without declaring a party affiliation. Most people, including those seeking elected office, have ideas about how government should carry out its role in serving residents. These ideas vary between conservatives (Republicans) and liberals (Democrats). Do you think residents should know the political affiliation of individuals running for office at the local level? How might this knowledge affect voting outcomes?

Voter Turnout in Local Elections

Voter turnout in Texas municipal elections is varied but tends to be low for several reasons. One reason is that some cities conduct local elections in off years. This means that some city elections take place when no state or federal legislative or executive elections are being held (off-off-year elections—for example, 2015, 2017, 2019, and 2021). Some take place when state elections and U.S. House of Representative elections are being held (off-year elections—for instance,

2022). And only one out of four municipal elections is held the same year as presidential elections (for example, 2020). A second reason is that many Texas cities hold their elections in May, rather than in November when most people expect elections to be held. Voter turnout rates in the City of Austin municipal elections, which are held in May, usually hover around 15 to 20 percent.[54] In the May 2021 municipal elections, 22.44 percent of registered voters voted.[55] A third reason is that many times the candidates' races are not contested. This has happened so often that a state law went into effect in 1991 allowing cities and school boards to cancel elections if no seat was contested. A fourth reason is the lack of media coverage in city elections. Most election news coverage of city races concentrates on mayors' races, and both electronic and print media of major cities ignore suburban city elections. Even local small-town or suburban newspapers virtually ignore city elections in their home communities, arguing that readers are not interested in local issues and races.

The lack of interest in municipal elections is disturbing because city government has such authority over so many aspects of people's daily lives, including streets and sidewalks, police and fire departments, building codes, speed limits, noise ordinances, and zoning and land use designations.

CORE OBJECTIVE

Taking Personal Responsibility . . .

Local government directly affects people in their daily lives. What can you do to improve local governance?

County Governments

Learning Objective: Describe county governments in Texas, including weaknesses and possible reforms.

county government

Local unit of government that is primarily the administrative arm of a state government; in most states, it does not provide urban-type services

The oldest type of local government in the United States is **county government,** an adaptation of the British county unit of government that was implemented in this country. County governments exist in all states except Connecticut, which abolished them in 1963, and Rhode Island (which never needed them). Louisiana calls counties "parishes," from the French influence, and Alaska calls them "boroughs." The number of counties varies greatly among the states. Of those states with counties or their equivalent, Hawaii and Delaware have the fewest (3) and Texas has the most (254).[56]

County governments were originally intended to be a subdivision, or an "arm," of state government to perform state functions at the local level. For example, voter registration, which is a state function, is handled at the county level. Most commonly, the county tax office is in charge of voter registration, although in some large counties a separate elections department may handle this function. Similarly, county governments issue marriage licenses, birth certificates, and automobile registrations, and they operate state courts. County governments act as an arm of the state in all these activities.

Besides performing state functions, county governments also provide local services. The level of services provided varies from state to state; counties in some states provide many local services. In Texas, however, counties provide only very limited local services. Generally, Texas counties provide road construction and repair, as well as police protection through the sheriff's department. Some urban county governments operate hospitals or health units, libraries, and parks.

In some states, urban counties are major providers of urban services. In Texas, city governments usually provide these services. Urban services include water supply, sewage disposal, planning and zoning, airports, building codes and code enforcement, mass transit systems, and fire protection. With few exceptions, Texas counties cannot perform these functions. Texas counties most closely resemble the traditional rural county governments that perform functions for the state: recording vital statistics, operating state courts and jails, administering elections, and maintaining roads and bridges. Texas counties can also help create rural fire protection districts. In Harris County, the government may help combine many smaller water and sewer districts into master water and sewer districts.

The distinguishing feature of county government is population. Of the 3,194 counties in the United States, most are rural with small populations; 725 counties have populations of fewer than 10,000; and 328 have populations of more than 250,000.[57] In Texas, 59 percent of the population lives in the 10 largest urban counties (see Table 7.3).

Urban Texans tend to identify with city governments rather than with county governments. People think of themselves as residents of Houston, not Harris County. Some city residents might not be able to name the county where they live. This stems in part from their identification with a service being provided, such as police protection. Residents of rural areas are more likely to identify with the county rather than the city, for many of the same reasons.

TABLE 7.3

The 10 Largest Counties in Texas, 2020

County (and Major City)	2020 Population
Harris (Houston)	4,738,253
Dallas (Dallas)	2,635,888
Tarrant (Fort Worth)	2,123,347
Bexar (San Antonio)	2,026,823
Travis (Austin)	1,300,503
Collin (Plano)	1,072,069
Denton (Denton)	919,324
Hidalgo (McAllen)	875,200
El Paso (El Paso)	841,286
Fort Bend (Sugar Land)	839,706
Total	17,372,399
Percentage of total population of Texas in the 10 largest counties	59%

Source: U.S. Census Bureau, *Annual Resident Population Estimates for States and Counties: April 1, 2010 to July 1, 2019; April 1, 2020; and July 1, 2020 (CO-EST2020), https://www2.census.gov/programs-surveys/popest/datasets/2010-2020/counties/totals/co-est2020.csv.*

The Structure of County Government

All Texas county governments have the same basic structure, regardless of the county's size. This structure mirrors the fragmented structure of state government. It can most accurately be described as weak or plural executive. Voters elect the heads of major departments of county government (see Figure 7.7). These provisions appeared in the constitution of 1876. The writers of this document distrusted appointive authority and trusted the electorate to choose administrators.[58]

The County Commissioner's Court

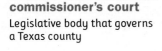

commissioner's court

Legislative body that governs a Texas county

In Texas, the governing body of county government is the county **commissioner's court,** made up of the constitutional county judge and four county commissioners. The county judge is elected at-large, and each commissioner is elected from a single-member district called a commissioner precinct. Like most other state officeholders, these officials are elected for four-year terms in partisan elections. Even though this body is termed the commissioner's court, it is not a court but a legislative body. Its duties include passing local ordinances, approving budgets and new programs, and overseeing county government.

The county judge presides as chair of the commissioner's court, participates as a full member in deliberations, and has a vote on all matters. The constitution assigns judicial duties to this office, but the occupant does not have to be a licensed attorney; the constitution states that the constitutional county judge must be "well informed in the law." In urban counties where the state legislature has created county courts of law, the constitutional county judge performs only very limited judicial functions. The judicial functions of constitutional county courts (described in Chapter 5) are transferred to the county courts of law, and the constitutional county judge acts as the primary administrative officer of the county.

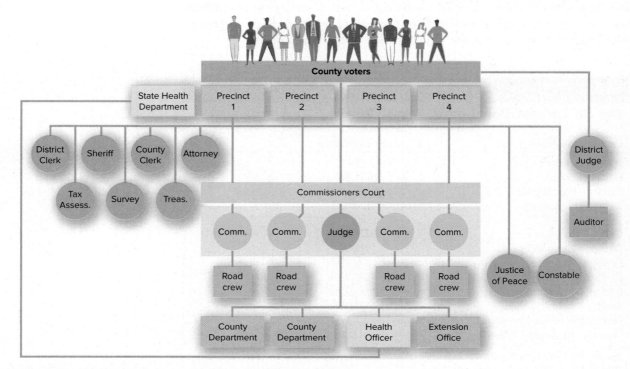

FIGURE 7.7　**Structure of County Government in Texas**

Like other legislative districts, commissioner precincts eventually became malapportioned. In 1968, the U.S. Supreme Court ruled that the one person, one vote rule applied to these election districts. The Commissioner's Court in Midland County claimed it was a court and not a legislative body, and therefore the one person, one vote rule did not apply. The U.S. Supreme Court disagreed and ruled that it was a legislative body and not a court, and that election districts had to be equally apportioned.[59] This means that each district should have roughly the same number of residents, or potential voters.

There are seven constitutionally prescribed county officers that voters elect: sheriff, district attorney, county attorney, tax assessor/collector, district clerk, county clerk, and county treasurer. These officials act as heads of departments of government. Some counties also have other minor elected officials, such as county surveyor and inspector of hides and wools (which was created to reduce cattle and sheep theft).

The County Sheriff

The **county sheriff** is elected countywide for a four-year term and is the law enforcement officer for the county. Sheriffs can appoint deputy sheriffs. In rural counties, the sheriff may be the primary law enforcement officer. In urban counties, city police departments carry out most of these duties, and the sheriff's primary duty may be to operate the county jail. In the smaller counties (those with fewer than 10,000 residents), state law allows the sheriff to act as the tax assessor/collector.[60] Some have suggested that combining sheriff and tax collector is a frightening leftover from Anglo-Saxon law, inspiring visions of Sherwood Forest, the Sheriff of Nottingham, and Robin Hood.

The voters also elect constables, who are law enforcement officers. Their primary function is to be court officers for the justice of the peace courts—delivering subpoenas and other court orders. Constables may also provide police protection in the precinct they serve.

county sheriff
Elected head of law enforcement in a Texas county

Focus On

Lupe Valdez: Dallas County Sheriff, 2005–2017

Lupe Valdez came onto the national scene when she ran as the Democratic contender for Texas governor in 2018, but she has a long history of public service before that, notably as the first Latina and one of the first openly LGBTQ county sheriffs in the state.[61]

The child of migrant workers, she was born in San Antonio and split her childhood between San Antonio and a farm in Michigan where her father and older siblings worked. While an undergraduate student in Kansas, she became a corrections officer. Later, she worked for the federal government in various law enforcement capacities. In addition, she went on to earn a master's degree in criminal justice and joined the Army Reserve. It was during these years that she realized her sexual orientation.[62]

As Valdez explained in a *Dallas Morning News* article, "Even in my dreams, I was never the princess. I was the one helping the princess. . . . When I

Lupe Valdez
Pat Benic/UPI/Alamy Stock Photo

(*Continued...*)

became aware of my sexuality, the struggle was with God. I came out late because I was too busy trying to get out of where I was. I didn't want to end up in the barrio."[63]

Eventually, she came to terms with her sexuality as a lesbian, and she "said she realizes she was accepted by God."[64]

Retiring from the Department of Homeland Security in 2004, she decided to run for sheriff of Dallas County. She won the primary and then the general election in a close contest.[65]

As sheriff, she believes "her greatest contribution was smashing intolerance in the department." She also was instrumental in improving jail conditions so that in 2010, Dallas County Jail finally passed federal inspection. During her tenure (she was reelected in 2008, 2012, and 2016), she also joined the Democratic National Committee and, at President Obama's behest, joined the fight for immigration reform.[66]

At the end of 2017, she retired to run for governor. Even though Greg Abbott ultimately won reelection, Valdez remains active in Democratic politics in the state.[67]

Critical Thinking Questions

1. Why do you think "smashing intolerance" would be particularly important to Valdez? What types of intolerance did she likely face?
2. What else did Valdez accomplish as county sheriff?

The County and District Attorneys

The county and district attorneys are the chief prosecuting attorneys for criminal cases in the county. The county attorney is at the county court level, and the district attorney is at the district court level. Each county has a county court and usually several district courts within the constituent districts that make up a given county. Not all counties have county attorneys. In counties with a county attorney, this office usually prosecutes the less serious criminal offenses before county courts, and the district attorney prosecutes major crimes before the district courts.

The County Tax Assessor/Collector

The tax assessor/collector is responsible for collecting revenue for the state and county. Before 1978, this office also assessed the value of all property in the county for property tax collection purposes. In 1978, these functions were transferred to a countywide assessment district. There are 254 of these tax appraisal districts in the state, and they are governed by a board elected by the governing bodies of all governments in the jurisdiction—counties, cities, school districts, and special districts. Although this office still has the title of assessor, few occupants serve in this capacity today. Most still collect county property taxes, sell state vehicle licenses and permits, and serve as voter registrars. The voter registration function is a carryover from the days of the poll tax.[68]

The County and District Clerk

The county clerk is the chief record keeper for the county; the clerk keeps track of all property records and issues marriage licenses, birth certificates, and other county records. Although normally the function of voter registration rests with the tax assessor/collector, in some counties this function has been transferred to the county clerk, who in all counties is responsible for conducting elections.

The district clerk is primarily a court official who maintains court records for county and district courts. The clerk schedules cases in these courts and maintains all records, acts, and proceedings of the court, along with keeping a record of all judgments. The district clerk also administers child support payments and maintains accounts of all funds derived from fines and fees collected by the office.[69]

The County Treasurer

The county treasurer is responsible for receiving, maintaining, and disbursing all county funds, including general revenue and special revenue funds. The county treasurer is the chief liaison between the commissioner's court and the depository banks, and the treasurer is responsible for maintaining a record of all deposits and withdrawals, as well as reconciling all bank statements. The county treasurer may also at times be designated as the chief investment officer for the county.[70]

The County Auditor

The district judge or judges in the county appoint the county auditor. The county auditor's responsibility is to oversee the collection and disbursement of county funds. The auditor reports to the district judge or judges. Counties with populations of less than 10,000 are not required to have auditors. In larger counties (with populations greater than 250,000), the auditor acts as a budget officer unless the commissioner's court appoints its own budget officer.[71]

Understanding Impact The government officials who work within the structure of county government have specific duties to the citizens of the county in which they serve. Texas has 254 counties. The majority of the state's population live in 1 of 82 metropolitan or urban counties. Little growth is projected for the remaining 172 rural counties in the state.[72] Based on the 2020 U.S. Census, Loving County has 181 residents and 16 other Texas counties, including Foard, have fewer than 1,500.[73] Consider the impact declining rural populations will have on county officials and their ability to provide their citizens with county services.

Weaknesses of County Government in Texas

The weaknesses in Texas county government can be broadly divided into (1) inherent weaknesses in the plural executive form of government and (2) the inability of county governments to confront many problems in urban areas.

As we have already seen, the plural executive structure of county government in Texas is a product of the nineteenth century and the general distrust of centralized executive authority. The plural executive structure lacks centralized authority, and the elected officials can, and often do, act quite independently of each other. Although the county commissioner's court does exercise some control over these department heads, it is primarily limited to budgetary matters. After a budget is approved, elected officials can make many independent decisions.

Elected officials also hire their own staffs. After each election, personnel at the county courthouse can change dramatically. For example, new sheriffs hire their own deputy sheriffs. The patronage ("spoils") system in some courthouses results in a less professional staff.

As indicated in our discussion of the judiciary in Chapter 5 and in the discussion of the commission form of city government in this chapter, elections are imperfect instruments for determining the qualifications of candidates, and voters do not always select the most competent person to administer departments. The appointment of department heads is more likely to result in the selection of competent persons. A lack of professionalism and competence is a frequently noted problem with officials in some counties.

In most (201 of 254) Texas counties, each county commissioner is responsible for road repair within the boundaries of the precinct in which the commissioner is elected.[74] As a result, there are four separate road crews, each under the

West Texas volunteer firefighters clean a fire unit at their headquarters on Friday, April 19, 2013. Only two days prior, the West fire department responded to a fertilizer company explosion that caused several fatalities and extensive damage to the community.

Ron T. Ennis/Star-Telegram/AP Images

direction of a commissioner. Although there is some sharing of equipment, duplication and inefficiencies are common. Commissioners have also been known to use their road crews to reward supporters with more favorable attention to road repairs that affect them directly.

County government was designed to meet the needs of and provide services to a rural population. In rural areas of the state, it still functions adequately. However, in large urban counties, this form of government has many weaknesses.

Inability to Provide Urban Services

The first of these weaknesses is the inability to provide urban-type services. Dense urban populations demand and need services that are unnecessary in rural areas. Usually, county governments are powerless under state law to provide even the most basic services common to city governments, such as water and sewer services. In the 1999 session of the legislature, Harris County received limited authority to assist in the formation of "master" water and sewer districts by consolidating many small suburban districts.

Citizens living on the fringe of cities are forced to provide these services themselves or to form other governments, such as a water district, to provide these services. In recent years, garbage (solid waste) collection and disposal have become a problem in the urban fringe areas. Many citizens must contract with private collectors for this service. Some counties help residents by providing collection centers, often operated by private contractors. In the area of fire protection, counties often help rural residents establish volunteer fire departments. However, counties are not permitted to operate fire departments. Each rural fire department goes its own way, and there is often a lack of coordination between departments. Training and equipment are generally below the standards of full-time city fire departments. Counties sometimes contract with city governments to provide fire protection for the county, although this practice has declined in recent years because the state has made it easier to form and finance rural fire districts.

Lack of Ordinance Authority

County governments also lack general ordinance authority. City governments in Texas may pass any ordinance not prohibited by state law, but county governments must seek legislative approval to pass specific ordinances. For example, county governments may not pass ordinances on land use (zoning) or building codes that regulate construction standards. A citizen buying a home in a rural area must largely depend on the integrity of the builder.

Even where counties have the authority to regulate activities, they often fall short. For example, counties received the authority to pass ordinances regulating the construction of septic systems. Some counties failed to pass such ordinances, and many failed to adequately inspect the installation of septic systems. In some counties, this function was transferred to the state health department in 1992.

Inequity of Financial Resources

Finally, a related problem with county governments is the inequity of financial resources and expenditures. A few counties have a sales tax, but most rely almost exclusively on the property tax. Most of this tax is paid by citizens living inside cities and not in the unincorporated, rural areas of the county. For example, in the tax year 2021 in Brazos County, the total taxable property was $19.74 billion. Most of this value ($15.61 billion) was located within the cities of Bryan and College Station, leaving only $4.13 billion in rural Brazos County.[75] Thus, most (79.08 percent) of the cost of county government was paid for with property tax money from the two cities. Although county residents pay little of the cost to operate county governments, they receive many services from them (such as road construction and repair and police protection) that the county does not provide to city residents. City residents receive these services from their city and pay city taxes. City residents are paying twice for services they receive only once. Most citizens do not notice this financial inequity.

Possible Reform of County Government

Since the 1930s, there have been suggestions to reform county government in Texas. The rhetoric often called for county government to be "brought into the twentieth century." In Texas, apparently all such reforms skipped the twentieth century and must wait for sometime in the twenty-first century. Whereas other states have modernized county governments, Texas has steadfastly refused all efforts for change. One suggestion that has been a frequent agenda item over the past 70 years is to allow for county home rule, which would allow the voters in each county to adopt a local option charter.[76] Voters could then approve any form of government not prohibited by state law; no county would be forced to change its form of government. This might result in the adoption of a strong executive form of government similar to the strong-mayor or council-manager forms popular with Texas cities. Even though this suggestion seems quite reasonable, many county elected officials in Texas have strongly opposed it because they see it as a threat to their jobs.

The Texas Association of Counties (TAC) is an umbrella organization that represents elected county officials—sheriffs, tax collectors, treasurers, judges, commissioners, and so on. The TAC has opposed granting county governments home rule. This group is politically powerful and has many supporters throughout the state. One group within the TAC, the Conference of Urban Counties (CUC), has shown mild support for home rule. The CUC represents 37 metropolitan county governments in Texas where home rule would have the greatest impact.[77] The CUC is not pushing home rule issues and is more concerned with representing the unique interests of urban counties.

County officials often have very provincial attitudes about the role of county government. The idea of expanding county services is foreign to many county officials. They seem content with the status quo. Prospects are dim for any great change in Texas county government in the short run. Urban counties will continue to face many problems that have only a mild impact on rural counties and will have to seek solutions to their problems that do not involve the major structural changes home rule would bring. Improving the professionalism of the staff might prove difficult because each elected county official can hire their own people. In some counties, officials place great emphasis on professionalism. Other officials reward faithful campaign workers with appointments. In rural counties, these jobs are often well paid and much sought after by supporters.

CORE OBJECTIVE

Thinking Critically . . .

Identify some of the problems facing county governments. What solutions would you propose?

Special District Governments

Learning Objective: Discuss special purpose districts.

special purpose district

Form of local government that provides specific services to citizens, such as water, sewage, fire protection, or public transportation

The biggest increase in government in Texas and the United States generally in the past 30 years or so has been in **special purpose districts** (not including school districts). Special purpose districts (also known as special purpose governments) have been referred to as shadow governments because they operate out of the view of most citizens. As the name implies, a special purpose district is a type of local government that is created to perform a specific set of duties or functions. Some districts are single function (such as fire) and others are multipurpose (such as water, sewer, and street repair). Some special districts (such as metropolitan transit districts) cover several counties, and others (such as the municipal utility districts) are very small, covering only a few acres.

Texas has 2,798 special purpose districts; only California and Illinois have more.[78] The primary reason special purpose districts are created is to provide services when no other unit of government exists to provide that service. Sometimes the need extends beyond the geographic boundaries of existing units of government. For example, flood control may transcend the municipal boundaries of any one city in particular, and the ability to coordinate among multiple city and county governments may be very difficult. Another good example is mass transportation. Dallas–Fort Worth, Houston, San Antonio, Austin, El Paso, and other metropolitan areas have created transit districts that serve several counties. Sometimes the service involves natural boundaries that extend over county lines.

In still other cases, the need for a service may be confined to a single county, but no government unit exists to provide the service. An excellent example of this is municipal utility districts (MUDs). These are multifunction districts generally created outside cities to provide water, sewage treatment, and other services. In Texas, these MUDs are created because county governments cannot provide these services. Finally, some districts are created for political reasons, when no existing unit of government wants to solve the service problem because of potential political conflicts. The creation of another unit of government to deal with a hot political issue is preferable. The

Gulf Coast Waste Disposal Authority, created to clean up water pollution in the Houston area, is a good example.

Special purpose districts are often an efficient and expedient way to solve a problem, but they can also generate problems. One problem for citizens is keeping track of the many special districts that provide services to them. For example, a MUD, a soil and water conservation district, a flood control district, a fire protection district, a metropolitan transit authority, a hospital district, and a waste disposal district can govern a citizen living in the Houston suburbs. Most citizens have trouble distinguishing among a school district, a county, and a city. Dealing with seven or more units of government is even more complicated and can lead to a lack of democratic control over local governments.

The governing boards of special purpose districts in Texas are selected in two ways. Multicounty special purpose districts (such as DART in Dallas and METRO in Houston) are governed by boards appointed by the governmental units (cities, counties) covered by the district. Single-county special purpose districts (such as MUDs and flood control districts) usually have a board of directors that voters elect.

Many special purpose districts have taxation authority and can raise local property taxes. The remoteness of these districts from the electorate, their number, and their potential impact on the lives of citizens raise questions of democratic control. The average citizen cannot be expected to know about, understand, and keep track of the decisions these remote governments make. The alternatives are to consolidate governments, expand cities through the annexation of land, or expand the power of county governments. None of these alternatives is generally acceptable. Citizens demand and expect local governments to be decentralized. This is true even if they have only limited ability to watch and control the actions of local government and the government is ineffective. Big government is something most Texans want to avoid.

School Districts

Article VII of the Texas Constitution gives the legislature the authority to "establish and make suitable provision for the support and maintenance of an efficient system of public free schools."[79] Although schools are subject to state control, especially in the areas of curriculum and financing, the administration of public education is largely the responsibility of the 1,073 school districts operating in the state.[80] Officially, all but one of the school districts in Texas are **independent school districts (ISDs),** which means that they operate independently of any city or county.

School districts are governed by a board of trustees who are elected to staggered terms of office (two, three, four, and six years) in nonpartisan elections. The board of trustees has no more than seven members and, although school districts may choose under certain circumstances to have trustees elected from single-member districts, trustees in Texas school districts generally are elected at large. The trustees set policy for the district and approve the budget, set tax rates, make personnel decisions, and approve construction and renovation contracts. The board is also responsible for hiring the superintendent, who may serve on contract for no more than five years.[81]

The superintendent is the chief executive officer of the school district and is responsible for planning, overseeing operations, evaluating education programs,

independent school district (ISD)
School district that is not attached to any other unit of government and that operates schools in Texas

and making annual performance appraisals of personnel. The superintendent reports to the board of trustees and provides policy and planning recommendations. The role of the school district superintendent is similar to the role of the city manager in the council-manager system of local government. Although the superintendent is the primary administrator who is responsible for the day-to-day operations of the district, they report to elected officials.

School districts have a profound impact on all citizens and as expected, issues in education can be highly polarizing. Many school boards are politicized, which increases the pressure on the superintendent. Issues facing school districts are discussed in Chapter 13.

How to

Speak Effectively

Communication, whether written, visual, or oral, is the process of transmitting information and ideas. Speaking is the most common form of daily communication. Learning to speak effectively enhances understanding and, in the case of persuasive speaking, can influence how the listener thinks.

Local governments or special districts often offer a public comment period during their regular meetings. The ability to speak effectively when engaging in this type of civic participation is essential as the time afforded each speaker is limited. Use these steps to speak more effectively.

Step 1: Identify your audience.
Consider the individuals who will be your audience. For example, if you speak during the public comment period at your local school board meeting, then your audience will be the school district's superintendent, its trustees (board members), and a group of citizens interested in school-related issues. In preparation, take time to learn the position of the individual members of the board on the matter that you intend to address. Knowing where others stand on your matter of interest will be particularly helpful in preparing your comments.

Step 2: Know your facts and values.
Most issues are a matter of *fact*, the acceptance of an observed condition, or *value*, the acknowledgment of what is right. Some issues are a combination of both. It is important to state your facts and values clearly to ensure you are transmitting accurate information and to avoid misunderstanding.

Step 3: Identify opposing points of view.
Develop your comments by addressing both sides of the issue. By preempting common objections to your position, you can acknowledge and respond to them during your speech. Recognizing opposing viewpoints and addressing them in a positive manner can enhance the persuasiveness of your comments.

Step 4: State your intent.
Let the audience know why you are speaking. For example, are your comments intended to bring attention to a matter of concern, to offer a solution to a problem, or to recommend a course of action? Clearly stating your intention allows the audience to consider your comments with an understanding of what you are trying to accomplish.

Understanding Impact Independent school districts exist throughout the state of Texas and serve a large portion of the state's population. School boards hire personnel and implement education policy. Board members to your local school district are elected, though voter turnout in generally very low. What can be done to increase voter turnout in school board elections?

Conclusion

Although local governments do not generate the same degree of interest that national and state governments do, they have extremely important effects on the daily lives of citizens. Without the services that local governments provide, modern life would not be possible.

In Texas, city governments are the principal providers of local services. Council-manager governments govern most major cities, a system that has brought a degree of professionalism to city government that is often lacking in county and some other units of local government. In many respects, the contrast between county and city government is remarkable. County governments have resisted change and seem content to operate under a form of government designed by and for an agrarian society. It is a paradox that council-manager city government and plural executive county government could exist in the same state, given the political culture. Economy, efficiency, and professionalism are not values supported by the traditional political culture of the state, yet they are widely practiced in council-manager government. It has been suggested that strong support from the business community in the state is one reason for the acceptance of council-manager government. Business leaders see the economy and efficiency of this form.

Summary

LO: Define general law cities and home rule cities.

City governments are municipal corporations, granted a corporate charter by their state. A city's charter provides the basic organization and structure of the city government and outlines the general powers and authority of its government and officials. Cities in Texas are chartered as either a general law city or a home rule city. The charters for general law cities are spelled out in state statutes, whereas citizens create charters for home rule cities.

LO: Define types of local government.

There are two basic forms of city government: mayor-council and council-manager. The mayor-council system has two variations: the strong mayor system and the weak mayor system. A third form of local government, the commission, is used by only a few cities nationwide; no city in Texas uses it, but it did play an important role in the development of local government in Texas. In the council-manager form, voters elect a mayor and city council; the mayor and city council appoint a professional administrator to manage the city. In the weak mayor-council form, the mayor shares power with the council and other elected officials. In the strong mayor-council form, most power rests with the mayor.

LO: Explain municipal elections in Texas, including a discussion of voter turnout.

The two main local election systems in Texas are at-large election systems and single-member district (SMD) systems. Cumulative voting and preferential voting also occur in some areas. In an at-large system, all voters in the city elect the mayor and city council members. In SMDs, the city is divided into election districts, and only the voters living in that district elect the council member from that district. In a cumulative voting system, each voter has votes equal to the number of seats open in the election. In a preferential voting system, voters rank the order of their preferred candidates for the city council. Voter turnout in Texas municipal elections is varied but tends to be low, especially when there are no national or state elections occurring at the same time.

LO: Describe county governments in Texas, including weaknesses and possible reforms.

County governments are local units of government and are primarily the administrative arms of a state government. In most states, they do not provide urban-type services. The level of services provided varies. In Texas, counties provide only very limited local services. There are major problems with county governments: (1) inherent weaknesses in the plural executive form of government and (2) the inability of county governments to confront many problems in urban areas. One suggested fix has been to allow for county home rule, which would allow the voters in each county to adopt a local option charter.

LO: Discuss special purpose districts.

Special purpose districts are a form of local government that provides specific services to citizens, such as water, sewage, fire protection, or public transportation. Independent school districts are one example. Many special purpose districts have taxation authority and can raise local property taxes. Some people see them as undemocratic because of their perceived distance from the voter, but they do provide much needed local services.

Key Terms

at-large election system
city manager
commissioner's court
commission form of government
council-manager form of
    government
county government
county sheriff

creatures of the state
cumulative voting system
extraterritorial jurisdiction (ETJ)
general law city
home rule city
incorporation
independent school district (ISD)
nonpartisan election

police power
preferential voting system
single-member district (SMD)
special purpose district
strong mayor form of government
unitary system of government
weak mayor form of government

Notes

[1] U.S. Department of Commerce, "Table 1. Population: Earliest Census to 2010; and Housing Units: 1950 to 2010," in *2010 Census of Population and Housing*, CPH-2-45, September 2012, https://www.census.gov/prod/cen2010/cph-2-45.pdf; Dulin, Matt, "2020 picture of Texas comes into focus: A diverse state dominated by major metros," Rice University: Kinder Institute for Urban Research, Sept. 13, 2021, https://kinder.rice.edu/urbanedge/2021/09/10/2020-census-texas-cities-counties (accessed April 5, 2022).

[2] Federal Advisory Commission on Intergovernmental Relations, *State and Local Rates in the Federal System*: A-88 (Washington, D.C.: U.S. Government Printing Office, 1982), 59.

[3] Terrell Blodgett, *Texas Home Rule Charters* (Austin: Texas Municipal League, 1994), 1.

[4] *Vernon's Texas Statutes and Codes Annotated*, vol. 1, 5.001–5.003.

[5] Texas Municipal League, *Handbook for Mayors and Council-members* (Austin: Texas Municipal League, 2019), 8, 15.

[6] *Vernon's Texas Statues and Codes Annotated*, "Local Government," vol. 1, 9.001–9.008.

[7] Texas Municipal League, *Handbook for Mayors and Council-members* (Austin: Texas Municipal League, 2019), 14.

[8] Ballotpedia, "Texas Home Rule Charter Provision Amendment, Proposition 7 (2013)," https://ballotpedia.org/Texas_Home_Rule_Charter_Provision_Amendment,_Proposition_7_ (2013) (accessed April 5, 2022).

[9] Type B and C general law municipalities can incorporate with 201 or more. Type A general law municipalities require 600 or more residents. See Texas Local Government Code Title 2, Subtitle A (Types of Municipalities), Chapters 5–8.

[10] *Vernon's Texas Statutes and Codes Annotated*, "Local Government," vol. 1, 7.005.

[11] David L. Martin, *Running City Hall: Municipal Administration in the United States* (Tuscaloosa: University of Alabama Press, 1990), 21–22; Scott Houston, "Municipal Annexation in Texas," Texas Municipal League, last updated July 2019, https://www.tml.org/DocumentCenter/View/1233/Annexation-Paper-TML-July-2019PDF (accessed April 5, 2022).

[12] Scott Houston, "Municipal Annexation in Texas," Texas Municipal League, last updated July 2019, https://www.tml.org/DocumentCenter/View/1233/Annexation-Paper-TML-July-2019PDF (accessed April 5, 2022).

[13] Attorney General of Texas, Opinion GA-0737, https://www.oag.state.tx.us/opinions/opinions/50abbott/op/2009/pdf/ga0737.pdf.

[14] Texas Municipal League, *Handbook for Mayors and Council-members* (Austin: Texas Municipal League, 2019), 12.

[15] Texas Municipal League, *Handbook for Mayors and Council-members* (Austin: Texas Municipal League, 2019).

[16] Ibid.

[17] Ibid.

[18] International City/Council Management Association (ICMA), "Municipal Forms of Government (2018–19)," https://icma.org/sites/default/files/Survey%20Research%20Snapshot_MFOG.pdf (accessed April 5, 2022).

[19] Bradley R. Rice, "Commission Form of City Government," *Handbook of Texas Online*, https://www.tshaonline.org/handbook/entries/commission-form-of-city-government (accessed April 5, 2022).

[20] National League of Cities, "Forms of Municipal Government," https://www.nlc.org/resource/forms-of-municipal-government/ (accessed April 5, 2022).

[21] City of El Paso, "Powers and Duties of the Mayor," https://www.elpasotexas.gov/mayor/powers-and-duties-of-the-mayor (accessed April 5, 2022).

[22] Richard Stillman, *The Rise of the City Manager: A Public Professional in Local Government* (Albuquerque: University of New Mexico Press, 1974), 15.

[23] For more information, go to icma.org and tcma.org.

[24] James A. Svara, *Official Leadership in the City: Patterns of Conflict and Cooperation* (New York: Oxford University Press, 1990), chaps. 2 and 3.

[25] Terrell Blodgett, *Texas Home Rule Charters* (Austin: Texas Municipal League, 1994), 30–31.

[26] Rebekah Herrick and Samuel H. Fisher III, *Representing America: The Citizen and the Professional Legislator in the*

House of Representatives (Lanham, MD: Lexington Books, 2007), 7.

27 Tim R. Sass, "The Determinants of Hispanic Representation in Municipal Government," *Southern Economic Journal* 66, no. 3 (January 2000): 609–30; Nicholas O. Alozie and Cherise G. Moore, "Blacks and Latinos in City Management: Prospects and Challenges in Council-Manager Governments," *International Journal of Public Administration* 30 (2007): 47–63.

28 W. Gardner Selby, "Few Hispanic Residents Elected to Austin City Council through History," PolitiFact, June 6, 2014, http://www.politifact.com/texas/statements/2014/jun/06/mike-martinez/few-hispanic-residents-elected-austin-city-council/.

29 Alice Barr, "Fort Worth Hispanic Leaders Pushing for New City Council Seats to Start Now," NBC DFW, May 19, 2016, http://www.nbcdfw.com/news/local/Fort-Worth-Hispanic-Leaders-Want-New-City-Council-Seats-to-Start-Sooner- 380194421.html; City of Fort Worth, "Population," http://fortworthtexas.gov/about/population/ (accessed April 9, 2020); City of Fort Worth, "Elected Officials," https://www.fortworthtexas.gov/government/elected-officials (accessed April 5, 2022).

30 Olivia P. Tallet, "Latino leaders plan lawsuit to change 'gross' underrepresentation in Houston City Council," Jan. 24, 2022 , Houston Chronicle, https://www.houstonchronicle.com/politics/houston/article/Latino-leaders-plan-lawsuit-and-citizen-drive-to-16798144.php (accessed April 5, 2022).

31 Eliza Relman, "Texans elect the first Republican mayor of McAllen, a majority Latino border city, in 24 years" June 7, 2021, Business Insider, https://www.businessinsider.com/texans-elect-the-first-gop-mayor-of-latino-majority-mcallen-in-24-years-2021-6 (accessed April 5, 2022).

32 Adriana Maestas, "Underrepresented in City Hall: A Look at U.S. Latino Mayors," *NBC Latino,* November 2, 2013, http://nbclatino.com/2013/11/02/underrepresented-in-city-hall-a-look-at-the-latino-mayors-in-the-united-states/.

33 Nicholas O. Alozie and Cherise G. Moore, "Blacks and Latinos in City Management: Prospects and Challenges in Council-Manager Governments," *International Journal of Public Administration* 30 (2007): 47–63; Abraham David Benavides, "Hispanic City Managers in Texas: A Small Group of Professional Administrators," *State & Local Government Review* 38, no. 2 (2006): 112–19.

34 NALEO Education Fund, "Latino Elected Officials in America," http://www.naleo.org/at_a_glance.

35 National Association of Latino Elected Officials, "2021 NALEO Directory of Latino Elected Officials," https://naleo.org/wp-content/uploads/2022/01/2021-National-Directory-Latino-Elected-Officials.pdf (accessed April 5, 2022).

36 Bradley Robert Price, *Progressive Critics: The Commission Government Movement in America, 1901–1920* (Austin: University of Texas Press, 1977), 12.

37 Ibid. 109.

38 Ibid. 85.

39 Ibid. 52.

40 City of Abilene, "City Council," https://www.abilenetx.gov/526/City-Council (accessed April 5, 2022).

41 For more information on Abilene's City Council, go to https://www.abilenetx.gov/526/City-Council.

42 For a good discussion of electoral systems in American cities, see Joseph Zimmerman, *The Federal City: Community Control in Large Cities* (New York: St. Martin's Press, 1972), chap. 4.

43 Blodgett, *Texas Home Rule Charters*, 46–47; City of Houston, "City Council," https://www.houstontx.gov/council/.

44 Abigail Thernstrom, "Redisricting, Race, and the Voting Rights Act," *National Affairs*, no. 3 (Spring 2010), http://www.nationalaffairs.com/publications/detail/redistricting-race-and-the-voting-rights-act (accessed April 5, 2022).

45 Abigail Thernstrom, "Redisricting, Race, and the Voting Rights Act," *National Affairs*, no. 3 (Spring 2010), http://www.nationalaffairs.com/publications/detail/redistricting-race-and-the-voting-rights-act.

46 Joseph F. Zimmerman, "The Federal Voting Rights Act and Alternative Election Systems," *William and Mary Law Review* 19, no. 4 (Summer 1978), http://scholarship.law.wm.edu/cgi/viewcontent.cgi?article=2413&context=wmlr.

47 James A. Svara, *Official Leadership in the City: Patterns of Conflict and Cooperation* (New York: Oxford University Press, 1990), 136.

48 Amarillo Independent School, "Cumulative Voting," http://p1cdn4static.sharpschool.com/UserFiles/Servers/Server_18929979/File/board/Elections/Cumulative%20Voting%202015.pdf.

49 Amarillo Chamber of Commerce, "Major Employers," http://www.amarillo-chamber.org/major-employers.html (accessed April 5, 2022).

50 For an extensive explanation of the county home rule efforts in Texas, see Wilbourn E. Benton, *Texas: Its Government and Politics*, 2nd ed. (Englewood Cliffs, NJ: Prentice Hall, 1966), 317–81.

51 *Vernon's Texas Statutes and Codes Annotated*, "Elections," 41.003.

52 For a discussion of San Antonio, see David R. Johnson, John A. Booth, and Richard J. Harris, *The Politics of San Antonio: Community Progress and Power* (Lincoln: University of Nebraska Press, 1983).

53 To learn more, go to https://www.texasmonthly.com/burka-blog/partisans-coming-cities-schools/.

54 Austin County Clerk, http://www.austintexas.gov/election/search.cfm.

[55] Travis County Clerk, "May 1, 2021," https://www.austintexas. gov/election/byrecord.cfm?eid=210.

[56] U.S. Department of Commerce, Bureau of the Census, "2017 Census of Governments: Government Organization," Table 2, https://www.census.gov/data/tables/2017/econ/gus/2017-governments.html.

[57] U.S. Census Bureau, Annual Resident Population Estimates for States and Counties: April 1, 2010 to July 1, 2019; April 1, 2020; and July 1, 2020 (CO-EST2020), https://www2. census.gov/programs-surveys/popest/datasets/2010-2020/counties/totals/co-est2020.csv.

[58] Gary M. Halter and Gerald L. Dauthery, "The County Commissioners Court in Texas," in *Governing Texas: Documents and Readings*, 3rd ed., ed. Fred Gantt Jr., et al. (New York: Thomas Y. Crowell, 1974), 340–50.

[59] *Avery v. Midland County*, 88 S. Ct. 1114 (1968).

[60] Texas Association of Counties (prepared by David B. Brooks), "Guide to Texas Laws for County Officials 2016," 114, https://www.county.org/member-services/legal-resources/publications/Documents/Guide%20to%20Texas%20Laws%20for%20County%20Officials.pdf (accessed April 9, 2020).

[61] Sarah Ruiz-Grossman, "Lupe Valdez Makes History in Texas by Winning Democratic Nod for Governor," *Huffington Post*, May 23, 2018, https://www.huffpost.com/entry/lupe-valdez-win-texas-democratic-primary-governor_n_5afcac91e4b06a3fb50d613c (accessed April 5, 2022).

[62] Gromer Jeffers Jr., "From Farm to Mansion? Lupe Valdez Relishes Underdog Role in Race for Texas Governor," Dallasnews.com, February 16, 2018, https://www. dallasnews.com/news/2018/02/16/from-farm-to-mansion-lupe-valdez-relishes-underdog-role-in-race-for-texas-governor/ (accessed April 5, 2022).

[63] Ibid.

[64] Ibid.

[65] Ibid.

[66] Gromer Jeffers Jr., "From Farm to Mansion? Lupe Valdez Relishes Underdog Role in Race for Texas Governor," Dallasnews.com, February 16, 2018, https://www .dallasnews.com/news/2018/02/16/from-farm-to-mansion-lupe-valdez-relishes-underdog-role-in-race-for-texas-governor/ (accessed April 9, 2020).

[67] See https://www.instagram.com/lupefortexas/ and https://twitter.com/lupevaldez

[68] Robert E. Norwood and Sabrina Strawn, *Texas County Government: Let the People Choose*, 2nd ed. (Austin: Texas Research League, 1984), 24. Also see John A. Gilmartin and Joe M. Rothe, *County Government in Texas: A Summary of the Major Offices and Officials*, no. 2 (College Station: Texas Agricultural Extension Service). For more information, see www.tacaoftexas.org.

[69] Texas Association of Counties, "District and County Clerk," https://www.county.org/About-Texas-Counties/About-Texas-County-Officials/%e2%80%8bTexas-District-Clerk.

[70] Texas Association of Counties, "County Treasurer," https://www.county.org/About-Texas-Counties/About-Texas-County-Officials/Texas-County-Treasurer.

[71] Texas Association of Counties, "County Auditor," https://www.county.org/About-Texas-Counties/About-Texas-County-Officials/%e2%80%8bTexas-County-Auditor.

[72] https://demographics.texas.gov/Resources/publications/2017/2017_08_21_UrbanTexas.pdf.

[73] U.S. Census Bureau, Annual Resident Population Estimates for States and Counties: April 1, 2010 to July 1, 2019; April 1, 2020; and July 1, 2020 (CO-EST2020), https://www2. census.gov/programs-surveys/popest/datasets/2010-2020/counties/totals/co-est2020.csv (accessed April 5, 2022).

[74] Texas Association of Counties, "Guide to Texas Laws for County Officials 2019," 4–10.

[75] Property tax records of the Brazos County Central Appraisal District, "Certified Values & Statistics, Historical Certified Totals, 2021 Certified Totals," https://www.brazoscad.org/tax-information/certified-values-statistics/ (accessed April 5, 2022).

[76] For an extensive explanation of the county home rule efforts in Texas, see Wilbourn E. Benton, *Texas: Its Government and Politics*, 2nd ed. (Englewood Cliffs, NJ: Prentice Hall, 1966), 317–81.

[77] https://cuc.org/.

[78] U.S. Census Bureau, *2017 Census of Governments—Organization*, Table 2, "Local Governments by Type and State, 2017," https://www.census.gov/data/tables/2017/econ/gus/2017-governments.html.

[79] Texas Constitution, art. VII, sec. 1.

[80] Ibid.

[81] *Texas Education Code*, Chapter 11 School Districts, sec. 11.201. and sec. 11.052.

CHAPTER 8

Public Opinion and the Media in Texas

Two terms that seem fairly concrete—"public opinion" and "the media"—are actually quite complex. This chapter aims to provide context to those terms and to demonstrate their importance to politics and public policy in Texas and in the United States as a whole.

Whereas Chapter 9 discusses citizens' formal role in the political process, this chapter discusses their informal roles: "the ways in which policymakers' perceptions of public opinion influence their decisions" and the role the media play in both facilitating and shaping this process.[1]

Public Opinion

Learning Objective: Explain the role of public opinion in U.S. and Texas politics.

Many academics have theorized what public opinion is and is not, from arguing "it simply doesn't exist" to "it exists but it's complicated." Some argue it is an illusion presented by the media, whereas others say it exists as an artifact of a complex sociocultural system; that is, American democracy.[2] To get at a definition, perhaps it's better to ask: What role does (or should) public opinion play in our democratic system?

What Is Public Opinion?

It is reasonable to assume that public intent is the most important determinant of what happens politically in a democracy. The American Founders were very aware of this concept, naming the legislature, the representative body, as preeminent. At the same time, however, the Founders doubted "the public's capacity to contribute constructively to political decision-making" and, therefore, in part, created the bicameral legislature to isolate decision makers from the masses and allow for focused deliberation. Over the years, politicians, theorists, and political scientists have argued over what role the public in general should play and how much influence it ought to have over policy. The reality, along with the debate, has transformed over time.[3]

Of course, we need to define what we mean when we say "the public." The term is not identical nor exchangeable with other terms that might describe the American citizenry, such as "the crowd" or "the masses." A public is characterized entirely by its communicative nature.[4] Whereas the activities of crowds and masses ostensibly take place outside the home, the activities of the public are the activities of the **public sphere,** a community's arena that allows individuals to freely discuss and identify societal problems and influence political action. "Unlike a mass, a public is self-aware and interactive" and engaged with current political and societal issues.[5]

When discussing public opinion, we are generally referring to a public engaged in **political communication** (through whatever medium) in the public sphere. For example, Table 9.5 in Chapter 9 shows that most of the other identified forms of political participation in which Texans engage are acts of political communication. In this less-formal political engagement, it is difficult for politicians and government bureaucrats to understand, and the media to accurately report, what the public wants.

With that in mind, what do we mean when we say **public opinion**? It turns out, unsurprisingly, that public opinion can mean a number of things, depending on who is discussing it, who is trying to measure it, and for what purpose it is being used. As identified in Table 8.1, there are five broad definitions: aggregation, majoritarian, interest group conflict, media/elite opinion, and fiction.

Each of these categories has implications for the ways in which public opinion can and/or should be taken into account. The measurers' perspective determines which type of public opinion they want to examine, influences the measurement tool they use, and colors their interpretation of the results.

Individuals form political opinions through a process called **political socialization;** that is, learning political attitudes and opinions through **agents of socialization.** Attitudes are how you feel about things; opinions are how you think about things. The process by which you acquire your attitudes and opinions is a process called socialization, and it begins the moment you are born. Generally, the first agent of socialization we encounter is the family, and it persists across time. The second agent is education, or schooling, which introduces the concept of civics and what it means to be a member of society. Primary and secondary education typically include the basics on how state and national governments function. Religious institutions provide normative understandings of what a good life should be and how community members ought to behave toward one another. Generational

public sphere

A community's arena that allows individuals to freely discuss and identify societal problems and influence political action

political communication

Communication in the public sphere concerned with social and political matters, encompassing all media and messages, between and among citizens, the media, and the governing elite; also an academic field of study that focuses on how information is disseminated and shapes the public sphere

public opinion

The aggregate (sum) of attitudes and opinions of individuals and groups on a particular topic

political socialization

The development of political attitudes and beliefs through agents of socialization, such as socioeconomic factors, family, religion, school, community, the media, and so on

agents of socialization

Family, teachers, peer groups, religious institutions, geographic location, class, gender, race/ethnicity, mass media; those societal forces and institutions that surround individuals from early childhood onward

TABLE 8.1	
Categories of Public Opinion	
Type	**Definition**
Aggregation	"The simple sum of many individual opinions"
Majoritarian	"The values and beliefs of the majority of citizens"; "people do pay close attention to the opinions of friends, coworkers, and neighbors and tend to conform to the majority opinion among their significant others"
Interest Group Conflict	"Groups are constantly engaged in a struggle to define social problems and provide solutions to them"
Media/Elite Opinion	"Projection of what journalists, politicians, and other 'elites' believe"
Fiction	"Rhetorical construction used so freely in our newspapers and on television as to be meaningless"

Source: Carroll J. Glynn, *Public Opinion* (Boulder, CO: Westview Press, 2004), 19–29.

effects describe the way in which your peer group may view an issue. Baby Boomers, for example, might feel very differently about same-sex marriage than Millennials do. Finally, the media are instrumental in crafting our view of reality and are, for the majority, the source of most of our information.

What might this mean for individual public opinion in Texas? The state's individualistic and traditionalistic political culture, as well as its predominantly Republican government and conservatively biased media coverage, affect individual Texans' opinions. For example, in a February 2019 poll by the University of Texas at Austin, just more than half of Texas respondents were in favor of a border wall between the United States and Mexico (52 percent), with 45 percent opposed. This reflected, in part, Donald Trump's campaign talking points and his popularity in the state as the Republican president at the time.[6] A more recent 2021 poll found that Texas Republicans remain highly aware of border security and are deeply unsatisfied with current President Biden's approach.[7] Texas Governor Greg Abbott has maintained support for the wall as the state's Republican voters continue to highly value border security. An individual's values, as shaped by these factors, affect "political thinking and direct individuals towards a specific mode of conduct."[8] Just as Chapter 9 discusses **socioeconomic factors** affecting voter participation during elections, so too do these agents of socialization affect political participation and communication more broadly.

How Can It Be Measured?

Public opinion is measured formally though voting (see Chapter 9) and informally through public opinion polls (surveys and focus groups) and the mass media.

Public opinion polling as we know it today began to emerge in the mid-1800s in the form of **straw polls.** Newspapers would set up outside of polling places and interview men (and, later, women) after they cast their vote. Much of the early polling era was characterized by these personal interviews, the results of which were published and shared with increasingly large audiences as newspaper circulation increased.

socioeconomic factors
Factors such as income, education, race, and ethnicity that affect voter turnout

straw polls
Unofficial, ad hoc personal interviews surrounding a formal vote

The 1920s and 1930s saw a convergence of changes. A growing concern over accuracy was accompanied by the founding of polling organizations, such as Gallup (originally the American Institute of Public Opinion) and Harris. Both employed more scientific methodologies, such as statistical sampling, and they could field large networks of interviewers to more accurately monitor national public opinion. It is important to note that just as Gallup and Harris were discovering national trends, so too was the public. The progress of communication technologies allowed citizens greater and faster access to information from an ever-widening geographic area.[9] In addition, the media were pushing for more data about their readers and listeners because they wanted to be able to sell those data to advertisers. The advent of broadcast media—radio and then television—as well as a swelling populace meant more advertising and an increased need to know who the members of the public were and what they wanted.

In the early 1970s, the cost of telephoning drastically decreased. In that same period, the relative complexity of political issues in the United States increased (civil rights, Vietnam, countercultures, culture wars), thereby increasing the need to more accurately take measure of the public's pulse.[10] Politicians began to take polling data seriously, particularly those related to presidential and gubernatorial administrations. The process of public opinion polling became more scientifically rigorous. Terms such as "population," "scientific sampling," "margin of error," and "response rate" became common language in political circles. Given the impracticality of surveying everyone, polling organizations began to use statistical methodology, the most important of which is probability sampling.

Suppose, for example, you want to find out what Texans think of toll roads. All Texas citizens are your population. But instead of phoning every single citizen, which would take far too much time and money, you decide to call a percentage of that population: That percentage is your sample. The tricky part is making sure that your sample is representative of the whole. In previous chapters, we've discussed types of representation. Here, descriptive representation is particularly important. You typically want your sample to be descriptively representative; that is, representative of your targeted population's demographics (sex, race, age, income levels, political values, and so on).

However a representative sample is determined (there are a variety of accepted methods), polling organizations must take into account a certain margin of error. Errors can crop up in a few ways: sampling error (the possibility for unrepresentative responses), total versus actual sample size (the possibility for respondents to answer some but not all questions), and response rate (the possibility for a large percentage of nonresponses). Pollsters make note of this margin of error by including a plus/minus percentage along with their results (that is, a survey's results or infographic summary will include a short statement like "The margin of error is +/−2%"). Still, as long as a poll is conducted scientifically and follows standard, accepted statistical methodology, it is considered more representative of a given population's political view or opinion than a nonscientifically captured survey.

In 2006, for example, to find out Texas opinion on toll roads, Kaethe V. Podgorski and Kara Kockelman of the University of Texas at Austin decided to use a telephone survey. They noted in their report that "in order to obtain 2,111 completed interviews, 53,625 calls were made to 18,750 phone numbers." Those total calls included partial interviews, nonresponses, and outright refusals. Still, overall, they discovered that within a margin of error of plus or minus 1 percent, 71 percent of Texans did not want to pay tolls on preexisting roads.

There are a number of ways you could measure Texas public opinion on toll roads. Scientific polling methods such as opinion surveys are usually favored and are typically conducted by phone (see Table 8.2).

Focus groups are also common ways to measure public opinion in Texas and elsewhere (see Table 8.3).

Less scientifically rigorous methods are still in use, such as the straw poll mentioned earlier, and **exit polls,** which are interviews with citizens just after they have voted in an election. These latter methods are subject to more

exit polls
Interviews of voters just as
they leave the polling center

TABLE 8.2

Surveys

Definition	"A research technique for measuring characteristics of a given population of individuals"
Process	1. Identifying a population
	2. Sampling that population
	3. Determining an instrument method (personal, phone, or mail interviews)
	4. Developing an interview instrument (typically some kind of questionnaire)
	5. Determining the type of analysis (quantitative)
Specific Types	1. Census survey, which counts the individuals within a population
	2. Sample survey, which interviews a nonscientific sampling of people within a population
	3. Probability sample survey, which interviews a scientifically determined sampling of people within a population; results can be extrapolated to overall population
	4. Panel survey, which reinterviews people to determine changes in opinion over time
Problems	1. Low response rates; people are not required to respond
	2. Biased sampling; those who respond may not be representative of larger population
	3. Leading questioning/poor questionnaire design
	4. Potential ignorance on issue being studied

Source: Carroll J. Glynn, Public Opinion (Boulder, CO: Westview Press, 2004), 75–84.

TABLE 8.3

Focus Groups

Definition	"Carefully planned discussions designed to obtain perceptions on a defined area of interest in a permissive, non-threatening environment"
Process	1. Identifying a population
	2. Sampling that population in small, random doses; typically fewer than 10 individuals at a time
	3. Developing an instrument (usually a written questionnaire with a few focused demographic questions)
	4. Talking with a moderator
	5. Determining the type of analysis (can be qualitative or quantitative)
Benefits	1. More flexible than surveys
	2. Make observable the dynamic forces of opinion formation through communication (its inconsistency and subjective construction over time)
	3. Allow for unanticipated responses in participants
	4. Can supplement survey research
Problems	1. Less quantitatively measurable
	2. Used less than survey methods

Source: Carroll J. Glynn, Public Opinion (Boulder, CO: Westview Press, 2004), 84–101.

push polls

Illegitimate, unscientific polling technique aimed at attacking a candidate or issue

controversy, particularly in how the media employ them during campaigns and potentially influence their audience[11] (a topic discussed later).

Push polls are considered outright illegitimate for two major reasons. Unlike other polls, push polls do not use scientific sampling. These pollsters typically try to telephone as many people as possible and, instead of maintaining some degree of nonpartisanship, they attack opposing candidates and ideas during the interview. Unfortunately, push polls are a reality of political life and are typically used by candidates to target potential voters, but also appear outside of campaigns aimed at specific issues.[12] For example, in January 1996, Texas attorney general Dan Morales became the target of a push poll by Public Opinion Strategies, a lobby/consulting group, aimed at reducing his chances for reelection. At the time, he was preparing to sue the four largest tobacco companies in the state. Although Morales proceeded with the lawsuit, the poll demonstrated that the tobacco companies could mobilize public opinion in their favor if they wanted to.[13]

As we can see, measuring public opinion is not a simple process, and much of it depends on who is doing the polling and the techniques they choose. Legitimate polling operations can give us a good picture of what people are thinking on important issues. The Texas Politics Project is one of the major legitimate Texas-based scientific polling operations. Some of its findings are shown in Figures 8.1, 8.2, and 8.3.

In Figure 8.1, UT/Tribune surveyed Texans on how they viewed Governor Abbott's performance. The bars graph shows spikes in the strongly approve and strongly disapprove categories. This reflects party affiliation. It is not surprising that Texas Republicans support the Republican governor while Texas Democrats overwhelmingly disapproved. This tends to be the norm. Party affiliation is a good indicator of how voters view the performance of major politicians in elected positions.

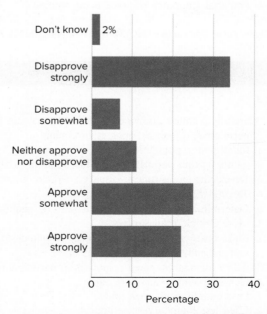

FIGURE 8.1 **Greg Abbott Job Approval Ratings (April 2022)**

Source: https://texaspolitics.utexas.edu/set/greg-abbott-approval-april-2022.

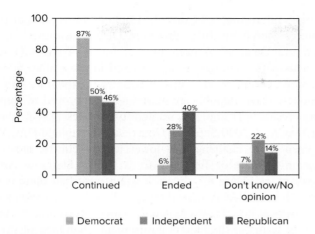

FIGURE 8.2   Should the U.S. continue to block deportation of "Dreamers"? (February 2021)

Source: https://www.texastribune.org/2021/03/03/texas-immigration-dreamers/.

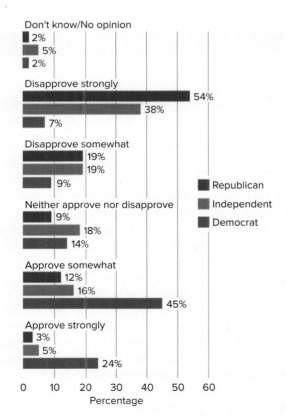

FIGURE 8.3   Federal Government Approval: Handling the Response to the Coronavirus (February 2022)

Source: https://texaspolitics.utexas.edu/set/federal-government-approval-handling-response-coronavirus-february-2022#party-id.

Perhaps more interesting is Figure 8.2. Immigration is a major issue in Texas and the country overall. In 2012, President Obama instituted an immigration policy called the Deferred Action for Childhood Arrivals (DACA), which allowed undocumented immigrants who arrived in the United States as minors to obtain a work permit to stay in the country. Democrats strongly support DACA. Although Texas Republicans have largely approved of Republican officials, such as President Trump who wanted to roll back DACA, they are deeply divided over DACA. A 2020 Supreme Court decision upheld DACA. Since then, there have been more challenges in lower federal courts, most significantly DACA Decision in State of Texas, et al., v. United States of America, et al. (2021).[14] However, as Figure 8.2 shows, it is apparent that there is more Democratic support to keep DACA than there is a Republican consensus to end it.

Figure 8.3 looks at how Texans regard the federal government. As can be seen in Figure 8.3, in terms of the federal government's handling of the coronavirus pandemic, the disapproval rate among Texas Republicans is much higher than the approval rate among Texas Democrats. Of course, approval ratings change over time. It is important to pay attention to such fluctuations.

These three survey questions take a snapshot in time. They paint a picture of how Texans view their state government, major issues, and our national government at a particular moment.

CORE OBJECTIVE

Thinking Critically . . .

Review Figure 8.3. Note that Joe Biden (Democrat) was the U.S. president at the time of polling. Why might Texas Democrats and Republicans display different levels of trust in the federal government in regards to the pandemic?

Why Is It Important?

"Democracy" means "rule by the people," yet many political scientists would say that in the United States, it means "majority rule." When we look at how our government actually operates, we see many elements that would seem undemocratic by that definition. Political scientist E. E. Schattschneider notes that "It is hard to see how anyone can formulate a satisfactory theory of public opinion without meeting this problem head on."[15]

Even though politicians are interested in public opinion and rely on information about it, they are not completely beholden to it. Nor do individuals always engage in political communication in the public sphere on every political topic. People can be ignorant on some issues and uninterested in others. Even politicians themselves cannot be fully informed or knowledgeable about everything that could possibly be relevant to governing. With that in mind, we return to the question posed at the beginning of this section: what is the role of public opinion in Texas and the United States as a whole?

Let's take a look at an example. Texans have been fairly rigidly opposed to most forms of marijuana legalization. But polls in recent years have shown, in aggregate, increasing support among the overall Texas population for expanding legal medicinal use of the drug. In 2021, a Texas Politics Project poll showed that 87 percent

How to

Interpret Polling Data

Polling is one of the most significant methods political scientists, journalists, legal analysts, politicians, and citizens use to interpret public opinion. Scientific polling is based on a random sample. A sample is a small group of individuals that the pollster questions and interviews to estimate the opinions of an entire population.

The sample must be entirely random in order to avoid bias. Bias in polls can happen when one geographic location, political ideology, political party, gender, race, ethnicity, class, age group, or any other faction is overrepresented or underrepresented.

Polling is a science. Unfortunately, not all polls are scientific, random, or legitimate. Polls that do not randomly select their participants may lead to significant bias. With this in mind, it is imperative to go over the steps to interpret data.

Step 1: Check the source.

Reliable polls seek out their participants; participants do not seek out the polling company. Therefore, the first step is to make sure that the poll comes from a legitimate company. Trustworthy and reliable polling companies are Gallup, Marist College, Quinnipiac University, CBS/New York Times, ABC/Washington Post, and NBC/ Wall Street Journal, among many others. If you come across a poll from a different company, go to the poll's website and research how it implemented the poll. Reputable polling companies should always have such information available to the public.

Step 2: Read the question. How is the question worded? What is the purpose of the question?

Sometimes you may misunderstand a poll because you misread it. Read the question carefully and slowly.

First, analyze the wording of the question. A good poll question is not supposed to sound as if it is favoring a particular position. Instead, the question should be neutral.

Second, analyze the choices to the question. Sometimes polls will provide only two choices, such as "Favorable" or "Not Favorable." Other polls may provide a third option, such as "Undecided," "Not Applicable," "No Opinion," or "Neutral." Still other polls may provide an even wider array of choices, such as five- or seven-point scales that range from "Very Favorable" to "Very Unfavorable."

Step 3: Analyze the data.

After you analyze the structure of the question, examine the results. Pay particular attention to the percentages next to each response option. If the question had more than two options, you may have to combine percentages. For example, suppose a question measuring the popularity of a certain politician shows that he or she is 42 percent Favorable, 50 percent Unfavorable, and 8 percent Undecided. Although the poll demonstrates that more constituents believe the politician to be unfavorable than favorable, it would be a mistake to believe that the majority of the sample believes the politician to be unfavorable because 8 percent of the respondents are undecided.

Step 4: Examine the dates the poll was taken, the sample error, and the sample size.

Always check the days when a poll was commissioned. Polls usually occur over a series of days. Moreover, there is sometimes a gap between when the interviews for the poll concluded and when the poll was released to the public. One of the limitations of political polls is that they are political snapshots of a particular moment. Poll participants can change their minds quickly because of evolving personal preferences, political events, natural disasters, national scandals or successes, or new and different personal experiences. Therefore, a poll taken two weeks ago may not be as instructive as a newly published poll.

Always check the sample error. This is a percentage of the poll's fallibility. Usually, even the best polls have a sample error of between 2 percent and 4 percent. In statistics, it is a statement of confidence, or a calculation based on a confidence interval. Pollsters calculate this by using a standard formula.

Finally, always check the sample size. A poll should have at least several hundred people. Statisticians have a mathematical method for determining what the minimum sample size should be based on the total population and the confidence interval they want to stay within. Without enough people participating in the poll, it becomes doubtful whether the poll's sample is truly representative of the intended population.

supported legalizing the use of marijuana (of which 27 percent was for medical use only, 31 percent was for small amounts with any purpose, and 29 percent was for any amount with any purpose).[16] A similar 2019 poll found that over 60 percent of Texans favor legalization and believe it should be taxed to fund public education.[17] This change encompasses two forms of public opinion: the aggregate opinion of Texas individuals and the majoritarian opinion of the Texas population. We can see that, in several polls over several years, the majority of the Texas population (that is, the majoritarian opinion) favors some form of expanded legalization, which has effects on politicians and government bureaucrats in the state.

This is evidenced by the fact that the number of dismissals for possession of small amounts has been increasing rapidly. An *Austin American-Statesman* study released in September 2016 on the five largest counties (Bexar, Dallas, Harris, Tarrant, and Travis) found that

> the rate of dismissal has risen since 2011, dramatically in some places. The trend also appears to be playing out statewide, where 23 percent of all misdemeanor marijuana cases were dismissed in 2011. In 2015, nearly a third were.[18]

Significantly, in January 2020, Austin's city council voted to "stop the APD [Austin Police Department] from citing and arresting people for [low-level] possession of marijuana cases they know will be rejected by prosecutors."[19] In addition, the state legislature has been seeing increased activity on the issue. During the 2019 session, the legislature legalized hemp in House Bill 1325, forcing a redefinition of marijuana. According to the *Texas Tribune*, "Before, marijuana was defined as parts of the cannabis plant, but now it is only those parts that contain more than 0.3% of tetrahydrocannabinol, the psychoactive ingredient in marijuana that produces a high. Cannabis below that level is now hemp."[20] This has resulted in increasingly fewer low-level possession arrests in the state overall due to the difficulty distinguishing between hemp and marijuana. Then, in 2021, the state passed HB 1535 which expanded medical use for people with any kind of cancer, chronic pain, and post-traumatic stress disorder.[21]

The political elite lead, but when conflict arises (such as on marijuana use and other political issues), public opinion affects the elite. This process happens through the media. The history of public opinion and its measurement is intrinsically tied to the history and functions of the media. It is a technological history as well as a social and political one.[22]

Understanding Impact What are your thoughts on the legalization of marijuana in Texas? If marijuana were legalized for medicinal use, what might be some of the consequences, particularly in terms of state regulation?

The Media and Their Functions

Learning Objective: Explain the functions of media in U.S. and Texas politics.

Although today people use the words "press" and "media" fairly interchangeably to refer to the media industry as a whole, at the time the Constitution and Bill of Rights were written, the Founders meant something a bit different. Freedom of speech was intended not just for journalists or "newsmongers," but for every-one. All citizens should be allowed to speak their mind, to give their opinion. Freedom of the press meant, literally, freedom to use the printing press, the technology itself. No one, and no opinion, should have more right or access to a printing press than any other. Over time, the meanings of the press and the media have broadened and overlapped significantly.

What Are the Media?

At the most basic level, the media are a set of technological "mediums" by which information is transmitted. **Mass media** transmit information to mass audiences. Yet it is clear that when we speak colloquially of "the media," we mean some-thing much more complex.

Political scientist Harold Lasswell's model "Who, Says What, In Which Channel, To Whom, With What Effect?"[23] is significant. Although the details and emphases from other models may differ, the basic questions are roughly the same as Lasswell's: Who is the sender? What is the message? Who is the audience? What is the method? These questions and the answers to them are part and parcel of what the term "the media" encompasses today. It is a complex system of mes-saging by private companies, journalists, citizens, and public institutions, all motivated by particular interests. These motivations can be economic, ideologi-cal, or professionally driven.

As such, the media serve three broad functions within their communities: (1) providing information, (2) shaping perception, and (3) acting as a link "between elected representatives and their constituents."[24]

Media as Sources of Information

First, the media provide **information.** Information is generally considered to be the coverage of goings-on in a community. Educating the public about commu-nity events strengthens social ties. Public service announcements about local parades, carnivals, or rummage sales allow community members opportunities to interact with their neighbors. The media play a vital role in sharing these events with the communities they serve.

Political scientist Thomas Patterson argues that the quality of information that citizens can directly access affects their interest in the news. **News** is defined as those stories that provide timely information about the important events or individuals in a community, state, nation, or world. News at the local level may often reflect more of an informational perspective, but will also include coverage of governmental decisions by city or county officials, criminal activity, or stories of public interest.

Hard news covers important events involving elected leaders, major domestic or foreign issues, or significant disruptions to daily lives. Conversely, the aim of **soft news** is to entertain; often, it includes special news features or human interest stories. Soft news can take the particularly negative tone of **critical journalism,** featuring embarrassing "gotcha" moments, typically seen in local newscasts, described as "the journalism of outrageousness."[25]

Arguably, as broadcasters compete for viewers and listeners, the temptation to shock viewers grows. Broadcasters can shock through the use of soft news that highlights increasingly critical or negative stories about elected leaders and policy issues. Political analysts Thomas E. Mann and Norman J. Ornstein

mass media
Means of communication that reaches many individuals

information
Messages provided that concern social events occurring or services available in a community to its members

news
Stories that provide timely information about the important events or individuals in a community, state, nation, or world

hard news
Factual, in-depth coverage of public affairs that contributes to citizens' understanding of political events and leaders in the public sphere

soft news
Information, presented as news, that serves to entertain, titillate, or overdramatize events but that lacks substance and value with respect to contributing to citizens' understanding of political events and leaders in the public sphere

critical journalism
A style of soft news that focuses on political scandal, vice, or mistakes of the government or politicians

contend that because of increased competition for an audience, the media have become increasingly focused on "sensationalism, extremism, and infotainment over information."[26] This presents a serious conundrum for Texans and other Americans seeking factual information. A 2021 Gallup poll found that only "7% of U.S. adults say they have 'a great deal' and 29% 'a fair amount' of trust and confidence in newspapers, television and radio news reporting... In addition, 29% of the public currently registers 'not very much' trust and 34% have 'none at all.'"[27] This lack of clear trust does not bode well for the levels of faith citizens have in governmental institutions overall.

How the Media Shape Perceptions

When faced with an array of complex information, citizens need to be able to discern which aspects of an issue are most relevant. The mass media act as gatekeepers of information. **Gatekeeping** is the process of filtering down all of what is happening in a given community into a specific set of news and then transmitting it to an audience. After the gatekeeper determines newsworthiness, it uses agenda setting, priming, and framing to transform the remaining information into news stories.

Agenda Setting   Bernard C. Cohen argued in 1963 that "the media are stunningly successful in telling their audience what to think about."[28] It could certainly be argued that the level of public interest in an issue is proportional to the amount of news coverage an issue receives and to which the public is exposed. Deciding what is news is a fundamental function of the media; it is defined as **agenda setting.** The media evaluate many issues that might go unnoticed and thrust them into the public sphere.

For example, in 2016, the Texas Department of Family and Protective Services' Child Protective Services (CPS) agency faced a public crisis that had begun more than a decade earlier, when the 82nd Legislature cut its funding significantly. Although the operations of this agency go largely unnoticed by the vast majority of Texans, agents working for CPS ensure children who are neglected or abused are protected or removed from harmful environments. The latest problems—including poor caseworker supervision, inadequate training, high caseloads, mounds of paperwork, and low salaries—meant that the agency faced high rates of turnover that hovered around 25 percent of its caseworkers, causing many children to fall through the cracks of the system. Chronically underfunded, a federal judge finally declared the Texas foster care system broken in the winter of 2015.[29] It was not until after the media covered a series of high-profile deaths of children across Texas that there was a storm of public outcry, and members of the Texas legislature, meeting in interim session during the summer, began reviewing CPS operations and problems. In this instance, the media served to set an agenda and force government action.

Since 2020, news on Covid-19 in particular overshadowed the foster care crisis in the state, leading to a continued lack of funds and loss of housing. A bill was introduced during a 2021 special legislative session to increase payments to foster families but was stalled by the time the session ended. The ongoing nature of the issue was not covered in the media nearly as much as during the 2015 ruling.[30]

gatekeeping

The process of filtering information and selecting what to transmit or not transmit as news

agenda setting

The power of the media to bring issues and problems to the public's attention

Regardless of the intent (journalists' or otherwise) behind media coverage of an issue, the fact that it remains in the headlines influences public opinion respecting the importance of that particular issue. The question is whether media coverage serves to invigorate democracy and public debate.

Priming   Related to agenda setting is the act of **priming** public opinion, an issue that people have studied since the early 1980s. Whereas agenda setting means the media influence what people see as newsworthy, priming provides a specific context and background through which audiences engage with a particular topic or story. For example, when the rodeo comes through town, the local media not only will announce it is happening but also will typically continue to bring it up over the period of time it is in town. That repetition of an issue or event over time is priming. It primes an audience to be aware that the rodeo is in town and also consider it important and/or interesting.

priming
The ability of the media to help shape public opinion respecting an event or a person in the public sphere

Framing   Additionally, the media **frame** issues by using perspective when reporting stories to the public. George Lakoff, a renowned cognitive linguist, studied why individuals attach themselves to particular political opinions and positions, especially where party affiliation is concerned. Lakoff argues that *how* the *story is told,* or what metaphors are selected, often shapes the public perception of what government chooses to do or not do about a policy problem. At times, this perception of a story can be irreversible, even after accurate but conflicting information comes to light. Although simply deciding *what* is news has a huge effect on public perception, *how* it is framed significantly influences public reaction to it. This is particularly true in political arguments. According to Lakoff, counterarguments become less effective in persuading an audience after an event or issue has been framed. Here, the opposition view has the added burden of not only discrediting the initial framing of the issue but also discrediting the issue itself.[31]

framing
The media's attempts to focus attention on certain events and place them within a context for meaning

For example, immigration is a huge issue for Texas and other states that border Mexico. Several studies over the years have indicated that newspapers from counties near the border tend to have an overall negative slant toward immigrants and include references to illegality, regardless of any liberal or conservative affiliation. In 2016, Simone Jasper of Elon University analyzed several Texas and Arizona newspaper articles from the summer of 2014 to see how their journalists framed stories, specifically about child immigrants from Latin America. She found that whereas the youth of the immigrants added a "victim" frame, the children were still referred to in a criminal context. This slanting further reinforces negative local community beliefs.[32]

Resonance   The reinforcement and magnification of existing beliefs about reality and commonality of events because of the presentation of reality by the media is called **resonance.** The media cultivate and influence the public's social reality and mirror society's culture back to the viewer.

resonance
The reinforcement and magnification of existing beliefs about reality and commonality of events because of the presentation of reality by the media

Media as Linkage Institutions and Political Actors

According to Harvard public policy theorists Matthew Baum and Philip Potter, "The traditional view of the media—especially in political science—as a mostly accommodating conduit for elite messages is built on a simplifying assumption that the media serve primarily as a linkage mechanism rather than as an independent, strategic actor in the policy-making process."[33] What they mean by "linkage mechanism" is that the mass media, as an institution in our democracy, traditionally act as a conduit for information up and down between the political elite (politicians and government bureaucrats) and their constituents.

It is apparent that the mass media, particularly the news media, are more than information providers.[34] Jan E. Leighley of Texas A&M notes that there are several models by which we might understand the mass media as political actors:

1. Reporters of objective fact: simple information conveyor belts
2. Neutral adversaries: watchdogs on government and on the political elite
3. Public advocates: strategic information conveyor belts whose purpose is to not only inform the public but also drive conversation in the public sphere toward important topics; actively seek to better society and maintain its financial independence
4. Profit seekers: businesses whose news outputs are products designed to make money; greater emphasis on sensationalism and infotainment
5. Propagandists: pushers of a particular individual/politician, product, or idea[35]

Each model affects the functions the media play in a community, and media institutions can play any of these roles at a given time. As McCombs et al. note, "the extent to which the public in aggregate has any opinion at all about a public issue or political candidate is strongly linked to patterns of news coverage."[36]

Understanding Impact Look again at the five models of mass media listed by Jan Leighly, and consider the primary purpose media fulfills in each of these models. Which of these purposes work well together? Which of them are potentially in conflict? How might those conflicts affect the public's ability to get trustworthy information?

Media Sources: Print, Broadcast, and Online

Learning Objective: Describe the various sources of media in Texas.

The media are typically categorized by type of message and type of medium. Entertainment, advertising, and news media differ in the type of *message* transmitted. Although they all can be mass media (messages transmitted to large audiences), they differ in content. The news media, in particular, operate as an institution within the public sphere, fulfilling a critical role by communicating information to the public so that something approaching public opinion can be formed.[37] Media professor Natalie Fenton insists that "news provides, or should provide, the vital resources for processes of information gathering, deliberation and analysis that enable democracy to function."[38] In many ways, the mass media determine what information the public receives.

In terms of *medium*, there are **print media** and **electronic media.** Print typically includes newspapers and magazines, both of which are still often

print media
Means of communication in the form of physically printed materials, such as newspapers, magazines, and pamphlets

electronic media
Means of communication that uses electronic equipment and can be analog or digital in nature

published on paper. Electronic media include both analog and digital transmission. Broadcast media (television and radio) are electronic media but are still distinct from the Internet and social media. Broadcast media function as one-to-many transmissions, whereas digital content transmitted online and through social media networks is often many-to-many transmissions. However, as time goes on, these distinctions become blurred as media companies increasingly publish their content on the Internet in addition to their original medium.

According to media theorist Marshall McLuhan, the form that the message takes shapes the way people receive the message. In addition, each medium contains within it the medium that came before.[39] For example, magazines, born out of newspapers, share events as written in the newspapers but include more pictures. Subsequently, television puts these events in motion and draws the viewer in even further. Generations have watched as the media brought the world into their living rooms. History and its events appear onscreen in color and with sound, and viewers become part of the story as their own perceptions, emotions, and reactions intertwine with the news of the day.

As technology has improved, methods of delivering the news have changed as well. First, radio and television changed the way people consumed information. Now, less than a century later, we receive information almost instantly. How citizens receive information affects their perception of what is news and even what is reality. Admittedly, this subject is a messy one.

Print Media: Newspapers and Magazines

Generations ago, Texans and other Americans came to rely on the print media to keep abreast of the goings-on in the global, national, and local communities. At its peak at the turn of the twentieth century, there were more than 17,000 printed newspapers across America.[40] Almost every town and city in America had at least one newspaper that was delivered to its readers' homes, sometimes twice daily.

Newspapers provide citizens with information about their local communities, politics and war, and domestic and international events. They conduct investigations and play a critical role in ensuring citizens are informed by exposing violations of trust by elected and appointed officials, earning the nickname "public watchdog."

Between 1813 and 1846, Texas was home to more than 85 newspapers. Texas's first newspaper (a single page with two columns) was the Spanish newspaper *Gaceta de Texas,* published in 1813. It was technically published in nearby Natchitoches, Louisiana, but its

Stereotyping. Curved forms of pages are made in a few minutes

Stereotyping, early 1900s mass printing technique using cylinder presses

Harry Ransom Center the University of Texas, Austin

dateline specified Nacogdoches, Texas. More newspapers cropped up soon after.[41] During the Texas Revolution, the *Telegraph and Texas Register* became the origin of the rallying cry, "Remember the Alamo!" Other newspapers reprinted the paper's reporting on the Alamo battle, spreading the information across Texas and the United States.[42]

It wasn't until 1842, however, that Texas would have a semiweekly paper when *The Daily News,* which still operates today as a morning paper, began publication in Galveston.[43] As the nineteenth century turned to the twentieth, newspapers increasingly became part of Texas's urban culture and were a force for urbanization and industrialization through the 1970s. Urban daily newspapers were frequently in symbiosis with their local business leaders and political elite. Patrick Cox, in his book *The First Texas News Barons*, argues that newspapers were, to a large degree, responsible for Texas's development of its unique blend of culture—urban, but also western with its cowboys and ranches, and southern in its conservative, traditional values.[44]

Table 8.4 identifies the top 10 daily newspapers in the state as of 2020 (exact numbers as of 2016). Today, the most widely circulated paper in Texas is the *Houston Chronicle,* which has a little over 149,000 in daily circulation. The next largest is the *Dallas Morning News,* which has 129,171 daily.[45] Both, however, have seen precipitous declines in subscriptions since 2013.

For decades, newspapers were the means people had of learning about issues and events, but papers have suffered from competition since the early twentieth century. Initially, the competition came from radio, which began offering news and entertainment in the 1920s. The real struggle for newspapers to remain viable would not come until the advent of television in the 1950s. By 1992, only 37 cities in the United States had separately owned, competing daily newspapers. See Figure 8.4 for a breakdown of the overall circulation of newspapers up to 2020.[46]

Although many Americans still rely on print media to access news, the demographic divide between Baby Boomers (those born between 1946 and 1964) and

TABLE 8.4

Top 10 Newspapers in Texas with Daily Circulation

Houston Chronicle	149,149
Dallas Morning News	129,171
Fort Worth Star-Telegram	91,469
San Antonio Express-News	85,971
Austin American-Statesman	85,018
Corpus Christi Caller-Times	42,472
El Paso Times	34,420
Focus Daily News (Desoto, TX)	33,678
The Baytown Sun	9,714
The Texas Tribune	—

Sources: Agility PR Solutions, "Top 10 Texas Daily Newspapers by Circulation," July 2021. https://www.agilitypr.com/resources/top-media-outlets/top-10-texas-daily-newspapers-circulation/ (accessed April 26, 2022); OfficialUSA, "Texas Newspapers," https://www.officialusa.com/stateguides/media/newspapers/texas.html (accessed April 26, 2022). Note: no circulation data for *The Texas Tribune*.

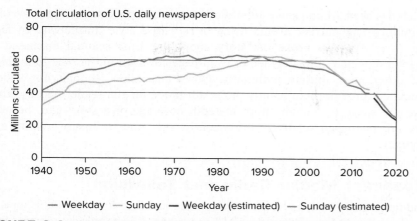

FIGURE 8.4   Total Estimated Circulation of U.S. Daily Newspapers

Source: Pew Research Center, "Newspapers Fact Sheet," https://www.pewresearch.org/journalism/chart/
sotnm-newspapers-total-estimated-circulation-for-u-s-daily-newspapers (accessed April 26, 2022).

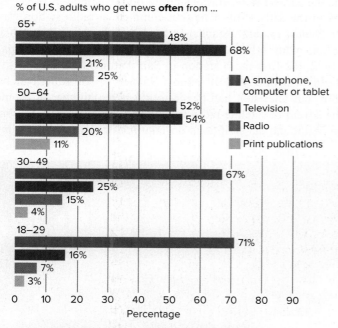

FIGURE 8.5   Americans' News Access by Platform

Source: https://www.pewresearch.org/fact-tank/2021/01/12/more-than-eight-in-ten-americans-
get-news-from-digital-devices/ft_2021-01-12_socialmedia_05/ (accessed April 26, 2022).

younger generations is quite stark. According to a 2020 Pew Research poll, only 3 percent of 18-to-29-year-olds get news from a print newspaper, whereas 25 percent of those age 65 and older do.[47]

Magazines are far fewer in number, and Texas boasts only two of note: *Texas Monthly* (see Figure 8.5), which began in 1973, and *The Texas Observer,*

investigative journalism
Deeply researched stories that uncover serious crime, corruption, or corporate wrongdoing

which has been around since 1954. Both magazines provide in-depth coverage of politics and current events using **investigative** style journalism. In fact, *The Texas Observer* broke the story about the Tulia scandal discussed in Chapter 6, which ultimately led to front-page coverage in the *New York Times* and other news outlets nationally. News magazines, though not widely circulated, provide significantly more substance for the reader because they have the space to include more in-depth coverage of a story and, because they are published relatively infrequently, the time to ensure quality and accuracy.

Broadcast Media: Radio and Television

Traditional radio stations have existed in America since the early 1920s, operating along the AM and, later, the FM bandwidths. Like television stations, they transmit information over the air. Radio broadcasts brought news and information into Americans' homes. Broadcasts provided new forms of entertainment as well, including music, live broadcasts of stories, and plays. It was, and is, also a way that government can connect directly with citizens.

In Texas, the earliest radio stations began on the campuses of UT Austin and Texas A&M in the early 1910s. The first commercial radio station was WRR of the City of Dallas, initially established for fire and police dispatch in 1920.[48] Not long after, many other commercial stations began popping up, including WOAI in 1922, the first radio station in San Antonio.[49]

By the end of World War II, almost 95 percent of American households owned radios, but television had begun to affect the number of listeners. More recently, the advent of satellite radio created very little stir, with minimal market penetration. Although subscriptions do continue to grow in small increments,

Early radio in the home was often listened to communally; the family gathered round.
PhotoQuest/Archive Photos/Getty Images

TABLE 8.5

Top 10 Radio Stations in Texas

Station	Format	Owner
1. KODA-FM	Adult Contemporary	iHeartMedia
2. KSBJ-FM	Christian	Hope Media Group
3. KLTN-FM	Regional Mexican	Univision Radio
4. KKHH-FM	Adult Hits	Audacy
5. KGLK-FM	Classic Rock	Cox Media Group
6. KMJQ-FM	Urban Rock	Radio One
7. KTBZ-FM	Alternative	iHeartMedia
8. KTRH-AM	News/Talk	iHeartMedia
9. KKBQ-FM	Country	Cox Media Group
10. KRBE-FM	Contemporary Hits	Cumulus Radio

Source: Nielson Ratings, https://ratings.radio-online.com/content/arb033. (accessed May 6, 2022).

by 2019 roughly 34.5 million adults, or only about 13 percent of the adult population in the United States, subscribed to satellite radio.[50]

Table 8.5 lists the current top listened-to stations in the Houston-Galveston area in March 2022. The range of programming reflects the demographic diversity of the region. The table also illustrates the tendency of a few large corporations to own a sizeable portion of the market.

Television, even more than radio, disrupted our relationship with print media and our perceptions of political reality. According to the Texas State Historical Association:

> The first television station in Texas, WBAP-TV, Fort Worth, began operating on September 27, 1948, carrying a speech by President Harry Truman; the station officially signed on two days later. By 1950 six stations were in operation in Texas, with three in the Dallas-Fort Worth area, two in San Antonio, and one in Houston. . . . In [1953] network broadcasting was made possible across the state through use of facilities of the Bell Telephone System, which had invested $10 million in Texas television cables and microwave relay stations.[51]

The November 1963 assassination of John F. Kennedy was a turning point in the evolution of broadcast media and the resulting effect on people's perception of the news. Anthropologist Thomas de Zengotita writes:

> Everyone became a participant/eyewitness to events on the world stage, past and present. . . . Reams of coverage, endless coverage, amazing coverage—in a way *more* compelling than if you had been there physically, because virtually you were there from so many different perspectives. . . . You had a sort of God's eye view.[52]

Studies from more than 20 years ago indicate that among the forms of media that existed, television provided the vast majority of citizens' information and news; however, print media's superior quality meant they overshadowed

President Kennedy in Dallas
Pictorial Press Ltd/Alamy Stock Photo

CNN effect

The effect of 24-hour broadcasts of live news media (CNN, MSNBC, Fox, etc.)

television media.[53] More recent research determined that television news remains the most effective single medium available for the acquisition of political information.[54] It is difficult to overstate how important television news media are as a linkage mechanism and political actor.

The **CNN effect** is a major factor in television's continuing importance.[55] Although the term is more typically heard in the foreign policy arena, it is applicable within a national context because these 24-hour news channels discuss issues that affect the country.

Local television news outlets have a slightly different focus, given their limited time slots. They tend to focus on recent sensational stories such as crimes, fires, or car crashes, as well as on entertainment-related programming, such as local sports and the weather. The percentage of such local content to the percentage of national news stories is variable, and is discussed later.[56]

Today, more than half of Americans still access information and news through television (national and local broadcasts); in fact, television continues to be a top daily news source for most Americans. In a 2020 Pew Research poll, 36 percent of Americans still relied on television to get their news.[57] CBS ranks as the highest network, in part because of its popular *60 Minutes* broadcast each Sunday. However, as Figure 8.6 illustrates, television viewing is in decline as most channels indicate a decline in overall viewership.

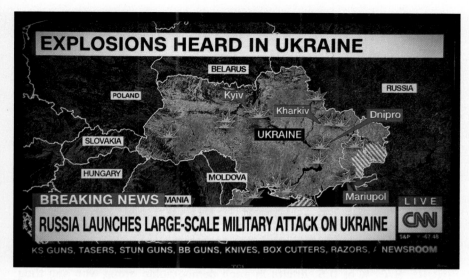

Viewers could tune into the Russian invasion of Ukraine 24 hours a day thanks to cable television news. This is known as the CNN effect.

Shiiko Alexander/Alamy Stock Photo

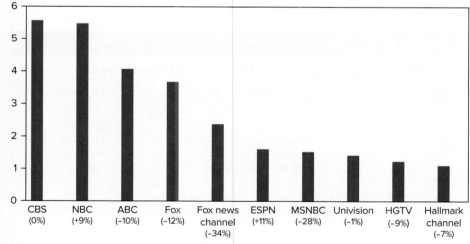

FIGURE 8.6   Top 10 Networks by Number of Viewers 2021 (in millions)

Source: Michael Schneider, "Most Watched Television Networks: Ranking 2021's Winners and Losers," *Variety,* December 30, 2021, https://variety.com/2021/tv/news/network-ratings-2021-top-channels-1235143630/ (accessed April 29, 2022).

In fact, older Americans are also increasingly utilizing the Internet for news acquisition. In Figure 8.7 we can see a marked increase in online use for higher age demographics, especially in the 65-plus range.

Still, while evidence shows that network viewership is declining, there are two major counterpoints. First, on average, Americans still spend roughly 5.5 hours a day consuming information through television.[58] According to the information in Table 8.6, TV market penetration in Texas is very high.

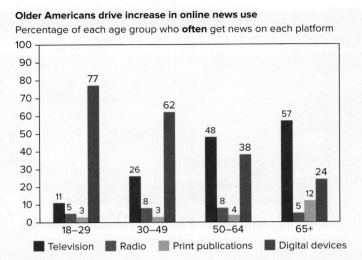

Older Americans drive increase in online news use
Percentage of each age group who **often** get news on each platform

FIGURE 8.7 % of U.S. Adults in each demographic group who say they prefer _____ for getting news

Source: Katerina Eva Matsa and Sarah Naseer, "News Platform Fact Sheet," Pew Research Center, November 8, 2021, https://www.pewresearch.org/journalism/fact-sheet/news-platform-fact-sheet/ (accessed April 29, 2022).

TABLE 8.6

TV Penetration % by Local Television Market (Texas)

Rank (U.S.)	Designated Market Area	Total Homes
5	Dallas–Fort Worth	2,962,520
8	Houston	2,569,900
31	San Antonio	1,031,180
38	Austin	912,400
83	Waco-Temple-Bryan	383,820

Source: OAAA, "2021 Nelson DMA Rankings," https://oaaa.org/Portals/0/Public%20PDFs/OAAA%202021%20NIELSEN%20DMA%20Rankings%20Report.pdf (accessed April 29, 2022).

Although Americans are accessing news through a variety of platforms, they do tend to express preferences respecting their level of trust based on the medium through which it is gathered and their political leanings. In Figure 8.8, more than half of both Democrats and Republicans expressed trust in local news organizations with a much wider partisan divide for national news outlets.

New Media: The Internet and Social Media Networks

The Internet has made people part of the news as it happens; citizens can comment on live streams, are provided opportunities to interact with events, and stories and perceptions are shaped by others viewing them as they unfold. Internet access changed many aspects of Americans' lives, and social

% of U.S. adults who say they have a lot or some trust in the information that comes from ...

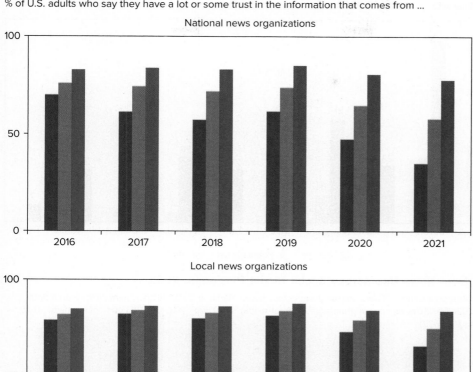

National news organizations

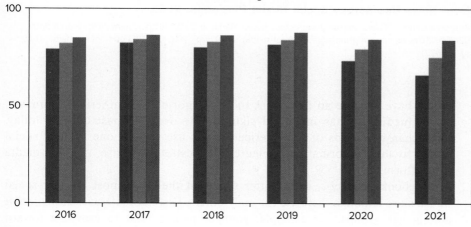

Local news organizations

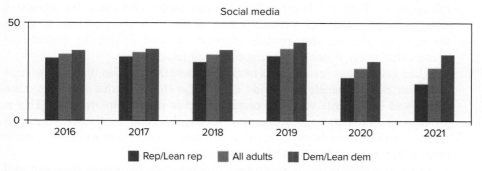

Social media

■ Rep/Lean rep   ■ All adults   ■ Dem/Lean dem

FIGURE 8.8   Wider partisan gaps emerge in trust of national and local news organizations, social media

Source: Jeffrey Gottfried and Jacob Liedke, "Partisan Divides in Media Trust Widen, Driven by a decline among Republicans," Pew Research Center, August 30, 2021 (accessed April 29, 2022).

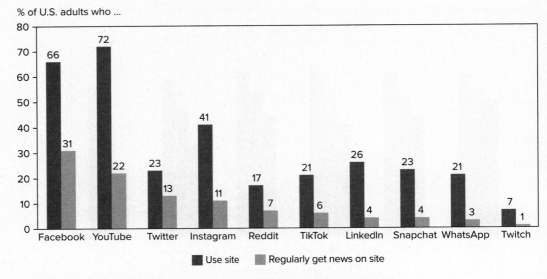

% of U.S. adults who ...

FIGURE 8.9 **News Use across Social Media Platforms, 2021**

Source: Pew Research Center, "News Consumption across Social Media in 2021," https://www.pewresearch.org/journalism/2021/09/20/news-consumption-across-social-media-in-2021/pj_2021-09-20_news-social-media_0-02/ (accessed May 3, 2022).

media have become an important tool for information gathering. Moreover, social media use has increased significantly over the past decade; today, more than two-thirds of all American adults use at least one form of social media to share information.[59] Figure 8.9 illustrates the use of social media by platform.

Facebook, YouTube, and Twitter represent the three most popular social media sites, although there are certainly others. Distinct preferences are present among age groups; for example, younger people tend to gravitate toward Instagram or Twitter.[60] These different social media sites present a disruptive element to the traditional forms of media in that they allow citizens to shape the news agenda, and they provide exposure to news outside the mainstream sources that many Americans are accustomed to accessing.

When using social media, users often self-select information that is consistent with their existing beliefs. The result is an "echo chamber" that amplifies those beliefs and leaves little room for dissenting or conflicting information. This is problematic for a diverse, democratic society because, as Cass R. Sunstein states, "[without] shared experiences, a heterogeneous society will have a much more difficult time in addressing social problems."[61]

This is particularly important to keep in mind given the rise of Facebook and Twitter. In a controversial move, Facebook changed the algorithms that prioritize content of a feed and limit the ability of news organizations to insert themselves.[62] These changes did not affect users' ability to share news, but the chances that users would see news from organizations with which they may disagree, be they liberal or conservative, were diminished. Here, your "friends, family, and acquaintances" decide what *is* news, and the echo chamber effect is exacerbated.

With increased cell phone use, many people with no journalism training have begun using YouTube as a means by which to share news as citizen journalists. **Citizen journalism** has emerged as a new form of journalism, often alerting traditional media sources to breaking news. It has grown out of the public's ability to use technology and the Internet to share information. Although YouTube, for example, provides the means by which citizens are able to get out information, often much more quickly than the news media can, it can be without context and lack the characteristics that represent work produced by professional reporters.

Where news is concerned, some significant issues exist with the use of YouTube. Although YouTube provides specific guidelines on how to properly attribute posted and shared videos, citizen journalists rarely follow those guidelines. Some users post dubious information, claiming it is news based on facts. Citizen journalists may provide more or different perspectives, or even cover events that traditional media has ignored, but there is always a risk that what they are providing is not factual or lacks context.

The issue of attribution notwithstanding, social media can allow people to share information when traditional media sources have refused or been unable to provide coverage to a story. For example, during one of the deadliest mass shootings in U.S. history at the Pulse nightclub in Orlando, Florida, social media sites, including Twitter and Facebook, were filled with news of the events as they unfolded, well before the police or news cameras arrived to intervene or to provide official coverage.[63] Similar use of social media occurred during the Las Vegas tragedy in October 2017 as well as after Texas's deadliest shooting in November 2017 at a church in Sutherland Springs.

Twitter is the third most popular social media sharing application, with more than 38 million accounts active daily in the United State alone.[64] Twitter users can send out more than 10 billion tweets in a day, but researchers at Carnegie Mellon University discovered in a survey that participants felt that barely more than one-third of the tweets reflected information worth reading. Those surveyed responded that the most "useless" information was the result of a tweet that did not share enough context to be understandable or worthwhile.[65] Although Twitter has the potential of providing relevant information to its users, like any other medium, the message must have substance and inform the user for it to be useful and valued.

In one instance, however, social media may have saved an innocent man from being falsely accused or perhaps even shot. Twitter brought the public news about the shooting deaths of five Dallas Metro Police officers in the summer of 2016 as a Black Lives Matter protest march in Dallas was occurring. In the confused aftermath, the Dallas police department tweeted a photo of a suspect. But citizens and other demonstrators were simultaneously posting photos and videos on Facebook and Twitter that clearly showed the suspect marching peacefully alongside others when the gunshots rang out. The suspect was not the shooter.[66]

Twitter use also played a role in the rise of Texas state senator Wendy Davis as a major political contender in the state as her filibuster of an anti-abortion bill went viral on the site in 2013. Over the course of a day, she garnered a significant online following with hundreds of thousands of retweets, an increase of over 40,000 followers, over 200,000 concurrent online viewers of her speech,

citizen journalism
The collection, dissemination, and analysis of news and information by the general public, especially by means of the Internet

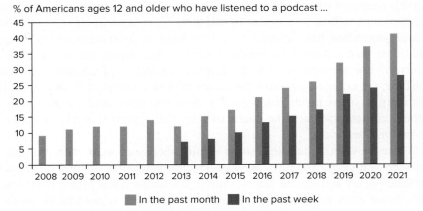

% of Americans ages 12 and older who have listened to a podcast ...

■ In the past month   ■ In the past week

FIGURE 8.10   Americans' Podcast Listening Habits

Source: Pew Research Center, "Audio and Podcasting Fact Sheet," https://www.pewresearch.org/journalism/fact-sheet/audio-and-podcasting/ (accessed May 3, 2022).

podcast

A digital audio file made available on the Internet for downloading to a computer or portable media player, typically available as a series, new installments of which can be received by subscribers automatically

streaming services

The transfer of music or video data over the Internet, generally through a subscription service provider

referendum

A direct public vote on a single political issue

and significant attention from both local and national media outlets across all media.[67] This popularity boost helped her gain a strong statewide standing and gave momentum to her 2014 campaign for governor, although she lost to Greg Abbott in the general election.

Podcasts, which became popular with the advent of Apple's iPod over a decade ago, represent another medium by which citizens obtain information. Podcasts range from short news segments to weekly installments covering a variety of topics, and some have become incredibly popular, particularly among Millennials. The most popular podcasts reflect content hosted by National Public Radio (NPR), such as *NPR News Now, Up First,* and *This American Life* and The New York Times's *The Daily*.[68] Figure 8.10 shows that podcast listening is increasing, though still lower than other forms of Internet or audio use.

Although traditional media face challenges from social media, it is clear that they can complement one another as individuals share information provided through network television, radio, and newspapers via their personal networks. What is perhaps more of a threat to traditional media's longevity are **streaming services** such as YouTube, Spotify, Netflix, and Amazon Prime. As more citizens begin moving away from commercial radio and television networks, a real possibility exists that these services will further erode broadcast media audiences. This is particularly relevant as more people have integrated smartphones into their daily lives. Although most social scientists today would argue that the medium (the physical means by we receive information) isn't everything, it certainly plays an important role. Our smartphones display information in certain ways and, therefore, affect how we perceive that information.

A recent example of how social media move the public occurred during the summer of 2016 after Britain voted to leave the European Union in a process nicknamed "Brexit" (for "British exit"). Twitter feeds lit up with calls for "#Texit," which would allow for a **referendum** for Texas to secede from the United States. During the Texas Republican convention, a few participants tried to force a floor vote on the issue.[69] Although there is much hope for the Internet and the potential for social media to invigorate democracy, early studies indicate that caution is in order.[70]

Focus On

Generational Differences in Information Consumption

As the Pew Center's data illustrate, Millennials and younger generations are more inclined to access news through the Internet, especially via social media platforms where they are three times more likely than Baby Boomers to access news.[71]

LeoPatrizi/E+/Getty Images

As of 2021, 72 percent of adults over 18 use at least one form of social media. Of those adults between 18 and 29, it's 84 percent. The age group 30 to 49 is at 81 percent; 50 to 64 is at 73 percent; and 65+ is at 45 percent.[72] Among younger users, Instagram has eclipsed Twitter though Facebook and YouTube still vastly outrank other platforms. Interestingly, in a 2020 survey, fully 65 percent of adults cite social media as an often used news source each week.[73]

Even with this conspicuous gap in the means of access, people across all generations are most likely to discover news by going directly to a news organization. For all groups, hearing directly from the reporting source is preferred to reading it as a social media post.

Critical Thinking Questions
1. Why do you think Instagram has begun to eclipse Twitter for younger social media users?
2. How well do social media provide news versus more traditional media such as newspapers and television?

A troubling paradox emerges if, in fact, three-quarters of Americans believe the media are biased in covering the news and providing information.[74] As the competition for "clicks" and advertising revenue becomes even more fierce, the quality of the news continues to deteriorate and the "medium becomes the message." For media to maintain an adversarial role to government within American democracy, their information, investigation, and analysis must explain complex issues, and the media must commit to substantial and accurate reporting of public affairs.

In 1969, Paul Baran, a computer engineer who is considered one of the Internet's earliest pioneers, penned an article on the effect new "electrical communications" would have on social values in America.[75] He predicted, with astonishing accuracy, that the rise of channel choice would create a decline of dialogue within the community and among individuals and groups with different ideological leanings and perspectives. This choice of channels would reflect not only the increase in options available to the viewer on television, but it would become further magnified with the advent of cable and satellite. Choice would increase again exponentially because of the Internet and the creation of a global community. Ironically, this increase in choice would lead to a decline in conversations among members in a community. The choices would create segregation into groups with like interests or viewpoints. As a result, these gaps of segregation (also called cleavages) would soon emerge, ultimately creating political instability.

Media's role then would be to provide a bridge between these cleavages so that, in societies, the overarching values that provide the "glue" would continue to bind even the most segregated groups. Baran cautioned that without some overlapping messages among these diverse media sources respecting the overarching principles of democratic theory, the ability for American (and Texan) media to function as those bridges would be questionable.

CORE OBJECTIVE

Taking Personal Responsibility . . .

What media sources do you consume? Print? Television? Social media? Which do you access most and least often? How might social media influence you differently than television?

Understanding Impact Consider the news sources you tend to access. Do you use sources from across the political spectrum, or do you primarily choose sources you know that you will agree with? Why do you make the choices you do? Now that you have read this section, are you considering any changes to the way you access news? Why or why not?

The Media in Political Campaigns

Learning Objective: Explain the role of the media in Texas political campaigns.

In no uncertain terms, "without media coverage, a candidacy is dead in the water for state and national elections." Name recognition is everything. The media—in various roles as fact reporter, neutral adversary, public advocate, profit seeker, and propagandist—make that name recognition possible and elections winnable.[76]

Traditional Media

Political campaign advertisements are the stuff that election seasons are made of. In 1992, Texas business executive Ross Perot spent $34.8 million of his own money—an equivalent of almost $60 million today—to purchase half-hour infomercials viewed by more than 16 million people.[77] It is estimated that for the 2016 election cycle, campaigns spent over $4 billion on television advertisements, and the fact is, they don't seem to matter much at the end of the campaign.[78] Candidates use **traditional media,** defined as conventional forms, such as television, print, radio, direct mail, and billboard signage, to connect with voters and get out their message, but this is expensive for a campaign. Candidates would prefer to rely on traditional media for free coverage when possible, and campaigns often schedule stump speeches, stage rallies, or agree to one-on-one interviews as opportunities for inexpensive or free exposure whenever they can.

One means of free exposure is the newspaper endorsement. In what was considered quite a coup, Hillary Clinton received the endorsement of the *Dallas Morning News*'s editorial staff in early September 2016.[79] This was the first time the paper had endorsed a Democrat in 75 years and, as a result, the endorsement itself garnered national attention.

Candidates purchase and produce several types of ads, posted on television and online. Specific formats and language vary across media, but these ads can all be classified into several broad types: positive, negative, and a combination. They can also focus on a candidate or a particular issue.[80]

Generally, a positive ad is designed to make the public feel good about the candidate or the party. In 1984, Ronald Reagan told viewers it was "morning

traditional media
The term associated with conventional forms of media, such as television, print, radio, direct mail, and billboard signage

Clinton, joined by Representative Joaquin Castro, greets crowds in San Antonio during her presidential bid in 2016.

Erich Schlegel/Getty Images

in America" in a commercial featuring scenes of a "middle America" town filled with happy people. In 1988, President George H. W. Bush saw "a thousand points of light." Others promise "fresh, bold leadership" or claim to have "common sense and uncommon courage." Still others, like gubernatorial candidate Clayton Williams, encourage listeners to "Share my vision." In 1998, Governor George W. Bush ran a number of TV spots that asked voters to support his effort to have every child read and become a productive member of society.

Positive candidate ads might try to depict the candidate as having saintly qualities: "Senator Smith is a Christian family man, Eagle Scout, Little League coach, Sunday school teacher, involved, concerned, committed, community leader who fights the people's fights. Let's keep him working for us." Others might take the form of testimonials from other citizens about the candidate. In a staged "person on the street" interview, the citizen says something like, "Senator Smith is the most effective leader this state has seen since Sam Houston. He's so effective it's frightening. He is committed to his job, and we need him to fight the coming battles with the liberals." In Texas, cattle and horses in the background can provide a down-to-earth backdrop for ranchers' "good ol' boy" testimonials.

Positive issue ads also tend to show the candidates taking "courageous" stands on issues everyone supports: sound fiscal management, planned orderly growth, good schools, open government, getting tough on crime, low taxes, and so on.

Negative ads, also called attack ads, play on voters' emotions by painting their opponent in a very unfavorable light. Former governor Rick Perry, running for secretary of agriculture in 1990, defeated Democratic incumbent Jim Hightower. In one of his commercials, Perry claimed that Hightower had once visited the home of Jane Fonda. Fonda is often used as a symbol for the radical war protesters of the 1960s because of her visit to Hanoi during the Vietnam War. When pressed for details on the visit, Perry said that Hightower had visited Los Angeles, and that Los Angeles was the home of Jane Fonda.

Attack ads have developed into a fine art. Newt Gingrich, former Speaker of the U.S. House of Representatives, extended the art when he used his GOPAC political action committee to help "train local Republican candidates." In 1990, GOPAC mailed a glossary of 131 words to more than 4,000 state Republican candidates. This glossary included a list of "optimistic positive governing words" that Republican candidates should use to describe themselves and a list of "contrasting negative words" they should use to describe their opponents. Republicans are described as "having common sense" and Democrats as "big-spending liberals."

Candidates use these types of advertisements because most often they work to the candidate's advantage. They plant a simple message in voters' minds that those voters carry into the voting booth. Many citizens do not spend much time studying issues or candidates' backgrounds and often depend on advertisements for information. Although the news media (which receive most of the money spent in campaigns) often denounce such ads, they do not refuse to run them. But occasionally these attack ads can backfire. They can come to be seen as illegitimate. Fact-checking organizations, such as PolitiFact, and fact-checking articles can minimize their impact. Or negative ads can unintentionally promote the candidate they are targeting.[81]

Digital Media

Candidates and campaigns purchase time and space on broadcast television, cable, radio, and print media outlets to provide citizens with information on their positions on issues. However, they have also begun to turn to digital media to create websites or social media sites, such as Facebook, YouTube, or Twitter, to share news and information with the public. Using these sites not only reduces the costs of campaigning but also gives them more precise control of what is covered, how it is covered, and who the message targets. By searching "campaign commercials" on YouTube, you can see a variety of these ads. To see how political ads have changed over the decades, compare recent ads with those for the 1956 Eisenhower presidential campaign.

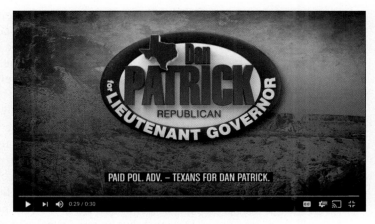

Then-senator Dan Patrick used YouTube to share political messages.
Dan Patrick/Dan Patrick for Texas Lt. Governor-TV ad "Texas Goes Sacramento"/Youtube

Further, in a geographically large state like Texas, digital media present a huge opportunity to save precious campaign dollars for more direct, capital-intensive efforts to get out the vote. As long as a voter has Internet access, these media options let campaigns save money and allow the message to spread far and wide, with little regard for coordination with network television or commercial media outlets.

Digital Campaigning and Citizen Participation

As the Internet evolved and social media sharing sites emerged, research began to focus on the specific influence social media had on citizens and their interaction with each other and their government. As candidates began using the Internet more often, the role of professional campaign consultants (particularly those with technical training) has become significantly more important to ensure that the message is professionally created and managed. The Internet gives campaigns the ability to control their message, connecting directly with the public without the interference or interpretation of the traditional media.

Connecting with the public directly is the most important advantage provided by the Internet; however, increasing interaction between candidates and their campaigns with the public is still no guarantee of winning an election. There have been many competing claims about the role the Internet plays in political engagement and participation. Some have argued that political participation would be transformed, and the influence of groups and elites would be diminished.[82]

Perhaps even more important is the claim that the Internet could reengage citizens or encourage apathetic voters to reconnect to the political system.[83] The argument largely rests on the assumption that people create online communities that would not only share political information but also create pressure on the communities' members to vote. Additionally, the input of members of the public becomes much more central; that is, "user-generated content suddenly became a far more potent campaign weapon than the slick ads created by media consultants."[84]

Facebook boasts over two billion users worldwide as of 2022. Recent research seems to indicate that particular activities on Facebook, like other social media sharing sites, helped create online communities. Further evidence suggests that, for some individuals, these online communities increased exposure to and discussion of political issues and events, which had a positive impact on its users' political participation.[85]

News, however, is not the only reason people use social media. Politicians and candidates running for public office use social media to connect *directly* to the public and voters. Social media allow elected officials to convey their message, unfiltered, to the world.

Ted Cruz was solicitor general of Texas from 2005 to 2008. In 2012, he ran a successful campaign for the U.S. Senate against Texas lieutenant governor David Dewhurst. Cruz had much less popularity, face recognition, and money than Dewhurst, but he ran a successful campaign thanks, in part, to his heavy focus on social media outreach. What did his campaign do? Politico notes the following:

> Weekly calls with supportive bloggers, who had access to the candidate throughout the race. Two full-time staffers focused on social media content, resulting in speedy responses to just about every tweet, Facebook comment and email. A microsite, cruzcrew.org, that empowered volunteers to take on tasks and print out campaign literature. The use of social media ads from the earliest days of the campaign to build a mailing list that is, in the words of Vincent Harris, the Cruz campaign digital strategist, "bigger than most of the failed Republican candidates for president."[86]

While this might seem the norm now, it wasn't at the time. Those strategies were developed in tandem with the growth of social media into what we have today. Of course, just like all forms of communication, there can be backlash. The Internet does not forget (at least for a while), and candidates who make statements or post comments or images may wind up facing criticism as a result of an inappropriate or ill-timed comment.

Texas lieutenant governor Dan Patrick was exposed to national scrutiny in 2016 when he tweeted what many saw as an inappropriate Bible verse following the deadliest mass shooting in American history.[87] At a gay club in Orlando, Florida, more than 50 people were killed and 50 others were injured. Not long after, Patrick's Twitter account released a prescheduled tweet of Galatians 6:7: "A man reaps what he sows." Although the tweet was apparently not intended to suggest that gay people were responsible for the shooting, its timing was unfortunate, and Patrick experienced negative publicity as a result.[88]

In practical terms, the rules for communicating with voters have changed. In large part, this is due to the proliferation of social media. Candidates and their campaigns who fail to use the power of social media sites such as Facebook and Twitter do so at their own peril.

CORE OBJECTIVE

Being Socially Responsible . . .

What responsibility do citizens have as social media participants within the context of political campaigns?

> **Understanding Impact** Many people complain about "gotcha" social media coverage that focuses on publicizing every mistake that candidates make. Do you think that is a fair complaint? Has the "gotcha" mentality gone too far, or is it important to hold public figures up to intense scrutiny? Explain.

Media Bias

Learning Objective: Describe bias in the Texas media.

Perceptions of Media Bias

From the time of the founding of the national government, Americans have expressed varying degrees of trust in their government. However, research indicates that citizens' levels of trust in the media, like their trust in government institutions, has decreased in most Western democracies.[89] In fact, a 2021 Gallup survey indicates that trust in the media is at one of the lowest points it has ever been since Gallup began asking about it in the 1970s.[90] This distrust has roots in an overwhelming amount of conflicting information and individuals' uncertainty in discerning what's true and what's not.[91]

Maxwell McCombs, a pioneer of media research, posited that someone attempting to study **media bias** would need years to make sense of the available data and refine a methodology to study them. That does not seem to stop anyone from presenting studies that say the media are biased, generally favoring one political party over the other.[92] Political scientist Tim Groeling, who specializes in studying political communication, proposes that two very specific types of bias exist in the media: selection bias and presentation bias.[93]

Selection bias results from several factors that affect media, including time, personnel, and budgetary constraints. The gatekeeping role of media is often what gives particular news sources their "slant." Many times, the media's selection of events may reflect partisan ideological positions on policy issues, matters of state, the economy, or the political parties themselves in terms of their decisions or actions taken.

Presentation bias occurs as a result of how a story is written or presented. The tone of a news story is crucial to understanding the framing taking place. This is where discussions emerge about the "echo chamber," which proposes that citizens self-select news sources that are in harmony with their own ideological positions and attitudes about government and policy. Contrary to what one might assume, however, there is no firm evidence that partisan media are making ordinary Americans more partisan.[94]

Still, according to Figure 8.11, in spite of perceived bias in the news, many Americans still believe that the media, and our trust in it, can improve.

Reality of Media Bias

In a landmark 1986 survey of journalists, researchers found that, overwhelmingly, journalists perceived themselves as being more liberal than both the

media bias
The actual or perceived failure of the media to report news objectively

selection bias
The systematic selection of particular news that presents a distorted view of reality

presentation bias
The act of writing or presenting news stories that reflect a significantly distorted view of reality, favoring one party over another in the case of political parties

% of U.S. adults who say___to improve the level of confidence Americans have in the news media

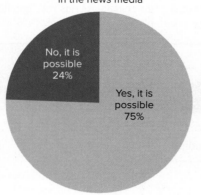

No, it is possible 24%

Yes, it is possible 75%

% of U.S. adults who rate the job news organizations have done covering the demonstrations to protest the death of George Floyd as ...

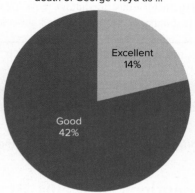

Excellent 14%

Good 42%

% who think the news media have covered the coronavirus outbreak ...

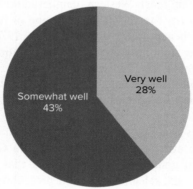

Very well 28%

Somewhat well 43%

FIGURE 8.11 How Americans View News Organizations

Source: Pew Research Center. "Americans See Skepticism of News Media as Healthy, Say Public Trust in the Institution Can Improve." https://www.pewresearch.org/journalism/2020/08/31/americans-see-skepticism-of-news-media-as-healthy-say-public-trust-in-the-institution-can-improve/

owners of the media and the public in general.[95] Other research points to bias as the result of journalistic norms, such as the dynamics of how journalists are expected to cover campaigns, the reliance on previous reporting to determine tone and information in subsequent work (for example, emulating other journalists), and pressures from market competition. Competitive editors of news outlets seeking to get the scoop can "make it all but impossible" for alternative framing of issues and candidates to break into the evening news or the front pages.[96]

Citizens consider information they receive directly from the media in light of their own ideological biases. Unfortunately, because individuals self-select news sources that are in harmony with their own perspectives and frequently reject those that are not, larger ideological gaps form among citizens. These

gaps lead to ideological segregation in social networks, which serves to increase bias in the media
as they seek to attract even larger audiences.[97]

Selection bias in the media and selective exposure of individuals is a particularly important issue
in Texas with many "red" (Republican) and "blue"
(Democratic) outlets solidifying their audience's
beliefs. The following "Tell the Truth! 2016" ad ran
during the Republican National Convention in the
2016 primary campaign season, repeating a popular
"red" media slogan.

Media bias plays a large role in the development
of public opinion. It reinforces political beliefs and
signals to audiences on matters of importance. At the same time, however, there
are legal limits on what is considered reasonable political communication. There
are limits on what the media can do, on the amount of bias displayed, and on
citizens' engagement in the public sphere.

2016 Republican National Convention ad campaign

FactCheck, American Press Institute, and Politifact

Understanding Impact Consider the issue of selection bias. Think of a hot-button topic such as abortion, Medicare
for all, or a Black Lives Matter protest. What type of story about this issue do you think a liberal-leaning media
outlet would feature? What type of story would a conservative-leaning media outlet feature? Judging from these
examples, how does selection bias by the media affect your understanding of major issues?

Regulating the Media

Learning Objective: Explain how the media are regulated in Texas.

Federal Regulation of Print and Broadcast Media

For the most part, print media are largely unregulated and given extensive
protection under the U.S. Constitution's First Amendment. However, this same
privilege does not exist for broadcast media. Traditional broadcast media use a
specific and limited spectrum of analog airwaves available for radio and television, and the Federal Communications Commission (FCC) limits who can
obtain broadcasting licenses. With the advent of satellite and cable technology,
as well as the Internet, regulation has changed over time.

Aside from laws that exist prohibiting the print media from printing **libelous**
or factually incorrect and defamatory information, there is little else that
impinges on print media's actions. The FCC is the regulatory body responsible
for issuing **regulations.** The Communications Act of 1934, which created the
FCC and empowered it to issue rules, also outlined how radio stations should
handle political advertisements. Today, many of those same rules apply. As a
consequence, and due to other factors, the public is often at a disadvantage
when determining whether media information is accurate.

libel
A published false statement
that is damaging to a private
individual's reputation

regulations
Administrative rules
implemented by governmental
regulatory agencies to guide
or prescribe specific conduct
by industry or business

Stephen Colbert explains super PACs to viewers in easy-to-understand terms.
Mark Wilson/Getty Images

One problem for the public arises around political advertisements. Because of campaign laws, advertisements that media sell—whether in print, radio, or television—must be sold at the lowest available rate. Media outlets have very little control over the content of these ads, even if they are misleading or false. The exception to this are ads placed by third-party groups classified as 501(c)(4)s, or super PAC, groups. In the 2010 *Citizens United* decision, the U.S. Supreme Court held that corporations and unions have a First Amendment right to spend unlimited funds on campaign advertisements, as long as these ads were not formally "coordinated" with any candidate. This ruling basically meant that the political speech rights of Americans and corporate entities are indistinguishable. Notably, super PACs had raised over $1 billion for the year's election cycle.[98]

Although these third-party and super PAC ads can be rejected for false or misleading information about issues or candidates, most are not. In a 2012 study conducted by the Pennsylvania University's Annenberg Public Policy Center, an overwhelming majority of political advertisements aired during the 2012 presidential election cycle were categorized as deceptive.[99] In the interest of the public and their duty to provide accurate information, broadcasters could refuse to air these misleading advertisements by third parties and super PACs, but they seldom do.

Another problem the public faces is that campaigns and interest groups can use newspaper stories or TV newscasts without permission as part of **fair use** even if they are presented in ways that distort their original intent. The danger here is when citizens see or hear the information in the news, and then see

fair use

Law that permits the limited use of copyrighted material without acquiring permission from the rights holders or hear the advertisement repeatedly, they will lose track of the original context and the new frame becomes the reality for viewers and listeners.

Yet another problem arises for the public when rules governing the media are not applied fairly. Several rules affect how the media treat political candidates and campaigns. The **equal time rule** requires broadcasters to provide equal air time to opposing views by candidates who seek the same political office. Broadcasters are prohibited from censoring anything said by the candidates or interests and, therefore, many media outlets choose not to provide airtime. The **right of rebuttal** states that a television or radio station cannot air an advertisement attacking a candidate without giving the target of the attack a chance to respond. This right, however, does not apply to print media. Media watchdogs groups such as Free Press and the Media Research Center have argued that the FCC has become lax in its enforcement of these rules, which is a disservice to the public. However, the FCC would argue that there has been tremendous growth in the media as well as access to sources through cable, satellite, and the Internet, the latter of which are not subject to the same degree of regulation that network television is, and many of these provide sufficient alternative views to counter false or misleading information.[100]

equal time rule
Provided that a broadcaster permitting one political candidate access to the airwaves must afford equal opportunities to all other such candidates seeking the same office

right of rebuttal
Candidates must be given an opportunity to respond to any criticism made by a media outlet

Federal Regulation of the Internet

Although there have been attempts in the past to regulate content on the Internet through action by Congress, it remains largely unregulated. In 2015, the FCC proposed rules regarding **network (net) neutrality,** which would ensure Internet service providers (ISPs) treat all available information equally and not block or slow down the delivery of content sought by consumers. In 2014, the United States Court of Appeals for the D.C. Circuit struck down the FCC's Open Internet Order in the case of *Verizon v. FCC*.[101] This ruling effectively ended network neutrality by disallowing the FCC to issue rules regulating ISP behavior that can result in ISPs—Spectrum (formerly Time Warner Cable), AT&T, Verizon, and so on—blocking or interfering with traffic on the web. That means, for example, a company can slow down its competitors or block political opinions with which it disagrees. There were no protections, including privacy, for Internet users because, unlike Google or Facebook, ISPs have direct control over the connections to the Internet and the devices used to connect to it. In 2015, the FCC reclassified broadband Internet transmission as a telecommunications service, which allowed it to regulate businesses that provide Internet service to the public.[102] Returning to court again, the United States Telecom Association sought to have this decision overturned, but in June 2016, ironically in front of the U.S. Court of Appeals for the D.C. Circuit, the court ruled against it.[103]

On December 14, 2017, however, those 2015 protections ended. The FCC, under Chair Ajit Pai, voted 3 to 2 to end the reclassification and remove the regulations put in place.[104] Still, the fight over net neutrality continues. The Trump administration attempted to litigate these state measures but the Supreme Court denied the FCC the ability to negate state-level net neutrality laws.[105] In July 2021, the Biden Administration requested the FCC return to those 2015 protections but, as of late 2022, the FCC Commissioners are deadlocked and Congress has not agreed on a possible federal net neutrality policy.[106]

network (net) neutrality
The principle that Internet service providers should enable access to all content and applications regardless of the source, and without favoring or blocking particular products or websites

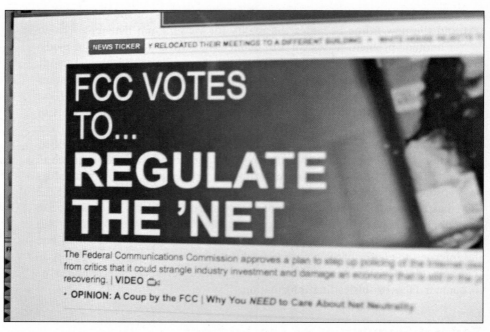

Regulating the Internet

Newsies Media/Alamy Stock Photo

Understanding Impact What are the advantages and disadvantages that would allow Internet service providers to regulate access and connection speed to certain sites on the web? Since the 2017 FCC action effectively ending net neutrality, have you had any personal experience, positive or negative, accessing sites through your service provider?

The Internet has also presented something of a conundrum for policy makers in terms of how to address obscene material because of the virtual impossibility of regulating it. The definition of what constitutes obscenity was originally established by the United States Supreme Court in *Miller v. California* (1973).[107] After several failed congressional attempts during the 1990s, the Children's Internet Protection Act (CIPA) became law in 2000. This act regulates the Internet through federal funding provided to elementary and secondary schools as well as public libraries. It requires these entities to ensure filtering systems are in place to prevent minors from gaining access to sexually explicit, obscene, or otherwise harmful materials online.

Many Internet service providers require users to agree to terms of service (TOS) that include general and specific prohibitions. This is true for social media sites as well. For example, Facebook cautions its users against posting material promoting a number of issues, such as direct threats, self-injury, bullying, sexual violence, or criminal activity.[108] Not only can Facebook administrators remove the content, violators can be put in "Facebook jail," which limits a user's ability to post or can result in account deletion. Twitter, YouTube, and other social media sites have similar statements for users.

Communicating Effectively . . .

Explain how the federal government regulates print and electronic media.

State and Local Regulation

While Article 6 of the U.S. Constitution grants supremacy to federal laws over state laws, states do still have authority to regulate specific aspects of the Internet. Under its **police powers,** many state laws, including those in Texas, have been amended to reflect changes in technology that have afforded criminals opportunities to access our personal information, stalk or bully victims online, target individuals for financial gain, or lure children into unsafe situations.

In 2009, the Texas legislature passed HB 2003, amending the Texas Penal Code to prohibit harassment, including "cyberstalking," "cyberimpersonation," and "cyberharassment." The new law added criminal harassment through electronic means to include repeated, unwanted electronic communications that have the intent of "harassing, annoying, alarming, abusing, tormenting, embarrassing, or offending." As the use of social media increased, cyberbullying, particularly among adolescents, has increased. Across the country, there have been repeated incidents of teenagers being harassed to the point of suicide.

Notably, in January 2016, 16-year-old David Molak, a student at Alamo Heights High School in San Antonio, Texas, committed suicide after prolonged bullying, the second such case since 2002. As a result, Texas senator José Menendez and other members of the Senate Criminal Justice Committee met during the 2016 summer interim session to discuss existing law and how to balance the issues of free speech with new, more insidious forms of bullying through social media. Menendez created a draft bill and submitted it to the legislature, aptly named "David's Law," during the 2017 session. The bill became law on June 9, 2017.[109]

> **police power**
> The ability afforded states under the Tenth Amendment of the U.S. Constitution to regulate behavior and enforce order within their geographic territories

Regulation within State and Local Agencies

Although Texas does not currently have a social media privacy law in place,[110] state and local agencies are creating internal rules. Social media present a huge opportunity for them to connect with their communities, and they have needed to come up with a set of guidelines for proper use.[111]

For example, Fuat Altunbas, for his dissertation at the University of North Texas, conducted a study on social media adoption and use by several police departments in the Dallas–Fort Worth area. He found that social media were increasingly used, and many departments take part in SMILE (Social Media, the Internet, and Law Enforcement), a national conference that aims to educate law enforcement on how to use social media and the Internet.[112]

In the past few years, more police departments have been using social media to help find criminals and provide updates on investigations and community events. Hewitt police department, for example, has #HewittHustle which is an ongoing reminder to help prevent car theft.[113]

Whose Media?

Learning Objective: Explain concerns about control of the media in Texas.

Who Owns the Media?

If, as James Madison said, "a marketplace of ideas" is what is required for a healthy democracy to function, how is that to occur if only a handful of companies serve as gatekeepers for information? Although the Internet certainly provides a vast array of information, recall that a majority of citizens still rely on television for their information and news. The 1996 Telecommunications Act, enacted under the promise of reduced costs to consumers, relaxed the limit on how many radio and television stations one company could own. The old limit was 12 percent of the national market; the new cap was 35 percent. The consequence of this law was that it allowed giant corporations to own hundreds of media outlets, ultimately creating a monopolistic flow of information in Texas and the United States as a whole (see Figure 8.12 for an overview of media ownership today).

The act has allowed a select few conglomerates to emerge as major providers of information, acting as large umbrellas for both traditional and digital media outlets. For example, Comcast owns many major brands (including NBC, MSNBC, Universal, and Telemundo) and has stakes in Hulu and more, with a market cap at roughly $261 billion. Disney has a cap of $321 billion. Time Warner, a huge conglomerate in its own right (HBO, Warner Brothers, and more), was recently incorporated into AT&T, becoming AT&T/WarnerMedia. In November 2017, the Justice Department filed a lawsuit to block the deal, but it lost the case in February 2019.[114] Most of what we see and hear can be traced back to these large national and international umbrella organizations.[115]

Not only is concentration happening nationally, but large conglomerates have also bought many Texas-owned media outlets. This overall concentration of ownership has consequences for Texas and for the news content Texans see.

In 2013, Dallas-based Belo Corporation sold its news stations—including Austin's KVUE-TV, Beaumont's KFDM-TV, Dallas–Fort Worth's WFAA-TV, Houston's KHOU-TV, and San Antonio's KENS-TV—to Gannett/Tegna (a media conglomerate also based in Virginia). In 2014, Virginia-based Media General, Inc. bought Austin-based LIN Media, leaving the city without any locally owned, or even Texas-owned, television news sources. This situation is happening across the state. What does it mean for the media (especially news media) that Texans consume? Most likely, it means less local news and a selection bias that is increasingly slanted toward national issues.[116]

Understanding Impact Newspaper readership is declining, as you learned in an earlier section, and television news is increasingly own by national media conglomerates. Considering these changes, what choices do you have if you want to learn about local issues?

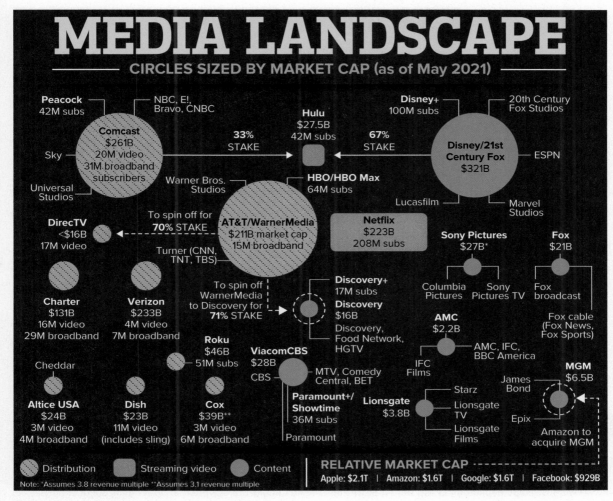

FIGURE 8.12   Who Owns the Media?

Adapted from Rani Molla and Peter Kafka, "Here's Who Owns Everything in Big Media Today: It Probably Won't Look Like This for Long," Vox, updated May 27, 2021, https://www.vox.com/2018/1/23/16905844/media-landscape-verizon-amazon-comcast-disney-fox-relationships-chart

The Future of Media

In February and March 2016, for the first time, both the Republicans and Democrats simulcast presidential debates in Spanish. With the Telemundo-CNN Republican debate, cohosted by Maria Celeste Arraras, the candidates faced questions that were of specific importance to the Latino community. These included President Obama's executive order for Deferred Action for Childhood Arrival (DACA) as well as the GOP's failure to appeal to Latinos on other issues. It was estimated that more than 500,000 viewers watched this debate through Telemundo's live stream. Univision's "El Debate Democratica," hosted in Miami at a local community college, was viewed by more than 2 million on Univision alone.[117] The question of media ownership is not about just ownership itself; it is also about who is consuming it. Consumers drive content as much as owners and producers do.

Telemundo is increasing its American viewership and ratings, edging out Univision in some markets.

Ken Wolter/Shutterstock

Focus On

Using the Media to Appeal to Hispanic Voters

The growing Hispanic population in the United States has finally caught the attention of both major political parties in America. Latinos make up approximately 18.5 percent of the U.S. population and 39.7 percent of the population in Texas. A little over 50 percent of Texas's Latino population is eligible to vote.[118] Spanish is the primary language in 40.3 million homes across the United States, and in Texas, roughly 30 percent of households speak Spanish. More specifically, 11.9 percent of Texas households speak primarily Spanish with limited English.[119]

Both George W. Bush and Al Gore stumped in Spanish while on the campaign trail in 2000, enlisted Spanish-speaking relatives to campaign on their behalf, and maintained Spanish-language websites, clearly attempting to capture the Latino vote.[120] Barely two years later, Texas's Democratic gubernatorial debate between Tony Sanchez and Dan Morales marked the first time in U.S. history that a major political debate was held in Spanish, indicating that the Democratic Party acknowledged the importance of the Latino vote, particularly in Texas.[121]

Telemundo, owned by NBC/Universal, and Univision represent the two largest Spanish-language programming providers in the United States. Telemundo owns 30 stations along with many other affiliates[122] and competes with Univision's 59 U.S. broadcast stations, 57 U.S. radio stations, and many other affiliates. See Figure 8.13 for a comparison of their viewership numbers in the United States.

In the fall of 2015, Telemundo unveiled its multiplatform voter information campaign #yodecido to target younger Spanish-speaking voters. The campaign's website provided a full complement of election coverage, focusing primarily on the 2016 presidential election. Using the #yodecido platform, Telemundo created a series of public service

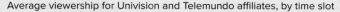

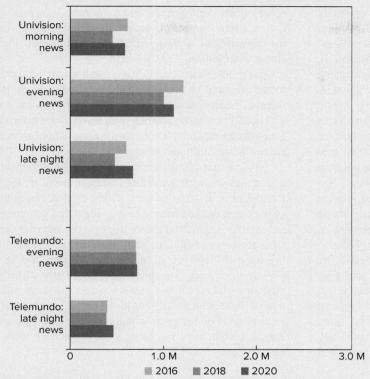

FIGURE 8.13 Univision and Telemundo Local Affiliates Viewership, by Time Slot

Source: Pew Research Center, "Hispanic and Black News Media Fact Sheet," State of the News Media 2021, https://www.pewresearch.org/journalism/fact-sheet/hispanic-and-black-news-media/(accessed May 3, 2022).

announcements and voter registration drives on a countrywide tour. These events were meant to provide spaces for interested young Hispanics to get involved, talk about their concerns, and discuss the candidates running for president. In 2020, Telemundo repeated the effort but renamed the website Decisión 2020.[123]

In the spring of 2016, Univision launched "Destino 2016." Like Telemundo's venture, "Destino 2016" was envisioned as a means to provide information and inspire young Latinos across the country to vote in the 2016 presidential election. One of the special projects for "Destino 2016" was "United Stories of America," a weekly broadcast that followed 16 Latinos across eight battleground states. These stories were presented by Jorge Ramos and Maria Elena Salinas, two of the most respected television personalities in the Hispanic community, and provided viewers a unique perspective on the lives of Latino and Latina Americans and the issues they faced as the country neared the presidential election. Four years later, the website featured a "Destino 2020" page.[124]

The Future of Univision and Telemundo Media Networks

In 2022, Univision merged with Televisa which is a large Latin American media corporation, allowing it to consolidate it's broadcast and streaming arms in Latin America and to reach into the United States more broadly.[125] The newly minted TelevisaUnivision is focusing on increasing streaming offerings over the next few years and has begun to grow its total viewership at a slightly higher rate than Telemundo.[126]

Telemundo, while having overall slightly lower viewership than Univision, has been increasing its audience among the 18-to-49-year-old demographic. It has a huge slate of programming geared toward them and plans on increasing ad revenue from Hispanic TV in general. Senior Vice President Dana Bonkowski noted recently that Telemundo "[has] been loyal to [its] plan of targeting a younger, bilingual audience."[127] The last few years has seen a large push into streaming, in particular utilizing YouTube and NCBUniversal's Peacock platform.[128]

Critical Thinking Questions

1. How effective do you believe the use of Spanish-language media outlets will be to target youthful Latino and Latina voters? Explain your answer.
2. How does the use of social media increase the likelihood of attracting Latino and Latina youth to the polls?

Conclusion

At its most basic level, public opinion is the aggregate (sum) of attitudes and opinions of individuals and groups on a particular topic. Individuals form political opinions through a process called political socialization, learning political attitudes and opinions through agents of socialization, such as family, education, religious institutions, generational effects, and the media. Public opinion is typically measured through surveys and focus groups using statistical methodology. It is important for government to know public opinion because when conflict arises (such as on marijuana use and other political issues), public opinion can help determine policy.

The media are part of our daily lives; media provide us with information and entertainment and help shape public opinion about what is or is not important in society. However, the role of media as adversary to government also requires accurate, substantive news. The media have evolved over their short history and continue to shape perceptions in the way they both select and present content to viewers. Even as the types of media sources available to citizens have expanded, there is rising concern about the consolidation of media outlets and the problems associated with bias as fewer and fewer outlets control more and more news information. Citizens rely on media to share information about what the government is doing in their communities, their states, their nation, and the world.

The media, both traditional as well as the new platforms provided by social media, have changed how political campaigns and politicians connect to citizens and voters and how governments at all levels share information with them. Today's citizens have a wealth of ways to access information and news.

To some extent, media can be regulated, but there are limitations on what government can prohibit or limit. Printed news is afforded very strong First Amendment protections, unlike its more heavily regulated contemporaries in broadcast and radio. Because the Internet contains elements of all of its predecessors, its regulation is the most difficult of all, given that we now live in a global community. The Internet (particularly with the birth of social media, which allow citizens to share information in printed forms) has given rise to new forms of journalism. For better or worse, it is clear that people are no less hungry for news today than they were a century ago.

Summary

LO: Explain the role of public opinion in U.S. and Texas politics.

There are five broad definitions of public opinion: aggregation of individual opinion, majoritarian, interest group conflict, media/elite opinion, and fiction. Individuals form political opinions through a process called political socialization; that is, learning political attitudes and opinions through agents of socialization such as family, education, religious institutions, generational effects, and the media. Public opinion is typically measured through surveys and focus groups using statistical methodology. It is important because when conflict arises (such as on marijuana use and other political issues), public opinion can help determine policy.

LO: Explain the functions of media in U.S. and Texas politics.

Media's primary role is to serve as a means by which citizens obtain information, news, and entertainment. The media prime, frame, and set the agenda for citizens as they consume information and news. Both hard and soft news provide readers, viewers, and listeners with a variety of stories that shape perceptions of the world around them and affect their daily lives.

LO: Describe the various sources of media in Texas.

The media include traditional forms, such as newspapers, magazines, broadcast outlets, and radio outlets. Cable and satellite television and radio emerged as alternatives to traditional media sources and have eroded viewers and readers. The Internet has brought new sources of media to citizens, including podcasts, blogs, social networking, and streaming audio and video.

LO: Explain the role of the media in Texas political campaigns.

The media shape and frame the processes and discourse of political communication as well as the society in which that communication takes place. Media have allowed more citizens to become active participants in political events and processes. Campaign advertisements are an important part of the election process and can affect how citizens vote. Negative attack ads can harm targeted candidates or backfire and benefit the targeted candidates.

LO: Describe bias in the Texas media.

Charges of media bias exist, but there is disagreement about its effect on the public. Selection bias, which reflects which stories are chosen, and presentation bias, which refers to the perspective from which a story is told, can both affect the substance of the information the public receives. There is some evidence to support the idea that bias in media is really a result of consumer demands and the self-selection of sources of information.

LO: Explain how the media are regulated in Texas.

Print media are the oldest form of information, and as such, they receive significant protection under the U.S. Constitution's First Amendment. Television and radio are more heavily regulated because of the limited resources available for broadcasting their messages to

the public. In terms of content, there are laws in place that regulate content with respect to obscenity, but political speech is more heavily regulated among broadcasters because of the nature of the medium and the speed with which information is provided. The Internet is the least regulated of all forms of media; however, there are laws that specifically reference criminal behavior, such as cyberbullying, stalking, harassment, and specific types of fraud. Attempts to regulate content contained on the Internet have been largely unsuccessful.

LO: Explain concerns about control of the media in Texas.

A few companies now control almost 90 percent of all prime-time viewing in the United States, and media consolidation is a concern for citizens across the globe. With media consolidation, there is a concern that there will be fewer alternative viewpoints shared with citizens and that media will be less able to fulfill the role of adversary to the government.

Key Terms

agenda setting
agents of socialization
citizen journalism
CNN effect
critical journalism
electronic media
equal time rule
exit polls
fair use
framing
gatekeeping
hard news
information

investigative journalism
libel
mass media
media bias
network (net) neutrality
news
podcasts
police powers
political communication
political socialization
presentation bias
priming
print media

public opinion
public sphere
push polls
referendum
regulations
resonance
right of rebuttal
selection bias
socioeconomic factors
soft news
straw polls
streaming services
traditional media

Notes

[1] Carroll J. Glynn, *Public Opinion* (Boulder, CO: Westview Press, 2004), *eBook Canadian Collection (EBSCOhost)*, Web. 21, September 2016, p. 291.

[2] George F. Bishop, *The Illusion of Public Opinion: Fact and Artifact in American Public Opinion Polls* (New York: Rowman & Littlefield), 1.

[3] Matthew A. Baum and Philip B. K. Potter, "The Relationship between Mass Media, Public Opinion, and Foreign Policy: Toward a Theoretical Synthesis," *Annual Review of Political*

Science 11 (2008): 39–65, https://www.researchgate.net/publication/228283589_The_Relationship_Between_Mass_Media_Public_Opinion_and_Foreign_Policy_Toward_a_Theoretical_Synthesis.

[4] Max McCombs, R. Lance Holbert, Spiro Kiousus, et al., *The News and Public Opinion: Media Effects on Civic Life* (Malden, MA: Polity Press, 2011), p. 1.

[5] Carroll J. Glynn, Susan Herbst, Mark Lindeman, et al., *Public Opinion,* 3rd ed. (Boulder, CO: Westview Press, 2015), p. 13.

[6] Texas Politics Project, "Support for Wall along Mexico Border (February 2019)," https://texaspolitics.utexas.edu/set/support-wall-along-mexico-border-february-2019 (accessed April 14, 2020).

[7] Heidi Perez-Moreno, "Immigration and border security remain top concerns of Texas voters, UT/TT Poll finds," *Texas Tribune*, June 28, 2021, https://www.texastribune.org/2021/06/28/immigration-border-security-ut-tt-poll/ (accessed April 15, 2022).

[8] Mira Sotirovic and Jack M. McLeod, "Values, Communication Behavior, and Political Participation," *Political Communication* 18 (2001): 273–300.

[9] Andrew Kohut, "But What Do the Polls Show? How Public Opinion Surveys Came to Play a Major Role in Policymaking and Politics," Pew Research Center, October 14, 2009, http://www.pewresearch.org/2009/10/14/but-what-do-the-polls-show/.

[10] Ibid.

[11] Herbert Asher, *Polling and the Public,* 8th ed. (Washington, D.C.: CQ Press, 2012), 22.

[12] Herbert Asher, *Polling and the Public,* 8th ed. (Washington, D.C.: CQ Press, 2012), 178–81.

[13] Shiela Kaplan, "Tobacco Dole: What Do Bob Dole's Telemarketer, His Chief California Strategist, and One of His National Co-chairs Have in Common? Big Tobacco," *Mother Jones,* May–June 1996, http://www.motherjones.com/politics/1996/05/tobacco-dole.

[14] U.S. Citizen and Immigration Services, "Consideration of Deferred Action for Childhood Arrivals (DACA)," https://www.uscis.gov/DACA (accessed April 15, 2022).

[15] E. E. Schattschneider, *The Semisovereign People: A Realist's View of Democracy in America* (Boston, MA: Wadsworth, Cengage Learning, 1975), 129.

[16] https://texaspolitics.utexas.edu/set/legalization-marijuana-june-2021 (accessed April 15, 2022).

[17] https://texaspolitics.utexas.edu/set/should-texas-legalize-marijuana-and-tax-it-fund-public-education-february-2019#overall (accessed April 15, 2022).

[18] Tony Plohetski, "Are Big Texas Cities Going Easier on Pot?," *Austin American-Statesman,* September 1, 2016, http://www.mystatesman.com/news/are-big-texas-cities-going-easier-pot/JCfWCatK0ne8lMJBrKMDXI/.

[19] http://www.texasmarijuanapolicy.org/2020/01/24/austin-no-more-arrests-for-small-amounts-of-marijuana/ (accessed April 20, 2020).

[20] Jolie McCullough, "Texas Leaders: Hemp Law Did Not Decriminalize Marijuana," *Texas Tribune.* July 18, 2019, https://www.texastribune.org/2019/07/18/greg-abbott-texas-leaders-hemp-marijuana-law/ (accessed April 20, 2020).

[21] Shawn Mulcahy, "A bill to expand Texas' medical marijuana program started moving in the Senate. Advocates worry time is running out.," *Texas Tribune*, May 20, 2021, https://www.texastribune.org/2021/05/20/texas-medical-marijuana-dan-patrick/ (accessed April 15, 2022).

[22] Carroll J. Glynn, *Public Opinion* (Boulder, CO: Westview Press, 2004), 61–62.

[23] H. D. Lasswell, "The Structure and Function of Communication in Society," in *The Communication of Ideas,* ed. L. Bryson (New York: Harper, 1948), 117.

[24] Jan E. Leighley, *Mass Media and Politics: A Social Science Perspective* (New York: Houghton Mifflin, 2004), 6.

[25] Matthew Carleton Ehrlich, "The Journalism of Outrageousness," *Journalism and Mass Communication Monographs,* No. 155 (February, 1996).

[26] Thomas E. Mann and Norman J. Ornstein, *It's Even Worse Than It Looks: How the American Constitutional System Collided with the New Politics of Extremism* (New York: Basic Books, 2013), 62.

[27] Megan Brenan, "Americans' Trust in Media Dips to Second Lowest on Record." Gallup. October 7, 2021. https://news.gallup.com/poll/355526/americans-trust-media-dips-second-lowest-record.aspx (accessed April 26, 2022).

[28] B. Cohen, *The Press and Foreign Policy* (Princeton, NJ: Princeton University Press, 1963), 13.

[29] *M.D. v. Perry* (S.D. Tex.) 01/19/2016 at pg 254, https://casetext.com/case/md-v-perry (accessed August 19, 2016).

[30] Reese Oxner and Neelam Bohra, "Texas foster care crisis worsens, with fast-growing numbers of children sleeping in offices, hotels, churches," *The Texas Tribune.* July 19, 2021. https://www.texastribune.org/2021/07/19/texas-foster-care-crisis/ (accessed April 26, 2022).

[31] George Lakoff, *Don't Think of an Elephant: Know Your Values and Frame the Debate* (White River Junction, VT: Chelsea Green, 2004), 109–10.

[32] Simone Jasper, "Framing of Children in News Stories about US Immigration from Latin America," *Elon Journal* (2016): 68.

[33] Matthew A. Baum and Philip B. K. Potter, "The Relationship between Mass Media, Public Opinion, and Foreign Policy: Toward a Theoretical Synthesis," *Annual Review of Political Science* 11 (2008): 39–65, https://www.researchgate.net/publication/228283589_The_Relationship_Between_Mass_Media_Public_Opinion_and_Foreign_Policy_Toward_a_Theoretical_Synthesis.

[34] Ibid.

[35] Jan E. Leighley, *Mass Media and Politics: A Social Science Perspective* (New York: Houghton Mifflin, 2004), 9–13.

[36] Max McCombs, R. Lance Holbert, Spiro Kiousus, et al., *The News and Public Opinion: Media Effects on Civic Life* (Malden, MA: Polity Press, 2011), 151.

[37] Craig Calhoun, ed., *Habermas and the Public Sphere* (Cambridge, MA: MIT Press, 1993).

[38] Natalie Fenton, foreword to *Media/Democracy: A Comparative Study,* by Alec Charles (Newcastle-upon-Tyne, England: Cambridge Scholars, July 2013), x.

[39] Marshall McLuhan, *Understanding Media: The Extensions of Man* (New York: McGraw-Hill, 1964), 8.

[40] U.S. Census Bureau, "Historical Statistics of the United States: Bicentennial Edition: Colonial Times to 1970, Part 1," https://www.census.gov/history/pdf/1850-1910newspapers.pdf (accessed July 19, 2016).

[41] Robert F. Karolevitz, *Newspapering in the Old West: A Pictorial History of Journalism and Printing on the Frontier* (New York: Bonanza Books, 1965), 139.

[42] Robert F. Karolevitz, *Newspapering in the Old West: A Pictorial History of Journalism and Printing on the Frontier* (New York: Bonanza Books, 1965), 141.

[43] Maury Darst, "Galveston News," *Handbook of Texas Online,* https://www.tshaonline.org/handbook/entries/galveston-news (accessed April 26, 2022); "The History of the Daily News," https://www.galvnews.com/site/the_daily_news.html (accessed April 26, 2022).

[44] Patrick Cox, *The First Texas News Barons* (Austin: University of Texas Press, 2005); Michael P. McDonald, "2022 General Election," United States Elections Project, https://www.electproject.org/2022g.

[45] Kantar Media, "U.S. Newspaper Circulation Summary (Ranked by Total Daily)," in SRDS Circulation 2018, p. 679 (accessed February 16, 2018).

[46] Pew Research Center, "Newspapers Fact Sheet," June 29, 2021. https://www.pewresearch.org/journalism/fact-sheet/newspapers/ (accessed April 26, 2022).

[47] Elisa Shearer, "More than eight-in-ten Americans get news from digital devices," January 12, 2021. https://www.pewresearch.org/fact-tank/2021/01/12/more-than-eight-in-ten-americans-get-news-from-digital-devices/ (accessed April 26, 2022).

[48] https://tshaonline.org/handbook/online/articles/ebr01.

[49] https://tshaonline.org/handbook/online/articles/ebw02.

[50] Statista, "Number of Sirius Holdings' Subscribers in the United States from 1st Quarter 2011 to 3rd Quarter 2019," October 2019, https://www.statista.com/statistics/252812/number-of-sirius-xms-subscribers/ (accessed May 8, 2020).

[51] https://tshaonline.org/handbook/online/articles/ect03.

[52] Thomas Zengotita, *Mediated: How the Media Shapes Your World and the Way You Live in It* (New York: Bloomsbury, 2008), 7.

[53] J. P. Robinson and M. R. Levy, "News Media Use and the Informed Public: A 1990s Update," *Journal of Communication* 46 (1996): 129–35.

[54] Michael A. Xenos, Dietram A. Scheufele, Dominique E. Brossard, et al., "News Media Use and the Informed Public in the Digital Age," paper presented at the American Political Science Association Political Communication Pre-Conference, Baton Rouge, LA, August 2012.

[55] "'The CNN Effect': How 24-Hour News Coverage Affects Government Decisions and Public Opinion," Brookings, January 23, 2002, https://www.brookings.edu/events/the-cnn-effect-how-24-hour-news-coverage-affects-government-decisions-and-public-opinion/.

[56] Jan E. Leighley, *Mass Media and Politics: A Social Science Perspective* (New York: Houghton Mifflin, 2004), 58–61.

[57] Pew Research Center, "News Platform Fact Sheet," November 8, 2021, https://www.pewresearch.org/journalism/fact-sheet/news-platform-fact-sheet/ (accessed April 29, 2022).

[58] Kaia Hubbard, "Outside of Sleeping, Americans Spend Most of their Time Watching Television," *U.S. News,* July 22, 2021, https://www.usnews.com/news/best-states/articles/2021-07-22/americans-spent-more-time-watching-television-during-covid-19-than-working (accessed April 29, 2022).

[59] Pew Research Center, "News Use across Social Media Platforms in 2021," https://www.pewresearch.org/journalism/2021/09/20/news-consumption-across-social-media-in-2021/ (accessed May 3, 2022).

[60] M. Duggan, N. B. Ellison, C. Lampe, et al., "Social Media Update 2014," January 2015, Pew Research Center, http://www.pewinternet.org/2015/01/09/social-media-update-2014/ (accessed September 10, 2016).

[61] C. Sunstein, *Republic.com 2.0.* (Princeton, NJ: Princeton University Press, 2007), 7.

[62] Farhad Manjoo, "Facebook, a News Giant That Would Rather Show Us Baby Pictures," *The New York Times,* June 29, 2016, http://www.nytimes.com/2016/06/30/technology/facebook-a-news-giant-that-would-rather-show-us-baby-pictures.html?action=click&contentCollection=Technology&module=RelatedCoverage®ion=Marginalia&pgtype=article (accessed September 3, 2016).

[63] Vanessa Borge, "Horrific Mass Shooting in Orlando Unfolds through Social Media," June 12, 2016, http://miami.cbslocal.com/2016/06/12/horrific-mass-shooting-in-orlando-unfolds-through-social-media/ (accessed September 17, 2016).

[64] Statista, "Number of Monthly Active Twitter Users in the United States from 1st Quarter 2017 to 4th Quarter 2021," October 2021. https://www.statista.com/statistics/970911/monetizable-daily-active-twitter-users-in-the-united-states/ (accessed May 3, 2022).

[65] Paul André, Michael S. Bernstein, and Kurt Luther, "Who Gives a Tweet? Evaluating Microblog Content Value," paper presented at the Conference on Computer Supported Cooperative Work, Seattle, WA, February 11–15, 2012, https://www.cs.cmu.edu/~pandre/pubs/whogivesatweet-cscw2012.pdf (accessed September 17, 2016).

[66] Will Oremus, "Twitter Exonerated This 'Suspect' in the Dallas Shooting: Why Didn't the Police Clear His Name?," *Slate,* July 8, 2016, http://www.slate.com/blogs/the_slatest/2016/

07/08/twitter_exonerated_suspect_mark_hughes_in_the_dallas_shooting_why_haven.html (accessed September 3, 2016).

[67] Caitlin Dewey, "Wendy Davis 'Tweetstorm' Was Planned in Advance," *The Washington Post,* June 16, 2013, https://www.washingtonpost.com/news/the-fix/wp/2013/06/26/this-tweetstorm-was-planned-in-advance/.

[68] Podtrac, "Podcast Industry Ranking Top 20 Podcasts US Audience: March 2022," http://analytics.podtrac.com/podcast-rankings (accessed May 8, 2020).

[69] Amber Phillips, "Texas Republicans Have Opted Not to Secede from the United States, After All," *The Washington Post,* May 13, 2016, https://www.washingtonpost.com/news/the-fix/wp/2016/04/19/the-texas-secession-movement-is-getting-kind-of-serious/ (accessed August 21, 2016).

[70] A. Ceron, "Internet, News, and Political Trust: The Difference between Social Media and Online Media Outlets," *Journal of Computer-Mediated Communications* 20 (2015): 487–503.

[71] Pew Research Center, "Millennials & Political News," June 2015, http://www.journalism.org/files/2015/06/Millennials-and-News-FINAL-7-27-15.pdf (accessed September 17, 2016).

[72] Pew Research Center, "Social Media Fact Sheet," April 7, 2021, https://www.pewresearch.org/internet/fact-sheet/social-media/ (accessed May 3, 2022).

[73] Pew Research Center, "Measuring News Consumption in a Digital Era," December 8, 2020, https://www.pewresearch.org/journalism/2020/12/08/assessing-different-survey-measurement-approaches-for-news-consumption/ (accessed May 3, 2022).

[74] Pew Research Center, "The Modern News Consumer," July 2016, http://www.journalism.org/files/2016/07/PJ_2016.07.07_Modern-News-Consumer_FINAL.pdf (accessed September 17, 2016).

[75] Paul Baran, "On the Impact of the New Communications Media upon Social Values," *Law & Contemporary Problems* 34 (1969): 244.

[76] Jim Willis, "The Media Effect: How the News Influences Politics and Government," in series *Democracy and the News,* ed. Jeffrey Scheuer (Westport, CT: Praeger, 2007), 93–94.

[77] Steven A. Holmes, "Candidate Perot Might Learn from Strategist Perot," *The New York Times,* October 29, 1992, http://www.nytimes.com/1992/10/29/us/the-1992-campaign-candidate-perot-might-learn-from-strategist-perot.html?pagewanted=1 (accessed August 20, 2016).

[78] Danielle Kurtzleben, "2016 Campaigns Will Spend $4.4 billion in TV Ads, but Why?," NPR, August 19, 2015, https://www.npr.org/sections/itsallpolitics/2015/08/19/432759311/2016-campaign-tv-ad-spending.

[79] *Dallas Morning News* Editorial Staff, "We Recommend Hillary Clinton for President," Opinion, September 7, 2016, http://www.dallasnews.com/opinion/editorials/20160907-we-recommend-hillary-clinton-for-president.ece (accessed September 12, 2016).

[80] Paul Freedman, "Thirty-Second Democracy: Campaign Advertising and American Elections," *Hedgehog Review* 10, no. 2 (Summer 2008): 48, *Supplemental Index,* EBSCO*host* (accessed March 17, 2017).

[81] Kim Fridkin, Patrick J. Kenney, and Amanda Wintersieck, "Liar, Liar, Pants on Fire: How Fact-Checking Influences Citizens' Reactions to Negative Advertising," *Political Communication* 32, no. 1 (2015), http://www.tandfonline.com/doi/full/10.1080/10584609.2014.914613?scroll=top&needAccess=true.

[82] Bruce Bimber, "The Internet and Political Transformation: Populism, Community, and Accelerated Pluralism," *Polity* 31 (1998): 1.

[83] Shyam Sundar, Sriram Kalyanraman, and Justin Brown, "Explicating Web Site Interactivity Impression Formation Effects in Political Campaign Sites," *Communication Research* 30, no. 1 (2003): 30–59.

[84] Morely Winograd and Michael D. Hais, *Millennial Makeover: MySpace, YouTube, and the Future of American Politics* (New Brunswick, NJ: Rutgers University Press, 2008), 113.

[85] L. Bode, "Facebooking It to the Polls: A Study in Online Social Networking and Political Behavior," *Journal of Information Technology & Politics* 9, no. 4 (2012): 352–69.

[86] Steve Friess, "Cruz's Secret: Mastering Social Media," July 31, 2012, http://www.politico.com/story/2012/07/contenders-secret-mastering-social-media-079213#ixzz4JtgYNNAS (accessed September 10, 2016).

[87] Patrick Svitek, "Dan Patrick Takes Heat for Posts after Orlando Shooting," *Texas Tribune,* June 12, 2016, https://www.texastribune.org/2016/06/12/patrick-criticized-tweet-after-orlando-shooting/ (accessed August 20, 2016).

[88] Dianna Wray, "Lt. Gov. Dan Patrick Reaps Tons of Criticism for His Social Media Post after the Orlando Shootings," *Houston Chronicle,* June 13, 2016, http://www.houstonpress.com/news/lt-gov-dan-patrick-reaps-tons-of-criticism-for-his-social-media-post-after-the-orlando-shootings-8477694.

[89] N. Couldry, S. Livingstone, and T. Markham, *Media Consumption and Public Engagement: Beyond the Presumption of Attention* (Basingstoke, UK: Palgrave Macmillan, 2010), 140–70.

[90] Megan Brenan, "Americans' Trust in Media Dips to Second Lowest on Record," October 7, 2021, Gallup, https://news.gallup.com/poll/355526/americans-trust-media-dips-second-lowest-record.aspx (accessed May 3, 2022).

[91] Uri Friedman, "The Trend Helps Explain Trump and Brexit. What's Next?," July 1, 2016, *The Atlantic,* http://www.theatlantic.com/international/archive/2016/07/trust-institutions-trump-brexit/489554/ (accessed September 10, 2016).

[92] Max McCombs, R. Lance Holbert, Spiro Kiousus, et al., *The News and Public Opinion: Media Effects on Civic Life* (Malden, MA: Polity Press, 2011).

[93] Tim Groeling, "Media Bias by the Numbers: Challenges and Opportunities in the Empirical Study of Partisan News," *Annual Review of Political Science* 16 (2013): 129–51.

[94] Marcus Prior, "Media and Political Polarization," *Annual Review of Political Science* 16 (2013): 101–27.

[95] Robert S. Lichter, Stanley Rothman, and Linda S Lichter, *The Media Elite* (Chevy Chase, MD: Adler & Adler, 1986).

[96] Elizabeth Skewes, *Message Control: How News Is Made on the Presidential Campaign Trail* (Lanham, MD: Rowman & Littlefield, 2007).

[97] Matthew Gentzkow, Michael B. Wong, and Allen T. Zhang, *Ideological Bias and Trust in Social Networks* (Cambridge, MA: National Bureau of Economic Research, 2015).

[98] OpenSecrets.org, "Super Pacs," https://www.opensecrets.org/pacs/superpacs.php (accessed March 13, 2018).

[99] Annenberg Public Policy Center, "High Percent of Presidential Ad Dollars of Top Four 501(c)(4)s Backed Ads Containing Deception, Annenberg Study Finds," June 20, 2012, http://www.annenbergpublicpolicycenter.org/high-percent-of-presidential-ad-dollars-of-top-four-501c4s-backed-ads-containing-deception-annenberg-study-finds/ (accessed September 17, 2016).

[100] Ian Gershengorn, "The Fall of the FCC's Personal Attack and Political Editorial Rules," *Communications Lawyer,* Spring 2001, http://www.americanbar.org/content/dam/aba/publishing/communications_lawyer/forums_communication_comlawyer_spring01_gershengorn.authcheckdam.pdf.

[101] 740 F.3d 623 (D.C. Cir. 2014).

[102] Rebecca R. Ruiz and Steve Lohr, "F.C.C. Approves Net Neutrality Rules, Classifying Broadband Internet Service as a Utility," *The New York Times,* February 26, 2015.

[103] Julia Jacobo, "Federal Appeals Court Rules in Favor of FCC Net Neutrality Rules," *ABC News,* June 14, 2016, http://abcnews.go.com/Politics/federal-appeals-court-rules-favor-fcc-net-neutrality/story?id=39854452 (accessed September 17, 2016).

[104] Associated Press, "FCC Votes along Party Lines to Repeal Net Neutrality Regulations," *Miami Herald,* December 14, 2017, http://www.miamiherald.com/news/nation-world/national/article189760309.html (accessed February 16, 2018).

[105] Jon Brodkin, "To Kill Net Neutrality, FCC Might Have to Fight More Than Half of US States," *Ars Technica,* February 16, 2018, https://arstechnica.com/tech-policy/2018/02/to-kill-net-neutrality-fcc-might-have-to-fight-more-than-half-of-us-states/ (accessed February 16, 2018); "Net Neutrality in the States," https://www.ncsl.org/research/telecommunications-and-information-technology/net-neutrality-legislation-in-states.aspx (accessed May 8, 2020).

[106] Congressional Research Service, "Net Neutrality Law: An Overview," November 22, 2022. https://crsreports.congress.gov/product/pdf/R/R46973 (accessed May 3, 2022).

[107] 413 U.S. 15, 24-25 (1973).

[108] https://www.facebook.com/communitystandards#criminal-activity.

[109] SBG San Antonio, "Gov. Greg Abbott Signs Anti-cyberbullying Legislation 'David's Law,'" news4sa.com, June 12, 2017, http://news4sanantonio.com/news/make-it-stop/gov-greg-abbott-signs-anti-cyberbullying-legislation-dubbed-davids-law (accessed February 16, 2018).

[110] http://www.ncsl.org/research/telecommunications-and-information-technology/state-laws-prohibiting-access-to-social-media-usernames-and-passwords.aspx.

[111] https://blog.ed.gov/2013/06/state-and-local-education-agencies-like-social-media/.

[112] https://digital.library.unt.edu/ark:/67531/metadc500211/m1/1/.

[113] Estephany Escobar, "Central Texas Police Departments Use Social Media as a Way to Prevent Car Burglaries," KXXV-TV, February 7, 2018, http://www.kxxv.com/story/37452959/central-texas-police-departments-use-social-media-as-a-way-to-prevent-car-burglaries; https://twitter.com/hewittpd1?lang=en.

[114] Matthew Belvedere, "AT&T CEO: Our Proposed $85 Billion Time Warner Deal Is Aimed at Competing with Netflix and Amazon," *CNBC,* February 9, 2018, https://www.cnbc.com/2018/02/09/att-ceo-stephenson-we-expect-to-win-approval-for-time-warner-deal.html (accessed February 16, 2018); Nathan Reiff, "AT&T and Time Warner Merger Case: What You Need to Know," *Investopedia,* December 7, 2018, https://www.investopedia.com/investing/att-and-time-warner-merger-case-what-you-need-know/ (accessed May 8, 2020).

[115] Alina Selyukh, "Big Media Companies and Their Many Brands—in One Chart," NPR, October 28, 2016, http://www.npr.org/sections/alltechconsidered/2016/10/28/499495517/big-media-companies-and-their-many-brands-in-one-chart (accessed June 13, 2017).

[116] Daniel Seed, "TV Station Ownership and Local News Content: A Content Analysis of the Austin, TV Market" (master's thesis, Texas State University, May 2015).

[117] Chris Ariens, "5.95 Million Watch Univision Democratic Debate," March 10, 2016, *Adweek,* http://www.adweek.com/tvnewser/5-95-million-watch-univision-democratic-debate/286804 (accessed August 21, 2016).

[118] QuickFacts: Texas, https://www.census.gov/quickfacts/fact/table/TX/POP010210 (accessed April 29, 2022); Luis Noe-Bustamante, Abby Budiman, and Mark Hugo Lopez, "Where Latinos Have the Most Eligible Voters in the 2020 Election," January 31, 2020, https://www.pewresearch.org/fact-tank/2020/01/31/where-latinos-have-the-most-eligible-voters-in-the-2020-election/ (accessed May 8, 2020).

[119] U.S. Census Bureau, "Selected Social Characteristics in the United States: 2020 American Community Survey 1-Year Estimates," https://www.census.gov/acs/www/data/data-tables-and-tools/data-profiles/ (accessed May 3, 2022).

[120] Stacey Counnaughton, *Inviting Latino Voters: Party Messages and Latino Party Identification* (New York: Routledge, 2005).

[121] Kris Axtman, "Que es Esto: Texas Debate in Spanish?," *The Christian Science Monitor,* March 1, 2002, http://www.csmonitor.com/2002/0301/p01s01-ussc.html (accessed August 20, 2016).

[122] NBCUniversal, "Telemundo Station Group," https://together.nbcuni.com/n/telemundo-station-group/; Televisa Univision, "About TelevisaUnivision," https://corporate.televisaunivision.com/our-company/ (accessed May 3, 2022).

[123] https://www.telemundo.com/noticias/noticias-telemundo/elecciones-eeuu-2020

[124] https://www.univision.com/noticias/elecciones-en-eeuu-2020.

[125] Sara Fischer, "Univision completes merger with Mexican media giant Televisa," *Axios,* January 31, 2022, https://www.axios.com/univision-completes-merger-with-mexican-media-giant-televisa-3bb0d191-20a1-49f8-92d4-8c492c67e41d.html.

[126] Bloomberg, "Univision CEO closes Televisa deal, promises new streaming push," *Los Angeles Times,* January 31, 2022, https://www.latimes.com/entertainment-arts/business/story/2022-01-31/univision-ceo-closes-televisa-deal-promises-new-streaming-push.

[127] John Consoli, "Telemundo's Rating Success Draws Media Buyer Attention," broadcastingcable.com, http://www.broadcastingcable.com/news/currency/telemundos-ratings-success-draws-media-buyer-attention/169429 (accessed February 16, 2018).

[128] Veronica Villafañe, "Passing 10 Million Subscribers, Telemundo Becomes Top US Broadcast Network on YouTube, Regardless of Language," *Forbes,* July, 2, 2020. https://www.forbes.com/sites/veronicavillafane/2020/07/02/passing-10-million-subscribers-telemundo-becomes-top-us-broadcast-network-on-youtube-regardless-of-language/?sh=18abd990378e (accessed May 3, 2022).

CHAPTER 9

Voting and Political Participation in Texas

O ne of the hallmarks of life in a democracy is people's ability to participate in politics. Voting is the most obvious way that citizens play a part in collective governance in a democracy. However, this is just one of many ways that people can participate in the public square. While people engage in politics to varying degrees, most people are not participating that actively in state and local politics, either here in Texas or around the country. Even though men and women are certainly social beings, it might be too optimistic to argue—as the ancient Greek philosopher Aristotle did—that we are naturally political animals. This chapter explores the ways in which Texans participate in politics, with special emphasis on voting behavior. It examines not

Volunteers register high school students to vote in Austin. Texas is seeing a rise in the diversity of young people registering and turning out to vote.

LM Otero/AP Images

only why voter turnout in Texas is so low today and has been in years past, but also the potential impact of low turnout on the quality of democracy in Texas.

Chapter Learning Objectives

- Explain political participation.
- Discuss voter turnout in Texas, including citizens' rights and responsibilities.
- Describe ways in which the state of Texas has, historically, restricted access to voting.
- Describe forms of political participation other than voting.

Political Participation

Learning Objective: Explain political participation.

political power

Influence on government based on some combination of numbers of people; wealth; social norms; ideas; force and violence; and government actions (including laws and regulations)

How do we effectively participate in a democracy? At the root of this question is the importance of understanding **political power** and how it works. To have political power in a democracy means that the people can influence the government to do what they would like it to do.[1] Other political actors, such as politicians, parties, and interest groups, also use political power to further their interests.

There are six types of political power: numbers, wealth, social norms, ideas, force and violence, and government actions (including laws and regulations).[2]

- When people participate in a democracy, most often their power is expressed in and magnified by the power of *numbers*. In other words, if many participants want a new law to be enacted, then that law is likely to come into being. Numbers can amplify the influence of other forms of power.
- The power of *wealth* is clear, not only in campaign contributions but also in how wealth as an influential socioeconomic variable enables participation.
- People can also influence political change with the two following powers: challenging *social norms* and modifying *ideas*. For example, political movements use teach-ins to educate people about problems.
- Individuals and groups may resort to using political *violence* and *force* to achieve their ends, but as a participation tool, they are generally not considered a constructive influence in a democracy. Political force is any type of display of aggression or brandishing of weapons without actual violence, but force often is perceived as belligerent behavior. Political violence at the hands of the government occurs too, but people consider it undemocratic.
- Finally, *government action* is how the government gets us to do what it wants through laws and regulations.

For citizens in a democracy, it is important to "see" when and how political power is working throughout the government and their lives. Government policy does not simply happen, nor is it created in a vacuum. For example, current policies in Texas that affect the quality of our daily lives result from historical and political influences, such as culture, social norms, and ideas. Policy choices and policy outcomes also reflect a story of who has power and who does not use their power effectively. Contemporary political actors, such as voters, political parties, and interest groups, also exercise power to create policies they desire. Political actors use their power throughout the policy-making process—not just at election time. Responsible citizens must understand how they individually have the power to influence policy and government. How does an individual contribute to the power of numbers?

Many individuals do not participate because they think they are powerless: they believe their vote does not count, their representative ignores them, or special interests control everything. They view their power in terms of themselves alone. This mindset is commonplace and shows a lack of understanding of political power in a democracy. The belief in individualism, for example, is a cultural influence that puts too much emphasis on the power of the individual, which is counter to how power works in a democracy. Individuals must participate, yes. However, the power from this individual participation is found collectively in the millions of individual votes counted together, thousands of individuals attending a march, or hundreds of individual signatures on a petition.

Interest groups and political parties understand the power of numbers. These actors even see citizens as voting blocs (demographic groups), not individuals. Therefore, if "we the people" are going to influence policies and governance, we must understand that we all have political power and that we all must use our power to influence the government throughout the political process. If we do not use our political power to influence the government and hold it accountable to our interests, other political actors will solidify their power by securing the passage of policies they want.

> **Understanding Impact** Now that you have learned about the types of political power and how they can be used to influence the government and policies, think about the political power of nonvoters. How do the government and democracy still exist and function even though so many people do not vote or participate in politics? The government does not stop making and implementing policies. When voting is low, in whose interest are policies most likely being made? How are those policies likely to affect the power of nonvoters? Does the lack of action by nonvoters have consequences for their own political power?

The vehicle for political power in a democracy is **political participation.** This refers to taking part in activities that relate to governance. While voting rates for Texans have increased in recent elections, voting is just one way to participate. Table 9.1 lists some common forms of non-electoral participation and the percentage of Texans who participate in these manners.

When people participate, it is important to understand which forms of participation will help them effectively reach their goals of influencing the government. The benefit of learning about power, Texas politics, and government institutions is that people can then choose the best participation methods for influence. Also, note that not all forms of political participation require the

political participation
All forms of involvement citizens can have that are related to governance

TABLE 9.1

Non-electoral Civic and Political Participation in Texas

Activity	Percentage Who Participated
Signed a petition	25%
Volunteered in the community	23%
Frequently discuss politics	23%
Avoided products for political reasons	17%
Contacted a politician	14%
Purchased products for political reasons	11%
Donated to a political cause	11%

Source: Annette Strauss Institute for Civic Life, "2018 Texas Civic Health Index," https://utexas. app.box.com/v/Texas-CHI-2018.

participant to be a citizen. What we know from history is that to bring about fundamental political change, making use of more than one power and more than one form of participation is necessary. The activities in Table 9.1 are not an exhaustive list. Many people are using online methods to engage in political activity, especially since the onset of the COVID-19 pandemic. A 2020 Pew Research Center survey shows that 36 percent of Americans publicly supported a campaign on social media in the 2020 election, and 10 percent attended online political rallies or campaign events.[3] This type of involvement is a fairly passive, and possibly not a very politically influential, means of participation. Indeed, *The Washington Post* recently noted that less burdensome or demanding "forms of advocacy, particularly those related to social media, are often derisively referred to as 'slacktivism' or 'armchair activism.'"[4]

In addition to looking at involvement in specific activities, we can examine levels and types of activities. Sidney Verba and Norman H. Nie, in their classic book *Participation in America,*[5] divide the population into several groups based on the types of participation and the intensity of involvement that citizens can have in the political process:

- Inactives, who take no part in politics
- Voting specialists, who confine their efforts to voting in elections
- Parochial participants, who become active in politics when the issue has a direct effect on them
- Campaigners, who like the activity and the controversial and competitive nature of political campaigns
- Communalists, who, while being active voters, avoid the combat and controversy of partisan campaigns and are attracted to other kinds of nonpartisan, noncontroversial community activity
- Complete activists, who get involved in all levels and kinds of activity, including voting, campaigning, lobbying officials, and participating in community affairs

In the past few years, there have been increasing rates of all forms of participation nationally. The 2020 elections had a voting rate of 66.2 percent—the highest national voting rate in over 120 years.[6] Campaign donations also increased. Small donations less than $200, which indicate more individual participation, increased to 27 percent from 19 percent in 2012.[7] Community organizing, organization formation, and protests also increased. Black Lives Matters protests had 15 to 25 million participants in 2020 alone.[8] Since the spring of 2020, there have been over 10,000 participants protesting state and city lockdown policies and other COVID-19 restrictions.[9]

However, since the 2020 presidential elections, participation and its role in democracy has been hotly contested. In the following 2021 state legislative sessions, 19 states passed 34 more restrictive voting laws. In contrast, 25 states passed 62 laws expanding voting access.[10] Debates about participation, mostly focusing on voting and elections, are increasingly controversial and partisan. What impact these new laws and debates will have on participation remain to be seen.

CORE OBJECTIVE

Taking Personal Responsibility . . .

What activities do you engage in that are related to governance? Which forms of political participation do you think are the most effective?

Voting in Texas

Learning Objective: Discuss voter turnout in Texas, including citizens' rights and responsibilities.

One of the most common forms of participation in politics is voting in elections. Amendments to the U.S. Constitution stipulate that the right to vote cannot be denied on the basis of race, ethnicity, gender, sex, failure to pay a **poll tax** (or any other tax), or age (as long as individuals are at least 18 years old).[11] Apart from these stipulations, states have considerable discretion to determine who is eligible to vote as well as what election system will be used within their borders.

Current Voting Requirements

In Texas today, any individual who is at least 18 years of age, a U.S. citizen, and a resident of the state may vote. The Texas Constitution excludes convicted felons currently serving time and those persons formally judged to be "mentally incompetent" from voting. Furthermore, the Texas Constitution states that voters must register before voting in an election.[12] As defined by the U.S. Census Bureau, **voter registration** is "the act of qualifying to vote by formally enrolling on an official list of voters."[13] Texans are required to register at least 30 days in advance to vote in a given election.

There are several ways to register in Texas. In general, it involves completing a paper form. Voter registration applications are available at libraries, high schools, post offices, and some state and county offices. Official applications can be requested, but not submitted, online. Applicants must provide either a driver's license number, a personal identification number issued by the Texas

poll tax
In place from 1902 until 1966 in Texas, a tax citizens were required to pay each year between October and January to be eligible to vote in the next election cycle

voter registration
The act of qualifying to vote by formally enrolling on an official list of voters

Department of Public Safety, or a partial Social Security number on the form. Applicants may then mail their completed form, with postage prepaid by the state, or personally deliver it to their local registrar's office.[14]

Alternatively, Texans may register to vote when they apply for or renew their driver's license. In 1993, the U.S. Congress passed the National Voter Registration Act (also known as the "Motor Voter Act") to facilitate voter registration. Though the law's provisions apply only to federal elections, they affect state elections as well because states use the same registration systems for both federal and state elections. Individuals applying for a driver's license can simultaneously submit an application to register to vote (or update their address for purposes of voter registration, if applicable).[15]

After their application is processed, individuals receive a voter registration certificate or card. This card specifies the precinct in which that individual will vote, based on the person's address. Each voter receives a new card every two years; the post office is instructed not to forward it if an individual has moved. If the card cannot be delivered to the addressee at the address on the card, it goes back to the voter registrar, and the voter's name is removed from the registration list. Individuals who move must re-register at their new address. Movers can change their address online only if they have relocated within the same county. Otherwise, they must submit a new paper form.[16]

On Election Day voters who have a government-issued photo ID must present it when they go to their polling place to vote.[17] (This requirement stems from the state's relatively new voter ID law, which we will discuss later in this section.) Even if individuals are listed on the voter registration roll, they must still provide this identification. Texans can present one of seven kinds of ID, including an election identification certificate that is available free of charge from the Department of Public Safety.[18] Subsequent to a 2016 court order, the state also provides accommodation for individuals who have been unable to get one of the seven forms of ID. Such individuals are not required to show a photo ID; instead, they can sign a declaration stating they had a "reasonable impediment" to obtaining a photo ID. Then they can show an alternate form of identification, such as a birth certificate, pay stub, utility bill, or bank statement. If a voter still does not have any of the approved forms of identification, then they may cast a provisional ballot that is counted if that individual reports to the county registrar's office within six days of the election with proper ID.[19]

There have been some attempts to make voting easier in Texas. For example, Texas allows early voting, either in person or by mail. With early voting, individuals go to any officially designated polling location, which is typically open between 4 and 17 days before an election, and vote as usual. Those who expect to be away from their county of residence on Election Day may vote early by mail. This process is sometimes called **absentee voting.** Although this practice began as a way to allow members of the military who were stationed outside of Texas to vote, it has since been extended to other individuals. Such voters must request or apply for their mail-in ballot before in-person early voting begins (that is, more than 17 days before the election). Marked ballots must be returned to the voting clerk and received by 7 p.m. on the date of the election (or if mailed from outside the United States, by the fifth day after the election). Military voters and citizens living overseas may use the regular vote-by-mail process; however, there is also a special process available only to military and overseas voters.[20]

absentee voting
A process that allows a person to vote early, before the regular election; applies to all elections in Texas; also called early voting

In 2019, Harris county instituted several election changes (with state approval) to make voting more accessible to voters. For the 2019 local elections, Harris County started its "Voter Your Way" initiative, providing open voting locations throughout the county and other voter benefits.[21] The Countywide Polling Place Program allows Harris County voters to vote at any approved polling place on Election Day—not just their assigned, neighborhood polling place. This means that if voting close to their workplace or school is more convenient on Election Day, voters can choose to vote at those locations instead. Counties are adapting to digital realities too. Harris County now provides real-time wait times for polling locations online, and voters can find the closest polling location to them or get directions texted to them (or sent through Facebook messaging). These online features work in tandem with being able to vote anywhere and allow voters to choose the best location given time constraints.

Focus On

Language Translation and Voting Rights for Asian Americans

The Voting Rights Act was extended in 1975 to include language provisions to protect the right to vote for voters with limited English proficiency. If a language group makes up 5 percent or more of a jurisdiction's total population, ballots and election information must be provided in that language.[22] For Harris County (the largest county in Texas, where 145 languages are spoken), election information and ballots are offered in English, Spanish, Vietnamese, and Chinese.[23] However, until a language group reaches that 5 percent threshold, the right to translation of election materials is the only option available, and finding a translation service is the responsibility of whoever needs it. As Harris County's Asian American population grows, there is more demand for translation of election materials and voting assistance, challenging county officials to figure out how to meet these needs and interpret Texas Election Code.

In the 2018 election, Korean translators volunteering to aid Korean American voters were barred from translating inside a polling place in the neighborhood of Spring Branch in Harris County.[24] The state upheld the county's decision to allow translators to offer help only 100 feet or more from the polling place.[25] The code does not allow anyone to offer translation services or voting advice inside the polling location nor within 100 feet of the entrance. As a right, however, voters can bring their own translators to help them vote, and their translator must sign an affidavit promising they are not trying to influence the person's choices.[26] Many voters new to voting do not know about this right to translation, the 100-feet rule, or the subtle difference between bringing a translator versus being approached by someone offering assistance.

Korean American civic groups and Harris County worked together to find ways to make election material translation easier for voters with limited English proficiency. Starting in 2019, Harris County began hiring more bilingual poll workers in high-demand Asian languages like Korean, Tagalog, Hindi, and Urdu.[27]

For the 2020 elections, Harris County announced the multilingual virtual poll worker system (MVP), which allows voters to video chat with a translator while voting.[28] The MVP as a policy solution was piloted to specifically address this translation need; the translation service offers 34 languages (including American Sign Language).[29]

Critical Thinking Questions
1. If you were a voter who needed translation help, would you prefer to bring your own translator or to seek help from someone outside the polling place at least 100 feet away? Explain your reasons.
2. Consider the number of languages spoken in Harris County and the importance of voters understanding the choices they must make. If you were a Harris County resident, would you support an expansion of the MVP system to include even more languages in the future? Why or why not?

In Comparison with Other States

Most states impose some restrictions on voting. Preregistration is one example of such a restriction. In most states, prospective voters must register by a certain deadline, typically ranging from 8 to 30 days, before an election. However, 20 states plus the District of Columbia currently have no pre-election registration requirements.[30] In states with **same-day registration,** voters show up at their polling place on Election Day, register on the spot (usually by providing identification and proof of residency), and vote. Research has shown that same-day registration results in greater turnout; states that have implemented same-day registration have turnout levels above the national average.[31] North Dakota has no voter registration whatsoever.[32]

Other factors related to voting restrictions include registration methods and identification requirements. All states provide paper registration forms upon request, but for added convenience, 42 states plus the District of Columbia also offer online voter registration. Oklahoma and Maine are still phasing in their online registration system.[33] As of 2022, 35 states including Texas have adopted voter ID legislation. These laws range from a strict requirement that voters show a photo ID to non-strict requirements that allow voters to provide some means of identification without a photo (such as a bank statement). The remaining states require no documentation to vote.[34]

Texas requires registration 30 days in advance of an election, does not offer online voter registration, and requires some form of identification to vote. Therefore, despite the recent weakening of its voter ID law, Texas appears to be demanding in terms of voting requirements and is considered the strictest in the nation.[35] But do these additional requirements actually deter people from coming to the polls and casting a ballot? Let's turn our attention now to the available data on how many Texans vote in elections.

Voter Turnout in Texas

There are several ways to calculate **voter turnout,** or the proportion of people who cast ballots in an election. One measure is the percentage of **registered voters** who cast a ballot. This statistic is commonly reported because it is simple to calculate and readily available to state elections divisions. However, there are drawbacks to using the percentage of registered voters to assess voter turnout. As discussed previously, registration requirements vary greatly among the states. These varying requirements (preregistration, same-day registration, or no registration) make it difficult to compare turnout rates across states using this method. In same-day registration states, for example, anyone who is eligible to vote can cast a ballot, whereas in other states voters must have been proactive enough to register ahead of time in order to participate. Furthermore, voter registration lists are not completely accurate and up-to-date; most contain "deadwood," or the names of individuals who are registered at a certain address but no longer live there.[36] This inaccuracy in the rolls distorts the count of registered voters in a precinct area.

A second measure is the percentage of the voting-age population that votes. **Voting-age population (VAP)** is defined as the number of people aged 18 and over. To calculate turnout using VAP, the number of people casting votes in an election is divided by the number of residents 18 years of age and older.[37]

same-day registration

Voters are allowed to register on Election Day; no preregistration before the election is required.

voter turnout

The proportion of people who cast ballots in an election

registered voters

Citizens who have formally gone through the process of getting their names on the voter registration list

voting-age population (VAP)

The number of people aged 18 and over

VAP is generally the preferred measure (and the one most often used by political scientists) because it discounts variations in state voting and registration requirements and makes it easier to compare states. However, there are problems with using VAP to express voter turnout as well. The voting-age population includes a sizable number of people who have met the age requirement but are nonetheless unable to register and vote. Reasons a person may be excluded from voting include not being a U.S. citizen, having committed a felony, having been declared mentally incapacitated, or not having met the state and local residency requirements for registration.[38] Measuring turnout by using VAP is distorted because these ineligible persons are counted in the figure, even though it is impossible for them to vote.

Voting during a pandemic still continues.

SeventyFour Images/Alamy Stock Photo

The *United States Elections Project* presents yet a third measure of voter turnout, based on the **voting-eligible population (VEP).** VEP is calculated by correcting VAP to eliminate ineligible groups, such as noncitizens and convicted felons.[39] Michael McDonald, the political scientist who pioneered the VEP measure, claims that "the most valid turnout rates over time and across states are calculated using voting-eligible population."[40] Using the VEP turnout rate (which, for the data shown here, is calculated by dividing the number of ballots cast for the highest office by VEP), participation in recent presidential elections appears higher than previously determined using the VAP measure. (In fact, McDonald has argued that "the much-lamented decline in voter participation" since 1971, based on VAP, is "entirely explained by the increase in the ineligible population.")[41] Some other political scientists have also recommended the use of VEP turnout rates but acknowledge that VEP data are not universally available at this time.[42] Table 9.2 compares voter turnout rates calculated according to these three methods. Note that using the percentage of registered voters who voted produces higher turnout rates than the other two methods; using the percentage of the voting-age population (VAP) who voted yields the lowest figures.

In general, Texans are not avid voters. As shown in Table 9.3, Texas consistently falls below the national average in terms of the percentage of the voting-eligible population participating in elections during the past 30 years. Texas's voter turnout also ranks at or near the bottom when compared to other states (see also Figure 9.1). Data from recent elections suggest, while there is an increase in turnout rates, there is still a continuation of this low-turnout trend. The Texas secretary of state reported that 11.3 million people, or 66.73 percent of registered voters, cast a ballot in the 2020 general election.[43] Voter turnout is still typically lower for midterm elections than in years when there is a presidential election at stake. The 2022 midterm elections saw a turnout rate of only 42.5 percent.[44] Party primaries for midterm elections and constitutional elections

voting-eligible population (VEP)

The voting-age population, corrected to exclude groups ineligible to vote, such as noncitizens and convicted felons

TABLE 9.2

Comparison of Percentage of Registered, Voting-Age, and Voting-Eligible Voters Voting in Texas Elections, 1988–2020

Year	Percentage of Registered Voters Who Voted	Percentage of VAP Who Voted	VEP Highest Office Turnout Rate
Presidential Election Years			
1988	66.2	44.3	50.1
1992	72.9	47.6	54.2
1996	53.2	41.0	46.5
2000	51.8	44.3	49.2
2004	56.6	46.1	53.7
2008	59.5	45.6	54.1
2012	58.6	43.7	49.7
2016	59.4	46.5	51.1
2020	66.6	51.5	60.2
Congressional and Statewide Election Years			
1990	50.6	31.1	35.3
1994	50.9	33.6	37.5
1998	32.4	26.5	29.9
2002	36.2	29.4	34.2
2006	33.6	26.4	30.9
2010	38.0	27.0	32.1
2014	33.7	25.0	28.3
2018	53.0	41.1	46.3

Sources: Texas Secretary of State, "Turnout and Voter Registration Figures (1970–Current)," http://www.sos.state.tx.us/elections/historical/70-92.shtml; Michael P. McDonald, "2018 November General Election Turnout Rates," *United States Elections Project*, 2018, http://www.electproject.org/2018g.

tend to have even lower turnout rates compared to presidential year elections or general elections overall. The 2021 Constitutional election had 8.75 percent of registered voters turn out.[45] The 2022 midterm election primaries had 17.5 percent of registered voters turn out.[46]

Tables 9.2 and 9.3 show the increased turnout rates for the country in the 2018 midterm elections. However, young people, in particular, made their mark with noteworthy gains in turnout. The Census Bureau notes that the difference in turnout rates between the 2014 and 2018 midterms for 18-to-29-year-olds was the largest voting increase of all age groups.[47] In Texas, the youth vote tripled from the 2014 to the 2018 midterm election.[48] Young people are increasingly becoming mobilized and using their power in numbers to influence politics and policy. This use of power does influence election outcomes: The Senate race between Republican incumbent Ted Cruz and Democratic challenger Beto O'Rourke was very close because of counties with large numbers of young Democratic voters, specifically young Latinos.[49] Nationally, 18-to-49-year-old (Generation X, Millennials, and Generation Z) Latinos make up 57.9 percent of the Latino electorate.[50] This makes the typical Latino voter a young Latino. As a testament to the growing political power and impact on election outcomes, in Texas, almost 400,000 new 17-to-18-year-olds were eligible to vote in 2020.[51]

The politics in elections leading up to the 2020 presidential election have been shaped by dealing with the novel coronavirus, or COVID-19. The usual

TABLE 9.3

Texas Rank as a Percentage of Voting-Eligible Population in National Elections, 1988–2020

Year	Texas Rank	National Turnout	Texas Turnout
Presidential Election Years			
1988	37	52.8	50.1
1992	40	58.1	54.2
1996	43	51.7	46.5
2000	41	54.2	49.2
2004	48	60.1	53.7
2008	48	61.6	54.1
2012	47	58.2	49.7
2016	47	58.8	51.1
2020	46	66.6	60.2
Congressional/Statewide Election-Only Years			
1990	41	38.4	35.3
1994	42	41.1	37.5
1998	47	38.1	29.9
2002	46	39.5	34.2
2006	48	40.4	30.9
2010	50	41.0	32.1
2014	48	36.0	28.3
2018	41	50.3	46.3

Source: Michael P. McDonald, "1980–2014 November General Election," 2015; "2016 November General Election Turnout Rates," 2016; and "2018 November General Election Turnout Rates," 2018, *United States Elections Project,* http://www.electproject.org/2016g.

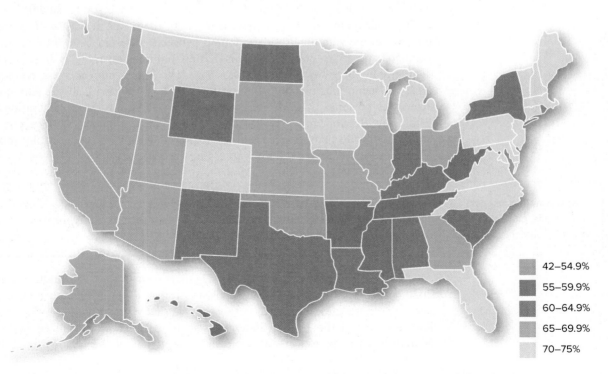

Legend:
- 42–54.9%
- 55–59.9%
- 60–64.9%
- 65–69.9%
- 70–75%

FIGURE 9.1   Percentage of Eligible Voters Voting in 2020 November General Election

Source: "2020 November General Election Turnout Rates," *United States Elections Project,* http://www.electproject.org/2020g.

March primary elections were moved to July, hoping to wait out the virus. The voter turnout during these elections reflect concerns about safety, the effects of changes in election patterns, and the high-profile competition among Democratic presidential candidates. The percent turnout to registered voters for the Republican primary was 12.44 percent, down 7.48 percent from 2016. The Democratic primary numbers improved slightly—up 2.84 percent—compared to 2016 in part because there was a presidential nominee to pick to run against President Trump in November 2020. However, there was a decrease overall of almost 160,788 voters from 2016.[52]

Turnout for the 2020 presidential election marked an unprecedented, positive trend for Texas. Historic turnout rates helped Texas move from 47th in the nation to 45th (including the District of Columbia), 6.6 percent points higher than the 2016 election.[53] Tables 9.2 and 9.3 show the 60.2 percent VEP. With a 66.6 percent turnout of registered voters, Texas almost broke its 1992 record (72.92 percent).[54] The highly contentious election between President Trump and Vice President Biden drew out numbers of voters. In the end, Texas voters chose President Trump with over a 5 percent lead over Vice President Biden.[55]

President Trump's win in Texas was not surprising given the majority of the state's voters have aligned with the Republican Party for many decades. However, the 2020 election did result in demographic and regional shifts for the Republican Party, namely the increase in the number of Latinos voting for President Trump in the Rio Grande Valley.

The Latino vote is not monolithic even though the majority aligns with the Democratic Party historically, and President Biden did ultimately win these counties in Valley. Part of this political diversity is seen in Latino Republican voters, which varies from 20 percent to 40 percent of the national Latino vote.[56] Cameron, Hidalgo, Starr, and Wallacy counties all had increases in the Latino vote for President Trump. Starr County voted 19 percent for President Trump in 2016 but increased to 47.1 percent in 2020; there was at least a 10 percent increase in the vote for President Trump between 2016 and 2020 for Cameron, Hidalgo, and Starr counties.[57] This Latino political diversity is based upon demographic diversity: of the Latinos who voted for Trump in these counties, most self-identify as racially white on the Census and specifically Tejano, characteristics of some Latinos who have lived in Texas for several generations.[58] While the Republican Party has been losing votes in many counties due to larger, statewide demographic shifts, the Republican Party successfully mobilized these more centrist, Latino voters in the Valley.

Understanding Impact: The number of registered voters is increasing for young people, Black Americans, Hispanic Americans, and Asian Americans in Texas. How might increased participation by these demographic groups influence election outcomes, political parties, campaign strategies, and subsequent policies?

Overall, despite the increase in participation seen in the 2018 midterms and 2020 presidential elections, Texas consistently has a lower voter turnout compared to other states. It is worth noting though, that voter turnout at the national level is lower in the United States than in most other industrialized nations. Moreover, participation in state politics is lower than at the national level and lower still at the local levels.

The Impact of Voting Restrictions in Texas

Overall, research shows that stricter voting laws and requirements do add barriers and decrease turnout for racial and ethnic minorities, low-income, senior citizens, and young voters but to varying degrees. For example, whereas voter ID laws affect Black Americans, they are less affected than other racial and ethnic minority groups. Black American community organizations and interest groups are better able to mitigate negative effects with education and mobilization efforts.[59]

Florida's Day Spring Missionary Baptist Church Pastor Marie Herring and lay leader Denise Grabbs lead Souls to the Polls voting mobilization efforts. Souls to the Polls is active in Texas and many other states mobilizing voters through religious institutions.

Steven Johnson/REUTERS/Alamy Stock Photo

The accuracy with which state government enforces voting requirements can also affect turnout. For example, concerned that non-citizens had been added to voting rolls by the Department of Motor Vehicles through its voter registration program, the Texas Secretary of State removed 95,000 names from the voter rolls in 2019.[60] A federal district court ordered Texas to stop this program as the majority of names on these rolls were those of naturalized citizens.[61] The secretary of state altered its procedures to comply with the court ruling. In 2021, the election officials sent 11,737 letters asking registered voters to provide proof of citizenship within 30 days or be removed from the rolls. Of the 2,327 individuals who have been removed from the rolls, 12 percent failed to provide adequate proof and 88 percent did not respond to the request within 30 days. Those removed from the rolls can still vote if they provide proof of citizenship at the polls.

The most recent attempt to make voting laws and requirements more strict is SB1, a law that went into effect in 2021 and increases voting access by lifting restrictions on mail-in ballots but prohibits some measures instituted by larger, urban counties to institute their own voting regulations.[62] For example, SB1 prohibits 24-hr voting polling locations and drive-thru voting, popular options for people of color, voters with disabilities or COVID-19 health concerns, and young people in urban areas in the 2020 election.[63] Absentee ballots now require driver's license numbers or the last four digits of Social Security numbers on the application form *and* return envelope. These numbers need to match voters' state records. Election officials cannot mail absentee ballots to voters unless voters have specifically requested one.[64] Proponents argue these measures safeguard election integrity. Opponents argue they present extra burdens that raise the costs of voting in terms of time, money, or political knowledge.[65] Another concern opponents have is that any misstep or unintentional mistake may lead to the inability to vote or even to being accused of fraud or a criminal violation.[66]

Other components of SB1 include protecting the free movement of partisan poll watchers at polling locations so they can be close enough to monitor voters, officials, and closing processes for the location. Poll watchers are also required to undergo training to prevent violations of voting rights. If they violate the law, poll watchers can be forced to leave voting locations, though the ability of election officials to prevent harassment of voters is diminished from previous laws.

In the context of a history of racially-motivated voter intimidation in the South, the concern is that poll watchers will be too close to voters and intimidate them. While most interactions with poll watchers are uncontroversial today, election officials have less legal recourse now. Another part of the law relates to voter assistance. Anyone assisting voters with disabilities or with language translation must now fill out a form before the election and take an oath to only help voters in the process of voting and not to influence their vote. Finally, SB1 requires that the Texas secretary of state check registered voters' citizenship status at the time of applying for and renewing their driver's license or voter identification card.[67]

The March 2022 primaries, the first elections conducted under the new SB1 laws, raised concerns about the new voter requirements with mail-in ballots. By the time early voting started, Harris County, the largest county in Texas, had to return almost 40 percent of mail-in ballots due to not writing in identification numbers in all the correct locations on the ballot and envelope or mismatched identification numbers. County elections offices return rejected ballots for voters to fix, and voters can cancel their mail-in ballot by voting in person or go to their county clerk's office within six days of the election to fix issues. Voters sometimes receive their ballot too close to the election or wait too long to return their ballot for this process to work, and there is no time to fix problems.[68] Moreover, it is logical to conclude that given the age requirement and proof of inability to vote on election day in order to receive a mail-in ballot, many voters cannot physically go to the polls or can easily get to county offices. Preliminary results show that more than 27,000 mail-in ballots were ruled as violating the new identification requirements in Texas—amounting to a 17 percent rejection rate across the 120 counties that contain the majority of the state's voters.[69] Of these ballots flagged for rejection and returned to voters, more than 18,000 ballots were not fixed *and* not counted in the election.[70]

Initial analysis shows this ballot rejection and potential disfranchisement are also correlated with race. Harris County reviewed its ballot rejection data, and the review demonstrates that areas in the county that are predominantly Black were 44 percent more likely to have mail-in ballots rejected than areas that are predominantly white. Black residents are the largest racial group in six of the nine zip codes in the county with the highest rates of rejected ballots.[71] This initial evidence suggests that more restrictive voting laws systematically disenfranchise specific demographics depending on the type of law. Some confusion follows any major change in voting requirements. The ultimate concern for democracy is finding the balance between maintaining election integrity and preventing systemic disenfranchisement.

The most recent developments for Texas voting laws include two federal court rulings that modify SB1. In July 2022, a federal judge overturned the section of SB1 that makes it a felony for people to have voting assistance beyond helping a voter read or mark the ballot. The federal court ruled that this section violated the rights of voters who need language help or extra assistance because of physical disabilities.[72] This case was initially brought by the Organization of Chinese Americans-Greater Houston. By August 2022, in a lawsuit brought by Latino and other voting rights interest groups like the League of United Latin American Citizens and Voto Latino, another federal court judge struck down the provision in SB1 requiring voters who use P.O. Boxes for addresses to provide extra proof of residency. The judge ruled this provision violated First Amendment rights, but Texas has appealed this ruling.[73] Given the significant controversy about SB1 and voting rights, there may be more revisions to SB1 as interest groups and the state continue to turn to the federal court's review of SB1's constitutionality.

Voter Fraud in Texas

Voting and election laws continue to be controversial in Texas, rooted in ideological and partisan conflicts. Following the 2020 presidential election outcomes, claims about electoral and voting fraud became widespread. These concerns led to election and voting law changes like Texas SB1. Proponents believe that some laws that allow for greater flexibility, such as mail-in ballots or same-day registration, open the door to voting fraud. Politicians in favor of stricter voting laws argue that they are necessary to combat voter fraud and to maintain trust in election processes and election results. Opponents argue that stricter laws are not necessary and that stricter laws add voting barriers for primarily racial and ethnic minorities, low-income voters, senior citizens, and young voters. Opinions largely follow partisan lines with Republican Party leadership supporting stricter laws and Democratic Party leadership not supporting stricter laws.[74]

However, Texas voters are not as polarized over this issue as party leadership. In a June 2021 Texas Politics Project poll before the September special session that passed SB1, 44 percent of voters, identifying as both Republican and Democrat, believe that voters rarely or never break election laws. Only 29 percent believe voters knowingly break election laws sometimes and 14 percent believe voters knowingly break election laws frequently. Figure 9.2 shows that there are partisan

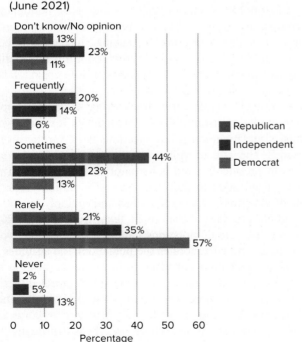

How often do voters knowingly break election laws? (June 2021)

FIGURE 9.2 Texans' opinions on how often voters knowingly break election laws

Source: June 2021 University of Texas/Texas Tribune Poll

Voting fraud

When voters intentionally break voting laws when they vote.

Electoral fraud

The intentional violation of election laws in any part of the process of elections.

variations, too.[75] What this data demonstrates is that while this is an issue driven by partisanship and party leadership, there is a disconnect between Republican- and Democratic-identified voters and their party leadership.

Is there fraud? Is there enough fraud to change the outcome of an election? Research and voting data show a complex reality. First, it is common to conflate, mix up, and use incorrectly the terms electoral fraud and voting fraud. **Voting fraud** occurs when voters intentionally break voting laws when they vote. There are several different kinds of voting fraud such as impersonation fraud during which someone pretends to be another voter and votes in their stead, multiple voting in which someone tries to vote more than once, and ineligible voting when some who does not have the right to vote, such as a convicted person or someone who does not live in the district, tries to vote.

Individuals often act alone, as was the case with Manual Rodriguez III, who used his grandfather's identity to vote in the 2014 general election in Edwards County even though he was not eligible to vote because he was still serving out parole.[76] Similarly, in the 2004 general election, Melva Kay Ponce in Bee County mailed in her recently deceased mother's mail-in ballot. Ms. Ponce's mother requested a mail-in ballot but died two days before receiving it; Ms. Ponce filled it in and mailed it back. A county voter registrar reported the ballot to the sheriff's office because they knew Ms. Ponce's mother had passed away.[77] Most examples of voting fraud are isolated incidents.

Electoral fraud is the intentional violation of election laws in any part of the process of elections. Since the process of elections is the responsibility of government institutions, violations of election laws encompass more government institutions and actors like election officials, candidates, politicians, poll watchers, interest groups, and political parties. Examples include vote-buying, ballot harvesting, voting machine tampering or hacking, misrecording or miscounting votes, hiding or damaging ballots, voter intimidation, misinformation, or manipulation, voter disenfranchisement and suppression, vote caging, false registration records, and campaign finance violations.[78]

The Texas Attorney General's office tracks fraud cases and conviction data.[79] An investigation of charges from 2004 to 2020 shows Texas charged 154 people with 534 counts of violating voting and elections laws, varying from mistakes to intentional fraud.[80] The rate of violations can be calculated by adding up the number of votes in presidential and gubernatorial elections (both primaries and general elections) from 2004 to 2020–93, 853, 678 million votes.[81] Then divide the 534 counts of violations by the total votes and multiply by 100. The percentage of voting and election laws violations in Texas from 2004 to 2020 rounds up to 0.0006 percent. This rate of violations indicates just how rare voting and electoral fraud is in Texas and corroborates the public opinion attitudes in Figure 9.2.

Sometimes, if mistakes do occur when there are close election results, courts order a new election for the sake of fairness and electoral integrity. New elections do not always mean there was fraud, as well. Overall, when examining data and case rulings, it is important to pay attention to words used that may indicate contexts other than fraud. There are checks throughout the election process that exist specifically to notice inconsistencies, address these errors, and prosecute alleged violations if necessary.

Since 2004, there have been 54 state and national elections in Texas.[82] Add in the hundreds of county, city, judicial, and special district elections and that sums to tens of thousands of individual races and election outcomes. Since 2004, there have been only five election outcomes affected by ineligible or illegal ballots. Courts examine if ineligible or illegal votes are counted, if these votes in question are more than the margin of victory between the top two candidates, and if it can be determined which candidates were voted for on these ballots. Table 9.4 highlights these cases and provides contexts for the elections in question. All of these instances are local elections with low turnout and close voting outcomes. The close races mean that any small amount of contested votes may overlap the margin of victory calling into question a clear winner. In this case, courts order new elections. In most of the elections below, the court does not charge people with intentional fraud even though ballots may be determined as ineligible or illegal.

Local elections are the most vulnerable because turnout is so low; even one ineligible or illegal ballot might necessitate a new election. In some of the cases in Table 9.4 that occurred before SB1's requirement of machines providing paper trails, new elections were required because courts could not determine for whom people voted. In elections with larger turnout, ineligible or illegal ballots do not affect election outcomes because they do not affect the margin of victory.

Intentionality is a key variable in a state with strict voting and election laws. There are trade-offs to increasing the stakes of voting. Mistakes increase because of the complexity of voting rules, and they are conflated with voting and electoral fraud. As more states make these voting mistakes violations of the criminal code, one concern is that this criminalization would decrease turnout rates even more because voters are afraid to accidentally violate the law.[83] Voter fraud and electoral fraud mean someone intentionally broke election laws to commit fraud and influence an election, and Texas is beginning to take steps to emphasize the differences in intention between mistakes and actual fraud. While the new voting law in Texas is controversial, it does decrease voting fraud from a second-degree felony to a Class A misdemeanor. Most importantly, SB1 added more specific language to differentiate between unintentional mistakes and intentional fraud.[84] This change in the language of the law does help to strike a balance between having strict laws that criminalize mistakes and identifying real fraud through due process.

Mistakes and fraud do occur by voters, election officials, and other political actors. However, intentional fraud is so rare that there only has been one 2014 election overturned in which courts convicted voters of fraud. Texas county governments conduct elections with integrity, and systems are in place to catch, investigate intent, and prosecute violations of voting and election laws.

Knowledge about election processes, when and how ballots officials count ballots, whether or not a county's voting machines yield paper trails or how votes are backed up, what the roles of local election officials are, and how long counties take to count votes after an election are points of departure to demystify the steps involved to ensure fair elections. The Texas state government provides all of these steps online for the sake of transparency through the office of the Secretary of State; county governments will also have the election process procedures available for the public to read.[85] Local election officials vet ballots through several steps that double-check identity, eligibility, and the number of ballots per voter, and if there are any concerns, county election offices forward complaints to the Secretary of State. If the Secretary of State finds merit, it

TABLE 9.4

Texas Elections Overturned Due to Ineligible or Illegal Ballots and Voting or Electoral Fraud

Election	Context	Intentional Fraud?	Outcome
2020 Brownsville ISD Board Elections[86]	24 ineligible mail-in ballots not caught by election officials	The court determined ballots ineligible or illegal for different reasons but fraud was not mentioned in the case.	The number of thrown-out votes was more than the number of votes to change the election outcome requiring a runoff election in 2022.
2018 Kleberg County, TX, run-off primary election for Justice of the Peace between Ofelia Gutierrez and incumbent Esequiel De La Paz[87]	Gutierrez requested a recount after losing the race by a small margin; the court threw out seven votes because they were by relatives of De La Paz who were not full-time residents of the precinct.	Court did not count the seven votes and determined them illegal, but no fraud charges were determined in the case.	The primary election court cases were not concluded by the time the general election occurred, so the primary run-off was never carried out. The county elections office allowed the original winner of the primary to run in the general election, De La Paz. He won the uncontested general election.
2018 Kaufman County, TX, Republican Primary County Court[88]	Dennis Jones initially beat Tracy Gray by one vote, and Gray challenged the outcomes claiming a ballot harvester illegally collected mail-in ballots.	The court determined that the mail-in ballots were not illegally collected. There were enough illegal provisional ballots due to voter registration mistakes to call into question the margin of victory. No one was charged with fraud.	The court ordered a special election and Gary won by over 400 votes.
2018 Mission, TX, run-off Mayoral election[89]	Armando O'Caña defeated incumbent Norberto Salinas, and Salinas challenged the outcome claiming the O'Caña campaign bribed voters, tampered with mail-in ballots, and illegally assisted voters at the polls.	Lower court ruled in favor of Salinas, but upon appeal, the 13th Texas Court of Appeals overruled the lower court in favor of O'Caña. The appeals court found that the evidence of fraud was not convincing.	The original run-off winner was determined to be the winner of the election.
2014 Woodlands Road Utility District[90]	Ten voters accused of fraud for registering to vote with an invalid residence just for voting purposes. Only 12 people voted in the election.	The court found four people guilty of fraud, though all maintained election officials told them they could use the address in question. One person appealed to the federal courts but the case was dismissed because of the statute of limitations.	The court reinstated the incumbents and overturned the election results. Four voters were convicted of fraud, two voters negotiated a plea deal for lesser sentences, and four voters were not charged at all (one of which had their case overturned by the Texas Court of Criminal Appeals because jurors were not reminded that intention to commit fraud has to be proven).

sends complaints to the Attorney General's office to investigate and support prosecution if local prosecutors deem it necessary. Overall, the Texas election process and procedures put many institutional mechanisms in place to ensure for us the legitimacy of elections and address potential fraud.

CORE OBJECTIVE

Thinking Critically . . .

How do you think the Texas voter ID law and recent attempts of making voting requirements more strict affect voter turnout in Texas? Where do you stand on these issues? Explain why you favor or oppose the changes in voter requirements in SB1.

Explaining Voter Turnout

Learning Objective: Describe ways in which the state of Texas has, historically, restricted access to voting.

How can we explain the relatively low levels of voting among Texans? For one thing, a significant portion of the state's population (namely, noncitizens and convicted felons currently serving time) is not eligible to vote. Including these ineligible groups in Texas's VAP inflates that figure and negatively exaggerates commonly cited turnout levels based on VAP. Even if we correct for this problem by using VEP to calculate turnout, however, the state's level of voter participation is still low. So what else accounts for low voter turnout in Texas?

Many other factors are involved. The political culture discourages participation. The traditionalistic political culture encourages participation of specific demographic groups to maintain power for the elites. Individualistic political culture places the responsibility of voting knowledge on the individual; the government does not try to make it easier for people to participate through education or laws. There is a legacy of restricted access to the ballot for many groups, and other social, economic, and political factors play a role. Of course, many of the factors that affect voter turnout in Texas are also connected to turnout levels across the country, and even around the world.

The Legacy of Restricted Ballot Access in Texas

Like other southern U.S. states, Texas has a history of restrictive voter registration laws for racial and ethnic minorities, known as Jim Crow laws. Jim Crow laws extended beyond the ballot box to create a racially and ethnically segregated society, which included separate schools, separate housing, separate economies, and separate political rights. In the past, these laws made it difficult to qualify to vote, and they limited avenues of meaningful political participation. The state's history of restricting access to voting is very much in keeping with its traditionalistic political culture.

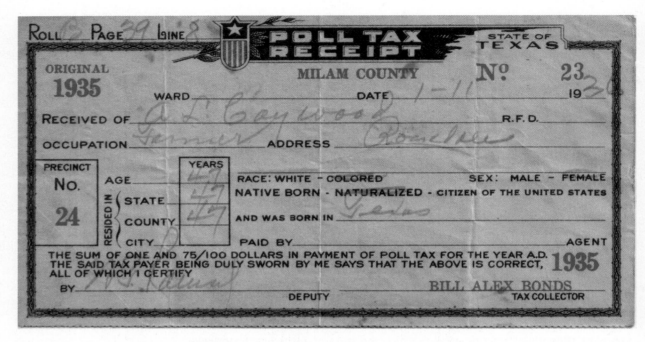

FIGURE 9.3 Original Poll Tax Receipt

Jerry Caywood

In 1902, the Texas legislature adopted, with voter approval, the payment of a poll tax as a requirement for voting. This law primarily targeted the Populist movement, which had organized low-income white farmers into a political coalition that threatened the establishment within the Democratic Party.[91] This tax ($1.75) was a large amount of money for poor farmers in the early 1900s.[92] The poll tax also restricted ballot access for Black Americans and Hispanics, who were disproportionately indigent as a group. The poll tax had to be paid each year between October 1 and January 31 for a person to be allowed to vote in the next election cycle. Figure 9.3 shows an original poll tax receipt.

The poll tax was in effect in Texas for about 60 years. In 1964, the passage of the Twenty-Fourth Amendment to the U.S. Constitution eliminated the poll tax as a requirement for voting in federal elections. However, Texas retained the poll tax as a requirement for voting in state elections.[93] In 1964–1965, 2.4 million Texans still paid the tax. In 1966, the U.S. Supreme Court invalidated Texas's poll tax.[94] The next election cycle proved how successful the poll tax had been in reducing the number of qualified voters. In 1968, the number of registered voters jumped by more than 1 million from the previous presidential election year, an increase of about 35 percent.[95]

Even after the poll tax was eliminated in 1966, Texas retained a very restrictive system of voter registration. It had an **annual registration** system, meaning voters were required to register each year between October 1 and January 31. Individuals were required to register at the courthouse, where they had also been required to pay the poll tax. (In most Texas counties, even today, the county tax collector is also the voter registrar.) For minorities, the trip to the courthouse could be an intimidating experience, so many avoided it.

annual registration

A system that requires citizens to reregister to vote every year

Following a 1971 court decision prohibiting annual registration systems,[96] the Texas legislature passed a very progressive voter registration law that eliminated annual registration and replaced it with a permanent registration system. **Permanent registration** is a system that keeps citizens on the voter registration list without requiring them to re-register every year. Easy voter registration procedures have been shown to increase the number of registered voters. In 1972, the first year Texas used a permanent registration system, voter registration increased yet again, by another 1 million (or nearly 28 percent) over the 1968 figure.[97]

Another past practice used by many southern states, including Texas, to block participation by Black Americans was the **white primary.** In 1923, the Texas legislature passed a law prohibiting Black Americans from participating in Democratic Party primaries. The U.S. Supreme Court declared this law unconstitutional.[98] In 1927, the legislature granted the executive committee of each political party the right to determine voter eligibility for primaries, thereby allowing the Democratic Party to exclude Black Americans.[99] In response, the U.S. Supreme Court again declared the legislature's role unconstitutional.[100] In 1932, bypassing the legislature entirely, the state Democratic Party convention adopted a resolution to hold a white primary.[101] This action prompted yet another U.S. Supreme Court challenge.[102] The Supreme Court's 1935 ruling stated that political parties were in fact private organizations and therefore could decide who was permitted to participate in the primary election. Finally, in 1944 the U.S. Supreme Court outlawed all-white primaries in southern states in *Smith v. Allwright,* a case that originated in Texas.[103]

As was common in many states, property ownership was also used to restrict the right to vote in Texas. These restrictions applied mostly to local elections, particularly bond elections. (In a bond election, voters decide whether to fund the building or renovation of schools or other large public works projects.) Part of Jim Crow laws sought not only segregation in housing, but also in access to housing loans to buy property.[104] The political issues in these local elections would be important to minority voters to improve their quality of life. Without the opportunity to vote in bond elections, they lose meaningful participation in such decisions.

The reasoning behind limiting voting to property owners was that property taxes provided the primary source of revenue for local governments, and renters supposedly did not pay property tax. However, enforcement of the property ownership requirement was difficult. Property ownership requirements were eliminated in the 1970s when permanent registration took effect in Texas.

For Hispanics, participation was discouraged by the Anglos in charge of local and state politics, and political participation came at a high cost.[105] The purpose of Jim Crow laws was to create and maintain the racial-ethnic hierarchy desired by traditionalistic political culture, and they affected all racial and ethnic minorities.[106] Hispanics were lynched as well as socially and economically segregated during this period.[107]

In South Texas and even bigger cities like San Antonio, boss control and political machines monitored and manipulated Latino voting.[108] A political boss is the same as a local political machine. *If* Hispanics were permitted to register and vote in an area, bosses often paid for their poll taxes in exchange for controlling *how* Latinos voted; they had to vote the way the machine dictated. Consequences for not voting as the boss insisted included violence or losing

permanent registration
A system that keeps citizens on the voter registration list without their having to reregister every year

white primary
From 1923 to 1945, Democratic Party primary that excluded African Americans from participating

National Anti-Suffrage Association Headquarters, 1911

Library of Congress Prints and Photographs Division [LC-USZ62-25338]

economic and social rights like land or employment.[109] The Texas Rangers were also often used to intimidate voters attempting to vote in predominantly Latino parts of town.[110] It was not until Supreme Court cases like *Hernandez v. Texas* (1954) that it was acknowledged that non–African Americans were discriminated against under Jim Crow laws and that the Fourteenth Amendment protects them from this discrimination too.[111] The Voting Rights Act 1970, 1975, 1982, and 1990 language extensions for non-English speakers finally made voting accessible to all Hispanics.[112]

The push for women's suffrage began at the state level. By 1915, 11 states had granted women the right to vote.[113] During the 1915 session, the Texas legislature considered granting women the right to vote, but the measure failed. In 1918, women were given the limited right to participate in primary elections. In 1919, Texas voters rejected a proposed amendment to the state constitution that would have granted women full suffrage. The following month, however, the state legislature ratified the Nineteenth Amendment to the U.S. Constitution, which outlawed any citizen from being denied the right to vote based on their sex. Texas was the first southern state to approve the amendment, which took effect in 1920.[114]

All these restrictions combined to prolong the state's tradition of limiting or even discouraging participation in elections. Although past restrictions have been removed from the law, and current access to voter registration is comparatively easy (and has increased the number of registered voters in the state), Texas still has low levels of political participation. As shown in Table 9.3 in the previous section, Texas recently ranked at or near the bottom of all states on voter turnout in elections. In time, the residual effect of restrictive practices may decline, but there are other factors influencing voter turnout such as current voting and election laws, as well as contemporary social and economic conditions.

Social and Economic Factors

socioeconomic factors

Factors such as income, education, race, and ethnicity that affect voter turnout

Rates of participation are also strongly affected by **socioeconomic factors,** such as education level, family income, and minority status. Well-educated people (those with a college education and/or postgraduate degree) are more likely to vote than are less well-educated people (those with a high school degree or less).[115] People of higher socioeconomic status are likely to be more aware of elections and to perceive themselves as having a high stake in election outcomes; therefore, they are more likely to vote. They are also more likely to contribute financially to political campaigns and become actively involved in elections and party activity.

Age is another factor that contributes to turnout. Young voters, particularly those aged 18 to 29, are less likely to vote than older adults.[116] They often have other interests, are more mobile, and may not perceive themselves as having an important stake in political outcomes. Although still lower than the turnout rate for the population as a whole, youth voting rates have increased recently, most recently in the 2020 presidential elections.[117] Issues like climate change, immigration, affordable education, and gun control have mobilized many young people to not only vote but also to participate in unconventional forms of participation like protests and boycotts. As generational cohorts, Generation X, Millennial, and Generation Z voters voted more than the Baby Boomers; these younger voters also make up the majority of the electorate.[118] Embracing this power in numbers and the ability to influence the outcomes of elections will further empower young people to influence the Texas government.

As Figure 9.4 shows, the 2020 presidential election turnout for all racial-ethnic minority groups was significantly lower than for non-Hispanic whites even though the numbers of all groups have increased.

Race is yet another factor in voting. Nationwide, racial and ethnic minority groups have historically voted and registered to vote in smaller proportions than non-Hispanic whites. However, a notable exception to this pattern emerged with regard to voting among Black Americans. In 2008, Black Americans both registered and voted almost at the same rate as white voters, aided by the candidacy of Barack Obama who became the first Black American to become president. In 2012, Black voting turnout was higher than non-Hispanic white turnout.[119] President Obama's candidacy did help increase turnout rates for Black voters,

FIGURE 9.4 **Voter Turnout in Texas in the 2020 Presidential Election, by Race**

Photo: SDI Productions/E+/Getty Images

Source of data: U.S. Census Bureau, https://www.census.gov/data/tables/time-series/demo/voting-and-registration/p20-585.html

but other factors contributed to this increase as well, like better party mobilization and targeted political media.[120] In the 2020 election, the percentage of Black Americans who voted in Texas fell below the percentage of white voters once again (56.3 versus 70.6 percent).[121]

The 2020 presidential elections drew out the highest turnout rates in the United States since the 1900 election–in 120 years.[122] The overall U.S. voter turnout rate rose to 66.2 percent, and the turnout rates for all demographic groups increased as well. Voting turnout in Texas rose 8.8 percent from 2016.[123] Table 9.5 provides a breakdown of Texas voter turnout and voter registration rates by gender, race, and ethnicity for the 2020 election. Demographic trends mirror larger national trends. The data show a gender gap–with significantly more women turning out to vote than men, White non-Hispanics had the highest turnout rates, followed by Black Americans, Asian Americans, and Hispanics of any race. Young Texans also increased their voting rates by 13 percent from 2016: from 28 percent in 2016 to 41 percent in 2020. Young Texans 18–29 years old had the highest increase in voting rates compared to all other demographic groups.[124]

Minority groups are younger than non-Hispanic whites, so part of this increase in voting intersects with the increase of voting by young people overall.[125] It is estimated that by 2022, one in three Texas voters will be younger than 30 and from a majority-minority racial or ethnic group.[126]

However, as shown by Figure 9.3, while there has been unprecedented growth in voting rates for racial and ethnic minorities, a voting gap remains across groups.

TABLE 9.5

Registration and Voter Participation by Race and Sex in Texas, 2020

	Total Population (in thousands)	Total Citizen Population (in thousands)	Total Registered (in thousands)	Percentage Registered (total)	Percentage Registered (citizen)	Total Voted (in thousands)	Percentage Voted (total)	Percentage Voted (citizen)
Total	21,485	18,581	13,343	62.1	71.8	11,874	55.3	63.9
Male	10,513	9,082	6,338	60.3	69.8	5,580	53.1	61.4
Female	10,972	9,500	7,005	63.8	73.7	6,295	57.4	66.3
White alone	17,042	14,760	10,734	63.0	72.7	9,612	56.4	65.1
White non-Hispanic alone	9,615	9,423	7,396	76.9	78.5	6,785	70.6	72.0
Black alone	2,700	2,502	1,759	65.1	70.3	1,521	56.3	60.8
Asian alone	1,239	821	521	42.1	63.5	482	38.9	58.7
Hispanic (of any race)	7,730	5,599	3,538	45.8	63.2	2,972	38.4	53.1
White alone or in combination	17,361	15,079	10,928	62.9	72.5	9,762	56.2	64.7
Black alone or in combination	2,890	2,692	1,882	65.1	69.9	1,636	56.6	60.8
Asian alone or in combination	1,355	937	601	44.4	64.2	546	40.3	58.3

Source: U.S. Census Bureau, April 2021.

Focus On

Increasing Voter Turnout among Hispanics

Hispanics constitute a burgeoning share of the national vote. In 2020, 16.6 million Hispanics and Latinos voted in the presidential election, representing a turnout increase of 30.9 percent from the 2016 election.[127] Moreover, the Hispanic electorate is projected to increase to 40 million by the year 2030. This massive increase will be fueled primarily by large numbers of young Hispanics reaching voting age (and secondarily by naturalizations).[128] In Texas, growth in the number of eligible Hispanic voters is expected to mirror that national trend.

Patricia Marroquin/Moment/Getty Images

As the Hispanic population continues to grow, Hispanics are beginning to play a bigger role in shaping the state's politics than ever before.[129] Analysis of election data shows that, historically, Hispanics have voted at much lower rates than Blacks and non-Hispanic whites.[130] Several socioeconomic factors contribute to lower voter turnout among Hispanics, including generally lower education levels and incomes. Texas is generally not considered to be a key state in presidential elections—something that can generate considerable interest in voting and the political process.[131] Other possible factors include the number of Hispanic candidates running for office and the candidates' efforts to engage the Hispanic community, including making campaign materials available in Spanish.[132]

However, in recent elections, the rate of Hispanics in Texas registering to vote and then actually voting has increased as the population changes. A big part of this changing story is understanding that the Hispanic electorate is young; 44 percent of the Hispanic eligible voters are Millennials, and millions of young Hispanics are becoming old enough to vote.[133] As previously discussed, young people in Texas are voting in record-breaking numbers, influencing election outcomes, political parties, and the Texas government.

The 2020 Census reports the Total Citizen Population for Latino 18–24-year-olds as 5.7 million with 2.3 million actually voting in the 2020 election.[134] Young Hispanics differ from older cohorts in that they are citizens and primarily speak English (almost 75 percent of U.S.–born Hispanics are Millennial and younger).[135] Another interesting population change is that Latinas vote more than Latinos; the largest gender gap between Latinas and Latinos is for 18-to-24-year-olds.[136]

Critical Thinking Questions
1. Discuss the factors involved in low, but increasing, voter turnout among Hispanics.
2. What do you think the future will bring with regard to Hispanic participation in elections?

Felony Conviction and Voting

Most states limit the voting rights of people convicted of a felony. Maine and Vermont are the only states that allow felons to vote even while they are in prison.[137] Texas prohibits persons convicted of a felony currently serving time, as well as those on probation or parole, from voting. However, felons in Texas may register to vote after they have served their sentence and completed their time on probation and parole.[138] According to the Sentencing Project, in 2020 there were 500,000 ineligible felons (2.8 percent of the voting-age population) in Texas who could not vote.[139] When one examines who makes up those affected by felony disenfranchisement, political power and demographics such as race, ethnicity, class, and gender are linked to lower rates of participation.

CORE OBJECTIVE

Being Socially Responsible . . .

Considering the discussion of political power and the socioeconomic factors that affect voter turnout, identify effective ways to increase civic knowledge in culturally diverse communities.

Party Competition and Gerrymandering

The lack of party competition in Texas for more than 100 years also contributes to the state's overall lower voter turnout. Studies have shown that party competition and the closeness of elections are important factors in voter turnout. (However, the effect of the latter is smaller than one might think.)[140] When there is party competition in a district, voters believe that their votes will actually "count," so they are more likely to show up at the polls and to participate in grassroots political organizations. Moreover, in competitive districts, both parties have a big incentive to increase voter turnout.[141] Texas does not have particularly politically competitive state government elections. Texans elected Republicans to all statewide offices from 2002 through 2022.[142] The state has also been solidly Republican in U.S. presidential elections. Furthermore, Texas has many noncompetitive seats, especially in the state legislature. It remains to be seen if this domination of state politics will be permanent. Although party competition has increased in recent years, the state has a long history of being a one-party state; consequently, voter turnout is lower than it might be with greater competition.

One issue that adds to the lack of party competition is gerrymandering. As demonstrated in Chapter 3, Texas has a history of gerrymandering, which means drawing district boundaries for political advantage. The *Texas Tribune* analyzed 2018 U.S. congressional districts in Texas and determined that 10 out of the 36 districts are competitive, 31 out of 50 Texas House districts are competitive, and 5 out of 31 Texas senate districts are competitive; these are increases from the 2016 elections.[143] While the races are becoming more competitive, for the most part, the districts across all types of elections are not competitive. Gerrymandering can lead to lower turnout because voters feel they are throwing away their vote if one party is always going to win because of gerrymandered district lines.

Other Factors Affecting Voter Turnout

Other factors can affect voter turnout in some elections. One is the timing of the election. Voter turnout is higher in November presidential elections than in midterm elections that do not elect a president or other statewide or national officeholders. For the most part, turnout for primary elections is even lower than for general elections. Also, local elections for city councils and school boards are generally not held in conjunction with general elections; in Texas, these are commonly held in May. However, efforts are currently being made to move these local contests to the fall. For example in 2012, Austin voters approved a proposition to move city elections from May to November.[144] More recently, in 2021, Austin voters chose to coincide mayoral elections with presidential election years to capture the attention of the largest and most representative electorate.[145]

Turnout in local elections is always lower than in other elections (despite the fact that the odds of casting a crucial or even tie-breaking vote increase as the number of people voting goes down). There are several reasons for this: local elections are less visible and receive less attention from the media, voters do not perceive these elections as important, and many of these races are not contested. In 1995, the Texas legislature proposed a constitutional amendment, which the voters approved, to change state law to allow cities and school boards to cancel elections if all races are uncontested. The governing body certifies the uncontested candidates as "winners." (Chapter 7 has more information on local elections.)

The day of the week an election is held can also affect voter turnout. Tuesday is the most common day for elections in the United States. This tradition dates back to 1845 when the U.S. Congress set the date for federal elections as the first Tuesday after the first Monday in November.[146] Local city and school board elections are often held on Saturday, which might appear to be a better day to hold elections than Tuesday because many people are off work and have time to vote. However, Saturday is also a departure from one's regular workday routine, and people might forget to vote or choose to devote the day to other activities, such as recreation or errands. Also, elections in the United States are generally held on a single day, with the polls typically being open for 12 hours. In contrast, many European countries hold elections over an entire weekend.

Election laws and trust in the election process matter, too. Longer election periods, early voting opportunities, and other ways that voting (and registration) can be made easier (such as voting by mail and increasing the number of polling places) might increase voter turnout. As political scientist Andre Blais notes, "It makes sense to assume that people are more prone to vote if it is easy."[147] Empirical evidence generally supports this intuition. However, a recent University of Wisconsin study of early voting offers a caveat. Kenneth Mayer, one of the study authors, found in this particular instance that early voting "actually causes voter turnout to go down."[148] Coauthor Donald Downs surmised that the existence of early voting might make voting on Election Day seem less important. It is not clear, though, whether this finding will be confirmed in other studies because scholars have generally found the opposite effect when it comes to making voting easier.

Trust in the election process also affects voting rates, though how, why, and when is still being studied by political scientists.[149] Trust in (or distrust of) government and leaders is a complicated concept to study. It usually results from several factors like individual behaviors, political leaders' behaviors,

Bexar County Precinct Chair Gina Sandoval registers people to vote for the Texas 2022 primary elections.

Ilana Panich-Linsman/The Washington Post/Getty Images

and institutional performance.[150] Political psychology research incorporates trust in political institutions as a part of the social capital and sense of efficacy people bring to their civic engagement.[151] Other research focuses on trust in political leaders.[152] Sometimes distrust because of institutional corruption, for example, leads to political alienation, which decreases participation rates.[153] At other times, distrust that arises as a result of increased government transparency (which is good for democracy) leads to people holding the government more accountable and increases participation rates.[154]

Trust in elections has been politicized since the 2020 presidential election, when President Trump contested the results of the general election. Texas passed stricter voting laws in 2021.[155] However, polling data from the Texas Politics Project at the University of Texas shows that the laws did little to change people's attitudes about trust in elections. A total of 76 percent of Republicans and 88 percent of Democrats believed that Texas elections were "very accurate" and "somewhat accurate" before the laws passed; a total of 73 percent of Republicans and 84 percent of Democrats believed that Texas elections were "very accurate" and "somewhat accurate" after the laws passed. While beliefs about election integrity in Texas are highly partisan, most Republicans, Democrats, and even independents believe that election results are accurate.[156]

Understanding Impact Now that you have learned about historical, institutional, and demographic factors that lead to low turnout in Texas, do you believe people should be concerned about the quality of Texan democracy? How does a legacy of low turnout or of laws preventing voting affect the political power and quality of life of those who do not vote? How can voters in Texas hold the government accountable to protect their right to vote and insist that the state maintain the integrity of elections?

Rationalist Explanations for Low Voter Turnout

A last reason for low voter turnout may be the realization by a number of voters that, at least in their individual cases, individual voting is irrational because (1) it does not meet the requirements of "strategic" or "instrumental" rationality (in the sense of voting being a purposeful act to influence an election), given the low probability of any single individual being the "marginal," "pivotal," or "deciding" voter in large-scale elections; and (2) the "consumption" or "expressive" value of voting does not outweigh the costs of participation (especially the cost of one's time). In other words, duty doesn't call, nor is the act of voting all that valuable relative to the costs for some segment of the population.

There is a long tradition of literature in political science and economics, starting with the path-breaking work of Anthony Downs, that makes these "rational choice" points. Scholars of voting often wonder, as Nobel Prize–winning economist Kenneth Arrow did, "why an individual votes at all in a large election, since the probability that his vote will be decisive is so negligible."[157] But since so many do—thus creating the so-called paradox of voting—we may want to ask not why so many don't vote but why so many people do vote! This is undoubtedly a more complicated question than we can fully answer here. However, one answer might be that individuals, like people who clap at the end of a movie or cheer in a football stadium full of people, gain expressive value from the act of voting.[158] It simply makes them feel better to express their preference for one candidate (or against another). An individual may also, consciously or not, want to signal to others that he or she is a good citizen or a serious person by being seen voting or by wearing a sticker from the voting facility. Or it could be that some individuals believe they have a real duty to participate in elections, especially given the price others have paid to secure that civil right.[159] There could be many reasons for people to vote, apart from narrowly strategic reasons. However, some people might choose not to vote for rational reasons. And it is worth asking why individuals pay less attention to and vote less often in local elections where they have a statistically greater chance of influencing the election.

Another rational reason some people may not vote is that they are satisfied with (or alienated from) the political system in general and do not feel the need to express themselves in favor of (or against) any particular candidate. Last, an admittedly small number of eligible citizens may be principled nonvoters who do not want to provide legitimacy to what they believe is an illegitimate system.

CORE OBJECTIVE

Communicating Effectively . . .

Write a one-page summary of the rationalist explanations for low voter turnout.

Other Forms of Political Participation

Learning Objective: Describe forms of political participation other than voting.

Although voting in an election is the most common form of political participation, people participate in politics in many other ways. You could be "involved" in politics by becoming a candidate for public office or by signing a petition or by writing a short letter to the editor of the local newspaper. Other forms of participation seen in Texas and the rest of the country include donating money to a campaign, volunteering for a campaign, supporting an advocacy group, contacting an elected official, attending a rally or protest, or using online social networks to support a candidate or group. A common goal of all these types of participation is to affect the decisions that governments make—either by electing certain people to office or by influencing those who are already in office.

A recent survey of Texas adults (see Table 9.6) sheds light on some of the ways Texans participate in politics.

Thanks to a greater reliance on the Internet by campaign fund-raising efforts, donating to a campaign has become one of the easiest ways to

2022 Republican candidate for the U.S. House of Representatives Mayra Flores at a March to the Border rally.

Bill Clark/CQ-Roll Call, Inc./Getty Images

TABLE 9.6

Popular Forms of Nonvoting Political Participation in Texas

Political Activity	%
Signed a petition	25
Avoided products for political reasons	17
Contacted a politician	14
Purchased products for political reasons	11
Donated to a political cause	11

Source: 2018 Texas Civic Health Index, p. 7, University of Texas at Austin, Moody College of Communication, https://moody.utexas.edu/sites/default/files/2018-Texas_Civic_Health_Index.pdf.

participate in politics. About 22 percent of respondents to the University of Texas poll reported making a political donation. According to OpenSecrets. org, a website run by the Center for Responsive Politics that tracks political contributions, individual Texans in increments of at least $200 donated more than $726 million to candidates, PACs, outside spending groups (including super PACs), and party committees for the 2020 funding cycle.[160] Texas placed third in the nation for the number of individual contributions to political campaigns. Republican candidates were the largest beneficiaries of these individual contributors, claiming 56.3 percent of all political contributions.[161]

However, political participation as a whole is still relatively low in the United States, and especially in Texas. Why don't more people participate in politics? Political scientists Henry Brady, Sidney Verba, and Kay Schlozman answer, "Because they can't, because they don't want to, or because nobody asked."[162] Participation in politics requires free time, expendable income, and political interest. The cost of participation in terms of time, in particular, is a crucial constraint. Involvement in social networks such as civic associations and

Tea Party activists head to a rally at the Texas State Capitol.

Ben Sklar/Getty Images

How to

How to Be Politically and Socially Responsible

Democracy is about people coming together to improve society. To have a high-quality democracy, citizens must use their political power to guide the government. This includes not only voting but also participating *after* elections.

Step 1: Know where to find election information.

To register to vote, go to the tax assessor's website for your county. You can print and mail a registration form. Once you are registered, you do not need to register again except if you move, if your name changes, or if you complete prison time.

To find election deadlines, ballot information, voting locations, and information on early voting, go to your county clerk's website. This site also has sample ballots for specific races, absentee ballots, and special information for military personnel and voters with disabilities.

As of 2020, Texas no longer has straight-ticket voting. This means you need alternative shortcuts to help you vote. Each political party has its own website with its party platform. Check out third parties, too!

In addition, look for nonpartisan, nonideological sources of information, such as the League of Women Voters. Interest group endorsements also provide a voting shortcut. Locate web pages of interest groups with which you agree, find a local chapter, and see their recommendations.

Finally, focus on what incumbents *actually do* in office, not just what they say or promise. Look at voting records and at any bills they proposed. The Texas Legislature Online has search options to help you do this. Also, note how or if your representatives respond to you.

Step 2: Fact-check information.

Know your news sources, and recognize shallow policy coverage, clickbait, and infotainment. Check out this resource: False, Misleading, Clickbait-y, and/or Satirical "News" Sources. Learn to identify political spin and fake news. Most important, diversify your news sources so you learn perspectives from across the political spectrum.

Make sure information is valid before you spread it on the Internet. Two main sites for fact-checking are Politifact.com and Snopes.com.

Step 3: Volunteer in the community or in politics.

Take time to discover your neighborhood's needs. Many organizations need volunteers: public schools, food banks, animal shelters, women's shelters, homeless shelters, religious organizations, and others. Start with a volunteer matching site, such as volunteermatch.org if you don't know where to begin.

Search event lists for local marches or community meetings. Take responsibility for organizing an event. Sending out event information on social media can help you find other volunteers quickly.

Finally, consider volunteering at the local party level. Contact local party organizations to find out how you can help their cause. They can also help you if you decide to run for political office!

---

churches, which enable people to interact and mobilize, also promotes political participation. These kinds of social networks also help people to develop "civic skills," or the ability to communicate and organize, which are important to political activity. Many Americans lack some or all of these resources for political participation. Another way to think about these material and non-material resources listed above is that they represent political power. Research by Bernard L. Fraga shows that turnout requires campaign voter outreach and demographic groups knowing the scope of their own political power.[163]

Does low political participation threaten American democracy? Although turnout in presidential elections has increased slightly in recent years (and, as political scientist Michael McDonald has argued, the supposed decline in voter participation since 1971 may not be as significant as once thought), it is still lower than in the 1950s and 1960s.[164] One concern with low turnout is policy and representation bias. Who votes, demographically speaking, influences who is in power and which policies are made. Voters' power—their ability to influence—increases. Those who do not vote—those who do not influence—have no sway over the power of representatives and their powerlessness compounds; moreover, nonvoters' policy interests can be ignored. When there is low turnout, majoritarianism does not guide democracy; democracy reflects only the interests of the numerical minority who participate, especially for local elections.

Other types of participation are also in decline. In his book *Bowling Alone,* Robert Putnam cites declining involvement in traditional civic associations as contributing to a loss of "social capital" in America. Social capital refers to the sense of shared purpose and values that social connection promotes, which Putnam and many others cite as necessary for a thriving democracy. Others are less pessimistic. Russell Dalton, for example, argues that the decline in traditional civic associations is accompanied by a rise in other types of participation that reflect the changing values of a younger generation.[165]

Understanding Impact Consider how effective different types of participation are in influencing the government to make policies you like. As you think about this, consider times when Texas was forced to make major political changes such as those related to civil rights. Do all types of participation influence equally? Which are more effective and why? Is voting enough to enact change, or do individuals and groups have to participate after candidates are put into power, too? Could how and when people participate increase their power?

Conclusion

The Lone Star State has chronically low levels of voter turnout in elections and low levels of participation in the political process in general. Many factors influence participation in voting and other political activities. Individual states determine who is eligible to vote within their borders, and some states, like Texas, have relatively strict requirements for voting. Some states also have a legacy of restricting access to the ballot and discouraging voter participation. Despite the removal of these restrictions and increases in voter turnout, voter turnout has not surged as much as some might have expected or hoped, suggesting that other factors may

play an important role in political participation. Social and economic factors, level of party competition, and other variables including the rational calculations of individuals are also involved. Moreover, political behavior can persist for generations (especially if there is a "habit component" to voting).[166] Demographic changes and increased party competition may affect voter turnout levels in the future. However, current low levels of participation are consistent with the traditional political culture of Texas. But recent elections indicate that turnout rates of young voters and Latinos are increasing incrementally.

Summary

LO: Explain political participation.

Political participation refers to all the ways in which citizens can be involved in governance. Voting in elections is the most obvious (but not the only) way that citizens take part in politics. We can discuss participation in terms of types of activities and degree or level of involvement.

LO: Discuss voter turnout in Texas, including citizens' rights and responsibilities.

Voter turnout is the proportion of people who cast ballots in an election. Regardless of the method used to calculate it, Texas has low voter turnout. Over the past 30 years, Texas has consistently fallen below the national average in terms of the percentage of the population participating in elections. The state's voter turnout also ranks at or near the bottom when compared to other states. In Texas today, any individual who is at least 18 years of age, a U.S. citizen, and a resident of the state may vote. Texans must register 30 days before an election and provide some form of identification in order to vote. Young voters and Latinos have seen recent increases in voting rates.

LO: Describe ways in which the state of Texas has, historically, restricted access to voting.

For part of its history, Texas required citizens to pay a poll tax each year to be eligible to vote in the next election cycle. After the poll tax was eliminated, Texas had an annual registration system, which required citizens to re-register to vote every year. Another restrictive practice was the whites-only primary. For a time, the Democratic Party in Texas prohibited African Americans from participating in primary elections. Boss and machine politics manipulated the Hispanic vote. All these practices have been invalidated by court decisions.

LO: Describe forms of political participation other than voting.

Although voting in an election is the most common form of political participation, other forms include donating money to a campaign, volunteering for a campaign, supporting an advocacy group, contacting an elected official, attending a rally or protest, or using online social networks to support a candidate or group. Alternatively, individuals might try to influence governmental decisions by running for public office, signing a petition, or writing a letter to the editor of the local newspaper.

Key Terms

absentee voting	poll tax	voter turnout
annual registration	registered voters	Voting Rights Act
election fraud	same-day registration	voting-age population (VAP)
permanent registration	socioeconomic factors	voting-eligible population (VEP)
political participation	voting fraud	white primary
political power	voter registration	

Notes

[1] Eric Liu, "How to Understand Power," TED-Ed, November 2014, https://www.ted.com/talks/eric_liu_how_to_understand_power?utm_campaign=tedspread&utm_medium=referral&utm_source=tedcomshare.

[2] Ibid.

[3] Andrew Daniller and Hannah Gilberstadt, "Key findings about Voter Engagement in the 2020 Election," Pew Research Center, https://www.pewresearch.org/fact-tank/2020/12/14/key-findings-about-voter-engagement-in-the-2020-election/.

[4] Aaron Smith, "Civic Engagement in the Digital Age," Pew Research Center, April 25, 2013, http://www.pewinternet.org/2013/04/25/civic-engagement-in-the-digital-age/. For raw data, see http://www.pewinternet.org/datasets/august-2012-civic-engagement/; Laura Seay, "Does Slacktivism Work?," *The Washington Post,* March 12, 2014, https://www.washingtonpost.com/news/monkey-cage/wp/2014/03/12/does-slacktivism-work/.

[5] Sidney Verba and Norman H. Nie, *Participation in America* (Chicago: University of Chicago Press, 1987).

[6] Michael McDonald, "National General Election VEP Turnout Rates, 1789-Present," accessed February 28, 2022, http://www.electproject.org/home/voter-turnout/voter-turnout-data.

[7] Ollie Gratzinger, "Small donors give big money in 2020 election cycle," OpenSecrets, October 30, 2020, https://www.opensecrets.org/news/2020/10/small-donors-give-big-2020-thanks-to-technology/.

[8] Larry Buchanan, Quoctrung Bui, and Jugal K. Patel, "Black Lives Matter May Be the Largest Movement in U.S. History," *New York Times,* July 3, 2020, https://www.nytimes.com/interactive/2020/07/03/us/george-floyd-protests-crowd-size.html.

[9] Carnegie Endowment for International Peach, "Global Protest Counter," last updated March 4, 2022, https://carnegieendowment.org/publications/interactive/protest-tracker?radiogroup=covid.

[10] Brennan Center for Justice, "Voting Laws Roundup: December 2021," January 12, 2022, https://www.brennancenter.org/our-work/research-reports/voting-laws-roundup-december-2021.

[11] These prohibitions are laid out in Amendments 15, 19, 24, and 26. See the Constitution of the United States, Amendments 11–27, http://www.archives.gov/exhibits/charters/constitution_amendments_11-27.html.

[12] *Texas Constitution*, art. 6, sec. 1-2. See http://www.statutes.legis.state.tx.us/Docs/CN/htm/CN.6.htm.

[13] U.S. Census Bureau, "Voting and Registration," revised February 10, 2016, http://www.census.gov/topics/public-sector/voting/about.html.

[14] Texas Secretary of State, "Texas Voting," http://www.sos.state.tx.us/elections/pamphlets/largepamp.shtml.

[15] Texas Department of Public Safety, "Application for Texas Driver License or Identification Card," http://dps.texas.gov/internetforms/Forms/DL-14A.pdf.

[16] Texas Secretary of State, "Texas Voting," http://www.sos.state.tx.us/elections/pamphlets/largepamp.shtml; VoteTexas.gov, "Your Voter Registration Card," http://www.votetexas.gov/register-to-vote/550-2/.

[17] VoteTexas.gov, "Required Identification for Voting in Person," http://www.votetexas.gov/register-to-vote/need-id/ (accessed September 3, 2016).

[18] Texas Department of Public Safety, "Election Identification Certificate (EIC)," http://www.txdps.state.tx.us/driverlicense/electionid.htm.

[19] Ibid.

[20] Texas Secretary of State, "Early Voting," http://www.votetexas.gov/voting/when/#early-voting; Texas Secretary of State, "Military and Overseas Voters," http://www.votetexas.gov/voting/#military-and-overseas-voters.

[21] Harris County Clerk's Office Election Division, "Election Day Polls & Ballot," https://www.harrisvotes.com/PollLocations.

[22] 89th Congress of the United States of America, "The Voting Rights Act of 1965, Public Law 89-110," http://library.clerk.house.gov/reference-files/PPL_VotingRightsAct_1965.pdf; Keith Ingram, "Minority Language Requirements," June 23, 2014, https://www.sos.state.tx.us/elections/laws/advisory-2014-13-minority-language.shtml.

[23] Houstontx.gov, "Top 25 Houston Languages," from *U.S. Census Bureau, 2010–2014 American Community Survey 5-Year Estimates*, houstontx.gov/ispeakhouston/top25HoustonLanguages2014.pdf.

[24] Emily Foxhall, "Korean Translator Alleges Harris County Election Judge Hindered Voters," *Houston Chronicle*, October 29, 2018, https://www.houstonchronicle.com/news/houston-texas/texas/article/Korean-translator-alleges-Harris-County-election-13343634.php#.

[25] Zach Despart, "Harris County Defends Decision to Ban Korean Translators from Spring Branch Polling Site," October 29, 2018, https://www.houstonchronicle.com/news/houston-texas/houston/article/Harris-County-defends-decision-to-bar-Korean-13346474.php.

[26] Texas Secretary of State, "Your Rights," 2012, https://www.votetexas.gov/your-rights/.

[27] Alexa Ura, "Translators Help Korean American Voters in Harris County Find Their Electoral Voice," *Texas Tribune,* November 26, 2019, https://www.texastribune.org/2019/11/26/how-korean-americans-lobbied-harris-county-bilingual-pollworkers/.

[28] Matt Harab, "Harris County Unveils New Polling Technology for Non-English Speakers," Houston Public Media, February 14, 2020, https://www.houstonpublicmedia.org/articles/news/harris-county/2020/02/14/360756/harris-county-unveils-new-polling-technology/.

[29] Ibid.

[30] National Conference of State Legislatures, "Same Day Voter Registration," September 20, 2021, https://www.ncsl.org/research/elections-and-campaigns/same-day-registration.aspx.

[31] Barry C. Burden, David T. Canon, Kenneth R. Mayer, et al., "Election Laws, Mobilization, and Turnout: The Unanticipated Consequences of Election Reform," *American Journal of Political Science* 58, no. 1 (January 2014).

[32] North Dakota Secretary of State, "North Dakota. . . . The Only State without Voter Registration," revised July 2015, https://vip.sos.nd.gov/pdfs/portals/votereg.pdf.

[33] National Conference of State Legislatures, "Online Voter Registration," July 26, 2021, https://www.ncsl.org/research/elections-and-campaigns/electronic-or-online-voter-registration.aspx#table.

[34] National Conference of State Legislatures, "Voter Identification Requirements: Voter ID Laws," January 7, 2022, https://www.ncsl.org/research/elections-and-campaigns/voter-id.aspx.

[35] Voting Rights Lab, "Showdown 2022: The State of State Election Law – and the Fights Ahead," February 2022, https://votingrightslab.org/wp-content/uploads/2022/02/VotingRightsLab-Showdown2022.pdf.

[36] Michael P. McDonald, "Why Not Calculate Turnout Rates as Percentage of Registered Voters?," Voter Turnout FAQ, *United States Elections Project*, http://www.electproject.org/home/voter-turnout/faq/reg.

[37] Thomas Holbrook and Brianne Heidbreder, "Does Measurement Matter? The Case of VAP and VEP in Models of Voter Turnout in the United States," *State Politics & Policy Quarterly* 10, no. 2 (Summer 2010): 157–79.

[38] U.S. Census Bureau, "Voting, People Eligible to Register," *Current Population Survey (CPS), Subject Definitions*, https://www.census.gov/programs-surveys/cps/technical-documentation/subject-definitions.html#voting.

[39] Ibid.

[40] Michael P. McDonald, "Why Should I Care If Turnout Rates Are Calculated as Percentage of VAP or VEP?," Voter Turnout Frequently Asked Questions, *United States Elections*

Project, 2016, http://www.electproject.org/home/voter-turnout/faq/vap-v-vap.

[41] Michael P. McDonald, "Voter Turnout Demographics," *United States Elections Project,* 2016, http://www.electproject.org/home/voter-turnout.

[42] Ibid.

[43] Texas Secretary of State, "Turnout and Voter Registration Figures (1970–Current)," http://www.sos.state.tx.us/elections/historical/70-92.shtml.

[44] Brian Miller, "Full 50 State 2018 Turnout Ranking and Voting Policy," *Nonprofit Vote,* April 10, 2019, https://www.nonprofit-vote.org/full-50-state-2018-turnout-ranking-voting-policy/.

[45] Ibid., 43.

[46] Mandi Cai and Sneha Dey, "Around 17% of registered Texas voters cast 2022 primary ballots, according to preliminary data," *Texas Tribune,* February 14, 2022, https://www.texas-tribune.org/2022/02/14/texas-primary-voting-turnout/.

[47] Jordan Misra, "Voter Turnout Rates among All Voting Age and Major Racial and Ethnic Groups Were Higher Than in 2014," United States Census Bureau, April 23, 2019, https://www.census.gov/library/stories/2019/04/behind-2018-united-states-midterm-election-turnout.html.

[48] "Youth Voter Turnout Analysis Shows Across-the-Board Increases in 2018 Midterms," TuftsNow, January 17, 2020, https://now.tufts.edu/news-releases/youth-voter-turnout-analysis-shows-across-board-increases-2018-midterms.

[49] "County by County, Young People of Color Key to Democratic Candidates in Close Races," CIRCLE: The Center for Information & Research on Civic Learning and Engagement, November 12, 2018, https://civicyouth.org/county-by-county-young-people-of-color-key-to-democratic-candidates-in-close-races/.

[50] Voto Latino, "The Latinx Voting Bloc Transformed 2020," accessed March 8, 2022, https://votolatino.org/understand-the-vote/.

[51] Matt Barreto, "Is Texas Turning Purple?," *Latino Decisions,* March 8, 2019, http://latinodecisions.com/wp-content/uploads/2019/06/SxSW_Texas_Purple.pdf.

[52] Ibid., 43.

[53] Michael P. McDonald, "2020 November General Election Turnout Rates," 2020, United States Elections Project, http://www.electproject.org/2020g.

[54] Ibid., 43.

[55] The Texas Secretary of State, "Texas Election Results," https://results.texas-election.com/races.

[56] Holly K. Sonneland, "Chart: How U.S. Latinos Voted in the 2020 Presidential Election," Americas Society/Council of the Americas, November 5, 2020, https://www.as-coa.org/articles/chart-how-us-latinos-voted-2020-presidential-election.

[57] Gaige Davila, "The Rio Grande Valley's political landscape is changing amid midterm, governor elections," Texas Public

Radio, December 28, 2021, https://www.tpr.org/border-immigration/2021-12-28/the-rio-grande-valleys-political-landscape-is-changing-amid-midterm-governor-elections.

[58] Jack Herrera, "Trump Didn't Win the Latino Vote in Texas. He Won the Tejano Vote: Understanding the Difference Will Be Key to Democrats Moving Past Their Faltering, One-size-fits-all Approach to Hispanics," *Politico,* November 17, 2020, https://www.politico.com/news/magazine/2020/11/17/trump-latinos-south-texas-tejanos-437027.

[59] Marjorie Randon Hershey, "What We Know about Voter-ID Laws, Registration, and Turnout," *PS* January 2009: 87-91; Bernard Fraga and Michael Miller, "Who Does Voter ID Keep from Voting?" updated January 1, 2021, https://www.dropbox.com/s/gbw7ldftbqu2jvv/Miller-Paper%201%20Voter%20ID.pdf?dl=0.

[60] Texas Secretary of State, "Secretary Whitley Issues Advisory on Voter Registration List Maintenance Activity," https://www.sos.texas.gov/about/newsreleases/2019/012519.shtml.

[61] *Texas League of United Latin American Citizens, et al. v. Whitley et al.,* https://texascivilrightsproject.org/wp-content/uploads/2019/02/Voter-Purge-MTD-Order.pdf.

[62] Office of the Texas Governor, "Governor Abbott Signs Election Integrity Legislation Into Law," September 7, 2021, https://gov.texas.gov/news/post/governor-abbott-signs-election-integrity-legislation-into-law.

[63] Alexa Ura, "Gov. Greg Abbott signs Texas voting bill into law, overcoming Democratic quorum breaks," *The Texas Tribune,* September 7, 2021, https://www.texastribune.org/2021/09/01/texas-voting-bill-greg-abbott/; Amy McCaig, "Drive-through voting is a hit with Harris County voters, according to newly released Rice U. survey," Rice University *Rice News,* August 24, 2021, https://news.rice.edu/news/2021/drive-through-voting-hit-harris-county-voters-according-newly-released-rice-u-survey; Peter Holley, "Meet the Harris County Voters Who Showed Up After Midnight to Cast a Ballot," *Texas Monthly,* October 30, 2020, https://www.texasmonthly.com/news-politics/harris-county-24-hour-voting/.

[64] SB1, Texas Congress 87(1), 2021, https://capitol.texas.gov/BillLookup/History.aspx?LegSess=871&Bill=SB1.

[65] Scot Schraufnagel, Michael J. Pomante II, and Quan Li, "Cost of Voting in the American States: 2020," *Election Law Journal: Rules, Politics, and Policy* (Dec 2020): 503–509.

[66] American Civil Liberties Union, "Block the Vote: How Politicians are Trying to Block Voters from the Ballot Box," August 17, 2021, https://www.aclu.org/news/civil-liberties/block-the-vote-voter-suppression-in-2020/.

[67] SB1, Texas Congress 87(1), 2021, https://capitol.texas.gov/BillLookup/History.aspx?LegSess=871&Bill=SB1.

[68] Ashely Lopez, "High Numbers of Mail Ballots are Being Rejected in Texas Under a New State Law," February 15,

2022, https://www.npr.org/2022/02/15/1080739353/high-numbers-of-mail-ballots-are-being-rejected-in-texas-after-a-new-state-law.

[69] Paul J. Weber and Acacia Coronado, "Texas Flagged 27,000 Mail Ballots for Rejection in Primary," *The Associated Press*, March 9, 2022, https://apnews.com/article/2022-midterm-elections-elections-austin-texas-voting-f28a41bf6482c-25299c99a8ea52734be.

[70] Nick Corasaniti, "Mail Ballot Rejections Surge in Texas, With Signs of a Race Gap," *The New York Times*, March 18, 2022, https://www.nytimes.com/2022/03/18/us/politics/texas-primary-ballot-rejections.html.

[71] Ibid.

[72] Taylor Goldenstein, "Court blocks new restrictions on voters' assistants in Texas," *Houston Chronicle*, July 20, 2022, https://www.houstonchronicle.com/politics/texas/article/Court-blocks-new-restrictions-on-voters-17318405.php.

[73] Democracy Docket, "Texas Residency Restriction Bill: Texas State LULAC v. Elfant," August 23, 2022, https://www.democracydocket.com/cases/texas-residency-restriction-bill/.

[74] Jayne C. Timm, "Georgia Republicans are pushing dozens of 'election integrity' bills. Black voters are the target, rights groups say," March 8, 2021, https://www.nbcnews.com/politics/elections/georgia-republicans-are-pushing-dozens-election-integrity-bills-black-voters-n1259687.

[75] Jim Henson and Joshua Blank, "The Deeply Polarized Public Opinion Context of Texas House Democrats' Flight to D.C. to Obstruct GOP Voting Laws," June 2021 poll update relating to voting and elections, https://texaspolitics.utexas.edu/blog/deeply-polarized-public-opinion-context-texas-house-democrats%E2%80%99-flight-dc-obstruct-gop-voting#part4.

[76] Edwards County Sheriff's Office, "Illegal Voting Arrest in Edwards County," Press Release, September 5, 2016, https://www.edwardscountysheriff.org/press_view.php?id=47.

[77] Houston Chronicle, "Two Are Indicted on Separate Voter Fraud Cases, Official Says," June 4, 2005, https://www.chron.com/news/houston-texas/article/Two-are-indicted-on-separate-voter-fraud-cases-1934806.php.

[78] A. David Pardo, "Election Law Violations," *American Criminal Law Review*, Volume 45 (2), 2008: 305–339.

[79] Office of the Attorney General of Texas, "Election Integrity," accessed May 6, 2022, https://www.texasattorneygeneral.gov/initiatives/election-integrity.

[80] Paul Livengood, "Yes, There is Voter Fraud in Texas. No, It's Not Widespread," KVUE ABC News Verify, July 14, 2021, https://www.kvue.com/article/news/verify/texas-voter-fraud-cases-verify/269-205e72be-17a1-4c34-8156-8321ff1ddd78.

[81] The Secretary of State of Texas, "Turnout and Voter Registration Figures (1970-current)," accessed May 6, 2022, sos.state.tx.us/elections/historical/70-92.shtml.

[82] Ibid.

[83] Jerrold G. Rusk and John J. Stucker, "6. The Effect of the Southern System of Election Laws on Voting Participation: A Reply to V. O. Key, Jr" In *The History of American Electoral Behavior* edited by Joel H. Silbey and Allan G. Bogue (Princeton: Princeton University Press, 2015): 198–250; Sari Horwitz, "Getting a Photo ID so You Can Vote is Easy. Unless You're Poor, Black, Latino or Elderly," *The Washington Post*, May 23, 2016, https://www.washingtonpost.com/politics/courts_law/getting-a-photo-id-so-you-can-vote-is-easy-unless-youre-poor-black-latino-or-elderly/2016/05/23/8d5474ec-20f0-11e6-8690-f14ca9de2972_story.html.

[84] Taylor Goldenstein, "Texas Republicans quietly reduced penalties for honest voting mistakes," *Houston Chronicle,* September 10, 2021, https://www.houstonchronicle.com/politics/texas/article/Voters-who-make-mistakes-get-a-break-with-new-16450334.php.

[85] Texas Secretary of State, "Laws and Procedures Pertaining to Local Election Officials (Cities, Schools and Other Political Subdivisions)," accessed May 6, 2022, https://www.sos.state.tx.us/elections/laws/local-laws.shtml.

[86] *Marisa F. Leal v. Minvera M. Peña*, No. 2020-DCL-06433, District Court of 107th Judicial District of Cameron County, TX (2020), https://texasscorecard.com/wp-content/uploads/2022/02/2020-DCL-06433-Findings-of-Fact.pdf; Rudy Mireles, "State District Judge to Order Brownsville ISD Runoff Election," January 26, 2022, https://www.krgv.com/news/state-district-judge-to-order-brownsville-isd-runoff-election/.

[87] *De La Paz v. Gutierrez*, No. 13-18-00377-CV, Court of Appeals 13th District of Texas Corpus Christi-Edinburg (2018), https://casetext.com/case/de-la-paz-v-gutierrez-1.

[88] Ray Leszcynski, "Judge sends Kaufman County race to special election after finding voter fraud but no way to determine winner," *The Dallas Morning News*, April 13, 2018, https://www.dallasnews.com/news/2018/04/13/judge-sends-kaufman-county-race-to-special-election-after-finding-voter-fraud-but-no-way-to-determine-winner/; note article title says fraud but article body presents different information.

[89] *Armando O'Caña v. Norberto Salinas*, No. 13-18-00563-CV, Court of Appeals 13th District of Texas Corpus Christi-Edinburg (2018), https://www.documentcloud.org/documents/5784450-13-18-00563-CV-V18563-O-Cana-v-Salinas-DC-FINAL.html.

[90] *Heath v. Paxton*, Civil Action No. H-21-0088, United States District Court for the Southern District of Texas Houston Division (2021), https://casetext.com/case/heath-v-paxton; Jay R. Jordan, "On Day of Heath's Arrest, Attorney Still Fighting for His Freedom," *San Antonio Express News*, February 7th, 2017, https://www.mysanantonio.com/neighborhood/woodlands/news/article/Woodlands-man-starts-3-year-sentence-for-10914586.php#photo-12326110.

[91] Robert A. Calvert and Arnold DeLeon, *The History of Texas* (Arlington Heights, IL: Harland Davidson, 1990), 212.

[92] The state tax was $1.50. The county was permitted to add 25 cents, and most county governments did so. See Article 7, Section 3 of the Texas Constitution, 1902.

[93] Robert A. Calvert and Arnold DeLeon, *The History of Texas* (Arlington Heights, IL: Harland Davidson, 1990), 387.

[94] *Texas v. United States,* 384 U.S. 155 (1966).

[95] Texas State Historical Association, "Voter Participation in Texas," *Texas Almanac,* http://texasalmanac.com/sites/default/files/images/topics/prezturnout.pdf.

[96] *Beare v. Smith,* 321 F.Supp. 1100.

[97] Ibid.

[98] *Nixon v. Herndon et al.,* 273 U.S. 536 (1927).

[99] Sanford N. Greenberg, "White Primary," *Handbook of Texas Online,* published by the Texas State Historical Association, http://www.tshaonline.org/handbook/online/articles/wdw01.

[100] *Nixon v. Condon et al.,* 286 U.S. 73 (1932).

[101] *Nixon v. Condon et al.,* 286 U.S. 73, 47 (1932).

[102] *Grovey v. Townsend,* 295 U.S. 45 (1935).

[103] *Smith v. Allwright,* 321 U.S. 649 (1944). Also, in *United States v. Classic,* 313 U.S. 299 (1941), the U.S. Supreme Court ruled that a primary in a one-party state (Louisiana) was an election within the meaning of the U.S. Constitution.

[104] Richard Rothstein, *The Color of Law: A Forgotten History of How Our Government Segregated America* (New York: Liveright, 2018).

[105] David Gutierrez, *The Columbia History of Latinos in the United States Since 1960* (New York: Columbia University Press, 2004), 425–30.

[106] Cynthia Orozco, *No Mexicans, Women, or Dogs Allowed: The Rise of the Mexican American Civil Rights Movement* (Austin: University of Texas Press, 2009).

[107] William D. Carrigan and Clive Webb, *The Forgotten Dead: Mob Violence against Mexicans in the United States, 1848-1928* (New York: Oxford University Press, 2013).

[108] Henry C. Garcia, *Rise of the Mexican American Middle Class: San Antonio, 1929-1941* (College Station: Texas A&M University Press, 1991); David Gutierrez, *The Columbia History of Latinos in the United States Since 1960* (New York: Columbia University Press, 2004), 425–30; Arnoldo De León, "Mexican Americans," *Handbook of Texas Online,* Texas State Historical Association, last modified January 26, 2017, http://www.tshaonline.org/handbook/online/articles/pqmue.

[109] Cynthia Orozco, *No Mexicans, Women, or Dogs Allowed: The Rise of the Mexican American Civil Rights Movement* (Austin: University of Texas Press, 2009), 34–39; Arnoldo De León, "Mexican Americans," *Handbook of Texas Online,* Texas State Historical Association, last modified January 26, 2017, http://www.tshaonline.org/handbook/online/articles/pqmue.

[110] Ibid.

[111] *Hernandez v. Texas, Oyez,* www.oyez.org/cases/1940-1955/347us475; V. Carl Allsup, "Hernandez v. State of Texas," *Handbook of Texas Online,* last modified August 3, 2017, http://www.tshaonline.org/handbook/online/articles/jrh01.

[112] Henry Flores, *Latinos and the Voting Rights Act: the Search for Racial Purpose* (Lanham, MD: Lexington, 2015), 27–31.

[113] George McKenna, *The Drama of Democracy: American Government and Politics,* 2nd ed. (Guilford, CT: Dushkin, 1994), 129.

[114] A. Elizabeth Taylor, "Woman Suffrage," *Handbook of Texas Online,* http://www.tshaonline.org/handbook/online/articles/viw01.

[115] Michael P. McDonald, "Voter Turnout Demographics," *United States Elections Project,* 2016, http://www.electproject.org/home/voter-turnout.

[116] Ibid.

[117] Center for Information and Research on Civic Learning and Engagement, "State-by-State 2020 Youth Voter Turnout: The South," March 30, 2021, https://circle.tufts.edu/latest-research/state-state-2020-youth-voter-turnout-south.

[118] Anthony Cilluffo and Richard Fry, "Gen Z, Millennials and Gen X Outvoted Older Generations in 2018 Midterms," Pew Research Center, Mary 29, 2019, https://www.pewresearch.org/fact-tank/2019/05/29/gen-z-millennials-and-gen-x-outvoted-older-generations-in-2018-midterms/.

[119] Michael McDonald, "Voter Turnout Demographics," U.S. Elections Project, accessed March 28, 2022, http://www.electproject.org/home/voter-turnout/demographics.

[120] Tasha Philpot, Daron R. Shaw, and Ernest B. McGowen, "Winning the Race: Black Voter Turnout in the 2008 Presidential Election," *The Public Opinion Quarterly* Vol. 73, No. 5, Understanding the 2008 Presidential Election (2009), pp. 995–1022.

[121] U.S. Census Bureau, "Voting and Registration in the Election of 2012—Detailed Tables," Table 4b, Reported Voting and Registration by Sex, Race and Hispanic Origin, for States: November 2012, http://www.census.gov/hhes/www/socdemo/voting/publications/p20/2012/tables.html.

[122] Michael McDonald, "National General Election VEP Turnout Rates, 1789-Present," United States Elections Project, http://www.electproject.org/national-1789-present.

[123] Drew Desilver, "Turnout Soared in 2020 as Nearly Two-thirds of Eligible U.S. Voters Cast Ballots for President," Pew Research Center, January 28, 2021, https://www.pewresearch.org/fact-tank/2021/01/28/turnout-soared-in-2020-as-nearly-two-thirds-of-eligible-u-s-voters-cast-ballots-for-president/.

[124] Center for Information and Research on Civic Learning and Engagement, "State-by-State 2020 Youth Voter Turnout: The South," March 30, 2021, https://circle.tufts.edu/latest-research/state-state-2020-youth-voter-turnout-south.

[125] U.S. Census Bureau, "Hispanic Heritage Month 2020," August 11, 2020, https://www.census.gov/newsroom/facts-for-features/2020/hispanic-heritage-month.html.

[126] Ashley Lopez, "Turnout among Young Texas Voters Exploded in 2018. Groups Want to Make It Even Bigger in 2020," *Texas Tribune*, September 24, 2019, https://www.texastribune.org/2019/09/24/young-texas-voter-turnout-exploded-2018-some-want-it-even-bigger-2020/.

[127] UCLA Latino Policy and Politics Initiative, "Vote Choice of Latino Voters in the 2020 Presidential Election Report," January 18, 2021, https://latino.ucla.edu/research/latino-voters-in-2020-election/.

[128] Jens Manuel Krogstad and Luis Noe-Bustamante, "7 Facts for National Hispanic Heritage Month," Pew Research Center, October 14, 2019, https://www.pewresearch.org/fact-tank/2019/10/14/facts-for-national-hispanic-heritage-month/; Paul Taylor, Ana Gonzalez-Barrera, Jeffrey S. Passel, et al., "An Awakened Giant: The Hispanic Electorate Is Likely to Double by 2030," Pew Research Center, November 14, 2012, http://www.pewhispanic.org/2012/11/14/an-awakened-giant-the-hispanic-electorate-is-likely-to-double-by-2030/.

[129] Mike Ward and Kevin Diaz, "Democrats Again Holding Out Hope That Latino Voters Will Make a Difference," *San Antonio Express-News,* https://www.expressnews.com/news/local/article/Democrats-once-again-holding-out-hope-that-Latino-12497869.php.

[130] Alexa Ura and Ryan Murphy, "Despite High Expectations for 2016, No Surge in Texas Hispanic Voter Turnout," *Texas Tribune,* May 11, 2017, https://www.texastribune.org/2017/05/11/hispanic-turnout-2016-election/.

[131] Ibid.

[132] Matt Stiles and Zahira Torres, "Texas Still Waiting for Latinos to Show Power at Polls," *Texas Tribune*, July 26, 2010, https://www.texastribune.org/2010/07/26/texas-still-waiting-for-latinos-to-vote/.

[133] Eileen Patten, "The Nation's Latino Population Is Defined by Its Youth," Pew Research Center, April 20, 2016, http://www.pewhispanic.org/2016/04/20/the-nations-latinopopulation- is-defined-by-its-youth/.

[134] U.S. Census Bureau, "Voting and Registration in the Election of November 2020," April 2021, https://www.census.gov/data/tables/time-series/demo/voting-and-registration/p20-585.html.

[135] Ibid., 133.

[136] "The Strength of the Latina Vote: Gender Differences in Latino Voting Participation," *California Civic Engagement Project Policy Brief Special Series: Issue Three*, October 2018, https://static1.squarespace.com/static/57b8c7ce15d5dbf599fb46ab/t/5bd98162562fa7963a63969c/1540981094145/UNIDOS+CCEP+Brief+3+Final+10+31+18.pdf.

[137] National Conference of State Legislatures, "Felon Voting Rights," January 4, 2016, http://www.ncsl.org/research/elections-and-campaigns/felon-voting-rights.aspx.

[138] Texas Secretary of State, "Effect of Felony Conviction on Voter Registration," http://www.sos.state.tx.us/elections/laws/effects.shtml.

[139] The Sentencing Project, "Texas Should Restore Voting Rights to 500,000 Citizens," February 2021, https://www.sentencingproject.org/wp-content/uploads/2021/02/TX-Voting-Brief.pdf

[140] See Andre Blais, "What Affects Voter Turnout?," *Annual Review of Political Science* 9 (2006): 119.

[141] Andre Blais, "What Affects Voter Turnout?," *Annual Review of Political Science* 9 (2006): 119; G. Bingham Powell Jr., "American Voter Turnout in Comparative Perspective," *American Political Science Review* 80, no. 1 (March 1986): 17–43.

[142] Texas Secretary of State, "Historical Election Results (1992–Current)," http://elections.sos.state.tx.us/index.htm.

[143] Shiying Cheng and Ross Ramsey, "Is Texas Really Going Purple? Our Heat Index Shows How Competitive Your District Was—and Is," *Texas Tribune*, June 4, 2019, https://apps.texastribune.org/features/2019/texas-turn-blue-voting-pattern-history/.

[144] Ballotpedia, "Municipal Elections in Austin, Texas (2014)," https://ballotpedia.org/Municipal_elections_in_Austin,_Texas_(2014).

[145] Ryan Autullo and Philip Jankowski, "Voters Say Yes to Switching Election Cycle for Austin Mayor, No to Adding Council District," *Austin American-Statesman*, May 2, 2021, https://www.statesman.com/story/news/2021/05/01/austin-election-results-propositions-homeless-camping-strong-mayor/7220640002/.

[146] Peter Grier, "Election Day 2010: Why We Always Vote on Tuesdays," *Christian Science Monitor*, November 2, 2010, http://www.csmonitor.com/USA/DC-Decoder/Decoder-Wire/2010/1102/Election-Day-2010-Why-we-always-vote-on-Tuesdays.

[147] Andre Blais, "What Affects Voter Turnout?," *Annual Review of Political Science* 9 (2006): 116.

[148] Julia Van Susteren, "Early Voting Has Little Effect," *Badger Herald*, October 2, 2012, http://badgerherald.com/news/2012/10/02/early_voting_has_lit.php.

[149] Richard J. Timpone, 1998, "Structure, Behavior, and Voter Turnout in the United States," *American Political Science Review* 92. no. 1 (1998): 145–58, https://doi.org/10.2307/2585934.

[150] Timothy E. Cook and Paul Gronke, "The Skeptical American: Revisiting the Meanings of Trust in Government and Confidence in Institutions," *The Journal of Politics* 67, no. 3 (August 2005): 784–803, https://doi.org/10.1111/j.1468-2508.2005.00339.x.

[151] Joshua Harder and Jon A. Krosnick, "Why Do People Vote? A Psychological Analysis of the Causes of Voter Turnout," *Journal of Social Issues* 64, no. 3 (September 2008): 525–49, https://doi.org/10.1111/j.1540-4560.2008.00576.x; Sari Sharoni, "E-Citizenship: Trust in Government, Political Efficacy, and Political Participation in the Internet Era," *Electronic Media & Politics* 1, no. 8 (July 2012): 119–35, https://ssrn.com/abstract=3342574.

[152] Luke Keele, "The Authorities Really Do Matter: Party Control and Trust in Government," *The Journal of Politics* 67, no. 3 (August 2005): 873–86, https://doi.org/10.1111/j.1468-2508.2005.00343.x.

[153] Jack Citrin and Christopher Muste, "Trust in Government," in *Measures of Social Psychological Attitudes, Vol. 2: Measures of Political Attitudes,* ed. J. P. Robinson, P. R. Shaver, and L. S. Wrightsman (New York: Academic Press, 1999); Sarah Birch, "Perceptions of Electoral Fairness and Voter Turnout," *Journal of Comparative Political Studies* 43, no. 12 (2010): 1601–22.

[154] Devra Coren Moehler, *Distrusting Democrats: Outcomes of Participatory Constitution Making* (Ann Arbor: University of Michigan Press, March 11, 2008).

[155] Office of the Texas Governor, "Governor Abbott Signs Election Integrity Legislation Into Law," September 7, 2021, https://gov.texas.gov/news/post/governor-abbott-signs-election-integrity-legislation-into-law.

[156] Jim Henson and Joshua Blank, "Polling Suggests Texas GOP-Led Election Reform Didn't Increase Overal Trust in State Election Results," January 6, 2022, https://texaspolitics.utexas.edu/blog/polling-suggests-texas-gop-led-election-reform-didn%E2%80%99t-increase-overall-trust-state-election.

[157] Kenneth Arrow, "The Organization of Economic Activity: Issues Pertinent to the Choice of Market versus Non-market Allocation," 1969, http://msuweb.montclair.edu/lebelp/PSC643IntPolEcon/ArrowNonMktActivity1969.pdf. I first saw this quoted in a draft paper by David P. Myatt titled, "On the Rational Choice Theory of Voter Turnout." There is an enormous amount of research on this question, starting with key works such as Anthony Downs, *An Economic Theory of Democracy* (New York: Harper and Row, 1957); Gordon Tullock, *Toward a Mathematics of Politics* (Ann Arbor: University of Michigan Press, 1967); and William Riker and Peter Ordeshook, "A Theory of the Calculus of Voting." *American Political Science Review* 62, no. 1 (1968): 25–42.

[158] For a review of the literature on "expressive" voting, see Alan Hamlin and Colin Jennings, "Expressive Political Behaviour: Foundations, Scope and Implications," *British Journal of Political Science,* 2011.

[159] Kenneth Arrow, "The Organization of Economic Activity: Issues Pertinent to the Choice of Market versus Non-market Allocation," 1969, http://msuweb.montclair.edu/lebelp/PSC643IntPolEcon/ArrowNonMktActivity1969.pdf.

[160] Center for Responsive Politics, "Texas State Summary 2020 Cycle," updated March 22, 2021, https://www.opensecrets.org/states/summary.php?cycle=2020&state=TX.

[161] Ibid.

[162] Henry Brady, Sidney Verba, and Kay Schlozman, "Beyond SES: A Resource Model of Political Participation," *American Political Science Review* 89, no. 2 (June 1995).

[163] Bernard L. Fraga, *The Turnout Gap: Race, Ethnicity, and Political Inequality in a Diversifying America* (New York: Cambridge University Press, 2018).

[164] See graph "Presidential Turnout Rates 1948–2012," Michael P. McDonald, "Voter Turnout," *United States Elections Project*, http://www.electproject.org/home/voter-turnout.

[165] Russell Dalton, *The Good Citizen: How a Younger Generation Is Reshaping American Politics* (Washington, D.C.: CQ Press, 2008).

[166] Many scholars have found this to be the case. See Andre Blais, "What Affects Voter Turnout?," *Annual Review of Political Science* 9 (2006): 123.

CHAPTER 10

Campaigns and Elections in Texas

Texas Learning Outcome

- Analyze the state and local election process in Texas.

Campaigns and elections are the heart of any democratic system and perform a number of important functions that make government work. Campaigns precede elections, often by a year or more, and are the process by which candidates seek the support of the electorate to vote them into office. Elections bestow legitimacy upon government; without them, all actions of governments are questionable. Campaigns and elections provide for an orderly transition of power from one group to another where, most importantly, the public perceives the newly elected government as legitimate. One of the great stabilizing forces in the American system of government has been this orderly

Texas delegates wave their hands during the final day of the Republican National Convention in Cleveland, Thursday, July 21, 2016.

Andrew Harnik/AP Images

transfer of power. Elections also allow citizens to express their opinions about public policy choices. By voting in elections, citizens express what they want the government to do. Elections are still the most essential element of any democracy, despite the fact that many citizens do not participate in them.

Chapter Learning Objectives

- Describe political campaigns in Texas, including the use of consultants and the role of money.

- Explain the election process in Texas.

- Discuss ballot forms in Texas.

- Discuss ballot access in Texas.

- Describe primary elections.

- Explain special elections.

- Describe the federal Voting Rights Act.

- Discuss absentee and early voting.

- Discuss ways in which the nature of elections has changed.

Campaigns

Learning Objective: Describe political campaigns in Texas, including the use of consultants and the role of money.

State senator Donna Campbell, R–New Braunfels, speaks at a Senate Finance Committee hearing at the Capitol in Austin, Texas, on July 23, 2017.

Jay Janner/Austin American-Statesman/AP Images

Campaign activity in Texas has changed considerably in the past two or three decades. These changes are part of a national trend. Early campaigns consisted of candidates engaging directly with citizens: making speeches and often pandering to the populace to garner votes. By the 1800s, however, the use of print media in campaigning was fairly common. Today, candidates for office rely on all forms of media to promote name recognition and their message.

The Role of the Media in Campaigns and Elections

In modern Texas, the media play a significant role in political campaigns. Reporters often follow candidates for statewide office as they travel the vast expanses of Texas. Political rallies are still held but are most often used to gain media attention and convey the candidate's message to a larger audience. Candidates hope these events will show a favorable image of them to the public.

Heavy media coverage can have disadvantages for the candidates. For instance, in 1990 Clayton Williams, the Republican candidate for governor, held a media event on one of his West Texas ranches. He and "the boys" were to round up cattle for branding in a display designed to portray Williams as a hardworking rancher. Unfortunately for Williams, rain spoiled the event and it had to be postponed. Resigned to the rain delay, Williams told the reporters, "It's like rape. When it's inevitable, relax and enjoy it." The state press extensively reported and commented on this remark, and it probably hurt Williams's chances with many voters and contributed to his eventual loss. The fact that his opponent was a woman (Ann Richards) helped magnify the significance of the statement.[1]

Similarly, in 1994, George W. Bush was the Republican candidate for governor running against incumbent Ann Richards. In Texas, the opening day of dove season is in September, and the event marks the beginning of the fall hunting season. Both Bush and Richards participated in opening-day hunts in an attempt to appeal to the strong hunting and gun element in the state. Unfortunately for Bush, he shot a killdeer by mistake rather than a dove. Pictures of Bush holding the dead bird appeared in most state papers and on television. He was fined for shooting a migratory bird. A Texas Democratic group in Austin produced bumper stickers reading: "Guns don't kill killdeer. People do." In 1998, Governor Bush did not have a media event for the opening day of dove season. He was so far ahead in the polls that even opening the issue could have resulted in nothing but a painful reminder.

Most campaign events are not as disastrous as the cattle-branding and dove-hunting incidents. Some gain attention and free media coverage for the candidate; however, free media attention is never enough. Candidates must buy time on television and radio and space in newspapers. In a state as large as Texas, this can be costly. Refer to Chapter 8 to learn more about the media and its role in national and state elections.

CORE OBJECTIVE

Being Socially Responsible . . .

What responsibility do you think the media have in covering campaigns and elections? Are the media living up to your expectations?

Political Consultants

Using professional campaign consultants is common in almost all political races. Most candidates need such professionals to help run their campaigns. If their opponents use professionals, candidates might face a disadvantage by not having one.

TABLE 10.1

Total Donated Money in State Campaigns from 2012 to 2020

Category	2012 Cycle	2014 Cycle	2016 Cycle	2018 Cycle	2020 Cycle
Total Itemized Contributions	$347,236,696	$152,825,947	$323,124,854	$295,940,533	$690,959,847
Total to Candidates and Parties	$234,143,043	$124,498,567	$243,108,450	$236,935,483	$ 612,757,577
Total to Democrats	$ 59,661,966	$ 31,431,684	$ 75,254,298	$ 94,773,254	$213,076,845
Total to Republicans	$ 171,537,509	$ 88,201,963	$ 161,941,643	$ 133,473,834	$ 387,677,154

Source: OpenSecrets Texas Profile, https://www.opensecrets.org/states/summary.php?state=TX.

focus group

Panel of "average citizens" who are used by political consultants to test ideas and words for later use in campaigns

Professional campaign consultants use many techniques. They take public opinion polls to measure voter reaction to issues so the candidate knows which stands will be most popular. They run **focus groups** in which a panel of "average citizens" reacts to issues or words. Consultants also help the candidate design advertisements and generally "package" the candidate to the voters. In 2002, then–lieutenant governor David Dewhurst filmed a TV spot for his consulting firm, praising its effectiveness in making him look professional. Go to Chapter 8 to learn more about public opinion polling.

Money in Campaigns

Using media advertisements, professional consultants, and a full-time paid campaign staff increases the cost of running for state office. The cost can run into the millions, even for a race for the Texas House of Representatives.

The amount of money spent in campaigns is increasing each election cycle. Much of this money comes from political action committees (PACs) and individual contributions to candidates. Note that donations can be hard or soft. Hard contributions are given directly to a candidate. Soft money contributions are given to a party or PAC for general purposes. Table 10.1 shows the total amounts of money contributed from 2012 to 2020. Note that the amount has gone up and down over time, with higher contributions on presidential election years.

As shown in Table 10.2, statewide races can be quite costly, and costs have continued to increase. Most of the money is coming from PACs, which obviously want something from government for their contributions.

A few candidates have been able to self-finance their campaigns. Vicente Gonzales primarily self-financed his campaign, won the 2016 general election, and became the U.S. Representative for Texas's 15th Congressional District. He self-funded approximately 76 percent of a total of $2.43 million.[2]

Money in campaigns has increased dramatically in recent years. Since the 2010 Supreme Court decision in *Citizens United v. Federal Election Commission,* campaign advertising by corporations and labor unions cannot be prohibited or restricted at the federal level.[3]

Money supplied by PACs obviously affects elected officials. At the least, PAC money buys the group access to the official. At the worst, PAC money buys the vote of the elected official. Distinguishing between the two is almost impossible.

TABLE 10.2

Top Five Candidates Total Contributions Raised in 2018

Race	Candidate	Total Contributions
Governor	Greg Abbott	$103,084,523.47
Lieutenant Governor	Dan Patrick	$ 19,698,820.41
Attorney General	Ken Paxton	$ 12,614,795.96
Texas House Rep District 21	Dade Phelan	$ 6,505,603.24
Land Commissioner	Dawn Buckingham	$ 3,896,780.69

Source: from https://www.transparencyusa.org/tx/candidates.

Most states, including Texas, have passed laws designed to regulate campaign finances. Many other states have passed laws limiting the amount of money that could be spent on campaigns, but the U.S. Supreme Court has invalidated these laws. (See Chapter 12 for more information on interest groups.)

Candidates sometimes lend themselves money that they can later repay with what are often called "late train" contributions. Special interest groups usually will not retire the debts of losers. The law limits the amount of money that a candidate can collect to retire campaign debts for each election (primary, runoff, general) to a total debt amount that is minus any cash on hand, money owed to the candidate by other entities, and personal loans over $250,000 (or $500,000 for gubernatorial candidates). Candidates will take out personal loans to fund a campaign with the hope and expectation that late contributions will help repay this debt. But it can backfire. Exceeding the personal loan limit rule makes it much more difficult for candidates to use late contributions and other funding to make up that loan debt. For example, in January 2022, a case between Texas U.S. Senator Ted Cruz and the Federal Election Commission went to the Supreme Court. Senator Cruz's team argued that the law's limit of debt repayment is at odds with his first amendment rights. Near the end of the 2018 campaign, he had loaned $260,000 and later received the limit of $250,000 in re-payment. The FEC has argued that the remaining $10,000 is to be considered a personal contribution. The Supreme Court ruled in Cruz's favor, striking the $250,000 limit on personal loan repayments.[4]

Today the regulation of campaign finances in Texas is limited to requiring all candidates and PACs to file reports with the Texas State Ethics Commission. All contributions over $50 must be reported with the name of the contributor (see Map 10.1). Expenditure reports must also be filed by the PAC treasurer before and after the election. The idea behind the reporting scheme is to make public the sources of the funds received by candidates and how the candidates spend their funds. Sometimes news media outlets closely examine these reports and give them significant media coverage, but this is not common. The best source for Texans' funds is Texans for Public Justice (www.tpj.org). For the most part, citizens must find out such information on their own, which is difficult for the average citizen. Texas has no limit on the amount of money candidates can spend on their statewide races.

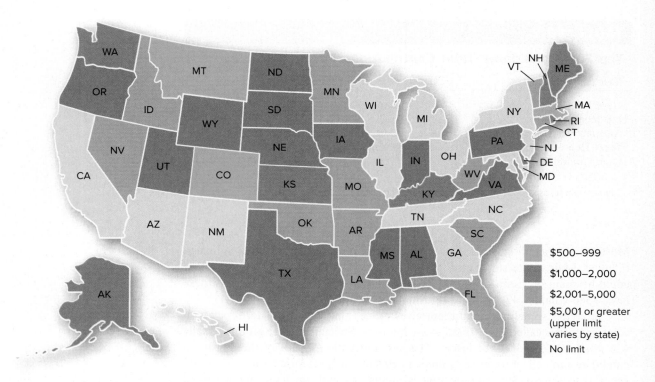

MAP 10.1 **Limitations on PAC Contributions in Statewide Races, 2021–2022** Some states differentiate between types of statewide office, typically separating gubernatorial, legislative, and "other" candidates. House and senate candidates may also be differentiated. For the purposes of this map, gubernatorial candidate limits were chosen if there was any differentiation whatsoever.

Source: National Conference of State Legislatures, "State Limits on Contributions to Candidates 2021–2022 Election Cycle," June 2021, https://www.ncsl.org/Portals/1/Documents/Elections/Contribution_Limits_to_Candidates_2020_2021.pdf.

CORE OBJECTIVE

Taking Personal Responsibility . . .

If you choose to contribute to a candidate's campaign, to what extent is the candidate obligated to you as a contributor? Should your contribution influence public policy? What about corporate contributions?

Understanding Impact The 2010 decision in *Citizens United v. Federal Election Commission* established that the federal government cannot prohibit or limit direct spending on campaign advertising by corporations or labor unions. Although the case applied to federal elections, it left the question unresolved as to the status of 24 states that had laws prohibiting such spending by corporations and labor unions.[5] For example, the Supreme Court ruled in 2012 that Montana's law limiting corporate contributions in support of a candidate or a political party was unconstitutional. Eight other states have repealed laws limiting or prohibiting such spending. Texas's election code provides that "a corporation or labor organization may not make a political contribution or a political expenditure that is not authorized by this subchapter."[6] The Texas legislature amended section 253.094 of the election code pertaining to corporate contributions in 2011. The amendment removed the ban on political expenditures and solely regulated direct campaign contributions.

How to

Get Involved with a Candidate or Issue

Politicians and policy makers establish and enforce rules governing our republic. They decide the type and amount of taxes we pay, regulate trade with foreign nations, provide for national security, and do many other things. Choosing elected officials is one of our most important civic duties.

Our system provides many ways for you to affect the political process. You can vote (our most basic civic duty), post on social media, try to persuade friends and family, contribute money, lobby elected officials, take part in protest marches, or volunteer to work on a candidate's campaign.

Working on a campaign is challenging, fun, and rewarding. If you take this route, you'll perform an important public service and emulate the people who have made America what it is today. The more you know, the more you may respect the process and the office. Here's a step-by-step guide to getting involved.

Step 1: Educate yourself.
Find an issue you want to support or oppose, or a candidate you enthusiastically support or oppose. Do research to be fully informed.

Step 1a: Learn about an issue that intrigues you.
Start with major media outlets. Try the *Texas Tribune*, or perhaps go to a national outlet, such as the *New York Times* or *Washington Post*. Look for information on people or organizations active in your area of concern. Once you've identified good sources, dig deeper to learn more. Visit websites promoting the issue you are investigating. Remember that educating yourself requires understanding the arguments you favor and the arguments you think you oppose. If you can't clearly and honestly articulate arguments on both sides of an issue, you don't really know it. Thoroughly learning the issues will make you a more effective advocate.

Step 1b: Learn about an individual who intrigues you.
If the person is already an elected official, go to his or her official website. You'll learn his or her positions on most issues. But don't stop there. If the person is in the Texas legislature, you can go to https://capitol.texas.gov/Home.aspx. From there you can go to a list of Texas House or Senate members to learn what legislation he or she has authored or supported. If your person of interest is not an incumbent, visit his or her campaign site to learn about positions on issues.

Step 2: Make an informed decision about what or whom you support.
Once you've learned what advocates want you to know about their issues or what politicians want you to know about themselves, remember to spend time finding out what the opposition says. Set aside emotional attachments for the moment, and take the time to appreciate what the folks you disagree with are saying. Otherwise, you may find yourself unable to answer legitimate questions about your position.

Step 3: Find a contact person and get in touch.
Once you've settled whom or what to support, find a way to volunteer. Campaign websites generally have a "get involved" page. In smaller races, such as a state House race, the candidate's web presence may be less sophisticated. In that case, you may find a contact person through the county political party site.

If you want to advocate for an issue, your research in the previous steps will have made you familiar with related organizations. Check their websites for "Contact Us" links. Many organizations are eager for recruits. Alternatively, those organizations may suggest ways you can work on your own or with others to achieve the goals you share.

Step 4: Follow through.
Effective advocacy takes hard work and persistence. That's why it helps to connect with like-minded individuals. They can share the workload and provide ongoing support. Stay focused on your goals, and keep working.

The Election Process

Learning Objective: Explain the election process in Texas.

Elections occur at regular intervals as determined by state and federal laws. All states conduct elections on two-year cycles. The date established by federal law for electing members of the U.S. Congress and the president is the first Tuesday after the first Monday in November of even-numbered years. States must elect members of Congress and vote for the president on this date. Most states also use this November date to elect governors, state officials, state legislators, and some local offices.

general elections

Regular elections held every two years to elect state officeholders

Texas holds **general elections** every two years. During nonpresidential years, voters elect candidates to statewide offices: governor, lieutenant governor, attorney general, land commissioner, agricultural commissioner, comptroller, some members of the Texas Railroad Commission and the Texas State Board of Education, and some members of the Texas Supreme Court and the Court of Criminal Appeals.[7] Before 1976, all nonjudicial officeholders served two-year terms. In 1977, the state constitution was amended to allow four-year terms, which began in 1978.

Every two years, voters also elect all 150 members of the Texas House of Representatives (for two-year terms), one-half of the members of the Texas Senate (for four-year terms), many judges to various courts, and local county officials.[8]

Understanding Impact Why do you think most states have chosen to also hold their statewide elections on the first Tuesday after the first Monday of November? How does consistency of dates impact voters?

Ballot Form

Learning Objective: Discuss ballot forms in Texas.

ballot form

The forms used by voters to cast their ballots; each county, with approval of the secretary of state, determines the form of the ballot

Each county in Texas decides the **ballot form** and method of casting ballots. The secretary of state's office must approve the method used to cast votes. That office has precleared some systems, and counties can choose any of these systems.

party column format

Paper ballot form where candidates are listed by party and by office

Texas counties formerly used paper ballots with a **party column format,** where candidates were listed by party and by office. The party that holds the governor's office was the first party column on the ballot. Being first on the ballot is an advantage—voters often choose the first name when all candidates are unfamiliar to them. The party column ballot also encouraged straight-ticket voting and was advocated strongly by the Democratic Party for many years. In recent years, straight-ticket voting has worked to the advantage of the Republicans in some elections, especially judicial offices.

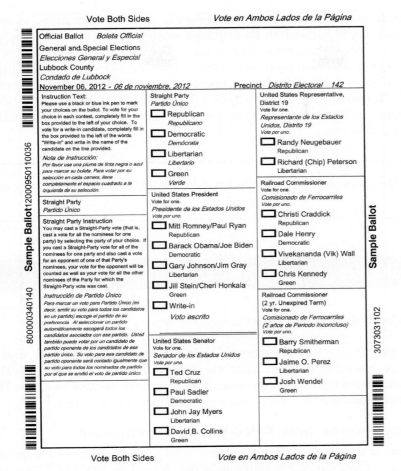

FIGURE 10.1 A Sample Texas General Election Ballot in Office Block Format

Source: Kaufman County, Texas; Texas Secretary of State, 2016; "2016 Nov. 08 General Election," Forney Votes, accessed August 2018.

Since the 2008 election, all 254 counties in Texas have used electronic voting systems. These systems were purchased with federal funds provided by the Help America Vote Act of 2002. The secretary of state must approve all electronic voting systems before counties can buy them. All counties are split fairly evenly between Electronic Systems Software (ES&S) and the Hart e-slate systems; only two counties use a different vendor specifically for their optical scanners only.[9]

Most computer ballots are in **office block format** (see Figure 10.1). This ballot form lists the office (such as president), followed by the candidates by party (such as Republican: Donald Trump, Democrat: Joseph R. Biden). Before each election, the ballot for each county system in Texas is available on individual county websites or the Texas secretary of state website.

Many people believe the office block format discourages straight-ticket voting, which we will discuss in Chapter 11. However, Texas law has allowed

office block format

Ballot form where candidates are listed by office with party affiliation listed by their name; most often used with computer ballots computer-readable ballots to enable voters to vote a straight ticket, as shown on the ballot in Figure 10.1. By marking a single place on the ballot, the voter could vote for all candidates for that party. The voter could then override this by voting in individual races. For example, a voter could vote a straight Republican ticket but override this by selecting some Democratic candidates. In 2017, Governor Greg Abbott signed a bill to eliminate straight-ticket voting beginning in September 2020, so Texas voters are unlikely to see a straight-ticket option again.

Understanding Impact How do you think the elimination of straight-ticket voting will impact elections? Explain your conclusions.

Ballot Access to the November General Election

Learning Objective: Discuss ballot access in Texas.

To appear on the November general election ballot, candidates must meet criteria established by state law. Each state has its own set of requirements. These criteria prevent the lists of candidates from being unreasonably long. The Texas Election Code specifies three ways for names to be on the ballot.[10]

Independent and Third-Party Candidates

independent candidate
A person whose name appears on the ballot without a political party designation

To run as an independent, a candidate must file a petition with a specified number of signatures. For statewide office, signatures equal to 1 percent of the votes cast for governor in the past general election are required.[11] For example, in the 2022 governor's race, a total of 7.96 million votes were cast.[12] An **independent candidate** for statewide office in 2022 has to collect at least 83,000 signatures. For multicounty offices, such as state representative, signatures equal to 5 percent of the votes cast for that office in the past election are needed. On average, 30,000 to 40,000 votes are cast in house races.[13] For county offices, signatures equal to 5 percent of votes cast for those offices are needed. This might seem like a large number of signatures, but the process is intended to weed out people who do not have a serious chance of being elected. Few candidates file for statewide office as independents. However, independents and third-party candidates often run in house and senate races. In the 2020 Texas House election cycle, for example, 21 people filed as Libertarians, two filed as Green Party members, and one filed as Independent for the 150 Texas house seats.[14] Even if these candidates declare a party, such as Libertarian, they may still be considered independents under the state election code.

Getting signatures on a petition is not easy. Each signer must be a registered voter and must not have participated in the primary elections of other parties in that electoral cycle. For example, persons who voted in either the Democratic or the Republican Party primary were not eligible to sign a petition to have

Ross Perot's Reform Party placed on the 1996 ballot. Signing the petition is considered the same as voting. This provision of state law makes it more difficult for independents to gather signatures and be placed on the ballot.

The 2006 governor's race in Texas was an exception to this. Carole Keeton Strayhorn, then comptroller, and Kinky Friedman, a country-western singer and mystery writer, qualified for positions on the ballot as independents. Friedman and Strayhorn suffered the same fate as most independent and minor party candidates: they did not win, but they pulled enough votes away from the Democratic candidate to upset the election outcome. Governor Perry won with a plurality of 38.1 percent, while Friedman won 12.6 percent and Strayhorn 18 percent. Chris Bell, the Democratic candidate, did better than expected with 30 percent. The role of these independent candidates was to help reelect the Republican governor who, after six years in office, managed to capture less than 40 percent of the votes.

Candidates who were defeated in the primary election may not file as independents in the general election for that year. This is the **"sore loser" law.** Write-in candidates are sometimes confused with people who file and are listed on the ballot as independents. The process of filing as a write-in candidate is a separate procedure. To be "official" **write-in candidates,** individuals must file their intention before the election. This is true for all elections, including local, city, and school board elections. If a person does not file before the election, votes for that person are not counted. For some state offices, a filing fee may be required to have a person's name listed on the ballot as a write-in candidate. The amount varies from $3,750 for statewide office to as little as $300 for members of the State Board of Education.[15] People sometimes write in choices such as "Mickey Mouse" and "None of the above." These are recorded but not counted. In 1990, nineteen write-in candidates filed for governor. Bubbles Cash, a retired Dallas stripper, led the pack with 3,287 out of a total of 11,700 write-in votes.[16]

"sore loser" law

Law in Texas that prevents a person who lost the primary vote from running as an independent or minor party candidate

write-in candidate

A person whose name does not appear on the ballot; voters must write in that person's name, and the person must have filed a formal notice that he or she was a write-in candidate before the election

CORE OBJECTIVE

Thinking Critically . . .

Explain the challenges that hinder minor party candidates from succeeding in statewide elections.

Party Caucus

The state election code defines a **minor party** (sometimes called a *third party*) as any political organization that receives between 5 and 19 percent of the total votes cast for any statewide office in the past general election. In the past 50 years, there have been four minor parties: the Raza Unida Party in South Texas in the 1970s,[17] the Socialist Workers Party in 1988, and the Libertarian Party and the Green Party in the 1990s and 2000s. Parties that achieve minor-party status must nominate their candidates in a **party caucus** or convention and are exempt from the petition requirement discussed previously. Currently, only the Libertarian Party and the Green Party qualify as minor parties in Texas.[18]

minor party

A party other than the Democratic or Republican Party; to be a minor party in Texas, the organization must have received between 5 and 19 percent of the vote in the past election

party caucus

A meeting of members of a political party to nominate candidates (now used only by minor political parties in Texas)

The Texas Libertarian Party logo

Texas Libertarian Party

primary election

An election used by major political parties in Texas to nominate candidates for the November general election

open primary system

A nominating election that is open to all registered voters regardless of party affiliation

closed primary system

A nominating election that is closed to all voters except those who have registered as a member of that political party

semi-closed primary system

A nominating election that is open to all registered voters, but voters are required to declare party affiliation when they vote in the primary election

semi-open primary system

Voter may choose to vote in the primary of either party on Election Day; voters are considered "declared" for the party in whose primary they vote

The Texas Election Code defines a *major party* as any organization receiving 20 percent or more of the total votes cast for governor in the past election. Only the Democratic and Republican parties hold this status today. By law, these party organizations must nominate their candidates in a **primary election.**

By definition, Texas has an **open primary system,** but this is a bit misleading because there can also be an argument for it having a semi-open system, as discussed shortly. Open primaries allow the voter to vote in any primary without a party declaration. The voter can vote as a Democrat and attend the Republican precinct convention or participate in any activity of the opposite party.

A **closed primary system** is currently used in nine states. This system requires voters to declare their party affiliation when they register to vote. They may vote only in the primary of their party registration. Most of these states have a time limit after which a voter may not change party affiliation before the election.

There are several important variations of open and closed primaries (see Table 10.3). A **semi-closed primary system** allows voters to register or change their party registration on Election Day. Independents may vote in the primary of their choice, but otherwise, registered members may vote only in their party's primary. In a **semi-open primary system,** the voter may choose to vote in the primary of either party on Election Day. After they request a specific party ballot, however, voters are considered "declared" for the party in whose primary they vote. If you vote in the Republican Party primary, you are in effect declaring that you are a member of that party. You may not participate in any activity of any other party for the remainder of that election year. For example, if you vote in the Republican primary, you may not attend the precinct convention of the Democratic Party. This also limits the voter in other ways. A top-two primary is somewhat different. All candidates, regardless of party, are placed on a single ballot. Depending on the state, a candidate can indicate a party affiliation or preference. At the end of the primary, the top two vote-getters, again regardless of party, move on to the general election.

Texas is, perhaps confusingly, also commonly labeled as having a semi-open system. Although Texas does have an open primary system, the state also restricts voters to a certain degree (though not to the extent of a more

TABLE 10.3

Primary Systems Used in State Elections

Closed Primary: Party Registration Required before Election Day

Delaware	Maryland	New York
Florida	Nevada	Oregon
Kentucky	New Mexico	Pennsylvania

Semi-closed Primary: Voters May Register or Change Registration on Election Day

Connecticut	North Carolina	South Dakota
Idaho	Oklahoma	Utah

Semi-open Primary: Voters Required to Request Party Ballot

Illinois	Iowa	Tennessee
Indiana	Ohio	Wyoming

Open Primary: Unaffiliated Voters May Vote in Any Party Primary

Arizona	Maine	New Jersey
Colorado	Massachusetts	Rhode Island
Kansas	New Hampshire	West Virginia

Open Primary: All Voters May Vote in Any Party Primary

Alabama	Minnesota	South Carolina
Arkansas	Mississippi	Texas
Georgia	Missouri	Vermont
Hawaii	Montana	Virginia
Michigan	North Dakota	Wisconsin

Top-Two Primary: One Ballot for All Candidates

California	Louisiana	Nebraska*
Washington		

*For nonpartisan legislative races only.

Note: Alaska has a top-four open primary which doesn't quite fit in the above categories.

Source: NCSL Elections Team, "State Primary Election Types," last revised January 5, 2021, https://www.ncsl.org/research/elections-and-campaigns/primary-types.aspx (accessed May 5, 2022).

by-the-book semi-open system). Voters in Texas do not have to declare a party, but when attending a primary, they must choose a ticket and pick only from the candidates in that party. After the primary is over, however, voters can cross party lines. In addition, when the next year begins, voters receive a new registration card and are free to vote however they choose. Texas might be best labeled as having a (semi-) open system.

In the past, Alaska, California, and Washington used a **blanket primary system.** This system allowed voters to switch parties between offices. A voter might vote in the Republican primary for the races for governor and U.S. House, and in the Democratic primary for the U.S. Senate race. The U.S. Supreme Court has ruled these unconstitutional (*California Democratic Party v. Jones*, 2000). California has adopted a top-two primary system. Alaska has adopted a top-four open primary system (this is exactly like a top-two simply with an expanded set of candidates who make it onto the final ballot).

blanket primary system
A nominating election in which voters could switch parties between offices

Washington State has adopted Louisiana's system of a nonpartisan primary for all statewide and U.S. House and Senate races. Under this system, all candidates are listed on the ballot by office. The voter can choose one candidate per office. If no person receives a majority, the top two candidates face each other in a runoff. This can result in two candidates from the same party facing each other in a runoff election.

> **Understanding Impact** As a voter, how are you affected by the type of primary the state choses? Do you like Texas's "semi-open" system, or would you prefer one of the other types of primaries described in this section? Explain.

Political Differences between Open and Closed Primary Systems

Learning Objective: Describe primary elections.

The primary system that a state uses may affect the party system in the state. Advocates of the closed primary system say that it encourages party identification and loyalty and, therefore, helps build stronger party systems. Open primary systems, they say, allow participation by independents with no loyalty to the party, which weakens party organization. There is no strong evidence that this is the case.

crossover voting

Occurs when voters leave their party and vote in the other party's primary

Open primaries allow **crossover voting.** This occurs when voters leave their party and vote in the other party's primary. Occasionally voters in one party might vote in the other party's primary in hopes of nominating a candidate from the other party whose philosophy is similar to their own. For example, Republicans have been accused of voting in the Democratic primary in Texas to ensure that a conservative will be nominated. This occurred in the 1970 U.S. Senate race when Republicans voted for the more conservative Lloyd Bentsen over the liberal Ralph Yarborough. Many voting precincts carried by Bentsen in the Democratic primary voted for Republican George H. W. Bush in the general election.

From 2006 to the present, more Texans have voted in the Republican primaries than in the Democratic primaries. Republicans claim that this is evidence that their party is the majority party. Some Democrats suggest that these differences in turnout are explained by the low levels of opposition in the Democratic primaries. Other Democratic Party leaders claim that many traditional Democratic voters cross over and vote in the Republican primary in an attempt to affect the Republican outcome. The truth is muddled. The Republican party is the dominant party; Democrats have been documented voting in the Republican primary. But there isn't enough data at present to suggest that makes a significant difference to the primary election outcome.[19]

party raiding

Occurs when members of one political party vote in another party's primary in an effort to nominate a weaker candidate or split the vote among the top candidates

Party raiding occurs when members of one political party vote in another party's primary; it is difficult to orchestrate. What distinguishes party raiding from crossover voting is that whereas crossover voting may be genuine (another party's candidate appeals to voters), party raiding is intentional and designed to nominate a weaker candidate or split the vote among the strongest contenders. Although there are often accusations of such behavior during primary elections, it is difficult to prove. Additionally, there have been attempts to organize party raids, but it is unclear whether they are effective. A notable example during the 2008 primary was Operation Chaos, in which popular conservative talk radio host Rush Limbaugh encouraged Republicans to vote in Democratic primaries for Hillary Clinton in order to weaken then-candidate Obama.[20] Obama won the primary and later went on to win the Presidency.

Runoff primaries are held in 10 states: Alabama, Arkansas, Georgia, Mississippi, North Carolina, Oklahoma, South Carolina, South Dakota, Texas, and Vermont.[21] A **runoff primary** is required if no candidate receives a majority in the first primary. Until the changeover to Republican dominance in the South, winning the Democratic Party primary was the same as winning the general election, and the runoff primary became a fixture, supposedly as a way of requiring the winner to have "majority" support. In reality, voter turnout in the runoff primary is almost always lower than in the first primary—sometimes substantially lower. The "majority" winner often is selected by a small percentage of the electorate—those who bother to participate in the runoff primary.

The Texas Election Code specifies that voters who voted in the primary election of one party may not participate in the runoff primary of the other party. Occasionally there have been charges that this has happened, as in a 1992 Democratic primary congressional race in Houston. The Houston congressional district had been drawn to "ensure" that a Mexican American could be elected, but the primary was won by an Anglo, Gene Green. His opponent, Ben T. Reyes, charged that Republicans had "raided" the primary and voted for Green. There was some evidence that this had happened, but it had not changed the results of the election. The current system of record-keeping and the difficulty of checking voter lists make it almost impossible to prevent such raiding or crossover voting from occurring in runoff primaries. A reform might be to require voters to sign a statement saying they had not voted in the opposition party's primary election. Another suggestion is to have computerized records at each polling place that election workers can check for this type of activity.

runoff primary
Election that is required if no person receives a majority in the primary election; primarily used in southern and border states

Understanding Impact What might occur if Texas went to a truly open primary? How might this affect voter turnout?

The Administration and Finance of Primary Elections

Learning Objective: Describe primary elections.

In the past, primary elections were considered functions of private organizations, and the state did not regulate them. As we will discuss in detail in Chapter 11, courts have ruled that political parties are not private organizations, and

filing fee

A fee or payment required to get a candidate's name on the primary or general election ballot

their functions are subject to control by state law. The Texas Election Code governs primary elections. It specifies the time and method of conducting primary elections. Runoff elections are usually held 30 days later.

Persons wanting to file for an office in the primary election must pay a **filing fee.** In 1970, court cases forced Texas to alter its filing fee system because the cost of filing for county offices had increased substantially. For example, the cost of filing for a countywide race in Dallas County was $9,000 in 1970. Adjusted for inflation, this would be $66,690 in 2022. In 1972, the state of Texas assumed part of the cost of financing primary elections. Filing fees are still required, but they are lower. Currently, the cost for filing for a many state-wide offices is $3,750. For state senators, it's $1,250 and for state representatives it is $750. For countywide races, the fee is either $2,500 or $1,250 or $750, depending on whether the county has more or less than 200,000 residents according to the 2010 census. Anyone who cannot pay the filing fee can still be placed on the primary ballot by filing a petition. For statewide office, about 83,000 signatures are required; for district or local office, signatures equal to 2 percent of the votes cast for that office in the past election are required (note, however, that the bare minimum is 500).[22] Some candidates file a petition as a campaign tactic to show they have broad support. Occasionally, petitioners also pay the filing fee just to play it safe and prevent a challenge to the validity of the petition.

Technically, primary elections are administered by the local party county chair and executive committee and by the state party officials at the state level. However, the Texas Election Code and the secretary of state oversee the administration of elections to ensure that the rules are followed, and the party has only limited discretion in the conduct of these elections. The secretary of state keeps a hotline open on Election Day so that citizens can report problems with an election, such as workers telling voters which candidates they should vote for.

Understanding Impact Do you agree with the state's decision to lower the cost of filing for office? What is the impact of such a policy on candidates and on voters?

Special Elections

Learning Objective: Explain special elections.

By Texas law, elections may be held in January, May, August, and November. Any election that takes place in January, May, or August is considered a special election. There are three types of special elections. The most common in Texas is selection of city council members and mayoral elections if they are not held in November. Most Texas cities hold municipal elections in May, but a few, including Houston, hold theirs in November. Also, all school board elections in Texas are in May.

A second type of special election may be called to decide on amendments to the state constitution. In the past 20 years, it has been common for the state legislature to arrange Texas constitutional amendment elections for January and August, when no other elections are usually held. Election turnout for constitutional amendment elections held in January, May, and August are usually much lower than such elections held in November.

A third type of special election occurs when only one contest is on the ballot. The governor calls these special elections to fill a vacancy caused by the death or resignation of a member of the Texas legislature or a Texas member of the U.S. House of Representatives or the U.S. Senate. Such special elections have played a very important role in Texas political history. For example, the death of Senator Morris Sheppard in 1941 led to a special election that pitted Governor W. Lee "Pappy" O'Daniel against Congressman Lyndon Johnson—an election that Johnson lost because of election fraud that O'Daniel supporters committed. In 1960, Senator Lyndon Johnson won reelection to the Senate and was elected to the vice presidency of the United States. Johnson resigned his Senate seat and in a special election the next year, John Tower became the first Republican to win a statewide office in Texas since Reconstruction, elected in part by liberal Texas Democrats.

> **Understanding Impact** Elections to decide constitutional amendments usually have very low turnout. What are the implications of having a small proportion of the population decide whether the Texas Constitution should be altered?

The Federal Voting Rights Act

Learning Objective: Describe the federal Voting Rights Act.

In 1965, under the leadership of President Lyndon Johnson, the U.S. Congress passed the Voting Rights Act. As previously mentioned in Chapters 7 and 9, this act has had extensive effects on the state of Texas and the conduct of elections. After being passed in 1965 and extended to Texas in 1975, the Voting Rights Act required preclearance by the U.S. Justice Department of all changes in the election procedures, including such aspects as ballot reform, the time and place of an election, and the method of electing legislators.[23]

Until 2013, the Voting Rights Act allowed the federal government to oversee the operation of elections at a state level. The greatest impact had been felt in southern states, where racial and ethnic minorities were formerly barred from participating in elections. When the U.S. Supreme Court struck down Section 4 of the Voting Rights Act in *Shelby County v. Holder* in late June 2013, certain states identified within the law no longer had to receive federal approval before changing any in-state voting procedure. Indeed, Texas and other states had been trying to legislate voter identification laws for several years without success. Once Section 4 no longer applied, Texas immediately put its voter identification laws into effect. They applied from November 2013 forward, though a court order modified their implementation for the 2016 election (see Chapter 9). The other sections of the Voting Rights Act are still functioning.

Focus On

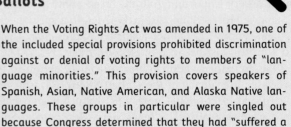

The Hispanic Population and Bilingual Ballots

Veronica G. Cardenas/REUTERS/Alamy Stock Photo

When the Voting Rights Act was amended in 1975, one of the included special provisions prohibited discrimination against or denial of voting rights to members of "language minorities." This provision covers speakers of Spanish, Asian, Native American, and Alaska Native languages. These groups in particular were singled out because Congress determined that they had "suffered a history of exclusion from the political process."[24] Before this, some jurisdictions had imposed a literacy test, in English, as a prerequisite for voting.

As a result of this law, localities must provide all election-related information—including ballots (regular, absentee, and sample), voter registration forms, voter instruction pamphlets, official notices of elections and polling place locations, candidate qualifying information, website information, and frequently asked questions at polling places—"in the language of the applicable minority group as well as in the English language."[25] This provision applies to all elections—federal, state, and local—from general and primary elections to school board elections and bond referenda. In addition, polling places must employ bilingual poll workers on Election Day, and bilingual employees must be available to answer voting and election-related questions in government offices. A precinct must comply with these requirements if it contains a significant number of minority language voters, which is defined as more than 5 percent of its voting-age citizens, or more than 10,000 voting-age citizens within the precinct, who speak a single minority language.[26]

Texas has been printing ballots in both English and Spanish statewide, as well as providing bilingual voting clerks in certain precincts, since 1975.[27] Texas Election Code specifies the method for identifying voters of Spanish origin or descent, using census data to determine the percentage of voters within each precinct who have Hispanic surnames. Precincts are required to provide bilingual election workers if 5 percent or more of their voters have Hispanic surnames.[28] (Incidentally, due to Voting Rights Act requirements,[29] a few counties in Texas must offer materials in other languages, in addition to English and Spanish. Harris County, for example, must also provide election materials in Vietnamese and Chinese.[30])

The legal requirement for bilingual ballots has generated controversy. Supporters have argued that such accommodations are necessary to give all citizens the opportunity to vote. Opponents have pointed to the cost, borne by local governments, of complying with these regulations, even when many jurisdictions are facing budget constraints.[31]

Critical Thinking Questions

1. What are bilingual ballots, and how does the provision requiring them relate to Texas and its Hispanic population?
2. Why might this legal requirement be generating controversy?

CORE OBJECTIVE

Communicating Effectively . . .

Do you think the Voting Rights Act requirement that Texas provide a bilingual ballot increases voter turnout? Construct an argument in favor of or against this provision of the Voting Rights Act.

Absentee and Early Voting

Learning Objective: Discuss absentee and early voting.

All states allow some form of **absentee voting.** This practice began as a way to allow members of the U.S. armed services, who were stationed in other states or overseas, to vote. In all but a few states, it has been extended to other individuals. In most states, persons who will be out of the county on Election Day may file for absentee voting.

In Texas before 1979, to vote absentee, voters had to sign an affidavit saying they would be out of the county and unable to vote on Election Day. They could also file for an absentee ballot to be sent to them if they were living out of state or in a hospital or nursing home. In 1979, the state legislature changed the rules to allow anyone to vote absentee without restrictions. In Texas this is called "early voting." Early voting now usually begins 17 days before an election and closes 4 days before the election.[32] During that period, polls are typically open from 7 a.m. to 7 p.m. Voters simply go to an early polling place and vote as they would on Election Day. It is important to note, however, that in 2019 the state adopted a law that effectively closed all polling locations that aren't open for the entire early voting period. This resulted in quite a few closures, most of which were in counties with large Black and Latino communities.

absentee voting
A process that allows a person to vote early, before the regular election; applies to all elections in Texas; also called early voting

Focus On

Early Voting Restrictions and Its Effects

Over the last 10 years, there has been a pattern of increasing early voting restrictions in southern states, including Texas. From 2012 to now, the number of polling stations has decreased and the number of voters per station has increased. *The Guardian* notes that, "In 2012, there was one polling place for every 4,000 residents. By 2018 that figure dropped to one polling place per 7,700 residents." For the 2020 election, additional closures were experienced, particularly in minority neighborhoods. More recently, in the 2022 primaries, there were staff shortages that led to intermittent closures of existing polling sites.[33] *The Guardian* did an analysis that resulted in the following conclusion: "The 50 counties that gained the most Black and Latinx

Melina Mara/The Washington Post/Getty Images

(Continued...)

residents between 2012 and 2018 closed 542 polling sites, compared to just 34 closures in the 50 counties that have gained the fewest Black and Latinx residents."[34]

This closure pattern culminated, as noted, in a law passed in 2019 that effectively closed rotating and mobile voting sites in the state. House Bill 1888, authored by Republican representative Greg Bonnen, stipulates that an early voting site must remain open every day of early voting in a single location. The bill passed via the Republican majority in the legislature and was signed by Governor Greg Abbott.[35]

It's important to note that not only are Black and Latinx communities affected. Rural counties have also been having issues, leaving some small towns without a single polling station. For example, Florence (a town in Williamson County) used to have a polling station for one day of early voting at City Hall. That station is no longer allowed, meaning there is effectively no early voting for that community. Rural county officials have to consolidate as best they can, leaving some of their smaller communities without a local opportunity. Urban counties, also affected, have to weigh the cost of keeping open previously mobile stations versus consolidating in a way that doesn't leave out particular neighborhood access.[36]

These restrictions have an economic impact. On average, Texans of color have lower incomes than do white Texans.[37] Similarly, on average, rural Texans earn only about 80 percent of what urban Texans earn.[38] As a result, the loss of polling places in minority and rural communities means that many Texans who are already at the lower end of the economic spectrum are being disproportionately affected by the loss of polling places. As their ability to vote is reduced, so is their ability to influence the policies that affect them economically.

Access to early voting is an ongoing issue. There have been some lawsuits over the last year, but the law remains in effect as of this writing.

Critical Thinking Questions

1. What are the benefits and drawbacks to having mobile and rotating early voting stations? How might these stations be abused?

2. What do you think are the effects of these closures? How much of a correlation is there to distance between polling stations and the number of ballots submitted in a given community?

The Changing Nature of Elections

Learning Objective: Discuss ways in which the nature of elections has changed.

Today, such issues as abortion, LGBTQ rights, women's rights, gun control, the environment, and health care dominate elections. Many people have very strong feelings about these issues and maintain their positions on these issues throughout their lives. Some individuals believe that their views are endorsed by God; often these "values voters" consider people who don't agree with them to be valueless. Others feel strongly that religion or majority opinion should never dictate what human rights are. Most of the time, neither side will compromise on such wedge issues. For example, in the 2004 presidential election, 14 states had anti–gay marriage propositions on the ballot. This turned out an impressive number of so-called values voters and infuriated supporters of gay rights.

Three changes in elections are worth noting. First, labor unions in the United States have declined as a voice in elections because of manufacturing jobs being shipped overseas and southern states that have antiunion (right-to-work) statutes, including Texas. Second, the Catholic and male votes, which used to be overwhelmingly Democratic, have migrated to the Republican Party because of such issues as abortion and gay rights. Many Catholics have allied with Christian fundamentalist groups, and many traditional old-line males have gravitated further to the right. And third, changes in the media have had an enormous effect on politics. Influential 24-hour news networks such as CNN, MSNBC, and Fox News, as well as email campaigns and political activity through social networking websites, have changed the way election campaigns are run and often strongly influence the outcome of elections (see Chapter 8).

Understanding Impact Traditionally, the democratic process has depended on opposing parties reaching a compromise to enact legislation that is tolerable to the majority. Do you think the current emphasis on appealing to "values voters" is an improvement on that system? Why or why not?

Conclusion

Campaigns and elections are essential to any democracy. As in other states, campaigns in Texas have become media affairs dominated by political consultants, targeted advertisements, and money (see Chapter 8). The rules governing the conduct of elections affect who is elected and which policies the government enacts.

For reasons discussed in Chapter 9, active involvement in politics in Texas is limited to a small number of citizens. The Anglo population dominates the electoral process and controls a disproportionate share of state offices. Most citizens choose not to participate in elections or the activities of political parties.

Summary

LO: Describe political campaigns in Texas, including the use of consultants and the role of money.

Political campaigns are large undertakings, requiring constant publicity, media expertise, and a lot of money. Reporters often follow candidates for statewide office as they travel. Political rallies are still held but are most often used to gain media attention. Professional campaign consultants help candidates design written and visual advertisements and generally "package" the candidate to the voters. Most campaign money comes from political action committees (PACs), with few legal limitations on what they can donate. Indeed, the regulation of campaign finances in Texas is limited to requiring all candidates and PACs to file reports with the Texas State Ethics Commission.

LO: Explain the election process in Texas.

All states, including Texas, hold general elections every two years. During nonpresidential years, Texas voters elect candidates to statewide offices: governor, lieutenant governor, attorney general, land commissioner, agri-

cultural commissioner, comptroller, some members of the Railroad Commission and the State Board of Education, and some members of the Texas Supreme Court and the Court of Criminal Appeals.

LO: Discuss ballot forms in Texas.

Ballot forms are the forms voters use to cast their ballots; each county, with approval of the secretary of state, determines the form of the ballot. Texas counties formerly used paper ballots with a party column format, with candidates listed by party and by office. This encouraged straight-ticket voting. Since the 2008 election, however, all Texas counties have used electronic voting systems, most of which use the office block format. This ballot form lists the office (such as president), followed by the candidates by party.

LO: Discuss ballot access in Texas.

To appear on the November general election ballot, candidates must meet criteria established by state law. The Texas Election Code specifies three ways for names to be on the ballot. To run as an independent, a candidate must file a petition with a specified number of signatures. A subset of independents, write-in candidates must pay a filing fee to legitimize their status. Major party candidates access the ballot through their party's primary election. Primaries can be open, closed, or a mixture of both. Texas has a semi-open primary.

LO: Describe primary elections.

Primaries are elections that major political parties in Texas use to nominate candidates for the November general election. They can be open (voters can vote in either primary and do not need to declare party affiliation), closed (voters must declare party affiliation when registering and can vote in that party's primary only), or a mixture of both. Open primaries, by nature, allow cross-over voting. This happens when voters leave their party and vote in the other party's primary. Crossover voting may be genuine (another party's candidate appeals to voters), but party raiding is designed to nominate a weaker candidate or split the vote.

LO: Explain special elections.

By Texas law, elections may be held in January, May, August, and November. Any election that takes place in January, May, or August is considered a special election. There are three types. The most common is selection of city council members and mayoral elections if they are not held in November. A second type of special election may be called to decide on amendments to the state constitution. A third type of special election occurs when only one contest is on the ballot.

LO: Describe the federal Voting Rights Act.

The Voting Rights Act of 1965 is a federal law aimed at preventing racial discrimination in the operation of voter registration and elections at the state level. It required preclearance by the U.S. Justice Department of all changes in the election procedures, including such aspects as ballot reform, the time and place of an election, and the method of electing legislators. When the U.S. Supreme Court struck down Section 4 of the Voting Rights Act in late June 2013, the primary method of enforcement, Section 5, was rendered useless and Texas immediately put voter identification laws into effect.

LO: Discuss absentee and early voting.

Absentee voting allows a person to vote before the regular election. It applies to all elections in Texas and is also called early voting. Early voting begins 17 days before an election and closes four days before the election. During that period, voters can either mail in a ballot or go to an early voting polling place.

LO: Discuss ways in which the nature of elections has changed.

Issues such as abortion, LGBTQ rights, women's rights, gun control, the environment, and health care dominate elections. Labor unions have declined. The Catholic and male votes, which used to be overwhelmingly Democratic, have migrated to the Republican Party because of such issues as abortion and LGBTQ rights. Influential 24-hour news networks, email campaigns, and political activity through social networking websites have also changed the way election campaigns are run and often influence election outcomes.

Key Terms

absentee voting	general elections	party raiding
ballot form	independent candidate	primary election
blanket primary system	minor party	runoff primary
closed primary system	office block format	semi-closed primary system
crossover voting	open primary system	semi-open primary system
filing fee	party caucus	"sore loser" law
focus group	party column format	write-in candidate

Notes

1 "Texas Candidate's Comment about Rape Causes Furor," *The New York Times,* March 26, 1990, http://www.nytimes.com/1990/03/26/us/texas-candidate-s-comment-about-rape-causes-a-furor.html.

2 OpenSecrets.org, "Self-Funding Candidates: Election Cycle 2016," https://www.opensecrets.org/overview/topself.php?cycle=2016 (accessed May 11, 2018).

3 *Citizens United v. Federal Elections Commission,* 558 U.S. 310 (2010).

4 Howe, Amy. (2022) "Court sides with Ted Cruz and strikes down campaign-finance restriction along ideological lines," Scotusblog. May 16, 2022. URL: https://www.scotusblog.com/2022/05/court-sides-with-ted-cruz-and-strikes-down-campaign-finance-restriction-along-ideological-lines/.

5 National Conference of State Legislatures, "*Citizens United* and the States," July 2016, http://www.ncsl.org/legislatures-elections/elections/citizens-united-and-the-states.aspx.

6 *Texas Election Code,* Title 15, Chapter 253, sec. 253.094.

7 The office of treasurer was also a statewide elected office. In 1996, the voters abolished this office by constitutional amendment. The state comptroller and other state agencies have taken over the functions of this office.

8 Texas House of Representatives, "Frequently Asked Questions," http://www.house.state.tx.us/resources/frequently-asked-questions/.

9 Texas Secretary of State, "Voting System Equipment by County (PDF)," updated February 2022, https://www.sos.state.tx.us/elections/forms/sysexam/voting-sys-bycounty.pdf.

10 The Texas Election Code can be found in full here: http://www.statutes.legis.state.tx.us/?link=EL.

11 Texas Secretary of State, "Running as an Independent Candidate in 2022," https://www.sos.state.tx.us/elections/candidates/guide/2022/ind2022.shtml.

12 Texas Secretary of State, "Turnout and Voter Registration Figures (1970–Current)," http://www.sos.state.tx.us/elections/historical/70-92.shtml.

13 Texas Secretary of State home page, http://www.sos.state.tx.us.

14 https://ballotpedia.org/Texas_House_of_Representatives_elections,_2020

15 Texas Secretary of State, "Procedures for Write-In Candidates in 2022," https://www.sos.texas.gov/elections/candidates/guide/2022/writein2022.shtml.

16 James A. Anderson, Richard W. Murray, and Edward L. Farley, *Texas Politics: An Introduction,* 6th ed. (New York: HarperCollins, 1992), 34.

17 The Raza Unida Party did not receive enough votes to qualify as a minor party but challenged this in court. The federal court sustained the challenge, and it was allowed to operate as a minor party.

18 *Ballotpedia,* "Ballot Access Requirements for Political Parties in Texas," https://ballotpedia.org/Ballot_access_requirements_for_political_parties_in_Texas (accessed May 5, 2022).

19 David Martin Davies, "Some Democrats are voting in the Texas GOP primaries. Will it make a difference?" February 28, 2022, Texas Public Radio, https://www.tpr.org/government-politics/2022-02-28/some-democrats-are-voting-in-the-texas-gop-primaries-will-it-make-a-difference (accessed May 13, 2022).

20 *Rush Limbaugh Show,* transcript March 12, 2008, "Rush the Vote: Operation Chaos," http://www.rushlimbaugh.com/daily/2008/03/12/rush_the_vote_operation_chaos.

21 National Conference of State Legislatures, "Primary Runoffs," http://www.ncsl.org/research/elections-and-campaigns/primary-runoffs.aspx (accessed April 24, 2018).

22 Texas Secretary of State, "Republican or Democratic Party Nominees," https://www.sos.texas.gov/elections/candidates/guide/2022/demorrep2022.shtml.

23 A court case in 1971 ended the early registration procedures in Texas (*Beare v. Smith,* 31 F. Supp. 1100).

24 U.S. Department of Justice, "Minority Language Citizens: Section 203 of the Voting Rights Act," https://www.justice.gov/crt/language-minority-citizens.

25 Voting Rights Act of 1965, Pub. L. 89-110, (see https://www.govinfo.gov/content/pkg/STATUTE-79/pdf/STATUTE-79-Pg437.pdf#page=1).

26 U.S. Department of Justice, "Minority Language Citizens: Section 203 of the Voting Rights Act," https://www.justice.gov/crt/language-minority-citizens; U.S. Department of Justice, "About Language Minority Voting Rights," https://www.justice.gov/crt/about-language-minority-voting-rights.

27 Texas Secretary of State, Election Advisory No. 2015-05, http://www.sos.state.tx.us/elections/laws/advisory2015-04.shtml.

28 Texas Election Code, Chapter 272, "Bilingual Requirements," http://www.statutes.legis.state.tx.us/Docs/EL/htm/EL.272.htm.

29 U.S. Census Bureau, "Voting Rights Act Amendments of 2006, Determinations under Section 203," *Federal Register,* October 13, 2011, https://www.federalregister.gov/documents/2016/12/05/2016-28969/voting-rights-act-amendments-of-2006-determinations-under-section-203.

30 Laurie Johnson, "Harris County Adds Chinese Language to Voting Materials," Houston Public Media, October 13, 2011, https://www.houstonpublicmedia.org/articles/news/2011/10/13/30496/harris-county-adds-chinese-language-to-voting-materials/.

31 "Federal Government Orders Bilingual Ballots in 25 States ahead of Elections," *Fox News,* October 14, 2011, http://www.foxnews.com/politics/2011/10/14/federal-government-orders-bilingual-ballots-in-25-states-ahead-elections.html.

32 Texas Secretary of State, "Early Voting," https://www.votetexas.gov/faq/early-voting.html.

33 Reese Oxner and Ureil J. Garcia, "Many voting locations throughout Texas did not open because of staff shortages," March 1, 2022, https://www.texastribune.org/2022/03/01/texas-primary-election-voting-location-closures/ (accessed May 12, 2022).

[34] "Texas Closes Hundreds of Polling Sites, Making It Harder for Minorities to Vote," *The Guardian,* https://www.theguardian.com/us-news/2020/mar/02/texas-polling-sites-closures-voting (accessed June 1, 2020).

[35] Katie Hall, "Texas Democratic Party Challenges Mobile Voting Ban in Lawsuit," *Statesman,* October 30, 2019, https://www.statesman.com/news/20191030/texas-democratic-party-challenges-mobile-voting-ban-in-lawsuit (accessed June 1, 2020).

[36] Alex Ura, "Texas Ended Temporary Voting Locations to Curb Abuse. Now Rural and Young Voters Are Losing Access," *Texas Tribune,* October 10, 2019, https://www.texastribune.org/2019/10/10/texas-temporary-voting-access-young-rural-voters/ (accessed June 1, 2020).

[37] Alex Ura and Annie Danial, "Incomes Continue to Rise, but Texans of Color Still Seeing a Gap," *Texas Tribune,* September 14, 2017, https://www.texastribune.org/2017/09/14/incomes-continue-rise-texans-color-still-face-gap/.

[38] Rural Health Information Hub, "Texas," https://www.ruralhealthinfo.org/states/texas (accessed June 3, 2020).

CHAPTER 11

Political Parties in Texas

- Evaluate the role of political parties in Texas.

P olitical parties are integral to government and politics in the nation and states, even though neither the U.S. Constitution nor the Texas Constitution mentions them. A **political party** is an organization that acts as an intermediary between the people and government, with the goal of having its members elected to public office. As you will see in Chapter 12, interest groups play a similar intermediary role but with a focus on policy rather than the election of its members. Traditionally, parties have vetted candidates, run campaigns, informed the populace on policy issues, and organized their members who are serving in office to ensure a measure of accountability.[1] As political scientists frequently note, parties play an important role in aggregating and articulating the preferences of citizens. Today, our representative government would not function without political parties.

> **political party**
> Organization that acts as an intermediary between the people and government with the goal of getting its members elected to public office

The founders of the United States did not favor parties, calling them "factions," because they saw these entities as pursuing special parochial interests instead of the interests of the country as a whole.[2] Even so, parties developed in the United States, largely because of the useful functions they provide in democratic politics. As early as the drafting of the U.S. Constitution, groups of like-minded political leaders and concerned citizens, Federalists and Anti-Federalists, joined in an effort to promote their ideas and influence voters. Except for a brief period in the first quarter of the nineteenth century, known as the "Era of Good Feelings," competitive parties have always existed at the national level.[3] For most of Texas's history, however, one party or the other has dominated the political process.

Political parties in the United States have never been strongly centralized. Throughout history, U.S. parties have consisted of coalitions of state parties. The most powerful party leaders arose from leadership positions in states that have large populations, extensive wealth, or both. Today, neither Texas nor the United States has strong parties, although partisan polarization has been increasing. Most candidates within parties self-select to run for office; once elected, they tend to toe the party line, as their voting patterns show. In Texas, neither party has a strong party organization or a strong grassroots organization. Candidates can act quite independently of either party.

Chapter Learning Objectives

- Describe the evolution of the political party system in the United States and in Texas.

- Explain the history of party realignment and one-party Republican dominance in Texas.

- Describe third-party movements in the United States and in Texas.

- Explain political party organization in Texas, including caucus and primary delegate selection systems.

How Parties Have Operated in the United States

Learning Objective: Describe the evolution of the political party system in the United States and in Texas.

In the past, parties performed many activities and functions. They also played a much more central role in our political system, which gave parties a great deal of power. Parties were particularly important when candidates relied more on traditional campaigns, which required more volunteers for activities such as door-to-door canvassing. But as campaigns have come to rely more on technology, campaigns, which today may be undertaken entirely in the control of the candidate, and not parties have become more prominent.

From the 1790s until roughly the 1970s, parties relied on party members and volunteers to perform a number of tasks related to elections and campaigns. These traditional party functions are sometimes called *labor-intensive politics* because, historically, the lack of communication and printing technologies (such as radio, television, the photocopier, and the personal computer) meant that parties had to enlist a lot of people or expend a lot of labor to accomplish these tasks.

- The parties selected candidates to run for office. Party leaders (most often elected officials) decided who would be put forward as candidates.[4]
- Parties organized candidates' campaigns. In the past, the parties controlled their candidates' campaigns. Parties sent party workers into neighborhoods to knock on doors and inform potential voters about the candidates and issues. Many times, the entire party slate would share the platform and speak at the same event.
- Parties could raise money directly and then distribute it to different candidates' campaigns. By controlling the purse strings, a party could keep its candidates in line and under control.
- Parties organized candidates' campaign rallies to allow candidates to meet and talk with voters. Before candidates campaigned for themselves, the party would produce campaign literature, arrange speakers on behalf of the candidates, and (from the early 1900s on) arrange speaking tours for the candidates.

This 1874 Thomas Nast cartoon is considered the origin of party symbols still in use today: Here, an elephant represents the Republican Party and a donkey (wearing a lion's skin) represents the Democratic Party.

Library of Congress Prints and Photographs Division Washington, D.C. 20540 USA [LC-DIG-ppmsca-15785]

- Inconceivable as it may be today, the parties—not local governments—printed election ballots.
- Starting in the 1930s, parties hired pollsters to conduct survey research for their candidates. Candidates were beholden to the party for such poll data.
- Finally, the parties ran the governments to which their candidates were elected. This was especially important after the introduction of the spoils system (or patronage system) around 1830. Under the spoils system, the victorious political party gave government jobs to party supporters. When Andrew Jackson won the presidency in 1828, recognized party members filled government positions. The higher the office was, the more important the party member chosen to fill it.

The role of parties in our political system has changed in many ways. For one thing, parties no longer designate a slate of candidates for office; rather, candidates self-select to run. Candidates generally assemble their own teams to manage their campaigns (or they hire professional political consultants to do this). Although parties still provide funding for campaigns, candidates might receive money directly from **political action committees (PACs)** (and, since the Supreme Court changed the rules in 2010, super PACs[5]) and donors. Also, some candidates fund themselves. In addition, local governments now prepare official ballots according to state specifications (although the party holding the primary still prepares the primary ballots),[6] and the merit system has, for the most part, replaced the spoils system. As a result of these changes, the influence of parties on the election process has declined. Since about 1970, there has been a shift from party-centered politics, in which parties provided the labor to mount effective campaigns, to more candidate-centered politics.

political action committee (PAC)

A spin-off of an interest group that collects money for campaign contributions and other activities

Understanding Impact Internet-savvy campaigns can reach more people more easily than ever before, creating opportunities for upstart candidates to get out their message and perhaps challenge entrenched political interests. But the Internet also creates an environment in which fake news and Internet trolls can thrive. Do you think the government should do more to police content on the Internet? What would be the First Amendment implications of such a government policy?

Political Parties Diminished

Learning Objective: Describe the evolution of the political party system in the United States and in Texas.

At the dawn of the twentieth century, a series of changes occurred in the laws regulating political parties and campaigns, changes that have continued up to the present day. As a result of these changes, which we will discuss in this section, parties are generally weaker today than at any other time during their history. This trend seems unlikely to change anytime soon.

To a large extent, parties have been weakened by political reforms, many of which came about during the Progressive Era (late 1890s to early 1920s). Reformers were very concerned about corruption and the influence of large urban political "machines," led by powerful men who controlled government jobs, contracts, and regulations. To reduce the power of the machines, reformers introduced measures that compromised the strength of political parties.

One way that parties traditionally maintained their power was through the voting system. Early in our country's history, some states used voice voting. According to this practice, eligible voters appeared at the courthouse, were called on by name, and then vocally announced their chosen candidate in front of onlookers. The lack of privacy and anonymity in this voting system made it easy for party members to intimidate or coerce voters. Those in a position of power (such as employers, landlords, and public officials) could pressure their subordinates to vote a certain way, and then witness their ballot casting to ensure compliance.[7] In states that used printed ballots, the parties themselves printed them, and they used techniques to identify how a ballot was cast. Often, the parties each used a different color of paper to make their ballots, and voters had to choose a ballot based on which party they wanted to support. As a result, voting was not private, as onlookers could easily determine which party's ballot a voter had put in the ballot box. Party members could intimidate and threaten retaliation for noncompliance.[8]

Texas's adoption of the Australian ballot in 1892[9] was intended to reduce these kinds of intimidation in elections by guaranteeing that the voting process would be both secret and uniform. Under this system, the government produced identical ballots. Each ballot listed all candidates running for office, not just those affiliated with a certain party.[10] Consequently, voters could mark and submit their choice in private, without fear of retribution, so long as they were allowed privacy in the voting booth.

Party bosses, however, continued to exercise influence over large groups of voters. Archer Parr, the "Duke of Duval County," and his son George built a Democratic Party machine by using jobs, bribes, and coercion. Parr, who, as "patrón" of a significant slice of south Texas, provided benefits to working class residents in return for a guarantee of their votes on election day.[11]

Not only was Parr able to guarantee that his workers would vote according to his instructions, he also managed other types of vote manipulation. In the 1948 Democratic primary election for U.S. Senate in Texas, Lyndon Johnson was in a runoff against Coke Stephenson. Johnson was trailing on the morning after the election, but the race was close enough to generate first one recount and then another. After several days, Johnson still trailed by more than 150 votes. Then, amazingly, 200 previously "uncounted" votes were discovered in Box 13 from Alice, Texas, which was inside the boundaries of the Parr political machine. Those 200 votes were recorded at the end of the voter list, written in different-colored ink, all in the same handwriting, and in alphabetical order! Those votes gave Johnson a victory by 87 votes out of almost a million cast.[12]

Another advantage of the Australian ballot was that voters could (if they wished) engage in "split-ticket" voting. In other words, they could vote for one party's candidate for one office and a different party's candidate for another office, all on the same ballot. The Australian ballot gained widespread use in the United States during the 1880s before Texas adopted it in 1892. By allowing voters to keep their votes secret, and by enabling them to split the ticket, ballot reforms decreased the influence of political parties on the voting process.[13]

Even with the Australian ballot, Texans could vote a straight ticket by checking the box for a preferred political party at the top of each ballot. A voter could thus easily vote for all the candidates of one party while still overriding that vote in individual races. Historically, Democratic voters in Texas used the straight-ticket option more often than Republicans. Straight-ticket votes accounted for 64 percent of the votes cast in the 2016 election in Harris, Dallas, and other large counties.[14] These urban areas tend to be Democratic strongholds. However, under the provisions of legislation opposed by Democrats but passed by the Republican majority and signed into law by Governor Greg Abbott after the 2017 Texas legislative session, Texas eliminated straight-ticket voting beginning in 2020.[15]

Another important area of party influence existed in the nominating process because party bosses selected candidates for office. To combat this aspect of party control, reformers introduced the concept of the direct primary. In direct primaries, all members of the party vote in an election, called a primary, to determine the party's nominee for an office. This practice was first adopted in Wisconsin in 1904.[16] Initially, it was difficult for candidates to gain access to primary ballots, but in the wake of the disastrous 1968 Democratic National Convention in Chicago (characterized not only by party divisiveness but also outright violence between protesters and police), the Democratic Party instituted substantial reforms. The Republican Party soon followed suit, and by 1972, the vast majority of delegates to party presidential nominating conventions were allocated as a result of primary elections. Party primaries are now used to select the nominees for all types of elected government positions, from justice of the peace to U.S. senator. As a general rule, delegates to party nominating conventions are allocated to candidates proportionally, based on results of the popular

The Spoils System Under Siege This Currier & Ives image argues for civil service reform by depicting Ulysses S. Grant with party supporters clamoring for government patronage.
Library of Congress Prints and Photographs Division Washington, D.C. 20540 USA [LC-DIG-pga-09549]

vote in primary elections. Some states use a caucus system to determine party nominations instead of conducting a primary. A caucus is a gathering at which party members publicly declare which candidate they will support and select delegates to attend the nominating convention.

Another way parties consolidated their power was through the spoils or patronage system, in which elected officials appointed faithful party members to government jobs. Reforms in this area gained wide support in the United States after the assassination of President James Garfield in 1881. A disappointed office seeker who had previously campaigned on Garfield's behalf shot him.[17]

The Pendleton Act of 1883 established a class of federal government positions, called the "civil service," that the government would fill on a merit basis as a result of competitive examinations instead of political appointments.[18] In addition, this employment continued regardless of which party held the White House.[19] Initially, only a small percentage of government positions were designated as civil service (nonpartisan) jobs and awarded by merit. However, Chester Arthur, the Republican vice president who succeeded to the presidency after Garfield's death, added more positions to the civil service rolls, as did each president thereafter through the end of the nineteenth century. By 1900, a majority of federal government positions were protected by the Pendleton Act. As the merit system replaced the spoils system, it undermined the connection parties had with government workers.

Reformers brought about other changes as well. They pushed for nonpartisan local elections to remove "political" considerations from municipal policy. They also championed the manager-council form of municipal government. This form of local government has no mayor. Instead, an elected city council hires a professional city manager to administer the departments and employees of the city.[20] (See Chapter 7 for a fuller discussion of this form of city government.) In the past, city governments had been a breeding ground for party talent development.

More recently, changes in the laws governing campaign finance have also lessened the influence of parties, albeit without achieving their intended goal of dampening the role of money in elections. In particular, *Citizens United v. Federal Election Commission* (2010) and *SpeechNow.org v. Federal Election Commission* (2010) eliminated, on free speech grounds, the legal prohibition whereby corporations were barred from spending money on political campaigns. Corporations can thus bypass political parties as they attempt to influence elections through independent expenditures such as via super PACs.[21]

Understanding Impact Campaign finance has been a perennial controversy in American politics. Many fear that too much money in campaigns creates at least the impression, if not the reality, of wealthy donors exercising excessive influence over politicians. However, courts have decided that campaign contributions are a facet of free speech, one of America's fundamental principles. Should there be stricter limits on campaign contributions? Or should freedom reign in elections, perhaps our most important democratic institution? Explain your answer.

CORE OBJECTIVE

Communicating Effectively . . .
Explain how political reforms have weakened political parties.

National versus State Parties

Learning Objective: Describe the evolution of the political party system in the United States and in Texas.

The United States does not have strong national parties; rather, it has 50 state party systems. Only two officeholders, the president and vice president, are elected on a nationwide basis. Even those are essentially state elections because voters in each state elect delegates to the Electoral College, which in turn elects the president and vice president. Whereas electors technically elect the president, today they in almost all cases vote for the winner of the statewide presidential vote, so in fact, the people actually do elect the president. However, after the November 2016 election, two Texas electors who had pledged to vote for Donald Trump chose instead to be "faithless electors." One cast a ballot for John Kasich and one for Ron Paul. Nationwide there were seven faithless electors in 2016.[22]

Having only two national offices weakens national parties and shifts power to state parties. The only time most people see anything resembling a national party organization is every four years, when Democrats and Republicans hold national conventions to nominate their candidates for president. Each of the 50 state party organizations can act independently of the others and of the national party organization.

A clear distinction exists between federal and state officeholders. At the federal level, Texas elects two U.S. senators and 38 U.S. representatives. The number of representatives from each state is determined by a process of **reapportionment** after each decennial census. Given Texas's significant population gains, its number of representatives, and therefore its number of electors in the Electoral College, increased by two, from 36 to 38, after the 2020 census.[23]

reapportionment
The process of allocating representatives to districts

Elected officials at the federal level spend most of their time in Washington, focusing on national, not state, policy. At the state level, Texans elect 31 state senators and 150 representatives to the state legislature. These state legislators focus on state issues. Occasionally, issues arise that cause federal and state legislators to work together. For example, state and federal officials worked together in response to the COVID-19 pandemic, ultimately bringing $16 billion in relief to Texas.[24] Most often, however, state and federal elected officials have different interests, agendas, and priorities.

Years ago, political scientist V. O. Key Jr. observed this about the state party system:

> The institutions developed to perform functions in each state differ markedly from the national parties. It is an error to assume that the political parties of each state are but miniatures of the national party system. In a few states that condition is approached, but . . . each state has its own pattern of action and often it deviates markedly from the forms of organization commonly thought of as constituting party systems.[25]

Professor Key's observation is as valid today as it was in the 1950s. State party systems vary widely, and often the only common link among them is the name *Democrat* or *Republican*.

Understanding Impact The framers of the U.S. Constitution intended that the Electoral College be free to choose the president and not be bound by a popular vote. They felt that electors would be better qualified to ensure "that the office of President will never fall to the lot of any man who is not in an eminent degree endowed with the requisite qualifications" (*Federalist Paper No. 68*). Should electors be obligated to vote in accordance with the popular vote in their state? The Supreme Court held in *Chiafalo v. Washington* (2020) that states may constitutionally bind their electors. Do you agree with this decision?

The Strength of State Party Organizations

Learning Objective: Describe the evolution of the political party system in the United States and in Texas.

States can be classified according to the strength of party organization within the state. In Texas, the Democratic Party dominated state politics for roughly 100 years following Reconstruction. During that period, the Republican Party was essentially absent except on a few occasions. In many elections, there was not even a Republican candidate on the ballot. However, the Republican Party in Texas has gained strength over the past 50 years. It now controls both houses of the Texas legislature, and it has captured the governor's office without interruption since 1994. Today, Republicans hold all statewide elected offices.[26]

Understanding Impact The last time any Democrat was elected to statewide office in Texas was 1994. Republicans have had a solid hold on Texas politics for a long time. However, a recent Gallup poll showed Republicans have only a 3 percent advantage in party identification.[27] Given the small gap in party preference, how do you think Republicans have maintained their dominance in statewide races? How might Republicans maintain this trend, and how might Democrats reverse it?

Party versus Ideology

Note that the Democratic and Republican Party labels do not necessarily indicate ideology.[28] **Ideology** is the basic belief system that guides political theory and policy. Different political ideologies are generally classified along a spectrum of conservative, moderate, and liberal. The Democratic Party in one state, for example, can be quite different ideologically from the Democratic Party in another state. For many years in Texas, the Democratic Party has had strong conservative leanings. The Democratic Party in Massachusetts, on the other hand, has a strong liberal orientation.

Even when the Democrats still controlled statewide offices and the state legislature, Texans had a tendency to support Republican candidates for president (see Table 11.1). In the past 18 presidential elections, Texas has

ideology
Basic belief system that guides political theory and policy; typically envisioned as falling along a conservative/moderate/liberal continuum

TABLE 11.1

Presidential Candidates Winning the Popular Vote in Texas (1952–2020)

Year	Candidate	Party
1952	Dwight Eisenhower	Republican
1956	Dwight Eisenhower	Republican
1960	John Kennedy*	Democratic
1964	Lyndon Johnson	Democratic
1968	Hubert Humphrey*	Democratic
1972	Richard Nixon	Republican
1976	Jimmy Carter	Democratic
1980	Ronald Reagan	Republican
1984	Ronald Reagan	Republican
1988	George H. W. Bush	Republican
1992	George H. W. Bush	Republican
1996	Bob Dole	Republican
2000	George W. Bush	Republican
2004	George W. Bush	Republican
2008	John McCain	Republican
2012	Mitt Romney	Republican
2016	Donald J. Trump	Republican
2020	Donald J. Trump	Republican

*Won the state by a margin of less than 50,000 votes.

Source: Texas Secretary of State, "Presidential Election Results," http://www.sos.state.tx.us/elections/historical/presidential.shtml.

voted Democratic only four times. In two of these cases, a native-son Democrat (Lyndon Johnson, who ran as Kennedy's vice president in 1960 and for president in his own right in 1964) was on the ballot. Hubert Humphrey, who had served as Johnson's vice president, won the state in 1968. Texans supported Jimmy Carter in 1976, partially because he was a southerner and partially due to backlash from the Watergate scandal. This strong support for Republican presidential candidates, even in times of Democratic dominance, reflects ideological differences that existed between the more conservative Texas Democratic Party and the more liberal national Democratic Party organization.

It may be that the common thread running through the state's political and electoral history is a generally consistent ideology. Despite the relative waxing and waning of the two major parties in Texas, the party offering a more conservative ideology has more often won the day. Even today, about twice as many Texans, when surveyed, describe themselves as conservative rather than liberal.[29]

CORE OBJECTIVE

Taking Personal Responsibility . . .

Examine your political values and compare them to the expressed values of both parties. Do your ideas about the role of government, politics, and policy align with one particular party? If so, which one?

Evolution of Political Parties in Texas

Learning Objective: Describe the evolution of the political party system in the United States and in Texas.

For a variety of reasons, as you learned earlier in this chapter, political parties in the United States are not particularly strong, either at the national or the state levels. In Texas, the two major parties have alternated dominance and weakness over time. So what happens in a political system in which parties are fairly weak?

Many political scientists believe that weakened parties lead to what is called *candidate-centered politics*. According to political scientists Jeffrey Cohen and Paul Kantor, with candidate-centered politics, prospective officeholders "emphasize their own talents, backgrounds, and characteristics rather than their association with either major party when running for office."[30] Indeed, the political history of Texas could be viewed as a chronological parade of personalities, intertwined with their respective ideologies and political parties. It remains to be see whether growing hyperpartisanship will reverse this trend toward candidate-centered politics and lead in the long term to increased identification with parties as a signifier of contrasting political beliefs.

Politics of the Republic of Texas

When the Republic of Texas was founded, the party system as we know it did not yet exist in Texas. Still, politics at the time were highly competitive. Two men, Sam Houston and Mirabeau Buonaparte Lamar, dominated the government of the Republic. Houston advocated annexation by the United States and peaceful relations with the Native American tribes of Texas, whereas Lamar envisioned a Texas empire stretching to the Pacific and initiated hostilities against the Native tribes. During the years of the Republic, Houston, Lamar, and their supporters competed for control of the Texas government. Because the Republic's constitution did not permit presidents to serve consecutive terms, elections revolved around the personalities of the two men and their surrogates. Texas politics of this era were dominated by strong political leaders instead of issues and public policy differences. This characteristic of Texas politics is still present today, though as partisanship has increased, policy differences, particularly "culture war" issues, have become more important.

Annexation and the Civil War Era

From U.S. annexation until the end of the Civil War, Texas's state politics clearly established a pattern of Democratic Party dominance. The Anglo settlers of pre–Civil War Texas were predominantly from the U.S. South; many were either slaveholders or sympathetic toward slaveholders, distrustful of the federal government, and convinced of the primacy of state sovereignty. During this period, Texas experienced a substantial expansion of its plantation economy.[31]

As a rule, Texas Democratic officeholders supported the southern position on issues dominating the United States during the Civil War era. A conspicuous exception to this was Sam Houston, who represented Texas in the U.S. Senate from 1846 to 1859 and served as governor from 1859 to 1861 as a Union Democrat. Houston voted for establishing Oregon as a free territory in 1848. He also argued successfully for the Boundary Act, a part of the Compromise of 1850, whereby Texas sold its right to territory now in New Mexico, Oklahoma, Kansas, Wyoming, and Colorado to the United States.

Houston's opposition to slavery deepened the cleavages between pro- and anti-Houston groups in the Texas Democratic Party that had existed since the early 1850s. Two factions arose in Texas: the pro-Houston faction, or "Jacksonians," and the newer, radical anti-Houston faction who called themselves the Constitutional Democrats. By 1857, the latter completely controlled the party. Houston ran for governor and lost that year, but in 1859, he ran for governor as an independent in an attempt to build up a Union Party, and he won. Houston campaigned against secession, but the people of Texas voted for it by more than a 3-to-1 margin in a popular referendum. Houston refused to take the oath of allegiance to the Confederacy, at which point the convention declared the governorship vacant and appointed the lieutenant governor to replace him. The Democratic Party would remain the sole party in Texas for the duration of the Civil War.

Sam Houston, governor of Texas, 1859–1861; U.S. (Democratic) senator from Texas, 1846–1859; president of Texas, 1836–1838, 1841–1844; Texas House of Representatives, 1839–1841; governor of Tennessee, 1827–1829; U.S. Representative from Tennessee, 1823–1827.

Library of Congress

The only period of one-party Republican dominance in Texas before the 1990s was during Reconstruction, when Edmund J. Davis was governor. Davis, a native of Florida, moved to Texas in 1848 and opposed secession in 1861. In 1869 he was elected governor in an election in which less than 50 percent of registered white citizens voted because of federal Reconstruction laws and a boycott by Conservative Democrats.[32]

The Republican Party was divided between Conservative Republicans and the Radicals under Davis. In his determination to protect the rights of freed formerly enslaved people, Davis instituted policies that were unpopular with both political parties. One such controversy was Davis's State Police. This police force employed formerly enslaved people and both former Union and Confederate soldiers. The force was given extraordinary powers and was entirely under Davis's control, which was considered excessive. Because of all these factors, the force was unpopular with many Texans. As we saw earlier, Texans tend to be conservative, regardless of their party affiliation. That was as true in the aftermath of the Civil War as it is today. Davis's administration was thus controversial for Democrats and Republicans alike and was especially a source of acrimony for former Confederates.[33]

V. O. Key Jr. observed that following the Civil War and the experiences of Reconstruction, southerners felt a very strong resentment toward the rest of the nation and the party that dominated it after the Civil War. This resentment bonded the South together as a unit, and in part because of controversial figures such as Governor E. J. Davis, it voted uniformly against Republicans.[34]

The One-Party Democratic Era in Texas

Reconstruction ended in Texas in 1874, and for more than half a century, Texas was a unified one-party Democratic state. When Davis lost his bid for reelection in 1873, the switch from Republican to Democratic control was swift. From 1874 until 1961, no Republican was elected to statewide office, and only a few were elected to other offices. In 1928, the state did vote for a Republican president, casting its Electoral College votes for Herbert Hoover. Notably, however, Hoover's opponent was Al Smith, a Roman Catholic from New York, whose candidacy suffered from anti-Catholic sentiment as well as opposition to the Democratic machine politics of Tammany Hall.

Certain factors were influential in deflecting Republican challenges and allowing the Democratic Party to dominate. Several third-party movements arose during the last three decades of the nineteenth century, and the conservative Democrats who controlled the party effectively destroyed all competition.

In 1877, the Greenback Party (initially, Greenback clubs) formed in the South and West in reaction to declining farm prices. In Texas, the Greenbackers recruited from the more radical farmers. They demanded currency expansion ("greenbacks") to drive up agricultural prices, and other Progressive priorities such as an income tax, the secret ballot, direct election of U.S. senators, better schools, and reduced railroad freight rates. In 1878, Greenbackers won 12 seats in the Texas legislature and even won a U.S. House seat.[35] But the Greenbackers faded quickly, replaced by the Populists.[36]

The People's Party—or Populists—had a large impact on the national Democratic Party (as depicted in the political cartoon on the next page) and

Swallowed! Political cartoon showing a python with the head of William Jennings Bryan, as the Populist Party, swallowing the Democratic Party donkey, 1900.

Library of Congress, Prints & Photographs Division [LC-DIG-ppmsca-25438]

the U.S. system as a whole, despite its short life. Formed in the early 1890s from the remnants of other agrarian reform groups, the Populists were primarily a farm movement but expanded their membership to include urban labor voters. The Populists were anti-elite and stood for a graduated income tax, direct election of senators, an eight-hour work day, and government ownership of the railroad.[37]

In Texas, the Populists were a "coalition of Anglo small farmers, Blacks, and labor," and currency issues predominated.[38] The national party had its greatest electoral success in the presidential election of 1892, when Populist candidate James B. Weaver of Iowa won four states and 22 Electoral College votes. Weaver and Texas gubernatorial candidate Thomas Nugent won about a quarter of the vote in the state. Despite its successes early in the decade, populism waned as an independent force in the country and in Texas because the Democratic Party adopted many of its planks and the national economy improved.[39]

> **Understanding Impact** This section describes populism as a political movement in the 1890s. "Populism" is a word used to describe politicians today as well, including "right populists" such as U.S. Senators Ted Cruz and Josh Hawley and "left populists" such as U.S. senator Bernie Sanders and U.S. Representative Alexandria Ocasio-Cortez. Given what you know, what do you see as the positives and negatives of populism? How can politicians on the right and the left both be thought of as populists?

Fractures in the Texas Democratic Party

As the Populists declined, the Progressives gained steam as the key reform movement. Despite its differences with the Populists, the Progressive movement did take up some Populist causes and carried them across the goal line in the early twentieth century. However, the Progressives did not share the anti-elitism and anti-centralism of the Populists. In fact, the Progressives embodied "a faith that educated and civilized individuals can, through the use of reason, determine what is best for society as a whole."[40] Thus it is not surprising that the Progressives favored elite (and national) management of government and the economy to lead the country forward. More specifically, Progressive causes included both political and economic reforms, such as women's right to vote, prohibition of the sale of alcohol, direct election of U.S. senators, antimonopoly efforts, and greater regulation of business, as well as progressive taxation and other egalitarian reforms.[41]

Women in Texas waged a long campaign to gain the right to vote, starting in the Constitutional Convention of 1868–1869. Minnie Fisher Cunningham was president of the Texas Equal Suffrage Association and a leader in the campaign nationally to adopt the Nineteenth Amendment to the Constitution, which gave women the right to vote nationwide. She and others like her continued the campaign until in 1919 Texas became the ninth state to ratify the amendment. Cunningham was also the first woman to run for the United States Senate from Texas.[42] Also in 1919, Texas ratified the prohibition amendment to the federal Constitution. The Progressive movement in Texas achieved goals that some in the conservative wing of the party had opposed.[43]

Though there was no effective challenge to Democratic dominance from outside the party, conflicts erupted within the party. Infighting took place among factions—the pro-business conservatives, liberals (including progressives, who were more critical of business and championed civil rights), and moderates. More people from minority groups joined the ranks of the Democratic Party over time, but the party's conservative element eventually found more in common with religious groups and those newly settled in Texas for economic reasons.

One might refer to this era in Texas as having shifted from a one-party Democratic to a two-party system, with the two parties being the conservative Democrats and the liberal Democrats. This split was most obvious with the rise of the Texas Regulars, a group within the Texas Democratic Party. The Regulars opposed FDR's New Deal and the growth of government championed by the more liberal national party. They also chafed at wartime economic restrictions. In the 1944 presidential election, they came up with an ultimately unsuccessful plan to take electors from Roosevelt in hopes of throwing the election into the House of Representatives, where a conservative southern Democrat—part of the group who would in 1948 become leaders of the segregationist Dixiecrats—would have a chance of being made president.[44]

A lack of competition from outside the party meant that general elections in November hardly mattered. Instead, the earlier Democratic Party primary election determined electoral outcomes. However, there was stiff competition between the conservative and liberal wings of the Democratic Party.

Writing about Texas political parties in 1949, V. O. Key Jr. observed: "In Texas the vague outlines of a politics are emerging in which irrelevancies are pushed into the background and the people divided broadly along liberal and conservative lines." This division, according to Key, was due to "personal insecurity of men suddenly made rich who are fearful lest they lose their wealth. . . . The Lone Star State is concerned about money and how to make it, about oil and sulfur and gas, about cattle and dust storms and irrigation, about cotton and banking and Mexicans."[45] Until the late 1960s, Texas politics revolved almost exclusively around personality and economic issues.

Party Realignment in Texas

Learning Objective: Explain the history of party realignment and one-party Republican dominance in Texas.

The long-running Democratic Party dominance of Texas politics did not last forever. Changes in voting behavior can transform the party system. Texas has undergone a significant change in the voting behavior of its citizens over the past 50 years. The name for this change is party realignment.

Realignment is "a decisive shift in the balance of power between political parties, creating new coalitions and leaving one party and one ideology with lasting dominance."[46] V. O. Key Jr. defined one type of realignment as "a movement of the members of a population category from party to party that extends over several presidential elections and appears to be independent of the peculiar factors influencing the vote at individual elections."[47] Another political scientist, Gerald Pomper, classified "realigning elections" as those "in which one party displaces the other as the majority party."[48]

Regardless of the particular definition used, the term "realignment" does not apply to a temporary deviation in voting behavior, such as when a lifelong party member crosses over to vote for the opposing party in a single election. Rather, realignment is a long-lasting change occurring on a large scale that affects the party landscape, as well as the relationship of the parties to each other. As the political landscape evolved from one of Democratic Party dominance to one of Republican Party dominance, such a change took place in Texas.

Political realignment can have many causes. In 1903, the Texas Democratic Party instituted the white primary, barring African Americans from participating in their primary. As this was a time of effective single-party Democratic control of Texas politics, the winner of the Democratic primary was virtually assured of winning the general election. Therefore, not being able to vote in the Democratic Party primary meant that African Americans in Texas had no meaningful vote at all. In 1944, in a case brought by Lonnie Smith, a Black dentist from Houston, the U.S. Supreme Court held that the white primary violated the Fourteenth Amendment equal protection rights of African Americans and banned the practice.[49]

Another important barrier to African American voting was the poll tax. The poll tax was added to the Texas Constitution in 1902 and required payment of $1.50 for the privilege of voting. Given that annual income averaged about $300 (roughly $6.00 a week), this was more than many Texans could afford to pay. After the poll tax was implemented, African American voting participation fell from 80 percent to about 15 percent, crippling the Texas Republican Party. The poll tax was not completely abolished until 1966.

When Congress passed the Civil Rights Act of 1964, Texas saw a large-scale shift of Anglo voters from the Democratic to the Republican Party. Conservative

realignment
"A lasting shift of party loyalty and attachment" (as defined by James L. Sundquist in *Dynamics of the Party System: Alignment and Realignment of Political Parties in the United States* [Washington, D.C.: Brookings Institute, 1983], p. 4)

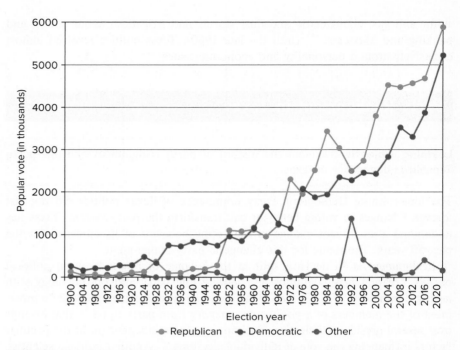

FIGURE 11.1 **Popular Vote by Party in Texas during Presidential Elections**

Source: Texas Secretary of State, https://www.sos.state.tx.us/elections/historical/presidential.shtml.

Texas Democrats were disenchanted with the national party apparatus responsible for passing the act.[50]

The graph in Figure 11.1 shows how Texans fled the Democratic Party and joined the Republicans in response to the twin shocks of the New Deal and passage of the Civil Rights Act of 1964.

Understanding Impact As you've seen, for many years Texas used a variety of tactics attempting to limit African American voting. Today some people argue that policies like Texas's photo ID requirement will have the effect of disenfranchising many voters, particularly racial and ethnic minorities. Others say such requirements are necessary to deter fraud, though no evidence of widespread fraud exists. Should a democracy be obligated to make voting as easy as possible, or should voters have to bear a burden of responsibility to exercise their voting rights? Does a state's history of pernicious voter discrimination mean it should have even more responsibility to improve accessibility of voting?

A Three-Party State

In the 1952 and 1956 presidential elections, many Yellow Dog Democrats (individuals who strongly identify as Democrats regardless of the party's ideological position) broke with tradition and voted for the Republican presidential candidate, Dwight D. Eisenhower. The leader of this movement was Governor Allan Shivers, the leader of the conservative faction of the Texas Democratic Party. This faction chose to dissociate from the New Deal/Fair Deal element of the national Democratic Party and from any candidate it might put forward.

In 1952, at the state Democratic Party convention, Governor Shivers persuaded the state delegates to endorse Eisenhower. The Texas Republican Party convention also nominated Shivers and most state-wide Democratic candidates as the Republican nominees. Thus, Shivers and most statewide office seekers were candidates for *both* political parties in 1952. This group became known as the "Shivercrats." The liberal faction of the Texas Democratic Party, still aligned with the national party, became known as the "Loyalists."[51]

This action, and a similar action in 1956, initiated the Texas tradition of supporting Republican presidential candidates while retaining Democratic Party dominance over state offices. Presidential politics in 1952 broke the tradition of **straight-ticket voting,** in which voters select candidates from the same party for all offices on the ballot—at least for the top offices on that ticket.

Through all this, the Republican Party became a legitimate political power in Texas for the first time since Reconstruction. The conservative and liberal wings of the state's Democratic Party were still in conflict, so Texas at this time looked like a three-party state: liberal Democrats, conservative Democrats, and Republicans.

Allan Shivers, governor of Texas, 1949–1957
John Dominis/The LIFE Picture Collection/Getty Images

The Election of John Tower

In 1960, Lyndon Johnson, the Democratic senior senator from Texas, ran for reelection to the U.S. Senate and won. At the same time, however, he was also John F. Kennedy's vice presidential running mate. Johnson's presence on the Democratic ticket temporarily halted Texas's movement toward the Republican Party. In 1961, after the Kennedy-Johnson victory, Texas held a special election to fill Johnson's seat. John Tower won this election, becoming not only the first Republican U.S. senator from Texas since Reconstruction but also the first Republican statewide officeholder in Texas since Reconstruction. Tower had won a plurality against a huge field of candidates in the initial round of voting, and then he claimed victory with a slight majority in the runoff election.

straight-ticket voting
Casting all your votes for candidates of a single party

Tower's election seemed to herald the beginning of a new era of two-party politics in the state. In the 1962 elections, Republicans managed to field candidates for many statewide, congressional, and local races. There were, for a variety of reasons, few successes. Some of these candidates were very weak, and some proved an embarrassment for the Republicans. Tower won reelection in 1966, 1972, and 1978, but it would be 17 years after Tower's first victory before another Republican won statewide office. Tower was frequently at odds with the

Elect
JOHN G.
TOWER
For U. S. Senator

**For Truly Texan
Representation
In Washington**

Campaign literature from Tower's election
Jimmy Tyler/Senator John G. Tower Archives, Southwestern University, Georgetown, TX

conservative wing of the Texas Republican Party—by supporting Gerald Ford over Ronald Reagan, for example—and ended up doing little to build the party statewide.[52]

A Two-Party State

For a time, Republicans had limited success in electing legislators and local officeholders. However, the election of Republican Bill Clements as governor in 1978 marked the real beginning of two-party politics in Texas. Governor Clements used his power to make appointments to boards, commissions, and judgeships, and to recruit people who would publicly declare their Republicanism. Some referred to these new converts as "closet Republicans" who had finally gone public. These appointments helped build the Republican Party in Texas and promote party realignment.

Clements's 1982 loss to Democrat Mark White was a blow to the Republicans because the party also had little success in winning other high offices. That year, the Democrats elected to statewide office included Ann Richards as state treasurer, Jim Hightower as agriculture commissioner, Gary Mauro as land commissioner, and Jim Mattox as attorney general.

Republicans bounced back and set the stage for today's Texas Republican Party in 1986, when Clements returned to the governor's office. He defeated White in what many termed a "revenge match," and he used his return to resume building the Republican Party in Texas. The political career of Governor Clements ended after his second term, largely because of his participation in the Southern Methodist University "Pony Express" football scandal. The school maintained a secret fund to pay SMU football players and their families. At the time, Clements was chair of the SMU Board of Governors as well as governor of Texas. He admitted knowing about the fund.[53]

The "Conversion" and Election of Phil Gramm

After four terms in office, John Tower announced he would not seek reelection to the U.S. Senate in 1984. Phil Gramm, the Democratic representative from Texas's Sixth Congressional District, used Tower's retirement to advance from the U.S. House to the Senate. Gramm had first been elected to the U.S. House of Representatives in 1978 as a Democrat. By early 1981, he had gained some national prominence for his work on the federal budget under Republican president Ronald Reagan. Gramm, who served as a member of the House Budget Committee, leaked Democratic strategy to the White House Budget Office.[54] Because of his disloyalty to the party and because of House rules, Gramm was not reappointed to another term on the Budget Committee.

Gramm used the loss of his committee seat as an excuse to convert to the Republican Party. In 1983 Gramm resigned his seat in the U.S. House. Outgoing Republican governor Clements called a special election, which was held one month after Gramm's resignation, to fill Gramm's seat. Because no other candidate could possibly put together a successful campaign in so short a time and due to the fit between his views and the state's conservative majority, Gramm

Former senator Gramm, with wife Wendy by his side
Kenneth Lambert/AP Images

easily won reelection to the same seat he had just vacated—this time as a Republican. In 1984, "fully baptized" as a Republican, Gramm won election to the U.S. Senate seat previously held by John Tower, thus continuing Republican Party control of one of Texas's two seats in the U.S. Senate. Gramm easily won reelection in 1990 and 1996 but chose not to run for reelection in 2002, ending a long career in Texas politics.

Texas Republicans Seize Control

In 1988, the Republican Party in Texas made significant gains, aided by Bill Clements's return to the governor's mansion and George H. W. Bush's election to the presidency. The party won four statewide offices. Three Republicans won election to the Texas Supreme Court, and Kent Hance was elected to the Texas Railroad Commission.

In 1990, Republicans captured the offices of state treasurer and agriculture commissioner and another seat on the state supreme court. The big setback for the Republicans in 1990 was the loss of the governor's office. Bill Clements did not seek reelection. Clayton Williams, a political newcomer, used his considerable wealth to win the Republican nomination. His campaign for governor was something of a disaster, and he lost to Democrat Ann Richards. Williams's loss, in a way, aided George W. Bush's 1994 gubernatorial and 2000 presidential victories. If Williams had won and served two terms, Bush could not have been elected governor until 1998, and this would have made it less likely for him to make a legitimate bid for the presidency in 2000.

In 1992, after serving as U.S. senator from Texas for 20 years, Democrat Lloyd Bentsen resigned to become secretary of the treasury under President

Ann Richards, governor of Texas, 1991–1995
Bettmann/Getty Images

Clinton. His resignation opened a path for Republican Kay Bailey Hutchison to capture Texas's second seat in the U.S. Senate, alongside Phil Gramm. Republicans thus held both of Texas's U.S. Senate seats for the first time since Reconstruction.

The One-Party Republican Era in Texas

The 1994 election marked the year that Texas went from its brief foray into two-party politics to a one-party Republican system. In 1994, the Republicans captured all three seats on the Railroad Commission as well as a majority of the seats on the state supreme court, and they retained control of the agriculture commissioner's office. They gained three additional seats on the state board of education, for a total of eight. In addition, George W. Bush was elected governor. When the dust cleared, Republicans controlled 23 of a total 27 statewide offices. Later elections solidified their position. After the 1998 elections, Republicans held all statewide offices. After the 2002 elections, Republicans held all statewide offices and were in the majority in both the Texas House and Senate (see Table 11.2). These victories substantially changed Texas party politics.

For realignment to have occurred, the shift in party affiliation must be enduring and of considerable magnitude. Therefore, party realignment cannot be confirmed unless a significant amount of time has passed, and the observed change was large in scope.[55] In retrospect, it seems clear that such a realignment has occurred in Texas. More than 20 years after the state converted to Republican dominance, Republicans still hold all statewide offices and the majority of state legislative seats. Today the state is as solidly one-party Republican as it had once been one-party Democratic.

TABLE 11.2

Total Offices Held by Republicans, 1974–2022

Year	U.S. Senate (2)	U.S. House (36)	Statewide Office (27)	Texas Senate (31)	Texas House (150)	County Office	Board of Education (15)
1974	1	2	0	3	16	53	—
1976	1	2	0	3	19	67	—
1978	1	4	1	4	22	87	—
1980	1	5	1	7	35	166	—
1982	1	5	0	5	36	270	—
1984	1	10	0	6	52	377	—
1986	1	10	1	6	56	504	—
1988	1	8	5	8	57	608	5
1990	1	8	6	8	57	717	5
1992	1	9	7	13	58	814	5
1994	2	11	13	14	61	900	8
1996	2	11	13	17	68	950	8
1998	2	11	18	16	71	973	9
2000	2	11	18	16	72	1,231	9
2002	2	15	27	19	88	1,327	10
2004	2	22	27	19	87	1,390	10
2006	2	22	27	19	81	1,410	10
2008	2	22	27	19	76	1,345	6
2010	2	26	27	19	101	1,356	6
2012	2	23	27	19	100	n/a	11
2014	2	25	27	20	97	n/a	10
2016	2	25	27	20	95	n/a	10
2018	2	23	27	19	83	n/a	10
2020	2	23	27	18	83	n/a	10
2022	2	25	27	19*	86	n/a	9†

Note: The number in parentheses at the top of each column represents the current total number of offices in that category. State Board of Education was not elected until 1988.

*19 as of November 17, with one race still undecided.
†9 as of November 17, with one race still undecided.

The Current Party System in Texas

Learning Objective: Explain the history of party realignment and one-party Republican dominance in Texas.

With Republican dominance firmly established in Texas, the state party system has remained fairly stable for several decades. After George W. Bush's rise to the presidency in 2000, his Republican lieutenant governor, Rick Perry, succeeded him in the governor's office. Perry was subsequently reelected for three full terms and became the longest-serving governor in Texas history (as well as one of the longest-serving state governors in U.S. history). After more than 14 years in office, Perry was succeeded by current governor Greg Abbott. Texas politicians have continued to attain prominence on the national stage as well; Perry and fellow Texans Ron Paul and Ted Cruz have all thrown their hats in the ring as Republican Party presidential candidates in recent years. Perhaps foreshadowing future shifts in Texas party dynamics, two Democratic politicians,

Beto O'Rourke and Julián Castro, both mounted long-shot campaigns for the presidency in 2020, as well. Both decided to end their candidacies early after they failed to garner significant support in an exceptionally crowded field.

Today's Texas Republicans

The Republican Party in Texas, like most dominant parties, has multiple, sometimes overlapping, wings with differing agendas. Two of the main wings are the social conservatives and the more pro-market, libertarian Republicans. However, traditional establishment and pro-business conservatives (some of whom might more accurately be called moderates in contemporary Texas politics), such as long-term speaker of the house Joe Straus (2009–2017), are also well represented in the diverse Republican caucus.

Traditionally, pro-business conservatives have been at the core of the Texas establishment. Their priorities were to keep spending and taxes low while limiting state government regulation of the economy. Their goal has been to foster a pro-business climate, even when a general free-market outlook was compromised by active government support of business. This has meant support for government spending on infrastructure, such as roads, highways, and port development and maintenance. But it has also meant more active efforts, such as special subsidies for companies like the Texas Enterprise Fund and the Texas Emerging Technology Fund.[56]

Of course, some due consideration is also given to the basic economic liberalism shared by the pro-market, libertarian Republicans. This economic liberalism is centered on a belief in the existence of an efficient, largely self-regulating market that functions best when government strongly defends property rights. But either because of the power of special interests or a principled position that sometimes the business climate needs a helping hand, the pro-business establishment Republicans have not generally been too particular about adhering strictly to the creed of economic liberalism. This, in turn, drives the more pure free-market libertarian Republicans to call some of the pro-business efforts "crony capitalism," inconsistent with true capitalism.[57]

The social conservatives focus on "culture war" issues and are troubled by a perceived decline of morality in Texas and the United States in general. These conservatives stress their pro-life stance against abortion, oppose LGBTQ civil rights (including same-sex marriage), support prayer in public schools (although this is not a consensus view even among social conservatives), and have pushed for teaching alternatives to evolution (such as creationism or intelligent design) in public schools. In *Obergefell v. Hodges* (2015), the U.S. Supreme Court dealt a blow to Texas social conservatives when it ruled that states may not ban same-sex marriage. Despite that ruling, two Texas conservatives pursued a lawsuit against the City of Houston, opposing its policy providing equal marriage benefits to all legally married couples, whether same sex or opposite sex. The suit, after years meandering through the courts, including a visit to the U.S. Supreme Court, was ultimately dismissed in 2021.[58]

The burgeoning strength of the social conservative wing of the Texas Republican Party was heralded in the July 2012 Republican primary for U.S. Senate when Tea Party candidate and social conservative Ted Cruz decisively defeated the pro-business conservative and establishment candidate (and then-lieutenant governor) David Dewhurst (57 percent to 43 percent).

Republican Ted Cruz first won election to the U.S. Senate in 2012; he retained his seat in 2018 despite stiff opposition by Democrat Beto O'Rourke.

Jabin Botsford/The Washington Post/Getty Images

Ted Cruz faced reelection in 2018. He won the Republican primary with no major opposition, but faced a serious Democratic Party challenger in U.S. Representative Beto O'Rourke. After a seesaw election night, Cruz held the seat for Texas Republicans by 2.6 percent, far below his 15.8 percent 2012 margin, and trailing Trump's 5.6% margin of victory in the state. Republicans celebrated holding the seat, and Democrats viewed the narrow margin as a hopeful sign for the future.

There is also a rising force in the Texas GOP—the more pro-market, libertarian Republicans who are as committed to personal liberty as they are to economic freedom and who challenge both the party establishment and the social conservatives. Indeed, Wayne Slater of the *Dallas Morning News* argues that the "real divide within the Texas GOP is between Christian conservatives who have been dominant in recent years and 'liberty' groups with a more secular view— those who believe government should set a moral agenda and those who want as little government as possible."[59] Some, including supporters of Kentucky senator and recent Republican presidential candidate Rand Paul (son of long-time Texas Republican congressional member Ron Paul), believe at the national level that these libertarian types represent the future of the Republican Party if it is to compete with the Democrats. It is unclear whether they can make serious inroads in the still relatively conservative Texas GOP or find a way to live together with more socially conservative Republicans in a "fusionist" party that somewhat mirrors the one that Ronald Reagan put together in the 1980s.[60]

During its heyday, the Tea Party brought together some pro-market libertarian Republicans and some social conservative Republicans. The group also included anti-establishment or more populist tenants who raged against the many problems they see coming from the political and cultural power centers on both coasts. Tea Party success in elections has dwindled, though.[61] Texas Republicans began to consider the Tea Party's influence a thing of the past.[62]

The waning power of the Tea Party was perhaps responsible for Donald Trump's winning the 2016 presidential race with a smaller percentage of the overall Texas popular vote, and a smaller margin of victory, than any Republican nominee since the 1996 Bob Dole vs. Bill Clinton race.[63] Trump's populist appeal elicits enthusiasm from that wing of the Republican Party, but business and social conservatives turned out less strongly. In the 2020 election, Trump carried Texas again, though again with a smaller percentage of the vote than other state-wide Republican races.[64] Despite missing coat tails from the top of the ticket, however, Republicans once again won every state-wide office and held onto their majorities in the Texas House and Senate. Maintaining those majorities allowed Texas Republicans to control the always-contentious decennial redistricting process,[65] and create districts favorable to Republican candidates for the next ten years.[66]

Today's Texas Democrats

In contrast with twentieth-century Texas Democrats, the state Democratic Party today appears to have less factional infighting because the vast majority of conservative Democrats have stampeded to the Republican Party.

Though their internecine warfare may be less pronounced than that between the Republicans' social conservatives and economic conservatives, Texas Democrats have their own divides, between more moderate "Blue Dog" Democrats and Progressives. While Blue Dog Democrats may be liberal in comparison to Republicans, supporting DACA, the Affordable Care Act (Obamacare) and LGBTQ issues, for example, their focus on fiscal responsibility, strong defense and border security[67] separates them from Progressives, whose focus is more on social safety net issues. Two Democrats in Texas's U.S. House delegation are members of the Congressional Blue Dog Coalition, and a third resigned his seat in 2022 to move back into the private sector.[68]

Tension between the center-left and progressive wings of the Texas Democratic coalition heated up during the 2020 presidential primary. Senator Bernie Sanders had been a favorite of progressives since his first campaign for mayor of Burlington, Vermont in 1981. After an unsuccessful run against Hillary Clinton for the Democratic Party presidential nomination in 2016, Sanders was in a strong position in the 2020 race. He was, in fact, leading in Texas presidential polls during the month leading up to the Texas Super Tuesday Primary.[69]

However, Sanders' lead was due in large part to splitting of the vote between more moderate Democratic presidential candidates. Many in the Democratic Party establishment feared splitting this moderate vote would hand the presidential nomination to Sanders, who, as a Democratic Socialist, they believed would likely be a weaker candidate against the incumbent President Trump.[70] After Joe Biden's strong showing in the South Carolina primary and just days before voting in Texas, three Democratic presidential candidates dropped out of the race and endorsed Biden. In what was called a "stunning turnaround,"[71] Biden won the state by almost 5 percentage points.

The progressive wing of the Texas Democratic Party in 2022 was hopeful that in Beto O'Rourke they had a candidate who could challenge Greg Abbott

Beto O'Rourke speaks with supporters at the Rise Up! rally in Austin, TX.
michelmond/Alamy Stock Photo

for governor of Texas. O'Rourke easily won the Democratic gubernatorial primary in 2022. He tread a progressive path on issues such as abortion, marijuana legalization, health care, voting rights and guns that provided plenty of fodder for Republican television ads. A Democrat had not won a state-wide election in Texas since 1994, and O'Rourke was unable to reverse that trend, losing decisively to the incumbent Greg Abbott.

Blue Texas?

Democrats have long viewed demographic realities in the state as cutting in their favor, though, particularly the relative increase in the size of the Hispanic population. The 2020 census documented Texas population growth enabling Texas to gain two more seats in its congressional delegation. As 95% of this growth was made up of people of color, chiefly Hispanic, and as communities of color tend to support Democrats, they believe they will be the beneficiaries of demographic change in the state.[72]

Democrats are hoping they will benefit from the influx of in-migrants from other states that could change the state's political culture. Many of these migrants may consider themselves "refugees" from more liberal states, though, and thus not be as much of a political benefit as the Democrats hope. And some liberal Democratic policy preferences may not be attractive to more socially conservative Hispanics.

Despite demographic trends, Democrats have struggled to win elections; no Democrat has been elected to statewide office since 1994.[73]

Democratic Party operatives were encouraged by Beto O'Rourke's close race in 2018 against U.S. senator Ted Cruz[74] and improved results in traditionally Republican Texas suburbs.[75] They also gained two seats in the Texas Senate and 12 seats in the Texas House. Given Democrats' success in the 2018 elections, they hoped to gain enough additional seats to secure a majority in the House and mounted a major effort to flip Texas "blue" in 2020.[76] (In recent years, Republicans have been associated with the color red and Democrats with blue.[77]) In 2020, however, while Republicans lost one seat in the Texas Senate, Texas House results left the party split unchanged, putting Republicans in a strong position heading into the 2021 Texas legislative session.[78]

So despite what Democrats believe are promising demographic trends, including a sharp uptick in Hispanic voting in 2020, as shown in Figure 11.2, a Democratic destiny for Texas is far from assured. As mentioned above, and as shown by Donald Trump's better-than-expected 2020 results in predominately Hispanic counties in South Texas, conservative Hispanics may not be as reliably Democratic as some have hoped. Additionally, many Texas Hispanics are too young to vote. The Hispanic under-18 population is the largest of any racial and ethnic group by far, and is projected to stay that way into the future.[79] Finally, the Republican Party also gets a vote in this war for the future. Republicans aren't likely to stand back and allow Texas to turn blue without a fight. They have already begun greater outreach efforts toward minorities.

Republicans demonstrated in the 2020 presidential race that they can successfully to appeal to Hispanic voters in Texas. Though President Trump performed less well than other state-wide Republican candidates, he overperformed expectations in several South Texas counties, losing by smaller margins than most observers anticipated, and even winning some traditionally blue counties.[80] Republicans will clearly not cede Texas based on demographic trends.

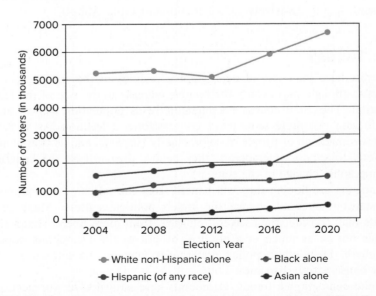

FIGURE 11.2 **Texas Voter Turnout by Race in Presidential Elections, 2004 to 2020**

Source: https://www.census.gov/topics/public-sector/voting/data/tables.2020.List_1863097513.html

Focus On

The Political Affiliation of Hispanics

Nerthuz/Shutterstock

Hispanic Texans are more likely to be affiliated with the Democratic Party than with the Republican Party. According to 2020 pre-election presidential polling data, about 29 percent of Texas Hispanics definitely intended to vote to reelect Donald Trump and about 56 percent definitely intended not to. For African Americans, the comparable numbers were 9 percent definitely would vote for President Trump and 81 percent definitely would not.[81] So while Hispanics prefer the Democratic Party, the numbers are within reach for Republicans who make an effective appeal.

This preference for the Democratic Party among Hispanics has not translated into Democratic victories at the polls. According to 2018 election exit polls, 69 percent of Hispanic voters chose the Democratic candidate, Beto O'Rourke, while only 30 percent voted for Ted Cruz, the Republican. This sizable Democratic advantage didn't deliver the election to O'Rourke, who lost a close race (50.9 percent to 48.3 percent). Still, while this result among Hispanics may have been partially a reflection of the individuals in the race, as opposed to strict party identification, a gap of that size must be troubling for Republicans.[82] Viewed from another perspective, Hispanic Texans are more likely to describe themselves as conservative or moderate than are Hispanics in California,[83] which encourages Republican strategists in Texas.

Many eyes are trained on how the Hispanic population will affect the future political balance in Texas. Polling shows that Texas Hispanics think the most important issue facing the state is, perhaps not surprisingly, immigration, which was cited by 19 percent of Hispanics statewide. The next most important issue was "gun control/gun violence" followed by border security, health care, and education.[84] The top results are not substantially different from the population as a whole, except that border security beats out gun control among the overall population.[85] Appeals to Hispanics, therefore, may not need to be very different from appeals to any concerned voter.

The Republican Party of Texas has made specific efforts to appeal to Hispanics, such as the formation of interest groups to recruit Hispanic candidates for office and the promotion of Hispanic leadership within the GOP. Texas Democrats, for their part, have outlined a strategy of increasing voter registration and turnout among Hispanics in the state. Perhaps the biggest challenge for Democrats who had hoped to turn Texas blue in 2020 was that polls showed an enthusiasm gap, with only 35 percent of Hispanic voters saying they were enthusiastic about voting in the 2020 election, versus 50 percent for the overall population and 60 percent for whites. Even the most well-crafted appeals to Hispanics from either Republicans or Democrats will make little difference in the future if those Hispanics don't turn out to vote.[86]

Critical Thinking Questions

1. Thinking back on what we have learned about voting patterns in Texas, what are the challenges each party faces in terms of recruiting Hispanic voters to their cause?
2. In light of anticipated demographic changes in the state, how do you think they will impact Texas's party system?

The fight for Hispanic voters will also be affected by whether the Republican governing majority is successful in maintaining Texas's general economic growth, as well as providing opportunities for the Hispanic community in particular. In November 2022, Republicans took a major step when Monica De La Cruz won the south Texas 15th U.S. House district, the first time a Republican had won the district. Coupled with 2020 Republican presidential candidate Donald Trump's unexpectedly strong performance among Hispanics, Republicans are hopeful that expectations among Texas Democrats that an increased Hispanic population will improve their chances of turning Texas blue will turn out to have been unfounded. As the 2024 presidential race heats up, Donald Trump already having officially kicked off his campaign, the eyes of political observers across the country will be turned toward Texas to see what happens in this growing demographic group.

For now, Democrats' hopes and Republicans' fears that Texas will turn blue seem unlikely, though demographics may cause the state to turn a shade of purple, Republicans and Democrats alike have an urgent electoral motivation to appeal to the Texas Hispanic population. Republicans will try to build on the success Donald Trump enjoyed on the border, and Democrats will try to maintain their traditional majorities among people of color.

Understanding Impact As you've learned, political party dominance in Texas has changed dramatically over the years. The same has been true for the nation as a whole. This section has described the potential for Democratic Party gains from increased Hispanic political participation, but also that Texas Hispanics see themselves as more conservative than Hispanics in other states, and thus possibly amenable to Republican outreach. What do you think the impact of the expanded Hispanic share of the Texas population will be? How should the political parties appeal to this increasingly influential population?

CORE OBJECTIVE

Being Socially Responsible . . .

What effect, if any, do factions have on enhancing or diminishing civic engagement? In your opinion, do factions promote acceptance of diverse opinions?

Third Parties in Texas

Learning Objective: Describe third-party movements in the United States and in Texas.

Although the story of Texas politics is mostly the story of two major political parties, third-party movements develop in Texas from time to time. (As we discussed earlier, because of the historic rift in the Democratic Party between the Shivercrats and the Loyalists, in Texas the question of what makes a third party is open for debate. Still, it is generally easy to identify third parties as distinct from Republicans and Democrats.) Some third parties are national, whereas others have been state based. At a national level, segregationist George Wallace used the American Independent Party to run for president in 1968 and managed to gain nearly 19 percent of the vote in Texas.[87] In the 1970s, the **Raza Unida (United Race)** Party ran

Raza Unida (United Race)

Minor party that supported election of Hispanic Americans in Texas in the 1970s candidates for several state and local offices, especially in South Texas. As a Raza Unida candidate, Ramsey Muniz managed to gain 6 percent of the vote for governor in 1972. Raza Unida tried to establish itself as an inclusive party in part by running a woman, Alma Canales, for lieutenant governor that year.[88]

The Libertarian Party has put forth candidates for statewide office in Texas for many years. It adheres to the principles of respect for individual rights, constitutionalism and the rule of law, personal responsibility, and limited government.[89] In general, Libertarian Party (LP) candidates do not receive more than a small percentage of the vote, especially because many Republicans also espouse the same principles. It is also the case that not all philosophical libertarians belong to the LP. Nobel Prize–winning economist Milton Friedman, for example, famously noted he was a "small-l" libertarian and a "large-R" Republican—meaning his party of choice was the Republican Party even though his principles were largely libertarian. The most successful Libertarian candidate for governor of Texas was Jeff Daiell, who received 3.3 percent of the vote in 1990.[90]

The LP has consistently maintained its status as a minor party in Texas and guaranteed its candidates' appearance on the ballot by garnering at least 5 percent of total votes cast in statewide races. But times are changing. The legislature in 2019 lowered the requirement from 5 percent in the previous election to 2 percent in any of the previous five elections, but added a requirement of filing fees or collection of signatures. Because Libertarian candidates gained over 2 percent in several statewide races in 2022, these new requirements will give the LP automatic ballot access through 2032 (five elections following the 2022 election) if they can afford to pay filing fees or gather enough signatures.[91] Despite its staying power, it is highly unlikely the LP will ever be a major electoral force in the state. This is partially because of the difficulty any third party has in establishing itself. Also, its platform so nearly resembles that of the Republican Party that voters tend to vote for the party they are more familiar with.

Texas industrialist Ross Perot ran as an independent candidate for president in 1992; he received about 22 percent of the statewide vote in Texas (see Table 11.3) as well as an impressive 19 percent of the national vote. However, he did not win any states and thus did not earn any electoral college votes.

The 2016 presidential race included a bid from Independent Evan McMullin, a former CIA clandestine agent (spy) who joined the CIA after the 9/11 terrorist attacks and worked undercover gathering intelligence about Al Qaeda and other extremist groups. His campaign was an effort by anti-Trump Republicans to win Utah, McMullin's home state, and possibly throw the election into the House of Representatives, where state Republican delegations would be free to choose their preferred candidate.[92] The strategy didn't work, but McMullin did receive over 42,000 votes in Texas, more than lesser-known third parties typically get.[93]

The Green Party of Texas, which advocates social justice, ecological sustainability, nonviolence, and political reform (including public financing of election campaigns), has been more active in recent years (see Table 11.4).[94] Under Texas's new ballot access rules, as described earlier, the Greens will have automatic ballot access, subject to paying the filing fee or collecting the necessary signatures, at least through 2026 because of having earned over 2 percent in the 2016 Texas Railroad Commission race.[95] Wherever they may end up on the ballot, the Greens (like other Texas third parties) are unlikely to occupy a prominent place in state politics,

TABLE 11.3

Texas General Election Results for President, 1992–2020

Year	Candidate	Percentage of Vote
1992	**Republican** George Bush/Dan Quayle	40.56%
	Democrat Bill Clinton/Al Gore	37.07%
	Independent Ross Perot/James Stockdale	22.01%
	Libertarian Andre Marrou/Nancy Lord	0.32%
1996	**Republican** Bob Dole/Jack Kemp	48.75%
	Democrat Bill Clinton/Al Gore	43.83%
	Independent Ross Perot/James Campbell	6.74%
	Libertarian Harry Browne/Jo Jorgensen	0.36%
2000	**Republican** George W. Bush/Dick Cheney	59.29%
	Democrat Al Gore/Joe Lieberman	37.98%
	Green Ralph Nader/Winona LaDuke	2.15%
	Libertarian Harry Browne/Art Olivier	0.36%
2004	**Republican** George W. Bush/Dick Cheney	61.08%
	Democrat John F. Kerry/John Edwards	38.22%
	Libertarian Michael Badnarik/Richard V. Campagna	0.52%
2008	**Republican** John McCain/Sarah Palin	55.45%
	Democrat Barack Obama/Joe Biden	43.68%
	Libertarian Bob Barr/Wayne A. Root	0.69%
2012	**Republican** Mitt Romney/Paul Ryan	57.16%
	Democrat Barack Obama/Joe Biden	41.38%
	Libertarian Gary Johnson/Jim Gray	1.10%
	Green Jill Stein/Cheri Honkala	0.30%

Continued

TABLE 11.3

2016	**Republican**	
	Donald Trump/Mike Pence	52.23%
	Democrat	
	Hillary Clinton/Tim Kaine	43.24%
	Libertarian	
	Gary Johnson/William Weld	3.16%
	Green	
	Jill Stein/Ajamu Baraka	0.80%
2020	**Republican**	
	Donald Trump/Mike Pence	52.17%
	Democrat	
	Joe Biden/Kamala Harris	46.40%
	Libertarian	
	Jo Jorgensen/Spike Cohen	1.11%
	Green	
	Howie Hawkins/Angela Walker	0.29%

Source: Texas Secretary of State, "1992–Current Election History," http://elections.sos.state. tx.us/elchist.exe.

One way third parties may exert influence is as a spoiler in a close election. The conventional wisdom is that Libertarians steal votes from Republicans and Greens steal from Democrats. If Texas's new ballot access rules increase the likelihood of either party's getting on the ballot, it could, with only a small percentage of the vote, change the results for Republicans and Democrats.[96]

To date, third-party candidates have not had much success getting elected in Texas. The rules governing elections in Texas, as in many other states, do not make it easy for third parties to gain access to the ballot. Even if third parties gain access, they still face an uphill battle to secure the financial resources necessary to run a successful high-dollar media campaign. Often the best a minor party can hope to do is to have its ideas picked up by a major party. Ross Perot is credited with focusing on NAFTA and on the need to balance the federal budget in his 1992 campaign. Echoes of this in the Republican Party were on display during the Donald Trump presidency, as he made reforming NAFTA one of his priorities. Ultimately, the U.S., Mexico and Canada signed the United States Mexico Canada Agreement (USMCA), which revised NAFTA in several ways.[97]

Democrats are struggling with how to respond to an increasing number of their voters who have adopted the progressive ideals of the Green Party, such as the "Green New Deal," even if they don't explicitly acknowledge the influence of Greens in their campaigns.[98]

Challenges for Third Parties

Why have third parties in the United States failed at the federal and state levels? Some scholars point to political and cultural consensus. The United States operates within a narrower ideological range than has most of the world in the past couple of centuries, and most Americans have agreed on the foundations of political order.

While it's true that the United States has for most of its history maintained a general centrist identity, since the 1990s (at least) there has been a trend away

TABLE 11.4

Texas Election Results for Governor, 1994–2022

Year	Candidate	Percentage of Vote
1994	**Republican**	
	George W. Bush	53.47%
	Democrat	
	Ann W. Richards	45.87%
	Libertarian	
	Keary Ehlers	0.64%
1998	**Republican**	
	George W. Bush	68.23%
	Democrat	
	Garry Mauro	31.18%
	Libertarian	
	Lester R. "Les" Turlington Jr.	0.55%
2002	**Republican**	
	Rick Perry	57.80%
	Democrat	
	Tony Sanchez	39.96%
	Libertarian	
	Jeff Daiell	1.46%
	Green	
	Rahul Mahajan	0.70%
2006	**Republican**	
	Rick Perry	39.02%
	Democrat	
	Chris Bell	29.78%
	Independent	
	Carole Keeton Strayhorn	18.11%
	Independent	
	Richard "Kinky" Friedman	12.44%
	Libertarian	
	James Werner	0.60%
2010	**Republican**	
	Rick Perry	54.97%
	Democrat	
	Bill White	42.29%
	Libertarian	
	Kathie Glass	2.19%
	Green	
	Deb Shafto	0.39%
2014	**Republican**	
	Greg Abbott	59.27%
	Democrat	
	Wendy R. Davis	38.90%
	Libertarian	
	Kathie Glass	1.41%
	Green	
	Brandon Parmer	0.39%

Continued

TABLE 11.4

2018	**Republican**	
	Greg Abbott	55.83%
	Democrat	
	Lupe Valdez	42.47%
	Libertarian	
	Mark Jay Tippetts	1.68%
2022	**Republican**	
	Greg Abbott	54.8%
	Democrat	
	Beto O'Rourke	43.8%
	Libertarian	
	Mark Tippetts	1.0%
	Green	
	Delilah Barrios	0.4%

Source: Texas Secretary of State, "1992–Current Election History," http://elections.sos.state. tx.us/elchist.exe.

from our more moderate roots and toward more strident partisanship. What were once fringe ideas are now becoming mainstream. Along with that move away from the center has been a growing hyperpartisanship that threatens to fundamentally reshape the nature of political debate in the United States.[99]

This growth in hyperpartisanship has been accompanied by a shift in the Overton Window, a gauge of what topics are accepted as being within the political mainstream. In recent elections, candidates tended to support NATO treaty commitments and international trade. However, Donald Trump cast doubt on his support for these positions, thus shifting the nature of "acceptable" political discourse toward the political extreme. It remains to be seen if the movement away from the middle will be permanent, or if this movement will enable third parties to gain traction with a broader slice of the public.[100]

Another important reason for the failure of third parties in the United States is the issue of voter identification. Most people grew up with the two major parties and identify themselves politically in reference to those parties.

The lack of proportional representation in state and national legislatures also hurts U.S. third parties. Many countries elect representatives based on the percentage of the national and provincial (state) vote that the parties receive. For example, if in Germany 35 percent of the votes are cast for a Christian Democratic candidate, then Christian Democrats will hold roughly 35 percent of the seats in the national, provincial, or state legislature. In contrast, the United States has single-member districts. A candidate is elected if they receive more votes than any other candidate and becomes that district's sole representative. Therefore, if people vote for a candidate who comes in second or third, their votes do not result in any seats in the legislature.

Another factor that hurts third parties is the fact that candidates can be elected to office by a plurality (winning the most votes but not necessarily more than 50 percent) rather than a majority (winning with more than 50 percent of the votes). Currently, Texas law requires that to win a primary election, a candidate must win a majority of the vote. But candidates in general elections in the United

States and Texas need to win only a plurality of the vote. If a majority were required, third parties and their candidates might be able to strike bargains with major parties to gain support of the major party for the third party's platform. This situation would likely lead to increased interest in those third parties.

The difficulty of third parties in single-member districts with plurality election rules is not surprising given **Duverger's law.**[101] This political science law tells us that the electoral system strongly conditions the type of party system that will result. Therefore, an electoral system in which candidates in single-member districts need only to win a plurality incentivizes parties to develop broad pre-election coalitions. It also disincentivizes narrower parties that cannot win a large vote share (and thus consistently fail to win any elections). Likewise, proportional representation systems create an incentive to form and vote for smaller parties, because they can win seats without winning pluralities or majorities and can even play a key role in coalition governments.

A fifth reason for third-party failure is that the two major parties legally limit access to the ballot. Republicans and Democrats are automatically on the ballot, but other parties need either to pay a substantial filing fee or submit petitions signed by one percent of voters in the previous race. For the next governor's race, for example, that would be 80,759 signatures,[102] and those signers must be eligible voters who have not voted in either the Republican or Democratic primaries. Third parties must therefore spend large amounts of money merely to qualify their candidates for the ballot. The two major parties have no such preliminary costs, so they are free to spend more on the actual campaigns.

Finally, the perception of third-party failure also contributes to the weakness of third parties. Many people think that a vote for a third party is wasted. Past failures reinforce the belief in future failures. No third-party candidate has ever won the U.S. presidency or the Texas governorship.

Third Party Factions in Major Parties

Few examples of third-party movements that have had an impact on state or national policy can be found in the late twentieth century to early twenty-first century. Instead, groups like the Tea Party emerge as a faction within a major party and attempt to influence that party. Indeed, the Tea Party explicitly tried to fight within the Republican Party. This strategy has met with mixed electoral results, but it has certainly led to a fight on "the Right" about the future of conservatism and the Republican brand.

Similarly, a group of Democratic Socialists with Senator Bernie Sanders as their standard bearer have fought to pull the Democratic Party further left in recent elections. Although he has served in the U.S. Senate as an independent, Sanders chose to seek the Democratic presidential nomination in 2016 and 2020 rather than make a more difficult third-party run as a Democratic Socialist.

As with the Republicans and their Tea Party influencers, the long-term impact of its more-extreme minority left wing on the Democratic Party as a whole remains to be seen. Still, in the short-term, the Democrats' progressive wing has made its way into the Democratic mainstream. Joe Biden has included some progressive priorities among his first-term priorities. He stopped spending for the Trump-era border wall and reversed President Trump's restrictions on immigration from some majority-Muslim countries. He made responding to climate change a priority, announcing a push to achieve net-zero carbon emissions by 2050.[103] These and other elements of Biden's early legislative agenda owe much to the progressive push within the party.

Duverger's law
A law in political science indicating that the electoral system strongly conditions the type of party system that will result

The fight for the soul of the Republican Party was on display in the 2017 session of the Texas legislature with the "bathroom bill" debate. Tea Party-backed lieutenant governor Dan Patrick was a vocal advocate for the bill, which would have barred transgender individuals from using public restrooms in schools and government buildings that did not match the sex assigned on their birth certificate. It also would have negated "trans-friendly" policies adopted by school districts and county and local governments across Texas. Backers of the law said it was needed to protect individual privacy, and to keep people from taking advantage of trans-inclusive policies to commit crimes. Opponents contended it was an attempt to "demonize transgender Texans."[104]

The 2017 regular session ended without the bathroom bill being passed. Governor Abbott added the bill to the call for a special session, some say as a result of pressure from Lieutenant Governor Patrick. Patrick and the right wing of the Republican Party strongly supported the bill, and House Speaker Joe Straus, the Texas business community, and anti-discrimination activists just as strongly opposed it, in part because supporters were unable to provide real-world examples of harm from transgender-inclusive policies in Texas or elsewhere. The bill passed the Patrick-led Texas Senate, but the House adjourned before taking up the bill for consideration.[105] Lieutenant Governor Patrick declined to bring the measure back to the legislature in the 2019 session, saying he'd "won the battle," a characterization challenged by LGBTQ activists.[106]

Acrimony between the conservative and business elements of the Republican Party continued during the 2018 Republican primary elections. In those races, the most conservative candidates did not seem to be able to take advantage of lingering anger over defeat of the bathroom bill.[107] As the 2020 primaries developed, any lingering intraparty animosity seemed to recede in anticipation of a bruising November general election race. As more moderate candidates generally had success at the ballot box in 2018 and 2020, divisive culture war issues took a back seat to more "bread and butter" politics.[108]

The 2021 legislative session, though, brought social conservatives' issues back to the fore. Conservative Dade Phelan, the new Speaker of the House, joined with Dan Patrick in the Senate, as the Texas legislature passed many of the priorities that had languished during the speakership of the more moderate Joe Straus. As the 2021 regular session ended, Governor Greg Abbott took to Twitter to announce that Texas had wrapped up the most conservative legislative in a generation.[109] After the third special session, Abbott could add more legislative victories, including newly-drawn districts resulting from decennial redistricting, and restricting transgender youth from participating in high school athletics according to their gender identity. Still, conservatives were disappointed that some other items, like election audits and steeper property tax cuts, didn't make it through the legislature.[110]

At the end of the 2021 regular session, Greg Abbott summarized his legislative victories.

Gov. Greg Abbott

Understanding Impact Some people believe the two-party system inevitably limits the success of other political agendas. These agendas might include a centrist party occupying the middle ground between Republicans and Democrats. But when we look at many other countries with multiparty systems, Americans are, on average, neither more dissatisfied nor mistrustful of our government than people in other countries. Therefore, it appears having more parties doesn't necessarily lead to more voter satisfaction. Would you support legal or party rule changes to help third-party candidates succeed? Why or why not? What kind of third party do you think could succeed in Texas? Why?

CORE OBJECTIVE

Thinking Critically . . .

For a variety of reasons, third parties do not currently have much effect on Texas politics. What measures might be taken to level the playing field for third parties and improve their competitiveness in elections?

Party Organizations

Learning Objective: Explain political party organization in Texas, including caucus and primary delegate selection systems.

Political parties in all states have both permanent and temporary organizations. Their structure is partly determined by federal and state law, but parties have relatively wide discretion in deciding specific arrangements. Also, rules established by the national Democratic and Republican Party organizations almost always dictate state party actions in selected areas, such as the number of delegates to the national convention and how those delegates are selected.

Texas Election Code determines many aspects of party activity, especially the conduct of primary elections. Earlier we discussed the whites-only

Bloomberg/Getty Images

TEXAS ✦ DEMOCRATS

Texas Democratic Party

How to

Communicate Effectively Using Graphics

Have you ever heard the old saying, "A picture is worth a thousand words"? The idea behind this statement applies to much more than just photographs. Some information is easier to understand when it is presented visually rather than through verbal description.

When you are writing a report or preparing a presentation, think carefully about how you might use graphics to communicate more effectively. Graphics include graphs, flowcharts, diagrams, cutaways, and even logos.

1. Choose the most appropriate graphic for your information.

If you are dealing with statistical information, you might decide to convey it using a graph or chart. Line graphs such as Figures 11.1 and 11.2, shown earlier in this chapter, are good for showing change over time. Bar graphs are useful for comparing relative sizes or amounts. Pie charts are used to show how a whole is divided into segments.

If you want to show a process, a flow chart is an appropriate graphic to use. A good example is Figure 3.2, which shows the steps the Texas Legislature must follow to pass a law.

If you want to use a graphic to establish an identity, consider creating a logo such as the two party logos shown earlier in this section. Notice that both logos incorporate the silhouette of Texas to establish immediately that these are *state* political parties.

2. Include all necessary information.

Whether you are using a graph, chart, flowchart, or some other visual, make sure you include everything that is necessary to help others interpret it. Consider including the following:

- Title
- Labels
- Explanatory caption or captions
- Source line
- Key to explain the use of colors or symbols
- A scale along the axes of a graph
- Arrows or leader lines to point out important features

3. Use design elements sparingly.

Don't overload your graphic with too many colors or font styles. Use only what you need to convey the information. Keep the visual as clean as possible to make it easy to interpret.

Also, remember that if you use printing on a colored background, be careful that there is enough contrast so the text is easy to read.

4. Review your visual before you publish or present it.

Make sure that you haven't left anything out. Double check any statistics to make sure you have used them correctly. Proofread all the text. If possible, ask a friend to review the graphic and let you know if he or she has any questions.

primaries in Texas, which excluded Black Americans from voting in Democratic Party primary elections and which the U.S. Supreme Court eventually outlawed. This situation is a good example of national or state actions restricting party activity. Parties are not free agents or purely private organizations, but quasi-public agents.

Each county in Texas is divided into election precincts, which form the smallest political subdivisions in the state. According to Texas Election Code, each precinct must contain between 100 and 5,000 registered voters, although exceptions to this minimum standard may be granted for rural areas.[111] Statewide there are just over 5,700 election precincts.[112] When voters register, they are assigned to a precinct-based polling place near their home. Polling places are normally in public buildings (such as schools, city halls, and churches), but they may be located in private buildings when no public building is available.

Permanent Party Organization

permanent party organization
Series of elected officials of a political party that keep the party organization active between elections

The **permanent party organization** within the state is a hierarchy of elected party officials who handle party business regularly. At the lowest level is the precinct chair; the highest level is the state chair.

The Precinct Chair

precinct chair
Party official elected in each voting precinct to organize and support the party

In March of even-numbered years, the Democratic and Republican Parties in Texas each hold a primary election. In addition to selecting which of their party's candidates will run in the general election in November, primary voters also elect a **precinct chair** and a county chair. The role of the precinct chair is to organize the precinct, identify party supporters, make sure they are registered to vote, turn out voters on Election Day, and generally promote and develop the interests of the party. In the one-party Democratic era in Texas, few precinct chairs actually performed these duties; generally, their only job was to serve as an election judge (the person who supervises the conduct of an election at a polling place) during primary and general elections. Except for areas that remain essentially uncontested for one party or the other, though, the role of the precinct chair has changed from election judge to party organizer at the grassroots level.

The precinct chair serves a two-year term. Any registered voter who lives in the election precinct may file as a candidate for precinct chair, and his or her name will be placed on the ballot. Occasionally these races are contested, but often candidates for precinct chair are unopposed. Write-in votes are allowed if a declaration of write-in candidacy has been filed.

The County Chair

county chair
Party official elected in each county to organize and support the party

The next office in the party hierarchy is **county chair.** Similar to that of the precinct chair, the role of the county chair is to organize the party at the county level. This includes voter registration, fundraising, candidate recruitment and education, and facilitating the election of candidates in the general election. Informally, the county chair's duties consist of representing the party in the county, being the official spokesperson for the party, maintaining a party headquarters (in some counties), and raising funds. Formally, the county chair is responsible for receiving formal filings from persons seeking to have their names placed on the party's primary election ballot, conducting the primary election, filling election judge positions, giving official notice of precinct and county conventions, and officially counting the ballots in the primary election.

The position of county chair is filled during the primary election for a two-year term. In large urban counties, the county chair is often a full-time employee of the party. Any registered voter who is a resident of the county may file for the office. In large urban counties, the race for this office is usually contested.

The County Executive Committee

county executive committee
Committee made up of a county chair and all precinct chairs in the county; serves as the official organization for the party in each county

The **county executive committee** is the next level in the permanent party organization. It is composed of a county chair and all precinct chairs within that county. The degree of organization of this committee varies greatly from county to county. In some counties, the executive committee is an active organization that works to promote the party's interests. In many counties, especially in rural areas, this committee is more an organization on paper that fulfills the formal duties of canvassing the election returns and filling vacancies in party offices when they occur. Occasionally, the committee might be called upon to fill a vacancy on the general election ballot if a nominee has died or has become ineligible to run between the time of the primary and the general election.

Many large metropolitan counties use, instead of the county executive committee, a district executive committee for these functions. This is an organizational convenience because these counties would otherwise have very large county committees. District committees are established based on state senatorial districts.

The State Executive Committee

The next level of permanent party organization is the **state executive committee.** The state executive committee consists of 62 members: one committeeman and one committeewoman from each of Texas's 31 state senatorial districts. Members of the state executive committee are elected at the state convention and serve two years; delegates to the convention gather by senatorial district and recommend representatives.

The state executive committee, guided by the chair and vice chair, provides leadership for the party. Its duties are very similar to those of the county chair and county executive committee in terms of organizing the party and overseeing primary elections. However, the state executive committee is also a policy-making body. It establishes rules, orchestrates the state convention, prepares the state party platform, and communicates with the national party organization. Both parties in Texas have permanent, full-time, paid professional staffs who do most of the work at the state level.

Being selected to serve on the state executive committee is considered an honor, usually reserved for those who have strong political ties and who have supported the party for many years. Occasionally, a maverick group will surface and take control of the party and elect its people, who might not be the longtime party faithful.

state executive committee
Committee, made up of one man and one woman from each state senatorial district as well as a chair and vice chair, that functions as the governing body of the party

The State Chair

The **state party chair** and state vice chair, one of whom must be a man and the other a woman, are also elected at the state convention. As stated earlier, their role is to guide the state executive committee. These officers are chosen by a majority vote of all the delegates in attendance. Historically in the Democratic Party, the state chair and vice chair were chosen by the governor or gubernatorial candidate, and the office of state chair was often filled by the governor's campaign manager. With the rise of the Republican Party and control of the governorship by the GOP, the state chair is no longer automatically chosen by the governor; however, the party's candidate for governor still has influence in the selection of the state party chair.

state party chair
Heads the state executive committee and provides leadership for the party

Temporary Party Organization

The **temporary party organization,** for both parties, consists of a series of conventions held in even-numbered years. These are the precinct, county or senatorial district, and state conventions. These conventions are not limited to elected party officials; rather, they are attended by a greater number of party supporters. Because these meetings last for only a brief period, they are said to comprise the "temporary" party organization.

temporary party organization
Series of meetings or conventions that occur every two years at the precinct, county, and state levels

Precinct Convention

Traditionally, the precinct convention was held on the same day as the party primary in March. This is still the practice in the Texas Republican Party. The

Democrats have started holding their precinct conventions on the morning of their county or senatorial district conventions.[113] Only individuals who voted in that party's primary are eligible to attend; all those who attend are considered delegates to the precinct convention. The polls usually close at 7:00 P.M., and for Republicans the precinct convention begins shortly thereafter, typically between 7:00 and 7:30 P.M. The precinct chair acts as temporary chair of the convention, verifying that attendees have voted in that party's primary, calling the meeting to order, and directing the election of "permanent" (for the term of the precinct convention) officers to run the remainder of the meeting. Sometimes, especially during presidential election years, there is contention over control of the convention's offices. In non-presidential-election years, though, attendance is usually very low, and control of the convention is generally not an issue.

After officers are elected, the convention's most important function is the selection of delegates to attend the county convention (or the senatorial district convention, in large metropolitan counties where there are multiple districts). The number of delegates a precinct sends to the county convention is based on party support in the precinct; the higher the party support, the larger the number of delegates. During presidential election years, many people are interested in attending the county convention, and seats can be hotly contested. In odd years, finding enough volunteers to attend the county convention can be difficult. Precinct conventions may also adopt resolutions in hopes of having them included in the party platform.

County or Senatorial District Convention

The county convention (or senatorial district convention), which is held on the third Saturday after the primary election and precinct convention, is similar to the precinct convention. Again, its most important function is to select delegates to attend the next higher convention level (in this case, the state convention). The number of delegates a county sends to the state convention depends on the county's support for the party's gubernatorial candidate in the previous election. The convention will also vote on resolutions received from precinct conventions to be sent on to the state convention.[114]

State Convention

The state convention normally takes place in June of even-numbered years. Generally, the convention is held in a major city. During presidential election years, the most important event is the selection of delegates to the national convention, at which the party's candidate for president will be nominated. During presidential election years, the convention also selects representatives (or electors) to serve in the Electoral College in the event their party's candidate wins the popular vote in Texas. At the state convention, Democratic delegates break into separate meetings by state senatorial district and choose electors. Republicans caucus by U.S. congressional district. These decisions are ratified by the convention as a whole. The party that wins the statewide popular vote sends its electors to meet in the state senate chamber in Austin on the first Monday after the second Wednesday in December following the election. On that date, electors cast their vote for their party's nominee for president.[115] Those chosen to serve in the Electoral College are generally longtime party supporters who can be relied on to vote for their party's candidate.

Even in nonpresidential election years, the state convention handles important party business, including choosing state party officers and adopting a platform, which is strongly influenced by resolutions adopted at the precinct and

Texas Republican Party state convention

Rodger Mallison/Fort Worth Star-Telegram/TNS/Alamy Stock Photo

county conventions. In addition, the convention elects individuals to serve on the national committee for either the Democratic or Republican Party. This committee provides leadership for the party at the national level.

Another notable function of the state convention is to provide a venue for state and national party leaders to speak to the assembled leadership of Texas's political parties.

> **Understanding Impact** Serving as an elector in the Electoral College process is an honor, recognizing long commitment to a political party. Sometimes, however, electors decide they cannot in good conscience vote in accordance with the popular vote; they become "faithless electors." The Framers of the Constitution intended that electors would be a protection against election of anyone not "eminently qualified" to be president (*Federalist Paper No. 68*). Do you think electors should be able to override the peoples' vote if they determine the winner is unfit? Or should they be obligated to cast their ballot in accordance with the vote, regardless of the winner?

Caucus and Primary Delegate Selection Systems

Learning Objective: Explain political party organization in Texas, including caucus and primary delegate selection systems.

Both major parties hold national conventions every four years to nominate a candidate for president. These conventions are perhaps the best-known institutions of American political parties. They attract national media attention and are usually covered from gavel to gavel. In elections before 1972, national conventions were frequently highly contentious, with candidates vying for votes from state delegates. Starting in 1972, state parties began to adopt binding primaries or caucuses. As a result, delegates are generally committed to support the winner of the state primaries, and the national conventions are thought of not so much as the time when candidates are selected but as the real kickoff of general election campaigns.[116]

Texas Presidential Primaries

The nominating process is complex, and the party's nominee is ultimately determined by the number of delegates supporting each candidate. Each state is allocated a certain number of delegates to the national convention based on party rules. To determine the delegates who will go to the national convention (where they will vote to determine the party's nominee), states hold a caucus, a **presidential primary election,** or a combination of the two.

presidential primary election

Election held every four years by political parties to determine voters' preferences for presidential candidates

Texas uses a primary system to determine most of the state's delegates to the national party conventions. Democratic and Republican presidential primaries are held every four years in March. In a **primary election,** voters go to their polling place (as they would in a general election) and cast a ballot for the candidate they prefer as their party's nominee. In very general terms, delegates are awarded to candidates based on the proportion of the popular vote they receive in their party's primary. However, delegate allocation is complicated, and not all delegates are allocated based on the statewide outcome. For Texas Democrats, a large number of delegates are allocated based on the primary outcome in each state senatorial district; the Republicans allocate many of their delegates by primary outcomes in each of the state's 38 U.S. congressional districts.[117] In addition, in the Democratic Party, some Party Leader and Elected Official (PLEO) delegates are "unpledged," or not committed to any candidate; these delegates may vote for any candidate they choose at the national convention, though they are barred from voting on the first ballot. These Democratic delegates are now called "automatic delegates," but they were previously known as superdelegates.[118]

primary election

An election used by major political parties in Texas to nominate candidates for the November general election

Until 2016, the Democratic Party in Texas used both a primary and a caucus to determine delegates to the national convention. In what was called the "Texas Two-Step," about three-fourths of Democratic delegates were allocated based on the outcome of the Democratic primary, while the other one-fourth was allocated based on caucuses.[119] After primary voting closed, primary voters could return to participate in their precinct convention (also called a **party caucus**). A caucus is a town hall–style meeting of party members. Delegates were distributed based on the number of supporters for each candidate who were in attendance. The more supporters of a particular candidate who were present, the more delegates that candidate would receive.[120] Therefore, a candidate's ability to mobilize and turn out large numbers of people was crucial for success at these caucuses.

party caucus

A meeting of members of a political party to nominate candidates (now used only by minor political parties in Texas)

The importance of voter mobilization within the two-step played a major role in the 2008 Democratic presidential primary election pitting Barack Obama against Hillary Clinton. Obama's Texas campaign aggressively recruited their voters to attend the caucus following the primary vote. Thousands of Obama voters showed up at precinct conventions, in many cases overloading the capacity of the system to deal with the crowds. At the end of the night, Clinton had won the primary vote by 50.7% to 47.4%. However, Obama's supporters in the caucuses outnumbered Clinton's by 56.2% to 43.7% and he ended the day with 99 delegates compared to 94 for Clinton, despite Clinton having won the vote.[121]

The national leadership for the Democratic Party deemed the two-step confusing to voters, so the state party eliminated the caucus.[122] Getting rid of the two-step system didn't solve all the problems associated with voting. Texas voters can still face other problems like long lines and too few voting machines in some locations.[123]

Political scientists have developed a measure called the "Cost of Voting Index" (COVI), using nine different criteria including regulations complicating registration and measures that decrease the convenience of actually voting on or before election day. In 2020, Texas ranked 50th of the 50 states, meaning that Texas is the most difficult state in the nation in which to vote.[124]

The Caucus System

Without presidential primary elections, all delegate preferences would be decided at conventions or caucuses. In states without presidential primaries, like Iowa, caucuses take on great significance. Because it is generally necessary to physically attend during the time of the convention, a well-organized group can dominate them. In 2008, Arkansas governor Mike Huckabee developed a strong grassroots organization and worked with local churches to win the most delegates in the Iowa caucuses. Churches were used as a rallying point before the evening caucus. Incentives such as potluck dinners, child-care services, and church buses that delivered voters to precinct conventions generated high turnout in support of the candidate.

A caucus system is a way of securing convention delegates that hearkens back to politics before the technological era. It requires an organization of active volunteers to produce results. If a candidate inspires large numbers of voters to show up at caucus locations around the state, they can win enough delegates to prevail state-wide, winning the most delegates to the national convention. Iowa in particular is an important caucus state, because it is first in the nation. A victory in Iowa can provide momentum, in the form of media attention and increased legitimacy, that can elevate a less well-known candidate into the ranks of real contenders for the nomination.[125]

If Texas were to change from a primary to a caucus system, different campaign organization and strategies would be required. Presidential primaries are mass media events that require big money and professional consultants. On the other hand, caucus systems require grassroots organization and dedicated volunteers. This demonstrates the importance of electoral rules in affecting political behavior and outcomes.

In Texas Republican state conventions since 1996, some Christian organizations have called for an end to primaries and a shift to the caucus system of selecting delegates. Because of religious groups' ability to organize and mobilize supporters, a caucus system would benefit them and allow them to control many delegates to the national convention. If this caucus were held early enough in the primary season, it might affect the outcome of the Republican presidential race. It would give the winner significant early exposure. That kind of exposure could lead the media to consider the winner more legitimate and could result in a swing of contributions and support.

Understanding Impact As you've learned, primaries and caucuses require different kinds of campaigning. Primaries favor candidates who have lots of money and consultants for statewide media coverage, while caucuses are better for "retail politics," with large groups of strongly motivated volunteers to get people to show up at caucus locations on the night of the election. Which of these systems is superior from the perspective of deciding who would have a better chance of winning a national presidential campaign? Which would better predict the candidate who would make a better president? Explain your answer.

Focus On

Religion in Texas Politics

Texas attorney general (and later governor) Greg Abbott at a monument inscribed with the Ten Commandments in front of the Texas State Capitol building

Jana Birchum/Getty Images

As you have seen in this chapter, most Texans are conservative, whatever political party they may be a member of. Most are also religious. Compared to the residents of other states, Texans are among the most likely to say that they believe in God and that religion is important in their lives.[126]

This religious fervor exercises an important influence on Texas politics. We've talked about the shift in control of Texas politics from Democrats to Republicans. As with any major change in society, this political change had varied causes. While the conventional wisdom says that the party shift occurred chiefly as a result of Democratic Party support for civil rights legislation opposed by conservative Republicans, some argue that the change started much earlier. They place the beginnings of the party shift during Prohibition and its subsequent impact on the 1928 presidential election, when "wet" (anti-prohibition) Catholic Al Smith, the Democratic candidate, lost Texas. No Democratic presidential candidate had ever lost Texas, and political activism among religious conservatives in the pulpit and the community was an important contributor to the outcome.[127]

Political and religious conservatism still combine to form the predominant ideology in Texas today. Of the 77 percent of Texans who identify as Christians, 44 percent believe that humans have always existed in their present form since creation, and 47 percent believe that the Bible should be taken as literally true, rather than as metaphor or philosophical teaching.[128]

And while, as we've said, conservatives tend to dominate Texas politics regardless of party, the Christian majority has a significant preference for the Republican Party. That preference is traceable to differences in the platforms of the two major parties. For example, more than half of Christians in Texas believe abortion should be illegal in all or most cases, and more than half oppose same-sex marriage, both traditional planks of the Republican Party platform.[129]

Today some conservative Republican judges argue that being required, as part of their official nonreligious judicial duties, to perform same-sex marriages violates their sincere religious beliefs.[130] Further, conservative Republican governor Greg Abbott originally excluded religious services from his spring 2020 stay-at-home order during the COVID-19 pandemic.[131]

Conservative Christianity has been a benefit to the growth and dominance of the Republican Party in Texas. But that doesn't mean it will always be that way. The youngest Texans, the future generation of voters, are the least conservative and the least religious of all Texans. How the parties reach out to them will largely determine the future of Texas politics.

Critical Thinking Questions

1. Both the U.S. and Texas Constitutions prohibit religious discrimination. The judges mentioned previously believe performing same-sex marriages would violate their religious freedom. But the couples seeking marriage believe the judges are unconstitutionally invoking religion to justify failure to perform their official duties, and thus are themselves both engaging in religious discrimination and failing to provide constitutionally mandated equal protection of the law. How do you think society should balance one person's right to exercise their religion with another's right not to be discriminated against?

2. Throughout American history, religion has been a strong influence in politics. Considering that young Texans are less affiliated with religion, do you think religion's influence will decline? How will this affect the major political parties?

Conclusion

U.S. political parties are not nearly as strong today as they were in the past. That may seem counterintuitive, given the frequency with which we hear the labels "Democrat" and "Republican" in the media. Political reforms during the Progressive Era significantly reduced the influence of parties. Yet they still play a vital role in our democracy.

The average citizen has little awareness of party organization at the state and local levels. The few active, elite members of the parties control this element of American politics. However, it is not very difficult to become part of this group. Any citizen with available time to devote to the party can become active at the precinct, county, and state levels. Most positions are not paid.

In the past, the state executive committees of both parties were likely to be part-time organizations with limited staff. Today, both parties have permanent headquarters, full-time paid professional staffs, and financial resources to help party development. They are actively engaged in organizing and building the party through voter identification and registration, candidate recruitment, candidate education, get-out-the-vote drives, and support of candidates during the general election.

What is the future of political parties in Texas? As we have seen, Texas has swung from being a one-party state to a state with significant support for both major parties. Now it is back to looking like a one-party state again, although today it's for a different party. Changing demographics provide Democrats an opportunity to turn Texas back in their direction. Recent elections provide some hints that such a change may happen. In 2016, President Trump won Texas by a smaller margin than did other recent candidates. In the senate race, Beto O'Rourke lost to Ted Cruz by only about 2.5 percent in 2018, and his coattails helped Democrats flip several U.S. House and Texas legislative seats from Republicans.

But such a change is far from ensured. After the 2020 general election, the Texas Republican Party continued to hold every statewide elected office. Republicans were energized and enthusiastically backed their 2016 winner, Donald Trump, delivering Texas's 38 electoral college votes to the Republican candidate once again. Republicans are raising money and registering voters, and they won't give up Texas without a fight. All we can say with certainty is that, like the Texas weather, Texas politics will change. In what direction that change will go and how long it will take are specifics that will likely surprise us, like a February hailstorm.

Summary

LO: Describe the evolution of the political party system in the United States and in Texas.

The United States has national and state political party systems that function fairly independently of each other. The United States does not have strong political parties. In fact, parties in the United States and Texas are weaker today than previously in our nation's history, thanks mainly to political reforms that took place during the Progressive Era. Because of this weakness, politics revolve primarily around candidates and their personalities.

LO: Explain the history of party realignment and one-party Republican dominance in Texas.

For about a century after the end of Reconstruction, Texas was a one-party Democratic state. Then, following a realignment (or shift in party loyalty among voting citizens), Texas became a one-party Republican state. Republicans currently hold all statewide offices and the majority in both the Texas House and Senate.

LO: Describe third-party movements in the United States and in Texas.

Third-party movements develop in the United States and Texas from time to time, but typically they are not very successful. Often the most a third party can hope to achieve is to have one of the major parties adopt its issues.

LO: Explain political party organization in Texas, including caucus and primary delegate selection systems.

Political party organization in Texas includes both permanent organizations (consisting of elected party officials) and temporary organizations (consisting of a series of conventions). State party organization has become more professional over time. Major parties in Texas use a primary (or election), rather than a caucus (or meeting of members of a political party), to nominate candidates for the November general election.

Key Terms

county chair
county executive committee
Duverger's law
ideology
party caucus
political action
    committees (PACs)

permanent party organization
political party
precinct chair
presidential primary election
primary election
Raza Unida
realignment

reapportionment
state executive committee
state party chair
straight-ticket voting
temporary party
    organization

Notes

[1] Theodore J. Lowi, Benjamin Ginsberg, Kenneth A. Shepsle, et al., *American Government: Power and Purpose*, brief 12th ed. (New York: Norton, 2012), 354.

[2] Washington's Farewell Address to the People of the United States, https://www.gpo.gov/fdsys/pkg/GPO-CDOC-106sdoc21/pdf/GPO-CDOC-106sdoc21.pdf.

[3] Library of Congress, "Creating the United States, Formation of Political Parties," https://www.loc.gov/exhibits/creating-the-united-states/formation-of-political-parties.html.

[4] Stephen S. Smith and Melanie J. Springer, "Choosing Presidential Candidates," The Brookings Institution, pp. 2–3, https://www.brookings.edu/wp-content/uploads/2016/07/reformingthepresidentialnominationprocess_chapter.pdf

[5] As discussed in the next section, two major cases decided in 2010 resulted in changes to regulation of campaign finance: *Citizens United v. FEC* and *Speechnow.org v. FEC*.

[6] Texas Election Code Section 52.002, http://www.statutes.legis.state.tx.us/Docs/EL/htm/EL.52.htm.

[7] Donald Ratcliffe, "The Right to Vote and the Rise of Democracy, 1787–1828," *Journal of the Early Republic* 33 (Summer 2013): 234–35, http://jer.pennpress.org/media/26167/sampleArt22.pdf.

[8] John Kenneth White and Daniel M. Shea, *New Party Politics: From Jefferson and Hamilton to the Information Age* (Boston: Bedford/St. Martin's, 2000), 58.

[9] Bobby Oliver, "TEXAS BALLOT REFORM: THE ADOPTION OF VOTER REGISTRATION AND THE AUSTRALIAN BALLOT SYSTEM, 1887–1892," https://search.proquest.com/openview/b806905f7f9af49ef0d523c8fcdc319a/1?pq-origsite=gscholar&cbl=18750

[10] Dan Balz, "The Mystery of Ballot Box 13," *The Washington Post*, March 4, 1990, https://www.washingtonpost.com/archive/entertainment/books/1990/03/04/the-mystery-of-ballot-box-13/70206359-8543-48e3-9ce2-f3c4fdf6da3d/.

[11] Bartee Haile, "Parr family ran the show in Duval County," *The Banner-Press*, October 18, 2019, http://www.brenhambanner.com/parr-family-ran-the-show-in-duval-county/article_abcbd882-bced-5fc0-9d32-f117350c16ee.html

[12] Ibid., 10.

[13] Jamie L. Carson and Jason M. Roberts, *Ambition, Competition, and Electoral Reform: The Politics of Congressional Elections Across Time* (Ann Arbor: University of Michigan Press, 2013), 53–54.

[14] Jolie McCullough and Ross Ramsey, "See the Straight-Ticket Breakdown in Texas' 10 Most-Populous Counties," *Texas Tribune*, November 11, 2016, https://www.texastribune.org/2016/11/11/texas-2016-straight-ticket-ballots/.

[15] Jolie McCullough, "Gov. Abbott Signs Bill to Eliminate Straight-Ticket Voting Beginning in 2020," *Texas Tribune*, June 1, 2017, https://www.texastribune.org/2017/06/01/texas-gov-greg-abbott-signs-bill-eliminate-straight-ticket-voting/.

[16] John Kenneth White and Daniel M. Shea, *New Party Politics: From Jefferson and Hamilton to the Information Age* (Boston: Bedford/St. Martin's, 2000), 59–60.

[17] Frank Freidel and Hugh Sidey, "James Garfield," *The Presidents of the United States of America*, White House Historical Association, http://www.whitehouse.gov/about/presidents/jamesgarfield.

[18] Pendleton Act (1883), http://www.ourdocuments.gov/doc.php?doc=48.

[19] John Kenneth White and Daniel M. Shea, *New Party Politics: From Jefferson and Hamilton to the Information Age* (Boston: Bedford/St. Martin's, 2000), 60.

[20] John Kenneth White and Daniel M. Shea, *New Party Politics: From Jefferson and Hamilton to the Information Age* (Boston: Bedford/St. Martin's, 2000), 63–64.

[21] SCOTUSBlog.com, "Citizens United v. FEC case," https://www.scotusblog.com/case-files/cases/citizens-united-v-federal-election-commission/; Federal Election Commission, "SpeechNow.org v. FEC," https://www.fec.gov/updates/speechnoworg-v-fec-appeals-court/.

[22] Scott Detrow, "Donald Trump Secures Electoral College Win, with Few Surprises," NPR, December 16, 2016, https://www.npr.org/2016/12/19/506188169/donald-trump-poised-to-secure-electoral-college-win-with-few-surprises.

[23] 2020 Census Apportionment Results, *The United States Census Bureau*, April 26, 2021, https://www.census.gov/data/tables/2020/dec/2020-apportionment-data.html.

[24] CBSDFW.com staff, "Gov. Greg Abbott Signs Bill Allocating Federal COVID-19 Relief Funds For Texans," *CBSDFW.com*, November 8, 2021, https://dfw.cbslocal.com/2021/11/08/gov-greg-abbott-signs-bill-federal-covid-19-relief-funds-texans/.

[25] V. O. Key Jr., *Politics and Pressure Groups*, 4th ed. (New York: Thomas Y. Crowell, 1958), 331.

[26] Texas Secretary of State, "Statewide Elected Officials," http://www.sos.state.tx.us/elections/voter/elected.shtml.

[27] Gallup Poll, "2017 U.S. Party Affiliation by State," https://news.gallup.com/poll/226643/2017-party-affiliation-state.aspx.

[28] That being said, the current relationship between party and ideology is fairly robust, and has been getting stronger. According to 2020 Gallup polls, a high percentage (75 percent) of U.S. Republicans identify themselves as conservative, whereas only 12 percent of Democrats consider themselves conservative. On the other hand, 51 percent of Democrats call themselves liberal, while only 4 percent of Republicans identify with that moniker. See https://news.gallup.com/poll/328367/americans-political-ideology-held-steady-2020.aspx.

[29] A 2018 Gallup poll found that 38 percent of Texans identified themselves as conservative, compared to 20 percent who described themselves as liberal. Self-described moderates made up 36 percent of the sample. See https://news.gallup.com/poll/247016/conservatives-greatly-outnumber-liberals-states.aspx.

[30] Jeffrey E. Cohen and Paul Kantor, "The Places of Parties in American Politics," in *American Political Parties: Decline or Resurgence?*, ed. Jeffrey E. Cohen, Richard Fleisher, and Paul Kantor (Washington, D.C.: CQ Press, 2001), 1–8.

[31] Randolph B. Campbell, "Antebellum Texas," *Handbook of Texas Online*, http://www.tshaonline.org/handbook/online/articles/npa01.

[32] Dale Baum, "Chicanery and Intimidation in the 1869 Gubernatorial Race," *Southwestern Historical Quarterly* 97 (April 1994), 34–54.

[33] Carl H. Moneyhon, "Davis, Edmund Jackson," *Handbook of Texas Online*, http://www.tshaonline.org/handbook/online/articles/fda37.

[34] V. O. Key, Jr. with Alexander Heard, *Southern Politics in State and Nation* (New York: Alfred A. Knopf, 1949), 7.

[35] Jack W. Gunn, "Greenback Party," *Handbook of Texas Online*, http://www.tshaonline.org/handbook/online/articles/wag01.

[36] Robert A. Calvert, Arnoldo De León, and Gregg Cantrell, *History of Texas* (Wheeling, IL: Harlan Davidson, 2002), 201–07.

[37] Jack M. Balkin, "Populism and Progressivism as Constitutional Categories—Part II," *Yale Law Journal*, 1995, https://jackbalkin.yale.edu/populism-and-progressivism-constitutional-categories-part-ii.

[38] Donna A. Barnes, "People's Party," *Handbook of Texas Online*, http://www.tshaonline.org/handbook/online/articles/wap01.

[39] Ibid.

[40] Jack M. Balkin, "Populism and Progressivism as Constitutional Categories—Part II," *Yale Law Journal*, 1995, http://www.yale.edu/lawweb/jbalkin/articles/popprog2.htm.

[41] John Halpin and Conor P. Williams, *The Progressive Intellectual Tradition in America*, Center for American Progress, April 2010, http://americanprogress.org/issues/progressive-movement/report/2010/04/14/7677/the-progressive-intellectual-tradition-in-america/.

[42] Patricia Ellen Cunningham, "Texas State Historical Association," *Handbook of Texas Online*, https://tshaonline.org/handbook/online/articles/fcu24.

[43] Lewis L. Gould, "Progressive Era," *Handbook of Texas Online*, http://www.tshaonline.org/handbook/online/articles/npp01; K. Austin Kerr, "Prohibition," *Handbook of Texas Online*, http://www.tshaonline.org/handbook/onlline/articles/vap01.

[44] George N. Green, "Texas Regulars," *Handbook of Texas Online*, https://tshaonline.org/handbook/online/articles/wet02

[45] V. O. Key, Jr. with Alexander Heard, *Southern Politics in State and Nation* (New York: Alfred A. Knopf, 1949), 225.

[46] George Packer, Is America Undergoing a Political Realignment?, *The Atlantic*, April 8, 2019, https://www.theatlantic.com/ideas/archive/2019/04/will-2020-bring-realignment-left/586624/

[47] V. O. Key Jr., "Secular Realignment and the Party System," in John Kenneth White and Daniel M. Shea, *New Party Politics: From Jefferson and Hamilton to the Information Age* (Boston: Bedford/St. Martin's, 2000), 148.

[48] James L. Sundquist, *Dynamics of the Party System: Alignment and Realignment of Political Parties in the United States* (Washington, D.C.: Brookings Institute, 1983), 9.

[49] The Texas Politics Project, *Smith v. Allwright: White Primaries*, https://texaspolitics.utexas.edu/archive/html/vce/features/0503_01/smith.html.

[50] Ben Philpott, "Why Is Texas So Red, and How Did It Get That Way?," KUT, http://kut.org/post/why-texas-so-red-and-how-did-it-get-way.

[51] Douglas O. Weeks, *Texas Presidential Politics in 1952* (Austin: University of Texas, Institute of Public Affairs, 1953), 3–4.

[52] Susan Eason, "Tower, John Goodwin," *Handbook of Texas Online*, https://tshaonline.org/handbook/online/articles/ftoss.

[53] Robert Reinhold, "Clements Offers an Apology over Payments to Athletes," *The New York Times*, March 11, 1987, https://www.nytimes.com/1987/03/11/us/clements-offers-an-apology-over-payments-to-athletes.html.

[54] David A. Stockman, *The Triumph of Politics: How the Reagan Revolution Failed* (New York: Harper & Row, 1986).

[55] James L. Sundquist, *Dynamics of the Party System: Alignment and Realignment of Political Parties in the United States* (Washington, D.C.: Brookings Institution, 1983), 5–6.

[56] Erica Grieder, "The Revolt against Crony Capitalism," *Texas Monthly*, February 18, 2014, http://www.texasmonthly.com/story/revolt-against-crony-capitalism?fullpage=1.

[57] Ibid.

[58] https://casetext.com/case/pidgeon-v-turner-2

[59] Wayne Slater, "Texas GOP Splits between Social Conservatives, Libertarians," *Dallas Morning News*, June 7, 2014, http://www.dallasnews.com/news/politics/headlines/20140607-texas-gop-splits-between-social-conservatives-libertarians.ece.

[60] Frank S. Meyer, *In Defense of Freedom* (Indianapolis, IN: Liberty Fund, 1996).

[61] Shannon Najmabadi, "After a Tough Election Night, 'a Wakeup Call' for the Texas GOP's Hard Right," *Texas Tribune*, November 8, 2018, https://www.texastribune.org/2018/11/08/after-tough-election-night-wakeup-call-texas-gops-hard-right/.

[62] Emma Platoff, "Empower Texans Helped Topple House Speaker Dennis Bonnen. Did It Further the Conservative Movement?," *Texas Tribune*, November 1, 2019, https://www.texastribune.org/2019/11/01/empower-texans-bonnen-help-conservative-priorities/.

[63] Texas Secretary of State, "Presidential Election Results," https://www.sos.state.tx.us/elections/historical/presidential.shtml.

[64] Texas Secretary of State, Texas Election Results, November 3, 2020 General Election, https://results.texas-election.com/races

[65] The Texas Tribune, "Redistricting Texas," https://www.texastribune.org/series/texas-redistricting-2021/

[66] Fivethirtyeight.com, "What Redistricting Looks Like In Every State," https://projects.fivethirtyeight.com/redistricting-2022-maps/texas/ (accessed April 3, 2022).

[67] Jessica Mendoza, "Centrist Democrats are back. But these are not your father's Blue Dogs.," *The Christian Science Monitor*, June 4, 2019, https://www.csmonitor.com/USA/Politics/2019/0604/Centrist-Democrats-are-back.-But-these-are-not-your-father-s-Blue-Dogs

[68] Blue Dog Coalition Members, https://bluedogcaucus-murphy.house.gov/members, (accessed 4/11/2022).

[69] Fivethirtyeight.com, "Presidential Polls: Who's Ahead in Texas," https://projects.fivethirtyeight.com/polls/president-primary-d/texas/ (accessed April 22, 2022).

[70] Nick Corasaniti and Jeremy W. Peters, "The 2020 Democratic Primary Is Giving Some Republicans Déjà Vu," *The New York Times*, February 27, 2020, https://www.nytimes.com/2020/02/26/us/politics/sanders-2016-presidential-primary.html

[71] Alex Samuels, "Joe Biden Wins Texas Primary in a Stunning Turnaround," *The Texas Tribune*, March 3, 2020, https://www.texastribune.org/2020/03/03/texas-2020-presidential-results-bernie-sanders-joe-biden/

[72] Alexa Ura, Jason Kao, Carla Astudillo, and Chris Essig, "People of color make up 95% of Texas' population growth, and cities and suburbs are booming, 2020 census shows," *The Texas Tribune*, August 12, 2021, https://www.texastribune.org/2021/08/12/texas-2020-census/

[73] Christopher Hooks, "What Beto Won," *The Atlantic*, November 10, 2018, https://www.theatlantic.com/ideas/archive/2018/11/beto-orourke-lostbut-profoundly-changed-texas/575521/.

[74] Ibid.

[75] Texas Politics Project, "Donald Trump Approval," https://texaspolitics.utexas.edu/set/donald-trump-approval-february-2020#location.

[76] Laura Egan, "Texas Dems Announce Largest-Ever Voter Drive in 2020 Flip Effort," *NBC News*, March 9, 2020, https://www.nbcnews.com/politics/2020-election/texas-dems-announce-largest-ever-voter-drive-2020-flip-effort-n1152646.

[77] Jodi Enda, "When Republicans Were Blue and Democrats Were Red," *Smithsonian Magazine*, October 31, 2012, https://www.smithsonianmag.com/history/when-republicans-were-blue-and-democrats-were-red-104176297/#ixzz2BSTncTH4.

[78] Texas Secretary of State, 2020 November 3 General Election, https://results.texas-election.com/races.

[79] Olga Garza, David Green, Spencer Grubbs and Shannon Halbrook, "Young Texans: Demographic Overview," *Texas Comptroller*, February 2020, https://comptroller.texas.gov/economy/fiscal-notes/2020/feb/texans.php.

[80] Ross Ramsey, "Analysis: Texans in many border counties voted for Donald Trump — and then for Democrats," *The Texas Tribune*, November 13, 2020, https://www.texastribune.org/2020/11/13/south-texas-donald-trump/

[81] The Texas Politics Project, "The University of Texas/Texas Tribune Poll Cross Tabulations," November 1, 2019, p. 73, https://texaspolitics.utexas.edu/sites/texaspolitics.utexas.edu/files/uttt_crosstabs_201910.pdf.

[82] "2018 Voter Poll Results: Texas," *The Washington Post*, November 30, 2018, https://www.washingtonpost.com/graphics/2018/politics/voter-polls/texas.html?itid=lk_inline_manual_10.

[83] Jay Root, "Against the Grain, G.O.P. Dominated on Election Day," *The New York Times*, November 8, 2012, http://www.nytimes.com/2012/11/09/us/gop-dominated-in-texas-on-election-day.html.

[84] The Texas Politics Project, "The University of Texas/Texas Tribune Poll Cross Tabulations," November 1, 2019, p. 15, https://texaspolitics.utexas.edu/sites/texaspolitics.utexas.edu/files/uttt_crosstabs_201910.pdf.

[85] Ibid.

[86] The Texas Politics Project, "The University of Texas/Texas Tribune Poll Cross Tabulations," November 1, 2019, p. 12, https://texaspolitics.utexas.edu/sites/texaspolitics.utexas.edu/files/uttt_crosstabs_201910.pdf.

[87] Ibid., 63.

[88] Teresa Palomo Acosta, "Raza Unida Party," *Handbook of Texas Online*, http://www.tshaonline.org/handbook/online/articles/war01.

[89] Libertarian Party of Texas, https://www.lptexas.org/.

[90] Ross Ramsey, "Analysis: Democrats Found Candidates, If Not Voters," *Texas Tribune*, June 4, 2014, http://www.texastribune.org/2014/06/04/analysis-democrats-found-candidates-if-not-voters/.

[91] Maria Mendez, "Texas' New Ballot Requirements Have Libertarians and Greens Confused ahead of Elections," *Dallas Morning News*, January 21, 2020, https://www.dallasnews.com/news/politics/2020/01/22/texas-new-ballot-requirements-have-libertarians-and-greens-confused-ahead-of-elections/

[92] Ryan Struyk and Shushannah Walshe, "How Evan McMullin Could Tip The 2016 Election," *ABC News*, November 4, 2016, https://abcnews.go.com/Politics/evan-mcmullin-tip-2016-election/story?id=43306776

[93] Ibid., 63.

[94] Green Party of Texas, "Green Party of Texas State Platform," http://www.txgreens.org/platform.

[95] Texas Secretary of State, "Race Summary Report, 2016 General Election," https://elections.sos.state.tx.us/elchist319_state.htm.

[96] Elizabeth Byrne, "Critics Say Bill Moving through Texas Legislature Designed to Aid GOP Reelection Bids," *Texas Tribune*, May 20, 2019, https://www.texastribune.org/2019/05/20/texas-bill-would-help-republicans-hurt-democrats-elections-critics-say/.

[97] Jen Kirby, USMCA, "Trump's new NAFTA deal, explained in 600 words," *Vox.com*, July 1, 2020, https://www.vox.com/2018/10/3/17930092/usmca-mexico-nafta-trump-trade-deal-explained

[98] Danielle Kurtzleben, "More And More Democrats Embrace The 'Progressive' Label. Here's Why," *NPR*, September 13, 2021, https://www.npr.org/2021/09/13/1035971261/more-and-more-democrats-embrace-the-progressive-label-heres-why

[99] Lee Drutman, "We Need Political Parties. But Their Rabid Partisanship Could Destroy American Democracy," Vox, September 5, 2017, https://www.vox.com/the-big-idea/2017/9/5/16227700/hyperpartisanship-identity-american-democracy-problems-solutions-doom-loop.

[100] Stephen Lange Ranzini, "The 'Overton Window' and How Trump Won the Nomination with It," *The Hill*, October 1, 2016, http://thehill.com/blogs/pundits-blog/presidential-campaign/298417-the-overton-window-and-how-trump-won-the-nomination.

[101] Chuck McCutcheon, "Speaking Politics Term of the Week: Duverger's Law," *Christian Science Monitor*, August 9, 2016, https://www.csmonitor.com/USA/Politics/Politics-Voices/2016/0809/Speaking-Politics-term-of-the-week-Duverger-s-law.

[102] Carla Astudillo, "Election results: How Texas voted in the November 2022 midterms," *The Texas Tribune,* November 8, 2022, https://apps.texastribune.org/features/2022/texas-2022-election-results/

[103] Meagan Vazquez, "Biden zeroes in on policy: Here are 6 top priorities," *CNN*, February 16, 2021, https://www.cnn.com/2021/02/16/politics/president-biden-top-agenda-priorities/index.html

[104] Alexa Ura and Ryan Murphy, "Here's What the Texas Bathroom Bill Means in Plain English," *Texas Tribune*, June 9, 2017, https://apps.texastribune.org/texas-bathroom-bill-annotated/; Chris Strangio, "Lawmakers in Texas Are Returning to the Capitol for More Anti-Trans Discrimination," *ACLU*, July 18, 2017, https://www.aclu.org/blog/lgbt-rights/transgender-rights/lawmakers-texas-are-returning-capitol-more-anti-trans.

[105] Alexa Ura, "Texas Bathroom Bill Appears to Be All but Dead in Special Session," *Texas Tribune*, August 11, 2017, https://www.texastribune.org/2017/08/11/texas-bathroom-bill-appears-be-all-dead/.

[106] Emma Platoff, "Dan Patrick Says He Won the Fight over the Bathroom Bill, but at Schools Not Much Has Changed," *Texas Tribune*, January 9, 2019, https://www.texastribune.org/2019/01/09/texas-lt-gov-dan-patrick-dismisses-need-bathroom-bill-2019/.

[107] Patrick Svitek, "'Bathroom Bill' Fizzles as Republican Primary Issue," *Texas Tribune*, February 6, 2018, https://www.texastribune.org/2018/02/06/bathroom-bill-fizzles-primary-issue/.

[108] Emma Platoff, "In Texas, a Chaotic Primary Yields Status Quo Results," *Texas Tribune*, March 4, 2020, https://www.texastribune.org/2020/03/04/texas-2020-primary-who-won-incumbents-moderates/.

[109] Greg Abbott, May 19, 2021, https://twitter.com/GregAbbott_TX/status/1398719208758956036?s=20&t=lLVSGFjgPDuwDIqQzKnV_w

[110] Berna Dean Steptoe, "After a regular session and 3 special sessions, what did the Texas Legislature get accomplished?," *ABC Channel 8*, October 23, 2021, https://www.wfaa.com/article/news/politics/inside-politics/texas-legislature-accomplishments/287-5b6f7a39-2588-4d47-a689-7ea7967f419b

[111] Texas Election Code, Sec. 42.006, http://www.statutes.legis.state.tx.us/Docs/EL/htm/EL.42.htm.

[112] "Live Results: Texas Presidential Primary 2020," *The New York Times*, March 5, 2020, https://www.nytimes.com/interactive/2020/03/03/us/elections/results-texas-president-democrat-primary-election.html .

[113] Regina Mack and Sierra Juarez, "Here's How Texans Can Get Involved in Their Party Conventions," *Texas Tribune*, February 7, 2018, https://www.texastribune.org/2018/02/07/heres-how-texans-can-get-involved-their-party-conventions/.

[114] Republican Party of Texas, https://www.texasgop.org/rpt-conventions/; Texas Democrats, http://www.txdemocrats.org/wp-content/uploads/2017/08/TexasDemocraticParty_Rules_170130.pdf page 14–15.

[115] *Legal Provisions Relevant to the Electoral College Process,* National Archives, https://www.archives.gov/electoral-college/provisions

[116] Josh Putnam, "Everything You Need to Know about How the Presidential Primary Works," *The Washington Post*, May 12, 2015, https://www.washingtonpost.com/news/monkey-cage/wp/2015/05/12/everything-you-need-to-know-about-how-the-presidential-primary-works/.

[117] Ibid.

[118] Texas Democratic Party, "So You Want to Be a Delegate for Your Favorite Presidential Candidate," April 23, 2019, https://www.texasdemocrats.org/blog/so-you-want-to-be-a-delegate-for-your-favorite-presidential-candidate-texas-democrats-2020-series/.

[119] Ally Mutnick, "Texplainer: What's the 'Texas Two-Step' and Why Is It Gone?," *Texas Tribune*, July 7, 2015, https://www.texastribune.org/2015/07/07/texplainer-whats-texas-two-step-and-why-it-gone/.

[120] Carolyn Feibel, "A Guide to Texas' Electoral Two-Step," *Houston Chronicle*, March 1, 2008, http://www.chron.com/news/politics/article/A-guide-to-Texas-electoral-two-step-1653159.php.

[121] Election 2008, Texas Nominating Contest Results, *New York Times*, https://www.nytimes.com/elections/2008/primaries/results/states/TX.html

[122] Ibid., 119.

[123] Alexa Ura, "Texas Voting Lines Last Hours after Polls Close on Super Tuesday," *Texas Tribune*, March 3, 2020, https://www.texastribune.org/2020/03/03/texas-voting-lines-extend-hours-past-polls-closing-super-tuesday/

[124] Scot Schraufnagel, Michael J. Pomante II, and Quan Li, "Cost of Voting in the American States: 2020," *Election Law Journal*, December 15, 2020, https://www.liebertpub.com/doi/10.1089/elj.2020.0666

[125] Candice Norwood, "Do Iowa Caucus Winners Become President? History Shows Mixed Results," *PBS News Hour*, February 7, 2020, https://www.pbs.org/newshour/politics/do-iowa-caucus-winners-become-president-history-shows-mixed-results.

[126] Pew Research Center, "*Belief in God by State*," https://www.pewforum.org/religious-landscape-study/compare/belief-in-god/by/state/; Pew Research Center, "*Importance of Religion in One's Life by State*," https://www.pewforum.org/religious-landscape-study/compare/importance-of-religion-in-ones-life/by/state/.

[127] William O'Connor, "*How Religion Turned Texas Red*," *The Daily Beast*, July 12, 2017, https://www.thedailybeast.com/how-religion-turned-texas-red.

[128] Pew Research Center, "Christians Who Are in Texas," https://www.pewforum.org/religious-landscape-study/state/texas/christians/christian/.

[129] Ibid.

[130] Kevin Krause, "Texas Judges Say Religious Beliefs Allow Them to Refuse Same-Sex Weddings," *Dallas Morning News*, March 20, 2020, https://www.dallasnews.com/news/courts/2020/03/20/texas-judges-say-religious-beliefs-allow-them-to-refuse-same-sex-weddings/.

[131] James Barragán, "Texas Governor, Attorney General Give Guidance on Permitted Religious Services," *Dallas Morning News*, April 1, 2020, https://www.dallasnews.com/news/public-health/2020/04/01/texas-governor-attorney-general-give-guidance-on-permitted-religious-services/.

CHAPTER 12

Interest Groups and Lobbying in Texas

You walk into a coffee shop seeking your favorite flavor of coffee. While waiting in line, you see that pastries are on sale today only. You decide to buy half a dozen. After paying for your food and drink, you wait to get a bag of goodness. The clerk says, "Sorry, but we are prohibited by city ordinance from putting your order in a single-use bag. Would you like to buy this lovely multipurpose canvas bag for $5.99?" You decline, even though you wonder how you can carry six pastries and a giant drink in your hands. Who in the world dictated that you could not have a bag? After spilling your drink and sitting on a pastry while getting in the car, you decide to find out.

You learn that the American Multiuse Bag Union of South Hampshire (AMBUSH) lobbied the city to prohibit businesses from providing single-use bags. How did they convince the city council to pass such an ordinance? Why did the retail association fail to block this interference in free enterprise? You decide we need to protect the right to carry our giant coffee and pastries in a bag.

You begin to search the Internet for information on single-use bags. An email to the retail merchant's association of your town provides you with the names and contact information for like-minded people. They are going to rally at city hall to urge the passage of an ordinance to restrict the interference of government in commerce.

However, what if instead of this scenario, you decide the bag ordinance is a wake-up call to protect the environment? You search for the website of the anti-single-use-bag association. The Texas Association of Keep the Earth (TAKE) is going to the same rally to convince the city council to keep the ordinance. After your experience with the coffee and pastries disaster, you recognize the importance of protecting both your car and the Earth from wasteful practices like single-use bags.

Can you alone change government policy? No, the American system requires the cooperation and support of others to adopt or retain public policy. Interest groups alter public policy or reaffirm public policy every day. Political scientists and others attempt to understand how this works. You can also discover the role that interest groups play in the formation of rules and regulations.

Among several possible responses to the dilemma of single-use bags, you could join an interest group. Active participation in politics as discussed in

interest group

An organization of individuals sharing common goals that tries to influence government decisions

political action committee (PAC)

A spin-off of an interest group that collects money for campaign contributions and other activities

James Madison, ca. 1821

National Gallery of Art, Washington

Chapter 9 (see the section titled "Political Participation") often requires linkage with an interest group. What is an interest group? Political scientist Brigid Harrison defines an **interest group** as an organization that seeks to achieve common goals by influencing government decision making.[1]

Some observers use "interest group" interchangeably with the term "lobby group," although lobbying is a specific activity or technique (discussed later) whereby interest groups attempt to influence legislation and government officials. In recent years, many political scientists call the groups "pressure groups" to denote the groups' role of pressuring government.[2] Sometimes people also use the term "PAC" to refer to interest groups. **Political action committees (PACs)** are organizations that collect and distribute money to candidates and, as such, are a more specialized kind of interest group. Often, broad-based interest groups have PACs associated with them. Interest groups are distinct from political parties in the sense that their members are not trying to gain election to public office. Another type of interest group, a 527 group, is a tax-exempt group organized under Section 527 of the Internal Revenue Code to raise money for political activities.[3] PACs and 527 groups are similar, but the IRS imposes restrictions that alter their focus. PACs support candidates whereas 527 groups organize to influence an issue, policy, appointment, or election at any level. Currently, 527s appear poised to overtake PACs as the primary vehicle to influence public policy.

Interest groups play an important role in a democratic society. They are capable of exerting positive and negative effects on political processes and outcomes. Public attention often focuses on the negative influences; however, interest groups and their activities are protected by the First Amendment to the U.S. Constitution, which provides for the people's right "peaceably to assemble, and to petition the Government for a redress of grievances."

Early observers of American politics realized the importance of these political associations. In 1787, James Madison (one of the key framers of the U.S. Constitution, who is often called the "father of the Constitution"), writing under the name Publius in *Federalist No. 10,* predicted that interest groups or factions would play a significant role in American politics. Madison believed that the diversity of economic and social interests in an "extended republic" would be so great, and so many factions would form, that no one group would be able to dominate.[4] Madison's observation regarding the diversity of national interests applies to most individual states as well—especially large and populous states such as Texas. Alexis de Tocqueville (a famous foreign observer of American politics and society), writing in 1835, commented on the formation of interest groups in American politics and their importance in increasing individual influence.[5] Tocqueville's observation to some degree confirmed Madison's predictions.

Chapter Learning Objectives

- Describe interest group typology.
- Discuss the various techniques interest groups use, including lobbying.
- Explain how interest groups are regulated.
- Describe the factors that influence interest groups' strength.

Interest Group Typology

Learning Objective: Describe interest group typology.

Considering the great diversity of economic and social interests in the country and the state, it would not surprise James Madison that a vast array of interest groups exists throughout the United States and in Texas. Interest groups may form for many reasons and may represent a diversity of interests. Many of these groups have both national and state organizations. The National Rifle Association (NRA), the U.S. Chamber of Commerce, Mothers Against Drunk Driving (MADD), and the National Education Association (NEA) are all examples of interest groups that are active on the national and state levels.

The diversity of interest groups applies not just to the range of topics they address, but also to their form of organization and other characteristics. For instance, some groups are permanent organizations with full-time, well-financed professional staffs; others are temporary organizations that fade out of existence after their issue is resolved. Groups advocating property tax reform, insurance reform, and amendments to state constitutions are examples of such temporary groups. Groups can represent a single person, a large number of people, a private company, an entire industry, or even government employees and officials.

There are three broad categories of interest groups (see Table 12.1). **Membership organizations** are private groups whose members are individual citizens or businesses. **Nonmembership organizations** represent individuals, single corporations, businesses, law firms, or freelance lobbies; their membership is not open to the general public. **Government organizations** represent local government (city, county, school board, special districts) as well as state and federal agencies. Membership in these organizations ranges from local elected officials (such as mayors and council members) to government employees (police officers, firefighters, and federal and state employees).[6] This type of group is also called a state and local interest group, or SLIG, and is discussed later in the chapter.

membership organizations
Interest groups that have individual citizens or businesses as members

nonmembership organizations
Interest groups that represent corporations and businesses and do not have broad-based citizen support

government organizations
Interest groups that represent state and local governments; also called SLIGs, for state and local interest groups

Membership Organizations

Membership organizations within the state represent a wide range of economic and noneconomic interests. One kind of membership organization, a **peak business association**, is an interest group devoted to statewide business interests. These groups primarily try to promote their members' interests, and they use a variety of means. While these groups favor policies that maintain the state's "good business climate," they also present a united front against policies they view as harmful to business and business owners. Examples of peak business associations include the state Chamber of Commerce, the Texas Association of Manufacturers, and the National Federation of Independent Business. These groups are often most active at the state level and are generally well financed.

Trade associations differ from peak business associations in that they represent more specific business interest sectors. Texas has many such groups. Two powerful trade associations are the Texas Oil and Gas Association, representing oil and gas producers, and the Texas Trucking Association, which represents the trucking industry.

peak business association
An interest group devoted to statewide business interests

trade associations
Interest groups that represent more specific business interests than peak business associations do

TABLE 12.1

Interest Group Typology

Type	Examples
Membership Organizations	
Business/Agriculture	
Peak business organizations (groups devoted to general business interests)	Texas Association of Business
	State Chamber of Commerce
Trade associations	Texas Oil and Gas Association
	Texas Trucking Association
Agricultural trade groups	Texas Farm Bureau
	Corn Producers Association of Texas
Retail trade associations	Texas Apartment Association
	Texas Automobile Dealers Association
Professional Associations	
Private sector organizations	Texas Medical Association
	Texas Trial Lawyers Association
Public sector organizations	Texas State Teachers Association
	Association of Texas Professional Educators
Organized Labor Unions	Texas AFL-CIO
Noneconomic Membership Organizations	
Racial and ethnic groups	NAACP
	League of United Latin American Citizens
Religious groups	Christian Coalition of America
	Interfaith Alliance
Public interest groups	MADD
	American Civil Liberties Union
	AARP
	National Rifle Association
Nonmembership Organizations	
Representing individuals or single businesses	Halliburton Company Shell Oil Company
	American Airlines
	United Airlines
Government Organizations	
State and local interest groups (SLIGs)	Texas Municipal League
	Texas Police Chiefs Association

Source: Charles Wiggins, professor emeritus of political science at Texas A&M University, class handout, 1999. Revised.

CORE OBJECTIVE

Thinking Critically . . .

Review Table 12.1. Are you a participant in a membership organization? If so, how does the organization represent your interests? If not, how are your interests represented at the state and federal levels of government?

Given the importance of agriculture to the Texas economy, it is not surprising that there are multiple types of agricultural interest groups. General farming interests are represented by the first type of agricultural interest groups. The Texas Farm Bureau, the largest farm organization in the state, represents large agricultural producers. The Texas Farmers Union, the oldest farm organization in the state, represents family farms and ranches. Commodity groups, such as cotton growers, cattle raisers, chicken raisers, and mohair producers, constitute the second type of agricultural interest group. Suppliers to the above-mentioned producers fall into the third type of agriculture interest groups. These groups include, for example, cotton gin operators, seed and fertilizer producers, and manufacturers and sellers of farm equipment.

Retail trade associations are another type of trade group. The primary goal of these groups is to protect their trades from state regulations that the groups deem undesirable and to support regulation and policies favorable to the groups' interests (what some would consider "rent seeking" behavior, as we discuss later in the chapter). Examples of retail trade groups are the Texas Apartment Association, the Texas Automobile Dealers Association, the Texas Restaurant Association, and the Beer Alliance of Texas.

Professional associations differ from trade associations in two ways: members typically hold a professional license issued by the state, and the state regulates their scope of practice. Some of the best-known groups in this category represent physicians (the Texas Medical Association) and attorneys (the Texas Trial Lawyers Association). Other organizations represent the interests of architects, landscape professionals, engineers, surveyors, plumbers, tax preparers, librarians, cosmetologists, funeral directors, athletic trainers, hearing aid dispensers, dentists, nurses, chiropractors, optometrists, pharmacists, podiatrists, psychologists, veterinarians, and many other professions.

Although medical, legal, and other aforementioned professions generally fall under the private sector, public school educators (who, ultimately, are government employees) are part of the public sector. There are multiple interest groups related to education. One such group is the Texas State Teachers Association (TSTA), the oldest educators' association in the state. TSTA is the state affiliate of the National Education Association (NEA), a national teachers' union.[7] The Association of Texas Professional Educators (ATPE) has no affiliation with any national organization and is currently the largest educators' group in the state.[8]

The Texas High School Coaches Association (THSCA) is an example of a specialized "educational" association. In a state where football is a Friday night tradition, this organization has some political clout. In 1984, the Texas legislature enacted the "no-pass/no-play" law, which required students to pass their classes or be barred from participating in athletic and other extracurricular events.[9] The THSCA formed a PAC to combat this rule.[10] Despite strong opposition, the "no-pass/no-play" legislation passed and remains in effect to this day.

In other states, groups representing state and local employees are classified as public-sector labor unions. However, Texas does not give public employees the right to bargain collectively.[11] **Collective bargaining** is a process of negotiation "between an employer and a group of employees so as to determine the conditions of employment."[12] If collective bargaining existed in Texas, organizations representing government workers would be able to force the government

retail trade associations
Organizations seeking to protect and promote the interests of member businesses involved in the sales of goods and services

professional associations
Organizations promoting the interests of individuals who generally must hold a state-issued license to engage in their profession

collective bargaining
Negotiations between an employer and a group of employees to determine employment conditions, such as those related to wages, working hours, and safety

to enter into such negotiations and reach an agreement. Because Texas public employees lack collective bargaining, public-sector employee organizations are merely professional associations rather than labor unions.

In many industrialized states, organized labor unions have traditionally been important and powerful interest groups, although their influence has declined in recent years. In Texas, private-sector labor unions exist; however, they are not powerful and represent only a small fraction of workers. Except in a few counties on the Texas Gulf Coast, where organized labor represents petrochemical and longshore workers, organized labor in Texas is very weak. According to the Bureau of Labor Statistics, only 3.8 percent of wage and salaried employees in Texas belonged to labor unions in 2021.[13] As in most of the South, strong anti-union feelings are very much a part of the traditionalistic/individualistic political culture.

Texas is one of 27 states with **right-to-work laws**.[14] According to these laws, "a person cannot be denied employment because of membership or nonmembership in a labor union or other labor organization."[15] Among other things, these laws prohibit union shops where all workers are required to join the union within 90 days of beginning employment as a condition of keeping their jobs (see Map 12.1). Federal law also prohibits compulsory union dues or membership.[16] Unions and employers may enter into "union security agreements." While unions may not require workers to join under those agreements, they can require them to pay for efforts by the union in collective bargaining action. Some states such as Texas, might prohibit the use of "union security agreements" and not

right-to-work laws
Legislation stipulating that a person cannot be denied employment because of membership or nonmembership in a labor union or other labor organization

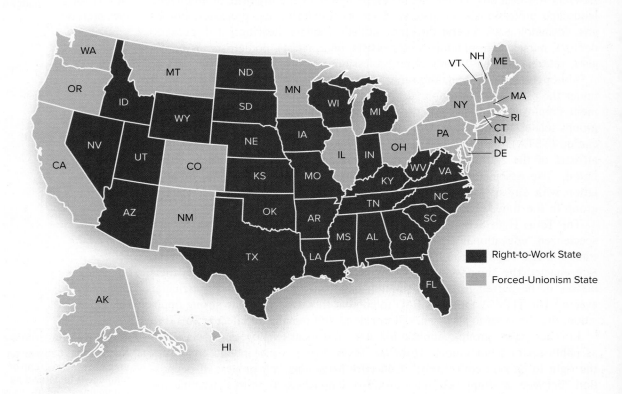

MAP 12.1   States with Right-to-Work or Anti-union Laws

allow employers to collect union dues from workers' paychecks. Compare this map with the political culture map in Chapter 1.

As previously stated, interest groups are not limited to focusing on economic interests; they can address social issues as well. One type of noneconomic organization relates to the special interests of minorities or ethnic groups. These organizations are primarily concerned with advancing their views on civil rights, discrimination, government services, and economic and political equality for those they represent. Hispanics are represented by a variety of groups including the **League of United Latin American Citizens (LULAC),** the oldest such group in the state. Other Hispanic organizations active in Texas include the Mexican American Legal Defense and Education Fund (MALDEF), the Mexican American Democrats (MAD), the Republican National Hispanic Assembly (RNHA), and the National Council of La Raza (NCLR). The National Association for the Advancement of Colored People (NAACP) played a significant role in the civil rights movement in Texas and continues to represent Black Americans in the state and throughout the country.[17]

Another type of social interest group focuses on religious issues. Religious groups have a long history in Texas. In the nineteenth century, fundamentalist Protestants in Texas, believing alcohol consumption to be immoral, supported the nationwide temperance movement to prohibit the production and sale of alcohol. They formed chapters of organizations such as the United Friends of Temperance and the Woman's Christian Temperance Union.[18] These religious groups advocated the passage of local option laws, allowing communities to vote on whether alcohol sales would be legal in their area. The local option elections persist to this day. As of August, 2021, five Texas counties were completely "dry," not permitting alcoholic beverage sales anywhere in the county while the other 249 counties have various options related to beer, wine, and spirits sales including on or off premise consumption.[19]

In recent years, too, fundamentalist Christian groups have been quite visible on the national stage and in Texas. Organizations such as the Christian Coalition of America oppose abortion and seek to end taxpayer funding of abortion and stem cell research.[20] Similar groups promote abstinence-based sex education, homeschooling, school prayer, and traditional marriage, among other issues. These groups have been somewhat successful in using government to promote their agenda.

The Texas State Board of Education (SBOE), which oversees some aspects of school policy statewide, including textbook selection and curriculum, is composed of 15 elected members. In 2020, the Texas Legislature passed SB3 which prohibited the teaching of critical race theory in public school. The SBOE will oversee the creation of new standards by Texas Education Agency (TEA) for social studies instruction.[21] Additionally, the SBOE in its role of selecting textbooks examined new sex education books.[22] These educational areas open the SBOE to lobbying by many interest groups.

Over the past several decades, the Catholic Church has become active in Texas state politics. This activity, primarily among Hispanic Catholics, is motivated by concerns about economic advancement, local services, and abortion. In San Antonio, the Catholic Church was a driving force behind the creation of Communities Organized for Public Service (COPS) in the 1970s.[23] This coalition of interest groups successfully challenged the Good Government League,

League of United Latin American Citizens (LULAC)
The oldest organization representing Latinos in Texas, established in 1929

An ACLU worker distributes literature

Brad Doherty/The Brownsville Herald/AP Images

a political machine that had dominated city elections for decades, and secured millions of dollars in funding for infrastructure and public services for low-income, primarily Hispanic areas of the city.[24] In the Rio Grande Valley, the Catholic Church was a driving force in the formation of Valley Interfaith. In the El Paso area, the Interreligious Sponsoring Organization was created to advance Hispanic interests. In 2012, the Catholic Church sued the federal government over the Affordable Care Act (also called "Obamacare"), alleging the new health care law violated religious freedom by mandating coverage of contraceptives and other drugs.[25] Several dioceses in Texas were among those filing suit. A 2016 Supreme Court case (*Zubik v. Burwell*) suggested a path forward in which the concerns of religious groups would be accommodated while the objective of the law in terms of contraceptive coverage would also be met. The Trump administration also issued rules that essentially allow groups with religious or moral objections to opt out of providing plans with such coverage.[26] The Biden administration did not revise the rules but indicated they would narrow the exceptions given to religious groups. Under the ACA, employers must provide free contraceptive unless they are an exempt entity.[27]

Public interest groups represent causes or ideas rather than economic, professional, or governmental interests. Many of these Texas organizations have national counterparts—for instance, Mothers Against Drunk Driving (MADD), the National Organization for Women (NOW), the National Right to Life Committee, the Sierra Club, the American Civil Liberties Union (ACLU), U.S. Chamber of Commerce, Common Cause, and the League of Women Voters. These groups usually limit their support or opposition to a narrow range of issues.

Nonmembership Organizations

Nonmembership organizations (which do not have active members but rather represent a single company, organization, corporation, or individual) form the largest category of interest groups. Even a cursory glance at the list of organizations registered with the Texas Ethics Commission in Austin reveals nearly 2,000 of these groups (see https://www.ethics.state.tx.us/search/cf/2020/CashOnHand_30BFeb20.html). For example, Bank of America and Valero Energy Corporation are both registered as active political committees (PACs) with the Ethics Commission. Many law firms also can act as "hired guns" available to represent a variety of interests in the state.

Government Organizations

In this typology, government organizations are considered separately from membership groups, even though some government organizations have active members. The members of these **state and local interest groups (SLIGs)** are government employees and officials; however, the interest groups represent the organization, not the interests of individual members.

The goal of these groups is to protect local government interests from actions of the state legislature, the governor, and state agencies. Examples include the Texas Municipal League, the Texas Police Chiefs Association, the Combined

state and local interest groups (SLIGs)

Interest groups that represent state and local governments, such as the Texas Association of Counties

Law Enforcement Association of Texas, the Texas Association of Fire Fighters, the Texas City Attorneys Association, the Texas Association of Counties, and the Texas Association of School Boards.

> **Understanding Impact** Interest groups play a critical role in the operation of governments. The interaction of interest groups with elected officials and the bureaucracy affects everyone's lives. Interest groups vary in many ways such as the size of membership, amount of money, and the policy areas they focus on. By recognizing the purpose and operation of various interest groups, we can better understand their influence. If you want to change public policy about single-use bags, for instance, what type of group should you contact? Do you think businesses use a different type of interest group to protect their interests than you would use for your interests?

Techniques Used by Interest Groups

Learning Objective: Discuss the various techniques interest groups use, including lobbying.

For interest groups to accomplish their goals, they must influence government and public policy decisions. How do they exert this influence? Interest groups use a variety of techniques to further their agendas; the type of technique employed depends on the type of group and the resources available to that group. The primary techniques that interest groups use are lobbying, electioneering, public education and grassroots lobbying, and litigation. Other tactics (not discussed in detail here) include petitions, protests, marches, and demonstrations.

Lobbying

Perhaps the best-known and most common technique used by interest groups is **lobbying.** According to the Texas Ethics Commission, lobbying involves "'direct communications' with members of the legislative or executive branch of state government to influence legislation or administrative action."[28] State law regarding lobbying does not apply to influencing local government officials. Local governments might have their own laws or ordinances regulating lobbying. Many stories circulate as to the origin of the term "lobbying"; one of the most common explanations is that legislators of the past did not have their own private offices. Because access to the chamber floor was limited to members of the legislature, those wanting to speak with legislators had to catch them in the lobby of the Capitol building or perhaps their hotel. One can find the American use of the term in the early nineteenth century. Regardless of the origin of the word, students of governmental behavior recognize the importance of individuals and groups attempting to influence public policy. Today lobbyists do not confine their activities to lobbies. The development of new communication tools has increased the ability of lobbyists to influence government.

Today, lobbying involves much more than the ambush-style meetings of the past. Because state and federal laws regulate lobbying,

lobbying
The practice of trying to influence members of the legislature, originally by catching legislators in the lobby of the Capitol

Citizens of Austin, Texas, attend and speak at a public hearing to discuss the future of Uber and Lyft ride-hailing services in the city at City Hall in downtown.

stock_photo_world/Shutterstock

it refers to a strictly defined set of activities. For instance, having a casual conversation with a member of the legislature is not lobbying.[29] However, if that conversation "is intended to generate or maintain goodwill for the purpose of influencing potential future legislation or administrative action, the communication is a lobby communication."[30] Likewise, publishing a newsletter to keep members of an interest group informed about legislative activities is not considered lobbying (even though legislators may read the group's newsletter).[31] The following activities, all aimed at convincing legislators to promote an interest group's agenda, are included in lobbying efforts:

- Contacting members of the legislature (in person or by phone, written letter, or electronic communication) to express support for or opposition to legislation
- Convincing members of the legislature to propose legislation (file a bill) favorable to the group
- Working with members of the legislature to draft legislation
- Testifying before a committee hearing about the effect of proposed legislation
- Encouraging members of an interest group to contact legislators (through email or phone campaigns, discussed later) regarding legislation[32]
- Issuing press releases and buying newspaper and television ads
- Providing written material to members of the legislature

This last activity serves a particularly important function in Texas politics. Interest groups often provide research findings to members of the legislature and their staffs. This information can obviously be self-serving, but it is often accurate and can be an important resource for busy state legislators. An interest group that produces high-quality research and information can have a positive impact on public policy. Over the years, several business-sponsored groups in Texas have developed a reputation for providing quality research and information to the Texas legislature. This desire to maintain integrity acts as a much-needed self-check on lobbyists' behavior.

Lobbying efforts take place throughout the year, although there are periods of particularly intense activity. Because the Texas legislature meets every two years for 140 days, most lobbying efforts are concentrated during the regular legislative session. However, lobbying does not stop when the legislature adjourns. All legislatures, including the one in Texas, perform some activities between regular sessions, and interest groups try to influence interim committees and other special activities of the legislature. Lobbyists also try to build knowledge and political capital between sessions. As two Texas lobbyists, Jim Grace and Luke Ledbetter, noted in the *Houston Lawyer,* "The session is simply too busy to build long-standing relationships while it is in progress. Only through continued hard work in the interim can you understand the personalities of the members, the unique needs of the constituents in their districts, and the issues about which they are passionate."[33] See Table 12.2 for Grace and Ledbetter's advice to fellow lobbyists.

Though lobbying is often thought of in conjunction with the legislature, the executive branch can also be lobbied. After a bill is passed, the governor has the option to sign it, veto it, or take no action (in which case the bill becomes

TABLE 12.2

Grace and Ledbetter's Rules and Tricks of the Lobbying Trade

1. NEVER lie to a member of the legislature.
2. Preparation. Preparation. Preparation.
3. Know what you don't know and be willing to admit it.
4. There are some things you can't control.
5. Information is the currency of the realm.
6. "Only speak when it improves the silence."[34]
7. Don't write it down (and especially don't put it in an email) unless you are comfortable waking up and seeing it as the headline on the front page of the *Houston Chronicle.*
8. The "Reply to All" button is not your friend.
9. Be prepared to forge strange alliances.
10. Compromise when you can; hold firm when you must.
11. Never ask members for a vote you know they can't take back to the district.
12. Be ever-present at the Capitol during session.
13. Know the calendar rules better than anyone else.
14. Money will never buy you a vote.
15. Treat everyone with respect.
16. Legislation (like water) takes the path of least resistance: do everything possible to make a staffer's life easier.
17. And finally, remember that "[n]o man's life, liberty, or property are safe while the legislature is in session."[35]

Source: Jim Grace and Luke Ledbetter, "The Lobbyist," *Houston Lawyer,* September–October 2009, 10, http://www.thehoustonlawyer.com/aa_sep09/page10.htm.

law without a signature).[36] Therefore, persuading the governor either to sign or veto a bill can be an important part of lobbying activity.

One example in which interest groups sought a gubernatorial veto occurred during the 2021 session. Texas House Bill 1927 would allow Texas residents to openly carry handguns in a holster or concealed without needing a permit, know as "Constitutional Carry." The Texas Municipal Police Association, Texas Police Chiefs Association, and police unions in Austin, Dallas, and Houston opposed the bill.[37] Guns Owners of America and other pro gun groups urged Governor Abbott to sign the bill.[38] The governor signed the bill into law. It is difficult to determine exactly how much the various interest groups influenced Abbott's decision.

After a bill goes into effect, a regulatory agency (typically part of the executive branch) must enforce the new law. As a result, lobbying can also be directed toward how much discretion or leeway an agency exercises in enforcing the law. Interest groups expend a great deal of effort to influence how agencies interpret and enforce regulations. If individuals friendly to the interest group are appointed to governing boards and commissions, enforcement of the law can be eased considerably.

Lobbyists can be classified into five types:

1. *Contract lobbyists* are hired to represent a client (an individual, group, or organization) and to try to influence the legislative process on behalf of that client. Many of these lobbyists represent more than one client.

2. *In-house lobbyists* are employees of a particular business or association, and they engage in lobbying as part of their job.
3. *Governmental lobbyists* and legislative liaisons work for a governmental organization and lobby as part of their job. They might not be required to register formally as lobbyists.
4. *Citizen or volunteer lobbyists* are nonpaid volunteers representing citizen groups and organizations. A good example is volunteers for Mothers Against Drunk Driving (MADD).
5. Finally, there are *private individuals*, usually with a pet project or issue. Sometimes called "hobbyists," these individualists act on their own behalf and do not officially represent any organizations.[39]

Lobbying is often looked down on by people worried about special interests taking precedence over the greater good. This is not a novel sentiment, as evidenced by Supreme Court Justice Noah Swayne's remark in *Trist v. Child* (1874) about such "infamous" employment: "If any of the great corporations of the country were to hire adventurers who make market of themselves in this way, to procure the passage of a general law with a view to the promotion of their private interests, the moral sense of every right-minded person would instinctively denounce the employer and employed as steeped in corruption, and the employment as infamous."[40] However, lobbyists (and interest groups in general) would counter that their actions are protected by the First Amendment to the U.S. Constitution, which guarantees "the right of the people peaceably to assemble, and to petition the Government for a redress of grievances."[41]

CORE OBJECTIVE

Taking Personal Responsibility . . .

Socrates suggested "know thyself," and Shakespeare's Hamlet admonished "to thine own self be true." It is important to know what your interests are and how they are represented in government. Consider what you have read in this chapter and determine how interest group efforts align with your personal interests. If they do not, what can you do to ensure that government addresses your interests or the interests of those who share similar values?

Electioneering

In addition to lobbying political leaders, interest groups devote considerable time and effort to try to influence the outcome of elections. Their goal is to help candidates who are sympathetic to the group's cause win public office. This type of activity is called **electioneering.** In pursuit of electioneering, an interest group's most important resource is money, usually contributed to campaigns and funneled to candidates through PACs. Some interest groups prefer to give money to other groups who, in turn, funnel the money to campaigns. At the national level, PACs—whether or not they are connected to a corporation, trade association, or labor union—are required to register with the Federal Election Commission at the time they are formed.[42] Historically,

electioneering
Various activities in which interest groups engage to try to influence the outcome of elections

TABLE 12.3

PAC Spending from 2000 to 2022

Election Cycle	No. of Active PACs	PAC Spending	Spending Increase from Previous Cycle	Percent Spending Increase
2000	865	$ 53,996,975	$ 2,453,155	5%
2002	964	$ 85,320,226	$ 31,323,251	58%
2004	850	$ 68,904,524	($ 16,415,702)	(19%)
2006	1,132	$ 99,167,646	$ 30,263,122	44%
2008	1,209	$ 119,561,861	$ 20,394,215	21%
2010	1,302	$ 133,466,187	$ 13,904,326	12%
2012	1,364	$ 126,367,460	($ 7,098,727)	(5%)
2014	1,421	$ 159,314,633	$ 32,947,173	26%
2016	1,950	$ 203,989,396	$ 44,674,763	28%
2018	2,225	$ 274,819,937	$ 70,830,541	34.7%
2020	2,006	$ 351,257,508	$ 76,437,571	21.8%
2022	1,828	$ 259,710,185* as of July 2022	N/A	N/A

Sources: Texans for Public Justice, "Texas PACs: 2008 Cycle Spending," April 2009, http://info. tpj.org/reports/txpac08/chapter1.html; "Texas PACs: 2010 Election Cycle Spending," August 2011, http://info.tpj.org/reports/pdf/PACs2010.pdf; "Texas PACs: 2012 Election Cycle Spending," October 2013, http://info.tpj.org/reports/pdf/PACs2012.pdf; "Texas PACs: 2014 Election Cycle Spending," February 2016, http://info.tpj.org/reports/pdf/PACs2014.pdf.; Transparency Texas, "Texas PACS 2016 Cycle Spending," 2016 Election Season, https://finance.transparencytexas. org/filers?e=2016-election-cycle; Transparency Texas, "Texas PACS 2018 Cycle Spending," 2018 Election Season, https://finance.transparencytexas/filers?e=2018-election-cycle; Transparency Texas (2018), PACS. https://www.transparencyusa.org/tx/pacs?cycle=2018-election-cycle

Transparency Texas (2020), PACS. April 2022 https://www.transparencyusa.org/tx/pacs?cycle= 2020-election-cycle

Transparency Texas (2022), PACS. April 2022 https://www.transparencyusa.org/tx/pacs?cycle= 2022-election-cycle

there were limits on how much money PACs could receive and distribute in a single year or election cycle, but those restrictions ended because of the *Citizens United* ruling by the Supreme Court.[43] (The section titled "Regulation of Interest Groups" discusses this in more depth.) See Table 12.3 for the amount of money contributed by the major PACs in Texas during recent election cycles. Note that the total amount spent by general-purpose PACs in the 2020 spending cycle was more than seven times the amount spent in 2000. During that period, PAC spending grew from $53 million to $351 million.[44]

Some writers have observed that PAC money has undermined party loyalty and weakened political parties in this country. Candidates no longer owe their loyalty to the party that helped elect them but to interest groups that funded them. Political action committees buy access in "an intricate, symbiotic relationship involving trust, information exchange, pressure and obligations. The inescapable fact is that resources, and especially money, are at least three-fourths of the battle in building and maintaining good relations and in securing the other essential elements that lead to access and influence."[45]

Eva Guzman served on the Texas Supreme Court before running for Texas attorney general.

Dylan Hollingsworth/Bloomberg/Getty Images

However, many political observers would argue that money doesn't guarantee outcomes in elections or in public policy debates. For example, Eva Guzman recently ran for the Republican Party nomination to be the Texas Attorney General. She enjoyed wide support from many Republicans and had significant political experience serving as a justice on the Texas Supreme Court. In addition, she raised more than a million dollars primarily from the interest group, Texans for Lawsuit Reform. Yet she only won 14 percent of the vote against the incumbent Ken Paxton. Incumbents, those who hold the office already, often win reelection.[46]

CORE OBJECTIVE

Communicating Effectively . . .

Review the information about Eva Guzman's bid. Identify the reasons that you believe she might have appealed to individual donors and at least one possible reason his candidacy did not take off. Share your ideas with another student.

Money may be among the most important tools for interest groups trying to influence an election, but it is by no means the only tool. The process of electioneering begins with candidate recruitment. Interest groups work to recruit candidates for office many months before an election. They encourage individuals who will be sympathetic to their cause to seek nominations in party primaries. This encouragement takes the form of promises of support and money in both the primary and general elections. Some interest groups might encourage both Democratic and Republican candidates to seek nomination in their respective parties. This covers their bets: regardless of which candidate wins, the interest group will likely have access and influence.

A number of other activities constitute electioneering. Interest groups can make a public endorsement, signaling to potential voters that a particular candidate is aligned with the group's interests. They can run television and newspaper ads detailing the records of officials or the virtues of a non-incumbent, or they can undertake voter registration drives and get-out-the-vote campaigns. Interest groups might also aid candidates by helping write speeches and organize rallies and by staging political events such as fundraisers. Some groups keep track of legislators' voting records and circulate "score cards" to members of the organization, suggesting members vote for or against certain candidates.

Public Relations: Public Education and Grassroots Lobbying

Interest groups also try to influence policy through public relations activities. The goal of these efforts is to influence public opinion on a particular issue and to create a favorable public image for the group. To achieve this goal,

What point does this cartoon make about the nature of campaign contributions?

Jeff Stahler/CartoonStock

organizations might sponsor an educational program or other forum where people discuss policy issues. In addition, they might publish and disseminate educational literature.[47] Obviously, information prepared and distributed by an interest group can be very self-serving and in some cases might even be called propaganda. Not all such information is wrong, but some filtering of the information by the public is necessary. Some interest groups might counter the information provided by a competing interest group. An interest group's credibility with the public can be compromised if the group provides inaccurate or misleading information.

Interest groups also try to mobilize their supporters to advocate for the organization, using a technique called *grassroots lobbying*. Grassroots lobbying is defined as a communication with the general public that attempts to influence specific legislation by expressing a view about that legislation and urging the public to act.[48] Such a "call to action" can take several forms, including asking individuals to contact their elected officials, providing names and contact information for pertinent representatives, or providing a means of communicating with representatives such as a postcard that can be mailed or an email link that can be used to send a message to a representative.[49] The goal of such email or phone campaigns is to generate a public response of sufficient magnitude that elected officials will act in accord with the group's wishes.

Aside from efforts to create a favorable opinion of themselves with the public, interest groups also try to curry favor with public officials. Inviting public officials to address organizational meetings is one strategy used to advance the group's standing in the eyes of these officials. Giving awards to officials at such gatherings, thanking them for their public service, is also a common technique.

Interest group tactics have changed.[50] Although entertaining members of the legislature remains very much a part of the process, the more unethical aspects of such entertainment occur less frequently today. Bribery of a public official is a felony punishable by 2 to 20 years in prison and a fine of up to $10,000.[51] Interest groups have moved away from unsavory practices and are more likely to rely on other tactics today.

Understanding Impact To influence public policy, interest groups must persuade decision makers such as governors or legislators to adopt their agenda. Interest groups use various techniques and strategies to move decision makers to act. How would you influence Texas legislators to send more money to college and universities in order to lower students' costs? Should you make compromises and/or deals with others so decision makers will accept your solutions to public problems?

Litigation

The court system provides another means for interest groups to advance their cause and influence policy. Interest groups sue individuals, organizations, or government entities "to safeguard the interests of their members [and] promote test cases or class action suits to secure judicial favor for a particular principle."[52] Interest groups sometimes sponsor litigation themselves, orchestrating and funding a lawsuit on behalf of their members. In other instances, groups file *amicus curiae* (literally, "friend of the court") briefs to try to influence court decisions. This occurs when the organization itself is not a party to the litigation but has an interest in the outcome of a case.[53] Research suggests that when they have submitted amicus briefs, interest groups have been quite effective in swaying courts in favor of a particular argument.[54] As political scientists Rorie Solberg and Eric Waltenburg stated, "the judiciary will be the scene of ever greater organized interest activity."[55]

Focus On

Hispanic Interest Groups

Hispanic interest groups have used Texas courts to advance the interests of their members. One notable example of this was in the case
Delgado v. Bastrop ISD. In the early twentieth century, many communities in Texas operated three separate, segregated school systems: one for white children, one for black children, and a third for
Hispanic children.[56] Although state laws at that time allowed segregation by race in public schools, children of Mexican descent were
considered Caucasian.[57] In 1948, attorneys for the League of United
Latin American Citizens (LULAC) filed suit on behalf of Minerva Delgado, the parent of a Hispanic student, against the Bastrop Independent School District and three other districts.[58] The lawsuit claimed
that the segregation of Hispanic children based on their national
origin was not justified by any law and that these children were
receiving a substandard education.[59] The court agreed and prohibited
the segregation of Hispanic students on separate campuses in Texas
public schools.[60]

James Steidl/Shutterstock

   Another lawsuit related to educational opportunity was *Edgewood ISD v. Kirby*. In 1984, the Mexican American
Legal Defense and Education Fund (MALDEF) filed a lawsuit on behalf of the Edgewood Independent School District in
San Antonio.[61] (The lawsuit named William Kirby, in his official capacity as Texas's Commissioner of Education, as the
defendant.) Because the main source of funding for public education in Texas is property taxes, school districts in
wealthier areas were able to generate higher revenues, and therefore they had more money available for education
than school districts in poorer areas. MALDEF's lawsuit alleged that the state's method of educational funding violated
the Texas Constitution and discriminated against students in poor districts. In 1987 (and again in 1989, following
appeals) the court "found that the state's public school financing structure was unconstitutional and ordered the
legislature to formulate a more equitable one."[62] Though controversy and lawsuits have persisted, the state's current
funding arrangement, based on redistribution of property tax wealth (discussed in detail in Chapter 14), is a legacy
of the *Edgewood* decision.

More Recent Hispanic Litigation

Groups like LULAC continue to go to court on behalf of Hispanics and other parties in Texas over key public policy
issues. For example, in 2019, the Texas League of United Latin American Citizens filed suit to block the state from
removing a large number of people from the voter rolls. Whitley's office claimed it had discovered about 95,000 possible non-U.S. citizens who had registered to vote in Texas. Civil rights groups contended that the Office of the Secretary of State along with Attorney General Ken Paxton's office targeted recently naturalized citizens who were still
listed in older state records as noncitizens. In response to the lawsuit, the state halted the voter purge, and Texas
Secretary of State David Whitley issued an advisory announcement to county-level officials to "take no further action
on any data files."[63]

Critical Thinking Questions
1. In what way might litigation be an effective way for interest groups to pursue the goals of their members?
2. What are the advantages and drawbacks of this approach for our system of government?

Regulation of Interest Groups

Learning Objective: Explain how interest groups are regulated.

Most states have laws regulating two activities in which interest groups engage: lobbying and making financial contributions to political campaigns (also known as "campaign finance"). In terms of lobbying regulations, organizations that have regular contact with legislators are generally required to register and file reports on their activities. Often these reporting requirements are weak, and the reports might not reflect the true activities of the organization.

Texas first attempted to regulate the activities of interest groups in 1907.[64] The Lobby Control Act prohibited "efforts to influence legislation 'by means other than appeal to reason' and provided that persons guilty of lobbying were subject to fines and imprisonment."[65] However, the statute was never enforced. In 1957, Texas passed a new law requiring lobbyists to register and disclose information about their activities; this law had many loopholes and was ineffective. Subsequent amendments to state law have called for more stringent reporting.

Texas Ethics Commission

State agency responsible for enforcing requirements for interest groups and candidates for public office to report information on money collected and activities

In 1991, the state created the **Texas Ethics Commission** to administer and enforce laws related to lobbying, political fundraising and spending, and financial disclosure by state officials (among other duties).[66] Under current rules, an individual, association, or business entity that crosses either the "compensation and reimbursement threshold" or the "expenditure threshold" while engaged in lobbying efforts must register as a lobbyist with the Ethics Commission. In other words, registration is required if a person receives, as pay and in reimbursed expenses for lobbying, a combined amount of more than $1,640 per quarter-year. Alternatively, persons must register if they spend more than $820 per quarter on gifts or other paid expenses for a state official or employee or their immediate families.[67]

The official list of registered lobbyists for 2022 included 1,416 persons and companies.[68] However, there are many exemptions from the registration requirement. Government employees who lobby as part of their jobs are not required to register as lobbyists. Journalists are not considered lobbyists, even though news media outlets may communicate directly with public officials and express opinions on government policy. Some businesses may avoid registration if all of their lobbying activity is reported by a registered individual (for instance, a lawyer who is representing that business). In addition, persons are not required to register if they are paid to lobby for less than 40 hours per quarter.[69] Thus, the total number of persons or entities who lobby is likely much higher than reported.

Regarding campaign finance, most states require some formal registration of PACs. In Texas, PACs must register with the Texas Ethics Commission, designate a treasurer, and file periodic reports regarding the group's contributions and expenditures. These reports must provide the full name and occupation of persons who donate more than $50 to the group during a given reporting period.[70] A statewide officeholder, member of the legislature or a specific-purpose committee are prohibited from receiving a political contribution during the period beginning 30 days before the start of a regular session and ending 20 days after the regular 140-day session.[71] Although corporations and labor unions are prohibited from giving money directly to campaigns, state law does not limit the amount individuals or PACs can contribute to candidates for statewide or legislative office.[72]

How to

Evaluate Sources

Many of us experience information overload. We have so much news available that it is difficult to absorb and process what we need to know and to differentiate the best from the inaccurate or misleading. Even the most careful scholarship may reflect certain biases, and motivated writers may be trying to "sell" you on their view rather than providing complete information. So it is important to understand how to evaluate sources. Let's explore the 5 Ws approach.

Who?

First ask who the author is and what his or her position and background are. Is the person considered an expert by way of advanced study, scholarly credentials such as a Ph.D., or relevant experience in the area? Has the author published widely in that area or with widely respected sources (see below)? Does the person have political, religious, social, or other characteristics or stances that could bias them?

Information is not necessarily false or biased merely because of who the speaker is or what views they hold. Judge arguments, ideas, or facts based on their logic, truth, or merit.

What?

What is the message? Is it meant to be a factual statement (such as the number of eligible voters in Houston) or an opinion (such as an argument for a particular understanding of the First Amendment)? How sophisticated is the information? Is it a well-supported argument that seems to follow logic and contain relevant facts?

When?

When was this message first published or distributed, and has it been updated since? A source examining party politics in Texas published in the 1970s would look at issues differently from one published today. However, that same source might be valuable if you are trying to understand historical trends. With newspapers, it is sometimes useful to know whether the version you are reading is the latest or an earlier account.

Where?

Where did you find this information? Is it in a widely respected news source, such as a "paper of record" in a city, state, or country? Examples include the *Houston Chronicle*, the *Dallas Morning News*, and *The New York Times*. If it is from a newspaper, is it in the front news section of the paper, or is it in the editorial section where opinion pieces appear? Does the story have a dateline (information on the time and place the reporter filed the story) beneath the headline? If so, was the story filed from the place being reported on, from a faraway capital city, or even from another country?

If the information is a scholarly article, was the information published in a double-blind, peer-reviewed academic journal? That means the article has gone through a vetting process to judge the quality of the scholarship. Other experts anonymously review the content without knowing who the author is, thus ensuring some objectivity. Examples include the *American Political Science Review* or *State Politics & Policy Quarterly*.

If the information is in a book, who published it and when? Is it from a university press, which means it has probably undergone a vetting process? Or is it from a trade press, which is a publisher that sells books to a general audience instead of to students and professors?

Of course, be on the lookout for bias, and apply the other questions to information presented in any of these sources.

Why?

Why is this article, story, or fact being told? Is it meant to educate or persuade? Or is it trying to sell you something or provide you with entertainment? There is a big difference in how you should view a technical source discussing the reliability of a certain car engine, an advertisement discussing the power of that engine, and a local car show in which people tell you about car engines.

Following this system can make you a more sophisticated evaluator of information. Failing to do so may make you a dupe of demagogues and propaganda.

In 2010, the U.S. Supreme Court, in *Citizens United v. Federal Election Commission,* removed previous restrictions by the federal government on PACs' ability to spend money on election campaigns. The case stated that "political spending is a form of protected speech under the First Amendment."[73] Therefore, the government cannot prohibit corporations and unions from spending money, through PACS, on "electioneering communications" such as television ads for or against a particular candidate.[74] This ruling opened the door to a greatly expanded role for PACs in elections. The *Citizens United* decision does not affect the Texas law prohibiting direct campaign contributions by unions and corporations; however, it allows these groups to establish PACs to fund election-related advertising.[75]

People have criticized the Texas Ethics Commission for "timid" and ineffective enforcement of the rules, but greater efforts have been made in recent years to ensure compliance.[76] Although reporting systems have improved, it is still somewhat difficult to find and summarize information on interest group activities.

The ethics of interest group activity vary from state to state, influenced by the political culture of each state. What is considered acceptable in a traditionalistic/individualistic state such as Texas may be viewed as corrupt in a state with a moralistic political culture. The late Molly Ivins, a well-known Texas newspaper writer and observer of Texas politics, once said that in the Texas legislature, "what passes for ethics is if you're bought, by God, you stay bought."[77] Despite Ivins's deprecating humor, her comment reflects the evolution of Texas lobbying activity over time. While Texas might continue to experience some political corruption, the incidents of that behavior have decreased from the "good ol boys' day."

Understanding Impact The U.S. Supreme Court ruled that campaign contributions are political speech protected by the First Amendment to the Constitution. The Court further ruled that a corporation is a person in this instance. Corporations can now give unlimited amounts of money to candidates. Texas adopted regulations requiring candidates to report donations and expenses. Should Texas citizens be able to give unlimited amounts of money to candidates? Should non-Texans be able to give money to candidates for Texas offices? Should there be limits on how much money interest groups can spend to influence politics?

Factors Influencing the Strength of Interest Groups

Learning Objective: Describe the factors that influence interest groups' strength.

Interest groups have a variety of resources available to them. Their resource base depends on the type of group, the number of members in the group, and who those members are. For example, the Association of Texas Professional Educators (ATPE) has strength because it has so many members (about 100,000, according to the group's website).[78] Thus, they represent a large potential voting bloc. On the other hand, the Texas Municipal League (TML), which represents Texas city officials, has a comparatively smaller membership of 1,169 out of about 1,220 Texas cities (as of early 2020).[79] However, the TML's membership includes influential public officials, such as mayors and council members. The TML has lists of representatives and senators keyed with local officials. The

TML contacts local officials and asks them, in turn, to contact representatives and senators regarding legislation.[80] Local elected officials can easily contact legislators, and those legislators will listen, even if they do not always respond. A recent shift in the attitude of many legislators points to a diminished status for TML as one of the most influential groups.[81] Many legislators, along with the lieutenant governor, are unhappy with TML members' opposition to efforts to lower property taxes. Lieutenant Governor Patrick argued, "Where do we have all our problems in America? In our cities—that are mostly controlled by Democrat mayors and Democrat city council members. That's where you see liberal policies. That's where you see high taxes."[82]

Students and their supporters rally at the state Capitol, the terminus of the "March for Our Lives" against gun violence in schools.

Alex Scott/Bloomberg/Getty Images

It is important to note, however, that some groups have difficulty recruiting members (or money) to their cause because of the "free-rider problem." All interest groups provide benefits, and individuals may derive benefits from an interest group's efforts regardless of whether they participate in the group's activities. Thus, it is rational for some people not to contribute to or work on the group's behalf because they will still benefit.[83] The larger the group and the more diffuse the possible benefits, the greater the possibility of the free-rider problem undermining the group's cause. On the other hand, smaller groups that seek more concentrated benefits are less likely to suffer from this problem.[84]

The status and size of an interest group are important determinants of power. Obviously, the presidents of large banks and corporations in Dallas, due to their status, can command the ear of most state senators and state representatives from the Dallas area. Groups with many members can use their numbers to their advantage by inciting a barrage of telephone calls and messages to legislators regarding legislative actions.

The total number of groups representing a particular interest may not be a valid indication of strength. For example, in recent years the number of groups representing business interests has multiplied dramatically, and the number of groups representing the interests of local government has grown very little. One might take this as a sign that business groups have grown in influence relative to governmental groups. However, growing numbers do not necessarily indicate increased influence. Instead, they may indicate the increased diversity of economic interests in Texas over the past several decades. Except for special districts, the number of local governments has not changed in the past 40 years, which explains the more constant number of governmental interest groups. Factors other than sheer numbers—such as leadership, organization, the geographic distribution of its membership, and money—determine the strength of an interest group. Other authors point to additional factors, such as economic diversity, party strength, legislative professionalism, and government fragmentation, to help explain an interest group's power.[85]

Leadership and Organization

Leadership quality and organizational ability can be important factors in the power of interest groups. Many interest groups hire former legislators to help them. Some groups are decentralized with a loose-knit membership, which makes mobilization difficult. Other groups, such as the Texas Municipal League, are highly organized, monitor legislation being considered, and can easily contact selected members to influence bills while they are still in committee. Between legislative sessions, the TML's policy committees meet to begin formulating a legislative program that will be put in place for the next legislative session.[86] These committees recommend positions on legislation that lawmakers are likely to consider in that session. Then the TML membership considers the committees' recommendations at an annual conference. The organization adopts stands on key items, and the TML's board finalizes those stands. This process gives the group's leadership a firm basis on which to act, and constant contact with all members is not necessary. TML contacts key members only when quick action is required.

Geographic Distribution

geographic distribution
A characteristic of some interest groups in that they have members in all regions of the state

Some groups have more influence than others because they have members throughout the state and therefore can command the attention of many more legislators. The Texas Municipal League, for example, has city officials in the district of every senator and representative. Texas bankers and lawyers are located throughout the state as well. Legislators might not listen to citizens from other areas of the state, but they certainly will listen to citizens from their own district. Legislators will also listen to local elected officials. Thus, having members that are geographically distributed across the state is a key advantage for interest groups. Obviously, some groups cannot have **geographic distribution.** For instance, commercial shrimp trawlers are limited to the Gulf Coast region of Texas.

CORE OBJECTIVE

Being Socially Responsible . . .

How can the geographic distribution of interest groups improve political awareness between culturally diverse populations?

Money

Interest groups need money to fund their lobbying, electioneering, and public relations efforts. Money is also an important resource for other, less obvious reasons. Interest groups able to hire full-time staff and travel to meet with legislators have more potential influence than those dependent on volunteers and part-time staff. As indicated earlier, some groups have no active members per se, but instead represent individuals, corporations, or businesses. With enough money, groups do not need dues-paying or contributing members to affect government policy. Some of these groups do a very good job of mobilizing nonmember citizens to their cause. Others are good at giving the appearance of doing so. For example, several major pharmaceutical companies and labor unions, including a large construction-industry union, created the Pharmaceutical Industry Labor-Management Association (PILMA). The interest group ran ads to defeat a Democrat-sponsored bill to lower drug prices. PILMA used various tactics to fight legislation to restrict rising drug prices. Tactics included buying print advertisements, mailing fliers to voters, and employing well-known union lobbyists. The group received most of its money from the pharmaceutical industry and had revenues of $4.3 million in 2019.[87] One writer has referred to such nonmembership groups, which lack a grassroots (spontaneous, community-based) organization, as **"astroturf organizations."**[88]

Economic Diversity

The economic diversity of a state can affect the strength of an interest group operating within that state. Highly industrialized states with a variety of industries generally have many interest groups. Because of the diversity and complexity of the state's economy, no single industry or group can dominate. The many interests cancel each other out, as Madison predicted they would in *Federalist No. 10.* In other states, a single or a few industries dominate the economy. For example, in Alaska, oil is still dominant. Coal mining dominates Wyoming's economy, providing much of the state's revenues. Copper mining was once the most prominent industry in Montana, and lumbering is still the primary industry in Oregon.

In the past, a few industries dominated the Texas economy: cotton, cattle, banking, and oil. Today, the Texas economy is more diversified, and the number of interest groups has grown accordingly. It is much more difficult for one or a few interests to dominate state politics. Nonetheless, the traditional industries still wield a lot of power.

Political Party Competition

The strength of political parties in the state can influence the strength of interest groups. States with two strong, competitive parties that recruit and support candidates for office can offset the influence of interest groups attempting to put their own candidates forward. Legislators in competitive party states might owe their election to, and therefore be more loyal to, their political party and be less influenced by interest groups. In Texas, a history of weak party structure has contributed to the power of interest groups.

Professionalism of the State Legislature

In Chapter 3, we defined a professional legislature as being characterized by higher legislative pay, longer sessions (such as no limits on the length of regular sessions), and more staff support.[89] In theory, well-paid legislators with professional staffs depend less on information supplied by interest groups, and the information exchange between lobbyists and legislators is reduced. The Texas legislature has improved staff quality in recent years; most members have full-time staff in Austin and their local offices. In addition, committee staff has increased.[90] The highest-paid staff member of the Texas Senate receives $280,000. The median salary for the Texas House is $43,000.[91]

Even so, Texas government continues to experience turnover due to working conditions and low pay. While the professionalism of the legislative staff has improved, political actions might lower the quality of the staff. For example, the Texas Legislative Budget Board (LBB) helps the legislature act more professionally by providing impartial financial analysis on which to base the budget. Lt. Governor Dan Patrick and Texas Speaker of the House Dennis Bonnen appointed Jerry McGinty as director of the LBB after a lengthy vacancy.[92]

The Texas Legislative Council also provides excellent staff assistance in research and information. This increased level of support has led to a rise in legislative professionalism in Texas; whether this has resulted in a corresponding decrease

astroturf organization
A political term for an interest group that appears to have many grassroots members but in fact does not have individual citizens as members; rather, it is sponsored by an organization such as a corporation or business association

Focus On

LGBTQ Interest Groups

The fight for LGBTQ rights has become an important force in U.S. soci- ety. From the founding of the United States, people have struggled to establish justice for all. Although Texas adopted the Fourteenth and Fifteenth Amendments, some private and public institutions did not observe the rights that these amendments guaranteed. Members of the LGBTQ community faced discrimination and legal penalties. In the past, Texas law labeled LGBTQ behavior such as sodomy as criminal and imposed prison penalties. Because of this, Texas activists recognized the importance of political and social action. As American culture changed, minorities worked to assert their constitutionally guaranteed rights.

Michelmond/iStock/Getty Images

The strength of LGBTQ interest groups comes from several factors. In the twentieth century, the civil rights movement took on new vigor. LGBTQ groups build on the techniques and tactics of other groups such as the NAACP.[93] Using electioneering, protest- ing, organizing, and litigation, LGBTQ interest groups worked to gain acceptance. For example, LGBTQ activists orga- nized groups in major cities such as Dallas, Houston, San Antonio, and Austin to promote political action with a goal of gaining equal rights in employment, housing, and public accommodations.[94] Texas groups linked with national interest groups, such as Human Rights Campaign, to influence national policy. One result is increased nonprofit, governmental, and corporate support for LGBTQ groups and their issues.

Litigation has led to the U.S. Supreme Court considering several cases involving LGBTQ status:

- In *Romer v. Evans* (1996), the Court ruled that laws could not single out LGBTQ people in order to diminish or remove their rights.[95]
- Texas statutes used to outlaw sodomy, including in a private, consensual, and intimate setting. The U.S. Supreme Court opinion in *Lawrence v. Texas* (2003) declared the state had no legitimate state interest that could justify its intrusion into the individual's personal and private life.[96]
- After the U.S. Congress passed the Defense of Marriage Act (DOMA) in 1996, several states including Texas adopted laws or state constitutional amendments defining marriage as a "legal union between one man and one woman as husband and wife." In a 5−4 vote, the U.S. Supreme Court ruled the DOMA violated the due process and equal protection provisions of the U.S. Constitution (*United States v. Windsor*, 2013).[97]
- *Obergefell v. Hodges* (2015) established the status of marriage for LGBTQ people. In a 5−4 vote, the Court relied on the equal protection provision of the Fourteenth Amendment to strike down laws denying marriage to LGBTQ couples.[98]
- *Masterpiece Cakeshop, Ltd. v. Colorado Civil Rights Commission* (2018) ruled that the bakery could bakery to refuse to make a wedding cake for a same-sex couple. In issuing this ruling, the Court weighed two conflicting rights, the free exercise of religion and the Fourteenth Amendment equal treatment clauses.[99]

Critical Thinking Questions

1. How has the majority opinion of the U.S. Supreme Court changed over time concerning LGBTQ rights?
2. Why are equal protection of the law and due process important in defining the rights of minorities in American society?

in the power of interest groups remains to be seen. However, there are potential costs, too; it is not automatically better to have a professional legislature rather than a citizen legislature. Moreover, there are also literal costs because professional legislatures require higher pay for lawmakers and more staff to support as well.

Fragmented Government Structure

Interest groups expend much effort trying to influence the administration of state laws. The degree to which they succeed depends in part on the structure of state government. If the government is centralized under a governor who appoints and removes most department heads, then interest groups will find it necessary to lobby the governor directly and the agencies indirectly.

Texas has a **fragmented government structure.** The governor of Texas makes few significant appointments of agency heads. Therefore, each interest group tries to gain access to and influence the particular state agency relevant to its cause. Often these agencies were created to regulate the industry that the interest group represents. For example, the Texas Railroad Commission, an agency originally created to regulate railroads, also oversees the state's oil industry. Historically, oil industry lobby groups have had great influence over the agency's three commissioners and their decisions.[100] In 1971, the *Texas Almanac* contained a full-page ad, paid for by the Texas Independent Producers and Royalty Owners Association and the American Association of Oil Well Drilling Contractors, thanking the Railroad Commission. The ad read: "Since 1891, The Texas Railroad Commission Has Served the Oil Industry." Following public outcry over the impropriety of a state regulatory agency "serving" a private industry, the revised ad in the 1974 edition of the Almanac read as follows: "Since 1891 The Texas Railroad Commission Has Served Our State."[101] In truth, similar relationships exist between many state agencies and interest groups.

The members of most state licensing boards (such as the State Bar of Texas, the Texas Medical Board, and the Texas Funeral Service Commission) are professionals in those fields and may also be members of a relevant interest group. These licensing boards were ostensibly created to "protect the public interest," but they often spend most of their time protecting the profession by limiting the number of persons who can be licensed and by creating rules favorable to the group.

For example, in Texas, cremation cannot occur until at least 48 hours after the time of death.[102] However, if a body is not buried within 24 hours of death, state law dictates it must be embalmed or refrigerated.[103] Supposedly, the reason for embalming is to preserve the body and protect the public from the spread of diseases. However, others have suggested that embalming prior to cremation is unnecessary and merely protects the profit margin of funeral directors doing the embalming. (In fact, a 2015 law made it a "deceptive" practice for funeral directors to suggest that embalming is required when refrigeration is available as an alternative.[104]) Still, the way these laws are written, including the waiting period for cremation, creates an opportunity for morticians to charge for additional services.

This situation illustrates how members of a profession or interest group can influence rule making in a way that favors the group, thereby influencing how much money members of the group can make. Another term for this type of practice is **rent seeking.** Rent seeking happens when individuals or groups try to secure benefits for themselves through political means.[105] Rent-seeking behavior can lead to great costs to society, not only in the obvious senses but also because of the opportunity cost associated with people using scarce resources (time, energy, human capital, money, and so on) to capture political benefits rather than for "productive endeavors."[106]

fragmented government structure
A government structure where power is dispersed to many state agencies with little or no central control

rent seeking
The practice of trying to secure benefits for oneself or one's group through political means

capture

The situation in which a state
agency or board falls under
the heavy influence of or is
controlled by its constituency
interest groups

When the relationship between a state agency and an interest group becomes very close, it is referred to as **capture.** In other words, the interest group has "captured" the agency. However, capture of the agency by the interest group is probably more the exception than the rule. Often, competing interest groups vie for influence with the agency and reduce the likelihood of capture by a single interest group. (The creation of the Public Utility Commission is a good example of this.)

In practice, policy is created through the combined efforts of interest groups, the state agency, and the legislative committee (with oversight of the agency). This process is called the "Iron Triangle." Figure 12.1 shows how the process works at the state level.

Understanding Impact Do you see particular pieces of legislation as promoting a common good or fixing a problem? Or do they often seem to benefit certain individuals or groups at the expense of others? Do the concepts of rent seeking and capture help you understand the political process? Explain your answers.

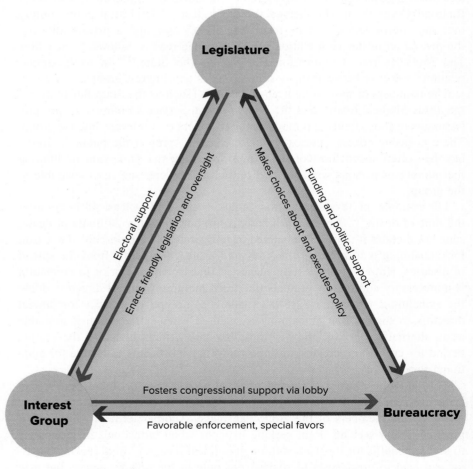

FIGURE 12.1   Often, a close relationship exists between the state agency created to regulate an industry, the legislative oversight committee, and interest groups. This relationship is sometimes called the "Iron Triangle."

Conclusion

Though often criticized (and sometimes rightly so), interest groups play a very important role in state politics. The First Amendment to the U.S. Constitution protects free speech and association, and interest groups are a necessary part of the political process. Government efforts to control interest groups are, and to many observers should be, limited. Knowing the tactics these groups use to influence government helps us understand politics.

The influence of interest groups, especially PACs, is likely to grow—especially if the size, scope, and budget of government continue to expand, thereby offering greater enticement for getting a piece of the pie or capturing a regulatory agency. In some campaigns, PAC money has essentially replaced the political party as a nominating and electing agent. The recent U.S. Supreme Court decision in *Citizens United v. Federal Election Commission,* by lifting a previous ban on direct PAC funding of certain types of political communication, has given PACs even more freedom to participate in election campaigns. In a mass-media age, little can be done to suppress the influence of interest groups.

Given the low levels of voter turnout and other forms of political participation in Texas, interest groups will likely continue to dominate state politics. The traditionalistic/individualistic political culture also supports such dominance. The present decentralized administrative structure in the state makes it easier for interest groups to influence state agencies. Because a reorganization of state agencies into a centrally controlled administration seems unlikely, this situation will persist for many years to come.

Summary

LO: Describe interest group typology.

There are three basic types of interest groups (or organizations of individuals with a shared goal that try to influence governmental decisions). Membership organizations are groups whose members are dues-paying individual citizens or businesses. Nonmembership organizations represent a single company, organization, corporation, or individual; their membership is not open to the general public. Government organizations represent the interests of local government as well as state and federal agencies.

LO: Discuss the various techniques interest groups use, including lobbying.

Interest groups use various techniques to promote their agendas, including lobbying, electioneering, public relations, and litigation. Lobbying involves direct communication with a member of the legislature or the executive branch in an effort to influence legislation or administrative action. Electioneering activities, such as making financial contributions to political campaigns, attempt to influence the outcome of elections. Interest groups engage in public relations activities to influence public opinion regarding a particular issue and to create a favorable image for the group. Groups may also protect their members' interests by filing lawsuits in court.

LO: Explain how interest groups are regulated.

Most states have laws regulating the activities of interest groups. The Texas Ethics Commission administers and enforces laws related to lobbying and campaign finance (political fundraising and spending). Individuals and organizations that have regular contact with legislators are generally required to register with the Ethics Commission and file reports on their activities. With regard to campaign finance, political action committees (PACs) must register with the Ethics Commission and file reports on the group's contributions and expenditures. The Supreme Court, in *Citizens United v. Federal Election Commission,* held that "political spending is a form of protected speech under the First Amendment"; therefore, corporations and unions cannot be prohibited from funding advertisements that support or oppose candidates.

LO: Describe the factors that influence interest groups' strength.

Many factors influence the strength of interest groups, including their status, the number of members they have, the quality of their leadership, their degree of organization, the geographic distribution of their members across the state, money, the economic diversity of the state, the presence of competitive political parties, the degree of professionalism of the state legislature, and whether government structure is fragmented or centralized.

Key Terms

astroturf organization
capture
collective bargaining
electioneering
fragmented government structure
geographic distribution
government organizations
interest group

League of United Latin American
  Citizens (LULAC)
lobbying
membership organizations
nonmembership organizations
peak business association
political action committee (PAC)
professional associations

rent seeking
retail trade associations
right-to-work laws
state and local interest groups
  (SLIGs)
Texas Ethics Commission
trade associations

Notes

1 Brigid Harrison, Jean Harris, and Michelle Deardorff. *American Democracy Now*, 6th ed. (New York: McGraw Hill Education, 2019), 227.

2 "Types of Advocacy Groups," OpenSecrets.org: Center for Responsive Politics, 2022, https://www.opensecrets.org/527s/types.php.

3 United States Internal Revenue Service, *Tax Information for Political Organizations,* https://www.irs.gov/charities-non-profits/political-organizations.

4 James Madison, The Federalist Papers, No. 10, U.S. Library of Congress, https://guides.loc.gov/federalist-papers/text-1-10#s-lg-box-wrapper-25493273

5 Alexis de Tocqueville, *Democracy in America*, trans. George Lawrence, ed. J. P. Mayer (Garden City, NJ: Anchor Books, 1969), 190–91.

6 Adapted from a typology developed by Charles Wiggins, professor emeritus of political science, Texas A&M University, College Station, 1999 (unpublished class handout).

7 Texas State Teachers Association, https://www.tsta.org/about_tsta/history/.

8 Association of Texas Professional Educators, "History of ATPE," https://www.atpe.org/en/About-ATPE/History-of-ATPE.

9 The University of Texas at Austin, "UIL Academic Requirements," 2022, https://www.uiltexas.org/academics

10 Texas High School Coaches Association, "Membership," http://thsca.com/membership.

11 Texas Government Code, Title 6, Subtitle A, Chapter 617, "Collective Bargaining and Strikes," https://statutes.capitol.texas.gov/Docs/GV/htm/GV.617.htm

12 Cornell University Law School Legal Information Institute, "Collective Bargaining," http://www.law.cornell.edu/wex/collective_bargaining.

13 U.S. Department of Labor, Bureau of Labor Statistics, "Table 5, Union Affiliation of Employed Wage and Salary Workers by State, 2020–2021 Annual Averages," https://www.bls.gov/news.release/union2.t05.htm.

14 World Population Review, "Right to Work States 2022," https://worldpopulationreview.com/state-rankings/right-to-work-states

15 Office of the Attorney General of Texas Ken Paxton, 2022, https://www2.texasattorneygeneral.gov/agency/right-to-work-laws-in-texas.

16 National Labor Relations Board "1947 Taft-Hartley Substantive Provisions." https://www.nlrb.gov/about-nlrb/who-we-are/our-history/1947-taft-hartley-substantive-provisions

17 Michael L. Gillette, "National Association for the Advancement of Colored People," Handbook of Texas Online, https://www.tshaonline.org/handbook/entries/national-association-for-the-advancement-of-colored-people

18 K. Austin Kerr, "Prohibition," Handbook of Texas Online, https://www.tshaonline.org/handbook/entries/prohibition

19 Texas Alcoholic Beverage Commission, "Wet and Dry Counties," https://www.tabc.texas.gov/texas-alcohol-laws-regulations/local-option-elections/.

20 Christian Coalition of America, "Christian Coalition of America's Legislative Agenda," https://cc.org/legislative-agenda/

21 Brian Lopez, "Republican bill that limits how race, slavery and history are taught in Texas schools becomes law," December 2, 2021, *The Texas Tribune,* http://texastribune.org/2021/12/02/texas-critical-race-theory-law/

22 Drew Knight, "Texas State Board of Education approves sex education changes for singular textbook publisher," November 19, 2021, KVUEABC, https://www.kvue.com/article/news/local/texas/texas-sboe-sex-ed-textbook-publisher-approved/269-ebdf4455-3275-4e86-aaf3-fc221cf4114a

23 Robert E. Wright, "Catholic Church," Handbook of Texas Online, http://www.tshaonline.org/handbook/online/articles/icc01

24 Cynthia E. Orozco, "Texas IAF Network," Handbook of Texas Online, http://www.tshaonline.org/handbook/online/articles/pqtpp

[25] Terry Baynes, "U.S. Catholic Groups Sue to Block Contraception Mandate," Reuters, May 21, 2012, http://www.reuters.com/article/2012/05/21/us-usa-healthcare-contraception-idUSBRE84K19R20120521.

[26] *Zubik v. Burwell*, 578 U.S. _____ (2016), http://www.supremecourt.gov/opinions/15pdf/14-1418_8758.pdf; Katie Keith, HealthAffairs, "The ACA Contraceptive Coverage Mandate Litigation: Where Things Stand and What Comes Next," https://www.healthaffairs.org/do/10.1377/hblog20190102.683454/full/.

[27] Shefali Luthra, "The ACA has a birth control guarantee. Senators are pushing for better enforcement." February 16, 2022, The 19th, https://19thnews.org/2022/02/aca-birth-control-out-of-pocket-enforcement/

[28] Texas Ethics Commission, "Lobbying in Texas: A Guide to the Texas Law," January 1, 2022, https://www.ethics.state.tx.us/data/resources/guides/lobby_guide.pdf.

[29] National Conference of State Legislatures, "How States Define Lobbying and Lobbyist," http://www.ncsl.org/research/ethics/50-state-chart-lobby-definitions.aspx.

[30] Ibid., 28.

[31] Ibid., 28.

[32] Internal Revenue Service, "Lobbying," https://www.irs.gov/charities-non-profits/lobbying; Texas Ethics Commission, "Lobbying in Texas: A Guide to the Texas Law," January 1, 2022, https://www.ethics.state.tx.us/data/resources/guides/lobby_guide.pdf.

[33] Jim Grace and Luke Ledbetter, "The Lobbyist," *Houston Lawyer,* September–October 2009, 10, http://www.thehoustonlawyer.com/aa_sep09/page10.htm.

[34] Chris Matthews, *Hardball: How Politics Is Played Told by One Who Knows the Game* (New York: Touchstone, 1988), 133.

[35] *Final Accounting in the Estate of A. B.*, 1 Tucker 248 (N.Y. Surr. 1866).

[36] Texas House of Representatives, "How a Bill Becomes a Law," http://www.house.state.tx.us/about-us/bill/; Texas Legislative Council, "The Legislative Process in Texas," https://tlc.texas.gov/docs/legref/legislativeprocess.pdf

[37] Christian Flores, "Law enforcement leaders voice opposition to bills allowing unlicensed carry of handguns.", April 13, 2021, https://cbsaustin.com/news/local/law-enforcement-leaders-voice-opposition-to-bills-allowing-unlicensed-carry-of-handguns

[38] Gun Owners of America, "Your gun rights are so close to a touchdown?," May 20, 2021, https://texas.gunowners.org/your-gun-rights-are-so-close-to-a-touchdown/

[39] Adam J. Newmark and Anthony J. Nownes, "Interest Groups in States," in *Politics in the American States*, ed. Virginia Gray, Russell L. Hanson, and Thad Kousser, 11th ed. (Glenview, IL: Scott Foresman/Little, Brown, 2017).

[40] As cited in Luigi Zingales, *A Capitalism for the People: Recapturing the Lost Genius of American Prosperity* (New York: Basic Books, 2012), 183.

[41] U.S. Constitution, Amendment 1.

[42] Federal Election Commission, "Help for candidates and committees," 2022, http://www.fec.gov/ans/answers_pac.shtml.

[43] "Citizens United v. Federal Election Commission," *SCOTUSblog*, http://www.scotusblog.com/case-files/cases/citizens-united-v-federal-election-commission/.

[44] Transparency Texas, "PACS", https://www.transparencyusa.org/tx/pacs.

[45] Clive S. Thomas and Ronald J. Hrebenar, "Interest Groups in State Politics," in *Politics in the American States*, ed. Virginia Gray, Herbert Jacob, and Robert Albritton, 5th ed. (Glenview, IL: Scott Foresman/Little, Brown, 1990), 154.

[46] Renuka Rayasam, "How Texas' flashy attorney general race fizzled out," Politico, February 24, 2022. https://www.politico.com/news/magazine/2022/02/24/texas-attorney-general-race-fizzled-out-00011164

[47] Ibid., 32.

[48] Cornell Law School Legal Information Institute, "26 CFR 56.4911-2- Lobbying Expenditures, Direct Lobbying Communications, and Grass Roots Lobbying Communications," https://www.law.cornell.edu/cfr/text/26/56.4911-2 (accessed March 2022).

[49] Ibid.

[50] Kay L. Scholozman and John T Tierney, "More of the Same: Washington Pressure Group Activity in a Decade of Change," *The Journal of Politics* 45, no. 2 (May 1983): 351–77.

[51] Texas Ethics Commission, "Lobbying in Texas: A Guide to the Texas Law," January 1, 2022, https://www.ethics.state.tx.us/data/resources/guides/; Texas Penal Code, Section 36.02, http://www.statutes.legis.state.tx.us/ Docs/PE/htm/PE.36.htm: Keith E. Hamm and Charles W. Wiggins, "The Transformation from Personnel to Information Lobbying," in *Interest Group Politics in the Southern States,* ed. Ronald J. Hrebenar and Clive S. Thomas (Tuscaloosa: University of Alabama Press, 1992), 170.

[52] Kim Lane Scheppele and Jack L. Walker Jr., "The Litigation Strategies of Interest Groups," in *Mobilizing Interest Groups in America: Patrons, Professions, and Social Movements,* ed. Jack L. Walker Jr. (Ann Arbor: University of Michigan Press, 1991), 158.

[53] "Amicus Brief," *Legal Dictionary*, http://legaldictionary.net/amicus-brief/.

[54] Richard L. Pacelle, John M. Scheb, Hemant K. Sharma, and David H. Scott, "Assessing the Influence of Amicus Curiae Briefs on the Roberts Court," *Social Science Quarterly* 99, no. 4(2018): 1253–66.

55 Rorie S. Solberg and Eric N. Waltenburg, "Why Do Interest Groups Engage the Judiciary? Policy Wishes and Structural Needs," *Social Science Quarterly* 87, no. 3 (September 2006): 558–72.

56 Cynthia E. Orozco, "Del Rio ISD v. Salvatierra," Handbook of Texas Online, https://www.tshaonline.org/handbook/entries/del-rio-isd-v-salvatierra.

57 V. Carl Allsup, "Delgado v. Bastrop ISD," Handbook of Texas Online, https://www.tshaonline.org/handbook/entries/delgado-v-bastrop-isd.

58 V. Carl Allsup, "Delgado v. Bastrop ISD," Handbook of Texas Online, https://www.tshaonline.org/handbook/entries/delgado-v-bastrop-isd; League of United Latin American Citizens, "LULAC's Milestones," http://lulac.org/about/history/milestones/.

59 Ibid., 57.

60 V. Carl Allsup, "Hernandez v. Driscoll CISD," Handbook of Texas Online, https://www.tshaonline.org/handbook/entries/hernandez-v-driscoll-cisd.

61 Teresa Palomo Acosta, "Edgewood ISD v. Kirby," *Handbook of Texas Online*, https://www.tshaonline.org/handbook/entries/edgewood-isd-v-kirby.

62 V. Carl Allsup, "Hernandez v. Driscoll CISD," *Handbook of Texas Online*, http://www.tshaonline.org/handbook/online/articles/jrh02.

63 Eli Watkins, "Texas Settles Lawsuit, Agrees to $450K Payment after Latino Group Accuses State of Intimidating Voters," *CNN*, April 29, 2019, https://www.cnn.com/2019/04/29/politics/texas-citizen-voter-citizenship-settlement/index.html.

64 Janice C. May, "Texas Legislature," Handbook of Texas Online, https://www.tshaonline.org/handbook/entries/texas-legislature.

65 Keith E. Hamm and Charles W. Wiggins, "The Transformation from Personnel to Information Lobbying," in *Interest Group Politics in the Southern States,* ed. Ronald J. Hrebenar and Clive S. Thomas (Tuscaloosa: University of Alabama Press, 1992), 152.

66 Texas Ethics Commission, "A Brief Overview of the Texas Ethics Commission and Its Duties," January 10, 2017, https://www.ethics.state.tx.us/data/about/Bethic.pdf

67 Ibid., 28.

68 Texas Ethics Commission, "2022 Lobbyists List," March 6, 2022, https://www.ethics.state.tx.us/search/lobby/loblistsREG2021-2025.php#R2022

69 Ibid., 28.

70 Texas Ethics Commission, "Campaign Finance Guide for Political Committees," January 1, 2022, https://www.ethics.state.tx.us/data/resources/guides/pac_guide22.pdf.

71 Texas Election Code, Title 15, Sec. 253.034, http://www.statutes.legis.state.tx.us/Docs/EL/htm/EL.253.htm#253.034.

72 National Conference of State Legislatures, "State limits on Contributions to Candidates, 2021-2022 Election Cycle," Updated June 2021 https://www.ncsl.org/Portals/1/Documents/Elections/Contribution_Limits_to_Candidates_2020_2021.pdf.

73 Ibid., 43.

74 Federal Election Commission, "Citizens United v. FEC (Supreme Court)," February 1, 2020, https://www.fec.gov/updates/citizens-united-v-fecsupreme-court/.

75 National Conference of State Legislatures, "Citizens United and the States," https://www.ncsl.org/research/elections-and-campaigns/citizens-united-and-the-states.aspx.

76 Jay Root, "Ethics reform not swept under the rug, but not sweeping either," *Texas Tribune,* June 1, 2017, https://www.texastribune.org/2017/06/01/ethics-reform-not-swept-under-rug-not-sweeping-either/

77 Molly Ivins, *Molly Ivins Can't Say That, Can She?* (New York: Random House, 1991), 58.

78 Association of Texas Professional Educators, "ATPE Membership," https://www.atpe.org/en/Member-Benefits.

79 Texas Municipal League, "About the Texas Municipal League," https://www.tml.org/318/Membership; Shannon Najmabadi, "'People Were Giving Us Lip Service': Texas Cities' Legislative Efforts Have Struggled This Year," *Texas Tribune*, May 14, 2019, https://www.texastribune.org/2019/05/14/texas-municipal-league-has-struggled-influence-lawmakers-year/.

80 Texas Municipal League, "The Texas Municipal League Program for 2020–2021," https://www.tml.org/Document Center/View/2374/TML-Legislative-Program-2021-2022.

81 Ross Ramsey, "Analysis: From homegrown culture warriors to tomorrow's Texas leaders.", December 13, 2021. https://www.texastribune.org/2021/12/13/texas-republican-local-elections/

82 Shannon Najmabadi, "'People Were Giving Us Lip Service': Texas Cities' Legislative Efforts Have Struggled This Year," *Texas Tribune*, May 14, 2019, https://www.texastribune.org/2019/05/14/texas-municipal-league-has-struggled-influence-lawmakers-year/.

83 Tyler Cowen, "Public Goods," *Library of Economics and Liberty*, 2012, http://www.econlib.org/library/Enc/PublicGoods.html.

84 Mancur Olson, *The Logic of Collective Action* (Cambridge, MA: Harvard University Press, 1971).

85 Thomas R. Dye, *Politics in States and Communities*, 7th ed. (Englewood Cliffs, NJ: Prentice Hall, 1991), 112–13.

86 Texas Municipal League, "2020 TML Legislative Policy Development Process," https://www.tml.org/Document Center/View/2141/2019-2020-Policy-Process-9220sh

87 Katie Thomas, "Labor Unions Team Up with Drug Makers to Defeat Drug-Price Proposals," *The New York Times*, December 3, 2019, https://www.nytimes.com/2019/12/03/health/drug-prices-pelosi-unions.html.

88 Molly Ivins, "Getting to the Grass Roots of the Problem," *Bryan-College Station Eagle*, July 13, 1995, A4. Copyright Molly Ivins. Reprinted by permission.

89 National Conference of State Legislatures, "Table 2. Average Job Time, Compensation and Staff by Category of Legislature," https://www.ncsl.org/research/about-state-legislatures/full-and-part-time-legislatures.aspx#side_by_side.

90 Luis Acuna, "Legislative Staff Salaries and the rising cost of living in Austin," Texas 2036, July 20, 2021, https://texas2036.org/posts/legislative-staff-salaries-and-the-rising-cost-of-living-in-austin/

91 Government Salaries Explorer, *Texas Tribune,* January 1, 2022, https://salaries.texastribune.org/state-comptroller-payroll/departments/house-of-representatives/ and https://salaries.texastribune.org/state-comptroller-payroll/departments/senate/.

92 Platoff, E. (2020, March 5). Jerry McGinty to head troubled Legislative Budget Board. *The Texas Tribune.* Retrieved from https://www.texastribune.org/2020/03/05/jerrymcginty-legislative-budget-board-director/.

93 Alan Brinkley, *American History*, 14th ed. (New York: McGraw Hill, 2011), 812–16.

94 Human Rights Campaign 2021, "Municipal Equality Index 2021," https://www.hrc.org/resources/municipal-equality-index

95 Tara Law, "9 Landmark Supreme Court Cases That Shaped LGBTQ Rights in America," *Time*, October 8, 2019, https://time.com/5694518/LGBTQ-supreme-court-cases/.

96 Ibid.

97 Ibid.

98 Ibid.

99 U.S. Supreme Court, "Masterpiece Cakeshop, Ltd. V. Colorado Civil Rights Commission," 2018, https://www.supremecourt.gov/opinions/17pdf/16-111_j4el.pdf

100 David F. Prindel, *Petroleum Politics and the Texas Railroad Commission* (Austin: University of Texas Press, 1981).

101 Richard H. Kraemer and Charldean Newell, *Texas Politics*, 2nd ed. (St. Paul: West, 1984), 79. Also see *The Texas Almanac and State Industrial Guide, 1970–71* (Dallas: A.H. Belo, 1970), 425; and *The Texas Almanac and State Industrial Guide, 1974–75* (Dallas: A.H. Belo, 1974), 19.

102 Texas Health and Safety Code, Sec. 716.004, https://statutes.capitol.texas.gov/Docs/HS/htm/HS.716.htm.

103 Texas Administrative Code, Section 203.48, https://texreg.sos.state.tx.us/public/readtac$ext.TacPage?sl=R&app=9&p_dir=&p_rloc=&p_tloc=&p_ploc=&pg=1&p_tac=&ti=22&pt=10&ch=203&rl=48.

104 Ibid.

105 David R. Henderson, "Rent Seeking," *Library of Economics and Liberty, 2012,* http://www.econlib.org/library/Enc/RentSeeking.html. Also see the pioneering works by Gordon Tullock and Anne Krueger, especially the latter's "The Political Economy of the Rent-Seeking Society," *American Economic Review* 64 (1974): 291–303.

106 Tyler Cowen and Alex Tabarrok, "The Opportunity Costs of Rent Seeking," http://mason.gmu.edu/atabarro/TheOpportunityCostsofRentSeeking.pdf. Also see Kevin M. Murphy, Andrei Scheifer, and Robert W. Vishny, "Why Is Rent-Seeking So Costly to Growth?," *AEA Papers and Proceedings*, May 1993.

CHAPTER 13

Public Policy in Texas

You are driving home late one night on a lonely city road. You come to an intersection with a stop sign. Do you stop? It is late, nobody is around, and no one will see your choice. Do you roll through as if the sign is a yield sign? Do you act as though you do not see any stop sign?

Let's change the situation. You glance across the intersection and see a law enforcement officer in a marked car. Now, what do you do?

After making this decision, you might also ask, "Who put the stop sign there in the first place?"

Somewhere, a government official decided that the intersection needed a stop sign (or two, or four). This is public policy in action. What information led to the placement of a stop sign? Considering that local governments generally do not have large sums of money, why is there a stop sign at that intersection? By placing the sign there, the local government is requiring you to make a decision. The government action is the result of many decisions. The police officer is there to make sure you stop. If you fail to stop, then you may experience an ever-increasing use of power to correct your behavior. Policy decisions by the government create consequences.

You may ask if the traffic department, the police department, a local citizen, or a series of accidents prompted the local government to act. Are there general policies requiring stop signs at intersections with certain characteristics? How many accidents are necessary to prompt action? Can one citizen mobilize a government to act? If 20 residents complain and call for a stop sign at an intersection, is that enough to make a change? Does the local government have a priority list for placing signs? There are so many questions to ask about one stop sign in an out-of-the-way place.

Political scientists try to answer these and many other questions about the actions of governmental organizations. Using their knowledge of political culture, governmental and non-governmental institutions, and theories of public policy, political scientists seek answers. But political scientists are not the only ones seeking to understand. Students, politicians and average citizens do too.

The state of Texas and its subdivisions act every day to create, adopt, and implement public policy. Bureaucrats and public officials consider input from

Texas state Capitol

Elijah E. Myers (American Architect 1832–1909)/CrackerClips Stock Media/Shutterstock

various agents as they create policies that are contained in laws, rules, statutes, edicts, regulations, and commonly accepted governmental behaviors.

public policy

"Whatever governments choose to do or not to do." —Thomas Dye

What is **public policy**? Experts disagree on an exact definition, but here are a few that may serve the purpose. Public policy involves the general public directly or indirectly. Policies adopted by private organizations, such as civic groups or youth sports groups, are not public policy. Public policy always includes government with its power of coercion and force. Public policy is a result of politics. One political scientist proposed a definition of politics as "who gets what, where, when, and how."[1] Another offered this definition of public policy: "a policy may usefully be considered as a course of action or inaction rather than specific decisions or actions."[2] One source defines public policy as "an officially expressed intention backed by a sanction, which can be a reward or a punishment."[3]

Every day, government actions and inactions affect people, businesses, and groups. The state of Texas and its various subdivisions channel, challenge, and control much of your life. Earlier chapters described government and its policies. This chapter discusses various key policies that Texas has adopted and implemented. Among them are public education, higher education, regulatory policies, and social policies. While the federal government generally controls some policy areas, Texas has also adopted policies in response to those national issues.

Political leaders must decide how to allocate money and resources. For instance, if lawmakers spend more on border security, they cannot spend as much on public health services unless they raise taxes. Lawmakers soon confront the reality of complex issues involving different political philosophies, limited resources, federal policy, and restrictions on state power.

In this chapter, we examine some of the most important areas of governmental action at the state and local levels. But first, let's discuss what the steps are in the policy-making process and how Texas compares to other states in terms of its overall policy ideology.

Chapter Learning Objectives

- Discuss the steps in the policy-making process.
- Discuss public policy areas in the Texas state government.

Steps in the Policy-Making Process: The "Policy Cycle"

Learning Objective: Discuss the steps in the policy-making process.

Why do policies change, and what are the key factors that lead to these changes (or lack thereof)? Political scientists have proposed various theories to account for changes in policy that range from slow, steady change to change driven by certain privileged stakeholders. Some of the most common explanations include the following:

- **Incremental change:** This theory suggests that most government officials and institutions make small, gradual changes.
- **Punctuated equilibrium:** Policy changes gradually and subtly, with sudden and violent change occurring only as the result of a catastrophic event.[4] For example, the state of Texas operated several juvenile detention facilities. In 2007, after reports surfaced about the abuse of inmates in a juvenile prison in Texas, the state closed the Texas Youth Commission.[5]
- **Multiple streams theory:** This theory suggests that the policy process contains three key streams. The first relates to problems. The second stream has to do with proposed solutions. The third stream has to do with politics, including the public mood and turnover of elected officials. The streams may run side by side, but only when they intermingle does policy change.
- **Policy feedback theory:** Often decision makers pick from a limited list of choices shaped by current politics and policies. Interest groups promote answers tied to their interests.[6]

How do policies change? In his book *Public Policymaking,* political scientist James Anderson published one of the first comprehensive attempts to define policy making as a process. In particular, he refers to this process as a "policy cycle."[7] He outlined the primary stages of the policy cycle as follows: problem identification and agenda setting; policy formulation; policy adoption; policy implementation; and policy evaluation (see Figure 13.1).

Let's look at each stage in the process and discuss some Texas-based examples.

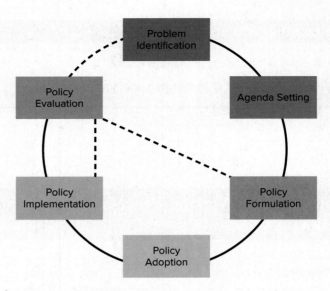

FIGURE 13.1 The Policy-Making Cycle

Problem Identification and Agenda Setting

This first step in the process may be the most important and most difficult. One group of political scientists described a garbage-can theory of organizational choice. In this theory, issues float around in the world like garbage in a can. Some issues land on the top of the pile and remain on top, while others fall on top but quickly sink to the bottom. Most issues move up and down in the garbage, seeking attention. Those demanding action may reach into the can to pull up the issue. Before any action can happen, the issue must arrive at the top and be plucked from the can onto the arena of public debate. People mine the issues, seeking to match their solution with an issue. If the government adopts their solution, they may gain power, money, and prestige. Other agents pull and push issues onto the stage of public attention to solve problems for their own groups. This may result in a particular group and its agent receiving much-needed public attention and funding.[8] Keep in mind that the garbage-can theory does not state that lawmaking is garbage. Instead, it describes a process that is more chaotic than most people realize.

Understanding Impact Leaders cannot attempt to solve all of society's problems at one time, so they identify which to focus on. An important current issue in Texas is the K–12 funding policy. Issues include *who* should pay for public education—parents, local taxpayers, or the State of Texas, and *how much* should each source of revenue pay. Texas taxpayers complain often about high taxes—both the state sales tax, which is one of the highest in the United States and property taxes. In 2019, Texas voters added a new state constitutional amendment making it harder to adopt an income tax. With local school districts relying on a mixture of property taxes, fees, and state funding to gain revenue, do we need a statewide education tax? Each student would receive an equal amount of funding from a common pool. Why or why not?

How to

Write Effectively

One role that citizens can play in a democracy is to help leaders identify the issues that are important to their constituents. Many people write letters, emails, or petitions to try to bring their concerns to their representatives' attention.

Your efforts to communicate with leaders will be more effective if you learn how to write well. Following the steps of the writing process will assist you in doing this.

1. Plan your message.
Before you write a word, consider what you want to say and how you want to say it. What topic do you want to write about? What point do you want to make, and do you need evidence to support your ideas? Is your purpose to inform or to persuade? Who is your audience? If you are writing to a legislator, for example, are they likely to agree or disagree with you? How are you going to send your message—by traditional mail, email, or some other method? You will need different strategies depending on the answers to these questions.

2. Research and organize your message.
Once you have decided on the topic and purpose of your message, look for any supporting evidence and data that you will need. For example, if your goal is to persuade the city council to put a stoplight at a particular intersection, then statistics about accidents at that intersection will help you make your case.

After you have your information, organize it by writing an outline. This is where the work you did analyzing your audience is helpful. If you are writing to someone you think will agree with your proposal, then you can use a direct pattern of organization. Start with your request

or proposal—"I am asking the city to put a stoplight at the intersection of Camden and Main"—and then give the arguments and evidence that support it.

If, on the other hand, you think you need to persuade someone who disagrees with you, use the indirect pattern of organization. Start with the evidence—"Did you know there were six fatal accidents at the intersection of Camden and Main last year?"—and build up to your request.

3. Write your draft.
Write out the first version of your message. Don't try to make it perfect; at this stage, you just want to get something down that you can work with.

4. Edit your message.
Read it over, and see if it makes sense. Are the ideas ordered logically? Do you need to rearrange the paragraphs? Are there places where the argument seems weak? Would it help to find more evidence? Are there places with too much detail that you could trim? Revise your message as many times as necessary to make it as strong as possible. Consider asking a friend to read it and make suggestions.

5. Proofread the message.
After you finish editing, read it carefully for spelling, grammar, and punctuation errors. You can use spell check and grammar check, but don't rely on them alone because such programs don't catch everything.

6. Send the message.
Once you are satisfied with your message, send it off by whichever channel you chose during the planning stage. Then wait to see if you receive a response.

Policy Formation

Political actors promote issues and solutions. Interest groups and bureaucrats supply decision makers with suggestions, information, and data. Politicians shape the proposed solutions into acceptable solutions. Rarely do decision makers and institutions adopt a solution without alteration.

Most solutions raised in the Texas legislature die in committee. Only a handful of bills become law after a journey through a system loaded with obstacles. Legislators must be careful when writing laws, rules, and regulations because the interpretation of a few words can result in a lawsuit. Frequently, citizens who observe the Texas legislature and its members are disappointed at what appears to be inaction. The observers join a large crowd of persons who seek action in legislative bodies across the United States.[9]

The policy formulation stage may lack analysis of the effects of the proposed policy or any alternatives (not to mention failure to consider the likely unintended consequences). This is due in part to the nature of legislative work: constituents complain and legislators react.

Responding to constituent complaints is a time-honored role for legislators—and something that many citizens expect of state and local decision makers. In some cases, legislators may propose legislation to correct a perceived problem based on anecdotal evidence from a single constituent. Legislators may react, not with great forethought, but instead because they know their constituents expect them to take some action.

This is not a recipe for careful policy design, especially in moments of crisis when the urge to "do something, do anything" is strong. However, the Texas legislature's biennial sessions help mitigate somewhat the problem of reacting under pressure without thinking.

Policy Adoption

Once a policy issue arises, decision makers wrestle with the exact wording of the policy and its acceptance by legitimate legal authorities. Legislators may offer a new policy in the form of a bill. They may receive sample bills from lobbyists or executive branch leaders. In a lengthy process of maneuvering, compromising, negotiating, and sometimes bullying, legislators adopt bills. These activities take place in Congress, state legislatures, city councils, school boards, and special districts. The chief executive may also have to approve the bill for it to become law.

In other cases, executive agencies, bureaus, and departments move through a process of proposing a policy, hearing public comments, amending the policy, and finally adopting it (or deciding not to adopt it). The adoption may not be over at this point. Sometimes interested parties may sue, contending that the policy is flawed or conflicts with the constitution or other laws.

For example, the 2020–2021 Texas legislature voted to establish a Broadband Development Office in the Texas comptroller's office. HB5 created the office and an account within the state general revenue fund to support this effort. The primary goal of the office is to develop a statewide plan to expand broadband service to rural areas and other unserviced locations. The plan includes a map of those locations. The House Research Office estimated it would cost 3.8 million dollars to fund the project. Meanwhile, the governor's office already has a Broadband Development Council. This example illustrates how decision makers recognize an issue and attempt to solve it. Of course, the new law does not guarantee an acceptable outcome to the public.[10]

Policy Implementation

Elected government officials often write laws with vague wording, allowing bureaucrats to decide the particulars of the policy. Even when the language in a law, rule, or regulation is clear and precise, those who carry out or use the policy may interpret it in an unintended manner. An example of a law considered vague by some is Senate Bill 4, the "sanctuary cities" law. Within the debates about immigration, the use of the term "sanctuary cities" varies in its meaning. States and counties adopt the practice of sanctuary cities in an effort to respond to federal law enforcement. Their response includes both informal and formal policies to limit cooperation or involvement with federal immigration enforcement laws. The Texas law forbids local entities from pursuing or endorsing "a pattern or practice that 'materially limits' the enforcement of immigration laws." Opponents of the law assert the use of the word "endorse" is vague. The law also contains penalties against officials, such as mayors or sheriffs, who fail to assist or cooperate with federal immigration officers. A federal court, the Fifth Circuit Court of Appeals, ruled in November 2017 that Texas could enforce more provisions of the law.[11]

In March 2018, the same court issued a ruling allowing enforcement of almost all parts of the law. It did say local officials could comment on the wisdom and enforcement of the law as allowed under the First Amendment of the U.S. Constitution.[12]

Students of political science may be surprised to find that laws are not always enforced and that agents of government take liberties with how they are implemented. Those responsible for administering the law may alter the policy because of limited resources, ignorance, misinterpretation, or disobedience.

In some cases, there is no policy implementation stage because the new policy is largely symbolic. For example, some critics contend the recent law establishing a doctor-patient relationship between infants who survive abortion addresses a situation that is so rare that the law is largely symbolic.

Policy Evaluation

In recent years, governments have tried to find out if a given policy fulfills its purpose. With computers and data analysis software, public policy analysts in and out of government seek to figure out the effectiveness, efficacy, and economics of a policy.

Of course, not all policy-making efforts include each step in the process. The cycle represents the ideal. In real life, there is often no policy evaluation—in other words, nobody tries to assess effectiveness after a policy has been implemented and then makes adjustments. Often policies are passed with no consideration of this need for review and change in the future.

In some cases, reversing a policy would be costly, requiring budget cuts elsewhere or tax increases. For example, the Texas state legislature has decided to increase the portion the state pays for the cost of public education. At the same time, however, state leaders proposed a Texas Constitutional amendment to reduce the property tax rate, which would reduce the income of K–12 school districts, which rely heavily on these taxes. The state legislature is unlikely to reverse its decision to provide a greater proportion of the cost of public education because that could lead to a public school funding crisis.

CORE OBJECTIVE

Taking Personal Responsibility . . .

How can you affect public policy decisions? At what point or points in the policy cycle could you voice your preferences? Use Figure 13.1, the policy-cycle graphic, to help you answer these questions.

Public Policy Areas in Texas State Government

Learning Objective: Discuss public policy areas in Texas state government.

Despite the ever-expanding range of issues over which the federal government has assumed control in the past half century or so, states still play an important role in legislating in certain policy areas and implementing a wide array of policies set at both the state and federal levels. States vary quite a bit in terms of policy output and outcomes. The 2020 elections did not signal a significant shift in the Texas political leadership as almost all statewide officials return to their elected position. The only notable change occurred in the Texas Speaker of House position with Dennis Bonnen choosing not to run again. Dade Phelan replaced Bonnen. At the national level, the election of Joe Biden and Kamala Harris has resulted in new U.S. Government policies. President Trump and the U.S. Senate also placed many new judges in United States Courts with four new U.S. Supreme Court justices. One might see shifts in U.S. policy in abortion, LGBTQ, immigration, health care, and environmental regulation areas. Chapter 14 focuses specifically on tax policy at the state level, an area in which states differ dramatically and meaningfully. The remainder of this chapter examines a number of other important policy areas in the state of Texas, including regulatory policy, health care policy, education policy, social policy, immigration policy, and water policy.

Regulatory Policy

First, let's consider Texas's regulatory policies toward business and put them in national perspective. In the United States, state governments regulate a range of activities that include the following:

- Life, property, and auto insurance (how much insurance companies can charge consumers, as well as their financial soundness)
- Internet service, wireless availability, and Internet speed, provided by local governments and other entities
- The court system (how friendly the process is to defendants or plaintiffs, often covered by the term "**tort** reform")
- Professions and occupations (requirements for getting and maintaining licenses to practice)
- Public utilities (electricity, natural gas, telecommunications, and cable television)
- Labor law (minimum wage, unemployment compensation, workers' compensation, collective bargaining between unions and employers, and so on)
- The environment, including land use (whether and how land can be developed or taken for a public purpose)
- Wind farms and other projects that some people may consider eyesores
- Fracking within municipalities

Texas's regulatory policies are usually considered pro-business. In fact, *Chief Executive* magazine rated Texas the best state for business in 2021 due to its stellar job creation, low taxes, and favorable cost of living for employees.[13] Texas has held

tort

"A civil wrong, recognized by law as grounds for a lawsuit, which can be redressed by awarding damages."

Source: Cornell University Law School, Legal Information Institute, *Wex Legal Dictionary.*

this top ranking for 15 consecutive years since the ratings began. The state's policy makers have fostered this pro-business environment in a number of ways.

For instance, Texas labor law tends to be anti-union and pro-employer. Texas has a right-to-work law that prohibits collective bargaining agreements between employers and unions from including clauses that require employees to pay agency fees to the union as a condition of employment. (See Map 12.1 for all right-to-work states.) Right-to-work laws tend to reduce the power of unions because many employees prefer to opt out of paying the agency fees while still receiving the benefits of collective bargaining. (Agency fees and union dues are slightly different. As one teachers' group explains: "An agency fee is a percentage of dues that the union determines is the amount it costs the union to represent you before your employer in the areas of bargaining, contract administration, and grievances.")[14] Another point supporting Texas's pro-employer reputation is that it is the only state not to mandate that employers purchase workers' compensation insurance in case of employees' injuries. Employers are allowed to opt for a "tort" model instead, in which injured employees can sue their employers for damages. Texas's labor laws have both benefits and costs. They probably raise business investment and levels of employment, but they also reduce the wages of those specific workers who would otherwise be represented by stronger unions.

Texas is also considered to be pro-business because of what state and local governments do to actively recruit and support businesses. Foremost among these are tax abatements and programs for special corporate subsidies. For example, Texas has no corporate income tax, which makes it attractive to business.[15] In addition, Texas and its various local entities use their taxing authority to encourage private business to move there. Tax abatements are an economic development tool to attract new businesses and encourage existing business to stay. A tax abatement means that the government is allowing a business to pay fewer property taxes or no property taxes for a specified period.

Proponents argue that businesses receiving tax abatements bring in money by boosting the area economy. Opponents argue tax abatements are an inefficient means of using scarce government resources. In spite of that criticism, cities and other local governments in Texas and across the United States continue to use tax abatements as they compete for business to relocate or remain in their zone.

As for corporate subsidies, the Texas Enterprise Fund, started by former governor Rick Perry in 2003, awarded grants to corporations for locating (or expanding) a business in Texas. It was created to attract businesses (and the jobs that come with them) to the state, and over the time it existed, provided companies with

Governor Greg Abbott at the New York Stock Exchange highlighting the friendly Texas business environment.

Mark Lennihan/AP Images

$609 million in incentives.[16] The website of the Office of the Governor notes that this "'deal-closing' fund" strengthened the state's economy by boosting capital investment and job creation.[17] (Even so, Governor Abbott opted to discontinue the Texas Emerging Technology Fund in 2015; this is discussed later.)

This amalgamation of pro-business policies has drawn the ire of both liberal Democrats and free-market libertarian Republicans. The former complain that the subsidy programs are, at best, funnels for "corporate welfare" and, at worst, "political slush-funds" for Republican politicians.[18] The latter criticize them on the grounds that they are examples of "crony capitalism" and inconsistent with true capitalism. As one journalist explained, these skeptics "argue that such subsidies aren't even good for business, because they amount to the government 'picking winners and losers,' thereby distorting potentially efficient markets: companies with a bad product may be artificially buoyed by the grants, and those that might otherwise succeed struggle to outlast their well-funded competitors."[19] Critics also point out that there isn't enough transparency in the incentive rewarding process.[20]

Governor Abbott has said he wants the government "out of the business of picking winners and losers." Governor Abbott proposed a new approach: ending the Texas Enterprise Fund and using those moneys to start up his University Research Initiative, a proposal the legislature approved in 2015.[21] Under that initiative, Texas government funds would be used to attract Nobel laureates and other world-renowned researchers to Texas universities.[22]

eminent domain

The process whereby the government can take private land for a public purpose with compensation

Texas has placed more restrictions on the use of **eminent domain** than most other states. Eminent domain is the process whereby the government can take private land for a public purpose with compensation. The U.S. Supreme Court case *Kelo v. City of New London* (2005) established that local governments may use eminent domain to transfer private property to other private parties so long as the government envisions public benefits from doing so. This decision was highly unpopular across the country, and many state legislatures rushed to place legal restrictions on this use of eminent domain. In most states, those reforms were mostly symbolic and left significant loopholes. Texas, however, enacted one of the more far-reaching reforms.

In 2011, Texas enacted SB 18, which updated the Texas Government Code to clarify the term "public benefits" and offer more protection to landowners. Controversies erupt when public entities take land for highways and roads. A battle is still ongoing between landowners and the advocates of a Dallas-to-Houston bullet train. The two sides disagree on whether a private corporation, Texas Central Railroad, may use eminent domain to build the train route and stations.[23] The Texas legislature has also heard testimony regarding the efforts of landowners to fight pipeline companies, electric utilities, public agencies, and other entities.

Texas has a history of rather burdensome licensing regulations, but reforms have recently been made in this area. Occupational and professional licensing regulations can be a barrier to employment and small business formation, as job seekers and would-be entrepreneurs must meet requirements in education and training, take examinations, and pay fees before they can get the government's permission to work. Traditionally associated with careers in medicine and law, occupational licenses are now issued for a wide range of workers, from contractors to hair stylists to athletic trainers. Strict requirements for obtaining a license reduce competition, economic opportunities for working-class people, and affordability for consumers, but they are often justified on grounds of public health or ensuring higher quality for the consumer.[24] On October 8, 2019, Governor Abbott sent an open letter to the heads of state agencies directing them to look for ways to reduce or eliminate occupational licensing burdens on individuals.[25] Other legislation reduced licensing requirements for low-income occupations as well. During the 86th Legislative session, the members passed SB 1995 requiring the establishment of a licensing office in the Texas governor's office with a director.[26] The new licensing office will provide oversight of Texas agencies that regulate various occupations. For example, hair braiding—an occupation that previously required 35 hours of training for licensure—was completely deregulated, meaning individuals no longer need to get a state license to braid hair or teach hair braiding.[27] This is an area of rare left-right agreement at the national level, as both leading Democrats and President Trump have argued for the scaling back of occupational licensing requirements that impair economic opportunity.[28]

An area where Texas was not so pro-business is its court system. The U.S. Chamber of Commerce evaluates states on the business friendliness (and, therefore, plaintiff unfriendliness) of their civil liability systems. In the 2019 survey, Texas ranked thirty-eighth, indicating that the state is comparatively unfriendly to businesses in this area and friendly to plaintiffs who sue businesses for, say, product-liability claims.[29] The private group, Texans for Lawsuit Reform, began a campaign to alter Texas Civil law. Begin in the 1995 Legislative session, the group and its allies have attempt to alter the business friendliness of Texas Court with restrictions on lawsuits and liability awards. Another private group, Texas Trial Lawyers Association, argue that Texans need protection from harmful persons and businesses.[30] People sue companies when a product or service causes injury and the company may be liable (in other words, to blame). For example, Texas and other states sued tobacco companies for selling harmful products.[31]

Health Care Policy

The federal government uses two programs to support people who need help paying for medical care: **Medicare** and **Medicaid**. Medicare provides funds to pay for doctor's office visits, hospital stays, and prescription drugs. The program provides funding for eligible people 65 or older and some people who have disabilities. The federal government gets the money for this program from payroll taxes.[32] If you have ever wondered why your paycheck includes deductions, this is one of the reasons. A person who is eligible for Medicare can use the program even if they are wealthy.

Many people confuse Medicare with Medicaid, a federal program for people of any age who have very low incomes. Both programs contain many rules and restrictions. Millions of Americans rely on one of the two programs to pay for medical care. The federal government sets most of the rules and regulations for the two programs and determines what is covered. Within its borders, the state of Texas manages and controls the administration of the programs with health care providers and doctors. In 2020, the Texas legislature authorized spending approximately $42 billion on health care each year for two years, and 34 percent of the Texas state budget focused on health care costs. For 2020, health care ranked as the second-highest area of government spending in Texas, after education.[33]

In 2010, Congress passed and President Obama signed the **Affordable Care Act (ACA)**, also known as "Obamacare," in an effort to reform health care and

Medicare
Federal program providing funds to pay for medical care to eligible people 65 and older and also some people who have disabilities

Medicaid
Federal government program to provide funds to pay for medical care for people of any age with very low incomes

Affordable Care Act (ACA)
A complex and detailed federal law to reform health care and extend coverage to more Americans

individual mandate

A controversial major provision of the Affordable Care Act requiring every person to buy and maintain health insurance coverage satisfying certain minimum standards or pay a tax

extend coverage to more Americans. One of the goals of this law was to expand Medicaid. After weathering multiple legal challenges (the state of Texas was among those that sued the Obama administration), most of the ACA was ultimately upheld by a 5–4 vote of the U.S. Supreme Court in 2012.[34] A major provision of the law as originally adopted was the requirement—known as the **"individual mandate"**—that every person buy and maintain health insurance coverage satisfying certain minimum standards; uninsured individuals had to pay a fee.[35] The 2012 Supreme Court ruling stated that although Congress's passage of an individual mandate to buy health insurance could not be justified under the Commerce Clause of the Constitution, it could be upheld as part of Congress's taxing power. However, the Court rejected the portion of the law involving expansion of Medicaid eligibility, arguing that this expansion would unduly "coerce" the states. As a result, states have discretion over whether to expand Medicaid benefits to individuals and families with higher income levels than those previously specified. Texas has not adopted this expansion to date.

Table 13.1 shows some key provisions of the ACA. Under the ACA, insurance companies cannot place an annual or lifetime limit on benefits, nor can they deny coverage to someone with a preexisting condition. Individuals can maintain

TABLE 13.1

Key Provisions of the ACA

Guaranteed Coverage	Health insurers cannot refuse to cover an individual because of current or prior health problems (called "preexisting conditions").
Benefit Standards	Health insurance policies must provide certain benefits, called "minimum essential coverage."
Individual Mandate	Individuals were required to buy health insurance or pay a fee (what critics contend is a tax) for not having coverage. This was eliminated for tax year 2019 and beyond, but some states still have their own state-based individual mandates.
Health Insurance Exchanges	Individuals who do not have health insurance through their employer or the government must buy coverage through a state or federal exchange (i.e., online "Health Insurance Marketplace").
Low-Income Subsidies	Individuals who buy coverage through an exchange and whose income is below a certain threshold are eligible for a government subsidy. In other words, the government pays a portion of that person's insurance premiums.
Medicaid Expansion	The income threshold used to qualify individuals for Medicaid coverage has been raised. (*Note:* States may opt out of this expansion and continue to use the prior income threshold to determine whether individuals qualify for their state's program.)
Coverage for Young Adults	Children can remain on their parents' insurance plan until age 26.
Annual and Lifetime Limits	Insurance companies cannot limit the dollar amount they would spend for most of an individual's covered benefits, either during a given year or during the entire time a person is enrolled in that insurance plan.

Sources: Mike Patton, "Obamacare: Seven Major Provisions and How They Affect You," *Forbes*, November 27, 2013, http://www.forbes.com/sites/mikepatton/2013/11/27/how-obamacare-will-change-the-american-health-system/#1d8423ab6593; U.S. Department of Health and Human Services, "Key Features of the Affordable Care Act by Year," http://www.hhs.gov/healthcare/facts-and-features/key-features-of-aca-by-year/index.html; Heather Long, "The Final GOP Tax Bill Is Complete. Here's What Is in It," *The Washington Post*, December 15, 2017, https://www.washingtonpost.com/news/wonk/wp/2017/12/15/the-final-gop-tax-bill-is-complete-heres-what-is-in-it/?n; https://obamacarefacts.com/obamacare-2020/.

coverage under their parents' insurance until age 26, and certain preventive services are available at no cost to the insured.

To help people without insurance find coverage, the government created a health insurance marketplace. Like many other federal programs, these marketplaces, or exchanges, were expected to be administered by the states. According to the law, state governments can opt to run their own exchanges, share a regional exchange with other states, or operate an exchange jointly with the federal government.[36] However, if a state refuses to set up an exchange, the federal government will step in and establish one. As of 2018, only 12 states and the District of Columbia were operating their own exchanges fully independent of federal assistance. Texas has declined to run its own exchange, meaning that Texans shopping for health insurance in the online marketplace use a federally run exchange.[37]

In late 2017, Congress eliminated the individual mandate by reducing the penalty to zero; this change went into effect for 2019. As a result, taxpayers no longer have to pay a penalty if they do not have insurance.[38] Also, on December 18, 2019, the U.S. Fifth Circuit Court of Appeals in New Orleans, Louisiana, agreed with an earlier district court ruling that the individual mandate is unconstitutional. The Court further remanded the case (returned it to the lower court) to Judge Reed O'Connor in a North Texas District Court for more analysis. Judge O'Connor had earlier ruled the entire ACA was invalid. He agreed with the plaintiff that if the individual mandate was unconstitutional, the entire law was invalid. This decision rests on the issue of **severability**. (Severability is a common provision in contracts. If one part of a law or contract is deemed invalid, it does not make the rest of the law or contract invalid. The invalid part is severed from the rest. In this case, O'Connor tried to establish the intent of Congress. Did Congress as a body want the law to stand even if the individual mandate was removed?) Texas and 19 other states argued in O'Connor's court that the individual mandate was so central to the law that, without it, the law was invalid and no longer enforceable as a tax. California and several other states argued against the Texas claim. The U.S. Supreme Court will probably hear this case in a few years.[39]

A key political goal for many Republicans both in Texas and Washington, D.C., was the repeal of the ACA. While various attempts to repeal the law have failed in the U.S. Senate, we have already seen that congressional Republicans were able to remove a key provision, the individual mandate. This disagreement between the Republicans and Democrats about how to approach health care illustrates the cycle of the public policy process. When Democrats controlled Congress and the presidency, they were able to pass the ACA into law. Once the Republicans gained control of Congress and the presidency, policy changed. This demonstrates an important element of a republic—that citizens can make policy change by electing different political representatives.

Perhaps not surprisingly for a conservative state, Texas's past two governors have firmly opposed the health care law. Former governor Perry denounced the ACA, calling its provisions "brazen intrusions into the sovereignty of our state."[40] Governor Abbott reiterated this objection, stating "Medicaid expansion is wrong for Texas."[41]

The Texas government's decision not to expand Medicaid has had a direct impact on Texans. According to the U.S. Census Bureau, in 2020 Texas had the highest percentage of uninsured people of all 50 states, at roughly 17.3 percent

severability
Capable of being divided into legally independent obligations

of the state's population. This not only exceeded the national average of 8.7 percent of the population without health insurance, it was also higher than the 15.5 percent uninsured rate for states that did not expand Medicaid.[42]

To qualify for Medicaid in Texas, you must meet strict guidelines. Current guidelines state that your pretax income must be less than $24,731 if you are an individual. If you are supporting a family of four, your income can be no more than $50,985. You must also be either pregnant, a parent or relative caretaker of a dependent child or children under age 19, blind, have a disability or a family member in your household with a disability, or be 65 or older. Undocumented immigrants do not qualify for Medicaid.[43]

Primary and Secondary Education in Texas

School District Financing

The state of Texas pays for part of the cost of public K–12 (also referred to as primary and secondary) education. Until the 2019 legislative session, the state's share of the cost of education had declined for 20 years, and local school districts have been forced to pick up a larger part of the cost.

Local taxpayers rarely know the total amount of sales taxes they pay, but property owners receive annual tax demands. Therefore, when taxpayers feel they are paying too much, property taxes jump into citizens' minds. In most cases, local school property taxes are the highest single tax that a property owner pays. Taxpayers complain frequently about these taxes to their elected state representatives.

Because the largest source of local funding is the property tax, some school districts have been better able than others to absorb the higher local share. Some school districts have a high per-pupil property tax base (so-called rich districts) and others have a low per-pupil property tax base (so-called poor districts). Although the state provides more funding to poor districts, this support does not eliminate the disparities that exist in the amount of money available to school districts on a per-pupil basis.

Teachers at the Texas Capitol protest proposed cuts to the education budget.

Eric Gay/AP Images

Differences in school funding became a statewide issue in 1968, when parents in San Antonio filed a lawsuit challenging the financing of schools in Texas. In that case, the U.S. Supreme Court ruled that unequal public school funding in Texas did not violate the equal protection clause of the U.S. Constitution.[44] In 1984, another lawsuit brought education finance to the forefront in Texas. *Edgewood v. Kirby* was filed in state district court, and because of the efforts of the Mexican American Legal Defense and Education Fund and the Equity Center in Austin, the Texas Supreme Court ruled the state's system of school finance unconstitutional in 1989.[45]

Changes in state law have lessened differences between school districts, but those differences have not disappeared. Most aid is aimed at providing the "basic foundations" of education. Wealthier districts can provide funds for so-called enrichments.

In 2016, the Texas Supreme Court found the current Texas school funding plan constitutional.[46] The ruling did not settle the discussion, however. In 2017, lawmakers appointed a 13-member commission to investigate possible solutions. Key leaders appeared to divide on the issue of more money versus better and more efficient use of the current level of funding.[47] Some suggest that the state use vouchers. Under this proposal, parents would receive a set amount of money they could use at any public or private school they choose. By 2019, state leaders had backed away from adopting vouchers. Speaker of the House Bonnen stated the Texas House would not pass a school voucher bill.[48]

In December 2018, the Texas Commission on Public School Finance presented its 165-page report.[49] The commission detailed 35 recommendations. Acting on the commission's report, the 86th Texas Legislative and its leadership identified the need to "reform" the state approach to funding Texas public schools. The legislature adopted about 1,100 bills related to K–12 public schools, with HB 3 deemed the most important. HB 3 attempts to achieve two overriding goals; reduce property taxes and redirect state money within the Texas public school system. In conjunction with HB 3, the Texas legislature also adopted SB 2. This bill stipulates that Texas local governments must seek voter approval to increase property taxes more than 3.5 percent a year, down from a cap of 8 percent. Texas political leadership pledged to shift some of the tax burden from local property owners to the State of Texas.[50]

CORE OBJECTIVE

Being Socially Responsible . . .

To what extent should the government of Texas be responsible for ensuring equal funding for wealthy school districts and poor school districts?

High-Stakes Testing

Local school districts must follow guidelines set by the State Board of Education (SBOE) and the Texas Education Authority (TEA). In effect, the TEA is the enforcement body for the SBOE and the state in general. According to the TEA's website, its organization is responsible for "assessing public school students on what they have learned and determining district and school accountability ratings."[51] To that end, basic mandatory standardized testing is administered to measure student and school performance. The Texas Assessment of Knowledge and Skills (TAKS) testing was the standard until 2012, when it was replaced by the State of Texas Assessment of Academic Readiness (STAAR) exam. STAAR is given to students starting in third grade and continuing throughout students' public school education. Elementary and middle school students are assessed in the areas of reading, math, writing, science, and social studies, and high school students take end-of-course (EOC) tests in English, math, science, and social studies.[52] Performance is classified as either advanced,

Focus On

Hispanics and Bilingual Education

Charles O. Cecil/Alamy Stock Photo

With the explosive growth of Texas's Hispanic population, bilingual education has become a vital issue. At one point, many Anglo-Texans objected to the use of tax dollars for bilingual education. Former governors Bush and Perry helped soften resistance to these programs and reached out to Hispanic voters in the state.

Texas law currently requires that bilingual education, as well as instruction in English as a second language (ESL), be offered as a means of improving understanding of English in students whose primary language is not English. More than 17 percent of Texas public school students receive such instruction.[53] According to the state code, bilingual education is "a full-time program of dual language instruction that provides for learning basic skills in the primary language of the students enrolled in the program" in addition to English instruction. (Typically, bilingual education involves students in a self-contained classroom being taught all academic subjects using a mix of Spanish and English.) ESL instruction consists of students being pulled out of mainstream classrooms for brief periods of "intensive instruction in English."[54] Bilingual education and/or ESL is required for school districts with at least 20 students who are English-language learners. There is continued debate over which instructional models offer the most effective, cost-efficient way to help non-English-speaking students become skilled at the English language.

Critical Thinking Questions

1. What are some arguments for and against the idea that public school students should achieve competence in the English language?
2. Explain whether current state mandates regarding bilingual education are appropriate and sufficient.

satisfactory, or unsatisfactory, and to graduate, students must achieve a cumulative score reflecting satisfactory performance in each subject area. Students are allowed to retake EOC exams for any reason.

Anecdotal evidence suggests that teachers "teach to the test" because of the central role that test scores play in the evaluation of public school districts.

Higher Education in Texas

Like other populous states, Texas has a large number of public higher education institutions serving a diverse population of students. Texas's public higher education system is composed of a vast network of 37 four-year institutions, 50 two-year districts (several with multiple campuses), 6 technical colleges, 3 state colleges, and 10 health-related institutions.[55] Along with K–12 public education, taxpayers pay part of the cost of public higher education. According to the Texas Higher Education Coordinating Board, the state of Texas appropriated $22.4 billion for higher education for 1.62 million students for 2021–2022. A large part of the money pays for non-instructional costs, such as retirement and group insurance, along with research programs.[56]

Tuition and Fees

For many years, the cost of college tuition and fees in Texas was very low and affordable for most people. In fact, nonresidents of Texas often found it cheaper to come to Texas and pay a small out-of-state fee than to attend college in their own state. In the 1970s, the legislature began to gradually increase tuition, tying the amount students paid to the number of semester hours taken. For most of the 1970s, the cost was $4 per semester hour (about $12 per course) with a few fees for labs attached to certain courses. Although this cost was very low, most students did not realize what a bargain it was for them.

As the cost of education rose, the state shifted tuition fees for students. In the fall of 2003, the average cost of tuition and fees for 15 credit hours was $1,934. Thereafter, from fall 2003 to fall 2022, average tuition charges at Texas public universities jumped to an average of $5,478 per semester.[57] After the policy changed, some constituents began to complain to legislators about the increases.

Much of the state budget is set by required spending due to entitlements within the state constitution, and state and federal laws. In other words, the legislature has very little say in how the money is spent. However, operating funds for higher education are not part of this **budget fix.** Higher education funds come from the non-restricted area of the budget and thus can be reduced.[58] Even as tuition costs have risen, the proportion of educational costs covered by state funding (on a per-pupil basis) has gone down.[59]

Whereas parents and students continue to exert pressure on universities to keep costs down, others suggest the costs of education are rightly borne by those who use the service and benefit the most, rather than taxpayers in general.

Tuition increases over the years have helped Texas schools stay competitive with institutions in other states. See Table 13.2 for a look at how tuition at a sample of schools compares with the costs of other state universities. It is worth

budget fix
State laws and constitutional amendments that set aside money to be spent on specific items; the best example is the state gasoline tax being committed to state highways

TABLE 13.2

2021–2022 Tuition Costs among Major Public Universities (First-Year Tuition and Fees for Undergraduates)

University	Residents ($)	Nonresidents ($)
University of Illinois, Urbana–Champaign	15,442	32,892
University of California–Los Angeles	13,258	43,012
University of Arizona	12,736	37,258
University of Colorado–Boulder	12,496	38,314
Texas A&M University	13,239	40,134
University of Texas at Austin	11,752	40,996
University of Alabama	11,620	31,190
State University of New York at New Paltz	8,523	18,433
Iowa State University	9,634	25,446
University of North Carolina–Chapel Hill	9,028	36,891
University of Mississippi	9,044	25,886
North Florida Community College	3,054	11,400
Tyler Junior College	2,962	4,762
Austin Community College	2,550	8,580
Lone Star College	2,160	4,848

Sources: College Tuition Compare, https://www.collegetuitioncompare.com/.

Focus On

How Educational Debt Affects Different Generations

Stock Photo World/Shutterstock

As expenses go up, colleges and universities need more revenue. One of the main ways they get this revenue is to increase tuition and fees. By law, institutions must provide cost information. Parents and students can compare costs among institutions, along with other indicators found in college guides.

Two-year colleges have the lowest prices, while for-profit institutions set the highest rates. Because of the high cost of attending colleges and universities, most students borrow money and seek scholarships. Often, students do not consider the long-term impact of paying for a college degree. With many first-generation students attempting to navigate the world of higher education without clear guidance and advice, students and parents too often take on a high debt load. One can find stories of persons paying for college after retirement because many parents sign loan documents for their dependents. Parents might take on substantial long-term debt to pay for their children's education.

The money people borrow for education generally comes from interest-bearing loans. In the early days of student loans, private financial institutions such as banks loaned the money at the current general interest levels. The U.S. government responded to demands for help from financially challenged students and parents by creating government-backed loans administered by the U.S. Department of Education. While the U.S. government offers lower-rate loans, students and parents must still pay interest. Over an extended period, the total cost grows as interest and fees are added to the money borrowed. Students cannot avoid loan obligations by declaring bankruptcy, and the U.S. government can garnish wages and take Social Security money to pay for loans that are in arrears.

Many years ago, political and community leaders subscribed to the idea that higher education benefited society in general. A well-educated population meant a better quality of life, along with a better economy at all levels. Today, many leaders ignore those benefits and claim students receive the main benefits of a degree. The cost burden shifted to students and parents. While colleges and universities raised tuition and fees to meet increased expenses, governments at all levels decreased financial support. According to the National Center for Education Statistics, the average cost of higher education more than doubled from 1985 to 2017.[60] As a result, current generations are running up higher student debt than did previous generations. The long-term impact of such debt affects students for many years by limiting their ability to buy a car or a house or start a business.

Critical Thinking Questions

1. Do you agree that education benefits the whole community and should therefore be supported by the government, or with the idea that it mainly benefits the student and should therefore be paid for by individuals? Support your answer with evidence and logic.
2. If you could recommend one policy for dealing with educational costs and debt to your elected officials, what would it be?

remembering that there are many Texas state colleges and universities with lower costs than the University of Texas and Texas A&M.

Curriculum and Degree Requirements

In recent years, the Texas legislature has made laws and rules that affect the curriculum choices of students, faculty, and university officials. The following are a few examples of these decisions.

According to state law, all state universities are required to offer a set number of courses in what is called the core curriculum. As of 2014, the core consists of 42 hours of fundamental component areas identified by the Higher Education Coordinating Board (which includes 6 hours of political science and 6 hours of history) plus an additional 6 hours identified by each institution, provided that the institution justifies that the courses meet at least 4 designated core objectives.[61] Core objectives include instruction in communication, critical thinking, personal responsibility, social responsibility, teamwork, and qualitative analysis. Students must complete these courses in order to graduate.

The total number of hours required for degree completion is limited to 120 hours for most bachelor's degrees. Before this change (which went into effect in 2008), most bachelor's degrees required at least 128 hours. The legislature wants students to graduate more quickly, thereby reducing the state's cost of higher education. In addition, if a student takes more than 120 hours, the university does not receive any state funding for these extra hours.

Students can receive a rebate of $1,000 if they graduate within three credit hours of the total number of hours required for their degree. The legislature forced this policy on universities but did not appropriate any money to cover the cost. Therefore, colleges and universities will likely use fees to fund the rebates.[62]

Undergraduate students pay in-state tuition rates up to a certain number of total hours in their undergraduate degree. After they have exceeded this number of credit hours (set by the legislature), a student must pay the out-of-state tuition rate.

Higher Education Funds

Operating budgets for institutions of higher education are part of the regular state budget, but higher education in Texas has other funds available for capital projects. (A capital project is a "long-term investment project requiring relatively large sums" of money, such as constructing a new building on campus.[63]) The **Permanent University Fund (PUF)** was established by the Texas Constitution of 1876 to support the University of Texas and Texas A&M University systems. The original endowment began in 1839 when the Republic of Texas set aside 221,400 acres of land, the income from which was designated to fund higher education. This land was located in East Texas and was rather good farmland. Because this land was valuable, the state legislature later transferred the endowment to approximately 2 million acres of land, thought to be of less value, primarily in West Texas. Ironically, in the early part of the twentieth century, oil was discovered in these new lands, and the income it generated became substantial over time.[64] The PUF monies are transferred into the available university fund (AUF). The AUF includes the revenue from the PUF plus additional funds from interests on funds, state appropriations, and other sources. Universities draw money from the AUF. As of 2020, the AUF held approximately $2 billion.[65] The University of Texas and some of its branch campuses receive two-thirds of the money generated by the PUF's investments, and Texas A&M, its branches, and its divisions receive the remaining one-third.[66]

Permanent University Fund (PUF)

State of Texas fund to support the University of Texas and Texas A&M systems as required by the Texas Constitution

According to this policy, other colleges and universities in the state did not receive any portion of these funds, and other universities began to pressure the Texas legislature for a share of the PUF fund. In 1984, the legislature proposed an amendment to the state constitution (subsequently approved by the voters) creating the Higher Education Assistance Fund (HEAF). Beginning in 1985, the legislature set aside annual appropriations of $100 million for this fund. This amount was later increased to $175 million. Today this fund provides $787.5 million each year for colleges and universities not supported by the PUF.[67]

As mentioned earlier, in 2015 Governor Abbott proposed and the legislature approved the establishment of the Governor's University Research Initiative. According to the Governor's Office, the initiative helps fund the recruitment of "prestigious, nationally recognized researchers . . . to Texas public universities."[68] By providing matching funds for universities to hire desirable faculty, the Governor aimed to elevate the status of Texas higher education and boost the state's economy through research advances. To create this fund, legislators diverted money from the scrapped Emerging Technology Fund.[69] Four Texas universities have used funds to hire researchers in several fields, including engineering.[70]

The authors of the Texas Constitution of 1876 saw a need for higher education in Texas and created the PUF. Later sessions of the legislature wanted to fund other institutions of higher learning and created the HEAF, and Governor Abbott created the Governor's University Research Initiative. The establishment of these funds is an example of public policy that makes education a high priority.

Access to Higher Education

From the 1950s to the 1970s, access to state colleges and universities in Texas had open enrollment. In other words, all Texas residents who had graduated from high school were automatically admitted without consideration of high school standing or standardized test scores. Nearly all students could enroll in the university of their choice.

In Texas and elsewhere, women and ethnic minorities did not enroll in numbers that matched their percentage in the general population. In 1967, only 19 percent of U.S. women between 18 and 24 enrolled in college, but 33 percent of the U.S. male population in that age range enrolled. Among all Black Americans, only 13 percent of women were enrolled in college in 1967. The percentage drops to 10.4 among African American women aged 18 to 24. Only 12 percent of Hispanic women in that age range attended college in 1967. By 1990, 31 percent of women 18 to 24 were enrolled in college, with 24.8 for Black American women and 16.2 for Hispanic women. According to the latest figures from the U.S. Census Bureau, 44 percent of the U.S. population of women aged 18 to 24 are enrolled in college, including 39.3 percent of Black American women and 41 percent of Hispanic women.[71]

In the 1980s many schools, particularly Texas A&M and the University of Texas, began to impose higher standards for admittance, using mainly SAT scores and high school class standing to make that determination. One result of this tightening of admission standards is that enrollment at the two Texas "flagship" universities, Texas A&M and the University of Texas at Austin, remains flat. Student enrollment across Texas has grown dramatically, but most of the increase has been at community colleges. The majority of higher education students are attending community colleges.

Higher enrollment standards conflicted to some degree with the aim of increasing minority enrollment at state colleges and universities. At the time, Hispanics and Black Americans were a growing minority of the state's population, but only about 20 percent were enrolled in colleges, and fewer were still in the top two state universities. Ethnic minority students were also underrepresented in law and other professional schools.

Many colleges and universities began affirmative action programs in an attempt to increase minority enrollment in colleges and universities. These programs prompted a lawsuit regarding the admission of minority students to the University of Texas law school. In 1996, the federal court ended affirmative action practices at the University of Texas law school in the *Hopwood* decision.[72] Texas attorney general Daniel Morales, himself a beneficiary of affirmative action programs while a student in Texas, applied the *Hopwood* decision to all state colleges and universities and effectively eliminated affirmative action admission policies across the state. Morales found that "Hopwood's restrictions would generally apply to all internal institutional policies, including admissions, financial aid, scholarships, fellowships, recruitment, and retention, among others."[73] Thus, under Morales's interpretation, *Hopwood* was extended to prevent race from being considered in areas beyond admissions. *Hopwood* was overturned in 2003 by a case originating in Michigan. The U.S. Supreme Court, in *Grutter v. Bollinger,* 539 U.S. 306 (2003), ruled that the U.S. Constitution does not prohibit tailoring standards to use race in an admissions decision or policy.[74]

The *Grutter* case focused on law school admission, not undergraduate admission to universities. The majority opinion stated that the university had a legitimate goal of promoting a critical mass of minority students within the law school. The opinion foresaw a time, perhaps 25 years in the future, when affirmative action policies would not be necessary to promote a diverse student population. Efforts to overturn the ruling continue, with several other cases brought to the courts by white student applicants, in Texas and elsewhere.[75]

Prior to *Grutter v. Bollinger,* the Texas legislature, in an attempt to solve the problems of minority representation and equal opportunity, changed admission standards at Texas universities and established that admissions decisions and financial awards could not be based primarily on standardized test scores such as the SAT, ACT, or GRE. Under the new policy, any student graduating in the top 10 percent of their high school class was granted automatic admission to any state college or university, without consideration of other factors such as SAT scores. This rule, known as the "**Top Ten Percent Plan**," had the greatest impact on the University of Texas, where 75 percent of the 2017 first-year student class was admitted under the Top Ten Percent rule.[76]

This Top Ten Percent rule was expected to increase ethnic minority enrollment by allowing students from inner-city high schools to attend the top schools in the state. Some evidence suggests that the Top Ten Percent rule has increased ethnic minority enrollment, especially at the University of Texas and to a lesser degree at Texas A&M. However, some high-performing students at better high

Hopwood **decision**
Decision by federal courts to end affirmative action in Texas schools; these programs had provided for special treatment for minority students in being accepted to colleges and professional schools

Top Ten Percent Plan
State law allowing students who graduate in the top 10 percent of their high school to attend any state college or university, without consideration of other factors. The law has been amended to allow only the top 6 percent.

schools might not be admitted. It is not unusual for students at a competitive high school not to place in the top 10 percent of their graduating class, even with a 1,500 or higher score on the SAT. Therefore, these students are not guaranteed admission to a Texas institute of higher education under the Top Ten Percent Rule. Conversely, some students from small rural schools, who have very low SAT scores, are able to gain admission through the same policy. The legislature allowed the state's top universities to lower the top 10 percent rule to the top 8 percent and then to the top 6 percent.[77]

The U.S. Supreme Court has considered the issue of race and university admissions in Texas not once, but twice, in recent years. In *Fisher v. University of Texas*, the Court ruled in 2013 that universities can use affirmative action in their admissions policies only if there is no other way to achieve diversity among the student body.[78] This ruling did not change the University of Texas's admissions policy, but the case was sent back to a lower court for consideration of whether the university had met this standard.[79] The case was again argued before the U.S. Supreme Court in 2015. In its 2016 ruling, the Court upheld the university's "consideration of race as part of its [admissions] process" as lawful.[80]

Understanding Impact Now that you have learned more about school funding in Texas, what opinions can you offer on it? In a paragraph or two, explain what changes you recommend for Texas education—either at the K–12 level or the college level. Think about funding, access, and admissions requirements.

Social Policies

Firearms Policies

Despite being a relatively conservative state, Texas has traditionally had more restrictive gun laws than many other states, including liberal states such as Vermont and Maine. However, some restrictions on the right to carry firearms that did exist have recently been lifted. In January 2021, legislation permitting the "open carry" of firearms went into effect in Texas. Under this new law, gun owners who are not in a prohibited class, such as felons are allowed to carry a loaded or unloaded handgun, in plain view, as long as it is in a holster.[81] Texas law still prohibits open carry on college campuses, but additional legislation that went into effect later in 2016 allows licensed individuals to carry concealed handguns on the premises of an institution of higher education.[82]

In Texas, colleges and universities may designate certain areas of the campus as off-limits for carrying handguns. Most of those areas involve dangerous equipment, athletic events, and the presence of children. The law bars university presidents from establishing "provisions that generally prohibit or have the effect of generally prohibiting license holders from carrying concealed handguns on campus." Three UT–Austin professors filed an unsuccessful suit to restrict handguns in classrooms and offices there.[83] Public institutions must allow **campus carry**, but private institutions are not required to participate.

Twenty-three other states have enacted legislation related to firearms on campus, presumably in response to campus shootings that have occurred in recent

campus carry
The right, protected by state law, for licensed individuals to carry concealed handguns on college campus except in certain prohibited areas

years.[84] In Texas, an initial permit to carry a firearm costs $40, and a required training course costs more than similar courses in other states.

LGBTQ Rights

Public opinion has changed rapidly on the issue of same-sex marriage, and the legal landscape regarding this issue looks radically different than it did just a few years ago. In January 2013, only 9 states and the District of Columbia allowed same-sex couples to marry, but by October 2014, 24 states and the District of Columbia allowed same-sex marriage. In 2015, the U.S. Supreme Court essentially ended the political and legal debate over this issue, ruling in *Obergefell v. Hodges* that state bans on same-sex marriage were unconstitutional.[85] All states are now required to issue marriage licenses to all couples, regardless of sexual orientation.

Before the Supreme Court ruling, Texas had a long-standing ban on same-sex marriage. In 1996 the U.S. Congress passed the federal Defense of Marriage Act (DOMA), which defined marriage as the union of one woman and one man and denied federal recognition of same-sex marriage. Texas amended its constitution in 2005 to prohibit same-sex marriage; the ban was initially proposed in the legislature and overwhelmingly approved by voters (76 percent in favor).[86] Many state bans followed the language of DOMA. Texas's amendment was actually a "Super-DOMA." It not only defined marriage as the union of one man and one woman but also denied legal status to any other type of relationship that approximated marriage (such as civil unions and domestic partnerships). Therefore, unmarried couples, including same-sex couples, could be (in the words of one legal scholar) "nothing other than complete legal strangers to one another."[87] Nineteen other states had similar amendments. In 2013, in the case *United States v. Windsor*, the U.S. Supreme Court struck down a portion of DOMA and declared that the federal definition of marriage was unconstitutional.[88] Although this ruling did not necessarily guarantee same-sex couples the right to be married (because individual states regulate marriage within their borders), it opened the door for state laws or constitutional provisions banning same-sex marriage to be challenged in court. In February 2014, a federal judge struck down the Texas state ban.[89] Meanwhile, the ability of gay and lesbian couples to marry remained on hold while the state appealed this decision.[90] This was finally resolved in *Obergefell.*

Individuals in Texas are allowed to adopt without consideration of their sexual orientation. Therefore, gay men and lesbians can adopt children; however, because only one partner in a same-sex couple can be listed on the child's birth certificate,[91] of these adoptions tend to be single-parent adoptions and may be followed by a second adoption by a same-sex partner. Some Texas courts have recognized same-sex second-parent adoptions, such as in *Hobbs v. Van Stavern* (2006) and *Goodson v. Castellanos* (2007).[92] In 2017, Texas enacted a law allowing adoption agencies to deny adoption based on religious doctrine.[93] Agencies affiliated with religious organizations might deny same-sex persons or couples access to adoption services. Critics have also expressed concern that persons from other religions might be denied.

No statewide anti-discrimination law protects members of the LGBTQ (lesbian, gay, bisexual, transgender, queer) community. However, some local governments in Texas, including the cities of Dallas, Fort Worth, Austin, and San

Antonio, have passed such laws. In 2015, Houston voters rejected a nondiscrimination ordinance by a vote of 61 to 39 percent.[94] Advocates of the ordinance sought protections for LGBTQ residents from being fired, evicted, or refused service due to their gender identity or sexual orientation. Opponents voiced religiously inspired arguments in addition to concerns about the rights of business owners.[95] The primary argument focused on fears of men entering female bathrooms using the "rights" from the nondiscrimination ordinance.

In 2017, Lieutenant Governor Dan Patrick and Texas Senate Republicans tried to enact a law to require people to select the bathroom that corresponds to the gender listed on their birth certificate. Moderate Republicans, Democrats, and business leaders opposed the measure. Speaker of the House Joe Strauss led the opposition in the House of Representatives. The opposition leaders argued passage of a "bathroom bill" would harm the business climate and economy of Texas. The bill did not pass.[96] In 2019, Governor Abbott, Lieutenant Governor Perry, and Dennis Bonnen (who succeeded Straus as Speaker) did not include the issue on their legislative agenda. Other issues such as public school finance took center stage instead of the "bathroom bill."[97]

Abortion Policies

In July of 2022, the U.S. Supreme Court issued a ruling in the case of *Dobbs v. Jackson Women's Health Organization*. The ruling overturned the long-standing 1973 *Roe v. Wade* decision that established the right to abortion. The *Roe v. Wade* case used the idea of a right to privacy. The Court's majority opinion stated that each state should decide public policy regarding abortion instead of the U.S. Supreme Court. The opinion also stated that there is no right to privacy within the U.S. Constitution. Further, Justice Alito opined that the Supreme Court should revisit various cases dealing with same-sex marriage, anti-discrimination laws, individuals' right to access contraceptives, and health insurance issues. The U.S. Supreme Court's majority opinion reinforced that the constitutional right to access contraceptives remains untouched.[98]

In 2020, the Texas Legislature passed Senate Bill 8, which altered the state's statutes on abortion. SB8 empowers private individuals to sue in Texas courts anyone or any entity that supports or aids a person seeking an abortion after around the sixth week of pregnancy. The State of Texas adopted into law provisions making doctors and other medical providers liable for criminal prosecution. Texas also has a "trigger law" that bans all abortions from the moment of fertilization.[99]

In response, some district attorneys in high-population urban counties have pledged not to prosecute providers. The Texas Attorney General stated his office would enforce Texas anti-abortion laws if district attorneys did not act. Activists on both sides of the question argue that overturning *Roe v. Wade* will essentially eliminate abortion access in Texas. The Texas laws only make an exception to save a pregnant patient's life or if they risk "substantial impairment of major bodily function." Texas law does not allow an exception for rape or incest. Medical providers face questions about whether a patient's condition requires an abortion to save their life or not. Doctors could face penalties as high as life in prison and fines up to $100,000. Patient cases have occurred where the person was sent home to allow their condition to worsen. Another issue involves patients traveling to other states that allow abortion services. Patients are traveling to the Republic of Mexico and New Mexico to seek an abortion. While

Public debate over abortion was not settled by the Supreme Court's 1973 decision in *Roe v. Wade.* At left, a group from Texas demonstrates their pro-life position at a march in Washington, D.C. On the right, abortion rights supporters express their dissatisfaction with new legal restrictions inside the state Capitol.

Vic Hinterlang/Shutterstock

Texas has not adopted a law penalizing those who travel to other states, several state legislature are considering passing travel bans, such as Kentucky. Texas regulates abortion-inducing drugs. Texas law requires a doctor's prescription to be provided during an in-person visit for the first seven weeks of pregnancy.[100]

Since the U.S. Supreme Court's decision, the number of abortions performed in Texas has dropped from around 50,000 a year to almost none. Activists in Texas have served in the fight to restrict abortion access, with several organizations playing prominent roles. Pro-choice organizations have also engaged in the political battle. Numerous lawsuits filed in state and federal courts have influenced public policy. While surveys indicated a majority of Americans support abortion access, the political fight is far from over. This fight illustrates the differences in public policy in Blue and Red states.[101]

CORE OBJECTIVE

Communicating Effectively . . .

Summarize the legislation that Texas has passed on abortion. Discuss the advantages and disadvantages of state involvement in this policy issue.

Immigration Policy

Immigration has become a highly publicized issue nationally, due in part to the surge of undocumented immigrants from Central America in recent years, and the widely debated question of whether to accept Middle Eastern refugees in light of the threat of terrorism. It is important to note that immigration policy is set at the federal level; however, due to its more than 1,200-mile border with Mexico, Texas understandably plays a very prominent role in how our country reacts to immigration. For many years, Texas elected political leaders have expressed frustration with the U.S. Government policies and actions to deal with large numbers of persons seeking entry into the United States. Over the last few years, the State of Texas has spent billions of dollars in efforts to affect supplement U.S. Government actions, such as deploying Texas National Guard troops to the Texas-Mexico border.

According to the Census Bureau, about 17 percent of Texas's population was made up of foreign-born persons.[102] Although the Census Bureau counts people who are present both documented and undocumented, it is important to distinguish between the two types of immigrants. Documented immigrants go through a process to become **lawful permanent residents**, also known as Green Card holders. The process for becoming a lawful permanent resident (LPR) differs depending on whether the individual is outside or inside the United States at the time of application, but it generally requires being sponsored by a family member or employer, submitting forms, paying fees, and sometimes even attesting that an individual will have adequate financial support when they are in the country.[103] Foreign citizens living outside the United States must first get an immigrant visa. Congress limits the number of immigrant visas issued each year. Individuals who are already living in the United States (including refugees) must apply for an "adjustment of status" to lawful permanent residency (LPR). Upon approval, LPRs have permission from the federal government to live and work in the United States indefinitely.[104] LPRs can subsequently apply for U.S. citizenship or naturalization. In 2020, 74,565 people in Texas obtained lawful permanent resident status, and 66,942 people were naturalized.[105] Undocumented immigrants, on the other hand, are those who have entered or remain in the country without having government permission; these individuals may also be referred to as unauthorized (what these individuals should be called has become controversial). According to the most recent figures available, the number of undocumented immigrants in the United States in 2022 was estimated at 11.36 million. As of 2019, 1.739 million undocumented immigrants were living in Texas.[106]

Although U.S. agents established new records of deportations under the Obama presidency, efforts by the Trump administration to reduce the flow of unauthorized entries into the country resulted in even more arrests and deportations. The governor and lieutenant governor of Texas supported requests from President Trump to use National Guard troops along the Texas-Mexico border, costing Texas millions of dollars. Governor Abbott has continued this policy with Texas spending more than a billion dollars.[107]

How does having a large population of undocumented immigrants affect the state financially? The Texas state comptroller first tried to answer that question in a 2006 report, which found that state revenue generated by undocumented immigrants (primarily from sales tax and other government fees) outweighed what the state government spent on services for this population. However, the Texas Comptroller's report notably excluded the cost of educating the children born in the United States with undocumented parents because these U.S.-born children are citizens. The report also acknowledged that local governments and hospitals bear a disproportionate share of the cost of educating, incarcerating, and providing health care for undocumented immigrants—costs for which localities are not compensated.[108] A 2020 study similarly concluded that undocumented immigrants benefit the U.S. economy by paying taxes and fees as they fill a need within the labor market while incurring costs to the education, hospital, and prison systems. The report estimated that in 2018, the net revenue earned from undocumented immigrants by the state of Texas

---

lawful permanent resident (also called Green Card holder)
Noncitizen who is legally authorized to live permanently within the United States

amounted to $420.9 million. For every dollar spent on public services for undocumented immigrants, they provided $1.21 in revenue.[109]

Recent research indicates that the Texas population continues to grow with changing in the demographics of the state. U.S. Census data from 2020 show 95 percent of the population growth involves "people of color" while the number of undocumented immigrants grows but the rate of growth has slowed.[110]

Undocumented immigrants are not eligible for federally funded programs such as Temporary Assistance for Needy Families, food stamps, or public housing in Texas.[111] However, they are eligible for K–12 education, emergency medical care, and other health services. In the 1981 case *Plyler v. Doe* (which originated in Tyler, Texas), the U.S. Supreme Court ruled that denying any individual the right to education violated the Equal Protection Clause of the U.S. Constitution. Therefore, all states are required to provide K–12 education for undocumented immigrants and their children.[112] In 2001, the state legislature passed HB 1403, also known as the Texas **DREAM Act** (which stands for Development, Relief, and Education of Alien Minors), and amended this law in 2005 with SB 1528. This legislation allows some undocumented students to be classified as residents for the purpose of paying in-state college tuition rates, provided they meet certain requirements (including at least three years of prior residence in Texas and a signed statement of intent to apply for lawful permanent resident status as soon as possible).[113]

Statistics on this population are hard to find because the subjects of inquiry are, quite literally, without documentation, and therefore their presence cannot be verified. Most figures are either estimated or not reported at all. For the fiscal year 2006, the Texas Comptroller of Public Accounts (a state agency) estimated the cost of providing services to undocumented immigrants at $1.16 billion. The costs to Texas and its local governments involve primarily three areas; education, healthcare, and incarceration. In 2018, estimates indicated the cost is approximately 2.02 billion dollars.[114]

Although border security is mainly the responsibility of the federal government, Governor Abbott has expressed his intention to bolster security along the state's border with Mexico. For instance, in 2015 state leaders committed $800 million in state funds (over a two-year period) to border security—approximately double the amount appropriated for equivalent periods of time previously.[115] In the next session, the Texas legislature again appropriated an additional $800 million. Governor Abbott and other leaders considered adding $100 million to those funds with an expectation the U.S. government would reimburse Texas. These funds have been earmarked for new technology, training of law enforcement agents, and the hiring of 250 additional state troopers to guard the border, among other things. The political leadership directed the money to continue the support of National Guard troops and state troopers along the border. In 2021, Governor Abbott and the Texas Legislature authorized the spending of approximately 2 billion dollars to support border security. Governor Abbott also mobilized elements of the Texas National Guard in operation Lockdown to support efforts to halt illegal border entry.

In the 85th Texas Legislative session, the most controversial bill, SB 4, labeled the Sanctuary Law, required law enforcement personnel and agencies to cooperate with U.S. government officials such as the Border Patrol. Critics such as the American Civil Liberties Union (ACLU) attacked the bill and other actions by the state legislature directed at immigration policy.[116]

DREAM Act
The Development, Relief and Education of Alien Minors Act, a Texas law that allows some undocumented students to be classified as residents for the purpose of paying in-state tuition rates

DAPA (Deferred Action for Parents of Americans and Lawful Permanent Residents)

Executive order issued by President Obama allowing non-lawful resident parents of U.S. citizens and lawful permanent residents to remain in the United States; companion order to DACA

DACA (Deferred Action for Childhood Arrivals)

An executive order issued by President Obama allowing some people who were brought illegally to the United States as children to stay in the country for a defined period; companion order to DAPA

Recent federal policy on immigration has mainly been to enforce existing immigration laws by capturing and deporting people who are in the country illegally. Legislation intended to reform the immigration system has not passed the full U.S. Congress. In the absence of congressional action, in 2014, President Obama issued an executive order that would have allowed certain individuals who are in the country illegally (but who are parents of U.S. citizens or LPRs) to avoid deportation and obtain work permits. This plan, known as Deferred Action for Parents of Americans and Lawful Permanent Residents, or **DAPA**, would have applied to 825,000 people living in Texas.[117] Implementation of this program was delayed, however, when 26 states (led by Texas) sued the administration. These states charged the president with the overreach of presidential authority and failure to enforce the nation's current immigration laws. In 2016, the U.S. Supreme Court issued a deadlocked decision (4–4) on this case, resulting in the blockage of the president's immigration program.[118] The Trump administration continued to send mixed signals on immigration programs such as DAPA. In the spring of 2020, the U.S. Supreme Court announced plans to review the plan.[119]

Texas attorney general Ken Paxton said he would join with other officials of other states to sue in federal court to halt the Obama-era Deferred Action for Childhood Arrivals (**DACA**) program. DACA was a companion to DAPA. The policy allows some people who were brought illegally to the United States as children to stay in the United States for a defined period and become eligible for a work permit.[120]

Key actors in the DAPA court fight have reappeared to battle over DACA. Texas political leadership seems to support the end of DACA. About 120,000 residents of Texas could be affected by DACA-related detention and deportation.[121]

Members of the U.S. Army install part of the fence along the border near Puerto Palomas, Mexico. The federal government is building a 745-mile fence along the U.S.-Mexico border to reduce the flow of illegal migrants into the United States.

Brandon Bell/Getty Images

President Trump focused on immigration policy in his campaign for president with the slogan of "Build a Wall" between Mexico and the United States. He promised Mexico would pay for the new wall. New executive orders from President Trump attempted to reduce or stop immigration from not only Mexico but other countries. Applying a health law from the 1940s found in U.S. Code Title 42 to the coronavirus pandemic, the Trump administration deported people seeking asylum to Mexico or their country of origin.

President Biden has faced criticism from those concerned about increased undocumented immigration and from others who accuse him of continuing some Trump era policies, such as hasty denials of asylum for refugees and the closing of the border to certain categories of refugees. The state of Texas is suing the United States in response to President Biden decision to restart a family unification program and to end the use of Title 42 of a public health act and the "remain in Mexico" plan.[122]

Water Policy

The Texas population is projected to grow 82 percent from 2010 to 2060, from 25.4 million in 2010 to 46.3 million in 2060.[123] To allocate water rights, the government measures the water in "acre-feet," which equals the amount of water needed to cover one acre of land in one foot of water.[124] Total water use in Texas from 2010 until 2060 will increase from approximately 18 million acre-feet to approximately 22 million acre-feet, representing a jump of 22 percent.[125]

Texas relies on **surface water** and **groundwater** to satisfy its tremendous demand. The state's freshwater derives from 1 natural lake, 187 human-made reservoirs of more than 5,000 acres in size, 14 major rivers, 3,700 streams, and 30 underground aquifers (a naturally formed underground reservoir) of varying sizes throughout the state.[126] Groundwater currently provides approximately 59 percent of the state's water demand; surface water totals 41 percent.[127]

Texas's first new major reservoir in 30 years, Bois d'Arc Creek Reservoir, was begun in 2018. In April of 2021, the officials began the process to impound (hold) water in the new reservoir. The new reservoir began supplying water in northeastern Texas in 2022. Several landowners losing land to the creation of the reservoir unsuccessfully sued to halt construction. The North Texas Municipal Water District can supply 82 million gallons of water per day in its firm yield.[128]

Water law relates to quantity and quality. One set of laws and policies determines who has the right to use a given quantity of water. The second set of laws and policies exists to keep water uncontaminated and suitable for human use.

With respect to surface water, the state of Texas owns the water, but citizens can obtain exclusive rights to use a certain quantity of water, expressed in acre-feet. Landowners with property next to a river have rights to withdraw limited quantities of water. Otherwise, the procedure for obtaining water rights in the publicly owned surface water is called "first in time, first in right," the same system used in most of the western United States.[129]

Texas treats groundwater as if it were a separate source, subject to its own rules. Whereas surface water is publicly owned, Texas treats the water underneath a landowner's property as private property.[130] This leads to strange

surface water
Water visible on the surface of the land; under Texas law, it is owned by the state of Texas

groundwater
Water that is within in the earth; under Texas law, it is private property controlled by the owner of the land under which it is located

results. For example, the law would define water in a river as publicly owned, but when the same body of water flows underground, the law defines it as privately owned. The "rule of capture" provides that, even before the landowner removes the water from the ground, it is private property. Any law that limits the landowner's property-right interest in groundwater could be construed as a regulatory "taking," for which a unit of government might have to compensate the property owner.[131]

Despite the legal definition of groundwater as private property, the Texas legislature has made efforts to regulate it. On the local level, groundwater conservation districts have limited powers over such issues as the spacing of wells and monitoring the quantity of water pumped.[132]

Texas faces a number of water-related challenges in the coming decades. Severe drought conditions in recent years have dealt a blow to surface water supplies. Declining river levels deprive coastal river mouths of the freshwater they must have to support multibillion-dollar commercial fishing and tourism industries. In 2013, Texas voters shifted $2 billion from the state's "rainy day fund" for water projects.[133] Since that time, Texas and the U.S. Government have increased funding for water resource development and treatment. In 2022, state appropriations were approximately 75 million dollars, supplemented by 23 million dollars from the U.S. Government to pay for a various projects.[134]

CORE OBJECTIVE

Thinking Critically . . .

Given the water-related challenges facing Texas, what measures would you recommend to ensure all Texans have access to water? What might be some negative or unintended consequences of your recommendations?

Conclusion

As this chapter shows, state and local government policy decisions affect a wide range of issues and areas of life. For good or bad, the Texas state government performs all these functions:

- Regulating business activity
- Providing welfare and educational services
- Managing the use of natural resources and land
- Restricting certain behaviors
- Protecting certain rights

Whether or not you are interested in public policy, public policy is interested in you! The legislature, the governor, and many state agencies, including the board of regents of your public college or university, can have a direct effect on your life and your education. Reading this book can help you become more aware of how the government of Texas affects your life and community.

Summary

LO: Discuss the steps in the policy-making process.

Political scientist James Anderson described the process by which public policy is made as a "policy cycle" with the following steps: problem identification and agenda setting; policy formulation; policy adoption; policy implementation; and policy evaluation. Often this process begins with a complaint by a constituent (problem identification), in response to which a legislator proposes legislation to correct the perceived problem (policy formulation). Depending on the specific policy-making effort, steps in this process may be omitted. For instance, there is often no policy evaluation (an attempt to assess effectiveness after a policy has been implemented to then make possible adjustments).

LO: Discuss public policy areas in the Texas state government.

Although the federal government has taken the lead with regard to many issues, states still play an important role in legislating and implementing a wide array of policies. Important policy areas in the Texas state government include regulations, health care, education, social policy (including LGBTQ rights), immigration policy, and water policy.

Key Terms

Affordable Care Act (ACA)
budget fix
campus carry
DACA (Deferred Action for Childhood Arrivals)
DAPA (Deferred Action for Parents of Americans and Lawful Permanent Residents)

DREAM Act
eminent domain
groundwater
Hopwood decision
individual mandate
lawful permanent resident (also called Green Card holder)
Medicaid

Medicare
Permanent University Fund (PUF)
public policy
Roe v. Wade
severability
surface water
Top Ten Percent Plan
tort

Notes

[1] Harold D. Lasswell, *Politics: Who Gets What, When, How* (New York: Peter Smith, 1950).

[2] Hugh Helco, "Review Article: Policy Analysis," *British Journal of Political Science* 2 (1972): 85.

[3] Theodore J. Lowi and Benjamin Ginsberg, *American Government: Power and Purpose* (New York: Norton, 1996), 607.

[4] Christopher M. Weible and Paul A. Sabatier, *Theories of the Policy Process*, 4th ed. (New York: Routledge, 2018).

[5] Michael Barajas, "Problems Hide in Plain Sight at Texas' Youth Lockups," *Texas Observer*, January 3, 2018, https://www.texasobserver.org/problems-hide-plain-sight-texas-youth-lockups/.

[6] Ibid., 4

[7] For his earliest attempt to do so, see James E. Anderson, *Public Policy-Making* (New York: Praeger, 1975). The most recent edition is James E. Anderson, *Public Policymaking: An Introduction*, 7th ed. (Boston: Wadsworth, Cengage Learning, 2010).

[8] Michael D. Cohen, James G. March, and Johan P. Olsen, "A Garbage Can Model of Organizational Choice," *Administrative Science Quarterly* 17, no. 1 (March 1972): 1–25.

[9] Paul Cairney, "12 Things to Know about Studying Public Policy," https://paulcairney.wordpress.com/2015/10/29/12-things-to-know-about-studying-public-policy/ (accessed June 4, 2022).

[10] Texas Legislature, House Bill 5 Analysis, House Research Office, https://hro.house.texas.gov/pdf/ba87r/hb0005.pdf#navpanes=0 (accessed April 10, 2022)

[11] Julian Aguilar, "'Sanctuary Cities' Law Hearing Draws Debate on Free Speech, ICE Detainers," *Texas Tribune*, November 7, 2017, https://www.texastribune.org/2017/11/07/texas-sanctuary-cities-law-hearing-draws-debate-free-speech-ice-detain/.

[12] Maggie Astor, "Texas' Ban on 'Sanctuary Cities' Can Begin, Appeals Court Rules," *The New York Times*, March 13, 2018, https://www.nytimes.com/2018/03/13/us/texas-immigration-law-sb4.html.

[13] "Up for Grabs: The Best and Worst States for Business 2021" *Chief Executive*, https://chiefexecutive.net/up-for-grabs-the-best-worst-states-for-business/

[14] California Teachers Empowerment Network, "CTEN's Frequently Asked Questions," http://www.ctenhome.org/faq.htm.

[15] Jonathan Tilove, "Greg Abbott: Franchise Tax Cut Will Usher in 'New Era of Job Growth,'" *Austin American-Statesman*, June 15, 2015, http://www.statesman.com/news/news/state-regional-govt-politics/abbott-franchise-tax-cut-will-usher-in-new-era-of-/nmdFt/.

[16] Go Big in Texas, "Texas Enterprise Fund," https://gov.texas.gov/uploads/files/business/TEF_Legislative_Report_2019_Final.pdf

[17] Office of the Governor Greg Abbott, "Economic Development and Tourism—Texas Enterprise Fund," http://gov.texas.gov/ecodev/financial_resources/texas_enterprise_fund/.

[18] Forrest Wilder, "The Future of 'Corporate Welfare' in Texas after Rick Perry?," *Texas Observer*, April 24, 2014, http://www.texasobserver.org/future-corporate-welfare-texas-rick-perry/; and see Dana Liebelson, "Rick Perry's $487 Million Corporate Slush Fund Doesn't Need Your Stinkin' Audit," *Mother Jones*, March 20, 2013, http://www.motherjones.com/politics/2013/03/rick-perry-texas-enterprise-fund-audit.

[19] Erica Grieder, "The Revolt against Crony Capitalism," *Texas Monthly*, February 18, 2014, http://www.texasmonthly.com/story/revolt-against-crony-capitalism?fullpage=1.

[20] Jess Fields, "An Overview of Local Economic Development Policies in Texas," January 2014, Texas Public Policy Foundation, http://old.texaspolicy.com/center/local-governance/reports/overview-local-economic-development-policies-texas.

[21] Matthew Watkins, "Legislature Replaces Emerging Technology Fund with University Fund," *Dallas Star-Telegram*, June 1, 2015, http://www.star-telegram.com/news/politics-government/state-politics/article22800357.html.

[22] Office of the Texas Governor, "Governor's University Research Initiative," Texas Economic Development. https://gov.texas.gov/business/page/guri.

[23] Dug Bugley, "Company Announces $14 Billion Deal to Build Texas Bullet Train, but Is Still Long Way from the End of the Line," *Houston Chronicle*, September 13, 2019. https://www.houstonchronicle.com/news/transportation/article/Company-announces-14-billion-deal-with-build-14437777.php.

[24] Morris M. Kleiner, *Licensing Occupations: Ensuring Quality or Restricting Competition?* (Kalamazoo: W.E. Upjohn Institute for Employment Research, 2006).

[25] "Governor Abbott's Letter to State Agencies," *Texas Tribune*, October 8, 2019, https://static.texastribune.org/media/files/e6764b8b39599daaef25659070c3f572/Abbott%20Oct.%20 8%20letter%20to%20agencies.pdf?_ga=2.212962268. 938238043.1574698851-1652735908.1574698851.

[26] Texas House Research Organization, *Focus Report*, December 18, 2019, https://lrl.texas.gov/scanned/sessionOverviews/major/major86.pdf.

[27] Texas Department of Licensing and Regulation, "Hair Braiding Deregulation," https://www.tdlr.texas.gov/cosmet/cosmetfaq.htm#braiding.

[28] Adam Thierer and Trace Mitchell, "Trump's Economic Report Absolutely Right about the Need for Occupational Licensing Reform," Real Clear Policy, February 27, 2020, https://www.realclearpolicy.com/articles/2020/02/27/trumps_economic_report_absolutely_right_about_the_need_for_occupational_licensing_reform_485345.html.

[29] U.S. Chamber Institute for Legal Reform, "2019 Lawsuit Climate Survey: Ranking the States," https://www.instituteforlegalreform.com/uploads/sites/1/2019_Lawsuit_Climate_Survey_-_Ranking_the_States.pdf.

[30] Texans for Lawsuit Reform, "Timeline of Reforms," https://www.tortreform.com/timeline-of-reforms/; Texas Trial Lawyers Association, "Good Laws. Good Lawyers. Great Association," https://www.ttla.com/?pg=aboutmain

[31] Texas Department of State Health Services, "Tobacco Settlement Information Overview," https://www.dshs.texas.gov/tobacco/settlement.shtm (accessed June 7, 2018).

[32] U.S. Centers for Medicare & Medicaid Services, https://www.medicare.gov/.

[33] General Appropriation Act for 2020–2021 Biennium, Regular Session, 2019, https://www.lbb.state.tx.us/Documents/GAA/General_Appropriations_Act_2020_2021.pdf.

[34] U.S. Department of Health and Human Services, "Read the Law," http://www.hhs.gov/healthcare/rights/law/index.html.

[35] HealthCare.gov, "The Fee You Pay If You Don't Have Health Coverage," https://www.healthcare.gov/what-if-i-dont-have-health-coverage/.

[36] National Conference of State Legislatures, "State Actions to Address Health Insurance Exchanges," http://www.ncsl.org/research/health/state-actions-to-implement-the-health-benefit.aspx#Exchange_Status_Map.

[37] Ibid.

[38] Heather Long, "The Final GOP Tax Bill Is Complete. Here's What Is in It," *The Washington Post*, December 15, 2017, https://www.washingtonpost.com/news/wonk/wp/2017/12/15/the-final-gop-tax-bill-is-complete-heres-what-is-in-it/?noredirect=on&utm_term=.f358a8b87dfa.

[39] Emma Platoff, "Individual Mandate Is Unconstitutional, Federal Appellate Court Rules in Texas-Led Affordable Care Act Lawsuit," *Texas Tribune*, https://www.texastribune.org/2019/12/18/5th-circuit-strikes-down-individual-mandate-obamacare/.

[40] Manny Fernandez, "Perry Declares Texas' Rejection of Health Care Law 'Intrusions,'" *The New York Times*, July 9, 2012,

http://www.nytimes.com/2012/07/10/us/politics/perry-says-texas-rejects-health-law-intrusions.html.

[41] Edgar Walters, "With Hospital Funds in Question, Abbott Holds Firm against Medicaid Expansion," *Texas Tribune*, April 20, 2015, http://www.texastribune.org/2015/04/20/hospital-funds-question-abbott-holds-firm-against-/.

[42] U.S. Census Bureau, Health Insurance Coverage in the United States: 2020, "Percentage of People without Health Insurance Coverage by State: 2020," https://data.census.gov/cedsci/profile?g=0400000US48; Rachel Garfield, Kendal Orgera, and Anthony Damico, "The Coverage Gap: Uninsured Poor Adults in States that Do Not Expand Medicaid," KFF, January 21, 2021, https://www.kff.org/medicaid/issue-brief/the-coverage-gap-uninsured-poor-adults-in-states-that-do-not-expand-medicaid/view/footnotes/

[43] Benefits.gov, "Texas Medicaid," https://www.benefits.gov/benefits/benefit-details/1640 (accessed April 16, 2020).

[44] Body Politic, "San Antonio Independent School District vs. Rodriguez," https://www.oyez.org/cases/1972/71-1332.

[45] Texas Supreme Court, https://nces.ed.gov/edfin/pdf/lawsuits/Edgewood_v_Kirby_TX.pdf.

[46] Texas Education Agency Office of School Finance, "School Finance 101: Funding of Texas Public Schools," September 2014, http://tea.texas.gov/Finance_and_Grants/State_Funding/Manuals/School__Finance_Manuals/; Texas Education Agency, Chapter 41 Wealth Equalization, http://tea.texas.gov/Finance_and_Grants/State_Funding/Chapter_41_Wealth_Equalization/Chapter__41_Wealth_Equalization/; For the Supreme Court of Texas decision, see http://www.txcourts.gov/media/1371141/140776.pdf.

[47] Aliyya Swaby, "Will Texas School Finance Panel Tell Schools to Do More with Less? Some Members Think It's Predetermined," *Texas Tribune*, March 16, 2018, https://www.texastribune.org/2018/03/16/school-finance-efficiency/.

[48] Alliyya Swaby, "In 2017, Top Texas Lawmakers Were Galvanized for 'Private School Choice.' This Year, Momentum Has Faded," *Texas Tribune*, January 23, 2019, https://www.texastribune.org/2019/01/23/momentum-school-choice-vouchers-texas-fades-2019/.

[49] Texas Commission on Public School Funding, "Funding for Impact: Equitable Funding for Students Who Need It the Most," https://tea.texas.gov/sites/default/files/Texas%20Commission%20on%20Public%20School%20Finance%20Final%20Report.pdf.

[50] Office of the Texas Governor Greg Abbott, "Governor Abbott Signs Pivotal Property Tax Reforms into Law," https://gov.texas.gov/news/post/governor-abbott-signs-pivotal-property-tax-reforms-into-law.

[51] Texas Education Agency, "Student Testing and Accountability," http://tea.texas.gov/Student_Testing_and_Accountability/.

[52] Texas Education Agency, "STAAR Resources," http://www.tea.state.tx.us/student.assessment/staar/.

[53] Office of the Governor Greg Abbott, "2016 Report to the People of Texas," http://gov.texas.gov/2016report/?utm_medium=social&utm_source=&utm_campaign=20160202_txgov-p-2016report_02022016_website&utm_con.

[54] Texas Education Code (TEC) §29.051–29.064—Bilingual Education and Special Language Programs, http://www.statutes.legis.state.tx.us/Docs/ED/htm/ED.29.htm#B.

[55] Texas Higher Education Coordinating Board, "2019 Public Higher Education Almanac," http://reportcenter.thecb.state.tx.us/agency-publication/almanac/2019-texas-public-higher-education-almanac/ and Texas Higher Education Data, http://www.txhighereddata.org/Interactive/Institutions.cfm (accessed April 17, 2019).

[56] Texas Higher Education Coordinating Board, "General Appropriation Act Overview, Table 3," https://www.highered.texas.gov/institutional-resources-programs/funding-facilities/formula-funding/funding-overviews/.

[57] College Tuition Compare, "2022 Tuition Comparison between colleges in Texas," https://www.collegetuitioncompare.com/compare/tables/?state=TX

[58] Texas Education Code, https://texas.public.law/statutes/tex._educ._code_section_54.017.

[59] Kate McGee, "Texas universities got more state funding this year than they anticipated — but they're still hoping for more support," *The Texas Tribune*, https://www.texastribune.org/2021/06/07/texas-higher-education-funding/

[60] National Center for Education Statistics, "Tuition Costs of Colleges and Universities," 2017, https://nces.ed.gov/fastfacts/display.asp?id=76.

[61] Texas Higher Education Coordinating Board, "Texas Core Curriculum," http://board.thecb.state.tx.us/apps/TCC/.

[62] Texas Higher Education Coordinating Board, "College for All Texans," http://www.collegeforalltexans.com/apps/financialaid/tofa2.cfm?ID=447.

[63] "Capital Project," BusinessDictionary.com, http://www.businessdictionary.com/definition/capital-project.html.

[64] Vivian Elizabeth Smyrl, "Permanent University Fund," *Handbook of Texas Online*, published by the Texas State Historical Association, http://www.tshaonline.org/handbook/online/articles/khp02.

[65] Legislative Budget Board, "Available University Fund," https://www.lbb.state.tx.us/Documents/SFC_Summary_Recs/86R/Agency_799.pdf.

[66] State Constitution, art. 7, sec. 18.

[67] Texas A&M University System, *The 86th Legislative Regular Session Cumulative Report*, p. 42, https://governmentrelations.tamu.edu/resources/86th_TAMUS_EOS.pdf.

[68] Office of the Governor Greg Abbott, "Governor Abbott Proposes to Eliminate Emerging Technology Fund; Establish

New University Research Initiative," January 29, 2015, http://gov.texas.gov/news/press-release/20479.

[69] Office of Governor Greg Abbott, *Governor's University Research Initiative Report,* https://gov.texas.gov/uploads/files/business/86th_Texas_Legislative_Session_GURI_Report.pdf.

[70] Ibid.

[71] U.S. Census Bureau, Current Population Survey, 1967 to 2017.

[72] *Hopwood v. Texas,* 78 F.3d 932 (5th Cir. 1996), cert. denied, *Texas v. Hopwood,* No. 95–1773 (July 1, 1996).

[73] Ibid.

[74] U.S. Supreme Court, *Grutter v. Bollinger,* Cornell Law School, Legal Information Institute, https://www.law.cornell.edu/supct/html/02-241.ZO.html.

[75] The Civil Rights Project, https://www.civilrightsproject.ucla.edu/legal-developments/court-decisions/race-conscious-admissions-policies-challenged-university-of-michigan2019s-affirmative-action-under-fire; John Schwartz, "Between the Lines of the Affirmative Action Opinion," *The New York Times,* June 24, 2013, https://archive.nytimes.com/www.nytimes.com/interactive/2013/06/24/us/annotated-supreme-court-decision-on-affirmative-action.html (accessed June 8, 2018).

[76] Mathew Watlins, "UT-Austin Changes Automatic Admissions Threshold from 7 to 6 Percent," *Texas Tribune,* http://www.texastribune.org/2017/09/15/ut-austin-raises-automatic-admissions-threshold-6-percent/.

[77] Matthew Watkins, "UT–Austin Changes Automatic Admissions Threshhold from 7 to 6 Percent," *Texas Tribune,* September 15, 2017, https://www.texastribune.org/2017/09/15/ut-austin-raises-automatic-admissions-threshold-6-percent/.

[78] Amy Howe, "Finally! The Fisher Decision in Plain English," *SCOTUSblog,* June 24, 2013, http://www.scotusblog.com/2013/06/finally-the-fisher-decision-in-plain-english/.

[79] Manny Fernandez, "Texas University's Race Admissions Policy Is Debated before a Federal Court," *The New York Times,* November 13, 2013, http://www.nytimes.com/2013/11/14/us/texas-universitys-race-admissions-policy-is-debated-before-a-federal-court.html.

[80] *Fisher v. University of Texas at Austin et al.,* Supreme Court of the United States, 2016, https://www.supremecourt.gov/opinions/15pdf/14-981_4g15.pdf; *SCOTUSblog* (*Supreme Court of the United States Blog*), *Fisher v. University of Texas at Austin,* http://www.scotusblog.com/case-files/cases/fisher-v-university-of-texas-at-austin-2/.

[81] Texas State Law Library, "Gun Laws," https://guides.sll.texas.gov/gun-laws/carry-of-firearms.

[82] Texas Department of Public Safety, "New Laws for Handgun Licensing Program," http://www.txdps.state.tx.us/rsd/chl/legal/newlegislation.htm.

[83] Lauren McGaughy, "Court Tosses UT Professors' Lawsuit against Campus Carry," *Dallas Morning News,* July 7, 2017, https://www.dallasnews.com/news/texas-legislature/2017/07/07/court-tosses-ut-professors-lawsuit-campus-carry-law.

[84] National Conference of State Legislatures, "Guns on Campus: Overview," http://www.ncsl.org/research/education/guns-on-campus-overview.aspx.

[85] National Conference of State Legislatures, "State Same-Sex Marriage Laws: Legislatures and Courts," December 2012, http://www.ncsl.org/issues-research/human-services/same-sex-marriagelaws.aspx; National Conference of State Legislatures, "Defining Marriage: State Defense of Marriage Laws and Same-Sex Marriage," October 2014, http://www.ncsl.org/research/human-services/same-sex-marriage-overview.aspx; National Conference of State Legislatures, "Same-Sex Marriage Laws," June 2015, http://www.ncsl.org/research/human-services/same-sex-marriage-laws.aspx.

[86] Office of the Secretary of State, Race Summary Report, "2005 Constitutional Amendment Election," http://elections.sos.state.tx.us/elchist117_state.htm.

[87] Daniel R. Pinello, "Location, Location, Location: Same-Sex Relationship Rights by State," *Law Trends & News,* 2009, American Bar Association, http://www.americanbar.org/newsletter/publications/law_trends_news_practice_area_e_newsletter_home/bl_feat5.html.

[88] Supreme Court of the United States, *United States v. Windsor,* http://www.supremecourt.gov/opinions/12pdf/12-307_6j37.pdf.

[89] Manny Fernandez, "Federal Judge Strikes Down Texas' Ban on Same-Sex Marriage," *The New York Times,* February 26, 2014, http://www.nytimes.com/2014/02/27/us/texas-judge-strikes-down-state-ban-on-same-sex-marriage.html#.

[90] Edgar Walters, "State Files Notice of Appeal on Gay Marriage Ruling," *Texas Tribune,* February 26, 2014, http://www.texastribune.org/2014/02/26/federal-judge-rules-texas-gay-marriage-ban-unconst/.

[91] Department of State Health Services, "Adoption: Frequently Asked Questions," http://www.dshs.state.tx.us/vs/reqproc/faq/adoption.shtm#question 4.

[92] National Center for Lesbian Rights, "Legal Recognition of Lesbian, Gay, Bisexual, and Transgender (LGBT) Parents in Texas," http://www.nclrights.org/wp-content/uploads/2013/07/TX_custody_pub_FINAL.pdf.

[93] Marissa Evans, "Senate Passes Religious Protections for Child Welfare Agencies," *Texas Tribune,* May 21, 2017, https://www.texastribune.org/2017/05/21/senate-passes-religious-protections-child-welfare-agencies/.

[94] Alexa Ura, Edgar Walters and Jolie McCullough, "Comparing Nondiscrimination Protections in Texas Cities," *Texas Tribune,* November 11, 2015, http://www.texastribune.org/2015/11/11/comparing-nondiscrimination-ordinances-texas/.

95 Alex Ura, "Bathroom Fears Flush Houston Discrimination Ordinance," *Texas Tribune*, November 3, 2015, https://www.texastribune.org/2015/11/03/houston-anti-discrimination-ordinance-early-voting/.

96 Lauren McGaughy, "The Texas Bathroom Bill Is Dead—for Now," *Dallas Morning News*, August 15, 2017, https://www.dallasnews.com/news/texas-legislature/2017/08/15/transgender-texans-cautiously-optimistic-bathroom-bill-declared-dead-now.

97 Alex Samuels, "A Fight over Paid Sick Leave Is Turning into a Fight over LGBTQ Nondiscrimination Ordinances," *Texas Tribune*, March 12, 2019, https://www.texastribune.org/2019/03/12/lgbtq-texas-advocates-SB-15-discrimination-ordinances/.

98 Texas Tribune Staff. "How the U.S. Supreme Court abortion ruling is already affecting Texas." *The Texas Tribune*. 2022, June 28. https://www.texastribune.org/2022/06/24/texas-abortion-law-supreme-court-ruling/

99 Ibid.

100 Ibid.

101 Ibid.

102 U.S. Census Bureau, "QuickFacts," http://www.census.gov/quickfacts/table/PST045215/00,48.

103 U.S. Department of State, "The Immigrant Visa Process," http://travel.state.gov/content/visas/english/immigrate/immigrant-process.html.

104 Randall Monger and James Yankay, "U.S. Lawful Permanent Residents: 2013," May 2014, Department of Homeland Security Office of Immigration Statistics, http://www.dhs.gov/sites/default/files/publications/ois_lpr_fr_2013.pdf.

105 Department of Homeland Security, Office of Immigration Statistics, "Profiles on Lawful Permanent Resident status: state 2020, Texas," https://www.dhs.gov/profiles-lawful-permanent-residents-2020-state; Department of Homeland Security, Office of Immigration Statistics, "Profiles on Naturalized Citizens: state 2020," https://www.dhs.gov/profiles-naturalized-citizens-2020-state

106 Steven A. Camarota and Karen Zeigler, "Estimating the Illegal Immigrant Population Using the Current Population Survey." *Center for Immigration Studies*. March 29, 2022. https://cis.org/Report/Estimating-Illegal-Immigrant-Population-Using-Current-Population-Survey. Migration Policy Institute. "Profile of Unauthorized Population: Texas." https://www.migrationpolicy.org/data/unauthorized-immigrant-population/state/TX

107 Edgar Walters, "Behind Closed Doors, Texas Budget Writers Add $100 Million for Border Surge," *Texas Tribune*, May 25, 2019, https://www.texastribune.org/2019/05/25/texas-budget-writers-add-100-million-border-surge-behind-closed-doors/.

108 Carole Keeton Strayhorn, "Undocumented Immigrants in Texas: A Financial Analysis of the Impact to the State Budget and Economy," December 2006, Office of the Texas Comptroller.

109 José Iván Rodríguez-Sánchez, UNDOCUMENTED IMMIGRANTS IN TEXAS: A COST-BENEFIT ASSESSMENT Undocumented Immigrants to Texas: A Cost-Benefit Assessment. May 2020, Baker Institute Rice University. https://www.bakerinstitute.org/media/files/files/47a234a5/usmx-pub-undocumentedresidents-050620.pdf

110 Alexa Ura, Jason Kao, Carla Astudillo, Chris Essig. "People of color make up 95% of Texas' population growth, and cities and suburbs are booming, 2020 census shows.", August 12, 2021, *The Texas Tribune,* https://www.texastribune.org/2021/08/12/texas-2020-census/

111 "Changes to 'Public Charge' Inadmissibility Rule: Implications for Health and Health Coverage," *Kaiser Health News,* August 12, 2019, https://www.kff.org/disparities-policy/fact-sheet/public-charge-policies-for-immigrants-implications-for-health-coverage/.

112 *Plyler v. Doe,* 457 U.S. 202 (1982).

113 Texas Higher Education Coordinating Board, "Overview: Residency and In-State Tuition," September 2008, http://www.thecb.state.tx.us/reports/PDF/1528.PDF.

114 Ibid., 109

115 Paul J. Weber, "Texas Approves $800 Million for Border Security," *PBS Newshour,* June 16, 2015, http://www.pbs.org/newshour/rundown/texas-approves-800-million-border-security/.

116 Mathew Simpson, "TX Legislature in Review: Immigrants' Rights," ACLUtx, June 17, 2019, https://www.aclutx.org/en/news/tx-legislature-review-immigrants-rights; Mexican American Legal Defense Fund, "MALDEF Expands Challenge to Texas SB4 'Sanctuary Cities' Law," December 17, 2019, https://www.maldef.org/2019/12/maldef-expands-challenge-to-texas-sb4-sanctuary-cities-law/.

117 Mark Hugo Lopez and Jens Manuel Krogstad, "States Suing Obama over Immigration Programs Are Home to 46% of Those Who May Qualify," February 11, 2015, Pew Research Center, http://www.pewresearch.org/fact-tank/2015/02/11/states-suing-obama-over-immigration-programs-are-home-to-46-of-those-who-may-qualify/.

118 Adam Liptak and Michael D. Shear, "Supreme Court to Hear Challenge to Obama Immigration Actions," *The New York Times*, January 19, 2016, http://www.nytimes.com/2016/01/20/us/politics/supreme-court-to-hear-challenge-to-obama-immigration-actions.html; *United States v. Texas,* Supreme Court of the United States. 2016, https://www.supremecourt.gov/opinions/15pdf/15-674_jhlo.pdf; Adam Liptak and Michael D. Shear, "Supreme Court Tie Blocks Obama Immigration Plan," *The New York Times*, June 23, 2016, http://www.nytimes.com/2016/06/24/us/supreme-court-immigration-obama-dapa.html.

[119] Brian Shyr, "White House Continues Efforts at Immigration Reform," *JacksonLewis Blog,* March 4, 2020, https://www.globalimmigrationblog.com/2020/03/white-house-continues-efforts-at-immigration-reform/.

[120] Emma Platoff, "Texas and Six Other States Sue to End DACA," *Texas Tribune,* May 1, 2018, https://www.texastribune.org/2018/05/01/texas-and-six-other-states-sue-end-daca/.

[121] Ibid.

[122] Uriel J. Garcia, Texas sues to block Biden administration from lifting Title 42, a pandemic-era health rule used to expel migrants, *The Texas Tribune,* April 22, 2022, https://www.texastribune.org/2022/04/22/texas-biden-title-42-lawsuit/. Uriel J. Garcia, Texas sues Biden administration to halt program that reunites Central American children with parents in U.S., *The Texas Tribune,* January 28, 2022, https://www.texastribune.org/2022/01/28/texas-paxton-lawuit-biden-immigration/.

[123] Texas Water Development Board, "Water for Texas: 2012 State Water Plan," http://www.twdb.texas.gov/publications/state_water_plan/2012/2012_SWP.pdf.

[124] www.merriam-webster.com/acrefoot.

[125] Texas Water Development Board, "Water for Texas."

[126] Ibid.

[127] Ibid.

[128] North Texas Municipal Water District (2022). Bois d'Arc Lake. https://boisdarclake.org

[129] Texas A&M University, "Texas Water Law," http://texaswater.tamu.edu/water-law.

[130] *Edwards Aquifer Authority v. Day,* 389 S.W.3d 814 (Tex. 2012).

[131] See Private Real Property Rights Preservation Act, www.oag.tx.us/AG_Publications/txts/propertyguide2005.shtml.

[132] Chapter 36, Texas Water Code. See also "Spotlight on Groundwater Conservation Districts," Environmental Defense, Austin, Texas, www.texaswatermatters.org.

[133] www.mysanantonio.com/news/article/Texas-part-of-growing-drought-in-U.S.-that-rivals-3711733; www.cbbep.org.

[134] Texas Water Development Board, "Annual Operating Budget for Fiscal Year 2022," https://www.twdb.texas.gov/publications/reports/administrative/doc/AOB_FY22.pdf

CHAPTER **14**

Financing State Government

Texas Learning Outcome

• Analyze state financing issues and policies in Texas.

A fundamental question in the realm of political science is, "What should government do?" Individuals answer this question in many ways depending on their **political values**, a set of beliefs about political processes and the role that government should play in our society. Any action that government takes requires an expenditure of resources—whether it is measured as an expense or by the amount of time it takes to reach a decision. Today much attention is on federal spending, but few citizens realize that state governments also spend large sums to supply services to their citizens. In 2019, state and local governments combined spent $3.3 trillion.[1] The federal government provides some funding to state and local governments in the form of grants, but state and local governments generate a large portion of their revenue from their own sources. Texas reported gross revenue totaling $247.9 billion in fiscal year 2022; $45.82 billion of that was from federal sources.[2] On average, Texas generates approximately two-thirds of its revenue.

> **political values**
> A set of beliefs about political processes and the role that government should play in our society

Because the Texas legislature meets in regular sessions every other year (biennially), it approves budgets for two-year periods (biennial budgets). In 2021, the legislature approved a budget of $264.8 billion for the fiscal years 2022 and 2023. Approximately one-third of the biennial budget revenue comes from the federal government. Thirty-two percent of those funds are allocated to Health and Human Services, the system that provides for state Medicaid recipients.[3] In the 2020–2021 biennium, Medicaid funding accounted for 81 percent of the total Health and Human Services funding request.[4]

Chapter Learning Objectives

• Explain why governments provide services to citizens.

• Describe sources of state revenue in Texas.

• Discuss the issue of equity in taxes in the United States generally and in Texas specifically.

• Discuss local taxes in Texas.

- Discuss nontax revenue sources in Texas.
- Describe Texas government expenditures.
- Identify and explain continuing issues in Texas state finance.

Why Do Governments Provide Services to Citizens?

Learning Objective: Explain why governments provide services to citizens.

Governments provide many goods and services to the public. For instance, there are more than 5,000 local government units in the state of Texas alone. They provide crucial services such as public education, water treatment, fire protection, policing, and health care. Why are these vital services often left to government to provide? Why can't we rely on private businesses to provide roads, bridges, flood control, or clean air? Markets often fail to provide these goods and services because of some unique characteristics shared by these types of goods, called **public goods**.

Characteristics of Public Goods

public goods

Goods or services characterized by the features of nonexcludability and nonrivalrous consumption; governments often provide these

nonexcludability

The inability to practically prevent people from receiving or enjoying a good or service due to nonpayment

nonrivalrous consumption

Situation in which the use or enjoyment of a good or service by a person or persons does not diminish the availability of that good or service for others to use or enjoy

nonexhaustion

The availability of a good or service for others to use and enjoy will not diminish (i.e., consumption is nonrivalrous).

The goods and services mentioned in the introduction to this section are all types of public goods. Pure public goods share two characteristics that distinguish them from private goods: they are both **nonexclusive** and nonexhaustive (also referred to as **nonrivalrous**).[5] Nonexcludability means that it is not practical to exclude people from receiving or enjoying the good or service due to nonpayment. In other words, it is not easy to separate payers from nonpayers. For instance, imagine that a city tried charging a fee for fire protection and responded only to calls from those who paid the fee. Now, suppose you have paid the fire protection fee, but your neighbor hasn't. The city could not deny fire protection to your neighbor who had not paid because protecting your house could require preventing or putting out a fire at your neighbor's. Likewise, putting out a fire in your house is fire protection to your neighbor and other houses near your home regardless of whether your neighbors pay the fee.[6]

The second characteristic of public goods is **nonexhaustion,** which means that use of a good or service by one individual does not diminish the availability of that good or service for others to use. Street lights offer a good example. Well-lit streets are a benefit that everyone in a community shares. Your benefiting from street lights on a walk home from a friend's house does not reduce the lighting available to the jogger who passes you on the sidewalk. Another example is flood control. A flood control system that protects your community offers the same level of protection to you as it does your neighbors and local businesses. The benefit you get from flood protection does not lessen the level of benefit that everyone else gets.

The two characteristics of public goods, nonexcludability and nonexhaustion, result in the failure of the free market to adequately provide public goods. If a

	Exhaustive	Nonexhaustive
Exclusive	**Social Goods** Education Libraries Subsidized housing Vaccinations	**Toll Goods** Broadcasting airwaves National parks Toll roads Toll bridges
Nonexclusive	**Common-Pool Goods** Aquifers Fisheries Forests Groundwater	**Pure Public Goods** Clean air National defense Pollution abatement Street lights

FIGURE 14.1 Characteristics of Public Goods

service is nonexclusive, then a business cannot prevent nonpayers, or **"free-riders,"** from enjoying the benefit of the service. In such a case, there is very little incentive for people to pay for the service, and if a business cannot charge a price that people will pay, there is no incentive for the business to provide the service. Also, if a service is nonexhaustive, the marginal cost (defined as the cost for the last unit produced) of delivering the service to more people is zero. As a result, any price a business would charge for the service would be too high (higher than zero), and too few people would pay.[7] Efficient pricing is impossible, and the end result is too few public goods provided and consumed if left to the private market.[8]

Although pure public goods share both the characteristics of nonexcludability and nonexhaustion, several subtypes share one feature but not the other (see Figure 14.1). Economists call these goods quasi-public goods.

free-rider
An individual or individuals who benefits from a good or service without contributing to the cost

Types of Public Goods

Many goods that government provides are not pure public goods. They may share only certain features of pure public goods, or there may be a broader societal purpose for ensuring availability. Three important subtypes are worth discussing: social goods, toll goods, and common-pool goods.

Social Goods

Social goods are goods and services that the private sector often provides, meaning they are exclusive and can be exhausted. However, government also provides these goods because there is a value to society in ensuring that everyone has access to such goods regardless of an individual's ability to pay. Governments ensure availability of these goods either by providing them for free or by subsidizing them. For example, in public education, it would be easy to separate payers and nonpayers, and we do—there are private schools for which parents often pay substantial amounts in tuition. However, we do not exclude any child from education for nonpayment, and thus we ensure access to free public education for all children. In fact, most states, including Texas, require students to attend school until they reach a certain age because it is believed that there is a broader public purpose or benefit to having an educated populace. Thus, government provides some services without charge because there is a benefit to society as a whole—a collective benefit.

Toll Goods

Toll goods (sometimes called club goods) are exclusive but nonexhaustive. Toll roads and toll bridges are the classic examples. It's possible to prevent non-payers from using certain infrastructure by controlling access and exit points, but your use of the toll road does not reduce the benefit to other people. Now, it takes only a moment to recall sitting in bumper-to-bumper traffic on a congested highway to realize an important caveat. Toll goods are often nonexhaustive only to a certain point. All roads, even toll roads, have a maximum volume of traffic that can be sustained before causing delays or hazardous conditions. The same is true for parks and beaches that can become crowded to the point of diminishing the benefit to more people. At the point of congestion and overcrowding, toll goods like toll bridges or parks are more accurately common-pool goods.

Common-Pool Goods

The last subtype of public goods are common-pool goods. Common-pool goods are public goods that are nonexclusive but exhaustive. Natural resources are generally common-pool goods. Either by nature or design, exclusion is impractical or impossible, and because all natural resources are finite, common-pool goods can be exhausted. Groundwater is a particularly important example in Texas considering that many parts of the state have been in some stage of drought since 2010. Groundwater is treated as private property, meaning that one has a right to drill and pump whatever water exists beneath one's private property (the rule of capture). There are some restrictions on the extraction of groundwater by landowners, but these restrictions are arguably weak. If water is pumped at a rate faster than the water supply can be replenished, then access to groundwater will become difficult in certain parts, and in some cases, wells and springs can run dry. Without effective regulation, it is unlikely that groundwater would be managed sustainably. (See Chapter 13 for more on Texas water policy.)

Willacy County Judge Aurelio Guerra meets with other government officials to secure federal and state funding for Raymondville's drain project that's part of the Rio Grande Flood Control System.

Courtesy of Rio Grande Guardian

Although some think the government provides too many services to far too many citizens, attempts to reduce services often result in protests from those affected. As we all know, everyone favors cutting budgets (and taxes), but no one wants his or her favorite program cut. Despite what services one would think could be cut, all services must be paid for (eventually), either with tax money or from service charges and fees.

CORE OBJECTIVE

Thinking Critically . . .

Which goods and services do you think state government should provide? Consider the consequences of your answer. What would be the possible impact to society? Who would benefit, and who would lose out?

Sources of State Revenue

Learning Objective: Describe sources of state revenue in Texas.

To pay for the many services a state government provides, that government must raise revenue from many sources. For state governments, the primary source of revenue is taxes that citizens pay, not money from service charges or fees. The amount of tax money available for any given state depends on the wealth of the citizens of that state. Some states, like some individuals, have a higher income capacity than others.

Evaluating State Tax

The measure of a state's potential to tax is called its **tax capacity.** This measure is a ratio of the per capita taxable resources of each state indexed to the per capita taxable resources of the United States as a whole, which is set at 100. States above 100 have a higher tax capacity, and states below 100 have a lower tax capacity.[9] Texas had a tax capacity index of 94.8 in 2019, meaning that it was just below the national average of 96.46.[10] Map 14.1 groups the 50 states by per capita tax capacity in 2019.

Whereas a state's tax capacity measures its potential to tax, a state's **tax effort** measures its level of taxation. Ideally, a state's tax effort is a measure of the amount of revenue collected relative to its tax capacity. The tax effort in Texas is low, meaning that Texas is taxing below its capacity and that tax collection is low relative to other states. Thus, overall, Texas is a low-tax state; however, it is a high-tax state in terms of its dependence on sales and property tax when compared to other states.

tax capacity
A measure of the wealth of a state or its ability to raise revenues relative to all other states

tax effort
A measure of the amount of revenue collected by a state relative to its tax capacity

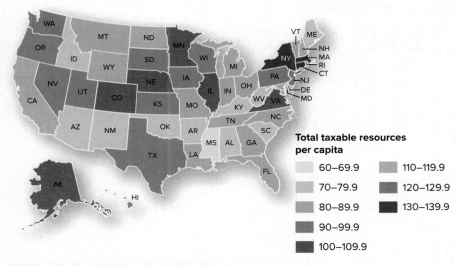

MAP 14.1 States' Tax Capacity, 2021

Source: U.S. Department of the Treasury, Resource Center, "Total Taxable Resources Estimates," September 2021, https://home.treasury.gov/system/files/226/TTR-tables-2021.pdf.

per capita tax

The total taxes raised in a state divided by the number of residents

tax exporting

The shifting of taxes to citizens in other states; a good example is Wyoming coal, which is exported to Texas to generate electricity

Another measure of state taxes is **per capita tax.** This is a simple measure obtained by taking the total taxes collected and dividing by the number of citizens in the state. Although this might be useful to know, it is not very informative about how much citizens actually pay in taxes. The primary point missed by the per capita tax measure is **tax exporting.** Sometimes taxes are exported to out-of-state residents, as the following paragraph explains.

Alaska and Wyoming rank near the top on per capita tax burden. However, much of this tax is from oil in Alaska and coal in Wyoming and is exported to residents of other states—tax exporting.[11] Anyone who has ever seen a coal train hauling Wyoming coal to Austin, San Antonio, or Houston has seen tax burden being exported from Wyoming to Texas. People use this coal to generate electricity, and consumers pay the tax when they pay their utility bills. Texas residents' tax contributions on that coal are then used to cover the costs of importing coal from Wyoming. In another example, Texas receives about $1 billion in taxes on oil production and natural gas each year. However, much of the final product is exported to other states, and so the taxes on these exports are being paid by the customers in other states—meaning part of the tax burden is exported rather than paid by Texans. Therefore, per capita tax is not a true measure of the tax burden on the citizens living in the state unless tax exporting is taken into account.

Thus, if you rank all states on per capita revenues, the data do not tell us much about the actual taxes that a state's residents pay. A somewhat better measure is to compare the 15 most populous states on the amount of revenue raised per $1,000 of personal income. This still does not overcome the issues of tax exporting, but at least it compares the larger states' taxes as a percentage of income. By comparison, Texas is the 4th-lowest tax state, 47th out of 50 (see Table 14.1).

TABLE 14.1

State Tax Revenue per $1,000 for 15 Most Populous States, FY 2020

Tax Revenue Rank among 50 States	State (by Population)	Per $1,000 of Personal Income	% of U.S. Average
16	California	$63.33	115.1%
47	**Texas**	**$38.01**	**69.1%**
48	Florida	$36.00	65.5%
12	New York	$64.86	117.9%
36	Pennsylvania	$52.13	94.8%
23	Illinois	$57.83	105.1%
38	Ohio	$49.30	89.6%
43	Georgia	$43.30	78.7%
30	North Carolina	$53.66	97.6%
32	Michigan	$53.37	97.4%
22	New Jersey	$58.80	106.9%
33	Virginia	$53.36	97.0%
24	Washington	$57.03	103.7%
39	Arizona	$49.10	89.3%
21	Massachusetts	$59.26	107.7%
	U.S. Average	**$55.00**	

Sources: U.S. Census Bureau; Texas Legislative Budget Board, *Fiscal Size-Up 2022–23 Biennium,* Figures 29 and 30.

Focus On

Asian American Tax Contributions

Asian Americans and Pacific Islander Americans make up roughly 5.2 percent of Texas's population, which is slightly lower than their proportion of the U.S. population overall (5.9 percent).[12] That percentage of the population is expected to grow to 10 percent by 2050, a rate of increase that now outpaces Hispanic population growth.[13] Yet, even as a relatively small demographic right now, they contribute significantly more in taxes than might be expected.

According to research done by New American Economy in 2015, Asian Americans and Pacific Islander Americans earned $783.7 billion in fiscal year 2019. Of that amount, $167.8 billion and $72.5 billion went to federal and state/local taxes, respectively. They also contributed significantly to Medicare and Social Security.[14]

Shutterstock

Additionally, Asian American and Pacific Islander immigrants earned and contributed substantial amounts—earning $612.1 billion and contributing $130.1 billion to federal taxes and $56.5 to state and local taxes.[15]

This high level of contribution is due to three major factors:

1. They have higher levels of educational attainment as a demographic than does the U.S. population as a whole. More specifically, as a percentage of population, more earn bachelor's degrees.
2. They have a higher percentage of working-age individuals than other demographics.
3. As a percentage of their demographic, more individuals hold jobs.[16]

Yuri Jang, Ph.D., in the School of Social Work at the University of Texas, created a survey in 2016 specifically asking Asian Americans in Austin about their quality of life and how well their health and social needs were being met.[17] Note that Austin has Texas's second-largest Asian American population, following Houston. The survey itself focused primarily on Chinese, Taiwanese, Asian Indian, Korean, Vietnamese, and Filipino Americans and immigrants. One of the main findings was that there are significant unmet health care (11 percent) and public transportation (20 percent) needs.[18] As a result, it would make sense for the city to invest resources in reducing language barriers for transportation and medical services—especially given the contribution this demographic group makes in local taxes.

Critical Thinking Questions
1. How would you summarize the factors that cause Asian and Pacific Islander Americans to contribute so much in tax revenue?
2. What economic arguments might you use to support the idea that Austin should reduce language barriers for Asian immigrants?

State Taxes in Texas

The most common, single sources of revenue for state governments are **consumer taxes**, such as sales and excise taxes on gasoline, tobacco, and liquor. Figure 14.2 shows the breakdown for Texas state tax revenue in 2020-2021, which totals $114.97 billion for the two-year period. As the figure shows, most revenue comes from consumer taxes paid by individuals when they make purchases. More than 80 percent of all tax revenue comes from consumer taxes (sales, motor vehicle sales, motor fuels, alcoholic beverages, tobacco taxes).

consumer taxes

Taxes that citizens pay when they buy goods and services—the most prominent example is sales taxes

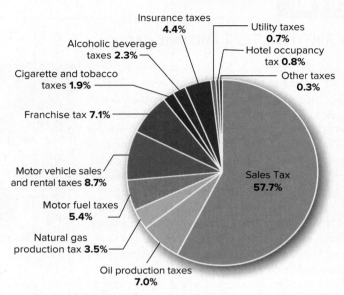

Where Your State Tax Dollars Come from 2018–2019 Biennium

- Insurance taxes **4.4%**
- Utility taxes **0.7%**
- Hotel occupancy tax **0.8%**
- Alcoholic beverage taxes **2.3%**
- Other taxes **0.3%**
- Cigarette and tobacco taxes **1.9%**
- Franchise tax **7.1%**
- Sales Tax **57.7%**
- Motor vehicle sales and rental taxes **8.7%**
- Motor fuel taxes **5.4%**
- Natural gas production tax **3.5%**
- Oil production taxes **7.0%**

FIGURE 14.2   **Total Tax Revenue in Texas, 2022–2023 Biennium: $135.9 Billion**

Source: Texas Legislative Budget Board, *Fiscal Size-Up 2020–21 Biennium*, Figure 26.

Because of high sales taxes, consumers and not businesses pay most of the taxes in Texas. Business taxes are limited, taking the form of a corporate franchise tax. When compared to taxes on consumers, business taxes are minimal. We will discuss that point later in this chapter.

Focus On

Tax Contributions of Hispanic Households

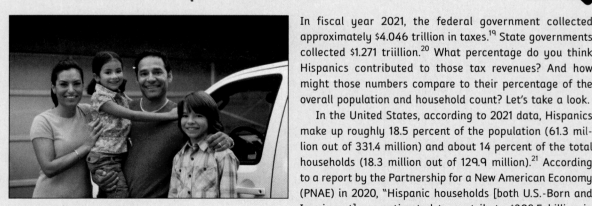

Siri Stafford/Digital Vision/Getty Images

In fiscal year 2021, the federal government collected approximately $4.046 trillion in taxes.[19] State governments collected $1.271 triillion.[20] What percentage do you think Hispanics contributed to those tax revenues? And how might those numbers compare to their percentage of the overall population and household count? Let's take a look.

In the United States, according to 2021 data, Hispanics make up roughly 18.5 percent of the population (61.3 million out of 331.4 million) and about 14 percent of the total households (18.3 million out of 129.9 million).[21] According to a report by the Partnership for a New American Economy (PNAE) in 2020, "Hispanic households [both U.S.-Born and Immigrant] are estimated to contribute $308.5 billion in federal taxes and almost $112 billion in state and local

TABLE 14.2			
Tax Contributions of Hispanic Households in Texas, 2019 (in billions)			
	All Hispanics	**U.S.-Born Hispanics**	**Foreign-Born Hispanics**
Federal Taxes	$32.6	$21.6	$10.9
State & Local Taxes	$18.7	$11.6	$ 7.1

Source: Partnership for a New American Economy, *Power of the Purse: Contributions of Hispanic Americans in Texas,* November 2021, https://research.newamericaneconomy.org/wp-content/uploads/sites/2/2021/11/NAE_TX-Hispanic-Spending-Power_2021.pdf.

taxes."[22] In addition, while U.S.-born Hispanics account for the majority of the total Hispanic population, just over 37 percent are immigrants.[23] Households headed by immigrant Hispanics contributed about 42.5 percent ($131.1 billion) of the total Hispanic federal tax payment.

For information on Texas, see Table 14.2.

It is also important to include the contributions of undocumented Hispanic immigrants (noncitizens) when looking at tax data. The Pew Hispanic Center notes that in 2014, roughly 11.3 million individuals were classified as undocumented immigrants and, of those, 49 percent were Mexican. Of the "5.6 million Mexican undocumented immigrants living in the U.S.," many are concentrated in "California, Texas, Florida, New York, and Illinois."[24] This is notable because of how much that population contributes in tax dollars. In a report released in 2017 by the Institute on Taxation and Economic policy, undocumented immigrants in general contribute "an estimated $11.74 billion" in state and local taxes.[25] In 2014, for example, Texas received more than $1.5 billion in state and local taxes from families headed by undocumented immigrants.[26]

Hispanics contribute significant tax dollars to federal, state, and local governments. According to the PNAE, "Federal taxes paid by Hispanic households go towards funding federal services—including the military, Social Security, and Medicare—that benefit all Americans."[27] At the state and local level, "Hispanic households help pay for critical local services like school districts, police and fire safety, local road and street maintenance, as well as emergency medical services."[28] Revenues at all levels of government increasingly depend on the relatively youthful Hispanic population, particularly as more move into the workforce.[29]

Critical Thinking Questions
1. Based on the data provided in Table 14.2, in Texas what percentage of all Hispanics' federal, state, and local tax revenues did U.S.-born Hispanics contribute?
2. As discussed in this chapter, all government services require an expenditure of resources. If all undocumented immigrants left Texas, what would be the likely consequence for state revenue?

Equity in Taxes

Learning Objective: Discuss the issue of equity in taxes in the United States generally and in Texas specifically.

Who should pay taxes? Should those who benefit from public services pay (**benefit-based taxes**), or should those who can most afford it pay? Some taxes are based more on the benefit a person receives, and others are based more on the **ability to pay.** For example, the excise tax on gasoline is an example of a tax based on benefit received rather than on ability to pay. A large portion of the gasoline tax goes to highway construction. The more gasoline people buy, the more tax they pay, and the more benefit they receive from using the streets and highways.

benefit-based taxes
Taxes for which there is a relationship between the amount paid in taxes and services received; motor fuel taxes are a good example

ability to pay
Taxes that are not based on the benefit received but on the wealth, or ability to pay, of an individual

For most taxes, other than the gasoline tax, showing direct benefit is problematic. Benefit received is more applicable to service charges and fees than to taxes. Sometimes the service charge covers the actual cost of providing the service, such as for garbage collection. In other cases, the service charge might cover only part of the cost of providing the service. College students receive most of the benefit from attending classes, and they pay tuition and fees to attend. In state-supported universities and colleges, however, tuition and fees paid by students do not cover all of the cost of a college education. Taxpayers pay some of the cost.

Generally, when individual benefit can be measured, at least part of the cost of the service is paid in the form of fees. People using a public golf course pay a greens fee, hunters pay for hunting licenses, and drivers pay a driver's license and tag fee. Often these funds go directly to the government unit providing the service. Taxpayers may pick up part of the cost. For example, greens fees that golfers pay often do not cover the total capital and operating costs of running a golf course. The difference comes from revenue from other sources, typically from property tax revenues.

Other taxes, such as the federal income tax, are based more on ability to pay. The higher your net income, the higher your income tax bracket, and the higher the percentage of your net income you pay in federal income taxes. Most taxes, especially at the state level, are not based on ability to pay.

Regressive and Progressive Taxes

regressive taxes

Taxes that take a higher percentage of income from low-income persons

progressive taxes

Taxes that take a higher percentage of income from high-income persons

proportional taxes

Taxes that take the same percentage of income from all citizens

Using the criterion of ability to pay, taxes are either regressive or progressive. A **regressive tax** takes a higher percentage of income from low-income people, and a **progressive tax** takes a higher percentage from higher-income people. The best example of a progressive tax is our federal income tax because individuals are taxed on their earned income in brackets. For example, individuals pay a higher percentage of tax on earned income based on income brackets of 10 percent, 12 percent, 22 percent, 24 percent, 32 percent, 35 percent, and 37 percent.[30] Examples of regressive taxes are those that adversely affect lower wage earners, including sales and property taxes that the state levies. Economists also talk about **proportional taxes,** in which the tax paid is a fixed percentage of each person's income. Examples of proportional taxes are difficult to come by but, in theory, are possible. Perhaps the best example of a proportional tax was the tax on earned income for Medicare (a federal program) before the 2010 Patient Protection and Affordable Care Act. After the passage of that federal law, the Medicare tax became slightly progressive because of the additional tax imposed on higher earners based on filing status. For example, married couples filing jointly paid more tax for Medicare if their combined earnings exceeded $250,000 per year.[31]

Texas has one of the most regressive tax structures of all the states (see Table 14.3). The Institute on Taxation and Economic Policy, a Washington, D.C., advocacy group, issues a report that ranks every state by the progressivity or regressivity of their tax systems. Texas made the "Terrible Ten" list in the 2018 edition, ranking second among all states.[32] It is worth noting that the top four—Washington, Texas, Florida, and South Dakota—do not levy a personal income tax, and 6 of the top 10 states get one-half to two-thirds of their tax revenue from sales and excise taxes.[33] Figure 14.3 shows tax revenue collected for major tax categories as a percentage of income by income group in 2018, As the figure shows, a Texas family in the lowest 20 percent of income paid

TABLE 14.3

The 10 Most Regressive State Tax Systems (2018)

Taxes as Shares of Income for Non-elderly Residents

	Taxes as a Percentage of Income		
Income Group	**Poorest 20%**	**Middle 60%**	**Top 1%**
Washington	17.80%	10.09%	3.00%
Texas	**13.00%**	**9.70%**	**3.10%**
Florida	12.70%	8.10%	2.30%
South Dakota	11.20%	8.70%	2.50%
Nevada	10.20%	7.40%	1.90%
Tennessee	10.50%	8.40%	2.80%
Pennsylvania	13.80%	11.00%	6.00%
Illinois	14.40%	12.30%	7.40%
Oklahoma	13.20%	10.50%	6.20%
Wyoming	9.60%	7.20%	2.60%

Source: Institute on Taxation and Economic Policy, *"Who Pays? A Distributional Analysis of the Tax Systems in All 50 States,"* October 2018, https://itep.org/wp-content/uploads/whopays-ITEP-2018.pdf.

about 13 percent of their income in taxes, whereas the national average for families in the lowest 20 percent of income was slightly less at 11.4 percent.

Figure 14.3 shows that, although all state tax structures are regressive, the tax structure in Texas is more regressive than average.[34]

The degree to which taxes are regressive or progressive depends on many factors. Regressivity and progressivity are affected not only by the mix

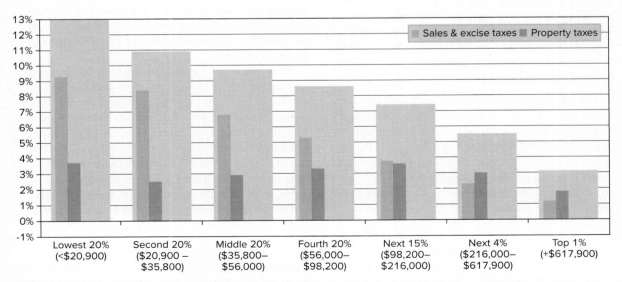

FIGURE 14.3 State and Local Taxes in Texas State and local taxes imposed on non-elderly taxpayers as share of income

Source: Institute on Taxation and Economic Policy, "Who Pays? A Distributional Analysis of Tax Systems in All 50 States," October 2018, https://itep.org/wp-content/uploads/whopays-ITEP-2018.pdf, 119.

How to

Interpret a Graph

Graphs are a visual representation of information or data along a vertical (*y*) axis and a horizontal (*x*) axis that shows the relationship between data. If you can't remember which axis is which, remember that "*y* goes to the sky."

The most common graphs are line graphs and bar graphs. Figure 14.3 is a bar graph. Follow these steps to interpret the data it presents.

Step 1: Read the title of the graph to figure out what information it shows.

Figure 14.3 shows the types of state and local taxes imposed on non-elderly taxpayers, divided into groups based on income level. The light yellow bars show the total percentage of income each group pays in taxes, on average. The other colored bars represent various specific taxes and what proportion of the taxpayers' income goes toward that tax. How can you tell which bar represents which tax? Check the key in the upper-right corner of the graph. The caption also tells you that the graph lists the taxes as a share (in other words, a percentage) of taxpayers' income.

Step 2: Identify the scale or units shown on the horizontal (*x*) axis and the vertical (*y*) axis.

In this case, the *x* axis represents income levels divided into seven categories or data sets, ranging from the lowest 20 percent of non-elderly taxpayers earning less than $20,900 per year to the top 1 percent earning more than $617,900 per year. The scale along the *y* axis represents taxes paid, ranging between 3 percent to plus 13 percent as a percentage of income.

Step 3: Analyze the information the graph presents.

Begin with the first set of data located closest to the intersection of the *x* and *y* axes. In this figure, that is the lowest 20 percent of non-elderly taxpayers, who earn less than $20,900 per year. (The < symbol means "less than." It looks a bit like an L, which makes the "less" part easier to remember. Some graphs use a > symbol that means "greater than.")

The tallest light green bar shows that sales and excise taxes take slightly more than 9 percent of this group's income, as shown on the *y* axis. The shorter orange bar shows that property taxes take 3.7 percent of this group's income. The yellow background colored bar represents the sum, right at 13 percent, of taxes that this group pays as a proportion of their yearly income.

Step 4: Interpret the relationship between information on the *x* axis and information on the *y* axis.

To understand this graph, you need to figure out how the income category (on the *x* axis) relates to the taxes paid as a percentage of income (on the *y* axis). To do this, repeat step 3 for each income level category. For example, review the light green bar that represents sales and excise tax in each income level. The first income level (less than $20,900 per year) shows slightly more than 9 percent. The second income level ($20,900 to $35,800 per year) shows slightly more than 8 percent; the third income level ($35,800 to $56,000 per year) shows slightly less than 7 percent; and the fourth income level ($56,000 to $98,200 per year) shows about 5.3 percent. The fifth income level ($98,200 to $216,000 per year) shows slightly less than 4 percent; the sixth income level ($216,000 to $617,900 per year) shows 2.3 percent; and the seventh income level (more than $617,900 per year) shows 1.2 percent.

Thus, you may conclude that non-elderly taxpayers earning less than $20,900 per year pay the highest amount of sales and excise tax as a proportion of their annual income. You may also conclude that non-elderly taxpayers earning more money per year pay less sales and excise tax as a proportion of their income. Therefore, the relationship between income level and taxes paid as a proportion of income is an inverse relationship. In other words, as one variable increases (income level), the other variable (taxes paid as a percentage of income) decreases.

tax base
The items that are subject to tax; for example, the items subject to sales tax

of taxes used in a state (income, sales, excise, property) but also by taxation rates and what is subject to tax. What is subject to taxation is called the **tax base.** For example, some states tax only unearned income (stock dividends and interest) instead of earned income (wages and salaries). Others do the opposite. Some states have a proportional rate for state income tax rather than a progressive tax rate. To be clear, Texas does not tax income.

With the sales tax, the tax base—what is subject to sales tax—is an important factor. If food and medicine are subject to a sales tax, then the tax is more regressive because these are commonly consumed goods for which lower-income earners would pay a higher percentage of their income in order to pay the tax. As of 2022, 32 states exempt food items, 44 exempt prescription drugs, and 9 exempt nonprescription drugs. Texas exempts legal and accounting fees from sales tax.[35] Wealthy people use these services more often than poor or middle-class people do, which makes the sales tax more regressive.

Some argue that taxes based on consumption are the "best taxes" because citizens have a choice to consume or not to consume. The less you consume, the smaller your tax burden. The degree to which this is true depends upon what is subject to tax. If many necessities of life, such as food, clothing, and medicine, are subject to tax, then the range of choice will be very limited, especially for low-income people who spend most of their income on such items. If, on the other hand, necessities are excluded and nonessentials are included, the choice theory has some validity. For example, if golf course fees, country club fees, accounting services, and legal fees are excluded, the argument that choice is a factor takes on a hollow ring. Table 14.4 shows rates of state and local sales taxes in the 15 most populous states.

TABLE 14.4

Comparison of State Tax Rates: 15 Most Populous States, 2022

State	Retail Sales Tax (Percentage)	Cigarette Tax Rate (Per Pack)	Gasoline Tax Rate (Per Gallon)
Arizona	5.6	$2.00	$ 0.18
California	7.25	$2.87	$ 0.511
Florida	6.0	$1.34	$ 0.19
Georgia	4.0	$0.37	$ 0.291
Illinois	6.25	$2.98	$ 0.392
Massachusetts	6.25	$3.51	$ 0.24
Michigan	6.0	$2.00	$ 0.272
New Jersey	6.625	$2.70	$ 0.421
New York	4.0	$4.35	$0.2535
North Carolina	4.75	$0.45	$ 0.385
Ohio	5.75	$1.60	$ 0.385
Pennsylvania	6.0	$2.60	$ 0.576
Texas	**6.25**	**$1.41**	**$ 0.20**
Virginia	5.3	$0.60	$ 0.262
Washington	6.5	$3.03	$ 0.494

Sources: Federation of Tax Administrators in Legislative Budget Board, *Fiscal Size-Up 2020–21,* p. 42, Figure 30; Janelle Cammenga, "State and Local Sales Tax Rates 2022," Tax Foundation, February 3, 2022, https://taxfoundation.org/publications/state-and-local-sales-tax-rates/; Ulrik Boesen, "Compare Tobacco Tax Data in Your State," Tax Foundation, July 22, 2021, https://taxfoundation.org/tobacco-tax-data-tool/; IGEN, "Gas Taxes By State for 2022," https://igentax.com/gas-tax-state/.

> **Understanding Impact** Regressive taxes adversely affect lower-wage earners. Although the state sales tax rate is fixed (6.25 percent) regardless of an individual's income, it is considered a regressive tax because the tax paid by lower-wage earners represents a higher proportion of their total income. As discussed in this chapter, sales tax is a vital source of revenue for Texas. Should the state consider other sources of revenue to pay for services delivered to Texans? If so, what sources would you recommend? How would these sources affect tax equity (fairness)?

Tax Shifting

tax shifting
Passing taxes on to other citizens

tax incidence
The person actually paying the tax

Another tax equity issue is the question of who actually pays the taxes, or **tax shifting.** Some taxes can be shifted from the apparent payer of the tax to others who become the true payers, or the **incidence,** of the tax. For example, a business may respond to a tax rate increase in three general ways: (1) by shifting the tax onto the consumer through increased prices; (2) by shifting the tax onto workers in the form of lower wages or fewer benefits; and (3) by absorbing the cost of the tax through lower profits to its owners or, in the case of publicly traded companies, in lower returns to investors.[36] No matter the approach, the goal of shifting the tax burden is achieved.

Students who rent apartments near their campus and who never receive a property tax bill provide another example of tax shifting. The landlord pays the tax each year; however, the landlord will try to pass along the property tax as part of the rent. Market conditions will determine when 100 percent of the tax is passed along to the renter and when the landlord has to lower prices and absorb part of the tax in lower profits.

Except for personal income tax, all taxes can be shifted to others, and market conditions will decide when taxes are shifted. People sometimes argue against business tax increases by advancing the argument that such increases will "simply result in higher prices to the customer." If taxes on businesses could always be shifted forward to customers as higher prices, no business would object to tax increases. Except for the inconvenience of collecting the tax and forwarding it to the government, there would be no cost involved. Obviously, taxes cannot always be shifted to the customer as higher prices, so businesses resist tax increases.

CORE OBJECTIVE

Being Socially Responsible . . .

Texas taxes prepared food items, but it does not tax unprepared food items (such as raw meats and fresh produce). Earlier in this chapter, you learned that individuals can be excluded from receiving services such as electricity if they cannot pay. Keeping this in mind, how does taxing prepared food affect our state's poorest citizens?

Local Taxes

Learning Objective: Discuss local taxes in Texas.

In addition to taxes collected at the state level, local governments in Texas also collect taxes from two primary sources—property tax and local sales tax. Almost all units of local government collect property tax. For school districts, the property tax is the single largest source of revenue, exceeding state contributions. For so-called rich school districts (where incomes and property values are generally higher than average), all of the cost of running local schools may come from the property tax. The property tax is also an important source of revenue for cities and counties. In addition, most cities, many counties, and all local transit authorities collect a local sales tax. In Texas, the local sales tax is fixed by state law at no more than 2 percent of the value of sales. Thus, in most urban areas in Texas, there is a 6.25 percent state sales tax plus a 2.0 percent local tax, for a total of 8.25 percent total sales tax.

There is effectively no state-level property tax in Texas. All but a small portion of property tax revenue collected goes to local governments. In calendar year 2019, the most recent year for which full data are available, local governments in Texas levied approximately $67.3 billion in property taxes, a roughly 5.5 percent increase from 2018 ($63.8 billion). Table 14.5 shows the property tax collections by local government type from 2015 to 2019. Texas local governments, especially school districts, are heavily dependent on property tax revenue. Texas is not a low-property-tax state. Table 14.6 shows the comparison with the 15 most populous states. Nationally, Texas has the sixth-highest property tax levied as a percentage of owner-occupied home value, and the third highest among the top 15.

Comparison of State and Local Tax Revenues

Local taxes are often lost in the focus on state revenues and expenditures. Over the past several decades, the legislature has paid for less and less of the cost of local government services, especially school districts. Figure 14.4 shows the total state and local tax revenue picture for Texas in 2019, "the most recent year for which complete property tax data is available."[37] As the figure shows, property taxes in Texas are almost half of all state and local revenues collected (45 percent). If the local sales tax is added to the local property tax, local tax revenues constitute 58 percent of total taxes collected in the state. Thus, local governments collect and pay just over half the total cost of government in Texas. If the current trend of the state spending less continues, local governments will be picking up a greater share of the cost of providing services to the citizens of the state.

The fact that local governments collect more than half of state and local revenues combined in Texas is an indication of the declining role of the state government in funding services, especially schools. This has been a trend in school financing for several decades and the root cause of much of the objection to property tax increases.

TABLE 14.5

Property Tax Collections by Local Governments in Texas, 2015–2019 (numbers in millions)

Type of Government	2015	2016	2017	2018	2019
School Districts	$28.18	$29.85	$32.13	$34.88	$36.25
City Governments	$ 8.38	$ 9.17	$ 9.73	$10.39	$ 11.15
County Governments	$ 8.69	$ 9.03	$ 9.53	$10.04	$ 11.00
Special Districts	$ 6.95	$ 8.03	$ 8.01	$ 8.47	$ 8.89
Total Property Tax	$52.20	$56.08	$59.41	$63.77	$67.29

Sources: Comptroller of Public Accounts in Legislative Budget Board, Fiscal Size-Up 2022–23, p. 48, Figure 41.

TABLE 14.6

Comparison of Property Tax Rates as Percentage of Owner-Occupied Housing Value: 15 Most Populous States, 2019

State	Revenue	Rank among 50 States
New Jersey	2.13%	1
Illinois	1.97%	2
Texas	**1.60%**	**6**
Ohio	1.52%	9
Pennsylvania	1.43%	11
Michigan	1.31%	13
New York	1.30%	14
Massachusetts	1.08%	18
Georgia	0.87%	25
Florida	0.86%	26
Washington	0.84%	27
Virginia	0.84%	28
North Carolina	0.78%	32
California	0.70%	34
Arizona	0.60%	39

Source: Janelle Fritts, "How High Are Property Taxes in Your State?," Tax Foundation, June 7, 2021, https://taxfoundation.org/high-state-property-taxes-2021/ (accessed May 26, 2022).

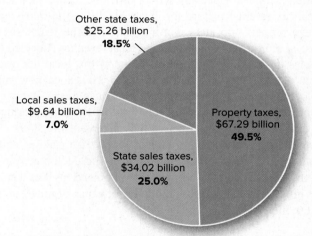

Other state taxes, $25.26 billion 18.5%

Local sales taxes, $9.64 billion— 7.0%

State sales taxes, $34.02 billion 25.0%

Property taxes, $67.29 billion 49.5%

Total Major Taxes: $136.21 Billion

FIGURE 14.4   Major Tax Revenue in Texas as a Percentage of Major Taxes in Texas in FY 2022

Source: Texas Comptroller Office in Legislative Budget Board, *Fiscal Size-Up 2022–23*.

Understanding Impact What role do you think the state should have in the financing of education? Of providing goods and services in general? Does it make sense for local government to be generating an increasing majority of revenue when, education expenditure, for example, remains an issue at both levels?

Nontax Revenue Sources

Learning Objective: Discuss nontax revenue sources in Texas.

Service charges and fees are a source of **nontax revenue** for state governments. Governments often impose service charges and fees when it is possible to exclude a person from receiving the service for nonpayment. When this exclusion is not possible, tax revenue usually finances the service. Figure 14.5 shows nontax revenue by source for the state of Texas in fiscal year 2022. Nontax revenue sources make up about half of state revenue. State governments get only a small percentage of their revenue from service charges and fees. In contrast, some local governments (especially cities) depend heavily on service charges and fees to finance their services. Cities usually impose service charges or fees for water, sewer, and solid waste collection.

The trend in recent years has been to increase service charges and fees as a way to increase revenue and avoid raising taxes. All students attending state colleges and universities in Texas have experienced these increases as higher tuition and service charges (see Chapter 13). In terms of total dollars in the state budget, the various service charges and fees provide 6.4 percent of total state revenue.

The state lottery and interest income generate about 2.8 percent of all (total) state revenue. Even though the Texas Lottery has been the most successful lottery in history in terms of total dollars raised, it contributes only a small portion of the state's total budget and will never be a significant player in providing revenue. In recent years, revenue from the lottery has declined.

As noted in the introduction, about one-third of the biennial budget revenue comes from the federal government. As shown in Figure 14.6, the largest part

nontax revenue

Governmental revenue derived from service charges, fees (tuition), lottery, and other sources

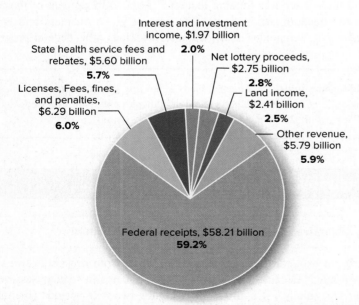

Interest and investment income, $1.97 billion
2.0%

State health service fees and rebates, $5.60 billion
5.7%

Net lottery proceeds, $2.75 billion
2.8%

Land income, $2.41 billion
2.5%

Licenses, Fees, fines, and penalties, $6.29 billion
6.0%

Other revenue, $5.79 billion
5.9%

Federal receipts, $58.21 billion
59.2%

FIGURE 14.5 Total Nontax Revenue for Texas in FY 2022: $98.29 Billion

Source: Texas Comptroller Office in Legislative Budget Board, *Fiscal Size-Up 2022-23*, p. 32, Figure 27.

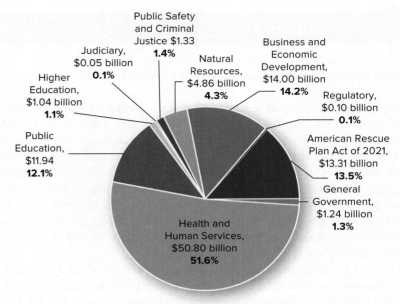

Total, All Articles = $98.53 Billion

FIGURE 14.6   Total Federal Funds Appropriated by State Function 2022–2023 Biennium

Source: Legislative Budget Board, *Fiscal Size-Up 2022–23*, p. 44, Figure 35.

of these federal funds goes to health and human services for Medicare or Medicaid payments and welfare payments. 51.5 percent of those funds are allocated to health and human services, the system that provides for state Medicaid recipients.[38] In the 2020–2021 biennium, Medicaid funding accounted for 69 percent of the total health and human services funding request.[39] About 13.2 percent of these federal funds go to education, and about 14.19 percent go to business and economic development. The remainder is divided among various other federal programs.

> **Understanding Impact** Much of Medicaid funding comes from federal funds. What are your thoughts on Medicaid as a societal good/service? What do you think of it comprising the lion's share of all health and human services funding? Does Medicaid have an impact on your life currently?

Expenditures: Where the Money Goes

Learning Objective: Describe Texas government expenditures.

The pattern of expenditures for Texas differs little from most states in terms of the items funded. Because the Texas legislature meets in regular sessions every other year (biennially), it approves budgets for two-year periods (biennial budgets). In May 2021, the legislature approved a budget of $264.8 billion for the fiscal years 2022 and 2023. In most states, three items consume most of the

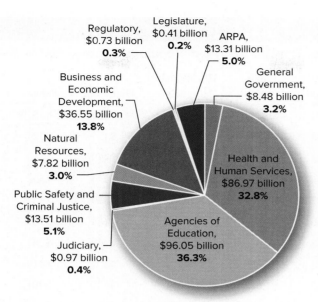

Total = $264.80 Billion

FIGURE 14.7 Total Appropriations by Function, 2022–2023 Biennium (numbers in billions)

Source: Legislative Budget Board, *Fiscal Size-Up 2022–23* p. 2, Figure 1.

state budget—education, health and welfare, and transportation. In recent years, an increase in the prison population has greatly increased the amount spent for public safety, which includes prison operations. Figure 14.7 shows the major expenditure items in the Texas 2022–2023 biennial budget.

Although education takes much of the state budget (about 36.3 percent), local school districts contribute about 60 percent of the funds for local schools. The state currently finances about 40 percent of the cost of elementary and secondary education. This is a decline in state contributions from a decade ago. The state's contribution has been steadily decreasing, and school districts have been forced to pick up a greater share of the cost of local education, which they are covering by assessing higher local property taxes.

Health and human services accounts for about 32.8 percent of the state budget and is funded primarily with federal grants to the state, as noted in the previous section. Texas contributes less than most states to the cost of providing these services. The Texas Constitution prohibits spending more than an amount equal to 1 percent of the state budget on welfare. These are the redistributive services discussed previously. Neither the tax structure nor the political culture supports such activities. Many students of budgeting have observed that a budget is a statement of policy in monetary terms. What and how much money a state spends largely expresses its priorities. The budget becomes a statement of the dominant values in the state. A comparison of Texas with other large industrial states on the primary budget items will tell us something about what Texans value.

As shown by examining the 15 most populous states, Texas ranks near the lower-mid range in expenditures for health and human services (Table 14.7). Although Texas spends a great deal of money in total dollars, it tends to spend

TABLE 14.7

State Government Expenditures Per Capita, 15 Most Populous States, Fiscal Year 2019

State (Population Rank)	Total	Education	Public Welfare	Health and Hospitals	Highways	Police	All Others
New York (4)	$15,667	$4,581	$4,067	$1,315	$727	$553	$4,424
California (1)	$13,156	$3,668	$3,397	$1,536	$490	$527	$3,466
Massachusetts (15)	$11,950	$3,203	$3,574	$513	$470	$350	$3,840
New Jersey (11)	$10,597	$4,036	$2,138	$620	$574	$407	$2,821
Pennsylvania (5)	$10,572	$3,417	$2,784	$844	$879	$337	$2,482
Washington (13)	$10,798	$3,580	$1,669	$1,512	$614	$307	$3,115
Ohio (7)	$9,637	$3,053	$2,533	$797	$518	$347	$2,387
Illinois (6)	$9,793	$2,981	$1,899	$499	$591	$449	$3,373
Virginia (12)	$9,346	$3,202	$1,658	$985	$636	$301	$2,563
Michigan (10)	$9,352	$3,138	$1,903	$1,014	$528	$278	$2,490
Texas (2)	**$8,650**	**$3,153**	**$1,428**	**$954**	**$836**	**$302**	**$1,978**
North Carolina (9)	$8,553	$2,578	$1,493	$1,534	$629	$334	$1,986
Florida (3)	$8,027	$1,982	$1,341	$882	$565	$440	$2,877
Georgia (8)	$7,280	$2,647	$1,247	$718	$420	$268	$1,980
Arizona (14)	$7,251	$2,202	$2,181	$224	$384	$351	$1,908
U.S. Average	**$10,171**	**$3,134**	**$2,256**	**$980**	**$617**	**$375**	**$2,790**
Texas as % of U.S. Average	85.05%	100.58%	63.02%	97.31%	135.60%	80.64%	70.89%

Source: The Urban Institute-Brookings Institution Tax Policy Center, "State and Local General Expenditures, Per Capita, FY 2019," August 27, 2021, https://www.taxpolicycenter.org/statistics/state-and-local-general-expenditures-capita (accessed May 26, 2022).

less than the average comparable state in per capita dollars for most items. In recent years, most of the growth in state expenditures has been driven by population increases alone. In terms of per capita expenditures, the state has remained at about the same level over the past decade.

The Budget "Fix"

The legislature is limited in the amount of discretion it has in spending money. Much of the state's budget (79.6 percent) consists of restricted funds that can be spent only for specific purposes as stipulated by constitutional provisions, enabling legislation, fund formulas, or by external providers such as the federal government. Although the legislature could change legislation and funding formula rules, these are often politically difficult. Generally, special interests have a strong attachment to these appropriations and will fight to maintain them. Table 14.8 shows how much of the state's budget is restricted, primarily as the result of funds being **earmarked** for specific programs (see Chapter 2).

earmarked revenue
Money dedicated to a specific expenditure; for example, the excise tax on gasoline funds highway infrastructure

TABLE 14.8

General Fund Restricted Appropriations, 2022–2023 Biennium

In Millions

Function	Appropriation	Percentage of Total Appropriation
Appropriations dedicated by constitutional provisions	$ 13,886.4	11.1%
Appropriations dedicated by statutory provisions	$ 41,012.5	32.7%
Appropriations influenced by federal law, regulation, or court decisions	$ 30,317.6	24.2%
Appropriations influenced by formulas	$ 14,688.7	11.7%
Total Restricted Appropriations	**$99,905.2**	**79.6%**
Nonrestricted appropriations	$ 25,568.9	20.4%

Source: Legislative Budget Board, *Fiscal Size-Up 2022–23*, p. 27-8, Figure 21.

Understanding Impact The Texas legislature meets biennially for 140 days, so the state's budget is for a two-year period. As noted in this section, most of the state's appropriations are restricted. What problems do you think may arise as a consequence of preparing a biennial budget with heavy restrictions on how money can be spent? Explain.

On the revenue side, many of the taxes and fees collected are either dedicated or nondedicated. Like restricted funds, **dedicated revenue** is specified for a particular purpose either by constitutional provision or state law. For example, the proceeds from the state lottery go to education, and the motor fuel tax goes primarily to state and local road programs. **Nondedicated revenue** is revenue available for general spending. The earmarking of revenues obviously limits the ability of the legislature to change budget priorities or to react to emergency situations. If one fund is short, movement of money from another fund may not be possible. Last year's budget becomes the best predictor of next year's budget. Changes in the budget occur incrementally, in small amounts, over a long period.

Table 14.8 indicates that most funds in Texas are fixed. Only 20.4 percent of general revenue funds are nonrestricted and, therefore, considered **discretionary funding.** This does not give the legislature much leeway in making changes in the budget without new legislation or constitutional amendments approved by the voters in a statewide election.

Remember, before constitutional amendments make it to voters on the ballot, they must be approved by two-thirds of members in both houses. That is not to say that amendments don't happen. After all, the constitution has been amended 520 times since 1876. However, it is telling that of the 91 amendments proposed since 2005, only 3 were amendments changing how dedicated revenue is apportioned. All were adopted. The latest, in 2019, dedicated certain sales and use tax revenue to the Parks and Wildlife Department (S.J.R. 24, Article 8 Section 7-D).

dedicated revenue
Money dedicated to a specific expenditure by constitutional provision or law

nondedicated revenue
Money available for general spending

discretionary funding
Those funds in the state budget that are not earmarked for specific purposes

CORE OBJECTIVE

Communicating Effectively . . .

Consider Table 14.8, which illustrates how specific appropriations are restricted. What percentage of funds is not restricted? How does restricting funds affect budget flexibility?

Continuing Issues in State Finance in Texas

Learning Objective: Identify and explain continuing issues in Texas state finance.

Over the past 20 years, Texas has experienced a number of fiscal shortfalls. The legislature has been forced to meet in special sessions, called by the governor, to correct these problems. Many of these solutions have been short-term fixes. An examination of several tax issues will help you understand the need for a long-term solution.

Tax Structure

During the last few decades, Texas has experienced various financial problems. During the 1980s, there were 10 special sessions of the legislature to attempt to correct revenue shortfalls. These shortfalls were caused primarily by a decline in the state economy because of a drop in oil prices from a high of $40 per barrel to a low of less than $10. The fiscal crisis was worsened by the state's tax structure. Texas is very dependent on highly **income-elastic taxes** (85 to 90 percent) that rise or fall very quickly relative to changes in economic conditions. This means that when the economy is growing or contracting, tax revenue grows or contracts proportionately with the growth or contraction in the economy. For example, as retail sales grow, the sales tax grows. Texas depends heavily on sales and **excise taxes,** which are highly income-elastic. The same is true for the tax on oil and gas extracted in Texas. As the price of oil increased on world markets, the economy of the state boomed, and tax revenue increased. When the oil bust came, the opposite happened, and Texas found itself extremely short of revenue. People quit buying goods and services subject to the sales and excise tax, and revenue fell accordingly. As the price of oil declined, oil revenue fell. Depressed oil prices also caused severe economic problems in Mexico and a devaluation of the peso. Fewer pesos flowed across the border, and some border communities had severe economic problems and declining local revenue along with the state revenue decline. The legislative response to revenue shortfalls is to cut expenditures. While reducing expenditures may provide a quick fix, it does not provide a long-term solution.

Figure 14.8 and Table 14.9 compare the tax dependence of the 15 most populous states. Texas is far more dependent on sales taxes than most other large states. Only Florida and Washington are about as dependent as Texas on consumer taxes. Washington, like Texas, lacks both a personal and a corporate income tax, and Florida lacks a personal income tax. Heavy dependence on consumer taxes makes for an income-elastic tax structure.

income-elastic taxes

Taxes that rise and fall quickly relative to changes in economic conditions; the Texas tax system is very income-elastic

excise tax

An excise tax is usually embedded in the price of a specific good or service and collected at the time of transaction. For example the excise tax on gasoline is part of the price paid per gallon of gasoline purchased at the pump.

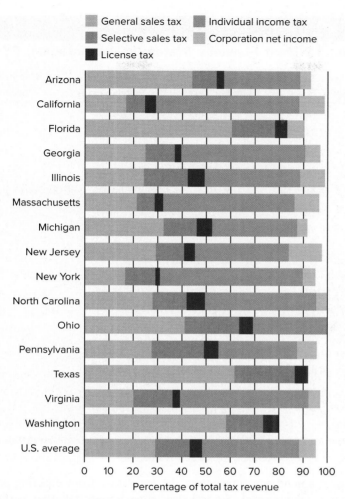

FIGURE 14.8 State Comparison, Percentage of Total Tax Revenue by Major Source in FY 2021

Source: U.S. Census Bureau, 2021 State Government Tax Tables: Detailed Table, https://www.census.gov/data/tables/2021/econ/stc/2021-annual.html (accessed May 26, 2022).

The Texas tax structure depends on highly income-elastic consumer taxes (such as sales and gasoline taxes). When there is an economic downturn, the state will again experience revenue shortfalls. The potential for these problems to occur again is great.

Is There a Personal Income Tax in the Future for Texas?

Texas, Alaska, Florida, Nevada, South Dakota, Washington, and Wyoming are the only seven states without any form of personal income tax. In addition, New Hampshire and Tennessee have a limited income tax on unearned income (dividends, interest, and capital gains). Being in such a limited company of states without an income tax is not troublesome to most Texans. Politically, there is great resistance to imposing such a tax. In 1992, the voters approved a

TABLE 14.9

Major Sources of Tax Revenue for 15 Most Populous States (in Percentages), FY 2021

State	General Sales Taxes	Selective Sales Taxes	License Taxes	Individual Income Taxes	Corporation Net Income Taxes
Arizona	44.12	10.12	2.97	31.38	4.35
California	16.91	7.74	4.55	58.96	10.52
Florida	60.58	17.54	5.09	–	6.91
Georgia	24.95	11.88	2.69	51.06	6.29
Illinois	24.18	18.11	6.88	39.38	10.32
Massachusetts	21.43	7.27	3.51	54.17	10.11
Michigan	32.50	13.75	6.33	34.85	4.35
New Jersey	29.31	11.60	4.55	38.54	13.64
New York	16.70	12.35	1.92	58.82	5.30
North Carolina	28.00	13.97	7.48	45.83	4.37
Ohio	41.23	22.22	5.81	30.54	0.02
Pennsylvania	27.67	21.57	5.96	32.23	8.16
Texas	**61.82**	**24.82**	**5.58**	**–**	**–**
Virginia	20.19	16.06	3.08	52.79	4.89
Washington	58.43	15.20	6.36	–	–
U.S. Average	**29.17**	**14.14**	**5.10**	**39.82**	**7.09**

Source: U.S. Census Bureau, *2021 State Government Tax Tables: Detailed Table,* https://www.census.gov/data/tables/2021/econ/stc/2021-annual.html (accessed May 26, 2022).

constitutional amendment preventing the legislature from enacting an income tax without voter approval. Several legislative leaders felt that without voter approval, the tax would never be imposed by the legislature.

Texas will face another fiscal crisis as long as it is so dependent on consumer taxes. What recourse is available to the state? During past crises, the problem of revenue shortfall was often solved by raising sales and gasoline taxes and by increasing fees. Can these taxes be tapped again? Texas has one of the highest sales tax rates, currently sitting at 6.25 percent. Only California, Indiana, Mississippi, New Jersey, Rhode Island, and Tennessee have reached 7 percent or more. Raising the rate might not be possible.

CORE OBJECTIVE

Taking Personal Responsibility . . .

Although few individuals would express a preference for higher taxes, given the information in this chapter about the goods and services the state provides and the revenue data presented in Figure 14.8 and Table 14.9, should Texans advocate for a personal income tax? Why or why not?

One suggestion, made by former Lt. Governor Bob Bullock and others, was to expand the base of the sales tax. Currently most services are not subject to a sales tax, most notably excluded are debt collection and processing fees. Politically, given the large number of attorneys in the legislature (35 percent), pushing such a change through the legislature might be difficult. The proposal was killed in several sessions of the legislature.

As of January 2022, the state tax on gasoline or motor fuel in Texas is at 20 cents per gallon, plus 18.4 cents in federal tax (38.4 cents total). The highest state gasoline tax is in California, at 86.55 cents per gallon including federal tax.[40] There might be room to raise the gas tax a few cents per gallon, but if prices at the pump continue to rise, the prospect of this happening is unlikely.

Over the past few decades, the tax Texas collects on oil and natural gas production, which is based on the market (dollar) value of the oil and gas extracted from the ground, has generally increased. This remains true even as we see dives and hikes in that market value. A recent dip was in early 2020 due to the COVID-19 pandemic. A more recent rise began in March 2022 due to the war in Ukraine and wide-sweeping sanctions against Russia. Even when global demand slows or increases due to international crises, the United States maintains or increases production, and Middle Eastern oil producers maintain their own output to keep their market share. As of May 2022, the price was roughly $110.33 per barrel.[41] The long-term price of a barrel of oil is very much tied to national and international factors. Still, the state can expect the amount of revenue available from extraction to increase over the long term, so long as there is oil and gas in the state to extract.

Texas has a form of corporate "income tax" that is called a **franchise fee.** Originally, it was assessed only on corporations doing business in the state. It did not apply to limited partnerships, corporations, limited liability companies, business trusts, professional associations, or business associations. Some businesses and corporations changed their structure to avoid the tax. The legislature was forced to eliminate many of these loopholes in 2007 and apply the franchise fee to most businesses in the state. As of 2022, the franchise fee was the third-largest source of tax revenue ($9.7 billion, behind sales and motor vehicle sales and rental taxes, which total $90.3 billion) in the 2022–2023 biennium.[42] The franchise fee seems to be a much improved source of business tax and may be filling the loopholes in the older franchise fee.

The franchise fee is rather complicated, but basically the tax is applied to the gross receipts of most businesses, with deductions allowed for some expenses such as wages, salaries, and employee benefits. Taxable entities with revenues of $300,000 or less owe no tax; however, all businesses must file a report. The tax rate is 0.5 percent for wholesalers and retailers and 1 percent for most other taxable entities. This tax is applied to most businesses in the state.

franchise fee
Major business tax in Texas that is assessed on income earned by corporations in the state

---

Understanding Impact Now that you have a better understanding of the tax structure in Texas, how revenue is produced and money expended, what do you think of the goods and services provided by your state and local governments? What local governments are you bound to? What services do they provide? What are the links between the taxes you pay on a day-to-day basis and the services you have access to as a resident?

Conclusion

Although the budget for the state of Texas is large in total dollars, the state ranks toward the bottom (46th) in terms of per capita expenditures.

What can you conclude about government financing in Texas? First, although Texas is rich in resources, its tax effort is low compared to its tax capacity. Texas has one of the lowest tax burdens of any state, which is in keeping with the political culture of Texas and the emphasis on limited government. Yet, despite Texas's low tax status, Texas has one of the most regressive tax structures. The state government relies on the regressive general sales tax, and the state does not have a personal income tax, which tends to be progressive in structure. It should be no surprise that the majority of states with the most regressive tax structures do not have a personal income tax.

Second, it is difficult to make major changes in the state's budget. Nearly 80 percent of the state's budget is fixed by constitutional, statutory, or federal mandates. About 38 percent of the state's budget is provided through transfer payments from the federal government, which means the state has less budget flexibility.

Finally, Texas will have to decide how best to manage growing fiscal challenges. The Texas economy continues to be one of the strongest in the country, with economic growth outpacing the national average. However, there is growing concern that state revenues will not keep pace with the demand for services such as transportation and education. Unlike the federal government, Texas, like almost all states, is required to balance its budget. It remains to be seen how the state will meet these challenges, although any changes to the tax structure are highly unlikely.

Summary

LO: Explain why governments provide services to citizens.

Markets fail to provide certain goods and services because of some unique characteristics shared by these types of goods, called public goods. Pure public goods are nonexclusive and nonexhaustive. Fire protection services are nonexclusive because even people who do not pay for them will benefit from them. Street lamps are nonexhaustive because one person using them does not decrease the supply of light for other people.

Some goods are quasi-public, and the government also provides them. These may share only certain features of pure public goods, or there may be a broader societal purpose for ensuring availability. There are three important subtypes: social goods (such as public education), toll goods (such as toll bridges), and common-pool goods (such as groundwater).

LO: Describe sources of state revenue in Texas.

For state governments, the primary source of revenue is taxes that citizens pay. The amount of tax money available for any given state depends on the wealth of the citizens of that state. State governments also levy consumer taxes, such as sales and excise taxes on gasoline, tobacco, and liquor. These account for the majority of all state tax revenue.

LO: Discuss the issue of equity in taxes in the U.S. generally and in Texas specifically.

A major question regarding taxes is who should pay, and why. Should those who benefit from public services pay taxes (benefit-based taxes), or should those who can most afford it pay the taxes? It is difficult to determine who benefits most from public and quasi-public goods. Generally, when individual benefit can be measured, at least part of the cost of the service is paid in the form of fees. Other taxes, such as the federal income tax, are based more on ability to pay. The higher your net income, the higher your income tax bracket, and the higher the percentage of your net income you pay in federal income taxes. Most taxes, especially at the state level, are based on benefits. Texas does not levy a personal income tax and has one of the most regressive tax structures in the country. This means that the poor are more heavily taxed than the wealthy.

LO: Discuss local taxes in Texas.

Local governments in Texas collect taxes from two primary sources—property tax and local sales tax. Almost all units of local government collect property tax. There is no state-level property tax, yet property tax accounts for a major percentage of total state revenue. The fact that local governments collect more than half of state and local revenues combined in Texas is an indication of the declining role of the state government in funding services, especially schools. In addition, most cities, many counties, and all local transit authorities collect a local sales tax (set at no more than 2 percent).

LO: Discuss nontax revenue sources in Texas.

Nontax revenue comes from service charges, fees (tuition), lottery, and other sources. Governments often impose service charges and fees when a person can be excluded from receiving the service for nonpayment. State governments get only a small percentage of their revenue from service charges and fees. However, some local governments, especially cities, depend heavily on service charges and fees to finance their services. Cities usually impose service charges or fees for water, sewer, and solid waste collection. Governments use nontax sources as a way to prevent tax increases.

LO: Describe Texas government expenditures.

A state's budget is a monetary expression of its politics. What and how much money a state spends largely depends

on its priorities. In Texas, education and health and human services are the main areas of expenditure, accounting for nearly 80 percent combined. The state currently finances about 40 percent of the cost of elementary and secondary education, though local governments are increasingly taking on that financial burden. Texas spends less on health and human services than most other states due to its regressive tax structure and political culture.

LO: Identify and explain continuing issues in Texas state finance.

Texas depends on income-elastic taxes that rise or fall quickly relative to changes in economic conditions. These kinds of taxes include sales and excise taxes and the tax on oil and gas extracted in the state, which make up a huge percentage of Texas's total revenue. For example, as the price of oil and gas rises and falls, so too does state revenue. When there is an economic downturn, the state has revenue shortfalls.

Key Terms

ability to pay	income-elastic taxes	proportional taxes
benefit-based taxes	nondedicated revenue	public goods
consumer taxes	nonexcludability	regressive taxes
dedicated revenue	nonexhaustion	tax base
discretionary funding	nonrivalrous consumption	tax capacity
earmarked revenue	nontax revenue	tax effort
excise tax	per capita tax	tax exporting
franchise fee	political values	tax incidence
free-rider	progressive taxes	tax shifting

Notes

[1] Urban Institute, "State and Local Expenditures," https://www.urban.org/policy-centers/cross-center-initiatives/state-and-local-finance-initiative/state-and-local-backgrounders/state-and-local-expenditures (accessed May 18, 2022).

[2] Texas Comptroller of Public Accounts, Annual Cash Report, Table 1: Statement of Cash Position, https://comptroller.texas.gov/transparency/open-data/dashboards.php.

[3] Legislative Budget Board, *Fiscal Size-Up 2022–23 Biennium,* Figure 1, https://www.lbb.texas.gov/Documents/Publications/Fiscal_SizeUp/Fiscal_SizeUp_2022-23.pdf.

[4] Texas Health and Human Services System, "Consolidated Budget Request 2020–2021," Figure 11.5, https://www.hhs.texas.gov/sites/default/files/documents/about-hhs/budget-planning/consolidated-budget-request-2020-2021.pdf.

[5] Cowen Tyler, "Public Goods," *The Concise Encyclopedia of Economics,* 2nd ed., ed. David R. Henderson (Indianapolis: Liberty Fund, Inc., 2007). Also available at http://www.econlib.org/library/Enc/PubligGoods.html. This is an effective general introduction to the concept, and it generally informs the treatment here. The classic work on the subject

of public goods is Paul A. Samuelson, "The Pure Theory of Public Expenditure," *Review of Economics and Statistics* 36, no. 4 (November 1954): 387–89.

[6] There is some debate on the classification of public goods. For example, see Nobel Prize–winning economist Richard H. Coase's classic piece, "The Lighthouse in Economics," *The Journal of Law and Economics* 17, no. 2 (October 1974): 357–76. For more on this debate, see David E. Van Zandt, "The Lessons of the Lighthouse: 'Government' or 'Private' Provision of Goods," *Journal of Legal Studies* 22, no. 1 (January 1993): 47–72; and William Barnett and Walter Brock, "Coase and Van Zandt on Lighthouses," *Public Finance Review* 35 (November 2007): 710–33.

[7] John L. Mikesell, *Fiscal Administration: Analysis and Applications for the Public Sector,* 8th ed. (Boston: Wadsworth, 2011), 5–6.

[8] Cowan, "Public Goods."

[9] J. Richard Aronson and John L. Hilley, *Financing State and Local Governments,* 4th ed. (Washington, D.C.: Brookings Institution, 1986), 37–40.

[10] U.S. Department of the Treasury, Resource Center, "Total Taxable Resources Estimates," September 2021, https://home.treasury.gov/system/files/226/TTR-tables-2021.pdf.

[11] Texas Research League, "The Rating Game," *Analysis 11* (August 1990): 2.

[12] U.S. Census, "QuickFacts: United States, Texas," https://www.census.gov/quickfacts/fact/table/US,TX/PST045219.

[13] Yuri Jang, "Asian Americans in Austin: Final Report of the Asian American Quality of Life (AAQoL) Survey," UT Austin School of Social Work, October 13, 2016, p. 3, http://www.austintexas.gov/sites/default/files/files/Communications/4.2_FINAL_AA_in_Austin_report_from_UT.pdf (accessed July 23, 2020).

[14] New American Economy, *Economic Contributions and Growth of Asian American and Pacific Islanders in the U.S.*, April 2021. https://research.newamericaneconomy.org/report/aapi-community-contributions-population-growth/ (accessed May 26, 2022).

[15] Ibid.

[16] New American Economy, *Power of the Purse: How Asian Americans and Pacific Islanders Contribute to the U.S. Economy*, October 2010. pp. 16-17, https://www.immigrationresearch.org/system/files/NAE-AAPI.pdf (accessed May 26, 2022).

[17] Ibid., 13.

[18] Yuri Jang, "Asian Americans in Austin: Final Report of the Asian American Quality of Life (AAQoL) Survey," UT Austin School of Social Work, October 13, 2016, p. 77, http://www.austintexas.gov/sites/default/files/files/Communications/4.2_FINAL_AA_in_Austin_report_from_UT.pdf (accessed July 23, 2020).

[19] U.S. Department of the Treasury, "Joint Statement by Secretary of the Treasury Janet L. Yellen and Acting Director of the Office of Management and Budget Shalanda D. Young on Budget Results for Fiscal Year 2021," Table 1, U.S. https://home.treasury.gov/news/press-releases/jy0428 (accessed May 26, 2022).

[20] U.S. Census Bureau, "2021 Annual Survey of State Government Tax Collections by Category Table," https://www.census.gov/data/tables/2021/econ/stc/2021-annual.html (accessed May 26, 2022).

[21] U.S. Census Bureau, "QuickFacts: Population Estimates, July 1, 2021 (V2021)," https://www.census.gov/quickfacts/fact/table/US,TX/PST045217; U.S. Census Bureau, "Historical Household Tables," Table HH-2. Households by Race and Hispanic Origin of Householder: 1970 to Present, November 2021, https://www.census.gov/data/tables/time-series/demo/families/households.html (accessed May 26, 2022).

[22] Partnership for a New American Economy, *The Economic Contributions of Hispanic Americans*, September 2021, https://research.newamericaneconomy.org/report/hispanic-spending-power-2021/ (accessed May 26, 2022).

[23] Ibid.

[24] Jens Manuel Krogstad and Jeffrey S. Passel, "5 Facts about Illegal Immigration in the U.S.," November 19, 2015, Pew Research Center, http://www.pewresearch.org/fact-tank/2015/11/19/5-facts-about-illegal-immigration-in-the-u-s/.

[25] Matthew Gardner, Sebastian Johnson, and Meg Wiehe, *Undocumented Immigrants' State and Local Tax Contributions*, Institute on Taxation and Economic Policy, March 2017, https://itep.org/wp-content/uploads/immigration2017.pdf.

[26] Matthew Gardner, Sebastian Johnson, and Meg Wiehe, *Undocumented Immigrants' State and Local Tax Contributions*, Institute on Taxation and Economic Policy, March 2017, p. 3, https://itep.org/wp-content/uploads/immigration2017.pdf.

[27] Partnership for a New American Economy, *Power of the Purse: How Hispanics Contribute to the U.S. Economy*, December 2017, p. 9, http://research.newamericaneconomy.org/wp-content/uploads/sites/2/2017/12/Hispanic_V5.pdf.

[28] Ibid.

[29] Charles P. Garcia, "Opinion: Want to save Social Security? Embrace Latinos," *CNN*, April 10, 2015, http://money.cnn.com/2015/04/10/news/economy/social-security-latinos/index.html.

[30] IRS.gov, "Tax Reform," https://www.irs.gov/newsroom/tax-reform (accessed May 8, 2018); Tax Foundation, "2022 Tax Brackets," https://taxfoundation.org/2022-tax-brackets/ (accessed May 27, 2022).

[31] IRS.gov, "What Is the Additional Medicare Tax?," https://www.irs.gov/newsroom/what-is-the-additional-medicare-tax (accessed May 26, 2022).

[32] Institute on Taxation and Economic Policy, "Who Pays? A Distribution Analysis of the Tax Systems in All 50 States," 6th ed. (Washington, D.C.: 2018), https://itep.org/wp-content/uploads/whopays-ITEP-2018.pdf (accessed May 26, 2022).

[33] Institute on Taxation and Economic Policy, "Who Pays? A Distribution Analysis of the Tax Systems in All 50 States," 6th ed. (Washington, D.C.: 2018), https://itep.org/wp-content/uploads/whopays-ITEP-2018.pdf.

[34] Ibid.

[35] Federation of Tax Administrators, "State Sales Tax Rates and Food & Drug Exemptions (As of January 1, 2022)," https://www.taxadmin.org/assets/docs/Research/Rates/sales.pdf.

[36] John L. Mikesell, *Fiscal Administration Analysis and Application for the Public Sector,* 8th ed. (Boston: Wadsworth, 2011), 355.

[37] Texas Legislative Budget Board, *Fiscal Size-Up 2022–23 Biennium,* p. 46, https://www.lbb.texas.gov/Documents/

Publications/Fiscal_SizeUp/Fiscal_SizeUp_2022-23.pdf (accessed May 26, 2022).

[38] Legislative Budget Board, *Fiscal Size-Up 2022–23,* p. 44, Figure 35.

[39] Texas Health and Human Services System, *Consolidated Budget: Fiscal Years 2020–2021,* https://hhs.texas.gov/sites/default/files/documents/about-hhs/budget-planning/consolidated-budget-request-2020-2021.pdf.

[40] American Petroleum Institute, "Gasoline Taxes," January 1, 2022, https://www.api.org/-/media/Files/Statistics/State-Motor-Fuel-Notes-Summary-january-2022.pdf?la=en&hash=F649022BA19339184C9ED8DAEFD26ABE8DEE2377 (accessed May 26, 2022).

[41] Nasdaq, "Crude Oil," https://www.nasdaq.com/market-activity/commodities/cl:nmx (accessed May 26, 2022).

[42] Legislative Budget Board, *Fiscal Size-Up 2022–23,* 35, Figure 26.

GLOSSARY

A

ability to pay Taxes that are not based on the benefit received but on the wealth, or ability to pay, of an individual

absentee voting A process that allows a person to vote early, before the regular election; applies to all elections in Texas; also called early voting

acting governor When a governor leaves a state, the position is held by the lieutenant governor, who performs the functions of the office

Adelsverein Society An organization that promoted German immigration to Texas in the 1840s

Affordable Care Act (ACA) A complex and detailed federal law to reform health care and extend coverage to more Americans

agenda setting The power of the media to bring issues and problems to the public's attention

agents of socialization Family, teachers, peer groups, religious institutions, geographic location, class, gender, race/ethnicity, mass media; those societal forces and institutions that surround individuals from early childhood onward

Anglo Here, refers to a non-Hispanic white North American of European descent, typically (but not exclusively) English speaking

annual registration A system that requires citizens to reregister to vote every year

appellate courts Higher-level courts that decide on points of law and not questions of guilt or innocence

appointive-elective system In Texas, the system of many judges gaining the initial seat on the court by being appointed and later standing for election

astroturf organization A political term for an interest group that appears to have many grassroots members but in fact does not have individual citizens as members; rather, it is sponsored by an organization such as a corporation or business association

at-large election system System where all voters in the city elect the mayor and city council members

attorney general Chief counsel to the governor and state agencies; limited criminal jurisdiction

B

Baker v. Carr Court case that required state legislative districts to contain about the same number of citizens

ballot form The forms used by voters to cast their ballots; each county, with approval of the secretary of state, determines the form of the ballot

ballot wording Description of a proposed amendment as it appears on the ballot; can be intentionally noninstructive and misleading to voters in order to affect voter outcome

benefit-based taxes Taxes for which there is a relationship between the amount paid in taxes and services received; motor fuel taxes are a good example

bicameral Legislative body that consists of two houses

biennial sessions Legislature meets every two years

bill of rights A list of individual rights and freedoms granted to citizens within a constitution

blanket primary system A nominating election in which voters could switch parties between offices

boards and commissions Governing body for many state agencies; members appointed by the governor for fixed term

budget fix State laws and constitutional amendments that set aside money to be spent on specific items; the best example is the state gasoline tax being committed to state highways

budgetary powers The ability of a governor to formulate a budget, present it to the legislature, and execute or control the budget

burden of proof The obligation associated with providing evidence sufficient to support the assertion or claim made by the individual bringing suit in a court of law

C

campus carry The right, protected by state law, for licensed individuals to carry concealed handguns on college campus except in certain prohibited areas

capture The situation in which a state agency or board falls under the heavy influence of or is controlled by its constituency interest groups

carpetbagger People who engage in political activities in a place they do not live. After the American Civil War, people from Union states and elsewhere went to the South to engage in politics and business. Southerners saw them as exploiters and called them "carpetbaggers" because of the type of luggage they typically used.

categorical grants Grants that may be used to fund specific purposes as defined by the federal government

ceremonial duties The expectation that a governor attends many functions and represents the state; some governors become so active at this role that they get caught in a ceremonial trap and neglect other duties

checks and balances Power granted by the Constitution to each branch of government giving it authority to restrain other branches

537

chief legislator   The expectation that a governor has an active agenda of legislation to recommend to the legislature and works to pass that agenda

citizen journalism   The collection, dissemination, and analysis of news and information by the general public, especially by means of the Internet

citizen legislatures   Legislatures characterized by low pay, short sessions, and fewer staff resources

city manager   Person hired by the city council to manage the city; is the chief administrative officer of the city

civil law   Defines private relationships as well as financial matters or damages to property committed by businesses or other individuals to a person

civil rights movement   A political movement, primarily in the 1950s and 1960s, that demanded equal civil rights for people of color

classical liberalism   An ideology that stresses the protection of individual rights, limited government, the rule of law, and a free market economy

closed primary system   A nominating election that is closed to all voters except those who have registered as a member of that political party

CNN effect   The effect of 24-hour broadcasts of live news media (CNN, MSNBC, Fox, etc.)

collective bargaining   Negotiations between an employer and a group of employees to determine employment conditions, such as those related to wages, working hours, and safety

commission form of government   A form of local government where voters elect department heads who also serve as members of the city council

commissioner's court   Legislative body that governs a Texas county

commute   The reduction in punishment for an individual convicted of a crime

comptroller of public accounts   Chief tax collector and investor of state funds; does not perform financial audits

conference committees   Joint committees of the house and senate that work out differences in bills passed in each chamber

constitution   The basic document that provides a framework for government and limits what the government can do

constitutional convention   An assembly of citizens that may propose changes to state constitutions through voter approval

consumer taxes   Taxes that citizens pay when they buy goods and services—the most prominent example is sales taxes

conviction   Following adoption of articles of impeachment by the lower legislative house, the senate tries the official under those articles; if convicted, the official is removed from office

council-manager form of government   Form of government where voters elect a mayor and city council; the mayor and city council appoint a professional administrator to manage the city

county chair   Party official elected in each county to organize and support the party

county executive committee   Committee made up of a county chair and all precinct chairs in the county; serves as the official organization for the party in each county

county government   Local unit of government that is primarily the administrative arm of a state government; in most states, it does not provide urban-type services

county sheriff   Elected head of law enforcement in a Texas county

creatures of the state   State governments create local governments, and all of local governments' powers come from the state government; there are no inherent rights for local governments independent of what the state grants them

criminal law   Statutory law that defines both the violation and the penalty the state will seek to have imposed upon the defendant

crisis manager   The expectation that a governor will provide strong leadership in times of a natural or human-made disaster

critical journalism   A style of soft news that focuses on political scandal, vice, or mistakes of the government or politicians

crossover voting   Occurs when voters leave their party and vote in the other party's primary

cumulative voting system   A system where voters can concentrate (accumulate) all their votes on one candidate rather than casting one vote for each office up for election

D

DACA (Deferred Action for Childhood Arrivals)   An executive order issued by President Obama allowing some people who were brought illegally to the United States as children to stay in the country for a defined period; companion order to DAPA

DAPA (Deferred Action for Parents of Americans and Lawful Permanent Residents)   Executive order issued by President Obama allowing non-lawful resident parents of U.S. citizens and lawful permanent residents to remain in the United States; companion order to DACA

dedicated revenue   Money dedicated to a specific expenditure by constitutional provision or law

delegates   Representational role of member stating that he or she represents the wishes of the voters

demography   The scientific study of a population

discretionary funding   Those funds in the state budget that are not earmarked for specific purposes

DREAM Act   The Development, Relief and Education of Alien Minors Act, a Texas law that allows some undocumented students to be classified as residents for the purpose of paying in-state tuition rates

dual court system   A judicial structure where there are two systems in place: federal and state. The federal court system deals with matters subject to federal law, as well as with interstate and international disputes. The state court system deals with almost everything else that falls within a given state's borders

due process clause   Clause in the Fifth and Fourteenth Amendments of the U.S. Constitution that requires states to treat all citizens equally and specifies that states must follow certain rules and procedures

Duverger's law   A law in political science indicating that the electoral system strongly conditions the type of party system that will result

E

earmarked revenue   Money dedicated to a specific expenditure; for example, the excise tax on gasoline funds highway infrastructure

economic regions   Divisions of the state based on dominant economic activity

electioneering   Various activities in which interest groups engage to try to influence the outcome of elections

electoral fraud   The intentional violation of election laws in any part of the process of elections.

electronic media   Means of communication that uses electronic equipment and can be analog or digital in nature

eminent domain   The process whereby the government can take private land for a public purpose with compensation

empresario   A person who contracted with the Spanish or Mexican government to recruit new settlers to Texas in exchange for the ability to claim land

enhanced punishment   The application of the next most serious penalty for repeat offenders

equal protection clause   Clause in the Fourteenth Amendment of the U.S. Constitution that requires states to treat all citizens equally

equal time rule   Provided that a broadcaster permitting one political candidate access to the airwaves must afford equal opportunities to all other such candidates seeking the same office

excise tax   An excise tax is usually embedded in the price of a specific good or service and collected at the time of transaction. For example the excise tax on gasoline is part of the price paid per gallon of gasoline purchased at the pump.

exculpatory evidence   Material evidence that could assist the accused in proving that they were innocent of the offense charged

exit polls   Interviews of voters just as they leave the polling center

exoneration   The official absolution of a false criminal conviction and release from incarceration

extra legislative powers   Legislative leaders serve on boards outside of the legislature

extraordinary session   A specially called meeting of the legislature, outside the regular session, to discuss specified matters

extraterritorial jurisdiction (ETJ)   City powers that extend beyond the city limits to an area next to the city limits

F

fair use   Law that permits the limited use of copyrighted material without acquiring permission from the rights holders

federal system of government   The division of powers between a national government and regional governments

felony   A serious criminal offense, punishable by death or incarceration

filing fee   A fee or payment required to get a candidate's name on the primary or general election ballot

focus group   Panel of "average citizens" who are used by political consultants to test ideas and words for later use in campaigns

fragmented government structure   A government structure where power is dispersed to many state agencies with little or no central control

framing   The media's attempts to focus attention on certain events and place them within a context for meaning

franchise fee   Major business tax in Texas that is assessed on income earned by corporations in the state

free-rider   An individual or individuals who benefits from a good or service without contributing to the cost

full faith and credit clause   Clause in Article 4 of the U.S. Constitution that requires states to recognize the judgments, legislation, and public records of other states

G

gatekeeping   The process of filtering information and selecting what to transmit or not transmit as news

general elections   Regular elections held every two years to elect state officeholders

general law city   City governed by a city charter, which state statutes created

geographic distribution   A characteristic of some interest groups in that they have members in all regions of the state

gerrymandering   Drawing district boundary lines for political advantage

government organizations   Interest groups that represent state and local governments; also called SLIGs, for state and local interest groups

graded penalties   Punishments that differ based upon the seriousness of the crime

grand juries   Juries of citizens that determine if a person will be charged with a crime

groundwater   Water that is within in the earth; under Texas law, it is private property controlled by the owner of the land under which it is located

H

hard news   Factual, in-depth coverage of public affairs that contributes to citizens' understanding of political events and leaders in the public sphere

home rule city   City governed by a city charter that local citizens created

Hopwood decision   Decision by federal courts to end affirmative action in Texas schools; these programs had provided for special treatment for minority students in being accepted to colleges and professional schools

Hunt v. Cromartie   Court case that ruled while race can be a factor, it can not be the primary factor in determining the makeup of legislative districts

I

ideology Basic belief system that guides political theory and policy; typically envisioned as falling along a conservative/moderate/liberal continuum

impeachment The process by which some elected officials, including governors, may be impeached (accused of an impeachable offense) by the lower house adopting articles of impeachment

in loco parentis Latin for "in the place of a parent"

income-elastic taxes Taxes that rise and fall quickly relative to changes in economic conditions; the Texas tax system is very income-elastic

incorporation Process of creating a city government

independent candidate A person whose name appears on the ballot without a political party designation

independent school district (ISD) School district that is not attached to any other unit of government and that operates schools in Texas

individual mandate A controversial major provision of the Affordable Care Act requiring every person to buy and maintain health insurance coverage satisfying certain minimum standards or pay a tax

individualistic subculture Government that benefits the individual rather than society in general

informal qualifications Additional qualifications beyond the formal qualifications required for men and women to be elected governor; holding statewide elected office is an example

informal rules Set of norms or values that govern legislative bodies

information Messages provided that concern social events occurring or services available in a community to its members

information or an administrative hearing A hearing before a judge who decides if a person must stand trial; used in place of a grand jury

initiative A process that allows citizens to propose changes to the state constitution through the use of petitions signed by registered voters; Texas does not allow constitutional revision through initiative

intake The procedures involved with the arrest and detention of an individual before a bail hearing

interest group An organization of individuals sharing common goals that tries to influence government decisions

intergovernmental coordinator The expectation that a governor works smoothly with other state governments

interstate commerce clause Article in U.S. Constitution that gives Congress the exclusive power to regulate commerce between the states; Congress and the courts determine what is interstate commerce

investigative journalism Deeply researched stories that uncover serious crime, corruption, or corporate wrongdoing

J

judicial powers The ability of a governor to issue pardons, executive clemency, and parole of citizens convicted of a crime

L

land-based economy An economic system in which most wealth is derived from the use of the land

land commissioner (LC) Elected official responsible for administration and oversight of state-owned lands and coastal lands

lawful permanent resident (also called Green Card holder) Noncitizen who is legally authorized to live permanently within the United States

League of United Latin American Citizens (LULAC) The oldest organization representing Latinos in Texas, established in 1929

Legislative Budget Board (LBB) State agency that is controlled by the leadership in the state legislature and that writes the state budget

legislative power The formal power, especially the veto authority, of the governor to force the legislature to enact his or her legislation

legislative professionalism Legislatures with higher pay, longer sessions, and high levels of staff support are considered more professional

Legislative Redistricting Board (LRB) State board composed of elected officials that can draw new legislative districts for the house and senate if the legislature fails to act

libel A published false statement that is damaging to a private individual's reputation

lieutenant governor Presiding officer of the Texas Senate; elected by the voters of the state

line-item veto The ability of a governor to veto part of an appropriations bill without vetoing the whole bill

lobbying The practice of trying to influence members of the legislature, originally by catching legislators in the lobby of the Capitol

M

magistrate functions Preliminary hearings for persons charged with a serious criminal offense

majority-minority Ethnic and racial minority groups make up a majority of the population of the state

mass media Means of communication that reaches many individuals

media bias The actual or perceived failure of the media to report news objectively

Medicaid Federal government program to provide funds to pay for medical care for people of any age with very low incomes

Medicare Federal program providing funds to pay for medical care to eligible people 65 and older and also some people who have disabilities

membership organizations Interest groups that have individual citizens or businesses as members

merit system, or Missouri system A system of electing judges that involves appointment by the governor and a periodic retention election

military powers Powers giving the governor the right to use the National Guard in times of natural disaster or civil unrest

minor party   A party other than the Democratic or Republican Party; to be a minor party in Texas, the organization must have received between 5 and 19 percent of the vote in the past election

misdemeanor   Less serious criminal offense, punishable by fine, incarceration, or both fine and incarceration

moralistic subculture   Government viewed as a positive force to achieve a common good for all citizens

multimember districts   Districts represented by more than one member elected to the legislature

N

name familiarity   Practice of voting for candidates with familiar or popular names; a significant issue in Texas judicial elections

necessary and proper clause (elastic clause)   Statement in Article 1, Section 8, paragraph 18 of the U.S. Constitution that says Congress can pass any law necessary and proper to carry out other powers

network (net) neutrality   The principle that Internet service providers should enable access to all content and applications regardless of the source, and without favoring or blocking particular products or websites

news   Stories that provide timely information about the important events or individuals in a community, state, nation, or world

noncompetitive districts   Districts in which a candidate from either party wins 55 percent or more of the vote

nondedicated revenue   Money available for general spending

nonexcludability   The inability to practically prevent people from receiving or enjoying a good or service due to nonpayment

nonexhaustion   The availability of a good or service for others to use and enjoy will not diminish (i.e., consumption is nonrivalrous).

nonmembership organizations   Interest groups that represent corporations and businesses and do not have broad-based citizen support

nonpartisan election   Election in which party identification is not formally declared

nonrivalrous consumption   Situation in which the use or enjoyment of a good or service by a person or persons does not diminish the availability of that good or service for others to use or enjoy

nontax revenue   Governmental revenue derived from service charges, fees (tuition), lottery, and other sources

O

objectivity   The appearance that courts make impartial decisions and not political ones

office block format   Ballot form where candidates are listed by office with party affiliation listed by their name; most often used with computer ballots

open primary system   A nominating election that is open to all registered voters regardless of party affiliation

ordinances   Laws passed by local governments

P

pardon   Grants forgiveness by the state for a conviction and requires that the convicted receive no punishment; does not erase the criminal record

parens patriae   Latin for "parent of the fatherland"

partial veto   The ability of some governors to veto part of a nonappropriations bill without vetoing the entire bill; a Texas governor does not have this power except on appropriations bills

partisan election   Method used to select all judges (except municipal court judges) in Texas by using a ballot in which party identification is shown

party caucus   A meeting of members of a political party to nominate candidates (now used only by minor political parties in Texas)

party chief   The expectation that the governor will be the head of his or her party

party column format   Paper ballot form where candidates are listed by party and by office

party raiding   Occurs when members of one political party vote in another party's primary in an effort to nominate a weaker candidate or split the vote among the top candidates

peak business association   An interest group devoted to statewide business interests

per capita tax   The total taxes raised in a state divided by the number of residents

permanent party organization   Series of elected officials of a political party that keep the party organization active between elections

permanent registration   A system that keeps citizens on the voter registration list without their having to reregister every year

Permanent University Fund (PUF)   State of Texas fund to support the University of Texas and Texas A&M systems as required by the Texas Constitution

petit juries   Juries of citizens that determine the guilt or innocence of a person during a trial; pronounced *petty* juries

plural executive system   System in which executive power is divided among several statewide elected officials

podcast   A digital audio file made available on the Internet for downloading to a computer or portable media player, typically available as a series, new installments of which can be received by subscribers automatically

police power   The ability afforded states under the Tenth Amendment of the U.S. Constitution to regulate behavior and enforce order within their geographic territories

policy liberalism index   A measure of how liberal or conservative a state is on some state policies

political action committee (PAC)   A spin-off of an interest group that collects money for campaign contributions and other activities

political communication   Communication in the public sphere concerned with social and political matters, encompassing all media and messages, between and among citizens, the media, and the governing elite; also an academic field of study that focuses on how information is disseminated and shapes the public sphere

political culture   A system of beliefs and values that defines the role of government and the role of citizens in that government

political gerrymandering   Drawing legislative districts to the advantage of a political party

political participation   All forms of involvement citizens can have that are related to governance

political party   Organization that acts as an intermediary between the people and government with the goal of getting its members elected to public office

political power   Influence on government based on some combination of numbers of people; wealth; social norms; ideas; force and violence; and government actions (including laws and regulations)

political socialization   The development of political attitudes and beliefs through agents of socialization, such as socio-economic factors, family, religion, school, community, the media, and so on

political values   A set of beliefs about political processes and the role that government should play in our society

poll tax   In place from 1902 until 1966 in Texas, a tax citizens were required to pay each year between October and January to be eligible to vote in the next election cycle

popular sovereignty   The idea that power granted in state constitutions rests with the people

populism   An ideology that emphasizes the role of government in economic concerns, while simultaneously supporting the government's role in upholding socially conservative values

precedent   An earlier legal decision by a court that can be used to decide similar cases in the future

precinct chair   Party official elected in each voting precinct to organize and support the party

preferential voting system   A system that allows voters to rank order candidates for the city council

presentation bias   The act of writing or presenting news stories that reflect a significantly distorted view of reality, favoring one party over another in the case of political parties

presidential primary election   Election held every four years by political parties to determine voters' preferences for presidential candidates

primary election   An election used by major political parties in Texas to nominate candidates for the November general election

priming   The ability of the media to help shape public opinion respecting an event or a person in the public sphere

print media   Means of communication in the form of physically printed materials, such as newspapers, magazines, and pamphlets

privileges and immunities clause   Clause in Article 4 of the U.S. Constitution that prevents states from discriminating against citizens of other states and requires those citizens to be treated in like manner

professional associations   Organizations promoting the interests of individuals who generally must hold a state-issued license to engage in their profession

Progressive Era   A movement in the late nineteenth and early twentieth centuries that sought increased federal and state government regulation to help wipe out economic, social, and political ills

progressive or modern liberal   An ideology that stresses the positive role of government intervention in the economy for the common and public good

progressive taxes   Taxes that take a higher percentage of income from high-income persons

proportional taxes   Taxes that take the same percentage of income from all citizens

public goods   Goods or services characterized by the features of nonexcludability and nonrivalrous consumption; governments often provide these

public opinion   The aggregate (sum) of attitudes and opinions of individuals and groups on a particular topic

public policy   "Whatever governments choose to do or not to do."—Thomas Dye

public sphere   A community's arena that allows individuals to freely discuss and identify societal problems and influence political action

push polls   Illegitimate, unscientific polling technique aimed at attacking a candidate or issue

R

racial gerrymandering   Legislative districts that are drawn to the advantage of a minority group

Raza Unida (United Race)   Minor party that supported election of Hispanic Americans in Texas in the 1970s

realignment   "A lasting shift of party loyalty and attachment" (as defined by James L. Sundquist in *Dynamics of the Party System: Alignment and Realignment of Political Parties in the United States* [Washington, D.C.: Brookings Institute, 1983], p. 4)

reapportionment   The process of allocating representatives to districts

recall   The removal of the governor or an elected official by a petition signed by the required number of registered voters and by an election in which a majority votes to remove the person from office

recidivism   The rate at which criminal offenders commit crime after they leave the state's custody

redistricting   The drawing of district boundaries

referendum   A direct public vote on a single political issue

registered voters   Citizens who have formally gone through the process of getting their names on the voter registration list

regressive taxes   Taxes that take a higher percentage of income from low-income persons

regulations   Administrative rules implemented by governmental regulatory agencies to guide or prescribe specific conduct by industry or business

rent seeking   The practice of trying to secure benefits for oneself or one's group through political means

reprieve   The temporary 30-day stay of execution the governor may grant

resonance   The reinforcement and magnification of existing beliefs about reality and commonality of events because of the presentation of reality by the media

retail trade associations   Organizations seeking to protect and promote the interests of member businesses involved in the sales of goods and services

Reynolds v. Sims   Court case holding that issues of representation are justiciable, and that one person's vote should be roughly equal in weight to another person's

right of rebuttal   Candidates must be given an opportunity to respond to any criticism made by a media outlet

right-to-work laws   Legislation stipulating that a person cannot be denied employment because of membership or nonmembership in a labor union or other labor organization

runoff primary   Election that is required if no person receives a majority in the primary election; primarily used in southern and border states

S

same-day registration   Voters are allowed to register on Election Day; no preregistration before the election is required.

secretary of state (SOS)   Chief election official and keeper of state records; appointed by the governor

selection bias   The systematic selection of particular news that presents a distorted view of reality

semi-closed primary system   A nominating election that is open to all registered voters, but voters are required to declare party affiliation when they vote in the primary election

semi-open primary system   Voter may choose to vote in the primary of either party on Election Day; voters are considered "declared" for the party in whose primary they vote

senatorial courtesy   The favor of the governor clearing his or her appointments with the state senator from the appointee's home district

separation of powers   Power divided among the legislative, executive, and judicial branches of government

severability   Capable of being divided into legally independent obligations

sine die   Legislature must adjourn at end of regular session and cannot continue to meet

single-member district (SMD)   District represented by one elected member to the legislature

social conservatism   An ideology that stresses the dangers of unregulated capitalism and supports relatively conservative social values

social contract theory   The idea that all individuals possess inalienable rights and willingly submit to government to protect these rights

socioeconomic factors   Factors such as income, education, race, and ethnicity that affect voter turnout

soft news   Information, presented as news, that serves to entertain, titillate, or overdramatize events but that lacks substance and value with respect to contributing to citizens' understanding of political events and leaders in the public sphere

"sore loser" law   Law in Texas that prevents a person who lost the primary vote from running as an independent or minor party candidate

speaker of the house   Member of the Texas House, elected by the house members, who serves as presiding officer and generally controls the passage of legislation

special purpose district   Form of local government that provides specific services to citizens, such as water, sewage, fire protection, or public transportation

special sessions   In Texas, sessions called by the governor to consider legislation proposed by the governor only

standing committees   Committees of the house and senate that consider legislation during sessions

stare decisis   The principle that court decisions depend on previous rulings of other courts; the term is Latin for "to stand by that which was decided before"

state and local interest groups (SLIGs)   Interest groups that represent state and local governments, such as the Texas Association of Counties

state executive committee   Committee, made up of one man and one woman from each state senatorial district as well as a chair and vice chair, that functions as the governing body of the party

state party chair   Heads the state executive committee and provides leadership for the party

statutes   Laws passed by state legislatures

straight-ticket voting   Casting all your votes for candidates of a single party

straight-ticket voting system   System that allows voters to vote for all candidates of a single political party by making a single mark and that has resulted in an increase in the number of Republican judges

straw polls   Unofficial, ad hoc personal interviews surrounding a formal vote

streaming services   The transfer of music or video data over the Internet, generally through a subscription service provider

strong mayor form of government   Form of local government where most power rests with the mayor

Sunset Advisory Commission   Agency responsible for making recommendations to the legislature for change in the structure and organization of most state agencies

supremacy clause   A clause that makes constitutional provisions superior to other laws

surface water   Water visible on the surface of the land; under Texas law, it is owned by the state of Texas

T

tax base   The items that are subject to tax; for example, the items subject to sales tax

tax capacity   A measure of the wealth of a state or its ability to raise revenues relative to all other states

tax effort   A measure of the amount of revenue collected by a state relative to its tax capacity

tax exporting   The shifting of taxes to citizens in other states; a good example is Wyoming coal, which is exported to Texas to generate electricity

tax incidence   The person actually paying the tax

tax shifting   Passing taxes on to other citizens

temporary party organization   Series of meetings or conventions that occur every two years at the precinct, county, and state levels

Tenth Amendment   Amendment of the U.S. Constitution that delegates or reserves some powers to the state governments or to the people

tenure of office   The ability of governors to be reelected to office and the term length

term limits   Limitations on the number of times a person can be elected to the same office in state legislatures

Texas Code of Criminal Procedure   The rules created by the Texas Supreme Court to govern the proceedings of trials in Texas

Texas Ethics Commission   State agency responsible for enforcing requirements for interest groups and candidates for public office to report information on money collected and activities

Texas Penal Code   The statutory law that defines criminal offenses and punishments in Texas

Texas Railroad Commission (RRC)   State agency with regulation over some aspects of transportation and the oil and gas industry of the state

Top Ten Percent Plan   State law allowing students who graduate in the top 10 percent of their high school to attend any state college or university, without consideration of other factors. The law has been amended to allow only the top 6 percent.

tort   "A civil wrong, recognized by law as grounds for a lawsuit, which can be redressed by awarding damages." *Source:* Cornell University Law School, Legal Information Institute, *Wex Legal Dictionary.*

trade associations   Interest groups that represent more specific business interests than peak business associations do

traditional media   The term associated with conventional forms of media, such as television, print, radio, direct mail, and billboard signage

trial courts   Local courts that hear cases; juries determine the outcome of the cases heard in the court

trial de novo courts   Courts that do not keep a written record of their proceedings; cases on appeal begin as new cases in the appellate courts

traditionalistic subculture   Government that maintains the existing political order for the benefit of a small elite

trustees   Representational role of a member that states that the member will make decisions based on his or her own judgment about what is best for voters

turnover   The number of new members of the legislature each session

U

unitary system of government   A system of government where all functions of government are controlled by the central/national government

V

voter registration   The act of qualifying to vote by formally enrolling on an official list of voters

voter turnout   The proportion of people who cast ballots in an election

voting fraud   When voters intentionally break voting laws when they vote.

voting-age population (VAP)   The number of people aged 18 and over

voting-eligible population (VEP)   The voting-age population, corrected to exclude groups ineligible to vote, such as noncitizens and convicted felons

W

weak mayor form of government   Form of government where the mayor shares power with the council and other elected officials

white primary   From 1923 to 1945, Democratic Party primary that excluded African Americans from participating

write-in candidate   A person whose name does not appear on the ballot; voters must write in that person's name, and the person must have filed a formal notice that he or she was a write-in candidate before the election

INDEX

H

S